STUDIES IN PRESOCRATIC PHILOSOPHY
Vol. I

The Beginnings of Philosophy

International Library of Philosophy and Scientific Method

EDITOR: TED HONDERICH

A Catalogue of books already published in the *International Library of Philosophy and Scientific Method* will be found at the end of this volume

Studies in Presocratic Philosophy
Vol. I

The
Beginnings of
Philosophy

edited by

David J. Furley

and

R. E. Allen

LONDON
ROUTLEDGE & KEGAN PAUL
NEW YORK : THE HUMANITIES PRESS

First published 1970
by Routledge & Kegan Paul Ltd
Broadway House, 68–74 Carter Lane
London, E.C.4

Printed in Great Britain
by Richard Clay (The Chaucer Press) Ltd
Bungay, Suffolk

ISBN 0 7100 6759 3

CONTENTS

CONTENTS

PREFACE

OUR thanks are due to the Clarendon Press for permission to publish article XII, which first appeared in the *Classical Quarterly*; to the Society for the Promotion of Hellenic Studies for articles II and IX and X, which first appeared in the *Journal of Hellenic Studies*: to the Harvard University Press for article VIII, which first appeared in *Harvard Studies in Classical Philology* and is here reprinted in shortened form; to the Johns Hopkins Press for articles XIII and XV, which first appeared in *The American Journal of Philology*; to the University of Chicago Press for article IV, which first appeared in *Classical Philology*; and to the editors of *The Journal of The History of Ideas*, *Gnomon*, *The Philosophical Quarterly*, *Mind*, *Hermes*, and *Annals of Mathematics* for articles I, III, V, VII, XI, and XIV respectively.

Professor Sir Karl Popper has asked that mention be made of his reply in *Conjectures and Refutations* to Professor Kirk's criticism of 'Back to the Presocratics' both in the body of this book and in this Preface.

R. E. A.
D. J. F.

INTRODUCTION

THIS volume contains articles on three subjects: (1) the nature of Presocratic thought in general; (2) the sources of our knowledge of the Presocratics; (3) the earliest philosophers, up to Heraclitus. A second volume will deal with Parmenides and his successors, as far as the Atomists, Leucippus, and Democritus.

We have tried to assemble a collection of essays which will be useful and interesting to students of the history of philosophy, the history of science, and classical literature. We have omitted articles with a strictly philological purpose and method, and aimed to please the Greek-less reader, although this has not always been possible. All the articles have appeared elsewhere, in the learned journals, but certain changes have been made here: (1) the article by Uvo Hölscher in Volume 1 and Hermann Fränkel's 'Parmenidesstudien' in Volume 2 have been translated from the original German; (2) J. B. McDiarmid's 'Theophrastus on the Presocratic Causes' and Gregory Vlastos's 'On Heraclitus' have been considerably abbreviated; (3) some articles have been revised by their authors; (4) Greek words and quotations have been translated into English whenever the nature of the article permitted this change. The place and date of the original publication of each article are mentioned in the Table of Contents. All non-trivial changes are marked by footnotes or in some other way.

The study of Presocratic philosophy has greatly increased in bulk and in depth during this century, and the rate of increase itself appears to be increasing. Where articles would suffice in the 1930s, we now have whole books, or even series of books, on individual philosophers. By comparison with some other branches of classical literature, there has been a rapid expansion, which has rendered some books and articles out of date. After considering several candidates, the editors have included no articles which were published before 1930, and few before 1940. We particularly regret omitting articles by W. A. Heidel and F. M. Cornford which were significant and progressive at the time of their publication, but appeared to us to be concerned with issues that are no longer alive now.

We have tried to include articles that are frequently discussed. Particularly in the first volume, we have often presented both sides of a case. This is not, in fact, a deliberate policy: we have not tried to be 'balanced'. We have simply chosen what seemed to us to be the best and most stimulating discussions of important problems—in so far as they are to be found in articles. This is, of course, an important qualification. For English-speaking students of the subject, the books by G. S. Kirk and J. E. Raven, *The Presocratic Philosophers* (Cambridge, 1957), and by W. K. C. Guthrie, *A History of Greek Philosophy* (Cambridge, Vol. I, 1962, and Vol. II, 1965) have been of the greatest significance. In selecting material for these volumes, we have avoided reproducing what is already easily available, and these authors are therefore under-represented. Indexes to both volumes will appear in Vol.II.

I

THE CHARACTERISTICS AND EFFECTS OF PRESOCRATIC PHILOSOPHY*

H. F. Cherniss

IT is only fair for you to be forewarned that I do not intend to present you with an exhaustive doxography, a list of the opinions and systems of all the important philosophers before Socrates, or to offer you a formula to which the meaning of all Presocratic philosophy can be reduced. My purpose is merely to suggest certain salient characteristics which, I believe, can help one to find one's way through the extant remains of Presocratic philosophy and to appraise at something like their real value the many formulae which have been offered, each as the only effective key to the understanding of those remains, and then to indicate how the Presocratic thinkers affected the character of subsequent philosophy.

This subsequent philosophy has unfortunately limited seriously and to some degree effectively prevented our direct approach to the Presocratics. We possess no single complete work of any of the Presocratic philosophers, and most of the scanty and disconnected fragments that we have are preserved only because they were quoted by post-Socratic philosophers for their own dialectical purposes or quoted by later commentators of those philosophers in illustration of the statements which they had made about the Presocratics. The result is that such direct quotations of the Presocratics as we do possess are almost entirely a selection determined by the interpretations and formulations of Presocratic philosophy by the post-Socratic philosophers for their own philosophical purposes, chiefly by Aristotle and to a lesser extent

* A lecture originally delivered at St John's College, Annapolis, Md., on 10 December 1948.

I

by Plato, by the Stoics, and by the Sceptics. The ancient accounts of Presocratic philosophy are prejudiced in the same fashion, since most of them depend ultimately upon Theophrastus' *History of Philosophy* and in that work Theophrastus interpreted the Presocratics not merely according to general Peripatetic formulae as might have been expected but usually in close dependence upon the particular formulations of Aristotle. In considering any so-called fragment, therefore, it is necessary not to be content to read it in isolation. One must take into consideration the whole context in which it has been preserved (a context which sometimes is as extensive as a whole book of Aristotle's *Metaphysics*), the ultimate source of that context if it can be discovered, and the possible reasons why this particular fragment was quoted or this particular interpretation adopted in this particular place. Such careful investigation, comparison, and reflection are necessary before one can feel even reasonably sure that one is ascribing to a Presocratic philosopher a conception or an attitude that was his own and not some later interpretation or deformation of it.

There is no more significant characteristic of a philosopher's thought than the kind of questions that he asks, the problems which he feels called upon to solve as contrasted with the assumptions that he makes; and it is just in this respect that the character of Presocratic thought is most thoroughly concealed and misrepresented as a result of the channels through which it has been transmitted. The doxographers listed the opinions of all philosophers as if they were all answers to the same questions asked in the same way; and each philosopher interpreted his predecessors, if he considered them at all, as if they had been trying to answer the same questions which he had posed for himself. Book A of Aristotle's *Metaphysics*, for example, which both directly and through Theophrastus had greater influence upon the subsequent ancient histories of philosophy than any other single work, interprets all previous philosophy as a groping for his own doctrine of fourfold causality and is in fact intended to be a dialectical argument in support of that doctrine,[1] which itself implies a question that could not have been formulated before Plato. Aristotle as a philosopher is, of course, entirely justified in inquiring what answer any of the Presocratic systems could give to the problem of causality as he had formulated it; but to suppose that such an

[1] Cf. *Metaphysics* 983 A 24–B 6 and 993 A 11 ff.

inquiry is historical, that is, to suppose that any of these systems was elaborated with a view to that problem as formulated by Aristotle, is likely to lead to misinterpretation of those systems themselves and certainly involves the misrepresentation of the motives and intentions of their authors.

It is in this same book of Aristotle's that Thales appears as the first of the 'material monists',[2] and this is the ultimate source of the convention which makes him the first identifiable figure in Greek philosophy. How, when, and from what origins Greek philosophy arose are questions which have excited interest, speculation, and controversy from the time of Aristotle to the present. Greek mythography, the Greek rationalistic spirit, the influence of Babylon or Egypt, the practical interests of the sea-faring and colonizing Milesians, mysticism, and interest in the form of divinity, each of these has been held responsible for the appearance in Ionia in the early sixth century B.C. of that systematic concern with the constitution and meaning of existence which is the essence of Greek philosophy. All of these various explanations, however, are based chiefly upon analogical arguments, the validity of which is highly dubious, and upon late Greek statements, which are themselves rather hypotheses and speculations than historical evidence. The lack of any real evidence for the resolution of this problem is emphasized by the paucity of genuine evidence concerning Thales himself. What Aristotle himself knew about Thales' opinions he says that he knew only by tradition; and this was very little and in its significance not at all clear. Thales declared, they say, that the earth rests upon water. So Aristotle in the *De Caelo*,[3] where he discusses the position and stability of the earth; in the passage of the *Metaphysics* to which I have already referred he states that this notion of Thales' followed from his doctrine that all things come to be from water.[4] This, at any rate, is a doctrine which Thales 'is said' to have held,[5] and on the basis of this Aristotle makes him a 'material monist'; but he does not tell us who said so. It might possibly have been Hippo, who held the doctrine himself and who may have sought in this way to lend it authority after the fashion of antiquity. Hippo is mentioned in this same passage,[6] and Aristotle here suggests as a reason why Thales decided that all things come to be from water an argument which

[2] *Metaphysics* 983 B 20–984 A 3.   [3] *De Caelo* 294 A 28–30.
[4] *Metaphysics* 983 B 21.   [5] *Metaphysics* 894 A 2–3.   [6] *Metaphysics* 948 A 3–5.

THE CHARACTERISTICS AND EFFECTS OF

elsewhere he ascribes to Hippo.[7] What we know of Aristotle's general method of interpreting his predecessors, however, and the specific purpose of his dialectical history in this book arouse the suspicion that Thales was not led from the general doctrine that all things come to be from water to draw the conclusion that the earth rests upon water, but conversely from the tradition which ascribed to Thales the notion that the earth rests upon water Aristotle inferred that he had made water the origin of everything. This suspicion is heightened by the fact that Plato does not mention Thales in connection with this doctrine in the passages where, attempting to establish the antiquity of the doctrine of flux, he facetiously ascribes it to Homer, Hesiod, and Orpheus on the strength of lines that make Ocean the origin of the gods.[8] To Plato Thales was one of the Seven Sages,[9] a man to whom tradition ascribed ingenious contrivances for the practical arts.[10] To Herodotus he was known for having advised the Ionians to form a confederation, for having foretold a solar eclipse, and (a tradition which Herodotus disbelieved) for having diverted the course of the Halys river which blocked the way of the army of Croesus.[11] Several passages of Aristophanes[12] show that the name 'Thales' had in the fifth century B.C. come to be used proverbially to indicate skill in such activities as surveying and engineering, a usage which reflects the same tradition as the later ascription to Thales of the introduction of geometry from Egypt[13] and of a work on navigation.[14] Such traditions, if taken seriously, can be used to support the thesis that Ionian philosophy grew out of an interest in practical techniques; but, on the other hand, those who insist upon finding the origin of that philosophy in mystical or theological motivations can appeal to the traditions according to which Thales first declared souls to be immortal,[15] asserted that all things are full of gods,[16] and ascribed a soul to the magnet because it moves iron.[17] The trouble is that tradition assigned these or similar statements to other philosophers or sages also,[18] that, strictly considered, the last two are not consistent with each

[7] *De Anima* 405 B 2–3. [8] *Cratylus* 402 B–C, *Theaetetus* 152 E and 160 D.
[9] *Protagoras* 343 A. [10] *Republic* 600 A. [11] *Herodotus*, i. 74, 75, 170.
[12] *Clouds* 180; *Birds* 1009. [13] *Frag. der Vorsok.*[5], i. 76, 10 ff.
[14] *Frag. der Vorsok.*[5], i. 80, 3 ff. [15] Choirilus *apud* D.L., i, 24.
[16] Aristotle, *De Anima* 411 A 7–9. [17] Aristotle, *De Anima* 405 A 19–21.
[18] Cf., e.g., Aristotle, *De Part. Animal.* 645 A 17–21; Plato, *Laws* 899 B where no author is given.

other,[19] and that quite contrary interpretations of these statements can be defended with equal force. To say that all things are full of gods, for example, may be to mean that all things are divine in a mystical or religious sense or equally to mean that *nothing* is, in the way that the author of the Hippocratic essay, 'On the Sacred Disease', asserts that all diseases are divine and all human, meaning that no disease is sacred in the religious sense at all.[20]

The fact is that about Thales' philosophy, if he had one, nothing was certainly known even in antiquity. He had become a kind of 'culture-hero' of philosophy; to his name were attached apophthegms and edifying anecdotes to illustrate, sometimes in contradictory fashion, the characteristics of the philosopher; and attempts were made to derive Greek philosophy through him now from foreign and again from indigenous sources by making him a pupil either of the Egyptian priests and the Chaldeans[21] or of Homer and Hesiod.[22] For all purposes of practical consideration Greek philosophy begins with Anaximander, and so it did in ancient times too. That is the kernel of truth in the artificial scheme of successions preserved in the first book of Diogenes Laertius,[23] according to which Ionian philosophy began with Anaximander, and Thales, though he is presumed to have been Anaximander's teacher, is listed not among the philosophers but among the sages.

Anaximander did write a book which was known to Apollodorus of Athens in the second century B.C.; and because of this, although only a few words of that book have been preserved for us, and because Anaximander had made a map which engaged the attention of Eratosthenes, so that his place in the geographical tradition is still discernible, we are not restricted for our knowledge of his work to the doxographical tradition alone. To Aristotle and to Theophrastus, and hence to the doxographies derived from Theophrastus, only those of Anaximander's statements were of interest which dealt with cosmology or natural science and appeared to have ontological or metaphysical implications; but study of the material that does not derive from this

---

[19] Cf. Cherniss, *Crit. Pres. Phil.*, p. 296, n. 26.
[20] Hippocrates, *Morb. Sacr.* xxi.   [21] *Frag. der Vorsok.*[5], 11 A 11.
[22] Probus *ad* Vergil., p. 21, 14 K (*Dox. Graec.*, p. 91 b); Heraclitus, *Quaest. Homericae*, Ch. 22; Theodoretus, *Graec. Aff. Cur.* ii. 9 (*Dox. Graec.*, 170).
[23] i. 13.

tradition has shown that Anaximander was not merely a physiologer in the Aristotelian sense and suggests that the orientation and the interests of the Ionian philosophy of Anaximander's time were far different from what Aristotle would lead one to believe.

Anaximander's purpose [24] was to give a description of the inhabited earth, geographical, ethnological, and cultural, and the way in which it had come to be what it was. His book began with a cosmogony and ended with a description of the contemporary world which was in a sense a commentary on the map of the inhabited world that he had charted; it proposed a theory of the origin of the earth and the heavenly bodies and their arrangement, explained the appearance of land-masses on the earth and of geological, geographical, and meteorological phenomena; and proceeded to account for the development of human life upon the land, the distribution of nations, and the origins and dispersion of civilization. The details of his theories aside, the startling and important features of his thought are its universality of scope, its freedom from anthropocentric orientation, and the strictly impersonal causal nexus which is assumed to hold together all objects and events. This is Ionian 'historia' in its full sense, the investigation of all existence without specialization or compartmentalization. Anaximander is at once astronomer and geographer, cosmogonist and genealogist, meteorologist, biologist, anthropologist, and historian—not any of them as profoundly as were the specialists to follow him but all of them equally in the service of the complete object of 'historia', knowledge of all the world as it is. Moreover, in this world, which is the object of his investigation, man has come to be under the same conditions and limitations as other objects; he is not something apart from the world but is of it and determined by it, not having been always such as he is now but having developed from animals of another kind,[25] animate beings themselves having developed from inanimate matter.[26] Nor is this world, or cosmos of earth, sun, moon, and stars unique; there is at any moment an unlimited number of such worlds, all of which arise from 'the unlimited', which encompasses them all, and into which all of them ulti-

[24] Cf. W. A. Heidel, 'Anaximander's Book, The Earliest Known Geographical Treatise', *Proc. Am. Acad. of Arts and Sciences*, Vol. 56, No. 7, April 1921.
[25] *Frag. der Vorsok.*[5], 12 A 10 and 30.   [26] *Ibid.*, 12 A 11 (§ 6) and 30.

mately pass away to be replaced by others which arise in the same fashion.[27] This 'unlimited', *to apeiron*, that from which all the worlds and all that is in them are separated out and into which they are again absorbed, is not a single unqualified substance from which entities are developed by qualitative change. The distinction of quality and substrate, the notion of alteration, and the logical conception of identity which makes a paradox of change had not even occurred to Anaximander; they are conceptions which were to come later and gradually, and they have to do with Anaximander's *arche* or 'reservoir' only in the sense that it involves them as problems which are as yet unrecognized. For Anaximander the *apeiron* was simply a boundless expanse of infinitely different ingredients so thoroughly mixed together as to be severally indiscernible in the mixture but which when segregated from the mixture are recognizable as all the differences of an articulated world;[28] it is like nothing so much as that 'limitless sea of dissimilitude' into which, in the myth of Plato's *Politicus*,[29] the cosmos is periodically in danger of sinking. A passage derived from Theophrastus[30] proves that Anaximander refrained from specifying further the nature of this reservoir of all existing things; but the designation that he chose for it, the adjective *apeiron* substantivized by the definite article, since it has the appearance of an abstraction, made it easy for Theophrastus to follow Aristotle[31] and, despite his better knowledge, taking *to apeiron* in Aristotle's sense of *arche* as a 'principle' or 'element' rather than in Anaximander's of 'source' or 'reservoir',[32] to interpret it in terms of Aristotelian prime matter as the substrate which is the indeterminate potentiality of all the properties, none of which it has actually.[33] Before Plato, however, both the name and the notion of abstract quality were unknown, and for all Presocratics what we call a quality was a characteristic which could not be considered separately from that of which it was characteristic.[34] *To apeiron* is in this respect no different from such a designation as *to thermon*. As the latter does not mean 'heat' in

[27] Cf. *Frag. der Vorsok.*[5], 12 A 9, 10, 11, 14, 17.
[28] *Crit. Pres. Phil.*, pp. 375–9.   [29] *Politicus* 273 D.
[30] *Frag. der Vorsok.*[5], 12 A 14 (i. p. 85, 5–6).
[31] Cf., e.g., *Physics* 204 B 22 ff. (*Frag. der Vorsok.*[5] 12 A 16).
[32] Cf. Heidel, *Class Phil.*, vii. (1912), 215–28.
[33] *Frag. der Vorsok.*[5], 12 A 9 a.   [34] Cf. *Crit. Pres. Phil.*, p. 362.

Aristotle's sense or ours, an abstract quality which cannot be anything other than itself, but that which is hot or all hot things, which being hot may yet at the same time have many other characteristics, so the former means that which is 'unlimited', though besides this significant characteristic it may have other characteristics too. The significance of the fact that Anaximander called his *arche* simply *to apeiron* without further specification or restriction is not that limitlessness or infinity exhausts its nature but that it is unlimited without restriction, unlimited in every sense of the Greek word, in extent, in multitude, and in kind, in short not that it is *potentially* everything being *actually* nothing but infinity, as the Peripatetic interpretation would have it, but that it is everything *in actuality*. Once this is recognized one finds no trouble but only consistency in the fact that the one Greek sentence of Anaximander's which has been preserved, if not in his own words at least in a paraphrase of Theophrastus', refers to the *apeiron* or rather to its ingredients in the plural number.[35] That is in itself a clear indication not only that the *apeiron* is not to be interpreted in the Peripatetic manner but also that the modern fashion of considering it to be a development of Hesiod's *chaos*[36] is equally erroneous, for the *chaos* of the *Theogony* is mere yawning emptiness,[37] whereas the *apeiron* is full and positive and active too, a congeries in continual motion, a motion which the doxographers tend to abstract[38] but which Anaximander really took for granted as one of the characteristics of all the ingredients of the *apeiron*, as is shown by Theophrastus' criticism that he provided no efficient cause but acted as if matter moves itself.[39] There is no description of this movement of the *apeiron*, and it may be that Anaximander gave none, though he apparently supposed that, once separated off, the sections of the *apeiron* were articulated as worlds in a vortex;[40] but he did assume that the *apeiron* must be in constant motion, that this leads to the separating-off which produces the articulation of worlds, and that consequently, whether directly

[35] *Frag. der Vorsok.*[5], 12 B 1 in its context, 12 A 9.
[36] Cf., e.g., Gigon, *Der Ursprung der Griechischen Philosophie*, pp. 30 and 61.
[37] Cf. *Theogony* 700; Jaeger, *Theology of the Early Greek Philosophers*, p. 13.
[38] Cf. *Frag. der Vorsok.*[5], 12 A 9 (i, p. 83, 12), 12 A 11 (i, p. 84, 5-6), 12 A 17 (i, p. 86, 20-5), and the extreme case 12 A 12.
[39] *Frag. der Vorsok.*[5], 12 A 14 (i, p. 85, 6-8).
[40] Cf. Burnet, *Early Greek Philosophers.*[3], pp. 61-2 on Heidel, *Class Phil.*, I (1906), 281.

by its own movement or indirectly through that of the articulated world or both, it also causes the reabsorption of these worlds into itself. This may be what he meant by the statement, if it is really his, that the *apeiron*, which he called ageless, deathless, and indestructible, encompasses and guides all things.[41] Ageless, deathless, and indestructible are traditional Greek epithets of the gods. Because Anaximander applied them to his *apeiron*, which guides all things, and Aristotle concluded that this is what is considered to be divine,[42] it has recently been contended[43] that there is a deep religious significance in Anaximander's conception, that he thought he had found a proof of the existence of Divinity, the general concept of which he first expressed, and that his system is in fact a theology, theogony, and theodicy in one. This is a conclusion which is at the very least unwarranted, even if Anaximander did say that what is divine is his *apeiron*, which is far from assured by the evidence, and call the articulated worlds 'gods', as the doxography reports.[44] The latter source in the same context ascribes to Thales the statement that god is the mind which fashioned all things from water,[45] a manifest fiction which casts suspicion upon the report concerning Anaximander's worlds. Among the sayings ascribed to Thales[46] is one that defines the divine as that which has neither beginning nor end. Such sayings are 'floating maxims' ascribed now to one sage and now to another; but they are undoubtedly old, and Aristotle probably had in mind nothing more than this traditional saying when he remarked that the unlimited is what is considered divine. In any case, Anaximander's *apeiron* is in no way conscious or personal and, if it guides all things, it does so in no voluntary sense. The worlds which are segregated from it are reabsorbed by it 'as needs must be', and Anaximander envisaged this repeated process as a settling and resettling of accounts among the ingredients of the

[41] *Frag. der Vorsok.*[5], 12 A 15 (i, p. 85, 17–21): ἀθάνατον καὶ ἀνώλεθρον alone *certainly* belong to Anaximander as does ἀγήρω in 12 A 11 (i, p. 84, 2).

[42] *Frag. der Vorsok.*[5], 12 A 15 (i, p. 85, 19–20) = *Physics* 203 B 13: the εἶναι of τοῦτ' εἶναι τὸ θεῖον depends upon δοκεῖ above and so need not be a quotation at all but an inference of Aristotle's supported by the specific quotation of the epithets which follows.

[43] Jaeger, *Theology of the Early Greek Philosophers*, pp. 31–7.

[44] *Frag. der Vorsok.*[5], 12 A 17 (Aetius, i. 7, 12; Cicero, *De Natura Deorum*, i. 10, 25).

[45] Cicero, *loc. cit.*; Aetius, i. 7, 11.   [46] *Frag. der Vorsok.*[5], i. 71, 20.

9

apeiron which by being reabsorbed into the common mixture make amends and requital to one another for injustice done 'in the fixed order of time'.[47] This is according to him the law of all nature, 'law' literally in the sense of a drastic process which continually redresses the balance among the constituents of existence, the *apeiron* being the common fund in which all accounts are equalized. If this is to be considered in relation to theology, it must be admitted to be a complete rejection of all that was traditional in Greek religion. It is the denial that natural order can be suspended by any supernatural being or force, the denial in fact that any supernatural being can exist, and the assertion that, if the divine means anything at all, it can mean only the system of nature ordered according to infrangible law.

This conception of nature as an all-inclusive system ordered by immanent law was Anaximander's most important legacy to subsequent thought. The universal sweep of Anaximander's genius had drawn a cosmological picture, the general outlines and major motifs of which determined the limits and the direction of all subsequent Presocratic speculation in this field; but the picture that he had drawn, if judged seriously by his own guiding principle, would obviously require greater elaboration and precision and rectification in detail and was most influential and most fruitful through the implicit problems to which it unwittingly called the attention of all who looked upon it with understanding. It is in this light that the achievement of Anaximander's younger townsman, Anaximenes, must be appreciated. Anaximenes apparently lacked the encyclopaedic interest which characterized Anaximander. At any rate, so far as is known, he confined his attention to cosmology and natural science—or better, natural history; but within this special field, applying with extreme rigour and consistency Anaximander's conception of nature, he devised a simple, elegant, and universal theory to account for those very aspects of the physical processes concerning which Anaximander's account was vague and unsatisfactory.

The numberless differences in the articulate world had not really been explained by Anaximander at all; he had simply supposed that they are all present in the reservoir of the *apeiron* from which they are separated out and into which they are again absorbed. He had not even considered what this process logically

47 *Frag. der Vorsok.*5, 12 B 1.

involves: the question of the existence of minute homogeneous particles, the determination of the specific character and form of such particles, the relation of the processes of segregation, aggregation, and dispersion; or the sufficient reason *why* any one of these processes should occur when and where it does 'in the fixed order of time'. To this last question Anaximenes offered no answer either; but he did attempt really to explain the existence of differences and to derive them from a single source by a single natural mechanism, for the operation of which he found evidence in the physical world about him. This was the mechanism of condensation–rarefaction. All change of every kind he regarded as the result of this one mechanism, in modern terms as a function of the variation of density. The air we exhale is a cold thing, if we compress it with our lips; if we relax our lips in exhalation, it is rarefied and becomes something hot.[48] If then it is compressed further, it should become water and finally earth and stones; but, if further rarefied, it should become fire.[49] These are definitely changes of one thing into another, not alterations of quality in a single substrate which remains identical;[50] but, since the most evenly distributed body and the most extensive is air and also because air as 'breath' is identified with the soul that 'holds living bodies together', Anaximenes made air, as it were, the manifestation of normal density and substituted it for the *apeiron* of Anaximander. That the theory was evolved within the frame of Anaximander's cosmology is clear from the fact that Anaximenes made this extra-cosmic air unlimited in extent, that the world is produced from it and reabsorbed into it, though by the new process of condensation and rarefaction, and that within the boundless air innumerable worlds are supposed to exist simultaneously and to pass away to be replaced by others.[51] The correction of Anaximander's system was far from being a mere detail, however; Anaximenes was obviously aware of its importance, for he applied his general theory of rarefaction and condensation with impressive consistency to all the details of his cosmogony, astronomy, geology, and meteorology. His analysis of all objects and events in the physical world as aspects and functions of a single

48 *Frag. der Vorsok.*[5], 13 B 2.
49 *Frag. der Vorsok.*[5], 13 A 7.
50 Cf. *Crit. Pres. Phil.*, pp. 379–80.
51 Cf. Aetius, ii. 1, 3 (*Dox. Graeci*, p. 327) and Burnet, *EGP*[3], p. 78.

quantitative process is the ultimate achievement that characterizes the orientation of Milesian philosophy.

It emphasizes at the same time the limitations of that philosophy, limitations which were to become important and stimulating problems for subsequent thinkers. Not even Anaximenes thought to give any sufficient reason for the universal process which he had derived, either in general or in its particular manifestations. The bodies which change into one another, including the boundless air, were assumed to be in constant motion. The doxographical report that he supported this with the reasoning that they would not change if they were not in motion[52] is probably a Peripatetic reconstruction; that motion is the natural state of all body seems to have been an unconscious assumption of his as well as of Anaximander's. At any rate, he did not bother to establish any reason for motion or any causal relation of motion to the stages of the natural processes which he elaborated. Moreover, the logical difficulties involved in Anaximander's ingredients of the *apeiron* are present in another form in the theory of Anaximenes, for the designation 'air' did not imply for him an identity which includes homogeneity, since the other characteristics of air, as of all bodies, depend upon the mechanical distribution of its parts and such a notion involves the logical difficulty of identifying the 'parts';[53] but Anaximenes was no more aware of this problem, upon which the Eleatic criticism first focused attention, than Anaximander had been before him. What was more obvious if not more important, the Milesians had succeeded in naturalizing man in the cosmos but had done it so thoroughly as to reduce him to a physical object on the same level as all other physical objects; and these physical objects Anaximenes had in fact, though unwittingly, dissolved. His notion that all things change according to a quantitative mechanism leads directly to the conclusion of physical relativism, for, if water is air that has been 'rearranged' by compression, air is also water that has been 'rearranged' by rarefaction, nothing is anything but a different degree of everything else, and only the process itself remains fixed.

This conclusion was drawn with radical thoroughness by Heraclitus. In the case of Heraclitus all the difficulties involved in the interpretation of the Presocratics are magnified and are, more-

52 *Frag. der Vorsok.*⁵, 13 A 7, § 2.   53 Cf. *Crit. Pres. Phil.*, p. 380.

over, further complicated by special factors. Whereas the Milesians had written in sober prose continuous treatises in which they attempted to give a systematic account of their subject, the book of Heraclitus, though written in prose, consisted of a series of apophthegms unconnected by any obviously logical transitions and expressed in an elaborate oracular style. Heraclitus apparently intended thereby to follow the example of the god whose oracle in Delphi, he said,[54] neither states anything nor conceals it but gives a sign. Such writing is difficult to interpret objectively but easy to quote for one's own purpose, particularly if one selects phrases that sound significant and quotes them without their context. Heraclitus was widely quoted in this fashion in antiquity; and a substantial number of these quotations is extant, in many cases different pieces of a single apophthegm quoted by different authors for different purposes and with different interpretations. Aristotle, fitting Heraclitus into his general scheme of Ionian philosophy, made of him a material monist who derived all the world from a single element but for this element chose fire instead of Thales' water, Anaximander's infinity, and Anaximenes' air. Nothing of this could have been guessed from the remarks of Plato to whom Heraclitus stood for the constant flux of all things and the everlasting accord of the discordant. The Stoics read into his book all their own doctrine including the endlessly recurring cycle of the articulation of the world from seminal fire and its destruction in conflagration; and the Christian writers turned him into a prophet of their own Last Judgment and the punishment by Hell-Fire. Still by weighing all these conflicting interpretations against one another and carefully comparing the many fragments of the apophthegms that are preserved it is possible to discern the intention and the main characteristics of Heraclitus' thought.

He believed[55] that he had discovered a truth which none of the teachers of men nor any of the mass of men had yet recognized although it manifests itself to everyone at every turn. Over and over again the extant fragments state the thesis that everything is itself and its opposite, all things are both one and many, because all things are in constant flux, a flux, however, that is not disorder but a harmony which, though hidden, far surpasses any sensible harmony. It is to signify this that he calls the world an

[54] *Frag. der Vorsok.*[5], 22 B 93.   [55] Cf. *Crit. Pres. Phil.*, pp. 380–2.

everlasting fire 'kindling according to measure and according to measure being extinguished'. Fire for him was neither a mere symbol of the universal process nor a substrate persisting as identical throughout its qualitative alterations. He speaks of it both as a token for exchange like gold in trade and as involved in change itself; and it was the easier for him in this case to identify the sign and the thing signified, since fire does appear to be the one existing phenomenon that is nothing but change. Even so the Buddhists used it, for whom there is no Being but only constantly shifting events in Becoming which is itself merely flux, flux of nothing.

Anaximenes had discovered that all the diverse entities in the world could be reduced to varying degrees of a single process, but he still retained the matter which changes and even clung to one phase of it as normal and so somehow more 'natural' than the others. Heraclitus simply followed his discovery to its logical conclusion, for it too implied that everything was one and many, one thing now and many things before or hereafter. It is then the process alone which really exists, and all the distinctions made by men are but fleeting phases of the process. If everything were smoke and all the other senses declared the single identity of all, the nose would still deny it and smell out differences; as it is, the senses assert that the world is a multitude of differences, whereas it is really one, the process that is fire.

Heraclitus is not to be understood, however, as simply continuing and extending Milesian philosophy. Even in developing the logical implications of Anaximenes' theory he radically altered its orientation; and despite any Milesian influence that can be discerned in the details of his pronouncements, the characteristics of his thought were entirely different from those of the Milesians and something entirely new. The difficulties that the doxographers found in extracting from his book a systematic natural history like that of the Milesians and the inconsistency of the accounts that they did produce are evidence that he had not intended to give what they insisted upon finding in his writings. We can still judge for ourselves the fashion in which his sporadic references to natural phenomena were used to construct for him a scientific doctrine. The doxographers state that he believed the apparent size of the sun to be its real size;[56] but fortunately the statement

[56] *Frag. der Vorsok.*[5], 22 A 1, § 7.

from which they elicited this notion of a reactionary astronomy is still preserved. Heraclitus had said: the sun you can cover with one human foot; but the boundaries of the soul you could not discover, though you trod every path, so profound is its measure.[57] This obviously was not meant to be astronomy at all; it has to do with the soul, not the sun, and goes to support the view of the ancient commentator Diodotus that the subject of Heraclitus' book was not natural science and that the references to natural phenomena in it had been introduced only by way of illustration.[58] Heraclitus was, in fact, not interested in 'historia' as such. He was willing to concede that one should investigate many things;[59] but he was scornful of erudition on the ground that it does not teach intelligence,[60] and with his usual picturesqueness of expression he first stated the limitations of the instruments of 'historia': the senses are bad witnesses to them whose souls cannot understand their reports.[61] It is not natural phenomena but the *meaning* of them that one must comprehend if one is to achieve wisdom; wisdom not information or learning is the goal of man, and Heraclitus condemned all those whose accounts he had ever heard because none of them had understood that wisdom is apart from everything else.[62] Yet the way of this comprehension is open to all men; he had achieved it by examining himself,[63] and it is possible for all men to know themselves and so to think soundly.[64]

The meaning behind phenomena that he had so discovered was not only that the whole world is a process and nothing else, a process that had no beginning and will never have an end,[65] but that all things are one[66] because the process has an ineluctable order, the order being a fixed proportion of change. This is the 'hidden harmony' that determines the phenomenal world which manifests and signifies it;[67] it is that which, being 'common', binds all the phases of the process together and renders the world intelligible to men if they will only open their eyes to it;[68] it is the

[57] *Frag. der Vorsok.*⁵, 22 B 3 and 45, and Fränkel, *AJP*, LIX (1938), 327.
[58] *Frag. der Vorsok.*⁵, 22 A 1, § 15.   [59] *Frag. der Vorsok.*⁵, 22 B 35.
[60] *Frag. der Vorsok.*⁵, 22 B 40.   [61] *Frag. der Vorsok.*⁵, 22 B 107.
[62] *Frag. der Vorsok.*⁵, 22 B 108.   [63] *Frag. der Vorsok.*⁵, 22 B 101.
[64] *Frag. der Vorsok.*⁵, 22 B 113 and 116.   [65] *Frag. der Vorsok.*⁵, 22 B 30.
[66] *Frag. der Vorsok.*⁵, 22 B 50.
[67] *Frag. der Vorsok.*⁵, 22 B 41 and 54; cf. 22 B 123.
[68] *Frag. der Vorsok.*⁵, 22 B 2; cf. 22 B 17 and 72.

divine law on which all human laws are nourished.[69] Heraclitus had, of course, no notion of positing a conceptual pattern apart from the world of phenomena; the latter for him *was* the pattern, and the very possibility of distinguishing them was not to be envisaged in the time of the Presocratics; but he for the first time in Western thought declared that reality is not the world that we perceive nor any part of it but a formula that is at once hidden and manifested by this perceptible process.

At least as significant for this first inclination of Greek thought in the direction of idealism is the revolutionary notion that the meaning of the world is to be discovered not by looking outward to phenomena but by probing one's own soul. In this case too Heraclitus did not distinguish two kinds of being. He did not separate the soul from the phenomenal world but thought of it as just another phase of the world process like the phases that are water and earth, in fact as fiery vapour which is a change from moisture and which changes into moisture again.[70] As fire, then, it is the purest or highest phase of the world-process, though even in this phase distinctions can be made and the soul that is dry is wisest and best.[71] The soul thus being part of the cosmic process and the best or clearest phase of it, it was no more than consistency for Heraclitus to call it also a profound formula or proportion that augments itself;[72] and one can understand how he may then have arrived at the notion that it should be possible to discover the meaning of the world by examining one's own soul, since it is the clearest phase of the ordered cosmic process. The soul, fire in this phase of the cosmic process, is supposed at the same time to be intelligent, of course;[73] and that should have raised the problem of the identity of subject and object and the puzzle of self-knowledge, but such questions did not occur to Heraclitus. What is important and new is, first, his assertion that introspection is a way of gaining knowledge about reality and, second, the ethical imperative that rings in all his words. Philosophy is no longer a matter of intellectual curiosity; it is a moral duty. It might seem that man, who is only a fleeting phase in the

[69] *Frag. der Vorsok.*⁵, 22 B 114.   [70] *Frag. der Vorsok.*⁵, 22 B 12 and 36.
[71] *Frag. der Vorsok.*⁵, 22 B 117 and 118; cf. *Crit. Pres. Phil.*, pp. 297–8, notes 29 and 31.
[72] *Frag. der Vorsok.*⁵, 22 B 115 and 45.
[73] *Frag. der Vorsok.*⁵, 22 B 118, cf. 41.

endless process of the world, need and can do nothing but resign himself to his lot; but Heraclitus insists, however inconsequently, that he can and should maintain his soul in a state of intelligence, understand the true nature of the world, and act in accordance with his knowledge.[74]

It has been suggested that the conception of geometrical proportion, which was so important to Heraclitus and the function of which in the cosmos he tried to indicate by expressing many of his apophthegms in that form, was in origin Pythagorean and was known to Heraclitus from that source.[75] Pythagoras is one of the persons attacked by name in the extant fragments of Heraclitus,[76] so that the latter knew or thought that he knew something about him and may very well, despite his antagonism, have adopted some notion of his or of his followers. Pythagoras himself wrote nothing; Plato knew him only as the institutor of a way of life;[77] and in the works of Aristotle he is scarcely mentioned and his name is never associated with any of the doctrines ascribed to his school.[78] A passage of Xenophanes[79] in which the doctrine of metempsychosis is ridiculed was supposed to refer to him, though his name is not mentioned there; and a fragment of Empedocles[80] celebrating an unnamed man who remembered ten or twenty of his incarnations was also taken in late antiquity to be a reference to Pythagoras. This theory of metempsychosis, which was to be adopted by Empedocles and later to be given a major role in European philosophy and poetry by Plato's integration of it into his philosophy, had been introduced into Greek thought before the time of Heraclitus, as the fragment of Xenophanes shows. If Heraclitus knew it as Pythagorean, it might well have been the source of his antagonism, for such a theory asserts the persistence of the individual soul and absolves it from participation in the process of cosmic change.

In one fragment Heraclitus calls Pythagoras 'the ancestor of swindlers';[81] in another[82] he brackets him with Hesiod and with Xenophanes and Hecataeus, condemning them all for lack of

[74] *Frag. der Vorsok.*[5], 22 B 2, 43, 44 (cf. 114), 73, 74, 112.
[75] Cf. Minar, *Class. Phil.* XXXIV (1939), pp. 337–40; Fränkel, *AJP*, LIX (1938), 321.
[76] *Frag. der Vorsok.*[5], 22 B 40, 81, and the doubtfully authentic 129.
[77] *Republic* 600 A.   [78] Cf. *Crit. Pres. Phil.*, p. 385.
[79] *Frag. der Vorsok.*[5], 21 B 7.   [80] *Frag. der Vorsok.*[5], 31 B 129.
[81] *Frag. der Vorsok.*[5], 22 B 81.   [82] *Frag. der Vorsok.*[5], 22 B 40.

intelligence despite their erudition. Hesiod's theogony, his differentiation of all the gods and cosmic powers and his failure to understand that all these are only different phases and aspects of one ordered process without beginning or end, was certainly what aroused the wrath of Heraclitus,[83] who was probably incensed against Hecataeus too more by his genealogies and their connections with gods and heroes than by the geographical and historical parts of his work. Xenophanes, a poet and rhapsode, who has become a figure in the history of Greek philosophy by mistake, could have been singled out for censure from among all other poets of his kind for only one reason. His historical poems could not have been unique, his references to natural phenomena were sporadic and made only for the sake of denying both the mythological and the subtly scientific explanations of them; he ridiculed metempsychosis and abominated the mythology of Homer and Hesiod as heartily as Heraclitus did, and like Heraclitus he waged incessant war upon the traditional theology and ritual of Greek polytheism. He maintained that God is one and not anthropomorphic in any sense,[84] a belief that so far might have made him not uncongenial to Heraclitus; but he also insisted that God never moves or changes,[85] and such a notion Heraclitus was bound to denounce with the utmost vehemence.

The theology of Xenophanes and the doctrine of metempsychosis arose outside of the main current of Greek philosophy. Both, greeted with scorn at first, were soon to exercise upon it intense though sporadic and tangential influence until finally they merged in the philosophy of Plato. The relations of early Pythagoreanism are even more nebulous, for there were no Pythagorean writings earlier than the time of Socrates and the later ascriptions of theories to the early school and to Pythagoras himself are quite untrustworthy. Unlike all other Presocratic thinkers the Pythagoreans formed communities whose ultimate purpose was moral self-improvement, and so a good deal of their concern was with the practice of a sort of mental and physical hygiene in which the discipline of silence and self-examination, taboos of various kinds, music, and mathematical studies were all ingredients. In their cosmological physics they seem to have adopted and accommodated to their own use the theories of the

[83] *Frag. der Vorsok.*[5], 22 B 57.   [84] *Frag. der Vorsok.*[5], 21 B 23.
[85] *Frag. der Vorsok.*[5], 21 B 26.

Milesians;[86] but the distinctive characteristic of their whole doctrine was the tenet that all things are numbers. Numbers they held to be groups of units, the units being material points between which there is 'breath' or a material 'void'; and they quite literally identified all phenomenal objects with such aggregations of points, without, of course, considering whether these material points were themselves divisible or not.[87] This was rather a materialization of number than a mathematization of nature, but it undoubtedly seemed to the Pythagoreans to be the only way of explaining the physical world in terms of those genuinely mathematical propositions which they had proved to be independently valid and which they therefore took to be the nature of the only reality that they could imagine, the reality of the physical world. The influence in many directions of this first crude step of mathematical physics was later to be enormous, as was the Pythagorean application of mathematical conceptions to astronomy. In a sense it was the first attempt to apply the results of purely deductive reason to natural philosophy, but it was too crude and too unconscious of itself to be fruitful at once; and so it was not from Pythagoreanism directly that the impetus which this method gave to Greek thought came.

According to one ancient tradition[88] Parmenides had been strongly influenced by a member of the Pythagorean sect. As his home was Elea in Magna Graecia, it is not unlikely that he was acquainted with the Pythagoreans; and the example of mathematical proof learned from them may have determined the rigorously deductive form of his argument and may have been the origin of his confidence in this method. Beyond any reasonable doubt, however, despite the recent fashion to deny it,[89] it was the book of Heraclitus that aroused Parmenides to protest and to formulate the argument which at first must have seemed to be a final check to all natural philosophy. It is clear enough that he

---

[86] Cf. *Crit. Pres. Phil.*, p. 398.   [87] Cf. *Crit. Pres. Phil.*, pp. 386–92.
[88] D.L., ix. 21; cf. Burnet, *EGP*³, p. 170.
[89] Cf. for example Gigon, *Der Ursprung der griechischen Philosophie*, p. 245, and Jaeger, *Theology of the Early Greek Philosophers*, pp. 101, 123, and especially 129. They do not follow Reinhardt and Abel Rey in placing Parmenides *before* Heraclitus but treat them as if they were entirely ignorant of each other. It is certain that Heraclitus, who attacked so many people by name, did not know Parmenides, for, if he had, he would certainly have attacked him first of all.

intended his criticism to apply not to Heraclitus *alone* but to *all* accounts of the world of change, those formulated by natural philosophers and those implicitly adopted by laymen alike. He says as much,[90] but his most virulently scornful description of the error that pervades all such accounts reproduces the peculiar and characteristic expressions of Heraclitus.[91] This is reasonable, for Heraclitus had made explicit what was implicit in all the theories of a changing world and had developed to the extreme of their logical consequences and as a positive doctrine the unformulated assumptions of naïve common sense upon which all the natural philosophers had hitherto unconsciously built. Parmenides saw this, that the opinions of all men were unconscious and unsystematic Heracliteanism and that in refuting Heraclitus he was refuting them all; that is why he employed the significant phrases of Heraclitus to characterize the opinions of men in general. Even the form into which Parmenides put his book bespeaks its origin as a protest inspired by the haughty words of Heraclitus. Parmenides was the first Greek philosopher, and apart from Empedocles who imitated him in this the only one, to express himself in poetry, poetry far different in tone from the *silloi* of Xenophanes, the epics of Homer, and the didactic poems of Hesiod and not to be understood as mere imitation of any of them. It is at least possible that he intended his hexameters themselves to be a reply and a reproach to Heraclitus' oracular and apophthegmatic style and that by using the most solemn and noble form of expression in the Greek tradition he meant to emphasize the seriousness and supreme objectivity of his own argument in contrast to the cryptic symbolism and sibylline tempestuousness of Heraclitus.[92] However it may be with the poetical expression, the proëm of Parmenides' book was certainly meant to contrast to the intuitional subjectivism of Heraclitus the universal objectivity that he claims for his own argument. This whole argument is the speech of an unnamed goddess whom he reaches by travelling on a road apart from the path of men[93] through the gates of day and night,[94]

---

[90] *Frag. der Vorsok.*[5], 28 B 1. 30; 28 B 8. 51–2, 55, and 61; 28 B 19. 3.
[91] *Frag. der Vorsok.*[5], 28 B 6 with Kranz's notes; cf. references in *Crit. Pres. Phil.*, p. 383.
[92] Cf. *Frag. der Vorsok.*[5], 22 B 93 and 92.
[93] *Frag. der Vorsok.*[5], 28 B 1. 27.
[94] *Frag. der Vorsok.*[5], 28 B 1. 11–14.

which Justice, the ineluctable Law of Being,[95] opens for him; and this goddess warns him to beware of the senses and to judge by *logos* alone.[96] Heraclitus too had bidden men distrust the senses and heed the *logos*; but this *logos* all were to find by introspection as he had, because it is common to all.[97] Parmenides, however, in effect denied that introspection is any more trustworthy than sensation, for the insight of men can be erroneous too;[98] for his own argument he claimed exemption from the possibility of human error by representing it to be the revelation of a goddess who is nameless and who dwells beyond the Law of Being. The *logos* that Heraclitus bade men heed declared all things to be one[99] because it was the formula of the incessant change of which they are part and which they would therefore discover within themselves; but the *logos* by which Parmenides is bidden to judge is independent of men and of the world—it is pure reason which is the sovereign canon of Being itself.

Everyone had assumed that something exists. The whole argument of Parmenides proceeds by applying the law of the excluded middle to prove that the identity of what *is* precludes the possibility of any characteristic except just *being*. This, he maintained, invalidates all the theories which, disregarding the fact that a thing is what it is, proceeded to talk about change as if not every object of thought and so every existing thing had either to be or not to be; here lies the decision, but to put the case is to answer it, for to think of anything is to think of it as being. The essential nature of Being, the inner necessity that a thing is identical with itself, holds it fast in bondage and allows it neither to come to be nor to pass away. The impossibility of any and all process is established by the logical consequences of identity.[100] As for all false notions of a world of difference and of change, the goddess lays bare the fundamental error that underlies them by showing that a whole plausible cosmology is derivable from the minimal error of positing two things that need not be identified.[101] This men do, in Heraclitean

[95] Cf. *Ibid.*, 28 B 1. 14 ff. and 28 B 8. 13–15 and 30–1.   [96] *Ibid.*, 28 B 7.
[97] *Frag. der Vorsok.*[5], 22 B 107. 50, 101, 2, and 72.
[98] *Frag. der Vorsok.*[5], 28 B 6. 5–6.   [99] *Frag. der Vorsok.*[5], 22 B 50.
[100] Cf. *Crit. Pres. Phil.*, pp. 383–4.
[101] *Frag. der Vorsok.*[5], 28 B 8. 51–4. For the correct interpretation of these lines cf. Jeanne Croissant, *Mélanges Desrousseaux*, pp. 99–104. Mlle Croissant does not mention Plato, *Sophist* 243 D–244 B, which proves her interpretation to be correct, if further proof were needed.

21

fashion believing that to be and not to be are the same thing and not the same;[102] and so the articulate world is simply the consequence of an erroneous human convention. Heraclitus had declared that the *logos* shows that all things are one; in a radical sense that he could not have contemplated the *logos* of Parmenides, not intuition but strict deductive logic, did conclude that, since nothing but Being can be, Being is all that is, an increate, imperishable, immobile, indivisible, homogeneous, and continuous unit that neither was nor will be but simply *is*.[103]

Once the argument of Parmenides had been stated, it was no longer possible to make the tacit assumptions and to leave undefined the indefinite conceptions with which all earlier philosophy had operated. The possibility of motion and multiplicity, the very possibility of the physical world had been impugned; and natural philosophy was forced to face the logical, epistemological, and metaphysical problems of identity and difference, of appearance and reality, of truth and error. The Parmenidean logic had rudely checked the course of Greek thought, but the check was also a mighty stimulus; and, working alternately as stimulus and corrective check, it determined the subsequent course of Presocratic philosophy which was in the main a series of attempts to save the world of nature without transgressing the rules of the new logic.

The most significant and fruitful of these attempts were the systems of Empedocles, Anaxagoras, and the Atomists. Empedocles[104] posited the existence of four physical bodies: earth, water, and fire (the three phases of Heraclitus' process) and air (for he had discovered that atmospheric air is a material body); and these four bodies, each with its own characteristics, were stated to be each identical with itself throughout, homogeneous, for ever unchanged, each equal to each, four physical copies, in fact, of Parmenidean Being. The mingling and rearranging of these bodies was to account for all the varied complexes of the articulate world without impairment of the identity of any real entity or infection of it with change; but, the bodies themselves being immobile in accordance with Parmenidean law, Empedocles raised to cosmic significance as two other entities the forces of Love and Strife, evidence for which he saw throughout the living

102 *Frag. der Vorsok.*5, 28 B 6. 8–9.   103 *Frag. der Vorsok.*5, 28 B 8. 3–49.
104 Cf. *Crit. Pres. Phil.*, pp. 398–9.

world, and supposed that their pervasion of the four bodies mingles them together and dissolves the mixture. Two forces were posited and not one because the Parmenidean law of identity seemed to require that the cause of mingling or of dissolution should not in either case have the contrary character as well. According to this scheme all that really exists is six entities, each conforming explicitly to the requirements of Parmenides' logic, and all together constituting the whole of existence, for there is nothing empty of them;[105] their mere mechanical rearrangement, proceeding from a thoroughly homogeneous mixture of the four bodies pervaded entirely by Love to their complete segregation when they are pervaded entirely by Strife and back again in an endless cycle, produces in each hemicycle all the possible complexes of an articulate world. Generation and destruction are expressly declared to be impossible, merely conventions of human language;[106] and all the multitudinous differences in the world are simply the external appearances of the various combinations of the identical roots.[107]

The gaping lacuna in Empedocles' construction was its neglect of the problem of the part and the whole; this is most obvious and painful in the 'thorough mixture' of the four bodies, for in this state it is apparent that these bodies must have minimal parts, but it also vitiates the construction at every step. Zeno, the follower of Parmenides, attacked Empedocles; and there are indications that in his attack he put his finger upon this sore point.[108] He had already counter-attacked the Pythagoreans who had sought to show that Parmenides' thesis in leading to a denial of multiplicity is self-contradictory; using against them their own dialectical method and proceeding from their own hypothesis of material points, Zeno had proved that the assumption of multiplicity entails contradictions more absurd than does the Parmenidean thesis, for one had either to make his multiple parts atomic or to assert the infinite divisibility of matter and the results of either choice are insoluble paradoxes,[109] the ghosts of which still arise periodically to haunt the conception of continuity in all its aspects.

It was objection to Empedocles' explicit assumption that the

[105] *Frag. der Vorsok.*[5], 31 B 14. [106] *Frag. der Vorsok.*[5], 31 B 8 and 11.
[107] *Frag. der Vorsok.*[5], 31 B 23. [108] Cf. *Crit. Pres. Phil.*, p. 95, n. 401.
[109] Cf. *Crit. Pres. Phil.*, p. 398.

Parmenidean law of identity need be asserted of only a limited number of bodies that produced the next important attempt, however, to reconcile natural philosophy with Eleatic logic. Anaxagoras,[110] who had been brought up in the Ionian tradition and in whom the older philosophy and the new logic of the West were first combined, objected that all so-called 'mixtures', even such things as hair and flesh, have characteristics of their own as unique as those of earth, water, air, or fire and so are in the same sense entities which must be eternally identical. Eleatic logic requires, he argued, that no new characteristic whatever be derived from any other; and therefore apparent change implies that everything be a mixture of everything else just as everything existed in the precosmical mixture of Anaximander. It was, in fact, this *apeiron* of Anaximander's that Anaxagoras adopted and sought to 'modernize' in accordance with the new logic. He consciously chose one horn of Zeno's dilemma and declared that matter is infinitely divisible, that there is no least part of *anything*, and that therefore everything must contain some of everything else. The motion of the *apeiron* could no longer simply be assumed as it had been tacitly assumed by Anaximander, although the complete mixture had to be set in motion if it was to be articulated. It had, however, to be moved by something other than itself and something which itself obeys the law of identity. On the other hand, since the process of separation on this theory need not be reversible, Anaxagoras felt it necessary to posit only one kind of motive entity instead of Empedocles' two; and the name that he gave to this entity was the source of his greatest influence upon later philosophy. Empedocles had derived his Love and Strife from the impulses that he saw manifested by all living creatures; Anaxagoras ascribed the origin of motion to *nous*, 'Mind',[111] and therewith introduced into Greek philosophy the potent notion that the natural world is somehow the result of reason, that reason is not a part of nature nor a product of it but different in kind from it and sovereign over it.

Anaxagoras like Empedocles reduced all change to local translation, which, since no void was admitted, was simply rearrangement; and, because the unit in the rearrangement retained its identity, this kind of change seemed to them not to transgress the logic of Parmenides. This Melissus of Samos, the last great

110 Cf. *Crit. Pres. Phil.*, pp. 400–1.   111 *Frag. der Vorsok.*,⁵ 59 B 12, 13, 14.

Eleatic critic, proved to be erroneous.[112] He impugned the mechanism of both systems by arguing that, if there is no void, there cannot be motion of any kind; but he went beyond this to prove that both systems restricted illegitimately the law of identity which they professed to respect. If the world exists, its very arrangement, he argued, can change no more than can any of the ingredients of that arrangement. Moreover, process of any kind implies a moment of initiation both temporal and spatial, and that moment involves the appearance of characteristics, at least of arrangement, that did not before exist. This being impossible, there can be no differentiation of any kind, from which it follows that what exists must be completely homogeneous and unlimited in extension. The very differentiation of material in the systems of Empedocles and Anaxagoras, therefore, is incompatible with the Parmenidean laws. That differentiation itself implies separation, and separation involves motion; but, motion being impossible, the one means of differentiation which had seemed to remain for those who accepted Parmenides' logic is shown to be inconsistent with it. Finally Melissus pointed out that, since even Empedocles and Anaxagoras had to deny the validity of the evidence of the senses in order to maintain the truth of their theories, the evidence of the senses cannot be adduced against the strict Eleatic position either, for it is in fact admitted by those who would maintain an articulate world of change that the logical laws are stronger than the evidence of sensation. It follows, then, from the very arguments of Empedocles and Anaxagoras that, if one were to assume a multiplicity of entities, each entity would still have to be what Melissus had declared the one Being to be.

Leucippus and his followers accepted this implied challenge.[113] Since there could be no motion without a void, they asserted the existence of a void, a physical non-being;[114] and, in as much as Melissus had shown that a commencement of motion contradicts the law of identity, they abandoned such forces as Anaxagoras' *nous* and, making explicit the old, naïve Ionic assumption, declared that constant motion is an unvarying characteristic of all matter. Melissus' proof of the necessary homogeneity of all matter they accepted; and, since the sensations could no longer be defended as true witnesses anyway, they denied that the characteristics

[112] Cf. *Crit. Pres. Phil.*, pp. 402–3.   [113] Cf. *Crit. Pres. Phil.*, pp. 403–4.
[114] Cf. *Frag. der Vorsok.*⁵, 68 B 156.

apparent in complex bodies had any existence at all. Anaxagoras, by asserting the infinite divisibility of matter, had laid himself open to Melissus' argument that he had no reason to assume difference save for the arbitrary division which involved an initiation of motion; the Atomists therefore accepted the other horn of the dilemma and assumed that the particles of matter are indivisible and unchangeable, differing from one another only in size and shape and, except for their motion, having no other characteristics at all. Since a consistent belief in the reality of characteristics had required Anaxagoras to assert that everything is in everything and Melissus had shown that this amounts to a denial of difference between the whole and the parts, these characteristics were useless encumbrances in a physical construction, and Leucippus simply denied their existence and explained the apparent differences of complex bodies as illusory epiphenomena of the real difference of the number, size, shape, arrangement, and position of atoms moving in the void.

The Atomic system was the last great construction of Presocratic philosophy. In a sense it can be envisaged as the first such construction, Anaximander's, purged of its indefiniteness and refined by the logic of Parmenides, the subsequent attempts to overcome the critique of Parmenides, and the rebuttal of those attempts by the Eleatic critics, Zeno and Melissus. For all its clarity and simplicity and elegance, however, Atomism had very little effect upon the philosophy to follow, for the later attempt of Strato to combine it with Aristotelianism was abortive and Epicurus' adoption of it reduced it to a utilitarian argument in support of his ethics. Its lack of influence may have been due in part to its rejection of the notion of law and meaning in the world of nature, in part to the fact that it was an arbitrary construction unsupported by evidence and containing within itself no possible sign of its own validity. What reason could it adduce for the assumptions on the basis of which it denied the conclusions of Parmenides? Not the evidence of the senses, for the senses, which give no indication that there are atoms and void, the Atomists denounced as untrustworthy witnesses. Democritus had to assume that there is a genuine knowledge of the mind that discerns the truth to which the bastard knowledge of the senses cannot penetrate.[115] Yet he must have felt uneasily that there is in

[115] *Frag. der Vorsok.*[5], 68 B 11.

the Atomic system no justification for such a distinction and no foundation for the intelligence which he had to assume; and he has left a fine ironical expression of that feeling, a snippet of a dialogue in which the senses, whose reports have been rejected as mere conventions by the mind that asserts the real existence of atoms and void, reply: 'Wretched Mind, who get your evidence from us and then try to overthrow us, our overthrow is your destruction.'[116]

Such a peripeteia in the drama of Greek thought had already occurred. Zeno and Melissus seemed to have shown not only that any possible natural philosophy but also all discursive thought on any subject could be proved self-contradictory by the use of Eleatic logic. The serious hope of accounting for the world on some cosmological principle consistently developed had been extinguished; and such sporadic attempts as were still made in this direction were like the last meaningless twitchings of a broken habit, unco-ordinated repetitions of a pattern of past meaning. Hippo of Samos and Diogenes of Apollonia, who sought to derive the articulate world, the one from water, the other from air, are our chief witnesses to the fact that there were still men who could talk as if Parmenides had never lived, witnesses also to the fact that men who are in the forefront of some specialized field of knowledge may in all others be uncritical traditionalists and inconsistent eclectics, for such were both of these men in philosophy, though both had done important and original work in biology and physiology. Others devoted themselves to some speciality such as mathematics or medicine and simply disregarded the fundamental difficulty with which science as a whole had been confronted; but the attitude of those who at this time claimed the ability and assumed the title of educating all the Hellenes was determined by that difficulty. The threat to reason that Democritus had so ironically made the senses deliver was carried out by Protagoras, against whose dictum that nothing is any more *so* than *so* he was himself constrained to argue at length.[117] Protagoras wrote a book attacking the Eleatic dogma of the unity of Being,[118] not with the purpose, however, of defending the possibility of an objectively true account of the physical world but in order to show that Eleatic logic can overthrow the Eleatic conclusions as well as the evidence of the senses, that there is con-

[116] *Frag. der Vorsok.*[5], 68 B 125.   [117] *Frag. der Vorsok.*[5], 68 B 156.
[118] *Frag. der Vorsok.*[5], 80 B 2.

sequently no objective canon, and that therefore what appears to be to anyone at any time has just as much and just as little valid claim to be *so* as what appears at any other time to him, when he is different, or to any other person. Parmenides had enthroned objective truth so far above men that it seemed to be inaccessible, useless, and a mere mocking negation of man and of his world. Protagoras expressly bade men desist from chasing such futile phantoms and reassured them that whatever appears to anyone to be true is true when it so appears, though one thing may be more useful than another: man himself, he declared, is the measure of all things.[119]

The pendant to the relativism of Protagoras was the nihilism of Gorgias, who seized upon the Eleatic method to prove that nothing whatever exists, that it is incomprehensible if it does exist, and incommunicable even if comprehensible.[120] So Eleatic Being, having engulfed the world, appeared to have swallowed itself; and Eleatic logic, having put an end to natural philosophy, seemed to have put an end to itself also. Something, however, was left. To Gorgias and Protagoras and their lesser fellows Eleatic logic, especially as it had been employed by Zeno, seemed to be an instrument for proving and disproving any proposition whatever, an instrument as if made to order for their purpose, which was the instruction of pupils in the art of argument as such. So much of positive influence the work of the Eleatics had upon the so-called Sophists, who, just because of their unconcern for any content, studied and developed and refined the purely formal aspect of Eleatic method and in so doing prepared the instrument of Socratic dialectic. This was the instrument, as the example of the living and dying Socrates was the inspiration, of Plato's genius, whereby the curse of Eleatic formalism was lifted from philosophy and the revelation of Parmenides was read aright; in the light of that revelation a cosmos was restored to man in which the *mind* of Anaxagoras, the endless process of Heraclitus, the wandering souls, which Empedocles could not deny and could yet not naturalize in his cyclical mechanism, all found their proper places. In the *Timaeus* Presocratic philosophy had its resurrection and transfiguration, the parts that were meaningless made meaningful in a whole that is far more than their mere summation.

[119] *Frag. der Vorsok.*[5], 80 B 1.   [120] *Frag. der Vorsok.*[5], 82 B 3.

II

WAS THE IONIAN PHILOSOPHY
SCIENTIFIC?

F. M. Cornford

[This paper was prepared by the late Professor F. M. Cornford
for the Joint Meeting of the Hellenic and Roman Societies held at
Oxford in the summer of 1942. It was read there in his absence
by Professor Gilbert Murray. To a suggestion that the paper should
be published in the *Journal of Hellenic Studies*, Professor Cornford
replied: 'The paper is a very short (and not very convincing)
summary of an argument which I am writing out at length in a
book which I hope to publish when times are easier*. I hoped to
get some criticism and discussion, but not being well enough
to attend, I did not gain much that way. Space in the *Journal* is
too valuable to justify this sort of advanced patrol work being
published as if it were a final statement with all the relevant
evidence.' After his lamented death, permission was obtained
from Mrs Cornford and from Mr W. K. C. Guthrie, his literary
executor, to publish the paper in the *Journal* with an explanation
of its origin and intention.]

This paper is concerned with a problem which has puzzled me for
many years. The Greek philosophers of the Ionian tradition, from
Anaximander to Epicurus, are commonly called specially
'scientific', in contrast with the Italian tradition started by
Pythagoras. Why is it, then, that their systems are cast in the form
of dogmatic pronouncements? It is not only that they describe,
with complete confidence, matters beyond the reach of observation, such as the origin of the world; but when they come to
matters of detail, they make assertions which could have been
upset by a little careful observation or by the simplest experiment.

* Published posthumously with the title *Principium Sapientiae* (Cambridge
University Press, 1952).

It has been argued—by Burnet, for instance—that this dogmatism may be only apparent. Our evidence is fragmentary, and comes largely from manuals compiled much later by men whose object was to discredit science for reaching contradictory conclusions, and by no means to record the methods employed to reach those conclusions. W. A. Heidel, too, thought that, if we possessed the philosophers' notebook, we should find that their results were obtained by methods akin to those of modern science, though with less awareness of the need for caution in experimental tests. Behind these arguments lies the assumption that the questions they asked themselves, the motives prompting their inquiries, and the quarter to which they looked for the sources of knowledge, were the same then as now. This assumption is naturally made by most historians of science. Looking back at the past from our own standpoint, they are interested in those features of ancient thought—atomism, for example—which have proved fruitful in modern developments. The archaic features are ignored or dismissed as pardonable errors in the infancy of science. But if our aim is to regain the standpoint of ancient speculation, we cannot afford to discard all elements foreign to our own ways of thinking; any more than the historian of religion can afford to dismiss as 'superstitious fancies' beliefs and practices which the civilized world has outgrown. Rather we should fix attention on these strange features and try to recover the attitude of mind that will account for them.

We are asked to believe that these Ionian systems were based on observation; that hypotheses were then framed by rational inference from observed facts; and that, sometimes at least, these hypotheses were checked by experiment, though with insufficient caution. Let us recall a few of the philosophers' statements and consider whether they could have been founded on such methods.

(1) Anaximander coolly asserted that the distance of the sun from the earth is precisely three times that of the fixed stars, and that the stars' distance is nine times the diameter of the earth. The earth itself is a cylindrical drum, three times as broad as it is high.

(2) A main feature of Anaximenes' system was his reduction of differences of temperature to differences of density: the hotter, the thinner; the colder, the denser. Water is the only substance which can easily be seen passing into vapour when heated and becoming solid when cooled. When water turns to steam, it expands; when

chilled into ice, it ought to contract into a smaller volume. But does it contract? If Anaximenes had put a jar of water outside his door on a frosty night, he might have observed that the water did not shrink when it turned into ice, but, on the contrary, split the jar. We may conclude that he never had recourse to this simple experiment. Nor is there any record of anyone testing his dogma in this obvious way.

(3) Empedocles explained respiration as a process whereby the warm air breathed out through the mouth is automatically replaced inside us by cold air drawn in through pores in the chest. Then the movement is reversed: the air inside, now heated, escapes through the same pores whereby it entered, and is replaced by cold air inhaled through the mouth. Plato adopts this theory. No one ever thought of sitting in a bath with the water up to his neck, to find out whether air bubbles could be observed passing through the water into his chest when he exhaled, and out again when he inhaled; and if not, whether his breathing was impeded.

Such tests would instantly suggest themselves today, not merely to a man of science but to any sensible person. Why did they not occur to the ancient philosophers, even when they were contradicting one another's theories?

They were, moreover, equally dogmatic on questions beyond the reach of observation, let alone experiment. They announced, with the same assurance, that the ultimate constituents of material things were water, or air, or the four elements, or atoms; and they described the process whereby an ordered world had arisen out of these elements. None of them had witnessed the process, or had the faintest conception of any method for isolating an element. Yet they narrate the history of the world from such beginnings as if it had happened before their eyes. Plato, whom our modern materialists despise as hopelessly unscientific, was the one philosopher who told the truth about ancient physics, when he said that it could be no more than a 'plausible tale'. That is exactly what all these Ionian systems were—an εἰκὼς μῦθος.

I suggest that the key to our problem lies in a difference of attitude towards the question of the *sources of knowledge* or wisdom. And here some light comes to us from the protest against the methods of philosophy, raised by doctors of the Hippocratic school. In an admirable survey of Hippocratic medicine, Heidel has pointed out that, in the medical art, a procedure was evolved which does go some way towards the methods of modern science. Doctors began to keep careful records of symptoms in individual cases; and from these they advanced to generalizations, and even to the rudiments of experimental procedure. Nearly all the experiments recorded in ancient literature were made by doctors.

Heidel, however, drew no distinction between the methods of medical science and those of philosophy. Hence he assumed, like Burnet, that the philosophers applied to their problems the inchoate scientific procedure of the doctors, and reached many of their conclusions by observation and experiment of which no record remains. Here, I believe, he was mistaken. There was, from the nature of the case, a radical distinction, and even opposition, between medicine and philosophy, in the way they approached such problems as they had in common.

Medicine was, from the outset, a practical art; indeed, it was the only practical art which, in ancient times, was impelled by its own needs to develop a scientific method. The doctor is a healer (ἰατρός), a craftsman in the public service (δημιουργός), a handworker (χειρουργός) in surgery. He is always dealing with an individual patient, and always with a practical purpose—to cure that patient. Hence (unlike the philosopher, speculating about the origin of the world) he starts by noting the symptoms of a particular case, to find out what is wrong, and needs to be put right. The application of a remedy is based on a generalization from accumulated experience—'This remedy has proved helpful in cases of this sort'—and it is experimental: 'Will it work in this case?' The doctor will be led on to speculate about the fundamental causes of disease and health. So at last he will arrive at the question of man's nature or bodily constitution—the elements and active or passive properties whose equilibrium needs to be restored by suitable treatment from outside.

Contrast with this procedure the route by which the philosopher approaches the nature of man. He starts with cosmogony. The questions implied (though they are answered rather than explicitly stated) are of this sort: What was the original state of things? What are the simplest constituents of all compound bodies? How can we give a natural explanation of 'what goes on in the sky and under the earth'? How did life begin? From such speculations about the remotest origins of the world the philosopher arrived

at accounts of the origin of plant, animal, and human life—
accounts predetermined by doctrines already laid down as to the
nature of the world as a whole. So, at the end, he came to the
point where his theories impinged on the domain of medicine.
The human body could only be composed of the same elements as
all other bodies—water, or air, or the four elements, or atoms. The
philosopher's 'physiological' theories (as we call them) were thus
dictated by their cosmological dogmas; and they were ready to
foist on the practical physician *a priori* accounts of the nature of
health and disease.

The characteristic reaction of the scientific doctor is vigorously
expressed in the treatise on *Ancient Medicine*. The author (who
may be Hippocrates himself) attacks all writers on medicine
who start from a groundless postulate or assumption, such as that
all diseases are caused by 'heat or cold or moisture or whatever
else they may fancy'. Such postulates, he says, may be inevitable in
dealing with 'problems beyond the reach of observation' (τὰ
ἀφανέα τε καὶ ἀπορεόμενα), such as 'what goes on in the sky or
under the earth'. There is no means of testing the truth of assertions made in this field. But medicine has long had a different
principle and method of its own, securely based on discovered
facts, which must be taken as the starting-point for further discovery. Philosophers like Empedocles have written about the
nature of things, how man came into being at the first, and of
what elements he was constructed. All this has no more to do with
medicine than with painting. Man's nature can be ascertained only
by discovering his reactions to food and drink and the effect of
habits in general on each individual. These effects will differ from
one individual to another. We must start with the observation of
particular cases.

The contrast could not be more clearly expressed. The philosopher descends from above to deduce the nature of man from
unproved postulates; the physician builds up his doctrine from
below, generalizing from particular observed facts.

My next point is that these two opposite approaches—the *a
priori* approach of the philosopher and the empirical approach of
the physician—are reflected in two opposite accounts of the
sources of knowledge or wisdom.

The empirical account is set forth (in *Met.* A 1) by Aristotle,
himself the son of a practising physician. It starts with the *senses*.

In the higher animals sensation gives rise to *memory*. In man repeated memories of the same thing result in a unified *experience*: 'This remedy benefited Callias in this disease, and also Socrates, and so on in many cases.' We then advance to the *generalization*: 'This remedy is good for all phlegmatic temperaments in burning fever.' Such generalizations constitute *Art*. For practical purposes experience may be sufficient, because the physician is curing not 'man' in general, but some individual who 'happens to be a man'. On the other hand, we associate knowledge or wisdom rather with art than with mere experience, which knows only the fact, not the reason. *Knowledge* in the full sense comes last, with the understanding of causes.

It is not for nothing that Aristotle's illustrations are all taken from the art of medicine. This empirical theory of knowledge had already been mentioned by Plato as having interested Socrates in his young days. Its author, in fact, was none other than the physician Alcmaeon of the early fifth century, who taught that man is distinguished from the animals by possessing understanding as well as sensation; that our sense-perceptions are centred in the brain; and that from them arise *memory, judgement* (or belief), and finally *knowledge*. Alcmaeon even tried, by dissection, to trace the 'pores' leading from the sense organs to the brain.

Here, then, in the practical art of medicine, we find the root of empirical epistemology—the idea that the senses are the ultimate source of knowledge, of that understanding which distinguishes man from the animals. There is no earlier trace of this view of knowledge. It was formulated when the doctors, under the influence of Ionian rationalism, were freeing their art from its magical phase and reflecting upon the procedure they actually followed in the successful advance of discovery.

If this view is correct, the first steps towards inductive science, as understood since the Renaissance, were taken by the physicians, in opposition to the philosophers. The medical art, morever, was the only art known in antiquity that was impelled to formulate a method based on observation and rudimentary experiment. It thus became the only 'natural science' (in our sense) that existed before Aristotle. When Aristotle set his three pupils, Theophrastus, Eudemus, and Meno, to write the history of earlier thought, he divided the field into (1) Metaphysics and Natural

34

philosophy, (2) Mathematics, and (3) Medicine. He felt, it would seem, the force of the Hippocratic contention that Medicine stood alone, with a starting-point and procedure of its own, opposed to those of the philosophers.

The alternative theory of the sources of knowledge was formulated by Plato; though I shall argue that it was by much the older of the two, and had all along been unconsciously assumed by the philosophers. It will account for their dogmatism.

It rests upon a very different conception of the nature and contents of *memory*. The empirical view we have just considered is materialistic. It starts from the tangible bodies outside us, which send off images to invade our senses and stamp impressions on the waxen tablet. At birth the tablet is blank. The impressions accumulate, like a vast unsorted heap of postage stamps. These are the sole contents of memory. Having got so far, the materialist has reluctantly to admit something suspiciously like a mind, with an entirely inexplicable power of sorting out the stamps and assigning them to their respective countries in an album. The album will symbolize knowledge; and the materialist will then try to forget all about the activity of the stamp-collector.

The memory implied in Plato's theory of *Anamnesis* is stored in a very different way. The senses have nothing to teach us: they are classed with the lusts of the flesh as a positive hindrance. Perfect knowledge can be enjoyed only by a disembodied spirit with no sense-organs at all. In this life knowledge is recovered from a memory which is not a record, inscribed since the moment of birth, of those personal experiences which are, of course, different for every individual. It is an *impersonal* memory, the same for all men. Its contents embrace the whole intelligible realm of eternal objects and truths, including all pure mathematics—the whole of knowledge worthy of the name. If this knowledge was ever acquired, it was acquired before the soul first entered a mortal body; but it is more likely that it is eternally possessed by the immortal soul. In this life it is latent; but no limit can be set to the amount that can be recovered by recollection, when the soul withdraws from the body and its senses to think by itself. The process of recovery is illustrated in the *Meno*, where the solution of a not very simple geometrical problem is elicited by questioning from a slave who has never been taught geometry. The doctrine, supported by fresh arguments in the *Phaedo*, forms the one substantial proof of pre-existence accepted by all parties in the first part of that dialogue.

It is instructive to attend to the more or less mythical associations and images surrounding *Anamnesis* in the *Phaedrus*. There the immortal soul is defined by its essential power of self-motion —the power of Eros. The three main forms of desire—the love of pleasure, the love of honour, and the love of wisdom (φιλοσοφία)— are typified by the winged chariot, drawn by the two horses of appetite and passion, and guided by the Intelligence, which alone is capable of seeing truth. The soul-chariots follow the gods in the procession compared to the procession of the already purified initiates to the final revelation at Eleusis. In the divine company, the soul, before incarnation, journeys outside the sphere of the visible heavens to the Plain of Truth, to learn there all the truth it can ever know. After its descent into a mortal body, some part of this knowledge can be regained by recollection, prompted by intimations of beauty shining through the veil of appearances. In this experience of the awakened love of wisdom, the soul is rapt into a condition of enthusiasm or ecstasy, declared to be on a footing with the divine madness of the seer inspired by Apollo, and of the poet inspired by the Muses. Neither seer nor poet has access to the truth of things while he is in his sober senses. And, like the seer and the poet, the philosopher needs to be rapt beyond this world of sensible experience and to recover a vision denied to the bodily eyes.

The imagery of the *Phaedrus* myth enables us to connect the theory of philosophic knowledge as drawn from memory with prophetic enthusiasm and the inspiration of the poet. To all three —seer, poet, and sage—their peculiar wisdom comes as a revelation—a light breaking in upon what we call the 'inner consciousness'. All three have laid claim to a spiritual faculty with access to an unseen world, beyond those limits of time and space which confine the body and its senses. The mantic inspiration of Apollo endowed the seer Calchas with knowledge of the *past* and the hidden *present*, as well as of the *future*: the whole pageant of events in time was unrolled beneath the prophet's vision. In dreams, moreover, the soul (as Cicero says) is 'called away from the contagion of its bodily associate, and remembers the *past*, discerns the *present*, and foresees the *future*; for the spirit is alive and in full vigour while the sleeper's body lies as if dead'. The knowledge disclosed to the poet by the daughters of Memory is equally extensive. In the second *Iliad* Homer calls on the Muses to 'put him in mind' of all who went to Troy: 'for ye are goddesses, and are present (πάρεστε) and know all things, while we only hear the report of fame and know nothing'. This means that the poet, when he is inspired, can see the past as an eye-witness present at the events he illustrates, no longer dependent on hearsay. So too the Muses who came to Hesiod on Helicon 'know how to tell many fictions that wear the guise of truth but know also how to declare the truth when they will'. The fictions are what we call creatures of 'imagination'; but what the Muses proceed to reveal to Hesiod is the truth about the remote past, the origin of the world and the birth of the gods. We should take these claims to supernormal knowledge more seriously than we do. For Homer and Hesiod they were already traditional and beginning to fade into a conventional artifice. But earlier they had been made quite literally. I suspect, indeed, that Homer felt as if he were not merely imagining, still less inventing, the scenes he describes, but seeing with the inward eye what had really taken place; just as Ion the rhapsode assured Socrates that, when he recited the parting of Hector and Andromache or the slaying of the Suitors, he was transported out of his sober senses and 'his soul believed that, in its rapt (ἐνθουσιάζουσα) condition, it was present at the events in Troy or Ithaca'.

Now the upshot of the *Phaedrus* myth is that knowledge of reality—the unseen nature of things—comes to the philosopher through the analogous exercise of a spiritual faculty called *nous*, having the same power to rise beyond the bounds of time and space, as the spectator of all time and all existence. The stages of this journey are enumerated in the *Symposium* and the central books of the *Republic*. It carries the soul all the way from the shadows of the Cave to the vision of the Good. The journey is always described in terms of progressive illumination, such as we inevitably use in speaking of intellectual discovery. All the great pioneers of thought have seen the light suddenly irradiate the intelligible pattern in an array of facts that had seemed disorderly and meaningless. This experience Plato equates with poetic and prophetic inspiration. Such moments of illumination come when thought has been extremely concentrated, shutting out the distracting influx of external impressions. A truth which has long been shaping itself breaks through into consciousness, and we seem to recognize something we have always known and had forgotten.

This theory of the sources of philosophic knowledge is no flight of Plato's fancy. It reproduces a serious belief far older than the empirical theory of Alcmaeon—a belief, moreover, which still flourishes in no small part of the world. In that phase of society when writing is unknown or confined to a small lettered class, the wisdom of the community is possessed and orally transmitted by persons of a type in which the attributes of seer, poet, and philosopher are united. Prophecy (in the wide sense) has been defined as the expression of thought, whether subjective or objective, and of knowledge, whether of the present, the future, or the past, acquired by inspiration and uttered in a condition of exaltation or trance. The artistic form of such utterance is poetry. Epic poetry, the literature of entertainment, preserves the history of the race and the great deeds of the men of old. Didactic poetry covers the origin of the world and of human institutions, the genealogical descent of families, catalogues, proverbial or gnomic wisdom, and information useful to the farmer and the sea-farer—all the elements combined in Hesiod.

Taught by the Muses, the poets are aware of no boundary separating the utterance of spiritual adventures and journeys to the unseen world from information about the right times for sowing crops or about the winds prevalent in certain seasons, which must have come from normal experience and observation. All this lore is vested in a class claiming mantic powers and universally respected as the most intellectual and gifted members of the community. Examples are: the *rishis* of ancient India, the druids in Gaul, the *filid* of ancient Ireland. Their successors today are found in the Siberian *shamans*, the seers of Polynesia (which is said to possess the richest oral literature in the world), the priests who taught Roscoe the history of Uganda, and so on. Such men are not witch-doctors or vulgar magicians or pathological neurotics. They are rather remarkable for health and sanity, and when not exercising their mantic powers, go about their business like anyone else.

Here I am relying on a great mass of evidence in Mr and Mrs Chadwick's survey of oral literature all round the outskirts of Mediterranean civilization, from Gaul and Ireland, across

Scandinavia and Siberia, to Polynesia, India, and North Africa. Their results are summed up in Mrs Chadwick's *Poetry and Prophecy*, a book which I earnestly recommend to all students of literature. I will quote one paragraph:

The fundamental elements of the prophetic function seem to have been everywhere the same. Everywhere the gift of poetry is inseparable from divine inspiration. Everywhere this inspiration carries with it knowledge—whether of the past, in the form of history and genealogy; of the hidden present, in the form commonly of scientific information; or of the future, in the form of prophetic utterance in the narrower sense. Always this knowledge is uttered in poetry which is accompanied by music, whether of song or instrument. Music is everywhere the medium of communication with spirits. Invariably we find that the poet and seer attributes his inspiration to contact with supernatural powers, and his mood during prophetic utterance is exalted, and remote from that of his normal existence. Generally we find that a recognized process is in vogue, by which the prophetic mood can be induced at will. The lofty claims of the poet and seer are universally admitted, and he himself holds a high status wherever he is found.

To understand the attitude of the early philosopher, we must see him as emerging from this composite figure of the mantic person. By Plato's time seer, poet, and sage had become distinct, but he divined their original affinity. He had before him a complete survival of the type in Empedocles. As philosopher, Empedocles narrated the past and future history of the cosmos; as prophet, he revealed the destiny of the soul and the means of purification; everyone admits his genius as a poet; and he called himself a god who had risen above the trammels of mortality. Earlier still, Heraclitus had denounced the 'learning of many things'. Searching himself, he found within him the *Logos* which he delivered in the oracular style of 'the Lord of Delphi, who neither explains nor hides the truth, but indicates it by a sign'. Pythagoras was the hierophant of philosophic mysteries, revealed only to the pure. Parmenides, from whom Plato inherited the image of the Soul-chariot, was borne by the horses of the Sun beyond the gates of day and night, to learn the nature of things from a goddess. The truth so revealed already came to him in the form of logical deduction from self-evident premises—the form in which the truths of geometry unfold themselves to *Anamnesis*. Parmenides is the prophet of Reason; and he sets the senses at defiance.

Yet earlier, in the sixth century, the wise men who shared with the poets the title σοφισταί were no doubt rationalists; but it is an anachronism to represent them as entirely sceptical and disillusioned men of science, starting afresh to study Nature by observation and experiment. They stood within the old tradition; and it is likely that Anaximander, for example, would look back to the cosmogony of Hesiod, and other cosmogonies of the same fundamental pattern, as the genuine revelations they claimed to be. In Hesiod's short account of the origin of the world, the mythical element is already reduced to the thinnest veil of allegory or metaphor. Anaximander had only to remove the last vestiges of poetical symbolism and to fill out the scheme with operant factors which seemed indubitably prosaic and natural.

The philosopher thus appears as the rationalizing successor of the poet-seer, relying at the outset on the traditional wisdom, confirmed by his own inward conviction. On the other hand, his rationalism was to bring him later into conflict with those two other figures, who had been taking their separate ways. The prosecution of Anaxagoras is believed to have been instigated by the seers, whose occupation as interpreters of omens would be gone, if philosophers were allowed to explain eclipses and earthquakes—'what goes on in the sky and under the earth'—as natural events and not signs of divine wrath. Diopeithes, whose decree forbade such atheistical heresies, was himself a seer. And in the moral sphere, the authority of the poets on matters of religion and conduct was threatened by the Sophists and Socrates. Among Socrates' accusers, Meletus figures on behalf of the poets, and it is with him that Socrates debates the religious count in the indictment. The quarrel between poetry and philosophy was carried further by Plato, to lengths which strike us as extravagant.

These rivalries throw light back upon the time when poet, seer, and sage were the same person. After they had become separate, the poet and the seer still claimed the inspiration of the Muses and Apollo. Plato revived the corresponding claim of the philosopher. But, as I have argued, this was no novelty. The philosopher has all along felt that his spirit was reaching out, beyond everyday experience, to an unseen realm of certain truth.

Against the prestige of this immemorial tradition, the protest of the physicians, with their empirical theory of knowledge, had little weight. Those very Hippocratic writers who object to the philosopher's empty assumptions, indulge in dogmatic pronouncements equally unfounded. 'All disease,' they will say, 'is due to lack of balance in the four humours.' Their only excuse is that the four humours can be seen and touched and dealt with, whereas no one has ever seen 'the hot' and 'the cold'.

If Aristotle had followed his father's profession and never joined the Academy, who can say how far he might have carried the empirical impulse of medicine into the whole field of natural philosophy? But he succumbed to the influence of the divine Plato; and no sooner were he and his master dead than they became authorities, whose intuitions rendered the study of brute fact superfluous. Thence onwards and all through the Middle Ages, the philosopher ranked once more beside the prophet, and the premises to which all knowledge must conform were furnished by the combined revelation of faith and reason. The empirical theory of knowledge has only raised its head again effectively in the last few centuries. It is a mistake to assume that it governed the speculations of ancient Ionia.

III

CORNFORD'S *PRINCIPIUM SAPIENTIAE**

Gregory Vlastos

ALL through his life Cornford was a dissenter. It is characteristic of him that he should turn in his later years against an assumption which he himself had first accepted along with the great majority of modern scholars: that the natural philosopher of Ionia, from Anaximander to the atomists, was 'scientific', in contrast with the religious philosophy of the Pythagoreans and the rationalistic philosophy of the Eleatics. Cornford had expounded just this notion in his early book, *From Religion to Philosophy* (London, 1912). Heretical in many ways, this work had taken for granted the orthodox view of the 'scientific' motives and nature of Ionian cosmology; it described the atomists, for example, as 'behaving exactly as a modern man of science would do, remodelling the hypothetical substance to "save appearances"' (p. 137). I do not know how long it was before Cornford came to question this view. He had certainly done so by 1931. His Inaugural Lecture in that year, *The Laws of Motion in Ancient Thought* (Cambridge), argues that this topic, the proper theme of physical science, was completely misconceived by the Presocratics, who tried to explain it by the supposed tendency of motion of 'like to like', a notion derived from the common sense of their own day and ultimately from the 'unacknowledged principles of magic' (p. 44) and mimetic rites. A few years later ('Greek natural philosophy and modern science', in *Background to Modern Science*, J. Needham and W. Pagel (eds.), Cambridge, 1938), he argued that the method,

* Cambridge, 1952. Minor revisions in this review have been made by the author.

42

objective, and motivation of Greek natural philosophy were all different from those of modern science: its method was marked by the neglect of experiment and indulgence in speculative dogmas unverifiable by observation; its objective was to understand 'what things really and ultimately are' (p. 10), instead of how they behave; and its motivation lacked the essential concern of the modern scientist, to understand nature for the purpose of furthering practical control. Cornford devoted the closing years of his life to the effort to round out and document this argument, and we can read the all but finished result in the present book. Its scholarship, unfortunately, is neither dispassionate nor precise. The book abounds in remarks which are opinionated tangents on the available evidence rather than sober conclusions from it. It nevertheless commands attention as the work of an imaginative man who has a rare power to challenge the mind of his reader. An exhaustive commentary on the mass of ideas it contains is quite impossible in this review, and I am anyhow not competent to discuss one of its important topics, the affinities between Greek cosmogonies and the creation myths of Babylonians, Canaanites, and others. All I can do here is to reckon, quite selectively, with those of its theses which bear directly on the nature, temper, and immediate origins of Presocratic cosmology.

The most vigorous part of Cornford's argument is in the opening chapter where he contends that the experimental method is foreign to the Presocratics. He points out, quite rightly, that the star example of a physical 'experiment' in the natural philosophers, the clepsydra, was not an experiment at all, in the proper sense of the word: Empedocles 'did not invent the clepsydra . . . with a view to testing the hypothesis that air has some substance, and then abiding by the unforeseen results of his experiments' (p. 6). Both the clepsydra and the inflated skins, to which Anaxagoras also appealed to confirm the same hypothesis, had been used in ordinary life long before this time. 'To draw a clear-sighted inference from familiar experience is not the same thing as to practise the experimental method.' Conversely, Cornford argues (pp. 6–7) that there are plenty of genuine experiments the *physiologoi* could have performed, if they were so minded: 'Had Anaximenes set a jar full of water outside his door on a frosty night and found it split in the morning, he might have found that ice fills

43

more space than water and revised his theory.'¹ He proceeds: 'The neglect is more remarkable because a similar experiment, made for another purpose, is recorded by a Hippocratic writer, *Airs, Waters, Places*, Ch. 8.'

But he fails to notice how very odd an experiment this is: it is designed to prove that 'freezing dries up and causes to disappear the lightest and finest' parts of water, because it is held to involve an *ekkrisis* of these from the heavier, darkest parts of water. This is a consequence of the theory of Anaxagoras (B 12, 15, 16) that the transition from a rarer to a denser state involves the segregation of the bright, dry, rare, warm from their opposites, dark, moist, dense, cold.² To show this our author would have had to measure the bulk of the frozen water and find whether this would be, as he expects, smaller than the bulk of the same water before it froze. What he does instead is only to measure the bulk of the water after it was melted (ὁκόταν δὲ λυθῇ, ἀναμετρεῖν) and compare this with the measure of the water originally poured into the vessel (μέτρῳ ἐγχέας). Such loss of water as he observed (it would be slight, but we need not question his report that he did observe it)

¹ But this conclusion is not so easy as Cornford fancies. The experiment might have been made, and its result taken to confirm the theory: 'So führen arabische Philosophen das Zerspringen der Flaschen, wenn Wasser in ihnen gefriert, darauf zurück, daß das Wasser sich dabei zusammenzieht und ein Vakuum entsteht, das aber nicht möglich ist. Daher wird die Flasche zerdrückt', E. Wiedemann, 'Uber das Experiment im Altertum und Mittelalter', *Unterrichtsblätter für Math. und Naturwiss.* 12, 1906, 122. Cornford does not seem to understand that, in the absence of the right kind of theory, experiment is not only useless, but may even be misleading, for it may be taken to prove the wrong thing: so it would be in this case, and so it did in several of the few recorded experiments of classical Greece, e.g. that of Anaximenes (B 1) designed to prove that compression reduces the temperature of air; that at Περὶ Σαρκῶν, c. 2, which purports to prove that water passes through the windpipe into the lungs in the course of drinking; that of Aristotle (*Hist. Anim.* 590 a 18 ff.; cf. *Meteor.* 358 b 35 ff.), allegedly proving that a certain quantity of 'fresh and drinkable' water will be found in a vessel of moulded wax submerged for 24 hours in sea-water.

² Of these, bright-dark occur explicitly in the *Peri aeron*, and the others are obviously implied; the mention of γλυκή in *Peri aeron* would not be foreign to Anaxagoras' thought (καὶ χροιὰς καὶ ἡδονάς at B 4; cf. Theophrastus, *De sens.* 28) nor that of κοῦφον (B 10 sub. fin.). That λιμναῖα waters are salty because their sweeter parts are evaporated by the sun, asserted earlier in the same chapter, is also a consequence of the same general theory, and was specifically held by Anaxagoras (A 90).

44

would be obviously due to evaporation, and would do nothing to confirm his theory.[3]

This single instance shows the difficulty in the proper conduct of even the simplest of experiments in the absence of a theory which gives the right direction to observation. It also brings out the fact that the Hippocratics, in spite of their occasional disclaimer of 'hypotheses', could not dispense with physical and physiological theories, and that the ones they invoked suffered from the same vices as those of the *physiologoi*. Cornford ignores this fact which leaps to the eye in reading any Hippocratic treatise except those which, like the *Epidemics*, restrict themselves to minute description of symptoms and attendant circumstances, or highly specialized essays, like *On Fractures*, which can afford to ignore the aetiology of disease. His thesis (Ch. 3) is that the empirical method, foreign to the philosophers, was discovered and followed by the physicians. This generalization is surely wrong. Those very treatises which start by denouncing a philosophical theory proceed a few pages later to propound a theory of their own, no less speculative in its own way, and directly or indirectly derived from the *physiologoi*. Thus *The Nature of Man* rejects the philosophical doctrine that 'the One and the All' and, consequently, man are just 'one thing' (Ch. 1), only to assert that man and, indeed, 'animals . . . and all other things' (Ch. 3) consist of just four things, 'being the same at all times alike' (Littré 6, 36, 13; cf. Emp. B 17, 34-5)—a theory which, as has been often remarked, is closely modelled on Empedocles. *Ancient Medicine*, which has such hard words for Empedocles, puts forward a theory of indefinitely numerous *dynameis*, none of them ever pure or 'by itself', whose very wording is reminiscent of Anaxagoras.[4] Both

---

[3] Heidel, '*The Heroic Age of Greek Science*' (Baltimore, 1939), 169, takes a kinder view of the experiment, but only by ignoring what our author himself says he is proving, and assuming instead that the author is proving 'the sublimation, or the immediate vaporization of ice without passing through the liquid state', which has no foundation in the text.

[4] Cf. ἐφ' ἑαυτοῦ γενέσθαι, ἐπ' ἑωυτοῦ ἐστιν, Anaxagoras B 6. 12, with ἐφ' ἑωυτοῦ, V. M. (= *Vetus Medicina*), Ch. 5. 14, 15 (Littré 1, 602, 14; 604, 15). Festugière (*L'ancienne médicine* [Paris, 1948], p. 53) adduces a number of instances of ἐφ' ἑωυτοῦ in other Hippocratic writings. But note that they refer to things like bread, meat, fish, honey, not to their constituent *dynameis*; the only two instances of the latter are, to my knowledge, Anaxagoras and V. M. There are other points of similarity: when things are mixed, says V. M., Ch. 14

authors, like so many of the Hippocratics, take the equitable balance of qualitatively opposite components as the norm of health, employing a pattern prominent in the thought of the *physiologoi*. Acute observers of medical symptoms as the Hippocratics certainly were, the stuff and temper of their theory is no different from that of the *physiologoi*. Cornford credits them with 'the beginnings of a genuinely experimental procedure' (p. 38). But if 'experimental procedure' is used with any rigour at all, we can ascribe it to the Hippocratics no more than to the *physiologoi*. In neither case were theories put forward as tentative hypotheses, whose fate would be determined by systematic experiment.[5] 'Le

[5] The word ὑπόθεσις is never used in this sense by the Hippocratics. It is singularly absent from their writings, though, by the beginning of the fourth century at the latest (Plato, *Meno* 86 e) it had been well established in geometry. Of the five instances in which it occurs, four are in V. M. (Littré 1,

they are not φανερά; only when something ἀποκριθῇ it becomes φανερόν. Anaxagoras has the same view; when things were all mixed together, οὐδὲν ἔνδηλον ἦν (B 1); in the ἀποκρινόμενα, each thing is ἐνδηλότατα those powers which preponderate in it. V. M. holds that the multiple powers which are in man are also in other things, not only in nutriments (Ch. 14, Littré 1, 602, 15 ff.), but καὶ ἐν σκύτεϊ καὶ ἐν ξύλῳ καὶ ἐν ἄλλοισι πολλοῖς (Ch. 15, Littré 1, 606, 11); so does, of course, Anaxagoras. That there is no absolutely unmixed thing in common to V. M. and Anaxagoras (who, however, would exempt mind), as also that there is relative ἀπόκρισις. V. M. speaks of the ἄκρητον as ἰσχυρόν (Ch. 14 passim); Anaxagoras says that Mind ἰσχύει μέγιστον because it is absolutely unmixed (B 12). Anaxagoras' curious doctrine that all sensation is accompanied by pain would make sense if he too held a doctrine of krasis whose disturbance λυπέει τὸν ἄνθρωπον (Ch. 14, Littré 1, 602, 13. 14), and assumed that the sensation of any quality involved the concurrent predominance of that quality in the organism. His only known medical doctrine (Aristotle, *De part. anim.* 677 a 5 ff.) is that χολή is the cause of acute disease; this agrees with V. M., which never mentions phlegma, but only (once) ξανθὴ χολή (Ch. 19, Littré 1, 618, 6).—I adduce all this detail because the possible relation of V. M. to Anaxagoras is generally ignored in the literature (but see W. H. S. Jones, *Hippocrates*, I [London, 1923], 5, and Festugière, *loc. cit.*). I should not infer that the author of V. M. subscribes to the whole of Anaxagoras' philosophy, which is absolutely precluded by his animus against 'all who have written peri physios' (Ch. 20). But he may have read one of Anaxagoras' physiological or medical treatises, or, failing this, been influenced by someone who had taken over parts of Anaxagoras' doctrine. That it was he who influenced Anaxagoras is chronologically most unlikely; an Ionian treatise which combats Empedoclean influence on medicine could hardly have preceded the formulation of Anaxagoras' theory.

médecin ancien,' writes the author of an admirably balanced recent study, 'n'envisage jamais à l'instar du savant moderne d'avoir à modifier son principe si l'expérience le contredit.'[6] Cornford thinks it significant that 'of all the recorded examples of anything resembling an experiment . . ., the great majority occur in the medical writers'.[7] Is it, really? Is there any reason to think that if the writings of the *physiologoi* had survived in any quantity, they would not have matched the few (a dozen at most) experiments recorded in well over a thousand pages of the extant Hippocratic literature?

Cornford also imputes to the Hippocratics (pp. 39-42), and denies to the *physiologoi*, what he calls the 'empirical theory of knowledge', i.e. the doctrine that all knowledge is derived from sensation. But this is not presented in any Greek text earlier than the *Phaedo* (96 b 5-9),[8] or any Hippocratic text other than *Precepts*, Ch. 1—which is so unmistakably Epicurean in both thought and language that it is worthless as evidence of a doctrine held by the

---

[6] L. Bourgey, *Observation et expérience chez les médecins de la collection Hippocratique*, Paris, 1953, 135.

[7] P. 38. For a survey of the records of experiments in the Hippocratics he refers to W. A. Heidel, *Hippocratic Medicine* (New York, 1941). He takes no account of Heidel's earlier book, *The Heroic Age of Greek Science* (Baltimore 1931); a study of the chapter on 'Experimentation' in this book, which covers instances in the historians and philosophers as well as the physicians, might have given Cornford a more balanced view of the subject.

[8] Cornford says that 'the author of this doctrine is known to be none other than the physician Alcmaeon' (41). All we can certainly ascribe to Alcmaeon on the basis of opinions explicitly referred to him (A 5-90) is the doctrine that the brain is the seat of sensation; we may infer that he held that the brain is also the seat of thought, since physical disturbances of the brain impair not only sensation (to which Alcmaeon referred to establish the connection of sensation with the brain, Theophrastus, *De sens.* 26) but also thought. There is nothing in the testimonia to establish that Alcmaeon taught that knowledge is the end product of a process which begins with sensation from which come memory and doxa and then, finally, through the 'stabilization' of memory and doxa, results in knowledge.

570, 1; 572, 4; 598, 3; 604, 13), in the pejorative sense of arbitrary, unverifiable philosophical theory. The other, in Περὶ Φυσῶν (Littré 6, 114, 18), is used of the author's philosophical theory that air is the single ἰδέη καὶ αἰτίη of all diseases (Ch. 2) as also the cause of all events throughout the universe (Ch. 3); ἀρχὴν ὑποθέσθαι is used similarly in Περὶ Σαρκῶν (Ch. 1, Littré 8, 584, 3) to refer to a cosmological theory which the author employs to explain the nature of man.

physicians independently of, and in opposition to, the *physiologoi*.[9] Aside from this, all that we find in the Hippocratics are the assumptions that the senses provide trustworthy cognitive data and that both thought and sensation are physical processes and thus depend on the physical state of the organism and its interaction with its physical environment. What is here that cannot be matched in the *physiologoi*? Alcmaeon's doctrine that the senses are 'channels' (πόροι) of understanding, so far from expressing a theory of knowledge hostile to that of the natural philosophers, is so congenial to them that it is immediately assimilated by Empedocles in *On Nature* (B 2; cf. A 36, 8). That none of them asserts an empiricist theory of knowledge does not convict them of discounting the value of experience as a source of knowledge; the very contrary is implied in their view that 'the intelligence of men grows according to what is present (to them)'.[10]

Cornford identifies quite correctly a doctrine of knowledge which would be certainly anti-empirical: that of *anamnesis*. Now the only philosophers to whom this can be imputed before Plato are the Pythagoreans and Empedocles in the *Katharmoi*; it can only be found in just those phases of Presocratic thought which are inspired by a theological dogma absolutely foreign to the *physiologoi*. Cornford wisely refrains from fathering *anamnesis* on the natural philosophers. But he argues that 'the reason itself, in which the philosopher trusted, had inherited its claim to immediate and certain apprehension of truth from the prophetic faculty of the inspired sage' (p. 159). The concept of 'inheritance' in this

[9] Cf. W. H. S. Jones, *Hippocrates*, I (London 1923), 306; L. Bourgey, *op. cit.*, p. 40 and n. 6. Cornford is misled by Heidel, *Hippocratic Medicine*, p. 73 and n. 43, who remarks that 'there is nothing in it that may not well have been said by any thoughtful Greek at the middle of the fifth century'; Heidel's references (*Dialexeis*, Ch. 9; *Phaedo* 96 a–b) simply do not bear him out.
[10] Emp. B. 106. Philosophers from whom one would expect a depreciation of sense-experience, like Heraclitus, surprise one by asserting just the opposite. Cf. B 1: the common experience of men, he believes, exemplifies the truths of his doctrine, and the trouble with the ἀξύνετοι is that ἀπείροισιν ἐοίκασι, πειρώμενοι καὶ ἐπέων καὶ ἔργων τοιούτων; so too at B 16 (reading ὁκόσοις ἐγκυρεῦσιν) and B 72. So too his saying that 'eyes are more exact witnesses than ears' (B 101 a); for the interpretation, see von Fritz, *Cl. Ph.* 40, 1945, 234. Emp. B 2 must be understood in the light of Heracl. B 1: the trouble with the experience of the common run of men is that it is too narrow, fleeting, and distraught—this kind of experience (οὕτως, 1, 7) cannot reveal to eye, ear, or mind the truth about the world.

48

context is so vague as to be almost meaningless. What sense is there, for instance, in the contention that Heraclitus is a 'successor' of the shaman? Certainly he believed that the reason of the philosopher is consubstantial with the reason of the universe, that the wise man can, and must, understand the '*gnome*' which steers all things through all things'. But if, as Cornford admits (p. 116, n. 1), Heraclitus was not an Orphic, and hence could not believe in any kind of knowledge derived from transmigration, what is there in his doctrine to match, or even approach, the shaman's claim that his spirit could wander throughout the universe to gather wisdom inaccessible to the senses and reasoning-powers of embodied spirits? Parmenides seems to come closer to this pattern: 'his journey to, or round, the heavens[11] recalls the heaven-journey of the shaman's ritual drama' (p. 118). But though Parmenides does present his doctrine in the guise of a religious revelation, he does not rest his claim to its truth on supernatural inspiration. His goddess does not say, 'Believe', but, 'Judge by reason' (κρῖναι λόγῳ, B 7, 5), appealing to an austerely logical demonstration, whose cogency is wholly rational; this is the exact opposite of shamanism. Consider finally the case of Epicurus. Cornford pounces on the ἐπιβολὴ διανοίας which, following Bailey,[12] he translates 'projection of the mind', with special reference to Lucretius (2, 1047) *animi iactus liber*, and comments: 'The Epicurean falls back upon a metaphor whose original meaning was that the mind has the power of escaping from the body and ranging at will on a flight into the unseen world' (p. 30). But there is absolutely nothing to show that this was the 'original meaning' of ἐπιβολὴ διανοίας; ἐπιβολή was never applied to mental functions, so far as we know, by anyone before Epicurus. And even if it had been, it would not prove at all that this was the

---

[11] 'Round the heavens' is not in B 1, nor even (strictly) 'to the heavens'; the journey is κατὰ πάντ' ἄστη and then to the 'gates of the ways of Night and Day', wherever these may be; our only clue to their location is the Hesiodic model (*Th.* 744), which puts them at the 'sources and limits' of Earth, Tartarus, Sea, and Sky, which must be under the earth.

[12] *The Greek Atomists and Epicurus*, (Oxford, 1928), pp. 559 ff. In all fairness to Bailey, he should not be charged with the view Cornford gets out of him, since Bailey recognizes, indeed stresses (p. 563), that ἐπιβολή is used of the senses no less than of the mind; from this it would surely follow that the term cannot mean anything like even a metaphorical 'escape' from the body, which would be absolutely senseless in the case of ἐπιβολὴ διανοίας.

meaning intended by Epicurus, any more than, e.g. one who uses the term 'substance' nowadays need do so with any reference to its original, Aristotelian sense. Had Cornford studied Epicurus' own use of ἐπιβολή, he would have seen that, so far from suggesting shamanistic detachment from the body, the term is employed in the crucial passages of just that mental function which concentrates thinking on the precise image which is 'stamped' upon the mind in sensation;[13] ἐπιβολή is not a lapse from Epicurus' exaggerated empiricism, but an assertion of it.

But if Cornford were persuaded to give up the shamanistic 'inheritance' of the *physiologoi*, he would still retort: 'But are they not all rationalists? Is not their cosmology in every case a "dogmatic structure based on *a priori* premises"' (p. 159)?—It is perfectly true that Presocratic *physiologia* rests on *a priori* premises, e.g. that the world results from the diversification of an originally undifferentiated state (the Milesians, Empedocles, Anaxagoras, the atomists); that nature is a realm of intelligible order (*dike* for Anaximander, *ananke-dike* for Parmenides, bare *ananke* for the atomists); that unalterable being persists throughout every process (Parmenides, Empedocles, Anaxagoras, the atomists). Without one or more of these premises, none of which can be reckoned as mere empirical generalizations, every Presocratic cosmology would collapse. But it is false to count the employment of such assumptions as evidence of hostility, or even indifference, to empirical inquiry. Had the Presocratics reached a greater degree of philosophical sophistication they might very well have argued that some *a priori* premises are the logical prerequisites of all scientific investigation. Since it would be obviously anachronistic to expect them to argue in this way, what we must ask is whether their rationalistic assumptions did imply in their own case any hostility to the use of sensory observation. The answer, surely, is that it did not. The injunction of Empedocles in *On Nature* (B 3, 9–13) to use eye, ear, tongue, and every other sensory 'channel of understanding' is one with which every one of the *physiologoi* would concur.[14] Their general attitude is well expressed in

---

[13] So at *Ep. ad Hdt.* 50 and 51. [Detailed examination of the Epicurean passages omitted.—Eds.]

[14] Empedocles would not even have troubled to assert this axiomatic assumption had it not been denied by Parmenides (B 7. 2–5). Yet Parmenides himself would accept it when he turned from the investigation of Being to

Heraclitus' dictum that 'eyes and ears are bad witnesses for men who have barbarian souls' (B 107); i.e. the senses themselves tell no lies; their testimony is truthful enough, if only the mind has wit enough to judge it correctly. Even Democritus' doctrine that sense-experience is 'bastard' knowledge does not imply the slightest hostility to its use for natural inquiry. The point of the doctrine is, of course, the denial that material bodies have 'secondary qualities', which may be good or bad philosophy, but is not inspired by, nor does it prompt, any depreciation of sensory observation in scientific inquiry: the founders of modern science, Galileo, Descartes, Boyle, Newton, held exactly the same doctrine. Democritus himself was an indefatigable investigator of natural, and even technological,[15] problems, where data would necessarily be supplied by the senses.

To locate that feature of Greek *physiologia* which did obstruct empirical inquiry, Cornford should have focused attention not on its theoretical load of *a priori* premises, nor even on its tolerance for generalizations which outrun observable fact, but on something quite different. That a natural theory should be an imaginative construct, rather than a mere record of detailed observations, is not a vice in empirical science, but the reverse;[16] this is exactly what a scientific theory ought to do, provided that it is formulated as a hypothesis testable by further observation. The vice of Presocratic theories of nature is precisely that they fail to conform to this proviso. All too frequently they are so loose in texture that it is hard to see how any relevant observation could either confirm or refute them. The conflicting claims of their general theories of the constitution of matter could not be adjudicated by observation: there is not a single observed or currently observable fact

[15] A point which needs to be stressed against Cornford's view that the natural philosophers had no interest in the control of nature (p. 43). The list of Democritus' writings includes Περὶ Γεωργίης (B 26 f., 28), and several works on applied science or the arts ('Εκπετάσματα, 11 q; Οὐρανογραφίη, 14 b; Γεωγραφίη, 14 c,; Πολογραφίη, 15 a; 'Ακτινογραφίη, 15 b; Περὶ Ζωγραφίης, 28 a; Περὶ Ρυθμῶν καὶ 'Αρμονίης, 15 c; medical essays, 26 b. c. d.)
[16] Cf. Claude Bernard: 'Of necessity we experiment with a preconceived idea', *Introduction to the study of experimental medicine*, English translation, (New York, 1927), p. 22.

physiologia; the theory of knowledge appropriate to the latter identifies thought with the κρᾶσις μελέων (B 16); μέλεα here = γυῖα in Emp. B 3, 13, i.e. the physical organism, including, of course, the sense-organs.

to which, e.g. Democritus could appeal to decide in favour of this theory against that of Anaxagoras or Empedocles.[17] Even their more specific theories are for most part undecidable by observation. Obvious as this may seem, Cornford shows little appreciation of it. Thus he thinks that Empedocles' theory of respiration 'could have been tested by anyone who would sit in a bath up to his neck in water and observe whether any air bubbles passed into, or out of, his chest as he breathed' (p. 6). But what is there in Empedocles' theory to imply that minute quantities of air passing through water out of (or into!) one's chest would cause bubbles? Nothing at all; bubbles or no bubbles, the theory would survive the bath experiment.

This is a relatively minor instance of the point at issue. One could find far more important cases where one would expect that known facts, or assumed facts, would clash with accepted theories, only to see, on second thoughts, that the clash would never be felt as such because of the vagueness of the theory. Thus even a child would know that earth or stones could be heated to a point far exceeding the normal temperature of water or air, so that they could actually ignite combustible substances in direct contact with them. Would not this contradict the theory which held its own for over a century in Ionia (Anaximenes, Diogenes) that hot bodies are formed by rarefaction, cold ones by condensation? So it would seem at first sight. But a closer look at the theory will show that there is nothing in it to require its proponents to admit that this phenomenon was contradictory of it. The theory is not cast in the form of a strict functional variation of temperature and density, comparable, e.g. to the inverse ratio of pressure and volume of gases in Boyle's Law. All that it says is that the hottest body, fire, resulted from the rarefaction of air, while successive degrees of condensation produced wind, vapour, water,[18] earth and stones. So stated it is undisturbed by any number of all-too-obvious facts, such that air, which is vastly rarer than earth, has

[17] Anaxagoras' question, 'How could hair come from that which is not hair, and flesh from that which is not flesh?' (B 10), is not at all an appeal to fact, but an assertion of an *a priori* principle, *sc.* that no substance could arise from, or perish into, any substance qualitatively different from itself. The facts of nutrition could be 'explained' by Empedoclean or atomistic theory as much (or as little) as by that of Anaxagoras.

[18] A 5 and 7 (3), Simplicius and Hippolytus, following Theophrastus. Cf. Diogenes A 5. 6. 9.

normally much the same temperature as earth, and does not need to be shaken in the least by the fact that earth can be both extremely hot and extremely dense at the same time. The theory does not exclude the possibility that while the temperature of air should correspond quite closely to its density (Anaximenes B 1), the temperature of other things, like earth and rocks should not. There is no *a priori* reason why earth and rocks, though very cold when first formed, should not be susceptible of high degrees of subsequent heating without impairment to their solidity.

If we are to understand why the *physiologoi*, in spite of their eagerness to use the senses for all they were worth, failed not only to use, but even to understand, the experimental method of modern science, we should focus attention on the form of their theories which made them such clumsy instruments of empirical research, as well, of course, as on the primitive state of their observational techniques, which forced them to rely so largely on qualitative data, unrefined by quantitative measurement. Cornford ignores this area of investigation in this book because he is much too preoccupied with his favourite theme of the religious origins of Greek cosmology. He wants to show that it was unempirical and unscientific, because its dominant concepts were derived, not from 'innocent observation of Nature' (p. 197), but from antecedent religious beliefs. But just what do these derivations come to?—Simply to the notion that great masses of the physical universe—Earth, Sea, Sky, Air—arose from an undifferentiated primal state, i.e. the first, and only the first, of the *a priori* premises I enumerated above (p. 50). This can be found in Hesiod's *Theogony*, though only in that passage which Cornford strangely enough completely ignores: that remarkable venture into cosmography at 736 ff., where the 'sources and boundaries' of Earth, airy Tartarus, Sea, and Sky are located 'all in a row' in Chaos.[19] Whether these lines were written by Hesiod himself, or by a later poet, the one thing that is certain is that they depict a conception not only different from, but quite incompatible with, the story of lines 116–32: the latter, as Cornford himself observes (p. 195), does 'not say that Earth was born of Chaos, but the

---

[19] See F. Solmsen, 'Chaos and "Apeiron"', *Stud. It.* N.S. 24, 1950, 235 ff.; H. Fränkel, *Dichtung und Philosophie des frühen Griechentums* (New York, 1951), pp. 148–9.

Earth came into being "thereafter"'; he might have added that they tell us that Uranos and Pontos are born of the Earth, which cannot be reconciled with the teaching of 736 ff. that they stem directly from Chaos itself. If Cornford is to make a case for a pre-philosophical cosmology 'already far advanced along the road to complete rationalization' (p. 225), he should have looked to just these lines, which are, in my opinion, by far the most likely source of Anaximander's *apeiron*.[20] But note how far short of 'complete rationalization' they fall. When he gets to these 'limits' of the universe the poet who wrote these verses feels that he also reached the limits of reason—and not only of human reason; the gods themselves 'shudder' at these limits, find them an 'awful marvel'. For Anaximander, on the other hand, the *arche* of the visible universe is not only intelligible in itself as a mixture of the physical opposites which compose the world, but is the source of

[20] The word, *apeiron*, is, of course, not directly applied to Chaos in the *Theogony*. But note the following similarities with Anaximander's *apeiron*:

(1) The immensity of its size: 'you would not reach its bottom even in a whole year that brings completion', vv. 740–1; cf. Solmsen, *op. cit.*, 247 (Cornford, 176 ff., doubts that 'infinite extension' is implied in Anaximander's *apeiron*, though for no good reason; but even if not strictly infinite, it would be vast enough. Cornford also thinks that it was 'conceived as spherical in shape', 176–7, for which there is no reason at all: the fact that round things are spoken of as *apeira* by the poets, does not imply that all unlimited things are conceived as round);

(2) that it is the source of Earth, Sky, Sea, and Air;

(3) that it is thought of as agitated by squalls (Θύελλα, v. 742)—Anaximander's *apeiron* is also (eternally) in motion, A 11 (2), 12;

(4) its immortality, indestructibility, is implied, since it is the source and boundary of Earth, Sky, etc., all immortal gods; moreover, Θεσπέσιον at v. 700 could also be construed as an epithet of Chaos (cf. Solmsen, *op. cit.*, 237).—Had Cornford paid attention to vv. 735 ff., or even to vv. 720 ff., he would not have made the mistake of imputing to Hesiod (194 ff.) the later notion that Chaos is the ' "yawning gap" between heaven and earth', which does not make sense at v. 116 (how could Chaos come into being as a gap between two things that don't yet exist?), and is contradicted by vv. 727–31 (the ἔσχατα γαίης are, where the Titans are imprisoned, obviously under the earth) and by vv. 736 ff. (how could the sources of Tartarus be above the earth?). Even at v. 700 (on which Cornford depends) does not strictly imply that the Chaos is between Heaven and Earth; the poet may only be saying that the great conflagration spread from Earth and Sea to their nethermost sources and beyond, as the din of the *theomachia* at *Iliad* 20, 56 ff., which shook earth and sea, reached down as far as Hades to frighten its king.

the intelligible order of this world, its 'governor', the guarantee of its 'justice'.[21]

Cornford does not intend to depreciate the unique achievement of 'Ionian rationalism':

'It was an extraordinary feat to dissipate the haze of myth from the origins of the world and of life. The Milesians pushed back to the very beginning of things the operation of processes so familiar as a shower of rain. It made the formation of the world no longer a super-natural, but a natural event. Thanks to the Ionians, and to no one else, this has become the universal premiss of all modern science' (pp. 187–8).

He might have added that the very concept of nature, as a domain of unitary, necessary, and intelligible order, was their own crea-tion, and that to this extent they may rightly be regarded the creators of the scientific world-view, in spite of the fact that they failed to understand and use the experimental method. When we have made full allowance for the unscientific form of so many of their theories, we must still give them credit for laying the con-ceptual foundations on which, nearly two millennia later, more skilful hands than theirs, equipped with better tools, intellectual and technological, could build the enduring edifice of natural science. This was their great bequest to the intellectual heritage of mankind, and this they did not derive from religious sources. If there were any sources for this at all, they were not religious but political, a topic to which Cornford never alludes in this book. In the work of his youth, *From Religion to Philosophy*, he had been fully alive to the social origins of Greek philosophical ideas, but had made the mistake of looking for them in the remote antecedents of primitive tribal life instead of the contemporary experience of the democratic polis. Elsewhere I have suggested that it is just this political experience which furnished the Presocratics with the conceptual pattern which they applied to the comprehension of nature as a rule of law, an autonomous, self-regulative, system, whose orderly 'justice' was guaranteed by the assumed 'equality' of its components.[22]

[21] For my interpretation of Anaximander, see *Cl. Ph.* 42, 1947, 168 ff. (below, pp. 73 ff.)
[22] *AJPh* 74, 1953, 361 ff.

C

IV

EQUALITY AND JUSTICE IN EARLY GREEK COSMOLOGIES[1]

Gregory Vlastos

THE early Greek notion of justice lends itself with seductive ease to application far beyond the bounds of politics and morals. To respect the nature of anyone or anything is to be 'just' to them. To impair or destroy that nature is 'violence' or 'injustice'. Thus, in a well-known instance, Solon speaks of the sea as 'justest' when, being itself undisturbed by the winds, it does not disturb anyone or anything.[2] The law of the measure is scarcely more than a refinement of this idea of one's own nature and of the nature of others as restraining limits which must not be overstepped.

Cosmic justice is a conception of nature at large as a harmonious association, whose members observe, or are compelled to observe, the law of the measure. There may be death, destruction, strife, even encroachment (as in Anaximander). There is justice none the less, if encroachment is invariably repaired and things are reinstated within their proper limit. This is the vantage-point from which the commentators have generally interpreted cosmic

---

[1] I regret that other obligations have prevented me from making the revisions and expansions of the argument of this paper that would be needed to make full use of valuable publications which have appeared since it was published. However, I have gone through the paper and have pruned away from its original text things which I now consider false or seriously misleading. In the section on Parmenides this resulted in drastic cuts and in some rewriting. Elsewhere it has involved some deletions (chiefly in the notes) and a few changes, chiefly verbal, in the text. For some later remarks on *isonomia* in Anaximander and Alcmaeon I may refer the reader to my 'Isonomia', *AJP*, 74 (1953), 337–66 at 361–3.

[2] Frag. 11 (Diehl). For the interpretation, see my 'Solonian Justice', *CP*, XLI (1946), 66, n. 18.

justice in the Presocratics. It is perfectly sound. But it leaves out
the additional postulate of equality; for, clearly, it is quite possible
to think of harmony and non-encroachment as a relation between
unequals. Solon so thought of it.[3] But the founders of Greek
scientific thought generally [4] made the opposite assumption: they
envisaged harmony in terms of equality. Cosmic equality was
conceived as the *guaranty* of cosmic justice: the order of nature is
maintained *because* it is an order of equals. To my knowledge, this
has never been established.[5] I propose to review the relevant
evidence and interpret briefly its historical significance.

I. MEDICAL THEORY

Greek medical thought offers two well-known formulae of
equalitarian harmony: Alcmaeon's definition of health as 'equality
(*isonomia*) of the powers' [6] and the conception of temperate climate
(κρῆσις τῶν ὡρέων) in *Airs, Waters, and Places* 12, as equality
(*isomoiria*) of the hot and the cold, the dry, and the moist.[7]
Isonomia and *isomoiria* here render explicit the equalitarian assumption implicit in the first principles of medical theory, *dynamis* and
krasis. The original meaning of *dynamis*, as Peck observes, is not

[3] Sce my 'Solonian Justice', pp. 78 ff.
[4] With the qualifications which we shall notice in the case of Heraclitus.
[5] But see the interesting material on 'equality in nature' collected by R.
Hirzel, *Themis* (Leipzig, 1907), pp. 308–11; and Werner Jaeger, *Paideia*, I,
104 (my references to this book here and throughout are to the English
translation [2nd edn; New York, 1945]).
[5] Alcmaeon Frag. B 4. (All references to Presocratic fragments are to H. Diels
and W. Kranz, *Fragmente der Vorsokratiker* [5th edn; Berlin, 1934–7]).
Isonomia means more than 'equality under the law'; it means, rather, 'equality
of rights' and thus implies equality of dignity or status among the citizens
(see, e.g., Herodotus, iii. 142, 3; Thucydides, vi. 38, 3). *Oligarchia isonomos*
(Thucydides, iii. 62, 3), possible as a form of speech, does not invalidate the
traditional association of *isonomia* with democracy. (I have discussed this
point at length in 'Isonomia politike' in *Isonomia: Studien zur Gleichheits-
vorstellung im griechischen Denken*, J. Mau and E. G. Schmidt (eds) Berlin,
1964.)
[7] These two pairs head the list of opposites in Aetius' report of Alcmaeon's
doctrine (*loc. cit.*). As for *isomoiria*, it means 'equality in portion', as, e.g., of
heirs inheriting equal shares of an estate (Demosthenes, xlviii. 19; Isaeus,
i. 2 and 35) and, therefore, 'equality in personal and social status or dignity',
e.g., *Iliad*, xv. 186–95, 209: Poseidon is Zeus's *homotimos* because he is his
isomoros.

'a substance that has power' but rather 'a substance which *is* a power, which can assert itself, and by the simple act of asserting itself, by being too strong, stronger than the others, can cause trouble'.[8] Its strength must, therefore, be 'taken away'[9] and thus 'moderated'.[10] And this is to be done not through repression by a superior but through counterpoise against an equal. This is the heart of the doctrine of *krasis*. Alcmaeon's *isonomia* of the powers is no more than its earliest-known statement at a time when interest still centred in the fact of equilibrium itself rather than in the specific nature of the equilibrated powers.

The kind of equality here envisaged can best be gauged from the methodology of 'Hippocratic' medicine. Observation, for all its acuteness, is mainly directed towards qualitative data, with only the vaguest quantitative base.[11] No effort is made to measure individual 'powers', generalize their observed values, and construct therefrom an equation, however crude. The existence of the equation is rather an outright assumption. If there is health, it is assumed that the constituent powers must be (1) in equilibrium and therefore (2) equal to one another, much as opposing parties in an evenly matched contest are assumed to be equal. This is exactly the sense in which equality figures in the medical treatises and, indeed, as we shall see, in the whole development of early cosmological theory from Anaximander to Empedocles. Powers

---

[8] In his introduction to Aristotle's *Generation of Animals* ('Loeb Classical Library' [1943], p. li). For a good example, see the definition of pathogenic *dynamis* in Π. ἀρχ. ἰητρικῆς xxii, 3–4 (*Hippocrates*, W. H. S. Jones (ed.), Vol. I ['Loeb Classical Library']) as the 'intensity and strength of the humours'. For 'strength' (ἰσχύς, ἰσχυρόν) see *ibid.*, Ch. 14; for 'strong' foods, *ibid.* Ch. 3–6; see also below, note 17; and cf. *Timaeus* 33 a: 'hot things and cold and all things that have *strong powers* . . .'

[9] Π. ἀρχ. ἰητρ. 16, 49: ἀφαιρεόμενον τὴν δύναμιν.

[10] Μετρίως, μετριότης, common through the Hippocratic writings. Ἴσως is sometimes added for emphasis (Π. φύσ. ἀνθρ. 3, 7–8 [Jones, *Hippocrates* Vol. IV]).

[11] The best clue to the observational roots of the doctrine of *krasis* (and its offspring, the doctrine of the humours) is the mention of 'unmixed' substances in stools (διαχωρήματα ἄκρητα, ἄπεπτα, often in Ἐπιδ. i and iii) and in vomit sputum, and urine (eg. Προγν. 12–14). The humours were, no doubt postulated to account for these unmixed substances: cf. the frequent association of 'bilious' with 'unmixed' in Ἐπιδ. i and iii; and, conversely, Προγν 13: 'the vomit is most useful when phlegm and bile are most thoroughly mixed together'.

are equal if they can hold one another in check[12] so that none can gain 'mastery' or 'supremacy'[13] or, in Alcmaeon's term, 'monarchy' over the others. Medical theory assumes this kind of equality even when it conceives *krasis* not as the equipoise of pairs of physical opposites (hot–cold, dry–moist, etc.) but as a many-valued blend of powers;[14] for here, too, the purpose of blending is to insure that 'no individual power is displayed'.[15] Should any power escape this blending and 'stand by itself',[16] it would be ominously 'strong' and thus create the 'monarchy' which constitutes disease.[17]

When we come to the '*krasis* of the seasons' we move directly into the area of cosmic justice; for medical thought is not content with the empirical fact that some climates are better suited than others (and thus more 'just') to human nature. It goes further to explain the harmony of human nature to its environment through an absolute cosmic fact, i.e. the harmony of the environmental forces with one another.[18] This is, in turn, construed as an equilibrium of opposites. But there is a difference. This *isomoiria*, unlike that of the body, can be grounded in an observable equation which is capable of strict quantitative expression—the equinox, when (1) day is equal to night, (2) all the hours throughout the day and night are equal to one another,[19] and (3) the sun

---

[12] Cf. Pseudo-Aristotle, *De mundo* 396 b 35, where *isomoiria* is paralleled by the expression 'no one of them is more powerful [πλέον δύνασθαι] than any other'; and this is, in turn, explained by adding, 'for the heavy is equally balanced [ἴσην ἀντίστασιν ἔχει] with the light, and the hot with the cold' (Forster's translation).

[13] Cf. Π. ἀ. ὑ. τ. 12, 18: 'nothing has violent supremacy' (μηδὲν ᾖ ἐπικρατέον βιαίως), as a parallel expression to '*isomoiria* prevails'.

[14] As, e.g., in the doctrine of coction in Π. ἀρχ. ἰητρ., which assumes 'innumerable' powers (καὶ ἄλλα μυρία [14, 33–4; 17, 9–10]) and lays down the principle that these 'become milder and better the greater the number [*sc.* of powers] with which they are mixed' (19. 53).

[15] *Ibid.* 19, 55–6.

[16] *Ibid.* 14, 37–8: αὐτὸ ἐφ᾽ ἑωυτοῦ γένηται. Cf. Π. φύσ. ἀνθρ. 10–11: ἐφ᾽ ἑωυτοῦ στῇ. Cf. below, note 141.

[17] Π. παθῶν 16 (Littré, VI, 224): 'for phlegm and bile, when concentrated [ξυνεστηκότα], are strong and dominate in whatever part of the body they establish themselves and cause much trouble and pain'.

[18] E.g., the physician Eryximachus in Plato, *Symp.* 188 a; cf. also *Laws* X. 906 c.

[19] These are the standard hours of scientific inquiry, the 'equinoctial hours', as over against the variable 'seasonal hours' (ὧραι καιρικαί) in popular usage (see Th. H. Martin, 'Astronomia' in Daremberg-Saglio, p. 485 a).

rises at a point midway between the northernmost and the southernmost risings of the year (i.e. the summer and winter solstices). That climatic *isomoiria* should be attended by these astronomical equalities was so impressive that the relation between the two was taken as one of causal implication. Thus the Island of Iambulus in Diodorus, ii. 56, 7 is endowed with a year-round equinox to validate its claim to the most temperate of climates.[20]

But if *isomoiria* belongs to the equinoctial seasons, a way must be found somehow to bring the rest of the year within the framework of equalitarian harmony. This was done through the idea of rotation in office, or 'successive supremacy' (ἐν μέρει or κατὰ μέρος κρατεῖν), among the powers. As in the democratic *polis* 'the demos rules by turn',[21] so the hot could prevail in the summer without injustice to the cold, if the latter had its turn in the winter. And if a similar and concurrent cycle of successive supremacy could be assumed to hold among the powers in the human body, then the *krasis* of man and nature would be perfect. Medical thought must have moved gradually towards this elegant tissue of assumptions.[22] In *Epidemics* i and iii we see the view that each season has its own 'constitution', which aggravates some diseases and relieves others.[23] *Airs, Waters and Places* goes into physiological details on the dependence of the healthy body on an ordered sequence of seasonal change, explaining how even good weather, if unseasonable, would be harmful (Ch. 10). Finally, that confident dogmatist, the author of *The Nature of Man*, produces the full-blown theory:

Man's body has always all of these [*sc.* four humors]; but as the seasons revolve they [*sc.* the humors] become now greater, now lesser, each in turn [κατὰ μέρος] and in accordance with nature. . . . At one time of the year winter is strongest; next spring; then summer; then autumn. So too in man at one time phlegm is strongest; next blood; next bile, first yellow, then the so-called black [7. 48–52 and 61–6].

[20] Aristotle, *Probl.* 942 B 37, ἡ ἰσημερίη ἔστι χειμών τε καὶ θέρος ἰσοκρατής.
[21] Euripides, *Suppl.* 406.
[22] Their earliest foundation was the commonsense business of adapting food, clothing, etc., to the prevailing weather: e.g. cold potions in the summer, hot in the winter (*Π. διαίτ. ὀξ.* 19 [Jones, *Hippocrates*, Vol. II]; cf. Heracleides of Tarentum *ap.* Athen. ii. 45 d).
[23] The *locus classicus* is 'Ἐπιδ. iii. 15.

II. EMPEDOCLES

Empedocles is our best bridge from medicine to philosophy proper. His thought was so congenial to the medical theorists of his time that, by all accounts, his influence upon them was enormous.[24] Even in the Aegean it was strong enough to draw the fire of the author of *Ancient Medicine*.[25] In his system man's flesh and blood is made up of the four world-components on the pattern of *isomoiria*; where this equality is imperfect, we get the deviations from perfect health and wisdom in man.[26] But in the cosmos the 'roots' are strictly equal among themselves;[27] and, since each of them is, like Parmenides' Being, eternally equal to itself,[28] cosmic justice is perpetually sure. Even at the zenith of the ascendancy of Strife,[29] when each of the four 'roots' would be 'unmixed' (Frag. B 35. 15) and thus, by Hippocratic norms, a 'strong substance', no harm could result, for none would be

---

[24] Wellmann (*Fragmente der sikelischen Ärzte* [Berlin, 1901], pp. 68 ff.) spoke of him as the 'founder' of the Sicilian school, and his statement has often been repeated. Neither Galen nor any other ancient authority goes so far (see the texts under Emp. Frag. A 3). However, it may well have been the influence of his four 'roots' that fixed the first two pairs of opposites in Alcmaeon's list (Frag. B 4) as the canonical *dynameis* in Sicilian medicine and even elsewhere (usually in combination with the doctrine of the humours as, e.g., in Diocles, Frag. 8 in Wellmann; *Π. παθῶν* 1 [Littré, VI, 208]; *Π. νούσων* i. 2 [Littré, VI, 142]; *Π. τόπ. τ. κ. ἀνθρ.* 12 [Littré, VI, 334]).

[25] Jaeger (*op. cit.*, Vol. III, Ch. I, p. 40) rightly warns against taking Empedocles as the sole butt of the polemic. Certainly, the scope of the argument is much broader. But it is none the less significant that Empedocles is the only opponent to be named. He clearly represents the objectionable influence of 'philosophy' in its most oppressive form.

[26] Emp. Frags. B 98, A 78, A 86 (Theophrastus, *De sensu*, 10–11).

[27] Emp. Frag. B 17. 27. Cornford (*From Religion to Philosophy* [London, 1912], p. 64) observed that Empedocles' roots are, like the three gods in *Il.* xv, 'equal in status or lot'. Actually, the equality of the roots is more thoroughgoing. In the *Iliad* it could be claimed for Zeus that he is superior in force and prior in birth (xv. 165 f.). Neither could be claimed for any of the Empedoclean roots.

[28] Emp. Frag. B 17, 35: ἠνεκὲς αἰὲν ὁμοῖα; and the thrice repeated αὐτὰ ἔστιν ταῦτα (Frags. B 17. 34, B 21. 13, B 26. 3).

[29] This ascendancy of Strife is never explicitly mentioned in the fragments. But it is a legitimate—indeed, unavoidable—inference from (1) the general principle of alternate dominance of Love and Strife and (2) the amply attested dominance of Love in the *Sphairos*.

stronger than any of the rest. Thus, even when Strife rules the World, equality is a sufficient preventive of 'injustice'.

Much has been written on what Empedocles really meant by the 'equality' of his elements. In one argumentative passage (*De gen. et cor.* 333 a 19–34) Aristotle professes to be in the dark as to whether equality in volume[30] or in 'power'[31] was meant; in another (*Meteor.* 340 a 14) he gives himself away, assuming the latter ($\ddot{\iota}\sigma\alpha$ $\tau\dot{\eta}\nu$ $\delta\dot{\upsilon}\nu\alpha\mu\iota\nu$ $\epsilon\dot{\iota}\nu\alpha\iota$) as a matter of course.[32] Aristotle's quandary in the first passage, even if only rhetorical, shows well enough that the distinction had not been settled by Empedocles. The second passage suggests just as well that 'power' was, nevertheless, uppermost in Empedocles' mind, as it certainly was for the medical writers.[33] Empedocles is not averse to spatial categories: Love is 'equal in length and breadth'.[34] But when he formally declares that the roots are equal, he immediately goes on to say that (1) they are of equal age, (2) each has its peculiar honour ($\tau\iota\mu\dot{\eta}$),[35] but (3) they rule in turn (Frag. B 17. 27–29).[36] Could we ask for more conclusive proof that not mere extension but 'power' (with its associated concept of 'honour') is uppermost? Points 2 and 3 state the principle of 'successive supremacy', whose significance in medical theory has just been explained; and they are introduced by Point 1, which rules out flatly the possibility that any of them could claim permanent supremacy in virtue of seniority rights.[37] Because of 1 the universe cannot be a

[30] $\kappa\alpha\tau\dot{\alpha}$ $\tau\dot{o}$ $\pi\sigma\sigma\dot{o}\nu$ (l. 20), purely extensive dimension; in *Meteor.*, 340 a 7–9, Aristotle speaks of $\ddot{o}\gamma\kappa\sigma s$, $\pi\lambda\hat{\eta}\theta\sigma s$, and $\mu\dot{\epsilon}\gamma\epsilon\theta\sigma s$.

[31] $\ddot{O}\sigma\sigma\nu$ $\delta\dot{\upsilon}\nu\alpha\tau\alpha\iota$ (l. 24). A third possibility, based on the distinction of $\pi\sigma\iota\dot{o}\nu$ and $\pi\sigma\sigma\dot{o}\nu$ (ll. 27 ff.), need not detain us here. In Empedocles and his predecessors *dynamis* anteceded this distinction and denoted either quality or quantity or else (more commonly) both.

[32] Empedocles is not named here; but it is generally agreed that the reference is to him.   [33] See above, p. 58.

[34] Emp. Frag. B 17. 20. Tannery was mistaken in taking this spatial expression as 'Empedocles' true thought' and discounting the dynamic *atalanton* in the preceding line as 'metaphorical' (*Pour l'histoire de la science hellène* [2nd edn; Paris, 1930], p. 314).

[35] Cf. Emp. Frag. B 30. 2: $\dot{\epsilon}s$ $\tau\iota\mu\dot{\alpha}s$ τ' $\dot{\alpha}\nu\dot{o}\rho\sigma\upsilon\sigma\epsilon$ (*sc.* $N\epsilon\hat{\iota}\kappa\sigma s$).

[36] With $\dot{\epsilon}\nu$ $\mu\dot{\epsilon}\rho\epsilon\iota$ $\kappa\rho\alpha\tau\dot{\epsilon}\sigma\upsilon\sigma\iota$ here (and also in Frag. B 26. 1) cf. Frag. B 30. 3: $\dot{\alpha}\mu\sigma\iota\beta\alpha\hat{\iota}\sigma s$ (*sc.* $\chi\rho\dot{o}\nu\sigma s$).

[37] See Peisthetaerus' argument in the *Birds* 471 ff.: the birds are 'prior to the earth and prior to the gods . . . being eldest, the kingship is rightfully theirs'. This is also the logic of Plato's long-winded argument in *Laws* X, tersely anticipated in *Tim.* 34 b-c.

'monarchy', for no power within it possesses the qualifying primogeniture. Because of 2 and 3 the universe must be characterized by *isonomia*, for it conforms to the democratic principle of rotation of office.

Thus Empedocles builds a universe to the specifications of Alcmaeon's formula of health; and in so doing he levels ancient inequalities which had been fixed by religious tradition. Zeus, heretofore 'king of kings, of all the blessed the most blessed, over all the mighty sovereign in might' (Aeschylus, *Suppl.* 524–6) is now merely one of the roots on a par with the 'unheard-of'[38] divinity, Nestis, so inconsequential that its very identity remains in doubt. As as for Strife—'unseemly', 'dreadful', 'evil', 'mad'[39]—every impulse of sentimental justice would urge its subordination to the power that makes all 'have thoughts of love and work the works of peace' (Frag. B 17. 23), 'queen Cypris', who in the golden age ruled alone in place of Zeus (Frag. B 128). But equalitarian justice rules otherwise. Were not Harmony matched with its perfect equal in Strife, there would be no created world, only the nondescript mixture of the *Sphairos*. It is only the strictly reciprocal power of Strife to undo the work of Harmony and 'prevail in turn' (Frag. B 17. 29) that makes a cosmos possible.[40] And, this equality once assured, the process works just as well backward as forward: whether Harmony or Strife has supremacy, the other will be 'rising up to [claim] his prerogatives' (Frag. B 30. 2), and a world will be born and destroyed in either case.

A lacuna in the argument so far is the apparent absence of any explicit reference to justice in the fragments; the word *dike* is never mentioned. My answer is that the reference to justice is none the less present; Empedocles' surviving words, if carefully examined, contain expressions which are charged with the imagery and notion of justice. Consider Fragment B 30 once again: Strife 'rose up to [claim] his prerogatives in the fulness of alternate time set for them [*sc.* Love and Strife] by the mighty

[38] Wilamowitz, *Glaube der Hellenen*, I (Berlin, 1931), 20.

[39] Emp. Frag. B 27 a, B 17. 19, B 20. 4, B 115. 15. Aristotle (*Metaph.* 1075, b 6–7) is shocked at the thought that Strife, the principle of evil (ἡ τοῦ κακοῦ φύσις), should be imperishable in Empedocles.

[40] The mutual interdependence between opposites is explicit in Π. φύσ. ἀνθρ. 7. 56–9: 'if one [*sc.* of the hot, cold, dry, moist] were to fail, all would disappear, for by the same necessity all were constituted and are nourished by one another' (translation adapted from Jones).

oath. . . .' (Burnet's translation). The fragment breaks off abruptly. But we hear of 'mighty oaths' again in Fragment B 115, where they 'seal' the 'decree of the gods'. Here 'oaths' represent the binding, inviolate, *necessary* character of that decree,[41] which is an 'oracle of *Ananke*'. But we know that in Parmenides *Ananke* and *Dike* perform the same function of holding Being fast 'in the bonds of the limit'.[42] We may thus infer that 'mighty oath' in Empedocles, like 'strong *Ananke*' in Parmenides, alludes to the orderliness of existence conceived under the aspect of justice. This inference is confirmed by three other terms in the fragment:

1. *'The "prerogatives"* (τιμαί) *of Strife.'*[43]—This tells us that the dominance of Strife is not lawless self-assertion but duly established right or 'office';[44] it is its 'rightful share' or 'just portion' (αἶσα).[45]

2. *'In the fullness of time'* (τελειομένοιο χρόνοιο).—'Time' here is no abstract measurement of the passage of events. It is the proper

[41] The oath was often thought so important an aspect of justice that ὅρκιον could be taken as equivalent to δίκαιον (Diogenes Laertius, viii. 33). Cf. θεῶν ἔνορκον δίκαν in Sophocles, *Ant.* 369.

[42] Parm. Frag. B 8. 14–15 and 30–1. Fränkel observes of *ananke* in Frag. B 8. 30: 'Ihr Tun wird dadurch begründet, dass das Gegenteil nicht θέμις sein würde' ('Parmenidesstudien', *Gött. Nachrichten* [1930], pp. 153–92, at p. 189 (see Vol. II of this collection). My heavy debt to this study will be evident throughout this paper).

[43] Cf. also Emp. Frag. B 17. 27.

[44] For the same association of the 'great oath of the gods' with the establishment of a 'prerogative' (γέρας) see Pindar, *Ol.* vii. 65: Τιμή, like γέρας, is the dignity of one's status in an ordered society (see Cornford, *op. cit.*, p. 16). The scrupulous observance of its claims to deference is the basis of justice. For a cosmological application of the idea, see Sophocles, *Ajax* 660 ff.

[45] Emp. Frag. B 26. 2: ἐν μέρει αἴσης. *Aisa*, like *moira*, originally 'share', derivatively 'appointed order' or 'destiny', and thus, on the assumption that what is fated to be is right, 'appropriate or right order' (cf. ὑπὲρ αἶσαν = ὑπὲρ δίκην). Empedocles rationalizes *aisa* exactly as Parmenides (Frag. B 8. 37) had rationalized *moira*, and Anaximander (Frag. 1) *chreon*. The latter means generally 'fateful necessity', such as attaches to the prediction of an oracle, but (like *aisa* and *moira*) could also mean 'right'. In Heraclitus (Frag. B 80) *chreon* is equivalent to *dike*; in Parmenides (Frag. B 8. 9, 11, 45) it stands for logicophysical necessity. Fränkel goes too far in excluding 'necessity' from the full meaning of *chreon*: 'Die Wörter des Stammes χρη- bezeichnen ein *Sollen* und *Schuldig Sein*, ein *Gebrauchen* und *Brauchbar Sein*, nicht ein Müssen und Unvermeidbar Sein' (*op. cit.* in note 42, p. 183). What else but 'Müssen und Unvermeidbar Sein' is the *chreon* of an oracle?

time-span allotted to Strife (as also to Love) in the cosmic order; it is a 'measure' whose observance is of the essence of justice.[46]

3. '*Alternate* (ἀμοιβαῖος) *time.*'—'Alternate time' specifies what kind of justice this is: the equalitarian justice of rotation of office.[47]

III. PARMENIDES

In Parmenides' Being the reference to justice is more explicit, and there is a stronger accent on its compulsiveness. There may be injustice among men, for they can overstep the limit of their own nature. There can be no injustice in Being, for its limit is an unbreakable 'chain' (Frag. B 8. 26 and 31) or 'fetter' (Frag. B 8. 14) which 'holds it fast'.[48] Justice or Necessity is thus spoken of as an active force—a wilful personification of the inexorable compulsiveness of logical inference, as it constrains our thoughts once we have found the right way to think about Being. And in the description of the object of our thought when so constrained we note, as the objective correlate of Justice, the fact that all Being is *equally* Being: 'it is all alike' and 'equal to itself₁ on all sides'[49] without distinction of 'greater' or 'lesser' [50] nor yet of more or less 'complete': it is 'complete all over (τετελεσμένον πάντηι) like the mass of a well-rounded sphere that is equally poised from the

---

[46] Cf. 'the ordering of time' in Anax. Frag. 1.

[47] Cf. above, note 36.

[48] See below, n. 133.

[49] Frags. B 8. 22: πᾶν ὅμοιον and B 8. 49: οἱ πάντοθεν ἴσον. *Homoion* and *ison* are so closely connected at this stage of thought that geometrical equality may be expressed by *homoiotes*: Eudemus *ap.* Proclus *In Eucl.* 251. 20–1, ἀρχαϊκώτερον δὲ τὰς ἴσας ὁμοίας (*sc.* Thales) προσειρηκέναι. For *homoios* with the sense of 'equal in rank or dignity', see Liddell and Scott, *Lexicon* (new ed.), *s.v.*, II.

[50] Parmenides' terms are suggestive of 'power', not mere volume (cf. above, p. 62); and they are charged with associations of dignity (cf. the τιμή of Empedocles' roots): χειρότερον, βαιότερον, and even ἧσσον (Frag. B 8, 24, 45, and 48) should be read in the light of the distinction in τιμή between the μεγάλοι and βαιοί, μέγας and σμικρός (e.g. Soph. *Ajax* 158–61) and μέγας and ὀλίγος (Callinus Frag. 1. 17). Note the force of ἐὸν ἐόντι πελάζει (clearly a play on the proverb ὅμοιον ὁμοίῳ πελάζει [Plato, *Symp.* 195 b]) following the repudiation of μᾶλλον and χειρότερον (Frag. B 8. 23–4). Fränkel has some valuable comments on all this; see especially his remark on μᾶλλον in Frag. B 8. 48: 'ein Adverb des Grades, nicht ein Adjektiv der Ausdehnung' (p. 192).

centre outwards in every direction (μέσσοθεν ἰσοπαλὲς [51] πάντηι)'. The image is that of an object whose motionless stability is due not to external fixtures or pressures, but to the symmetrical distribution of its own internal forces.[52] The absolute 'self-equality' of Being leaves no scope for anything within it which, by preponderating, could introduce injustice.

The notion of equality is also prominent in the cosmological appendix which makes sense of the quasi-truth and quasi-being of the world of 'mortal opinion'. The general formula of this cosmology is that there are two forms, Fire and Night, each of them as self-identical[53] in its own way as is Being itself, and that these two forms are 'equal'.[54] The meaning of this equality, unspecified in the physical fragments, may be interpreted in the light of Parmenides' use of 'equal'[55] in a dynamic sense as an alternate for 'equally poised'[56] in the doctrine of Being, and of Alcmaeon's concept of 'isonomia of the powers'. In the equipoise of physical opposites in the world of becoming Parmenides would thus find a material parallel to the internal equipoise in Being. This would explain why he thinks of the mock world of Fire and Night as a cosmos,[57] falling, like Being itself, under the sway of Just Necessity.[58]

[51] A term expressive not of extensive but of dynamic equality: παλές from πάλλω 'to shake, poise, sway, brandish, wield (a spear, or missile); in pass., to throb, vibrate, beat; to shake (lots) together', R. J. Cunliffe, *A Lexicon of the Homeric Dialect* (London, 1924), s.v. Cf. its use by Plato in *Tim.* 62 e, στερεὸν κατὰ μέσον τοῦ παντὸς ἰσοπαλές (almost certainly an echo of μέσσοθεν ἰσοπαλές in Parmenides, which is quoted by Plato in *Soph.* 244 e, by Aristotle in *Phys.* 207 a 17) to denote a solid *with an equal tendency* to move in any given direction away from the centre. Herodotus (v. 49. 8) uses it of opposing states so evenly matched in strength that neither could count on a victory over the other, and (i. 82. 4) of contending armies stalemated in a battle.

[52] Fränkel: 'Den Gegenstand des Vergleichs bildet nicht die Rundheit . . . , sondern das ausgeglichene Kräftespiel (ἰσοπαλές) in einer so verteilten Gewichtsmasse (ὄγκος)' (*op. cit.*, in note 42, p. 191).

[53] Frag. B 8. 57: ἑωυτῶι πάντοσε τωυτόν.

[54] Frag. B 9. 4: ἴσων ἀμφοτέρων.

[55] Above, note 49.

[56] Above, notes 51 and 52.

[57] Frag. B 8. 60: διάκοσμον ἐοικότα.

[58] Cf. the *Ananke* which 'drove and fettered it [*sc.* the embracing Ouranos] to hold the limits of the stars' (Frag. B 10. 5–7 [Cornford's trans.]) with the *Ananke-Dike-Moira* whose 'fetters' hold the limits of Being itself.

IV. HERACLITUS

Just as the self-identity of Truth and Being *is* justice for Parmenides, so the 'strife' of Becoming *is* justice for Heraclitus.[59] Here, too, we find, among the mediating concepts, necessity (*chreon*)[60] and measure: 'The earth is poured out as sea, and is measured according to the same *logos*[61] as before it becomes earth' (Frag. B 31). 'Strife' *is* justice because, through the very conflict[62] of the opposites, the measure will be kept. This means (1) that in every transformation the fire which is 'exchanged'[63] remains constant and (2) that the distribution of fire among the opposites is also constant: 'The way up and down is one and the same' (Frag. B 60), which I take to mean that the sum total of 'upward' changes in the universe equals the 'downward' ones,[64] so that the middle term, water, is exactly divided between the two ways, half of it 'turning' to earth and the other half to fire.[65]

Much could be said of the similarities of this design to the Empedoclean. Both are inspired by the principle of the 'hidden' harmony (Frag. B 54) of Harmony itself with its own opposite, Strife,[66] achieved in both systems by assuming that these, like

---

59 Frag. B 80: καὶ δίκην ἔριν.

60 Frag. B 80: κατ' ἔριν καὶ χρεών.

61 E. L. Minar, Jr., rightly calls attention to the primary significance of *logos* as 'computation, reckoning' ('The Logos of Heraclitus', CP, XXXIV [1939], 323).

62 Frag. B 36: each lives the other's death.

63 Frag. B 90: and see the parallel passages to this fragment in Bywater's edition of Heraclitus (Frag. 22 there).

64 Philo (*De incorr. mundi* 108–9) puts much the same interpretation on this fragment. He speaks of 'reciprocation [ἀντέκτισις] and interchanges according to the standards of equality and the bounds of justice'. He also speaks of the interchanges as isonomia (112; cf. also ἰσοκρατὴς ἡ τῶν στοιχείων μεταβολή [116]; and a similar passage in *De cherubim* 109–12, esp. 110: ἀντίδοσίν τινα καὶ ἀντέκτισιν πάντα ὑπομένοντα . . .). Philo here is not merely echoing Stoic doctrine, though his immediate source may be Stoic, for he is arguing against the Stoic ἐκπύρωσις; and he has a fair knowledge of Heraclitus, as one can see from his quotations and allusions. See further, below, note 129.

65 Frag. B 31 a, following Burnet's interpretation (*op. cit.*, p. 149).

66 The prototype of this idea, I surmise, was Anaximander's *dinos*. The effect of *dinos* and *dinesis* is to unsettle the established order of things: κυκάειν, ταράττειν (e.g. Plato, *Crat.* 439 c; Aeschylus, *Ag.* 987; Pindar, *Pyth.* 9. 38; Emp. Frag. B 110. 1). Thus the *dinos* shook the *apeiron* out of its proper state, the *krasis* of the opposites. But, strangely enough, the effect of this unsettling

all other opposites, balance.[67] But there are important divergences both in structure and in intention; and these are material to the role of equalitarian justice in the two cosmologies. The structural differences are mainly two: (1) the universe has not yet been parcelled out into six separate sets of Parmenidean being; nor (2) has its history been marked off into separate epochs of successive supremacy. Because of (1) it would be useless to look for the formal equation of physical roots. Everything in Heraclitus' world is in process; instead of equality between substantives of permanence, we find reciprocity between verbs of change. For everything 'turning' one way, something else is 'turning' the opposite way: 'cold things grow hot, the hot grows cold; the moist grows dry, the dry grows moist' (Frag. B 126).[68] Because of (2) the world is not made and unmade in alternate eons;[69] generation and destruction are concurrent and constant, hence the form of the world is also constant. Fire, 'kindled' by 'gathering' into its own substance a measure of fuel, is also 'extinguished' by 'scattering abroad' the same measure of light.[70] This measured

[67] The assumption that not only Love–Strife but the four 'roots' as well are conceived as opposites by Empedocles may be questioned. But see Emp. Frag. B 21. 3–6: fire is 'bright and warm', while water is 'dark and cold'; the earth is 'closed-pressed and solid' while—if we may fill in the fourth term which does not occur in the context—the air would be rare and light (as, e.g., in Parm. Frag. B 8. 56–9, 'rare' and 'light' appear as the opposites to 'compact' and 'heavy').

[68] Cf. the τροπαί of water, equal parts turning in opposite directions (see above, note 65).

[69] Burnet's argument against the ascription of the periodic conflagration to Heraclitus has been strengthened by Reinhardt, *Parmenides* (Bonn, 1916), pp. 169 ff. A further points may be added: Philo (cited above, note 64) quotes Heraclitus *against* the Stoic conflagration.

[70] Combining Frags. B 30 and B 91; cf. Aristotle, *Meteor.* 355 a 4–5: fire 'can live only as long as it is fed, and the only food of fire is moisture'; and cf. Galen in Hippocrates, Π. φύσ. ἀνθρ. i. 39: 'and fire . . . manifestly needs moisture for its nourishment, as the flames of [oil-] lamps show'. The last point has not always been understood, even by close students of Greek

was not chaos but cosmos. To Heraclitus this must have seemed a perfect instance of the 'hidden' harmony and the unity of opposites. Though the *dinos* has no place in his own cosmology, he does refer to an analogous instance in Frag. B 125 (Frag. 84 in Bywater); and the point is still clearer in the form in which the fragment is quoted by Alexander Aphrod. (cited by Bywater, *ad. loc.*): ὁ δὲ κυκεών, ὥσπερ καὶ ʿΗράκλειτός φησιν, ἐὰν μή τις ταράττῃ, διίσταται.

give-and-take accounts for the permanence of the world which 'was and is and is to be'.[71]

But there is another difference which may well be intentional: the words 'equal' and 'equality' never occur in the fragments.[72] To express the harmony of the opposites Heraclitus does not say that they are equal but that they are one;[73] to express their equivalence he says that they are 'the same thing'.[74] This is no verbal accident. It is true to a pattern of thought which separates him from Anaximander (as well as from Empedocles) and brings him closer to Anaximenes: the physical opposites are all explained as modifications of one of them; they are thus literally 'the same thing'.[75] This One is the 'common' thing throughout the universe.[76] And, since it defines the measure of every process (Frag. B 90), Heraclitus thinks of it as the 'one divine law', all-powerful,

---

[71] See Reinhardt, *op. cit.* in note 69, p. 176, n. 2: 'Die Worte ἦν τε καὶ ἔστι καὶ ἔσται [Frag. B 30] formellhaft, ein Ausdruck für die Unveränderlichkeit', and citations.

[72] Nor *homoion* and *homoiotes*.

[73] E.g., Frags. B 50: 'all things are one', and B 67, 'god', is day–night, winter–summer, war–peace, surfeit–hunger.

[74] E.g., Frag. B 88: the equivalence of contraries is shown through the fact that *a* μεταπεσόν becomes *not-a*, and *not-a* πάλιν μεταπεσόν becomes *a*; the logical upshot is that *a* and *not-a* are 'the same thing'. Alternatively, Heraclitus will say that *a is not-a*—Frag. B 62: 'immortals [are] mortals, mortals [are] immortals, etc.'. Finally, he will say that a thing is 'one and the same' as its opposite (e.g. Frag. B 60, of the upward and downward ways, where what he means is obviously not identity but equivalence).

[75] Anaximenes' wording is, of course, lost to us; but that of his fifth-century follower, Diogenes of Apollonia, agrees verbally with Heraclitus—Frag. B 2: πάντα τὰ ὄντα . . . τὸ αὐτὸ εἶναι . . . τὸ αὐτὸ ἐὸν μετέπιπτε πολλαχῶς. To be sure, there is a difference: Unlike Anaximenes' (and Diogenes') air, Heraclitus' fire is not an original substance *from* which the world evolved, but the 'ever living' power *in* the world (Frag. B 30). On the other hand, the two systems are precisely similar in that the 'one' appears in the world in a double role: it is itself one *of* the opposites, yet it explains the unity *in* all the opposites; it is both one *among* the many and the one which *is* the many.

[76] See below, note 84. Heraclitus uses ξυνόν as an alternate to ταὐτόν to express the equivalence of opposites as, e.g., in Frag. B 103.

---

science (e.g. Tannery, *op. cit.*, p. 175); yet that is what accounts for Heraclitus' triad fire–water–earth on the way up and down: fire and moisture ('water') are juxtaposed in 'concordant discord' (Plato, *Symp.* 187 a); fire is fed by its 'enemy' (cf. Aeschylus, *Ag.* 650–1).

all-sufficient, all-victorious (Frag. B 114). It is the 'thought which governs all things through all things' (Frag. B 41).[77]

Should this doctrine of the One 'governor' of the universe be interpreted in line with the 'aristocratic' politics with which Heraclitus is commonly credited in the textbooks?[78] It is clear enough that he was a misfit in Ephesian politics.[79] This is in striking contrast to Anaximander, Parmenides, and Empedocles, all of whom seem to have held posts of authority and influence in their respective states.[80] But from this we cannot jump to the conclusion that Heraclitus was a partisan of aristocracy in its relevant, historical sense.[81] His tirades against the 'many' follow logically enough from his basic conviction that they are philosophically benighted.[82] But the philosopher's contempt for the folly of the crowd is not peculiar to Heraclitus. Parmenides

[77] Anaximenes' air no doubt performed a similar function (Anaximenes Frag. B 2; Diogenes Frag. B 5).

[78] E.g., J. B. Bury, *History of Greece* ('Modern Library' edn; New York, 1937), p. 305: 'he was an aristocrat in politics'. Zeller, *History of Greek Philosophy*, English translation (London, 1891), II. 99: 'he hates and despises democracy'; this position remains unqualified in the sixth German edition by Nestle (1920).

[79] We can infer as much from Diogenes Laertius (ix. 1–6), without taking too seriously his various stories. There is no reason to doubt the fact that Heraclitus renounced a hereditary *basileia* in favour of a brother (Antisthenes of Rhodes *ap.* Diogenes Laertius, ix. 6); but the facile interpretation of the motive (μεγαλοφροσύνη) is another matter. Temperament and politics aside, would his attacks on the mysteries (Frag. B 14) and the purification ritual (Frag. B 15) be compatible with the discharge of the duties of a priestly office?

[80] Anaximander Frag. A 3; Emp. Frag. A 1 (Diogenes Laertius, viii. 64, 66) and Bignone, *Empedocle* (Turin, 1916), pp. 78–9; Parm. Frags. A 1 (Diogenes Laertius, ix. 23) and A 12; a commercial city, founded by Ionian émigrés, Elea was probably a democracy.

[81] Diogenes Laertius' statement (ix. 2) that Heraclitus declined the invitation to 'give laws' to Ephesus is unsupported by creditable authority. If true, it would only suggest that the demos did *not* think him an aristocratic partisan.

[82] Jaeger (*op. cit.*, I, 180 ff.) rightly insists on the unity of theory and practice in Heraclitus. Wisdom (*sophie*) includes both 'word and act' (ἔπη—ἔργα [Frag. B 1]; λέγειν—ποιεῖν [Frags. B 112 and B 73]). The many who live like dreamers, each in his private world (Frags. B 89, B 73), cannot 'follow the common' (Frag. B 2). This indictment cuts across class lines. The 'many' are not the demos but all who fail to meet the austere standards of Heraclitean wisdom, including the illustrious company of Homer, Hesiod, Archilochus, Pythagoras, Xenophanes, Hecataeus (Frags. B 40, B 42).

shared it; and so did Empedocles, whose loyalty to democracy is well attested.[83] What is peculiar to Heraclitus is, rather, the doctrine of the 'common': truth is the 'common'; the world is 'common';[84] and in the state, law is the 'common'.[85]

This concept of the state as a community, united by a common stake in a common justice, is perfectly compatible with democratic politics. Early in the sixth century it had inspired the Solonian reform programme.[86] It survived throughout the fifth century and into the fourth as a cherished doctrine of Athenian democracy.[87] Thus the doctrine of law as 'common' remains constant throughout a period of sweeping change *within* the democratic tradition. The vital choice in democratic politics in Heraclitus' day was whether to accelerate or to resist this development; whether to press forward toward the radical equalitarianism of the lot and 'ruling in turn' or else adhere to the earlier democracy, predicated, as in Solon, not on equal dignity but on common justice.[88] If our meagre evidence permits any hypothesis concerning Heraclitus' political sympathies, it would be that he favoured the limited democracy of the past. This is in line with his known admiration for Bias of Priene, who figures in the tradition

[83] Cf. 'mortal opinion' in Parmenides (Frags. B 1. 30, B 8. 51, B 19. 1–3) and Empedocles (Frags. B 2. 7–8, B 3, 1, etc.). Contempt for the ignorance of the public (cf. Hecataeus of Miletus Frag. 1 a; II. ἱερῆς νούσου 1. 3–5) need not of itself imply rejection of democracy except on the further assumptions that (1) this ignorance is incurable and (2) the enlightened would fare better under some practicable alternative to democracy.

[84] Cf. Frags. B 89, B 30. In Frag. B 80, *xynon* bears the same relation to *dike* and *chreon*, as 'war' to 'strife': the 'common' in Heraclitus denotes the same category of rational necessity which appears as *ananke-dike* in Parmenides.

[85] Frag. B 114. Here the law is clearly the 'common' thing in the *polis*, and as such the source of its strength. Hence 'the demos must fight on behalf of the law as for the city-walls' (Frag. B 44), i.e. as for the supreme condition of its common freedom. Similarly, in Frag. B 43, '*hybris* must be extinguished even more than a conflagration', the reference is again to a *common* peril.

[86] See my 'Solonian Justice', pp. 68–75 and 82–3.

[87] E.g., Euripides, *Suppl.* 430–2; Demosthenes, xxi. 30 ff.

[88] Solon's common justice does imply 'equal' laws (Frag. 24. 18 [Diehl]; literally, 'like', ὁμοίως, but see above, note 51). But these equal laws do not annul the vested inequalities in dignity between the social classes. Solon clearly thinks of himself as conserving the difference in 'honour' and 'prerogative' between the demos and their social superiors (Frag. 5 [Diehl]). His rejection of *isomoiria* in land is a corollary (Frag. 23. 21 [Diehl]).

as an early democratic statesman.[89] Indeed, Heraclitus' saying, 'the many are bad' (Frag. B 104), is also traditionally ascribed to Bias.[90] And Heraclitus' doctrine that the city 'strengthens' itself through the law has an obvious affinity to Bias' reputed saying that 'the strongest democracy is the one wherein all fear the law as their master'.[91]

From this perspective we should interpret those fragments in Heraclitus which exalt the 'one' against the 'many'.[92] The core of his politics is the supremacy of the 'common'—law. 'And it is law, too, to obey the counsel of one' (Frag. B 33) can only mean: the will of 'one' is law only when it expresses the 'common' to which all (including the 'one') are subject.[93] So, too, we must think of the cosmic supremacy of fire in Heraclitean physics, not as the predominance of a single power but as the submission of all powers to a single law. For if we think of fire as itself one of the powers, then it must keep its equal place among the rest. Thus

[89] There is good evidence of his repute as a 'pleader' (Hipponax Frag. 79 [Bergk]); this suggests that, whatever his political power at Priene, it was not above the law. Plutarch (*Moralia* 862 d) lumps his career with that of Pericles as examples of praiseworthy statesmanship. Of Priene's constitutional history we know next to nothing. But it is fair to assume that early in the sixth century its constitution, like that of other commercial Ionian cities, was at least moderately democratic.

[90] Diogenes Laertius, i. 88.

[91] Plutarch, *Moralia* 154 d. The obvious comparison is with Demaratus' words to the Persian king in Herodotus, vii. 104: 'Law is their despot, whom they fear much more than your men fear you.' This doctrine of δεσπότης νόμος sounds—and is—Spartan. But it is not opposed to democracy as such, but to Persian absolutism; it is matched in Aeschylus (e.g. *Eum.* 516–27 and 698–9). Its broader formulation in Demaratus' first speech to the king (Herodotus, vii. 102)—'virtue is acquired, wrought of wisdom and strong law'—is explicitly applied to 'all Greeks'. It could certainly be taken as the maxim of both Solonian and Heraclitean morality.

[92] Frags. B 49, 99, 110, 121. This point of Frag. B 121 should not be blunted by rendering ὀνήϊστος 'best' or 'worthiest', as in Cicero (*nemo de nobis unus excellat*) and subsequently in the textbooks. Hermodorus' intrinsic worth is not in question here. Heraclitus' point is that the Ephesians are losing the man who would be pre-eminently useful to the community and thus *to themselves*.

[93] The form of this fragment suggests the possibility that it is a qualifying antithesis to a preceding generalization: e.g. law is common counsel (cf. Frags. B 114, B 2, B 113), but 'it is law, too, to obey the counsel of one'. At any rate, a comparison with Frag. B 114 shows that the ultimate 'one' on which all human laws rest is the 'common mind' (= 'the one divine law').

water is absolutely impartial as between fire and earth, its two neighbours (and enemies) on the way up and down: it dies into earth as much as into fire; it lives from fire as much as from earth. Or if, conversely, we think of fire not as one of the many but as the One which *is* the many, then fire is not a separate power lording it over the rest; its justice is simply the common measure in all the powers. If everything is fire, then the 'government' of fire in the cosmos is cosmic self-government.[94]

V. ANAXIMANDER

We must reckon, finally, with the oldest and most controversial text in Presocratic philosophy, Anaximander's Fragment 1:

And into those things from which existing things take their rise, they pass away once more, 'according to just necessity [*chreon*]; for they render justice and reparation to one another for their injustices according to the ordering of time'.[95]

Any responsible interpretation of these words calls for justification; and this involves unavoidably the evaluation of certain Aristotelian texts which form our most important collateral evidence. I have left this last so as to approach it in the light of Heraclitus, Parmenides, Empedocles, and the medical writers: their thought-forms are safer guides to Anaximander than are the categories of Aristotelian physics. Yet, even so, we must respect what we know of the development of Presocratic thought and guard against reading into Anaximander atomic physics or Parmenidean logic.

---

[94] The Greek term αὐτόνομος (below, note 139) fits Heraclitus' thought exactly: the universe is 'a law unto itself'; its law is inherent in its own nature, not imposed upon it by a superior.

[95] Diels–Kranz start the citation with ἐξ ὧν. But Burnet's (*op. cit.*, p. 52, n. 6) and Heidel's ('On Anaximander', *CP*, VII [1912], 212–34, at 233) doubts with regard to τοῖς οὖσι, γένεσις, and φθορά in the first clause have never been properly answered. Φθορά is particularly open to suspicion. It never occurs as an abstract noun in any Presocratic fragment (Democritus Frag. B 249 has an obviously different meaning). Parmenides, whose polemic against the Ionians reflects their terminology, uses ὄλεθρος (and the verb, ὀλλύναι). That Anaximander, too, would use ὄλεθρος instead of φθορά is probable from ἀνώλεθρον in Arist. *Phys.* 203 b 14, quoting Anaximander, in place of ἄφθαρτον in l. 8, where Aristotle is using his own words. As for φθορὰν γίνεσθαι for φθείρεσθαι, is this likely at this stage of philosophic prose?

A. *Equality of the Opposites*

Aristotle writes:

Some people make not air or water the infinite, but this [*sc.* 'something distinct from the elements']⁹⁶ in order that the other elements may not be destroyed by the element which is infinite. They are in opposition to one another—air is cold, water is moist, fire hot. If one were infinite, the others would have been destroyed by now. As it is, the infinite is something other than the elements, from which they arise [*Phys.* 204 b 24–29].

Anaximander is not named here. But the identification is made in Simplicius, and there is no good reason to question it.⁹⁷ What the argument aims to prove is fortunately clear enough from independent evidence. We know that the first generation or two of Ionian thought *did* turn one of the opposites into the boundless source of everything else. This is obvious for Anaximenes' air. In the case of Xenophanes, we have his own words, off-hand, untechnical, and all the more valuable on that account: the earth has its upper limit just where you see it, 'next to your feet'; as for its lower limit, there is none, 'it goes on endlessly' (εἰς ἄπειρον ἱκνεῖται [Frag. B 28]).⁹⁸ Thales' water, too, must have been as endless as Xenophanes' earth and in the same sense: it must 'go on endlessly', for it supports the earth, while no provision is made for its being

---

⁹⁶ *Phys.* 204 b 23–4: τὸ παρὰ τὰ στοιχεῖα. The phrase serves well enough to distinguish Anaximander's *arche* from its derivatives. Aristotle's interpretation of the phrase—as a 'sensible body' which ought to be 'present in our world here' (ll. 32–4)—may be disregarded; it is clearly not Anaximander's own thought but a construction which Aristotle puts upon it for polemical purposes.

⁹⁷ Cherniss rejects it as 'the peculiarly Aristotelian argument of the necessary equilibrium of contrary forces' (*Aristotle's Criticism of Presocratic Philosophy* [Baltimore, 1935], p. 376), referring to *Meteor*, 340 a 1–17. But the latter is itself an Aristotelian adaptation of the old physical and medical doctrine of ἰσονομία τῶν δυνάμεων. Hence (and also in *Phys.* 204 b 14–18) Aristotle enriches the argument with various other notions of his own; these are absent from *Phys.* 204 b 23–9, especially the distinction between 'power' and 'bulk', which is foreign to the medical literature and the earlier philosophers (see above, p. 62).

⁹⁸ Aristotle (*De caelo* 294 a 22) paraphrases Xenophanes' doctrine as follows: ἐπ' ἄπειρον αὐτὴν [*sc.* the earth] ἐρριζῶσθαι. Xenophanes seems to be combating the Hesiodic view that the γῆς ῥίζαι start somewhere, i.e. from Tartarus (*Theog.* 728).

supported, in turn, by anything else.[99] Thus, in denying infinity to any of the opposites, Anaximander was going against the general trend. He could only have done so for a good reason. The argument in *Phys.* 204 b 24–9 supplies the reason: to safeguard the equilibrium among the opposites.

That the main components of the universe are equal was an old tradition in popular cosmology. In *Iliad* xv it is implied that the heavens, the sea, and 'the murky darkness' are equal, since their respective lords are equals in 'rank' and 'portion'.[100] In Hesiod earth and heavens are declared equal (*Theog.* 126); and the distance between heavens and earth is equal to that between earth and Tartarus (*ibid.*, 719–25). Such ideas are mainly without even a semblance of physical justification.[101] They boldly read into the universe that feeling for symmetry and balance which makes the *Odyssey* speak of a well-made ship as 'equal'[102] and of a wise, balanced mind also as 'equal'.[103] Anaximander's own cosmology is designed with just such a sense of aesthetic symmetry, with equality as the main motif: the intervals between each of the infinite worlds are equal;[104] the intervals between earth, fixed stars, moon, and sun are also equal;[105] earth and sun are equal;[106] the two land-masses of the earth—Asia and Europe—are equal, and the two great rivers in each are equal and divide the regions

[99] That the earth floats on water is well attested (Thales Frags. A 13, A 14, and A 15) and a surer ground of inference than the conflicting tradition on the question as to whether or not Thales' water was boundless (Theophrastus *vs.* Simplicius in Thales Frag. A 13). Anaximander may well have been the first to *name* his *arche* 'Boundless' (so Theophrastus *ap.* Simplicius, *Phys.* 24, 15–16).

[100] See above, note 7; and Cornford's discussion of this passage in *From Religion to Philosophy*, pp. 15–16.

[101] Only for the equality of heavens and earth in *Theog.* 126–7 can one conjecture a rough appeal to observable fact, i.e. the apparent coincidence of the visual horizon with the base of the celestial hemisphere.

[102] xi. 508, κοίλης ἐπὶ νηὸς ἐίσης. The most striking example of this use of equality to express geometric symmetry is the definition of the straight line in Euclid: ἥτις ἐξ ἴσου [i.e. symmetrically] τοῖς ἐφ᾽ ἑαυτῆς σημείοις κεῖται.

[103] xi. 337, φρένας . . . ἐίσας.

[104] Aetius, ii. 1. 8.

[105] From the data in Hippolytus, *Ref.* i. 6, 5; Aetius, ii. 20, 1, and ii. 21, 1, with Tannery's reasonable conjectures (*op. cit.*, pp. 94 f.).

[106] Aetius ii. 21, 2. Strictly speaking, this means that the diameter of the circular vent of the sun-ring which constitutes the visible sun is equal to the diameter of the earth.

through which they flow into equal parts.[107] To cap all this with the equality of the opposites which constitute this world would be in fine harmony with the whole design. The argument in *Phys.* 204 b 24–9 takes us beyond this aesthetic presumption into physical reasoning: if one of the opposites were boundless, it would not only mar the architectonic elegance of the cosmology but would positively 'destroy' the other opposites.[108] Why so? Because—as we know from Fragment 1—the opposites are constantly encroaching upon one another. If one of them were limitless, there would be no stopping it by the rest, singly or in combination, for they are all limited. Its encroachment would continue until the rest were destroyed.

B. *Justice in the Boundless*

We may now settle accounts with the older interpretation of Fragment 1: that the very existence of the cosmos is itself an injustice against the Boundless, to be expiated by reabsorption.[109] This was the general view before the restoration of the words 'to one another' (ἀλλήλοις) in the second clause; thereafter, it was left without firm foothold in the text and has been largely abandoned.[110] What still gives it a measure of plausibility is the sug-

---

[107] All this, of course, on the assumption that the geography of 'the Ionians' in Herodotus, iv. 36 and ii. 33 is substantially derived from Anaximander (via Hecataeus) and conserves his accent on equality (see Jaeger, *op. cit.*, l. 155–6).

[108] Cf. the association of encroachment ('injustice') with 'destruction' by Eryximachus in Plato, *Symp.* 188 e.

[109] Jaeger observes (*op. cit.*, p. 159) that this is not a Greek idea. Certainly, it is alien to the Presocratics. The least objectionable version of the view is in O. Gilbert, 'Spekulation und Volksglaube in der ionischen Philosophie'. *Arch. f. Religionswissenschaft*, XIII (1910), 312. He thinks that the divine energy 'stuft sich, je weiter es sich von dem Urquell der Gottheit [*sc.* the Boundless itself] entfernt, mehr und mehr ab'. Even so, I see no good reason for reading this Neo-Platonic notion into Anaximander. Hippolytus, *Ref.* i. 7, 1 (*Doxogr. Graeci* 560, 13–15), to which Gilbert appealed, does not bear out the interpretation he put upon it.

[110] Diels clung to it to the end (see 'Anaximandros von Milet', *Neue Jahrbücher f. d. klass. Altertum* [1923], p. 69). For a more recent defence, see Mondolfo, *Problemi del pensiero antico* (1935), Ch. II; also his 'La Giustizia cosmica secondo Anassimandro ed Eraclito', *Civiltà moderna* (1934). He argues that, because 'injustice' is normal (he compares war and strife in Heraclitus), existence is inherently unjust ('La Giustizia', p. 416), and thus a collective sin against the 'universal law of harmony and unity' (*ibid.*, p. 418).

gestion in the first clause that 'reparation' is somehow connected with 'passing away';[111] how can things 'render justice and reparation *to one another*' in a process which destroys their very existence? Unless this paradox can be resoved, we shall find ourselves drifting back into the older view, even after formally abandoning it; we shall be constantly tempted to think of the Boundless itself as the payee of the 'damages' and, consequently, as itself the victim of the original injustice.

We may approach the answer by way of the little-noticed fact that the fragment refers *in the plural*[112] to the matrix from which all things arise and to which they all return. This is strange, for the reference is obviously to the Boundless; and this is plainly singular. The shift to the plural can mean only that in this context the Boundless is explicitly thought of as a plurality.[113] This is in

[111] I follow Cherniss (*op. cit.* in note 69, p. 376) in assuming that the first clause, though probably only paraphrased (see above, n. 86), does convey the substance of Anaximander's thought. We would save ourselves a good deal of exegetical trouble by assuming (with Heidel, 'On Anaximander', pp. 233—4) that the thought, as well as the wording, is not Anaximander's but Theophrastus'.

[112] Cherniss (*op. cit.* in note 69, p. 377) observes that the standard translations obscure this point by turning the plural of the original (ἐξ ὧν . . . εἰς ταῦτα . . .) into the singular. Thus Burnet translates: 'Into that [= εἰς ταῦτα] from which [ἐξ ὧν] . . .'

[113] Cherniss (*loc. cit.*) infers an unlimited plurality. From Simplicius' statement, 'opposites are hot, cold, dry, moist, and the rest' (*Phys.* cl. 24–5), we may infer that Anaximander assumed a great number of opposites (as did Alc-

But this misses the whole point of the equation of reparation and encroachment which insures that, on balance, existence is always 'just'. Mondolfo writes of Heraclitus: 'Generated and existing only through war, individual things exist through each other's destruction and thus through *hybris*' (*ibid.*, p. 416). But *hybris* is not in Heraclitus, except in Frag. B 43, where the reference is not cosmological. As for war and strife, whatever we may think of them, they passed at the time for perfectly proper instruments of justice— so much so that νεῖκος could stand for action-at-law (e.g. *Od.* xii. 440; Hesiod, *Op.* 232); ἔρις could mean simply 'cause' (e.g. Aeschylus, *Suppl.* 644–5: ἀτιμώσαντες ἔριν γυναικῶν); and even participation in *stasis* could be made a matter of statutory obligation by Solon (Arist. *Ath. pol.* xiii. 5; Plut. *Solon* xx. 1). As I have argued in the text, because inverse processes of 'strife' balance in Heraclitus, his own statement that 'strife is justice' makes sense: from 'god's' standpoint there is no injustice (Frag. B 102). His system not only expels *hybris* and injustice from the cosmos but employs strife as an essential instrument in their expulsion.

line with what Aristotle tells us in *Phys.* 187 a 20–2, where he speaks of Anaximander's opposites (ἐναντιότητας) as being 'contained in' (ἐνούσας) the 'one' and issuing from it by a process of 'separation' (ἐκκρίνεσθαι). Burnet ruled against this statement as 'not even a paraphrase of anything Anaximander said'.[114] But his objection to Aristotle's word for 'contained in' (ἐνεῖναι) as 'unhistorical'—his only definite reason for the sweeping condemnation of the text—is completely unfounded. The same word occurs frequently in the Presocratics and the medical literature with the very sense required in the present context, i.e. the relation of any ingredient to the compound of which it forms a part.[115] As for the other terms used here by Aristotle—'separation' and 'oppositions'—both refer to characteristic concepts of Ionian medicine and physics and accord perfectly with what we know of Anaximander's system. The 'opposites' are obviously 'the hot, cold, dry, moist, and the rest' (Simpl. *Phys.* 150. 24), which are the main components of his cosmology. 'Separation' is the basic cosmogonic category of Ionian thought, the process by which 'the heavens and all the infinite worlds' are formed in Anaximander.[116]

---

[114] *Op. cit.*, p. 57, n. 1.

[115] For the Presocratics, see Kranz's *Wortindex*, *s.v.* ἐνεῖναι. For the medical literature see, e.g., II. ἀρχ. ἰητρ. 14, 29, 31; 16, 6; see also instances cited by H. C. Baldry in 'Plato's "Technical Terms",' *CQ*, XXXI (1937), 141–50, at 146.

[116] Pseudo-Plutarch, *Strom.* ii. For a good discussion of 'separation' see Heidel, 'On Anaximander', pp. 229–32. But Heidel's suggestion that ἐκ τοῦ ἀιδίου in Pseudo-Plutarch means 'from eternity' has not found favour. The correct rendering of the whole phrase (*Doxogr. Graeci* 579, 13–14) seems to me to be: 'something productive of hot and cold was separated off from the eternal' (adapted from Burnet's translation). That the process which generates the hot and the cold should be spoken of in the passive voice as itself 'separated off' sounds strange perhaps; but cf. Democ. Frag. B 167: δῖνον ἀπὸ τοῦ παντὸς ἀποκριθῆναι. 'Productive of hot and cold' may also seem strange, since both are 'contained in' the Boundless; but I think this sufficiently explained in the suggestion which I make in the following paragraph: hot and cold, being perfectly 'blended' in the Boundless, emerge as distinct, recognizable powers only after the 'separation'.

---

maeon: 'the wet, dry, cold, hot, bitter, sweet, *and the rest*' [Frag. B 4]). But to say that he assumed an *infinity* of opposites goes beyond our evidence and leaves unexplained the practice of Aristotle and his school, who regard this as the innovation of Anaxagoras (e.g. Theophrastus *ap.* Simplicius, *Phys.* 27. 4).

There is, none the less, a residual problem here: If the *apeiron* is a compound of opposites, why should Aristotle think of it as 'one' and contrast it as such with the 'one and many' of Empedocles' *Sphairos* and Anaxagoras' primitive mixture?[117] The answer is surely that Empedocles and Anaxagoras both thought of their original compound as made up of Parmenidean bits of Being, eternally self-identical in the mixture as in the world which issues from it.[118] This is just what we cannot ascribe to Anaximander without anachronism: he thought of his Boundless as 'one' in a far more intimate sense than would have been possible for a physicist schooled in Parmenidean logic. That logic compelled Empedocles to revise the basic concept of *krasis* and to think of it as a mere juxtaposition of minute particles.[119] For the unreformed doctrine of *krasis* we may look to the anti-Empedoclean *Ancient Medicine*, which speaks of a compound in *krasis* as 'one and simple'.[120] This seems to be our best clue to the sense in which Anaximander's Boundless is 'one': it does 'contain' the 'opposites'; but these are so thoroughly mixed that none of them appears as single, individual things.[121] This would explain why Aristotle and his school commonly refer to Empedocles' principles (*archai*) as six and to Anaxagoras' as infinite in number, while they invariably speak of Anaximander's principle as one.[122]

---

[117] *Phys.* 187 a 21–22.

[118] This leads to at least two fundamental differences from Milesian doctrine: (1) generation, the prime category of Milesian physics, is now denied (Emp. Frag. B 8; Anaxag. Frag. B 17); (2) the opposites themselves usurp the role of the Milesian *arche*: they become 'roots' and 'seeds', are thus the 'source' (πηγή) of mortal things (Emp. Frag. B 23, 10), and, in Empedocles, are endowed with the divinity which the Milesians had assigned to the *arche*.

[119] Galen's commentary on Hipp. Π. φύσ. ἀνθρ. 15 (cited in Diels–Kranz under Emp. Frag. A 34): οὐ μὴν κεκραμένων γε δι' ἀλλήλων [the Hippocratic doctrine] ἀλλὰ κατὰ σμικρὰ μόρια παρακειμένων. Empedocles was followed by the atomists: Alexander Aphrod. *De mixtione* 2 (cited in Diels–Kranz under Democ. Frag. A 64).

[120] Frag. 14. 55–7: εὖ τε κέκρηται καὶ . . . ὅλον ἕν τε γέγονε καὶ ἁπλοῦν. Contrast this with Aristotelian usage, where κεκραμένον and ἁπλοῦν appear as contraries (*De sensu* 447 a 18).

[121] In Hippocratic terms, 'no individual power is displayed' (see above, note 11).

[122] With the single exception noted above: the plural ἐξ ὧν . . . εἰς ταῦτα . . . in Frag. 1.

And it would further explain what we must understand by the Aristotelian term 'indeterminate' (φύσις ἀόριστος) as applied to Anaximander's Boundless. Just as in a Hippocratic compound in *krasis* the individual opposites are 'not apparent',[123] so neither are they in Anaximander's Boundless: no part of the compound, no matter how minute, being either hot or cold or dry or moist, etc., the whole is just what Aristotle would call 'indeterminate'.[124]

On this interpretation we can explain the strictly reciprocal nature of injustice and reparation in Fragment 1. In the Boundless itself, which is perfectly blended, no power can dominate another and thus commit 'injustice'. Only when the world-forming segregation occurs can separate powers show up. Thereafter, wherever one of these is strong enough to encroach upon another, 'injustice' will result. When the world is, in due course, re-absorbed into the Boundless, the opposites are *not* destroyed. They do *not* cease to exist. They are only blended once again, and their equilibrium is perfectly restored. And this must entail a process of 'reparation', where unjust gains are disgorged and unjust losses fully made up. Thus at no time is there either injustice against the Boundless or reparation to it. Reabsorption into the Boundless is only the process which insures full reparation among the opposites themselves; the damages are paid not to the Boundless but to *one another*.

C. *Justice in the World*

But what of the interval between generation and dissolution? Are we to suppose that the life-history of the world is a series of encroachments, unchecked until a judgement day at the very end? Such a supposition would go against every canon of Presocratic physics. If becoming were a theatre of injustice without reparation, it would be not cosmos but chaos, and the elegant pattern of balanced equalities in Anaximander's world would collapse. But such a possibility is precluded by the structural elements of Anaximander's own cosmogonic process. The opposites, balanced

[123] E.g. *Ancient Medicine* xvi. 35; when the powers are 'mixed and blended with one another, they are neither apparent [φανερά] nor do they hurt a man; but when one of them is separated off and stands by itself [see above, note 18], then it is apparent [φανερόν] and hurts a man' (translation adapted from Jones).

[124] For Aristotle determination is primarily qualitative, not quantitative; e.g. *Metaph.* 1063 a 28: τὸ ποιὸν ὡρισμένης φύσεως, τὸ δὲ ποσὸν τῆς ἀορίστου.

in the Boundless, issue from it *together* in balanced proportions.[125] It follows that the hot in a given world will be no stronger than the cold, and so for the other opposites. Moreover, since the world is 'encompassed' by the Boundless,[126] nothing can enter or depart to upset the balance fixed upon the opposites in the process of generation.[127] Thus the Boundless 'governs' the world throughout its growth and decline. This is never a matter of direct action by the Boundless upon the inner structure of the world, for the whole of the cosmology is delineated in terms of the interaction of the opposites themselves upon one another. The Boundless 'governs' by 'encompassing',[128] i.e. by safeguarding the original equality of the opposites with one another.

[125] Cf. Fränkel, *op. cit.*, p. 184: 'nichts Einzelnes werdend aus dem *apeiron* heraustritt, sondern nur gemeinsam die Gegensätze'.

[126] Aristotle, *Phys.* 203 b 11–13: 'and it encompasses all things and governs all things, as those assert who do not recognize other causes besides the Boundless, e.g. *nous* or love'. The terms of reference apply definitely, though not exclusively, to Anaximander. Cf. also Hippolytus, *Ref.* i. 6, 1 (*Doxogr. Graeci* 559. 18).

[127] For the atomists, matter inside and outside a 'world' was homogeneous; hence the *exitus introitusque* through the *spiracula mundi* (Lucretius vi. 492–4; cf. i. 999–1001; i. 1035–51; ii. 1105 ff. See also Democ. Frag. A 40 = Hippolytus, *Ref.* i. 13. 4; Leucippus Frag. A 1 = Diogenes Laertius, ix. 32). Similarly, Anaximenes' world could 'breathe in' the outside air, which was the same stuff as the air within. For Anaximander, on the other hand, the Boundless is unassimilable, unless duly separated out; and there is no hint in our sources that this separation could occur except at the appropriate stage of world-formation. This would seem to invalidate Heidel's assumption ('On Anaximander', pp. 227–8) of cosmic respiration in Anaximander.

[128] And thus performs the function which Parmenides would later assign to *Dike-Ananke*, i.e. it holds the world fast 'within the bonds of the limit' (see Parm. Frags. B 8. 31, and B 10. 5–7, bearing in mind that περιέχειν = ἀμφὶς ἔχειν. Parmenides internalized—to Being in Frag. B 8, to the Ouranos in Frag. B 10—this function of 'holding the limits' which Anaximander's Boundless performs by surrounding each world from the outside). But to 'hold the limits (or ends) of all things' had been the divine prerogative (e.g. Semonides of Amorgus Frag. 1. 1–2 [Diehl]; Solon Frag. 16 [Diehl]). Hence the point of Aristotle's reference to the σεμνότης of the Boundless: τὸ πάντα περιέχον (*Phys.* 207 a 19; cf. the ancient tradition in *Metaph.* 1074 b 2: 'that the divine encompasses the whole of nature'). The connection between 'holding the ends' and 'governing' need not be laboured. But it may be worth noting that (1) boundlessness as such conveyed the idea of inescapability (e.g. Aesch. *Suppl.* 1049–50); (2) even ἔχειν alone could mean 'to hold to the course, guide, steer' (Liddell and Scott, *s.v.*); (3) περιέχειν has also the sense 'surpass, excel' and 'overcome in battle' (*ibid.*, *s.v.*).

If this equality is maintained, justice is assured, for no opposite will be strong enough to dominate another. When encroachment occurs, it will be compensated by 'reparation', as, e.g. in the seasonal cycle the hot prevails in the summer, only to suffer commensurate subjection to its rival in the winter. We have already met this ordered sequence of 'successive supremacy' in the medical writers and Empedocles. And, although our evidence is not sufficient to establish it conclusively in the case of Anaximander, we can impute it to him with considerable likelihood.[129] In any case we can assume with perfect confidence that, while reabsorption into the Boundless would be the complete and absolute end of all injustice, nevertheless overall justice is preserved throughout the life-process of the world despite the occurrence of injustice; and this by the equation of reparation to encroachment, which is itself assured through the invariant equality of the opposites.

Every student of Greek science must feel how profound was the debt of subsequent cosmology to Anaximander. His were the seminal ideas of the whirl, the infinite worlds, the unsupported earth, the conception of sun and stars as huge, free-swinging masses rather than fixtures on a copper dome. Yet more important than these and his other physical hypotheses was his philosophical concept of nature as a self-regulative equilibrium, whose order was strictly immanent, guaranteed through the fixed proportions of its main constituents. Once established, this idea becomes the common property of classical thought. It is shared by minds as diametrically opposed as Lucretius,[129a] on the one hand, and the pious author of the *De mundo*, on the other.[130] In Anaximander we

---

[129] Heidel 'On Anaximander', pp. 233–4; also *Proc. Amer. Acad.* XLVIII (1913); 684–5. To the parallels cited by Heidel add Philo, *De incorr. mundi* 108 ff., which explicitly uses the cyclical exchanges of the seasons to illustrate 'reciprocation between the four powers'.

[129a] On *isonomia* in Epicurean atomism see below, note 156.

[130] His explanation of the imperishable order of nature through the *isomoiria* and successive supremacy of the opposites comes strikingly close to Anaximander's (see citation above, note 12; and 397 b 6–7). Cf. Philo (above, note 64); Ocellus Lucanus 22. ἀντιπαθεῖς οὖσαι [*sc.* the four 'powers'] μήτε κρατῶσιν εἰς τέλος αὐταὶ αὐτῶν μήτε κρατῶνται αὐταὶ ὑπ' αὐτῶν; Seneca, *QN* iii. 10, 3: 'omnium elementorum alterni recursus sunt; quicquid alteri perit, in alterum transit; et natura partes suas velut in ponderibus constitutas examinat, ne portionum aequitate turbata mundus praeponderet'.

can trace it back to its source in the political assumption that justice was an affair between equals[131] and that its settlement involved an equation of compensation to injury.[132]

VI. THE NATURALIZATION OF JUSTICE

When Parmenides speaks of *Dike-Ananke* holding Being fast in the bonds of the limit, his words echo Hesiod and Semonides, who speak of fate as a 'bond of unbreakable fetters';[133] but his thought is far from theirs. In Hesiod and Semonides the source of the compulsion is external to the thing compelled. In Parmenides the compulsion is immanent. The first is a non-rational concept of *ananke*: the determining agency remains hidden from human reason. The second is so thoroughly rational that *ananke* merges with *dike*, and *dike* with logicophysical necessity: the order of

[131] As Heidel observes; '*dike* obtains between peers', ('On Anaximander', p. 234).

[132] To 'get justice' was literally to 'get (back) the equal' (ἴσα ἔσσεται [*Od.* ii. 203]). To 'give justice' (δίκην διδόναι) was, again literally, 'to pay the equal' (ἴσην ἔτισεν [Sophocles, *OT*, 810]). The underlying principle is that of an *exchange*: equal value rendered for value taken. The same words apply to the closure of a commercial transaction, like barter, sale, or loan, and to the satisfaction of justice:

ἀμείβω,	ἀνταμείβομαι,	ἀμοιβή,	ἀνταμοιβή·
ἀλλάσσω,	ἀνταλλάσσω·	ἀπόδοσις,	ἀνταπόδοσις.

This pattern of thought was capable of indefinite generalization. It was popularly applied to physical sequences where one event was regularly followed by (and thus 'exchanged for') its reciprocal: e.g. the cycle of birth and death (*Phaedo* 71 e–72 b); waking and sleeping (*Phaedo* 72 b); the succession of day and night (e.g. Hesiod, *Theog.* 749); the cycle of the seasons (Philo, *De incorr. mundi* 109); hoofs that strike the ground in turn (Pindar, *Pyth.* iv. 226); land, plowed and left fallow in turn (Pindar, *Nem.* vi. 9). Scientific thought used this pattern to join events which had either been left unconnected (like evaporation and precipitation [Aristotle, *Meteor.* 355 a 28]) or else had not been clearly grasped as strict equations by the popular mind (like breathing in and breathing out [Plato, *Tim.* 79 e 7–8]; or the stretching of a lyre string and the vibration when released [Aristotle, *Mech. probl.* 803 a 31]). But the uniformity of nature as a whole could also be construed as just such a reciprocity among its basic components. Anaximander so construes it in Frag. 1.

[133] Hesiod, *Theog.* 615: ἀλλ' ὑπ' ἀνάγκης | . . . μέγας κατὰ δεσμὸς ἐρύκει. Semon. 7. 115 (Diehl): δεσμὸν ἀμφέθηκεν ἄρρηκτον πέδης. Parm. Frag. B 8. 14: (οὐκ) ἀνῆκε Δίκη χαλάσσασα πέδῃσιν, | ἀλλ' ἔχει. Frag. B 8. 31: πείρατος ἐν δεσμοῖσιν [sc. Ἀνάγκη] ἔχει, τό μιν ἀμφὶς ἐέργει.

nature is deducible from the intelligible properties of nature itself. We may speak of this transition, the work of Anaximander and his successors,[134] as the naturalization of justice. Justice is no longer inscrutable *moira*, imposed by arbitrary forces with incalculable effect. Nor is she the goddess *Dike*, moral and rational enough, but frail and unreliable. She is now one with 'the ineluctable laws of nature herself';[135] unlike Hesiod's *Dike*, she could no more leave the earth than the earth could leave its place in the firmament.

Thus the naturalization of justice transformed her status and added immeasurably to her stature. But it also transformed nature. These 'ineluctable laws of nature', what were they prior to Milesian physics? Behind the massive stability of heaven and earth had lurked a realm of arbitrariness and terror. The uniform motions of sun and moon could be inexplicably broken by an eclipse;[136] the fertility of earth and womb might mysteriously fail; children could be born 'unlike those who begat them, but monsters';[137] these and a thousand other things could be thought of as lesions in natural order, special interventions of Zeus and his instruments, vindicating the authority of the supernatural by suspending or reversing the ordinary course of nature.[138] The adventurous reason of Ionian science charted this realm of magic, detached it from the personal control of supernatural beings, and

[134] For Solon's contribution, see Werner Jaeger, 'Solon's Eunomie', *Sitzungsber. Preuss. Akad. d. Wissenschaften* (Berlin, 1926); and *Paideia*, Vol. I, Ch. VIII and also p. 158 in Ch. IX. Yet the old magical conception of justice survives in Solon, side by side with the new (see my 'Solonian Justice', pp. 76–8).

[135] Maurice Croiset in a brilliant comment on Solon Frag. 3 (Diehl): 'La Morale et la cité dans les poésies de Solon', *Compt. rend. Acad. d. inscrip. et belles lettres* (Paris, 1903), p. 587.

[136] Archil. Frag. 74 (Diehl); Pindar, *Paean* 9. 1–21. But it is worth noticing that Archilochus takes the eclipse not as the operation of a superior type of order, obscure but unquestionable, but rather as a threat against *all* order. He identifies order implicitly with nature (even though everything comes under the power of Zeus). His very consternation at the thought that a natural uniformity could be broken is a confession that he has lost faith in magic as a realm of order in its own right. This is a more enlightened attitude than Pindar's, whose main reaction is fear at the calamities that the eclipse may portend.

[137] See Hesiod, *Op.* 225–45, and parallels cited *ad loc.* in Mazon's edition; further parallels mentioned in my 'Solonian Justice', notes 9 and 10.

[138] For the supernatural sanctions of the pre-Solonian concept of justice see my 'Solonian Justice', pp. 65–6.

integrated it into the domain of nature. All natural events, ordinary and extraordinary alike, were now united under a common law.

The equality of the constituents of this new commonwealth of nature was of the essence of the transformation, for it meant the abolition of distinctions between two grades of being—divine and mortal, lordly and subservient, noble and mean, of higher and lower honour. It was the ending of these distinctions that made nature autonomous and *therefore* completely and unexceptionably 'just'. Given a society of equals, it was assumed, justice was sure to follow, for none would have the power to dominate the rest.[139] This assumption, as we have seen, had a strictly physical sense. It was accepted not as a political dogma but as a theorem in physical inquiry. It is, none the less, remarkable evidence of the confidence which the great age of Greek democracy possessed in the validity of the democratic idea—a confidence so robust that it survived translation into the first principles of cosmology and medical theory.[140]

Of the four *physiologoi* we have studied, Heraclitus alone appears estranged from democratic politics. His interest in the current belief in equality is not so much to vindicate as to qualify and correct it. It is therefore significant that there should be no

[139] For the political import of this idea, see II. ά. ύ. τ. 16 (also 23, 30 ff.; and cf. Herodotus, iii. 80. 3–6, iii. 142. 3, v. 78). The benefits of democracy are inferred here from the fact that under it men are *autonomous* (II. ά, ύ. τ. 16. 10; cf. 16. 35 and 23. 37). This is not merely the formal power to issue laws but the more fundamental power to order one's own life without domination by an 'alien power' (16. 36).

[140] Professor Kurt von Fritz raises an important question (by correspondence): May not the political equivalent of cosmic equality be the idea of balance of power between classes or governing bodies (as, e.g., kings, ephors, senate, *apella* in Sparta) rather than the idea of equality between individual citizens? Only the latter, of course, would be characteristic of democracy in its mature form. The answer, it seems to me, is in the idea of 'rotation of office', which (1) applies to individual citizens rather than to classes or governing bodies; (2) is decisively democratic as a general constitutional practice; and (3) implies equality of 'honour' (τιμή) or status. This, as we have seen, Empedocles explicitly asserts of the cosmic powers. There is no reason to believe that Parmenides or Anaximander thought of the powers in any other sense. On the contrary, everything we have seen of their respective cosmologies implies perfect equality of status among the basic constituents of their cosmos.

mention of equality in his physical fragments. The equalitarianism of his physics, such as it is, seems imposed upon the author as a structural necessity rather than as a conscious choice. Order he must have, and he knows of no other way of getting it than by enforcing the equal submission of all powers to the 'common' law. Thus Heraclitus in his own way remains within the general framework of equalitarian physics; certainly, he makes no effort to break with that tradition. The attempt first comes with Anaxagoras' doctrine of *nous*, which, unlike Heraclitus' fire, is 'mixed with nothing, but is alone, itself by itself',[141] and has therefore absolute,[142] one-sided dominion over the 'mixed' forces of nature. But this revolt proved abortive. It was Plato, the bitter critic of Athenian democracy, who carried through the intellectual revolution (or, more strictly, counter-revolution) to a successful conclusion; and Aristotle followed, though with hesitations and misgivings.[143] In their systems we find at last the explicit and thoroughgoing negation of Anaximander's equalitarian universe.

The attributes of divinity are now reserved to one set of superior entities, which alone are perfect, 'prior',[144] sovereign,[145] ageless, incorruptible. Nature is no longer a single mechanical system, composed throughout of the same stuff, ordered throughout by the same laws of motion. It breaks apart into a 'hither' and a

---

[141] Frag. B 12: μέμεικται οὐδενὶ χρήματι, ἀλλὰ μόνος αὐτὸς ἐπ' ἑωυτοῦ ἐστιν. For the same expression in Hippocratic treatises see above, note 16. In medical thought the state of isolation is a sign of *dis*order; in Anaxagoras' *nous* it accounts for *order*. There could be no more striking evidence of the clear-cut negation of Ionian categories. The Platonic Form conserves this feature of Anaxagoras' *nous*: it is αὐτὸ καθ' αὐτό, and thus ἄμεικτον, καθαρώτατον.

[142] Αὐτοκρατές, Frag. B 12. Cf. Plato, *Crat.* 413 c: αὐτοκράτορα γὰρ αὐτὸν ὄντα (*sc.* Anaxagoras' *nous*).

[143] For Plato, see my 'Slavery in Plato's Thought', *Philosophical Review*, L (1941), 289–304. Sec. I. Herodotus had registered the conviction that 'monarchy' is *unjust in principle*, i.e. irrespective of the personal merits of the incumbent; it would produce *hybris* even 'in the best of all men' (iii. 80. 3). Plato and even Aristotle, on the other hand, hold that, given a man sufficiently superior in virtue, he should be 'sovereign over all' as a matter of justice (*Pol.* 1284 b 28 ff., 1288 a 15 ff.).

[144] See above, note 37.

[145] Bonitz, *Index Arist.*, s.v. Κύριος. The term conveys the nearest Greek equivalent to the modern concept of political sovereignty.

'yonder'.[146] The first, thinks Aristotle, consists of the familiar Ionian opposites; the other, of 'something beyond the bodies that are about us on this earth, different and separate from them, the superior honour of its nature being proportionate to its distance from this world of ours'.[147] There are two types of motion, each simple and incommensurable with the other: the circular motions of the 'more honourable' bodies, which are 'perfect' and undeviatingly uniform; the rectilinear, 'imperfect', and 'wandering' motions which occur only in the 'lower' regions.[148] *Dike* and *ananke*, logical reason and physical necessity, which had merged in the Presocratics to banish disorder from the physical universe, are now separated.[149] For all its teleological subordination to the 'good', matter remains a residual principle of evil and disorder.[150]

From the polemics of *Laws* X, one would never guess that any

[146] Note Plato's use of τόνδε τὸν τόπον, ἐνθάδε versus ἐν θεοῖς, ἐκεῖσε, ὁ τῶν κακῶν καθαρὸς τόπος (*Theaet.* 176 a 7–8, b 1; 177 a 5), and Aristotle's use of τὰ ἐνταῦθα (*s.v.* Bonitz, *Index*), τὰ παρ' ἡμῖν versus τἀκεῖ, ἡ θειοτέρα οὐσία.

[147] *De caelo* 269 b 13–17 (Stock); cf. *ibid.* 269 a 31–3, and *Meteor.* 339 a 11. Abstracting from Aristotle's 'fifth' element, one finds a comparable, though weaker, distinction in Plato: in the heavens the four elements are 'purer', 'nobler', etc., than they are 'here' (*Phil.* 29 b–d; *Phaedo* 109 b–111 b, esp. 110 a), presumably because 'there' they are free of the six wandering motions (*Tim.* 34 a). In *Laws* xii. 967 c (cf. x. 886 d–e) the view that there are 'stones or earth' in the stars is denounced as criminal atheism.

[148] For the effects of this bifurcation on Aristotelian dynamics, see W. D. Ross, *Aristotle's Physics* (Oxford, 1936), p. 33. Ross points out that in *Phys.* 244 a 1–3 (he might have added *Meteor.* 370 b 20–8) there is, nonetheless, a true analysis of circular motion as the resultant of two inverse rectilinear motions. The history of thought offers no better example of a great thinker, hitting on a scientific explanation of revolutionary import, yet missing its significance because of the blinkers of a metaphysical dogma.

[149] See my 'Slavery in Plato's Thought', p. 296; to the references there cited add *Soph.* 265 c: αἰτίας αὐτομάτης καὶ ἄνευ διανοίας φυούσης ἢ μετὰ λόγου etc.; and *Laws* XII 967 a: ἀνάγκαις . . . οὐ διανοίαις. In Aristotle the contrast of the 'good' and the 'necessary' cause is analogous to the contrast of 'rational' and 'material' (*Phys.* 200 a 14: ἐν τῇ ὕλῃ τὸ ἀναγκαῖον, τὸ δ' οὗ ἕνεκα ἐν τῷ λόγῳ. *De part. anim.* 663 b 22–3; ἡ ἀναγκαία vs. ἡ κατὰ λόγον φύσις).

[150] See my 'Disorderly Motion in the *Timaeus*', *CQ*, XXIII (1930), 71–83, at 80 and 82, n. 3. Hence natural science can only be a 'likely tale'. And even Aristotle holds categorically that there can be no science of the indeterminate (*An. post.* 32 b 18); cf. the role of the indeterminateness of matter (ἡ τῆς ὕλης ἀοριστία) in *De gen. anim.* 778 a 7, and cf. also *Met.* 1010 a 3, 1049 b 2.

of Plato's materialistic opponents[151] had believed that 'all human laws are nourished by the one law divine' and had thought of this justice in the nature of things not as impersonal order but as a 'thought that steers all things through all things'.[152] But Plato

[151] Plato here is intent on exposing the basic error of 'all the men who have ever handled physical investigation' (891 c [Bury]). He has in mind the most mature physical systems, including atomism; but he draws no fine distinctions and makes no honourable exemptions, for he is convinced that all those who sowed the materialist wind must be held responsible for the whirlwind, i.e. the conventional theory of justice. Tate (*CQ*, XXX [1936], 48–54) has argued that the butt of Plato's polemic is Archelaus and his fourth-century followers. Certainly, Archelaus meets the double imputation of materialist cosmology and the conventional theory of justice and thus falls within the scope of Plato's polemic. But that a second-rate thinker should be singled out as *the* representative of materialist physics seems unlikely; and as for his 'followers', we know nothing about them. I think Tate forces the meaning of νέων καὶ σοφῶν in 886 d. Since ἀρχαῖοι here clearly refers to the theogonies (886 c; cf. Arist. *Meteor.* 353 a 34), νέοι can only mean the more 'modern', though scarcely contemporary, cosmogonies of scientific physics (cf. *Meteor.* 353 b 5; and *Met.* 1091 a 34–1091 b 11: ποιηταὶ ἀρχαῖοι versus ὕστεροι σοφοί); what is contemporary for Plato is the influence of this trend of thought. Tate further restricts unnecessarily the reference of the doctrine that the heavenly bodies are 'earth and stones'; this applies to Democritus (Frag. A 39) as much as to Anaxagoras. Tate appeals to 895 a to show that 'Plato cannot be arguing against atomism, according to which motion is eternal and had no beginning' (p. 53); but note the force of οἱ πλεῖστοι τῶν τοιούτων. The frequent inveighing against 'chance' and 'necessity' must have Empedocles and Democritus in mind, if we may judge from the reference of similar arguments in Aristotle (for Democritus see the passages in Diels–Kranz, Frags. A 65–A 70). And, since Empedocles was not known for his political theory (Frag. B 135 to the contrary notwithstanding), the sequel to materialism that 'politics shares little with nature, much with art' (889 d) must surely include Democritus (and *his* followers, whose existence is not a matter of conjecture). Plato's concession that politics, on this view, does have a 'small' share with nature fits Democritus, who would insist (against the out-and-out conventionalists) that art is itself a product of material necessity and 'makes' nature (Frag. B 33; cf. Nausiphanes Frag. B 2. 18. 3). Incidentally, Anaxarchus (Frags. A 3 and A 5) shows the kind of objectionable politics that could be associated (rightly or wrongly) with the Democritean school and thus lends some plausibility to the worst that Plato imputes against the wicked materialists in 890 a.

[152] Heracl. Frag. B 41. 'Governs' connects this fragment with Anaximander (see above, note 128). Xenophanes (Frag. B 25) and Empedocles (Frag. B 134) speak explicitly of a divine 'mind'; and Parmenides' Being was also, no doubt, conceived as mind on the principle of the identity of thought and being. Needless to say, in all this the accent falls not on spiritualizing nature

is right in accenting the difference and neglecting the agreement. His early predecessors had endowed physical nature itself with the attributes of reason, including justice and thought. They had been so absorbed in the discovery that nature was rational that they never stopped to distinguish between the categories of intelligibility and intelligence.[153] That distinction is foreign to archaic thought and language, as we can see from the systematic ambiguity of words like *logos*, *gnome*, and *nous*.[154] In Plato and Aristotle, on the other hand, the identification of rational thought and rational thing is deliberate. It is achieved not by rationalizing material nature but by degrading matter to the realm of the irrational, the fortuitous, and the disorderly.

W. A. Heidel, who was much preoccupied by this momentous transformation, took a strangely fatalistic view of the transition: 'The transfer of the functions and attributes of the ancient gods to *physis* by the philosophers of the sixth and fifth centuries eventually so charged nature with personality that the Socratic teleology was a foregone conclusion'.[155] The atomist system proves that this development was anything but a 'foregone conclusion'—that the

---

[153] On the contrary, they made, all too confidently, the opposite assumption —that 'all things have thought' (πεφρόνηκεν ἅπαντα [Emp. Frag. B 103; cf. Frag. B 110. 10]). There is every reason to believe that this is the general assumption among the Presocratics; cf. the identification of thought with the *krasis* of the elements in Empedocles and Parmenides and of soul with fire in Heraclitus and air in Anaximenes.

[154] Λόγος, 'accounts', both in the active sense of account*ing* (λόγος as speech and/or thought) and in the objective sense of the character of things which makes them capable of being so account*ed* (λόγος as mathematical proportion, etc., which can be in physical objects themselves [Leucip. Frag. B 2: πάντα ἐκ λόγου τε καὶ ὑπ' ἀνάγκης]). Similarly, γνώμη could also be used to mean not only the *cognoscens* but also (though rarely) the *cognoscendum*, e.g. the well-known κακῶν γνώμας in *Theog.* 60, where γνώμας has exactly the same sense as the σήματα of fire and night in Parm. Frag. B 8. 55 ('Merkzeichen' [Diels–Kranz]). As for νοῦς, Liddell and Scott cite Herodotus, vii. 162: οὗτος ὁ νόος (sense) τοῦ ῥήματος.

[155] Περὶ φύσεως, *Proc. Amer. Acad. Arts and Sciences*, XLV (1910), 79–133, at 94–5.

---

but on naturalizing spirit. In Anaximander the Boundless itself has the properties of the gods (Frag. 3). In Heraclitus the governing mind is still plain fire (Frag. B 64). In Xenophanes, God is described in words which Paramenides applies unchanged to his Being (cf. Xen. Frag. B 26: ἀεὶ δ' ἐν ταυτῷ μίμνει with Parm. Frag. B 8. 29).

natural evolution of Presocratic thought was not toward the ever increasing personalizing of nature, but the reverse. From their Ionian predecessors Leucippus and Democritus inherited the universe of homogeneous construction and immanent necessity which had been reared with the scaffolding of cosmic equality and cosmic justice. The structure completed, the scaffolding could be dropped. The intelligible order of nature is as secure in this new system as it had ever been in the earlier ones: 'nothing happens at random, but everything from a reason and by necessity' (Leucippus Frag. B 2). But no effort is now made to ground this order in *isonomia*.[156]

Compared to Anaximander's, the design of the Democritean universe is indifferent to equality: The infinite worlds are unequal in size and power and at unequal intervals from one another.[157] Earth, sun, moon, and stars are also, no doubt, unequal in size and at unequal intervals.[158] As for the earth, its breadth and length are unequal,[159] and the northern and southern halves of the cylindroid are unequal in weight.[160] Cosmic equality has lost its importance, for cosmic justice no longer makes sense. Justice is now a human device; it applies solely to the acts and relations of

[156] We do meet this principle once again in Epicurean atomism: Cicero, *N.D.* i. 19, 50; ... ut omnia omnibus paribus paria respondeant. Hanc *isonomian* appellat Epicurus, id est aequabilem tributionem. Cf. also the notion of successive supremacy of opposing forces in nature in Lucretius ii. 567–76, nunc hic nunc illic superant ... et superantur item.

[157] Hippolytus, *Ref.* i. 13, 2 and 3 (Democ. Frag. A 40). Hence the destructive collisions between worlds, 'the greater overcoming the lesser', (Aetius, ii. 4, 9 = Frag. A 84). Moreover, the worlds are dissimilar in contents: 'in some there is no sun nor moon, in others larger ones than ours, in still others more [*sc.* than one sun and moon] ... and there are worlds devoid of animals, plants, and all moisture' (Hippolytus, *loc. cit.*).

[158] The first I infer from (1) the general gravitational theory, which entails that the largest bodies are sifted towards the centre and (2) the fact that sun and moon were originally composed of a substance that 'resembled the earth' (*Strom.* 7 = Frag. A 39). As for the intervals, the only definite statement is Hippolytus, *Ref.* i. 13, 4 = Frag. A 40: 'neither is the height of the planets equal'; but even this would be enough to spoil the symmetry of Anaximander's scheme.

[159] Frag. B 15 (Agathemerus i. 1, 2); Frag. A 94 (Eustathius, schol. to *Iliad* vii. 446).

[160] The south being more temperate, 'the earth is weighed down in that direction, where it has an excess of produce and growth' (Frag. A 96 = Aetius iii. 12. 2).

conscious beings. It is not arbitrary, for it is rooted in the necessities of man's nature and environment. But neither does man find it in the universe as such; it is a product of civilization and art.[161] Justice is only the form which the immanent order of nature achieves in the mind and works of man. Justice is natural, but nature is not just.

[161] See Frags. B 172–3: 'good' and 'evil' are not in nature as such, but in what man does with nature through the power of his art and its 'teaching'. For the application of this principle to the origin of human civilization, see Democritus Frag. B 5. The validity of this material as a source of Democritean ideas has been disputed; but see 'On the Pre-history of Diodorus', *AJP*, LXVII (1946), 51–9.

V

THEOLOGY AND PHILOSOPHY IN EARLY GREEK THOUGHT*

Gregory Vlastos

I

WHEN one reads the Presocratics with open mind and sensitive ear one cannot help being struck by the religious note in much of what they say. Few words occur more frequently in their fragments than the term 'god'.[1] The style itself in certain contexts is charged with religious associations; the rhythm and sentence structure of certain utterances is unmistakably hymnodic.[2] In Parmenides and Empedocles the whole doctrine of Being and Nature is put forth as a religious revelation. The major themes of all the *physiologoi*—the creation of the world, the necessity of its order, the origin of life, the nature of the soul, and even such things as the causes of winds, rain, lightning and thunder, rivers, meteorites, eclipses, earthquakes, plagues—were matters of vivid religious import to their contemporaries. Lightning, thunder, a storm, an earthquake were 'signs from Zeus' ($\delta\iota\sigma\sigma\eta\mu\dot{\iota}\alpha\iota$) that could stop a meeting of the Law Courts or of the Assembly;[3] religious

* Minor revisions have been made by the author.

[1] See the word-index in H. Diels and W. Kranz, *Fragmente der Vorsokratiker*, 5th edn, (Berlin, 1934–7) (all subsequent citations of Presocratic fragments refer to this work), s.v. *theos*: eight columns of listings, against six for *physis*, less than six for *kosmos*.

[2] See Ed. Norden, *Agnostos Theos* (Leipzig, 1913), p. 164; K. Deichgraeber, 'Hymnische Elemente in der philosophischen Prosa der Vorsokratiker', *Philologus* 88 (1933); and now W. Jaeger, *Theology of the Early Greek Philosophers*, (Oxford, 1947), *passim*.

[3] For the evidence, see, e.g. O. Gilbert, *The Constitutional Antiquities of Sparta and Athens*. English translation (London, 1895), p. 292, notes 3 and 5.

92

feeling for an eclipse could overrule military intelligence to cause the greatest disaster ever suffered by Athenian arms.[4] The philosophers who took the 'natural' view of these things could not be indifferent to the religious bearing of their conclusions. To think of them as mere naturalists, bracketing off their speculations from religious belief and feeling, would be to take a very anachronistic view of their thought.

Now it is just this view that was upheld quite belligerently by Burnet,[5] whose *Early Greek Philosophy* has gone through four editions since its first publication in 1892 to become the most influential guide to the study of the origins of Greek thought in the English-speaking world. Burnet explained away the term 'god' in the Presocratics as a 'non-religious use of the word' (p. 14); and though perhaps he never thought through the meaning of this remarkable expression, the general point of his contention is clear enough. Like many a god and goddess in Hesiod, he argued, the 'gods' of the philosophers are not 'objects of worship' but 'mere personifications' of natural phenomena. Now it is true that the *physiologoi* maintained in all their thinking a singular independence from the public cult. If this were all that Burnet had in mind, his contention would be not only true but, as I shall argue shortly, absolutely fundamental to the proper understanding of their religious ideas. But Burnet went far beyond this when he claimed that they themselves attached no religious import to those ideas which they proclaimed in open or tacit defiance of the prevailing faith. It is true, of course, that their primary object is to understand nature, not to reform religion. When they discuss religious concepts, they are generally content to leave religious practices alone. But even this statement has important exceptions, and though one of them fits Burnet's thesis, the rest go dead against it.

In Empedocles it is the mystic, not the *physiologos*, who is exercised about the cult. His heart-wringing appeals for a religion undefiled by animal sacrifices and the eating of beans are inspired by the Orphic piety of his *Purifications* which admits of no rational connection with the scientific temper and doctrine of his work *On*

---

[4] Thucydides, 7. 50. 4.
[5] In a good cause; he was combating the error, then prevalent in some quarters, 'of deriving science from mythology' (p. 14).

Nature.[6] But in Xenophanes we find something quite different. When he calls nature 'God'[7] he is asserting no 'mere' personification, but a doctrine which has urgent religious relevance, since it prompts him to attack the traditional beliefs as both irrational and irreverent.[8] It is impious, he says in effect, to speak about the gods as Homer and Hesiod do, implying that *his* doctrine sets general standards for pious utterance. Heraclitus goes much further when he blasts away not only at what people say about the gods, but at what they do in their most sacred rites.[9] Such modes of worship offend not only his reason, but his religious sense; they are not only 'madness' (B 5, B 16), but sacrilegious madness, 'unholy mysteries' (B 14). There is a strong implication here that there can and ought to be a different form of worship which would qualify as 'holy'; and this is confirmed by a passage in Iamblichus: 'I distinguish two kinds of sacrifice: first, those of the completely purified, such as would happen rarely with a single individual, as Heraclitus says, or with a handful of men; secondly, the material . . .'[10] We need not take this as a wilful preference for

[6] See below, Section V. On the relation of Empedocles's *Purifications* to Orphism see e.g. W. Kranz, 'Vorsokratisches III', *Hermes* 70 (1935) at pp. 112–15.

[7] Aristotle, *Met.* 986 b 24, 'looking at the whole *ouranos*, the One, he said, is god'.

[8] B 1. 13–14, 'Pious (εὔφρονας) men must first hymn god with reverent (εὐφήμοις) myths and pure words'. Which myths he considered *ir*reverent is clear from lines 21–3 of this fragment and B 11, B 12. My translation of εὔφρονας differs from the usual renderings ('joyful' in Burnet and Kathleen Freeman), but is justified both by the context and by such usage as in Aeschylus, *Choephoroi* 88, πῶς εὔφρον' εἴπω, πῶς κατεύξομαι; εὐφήμοις = 'auspicious, of good omen' (Liddell and Scott, s.v.). Here, as in the following 'pure' (καθαροῖσι), Xenophanes is reinterpreting current religious terms, transposing them into the framework of his own rational religious beliefs. The word 'god' in the citation is not necessarily the One God of his philosophy of nature. As Grube observes in another context (review of Jaeger's *Paideia* in *American Journal of Philology*, 78 [1947], 211, n. 17), 'ὁ θεός no more implies the existence of one God than ὁ ἄνθρωπος the existence of only one man. . . . Both are generic'. This is quite clear here, since the fragment shifts to 'gods' in line 24. The relation between the 'One God' and the many 'gods' in Xenophanes is obscure. All we can get from the fragments is that the moral, non-anthropomorphic properties of the 'One God' are normative for the 'gods' as well.

[9] Attacks on purificatory rites and on image-worship, B 5: on the mystery cults, especially those of Dionysus, and magicians, B 14, B 15.

[10] B 69; omitted in Burnet.

solitary worship. It is more likely an expression of Heraclitus' despair of the capacity of the 'many' to understand what he was talking about and to act accordingly. In any case, it is clear that the 'divinity' of his World Order[11] is seriously meant as a genuine religious object which *could* be worshipped by the enlightened.

Nor will Burnet's appeal to Hesiod support his thesis. Certainly many divinities of the *Theogony* were not worshipped; but the same could be said of scores of figures in the traditional mythology which no one would term 'non-religious'. A Greek might know of no local cult to Sun or Moon, and might even think with Aristophanes[12] that none existed throughout the whole of Greece, and still be outraged by a denial of their *bona fide* divinity.[13] Certainly, too, many of Hesiod's figures are personifications of natural or human phenomena; but to say they are 'mere' personifications is to confuse the issue. What is there more typical of Greek religion than the personification of winds, springs, rivers, earth, season, graces, love, victory, justice, peace, etc., whose religious vitality is attested in the cult?[14] It is not Hesiod's verse that personifies everything from Lightning and Thunder to Sleep and Fear and Rumour, but the religious attitude of his people who feel the world as the theatre of super-natural and super-human forces. When Hesiod fills out the divine genealogies with innumerable persons, some of whom doubtless never figured in earlier mythology, he is simply pursuing the logic of this animistic view of nature and life. They all belong to the same 'race' as the gods of the cult, they all have some share, great or small, of that mysterious power which exalts divine beings above the rigid limits of natural necessity.[15]

[11] B 67, B 102, B 114, and see H. Fränkel, 'Heraclitus on God', *Trans. Amer. Philol. Ass.*, 69 (1938), 230–44.

[12] *Peace* 406 ff.

[13] Cf. the decree of Diopeithes, Plutarch, *Pericles* 32; and Plato, *Ap.* 26 de.

[14] See L. R. Farnell, *Cults of the Greek States* (London, 1909), Vol. 5, Ch. 11 and notes. When Aristophanes jokes, 'pour a libation to Stupidity' (*Knights* 221) he is not even lampooning this habit of mind; he is just taking it for granted.

[15] See below, note 90; and cf. E. Ehnmark, *The Idea of God in Homer* (Upsala, 1935) p. 11: 'the criterion of divine power is its supernatural power'. Jaeger (*op. cit.*, above, note 2) holds that Hesiod's gods 'are really subject to what we should call natural law' because they have all been 'generated by the mighty power of Eros'. The premise goes a long way beyond anything in

And this is precisely what, on any theory, Heraclitus (for example) did *not* mean, when he called his World Unity 'god'. What then *did* he mean? Burnet's theory stops him from so much as asking the question, and leaves him with a blind spot for that part of Presocratic thought which is its unique contribution to religion. Thus he can see no more in Xenophanes than a denial of 'the existence of any gods in the proper sense'; the words 'One god' mean 'No god but the world' (p. 128). The result has the effect of a distortion. It turns the Presocratics into purely 'scientific' thinkers, ignoring the fact that, for better or for worse, their 'science' was far more (and less) than science, in our sense, has any business to be.[16] Doubtless their concept of nature as a self-enclosed, self-regulative system is the intellectual foundation of science, and they who built it out of incredibly inadequate materials have every right to be considered pioneers of the scientific spirit. But neither can we forget on this account that those who discovered this concept of nature believed that they found in it not only the principles of physical explanation but also the key to the right ordering of human life and the answer to the problem of destiny. They began with the faith that nature itself was animated[17] by that Wisdom and Justice which the most enlightened conscience of their race had imputed to Zeus. So long as this faith

[16] This is recognized by Burnet himself in a remarkable passage. In *Greek Philosophy* (London, 1914), pp. 11–12, he notes that Greek philosophy 'is dominated from beginning to end by the problem of reality (τὸ ὄν)', a problem 'which at once takes us beyond science', and adds: 'Greek philosophy is based on the faith that reality is divine. . . . It was in truth an effort to satisfy what we call the religious instinct.' Here is impressive evidence that the vision of this great scholar was not blinkered by his theory. Had he pursued this line of thought he would have forestalled my objections. Unfortunately he did not; on p. 29 of this later book he repeats, almost verbatim, the statements, made many years before in *Early Greek Philosophy*, which I have criticized here.

[17] I use the word advisedly. See my 'Equality and Justice in Early Greek Cosmologies', *Classical Philology* 42 (1947), 177 and notes (above, pp. 87–89).

the *Theogony*, where Eros gets five lines altogether (120–3, 201–2). But even if we choose to read the potency of Eros into every 'birth' in the *Theogony*, we are still a long way from 'natural law', in a realm where the natural pattern of sexual generation can be broken *ad libitum* without occasioning the slightest surprise, as e.g. in the birth of Athena, or the birth of Erinyes, Giants, Nymphs, and Aphrodite (183 ff.), to say nothing of the (presumably asexual) generation of the originals, Chaos, Earth, Eros himself, and Night.

lived they could transfer to nature the reverence hitherto reserved for Zeus and could therefore call nature 'god' without indulging in an empty figure of speech.

II

There is a kind of poetic justice in the fact that Professor Jaeger's *Theology of the Early Greek Philosophers* should have been delivered as the Gifford Lectures (1936) at St Andrews where Burnet had held for many years the chair in Greek. It is not polemical in tone, and there is no mention of Burnet except at incidental points where Jaeger agrees with him as often as not. But it is doubtless the strongest reply Burnet's thesis has yet received,[18] and it is all the more telling for keeping clear of the fanciful speculations that marred earlier statements of the anti-thesis.[19] It works with the sound methodological principle that Presocratic philosophy is generally marked by close-knit coherence and should therefore be studied 'as an indivisible organism, never considering the theological components apart from the physical or ontological' (p. 7). Coming as it does from one of the foremost living students of Greek thought, it cannot fail to command attention. It will remain for years to come one of the 'standard' books with which every student of the Presocratics will have to deal. Such a work does not lend itself to summary, and does not need it. The many insights by which it illuminates and enriches our understanding of the first chapter of Western philosophy can best be appreciated by those who will read the book as a whole, with the leisureliness and care it invites and deserves. I shall therefore forgo here any thought of surveying its positive contributions and keep to a more limited and somewhat invidious task. I wish to discuss briefly

[18] For a sample of the clash compare their views of Xenophanes. Burnet: 'He would have smiled if he had known that one day he was to be regarded as a theologian' (*Early Greek Philosophy*, p. 129); Jaeger: 'only as a theologian can he be really understood' (p. 49).
[19] I am thinking particularly of K. Joel's *Der Ursprung der Naturphilosophie aus dem Geiste der Mystik* (Jena, 1960), whose title tells its own tale, and F. M. Cornford's *From Religion to Philosophy* (London, 1913), the early work of a great scholar which over-works the hypothesis that the categories of Greek philosophy were 'already implicit' in Greek mythology, and is further misled by uncritical borrowings from the then fashionable school of French sociology. It remains for all its faults a valuable, suggestive study.

those aspects of the author's thesis which strike me as open to grave objection. The critical tone of my remarks will not be misunderstood, I hope, as any reflection on the solid value of the work.[20] It is merely incidental to the expression and documentation of an alternative point of view which agrees with Jaeger against Burnet about the authenticity of the religious component in Presocratic thought, but prefers to interpret it along somewhat different lines.

My main question springs out of the very use of the word 'theology' both in the title and constantly throughout the book as a description of the religious ideas of the Presocratics. The word, of course, means no more than 'account of god' and could be so applied to any doctrine of divinity. But the historian of ideas must scruple to use fundamental terms without regard to their exact historical fitness. He must ask himself in this connection: Would the *physiologoi* themselves have used the word of their own speculations about divinity? We know that Aristotle so terms his metaphysics *qua* science of divinity,[21] and may assume that Plato would not be averse to have his arguments about the existence and providence of the gods described as 'theology'.[22] But we also

[20] One's best testimony to the value of the work of a serious scholar is to take it seriously, either by way of assimilation or else by way of criticism where one is compelled to disagree. The former I have done repeatedly in earlier published work, expressing my personal indebtedness to Jaeger for many things I have learned from him, and will do so again both in this paper and hereafter.

[21] *Met.* 1026 a 19; 1064 b 3.

[22] Jaeger holds that the very word *theologia* was coined by Plato (and adds, here unconsciously controverting the major thesis of his own book, 'and he [Plato] evidently was the creator of the idea', p. 4). But Plato is a fastidious linguist. When he makes up a word he is very self-conscious about it (e.g. at *Theaet.* 182 a). There is no hint of terminological innovation at *Rep.* 379 a; the word is introduced by Adeimantus (not Socrates) as a variant for 'tales about the gods': Socrates, 'The founders ought to know the canons (*typous*) in accordance with which the poets should tell their stories (*mythologein*) [*sc.* about the gods] . . .'; Adeimantus, '. . . What then are the canons for stories [or, accounts] about the gods (*typoi peri theologias*)?' The casualness with which the word is used here (and, curiously enough, never again in Plato in contexts such as *Laws* X where we should most expect it had it been 'coined' to indicate 'the importance from Plato's point of view of the mental attitude which it tries to express,' Jaeger, p. 194) suggests that it was in common use at the time. And I see no good reason for doubting that those who 'spoke about the gods' (*hoi legontes peri theon*, Plato, *Laws* 886 c,

know that neither Aristotle nor Plato assumed so much for the natural philosophers who preceded them. As Jaeger observes of Aristotle, 'in historical contexts . . . he used the term to designate certain non-philosophers such as Hesiod and Pherecydes, whom he contrasts sharply with the oldest genuine philosophers or physicists';[23] and Plato's practice is quite similar.[24] The basis of the contrast in Aristotle's mind seems to be mainly that the theologians talk myth, while the philosophers speak the rational language of natural inquiry. Jaeger would then seem to be on safe ground in taking this over, and so juxtaposing to the mythical theology of the older poets the rational or natural theology of the philosophers. But Aristotle never talks that way. As a *historical* term, 'theology' for him (and for his school) has a clearly marked denotation which excludes the *physiologoi*. Why so? The answer is not to be found in Aristotle, who never stopped to analyse the problem.[25] We can get at it only by looking at the actual work of the theologians themselves, beginning with Hesiod whose fully preserved text and well known impact on Greek thought gives us our best basis for judgement.

[23] He adds a little further: 'Eudemus [of Rhodes, the first writer of a history of theology] would never have included his master Aristotle, the creator of metaphysics or theology in the philosophical sense, among the theologians', p. 5; still less would he have included Anaximander or Anaxagoras.

[24] At *Laws* X. 886 c-d he distinguishes between (*a*) those who 'speak about the gods' and propound 'theogonies' and (*b*) those 'recent wise men' (νέων καὶ σοφῶν) whose cosmology is materialistic, further identified later at 891 c as 'all the men who have undertaken natural investigation'. The distinction, assumed at the beginning, is rigorously observed in the body of the ensuing argument which explicitly ignores the former (886 d) to concentrate on the refutation of the latter (886 e ff.).

[25] Neither did Plato. But his practice comes much closer to what, I shall argue, is the real difference, taking it for granted that the theologians are talking about the gods of the cult (cf. *Tim.* 40d–41a) while the *physiologoi* are either downright atheists or else deny (the primary assumption of the cult) that the gods 'care for human affairs' (886 e).

---

of the theogonists; cf. Empedocles B 131, *amphi theon . . . logon*, of his own theogony) would be referred to as *theologoi* long before this time; similar compounds with -*logos* such as *chresmologos, meteorologos*, occur in fifth-century texts; Philolaos B 8, if genuine, would settle the point. Whether *theologia* was used as the title of any of the sixth-century theogonies (as Diels assumes, e.g. in the case of Pherecydes) is a different, and secondary, question, which cannot be settled from the available evidence.

When Herodotus (2. 53. 2) speaks of those who 'composed a theogony for the Greeks and gave the gods their names and divided their honours and occupations and designated their forms', he gives pride of place to Hesiod.[26] His very wording here echoes the *Theogony*: 'Tell how at the first the gods and earth came to be, . . . and how they divided their wealth and shared their honours.'[27] The gods Herodotus is thinking about are quite specifically the gods of Greek worship. Hesiod's range is broader. It takes in gods whose connection with the cult is marginal, indeterminate, or wholly non-existent. But the ultimate concern of the *Theogony* is with the major deities of the cult, 'the gods, givers of good things'.[28] The great drama of the *Theogony* turns on the 'struggle for honours'[29] between Titans and Olympians. It tells how the former lost to the latter just that 'wealth' and 'honour' whose possessors qualify as cult gods by virtue of having 'good things' to give to those who honour them with sacrifice, libation, and prayer.

There is no need to slight in this connection the cosmogonic and cosmological interests of the *Theogony*. An adventurous mind could hardly inquire into the origin of the gods without passing over into the kindred question of the origin of the world. This would come all the more naturally to one who thinks, as Hesiod does, of the four main articulations of nature, Earth, Sky, Sea, and Night, as themselves divine beings, whose generation accounts at one stroke for both the origin of the physical universe and the generation of the whole 'race' of the gods. Thus theogony broadens out easily into cosmogony, and even passes at times into pure cosmology, as in the famous description of the geography of the universe (720 ff.), with equidistant intervals from Sky to Earth and from Earth to Tartarus, and its remarkable account of the

[26] An earlier testimony of the crucial role ascribed by the Greeks to Homer and Hesiod in the shaping of the popular creed comes from Xenophanes, who makes them the main butt of his attacks (B 11, B 12).

[27] 108 ff.; I follow Solmsen (*Hesiod and Aeschylus*, Ithaca, 1949, p. 8, n. 7) in accepting the genuineness of vv. 111–14. For 'honour', 'gift' (τιμή, γέρας, δῶρον), 'lot' (μοῖρα) among the gods, see also vv. 74, 204, 393–9, 413, 882, 885.

[28] Vv. 46, 111; also 633 and 644 where the 'givers of good things' are clearly identified with the Olympian faction.

[29] V. 882. In Homer (*Iliad* xv. 165 ff.) the 'lots' and 'honours' of the gods are fixed by primordial *moira*. In Hesiod they have to be fought for and apportioned as spoils of war.

'sources and limits' in Chaos of Earth, Sky, Sea, and Tartarus (736 ff.). One may recognize all this, and still assert that the great bulk of the epic is not cosmology or cosmogony, but theogony and theology.[30] Its primary purpose is twofold: first, to sort out the motley mass of divinities, both the ones that Hesiod found ready-made in cult and those added by his own inspired fancy, into well-defined stems of descent; and secondly, to vindicate the reigning order among the gods. The latter not only establishes the supremacy of the gods of the cult over all the rest, but ends the quarrelsome anarchy of the Homeric pantheon and assures law and order on Olympus under the stern authority of Zeus. Hesiod's audience is now assured that each cult god has and keeps his proper province, so that each may be worshipped without risking offence to his peers and thus causing more trouble than he is worth.

This is what makes Hesiod's work a theology in a sense which cannot, by any stretch, take in the *physiologoi*. It is not merely that his forms of thought are mythical, his standards of rationality more primitive, his conclusions more traditional than theirs. All these things are true, but do not get at the heart of the difference, which is just this: the divinity of the *physiologoi* has no direct connection with the public cult, and is indeed so independent of it as to leave the very existence of the cult-gods in doubt and expose the most sacred ritualistic acts to Heraclitus' scornful rejection.[31] Hesiod's teaching of divinity, on the other hand, puts the objects of the public cult at its centre. The information it conveys and the assurance it offers about the divine order make the acts of the cult sensible propositions to a thrifty, calculating, peace-loving worshipper, such as Hesiod himself and the rural public to which he

---

[30] Cf. Solmsen, *op. cit.*, p. 58: 'it is wrong to call the *Theogony* a cosmogonic poem'; and p. 104, n. 6: while the Presocratics 'are anxious to find a condition of *dikē* and *eunomiē* in the world of the physical elements, . . . Hesiod had restricted these "ideas" to the dispensation of Zeus and to human society. . . . In this important respect the Presocratics may be said to have destroyed the Hesiodic pattern.'

[31] The average man would at least gather from the teaching of the *physiologoi* that it makes the worship of the traditional gods perfectly pointless. Cf. the reaction of Strepsiades (Aristophanes, *Clouds* 425–6), when converted to the new philosophical divinities: 'I absolutely will not talk to the other gods, not even if I run into them on the street; I will not sacrifice, nor pour libations, nor offer frankincense to them.'

spoke.[32] What the 'Greeks' got from his *Theogony*—not later philosophers, like Aristotle, who regarded it so patronizingly as uncouth, archaic cosmology, but the people at large who read it as a religious text—was a creditable and satisfying account of the gods they worshipped.

III

It is just this relation to the public cult that Jaeger ignores in his account of Hesiod's theology[33] and systematically belittles when he gets to the theogonies which are contemporary with the first generations of Presocratic philosophy. His thesis here is that these 'theogonic writers cannot be understood except in the light of their close reciprocal relationships with the philosophers of their own period' (p. 57). Now we do not know what influence, if any, these theogonies had on the philosophers, nor does Jaeger profess to tell us.[34] Nor is there any evidence of philosophical influence

[32] Hesiod's work is not, of course, apologetics for the cult; none would be needed where no doubt of its validity has yet arisen. But when he comes across a specific feature of the cult which must have struck him and his hearers as decidedly queer, he is ready to explain away the difficulty with an aetiological myth: vv. 533 ff., and Solmsen, *op. cit.*, pp. 48–9, for the interpretation of the Prometheus story as an aetiological myth.

[33] Though not in *Paideia* (Vol. I, 2nd English edn, [New York, 1945], p. 65), where he was not preoccupied with the thesis of the present book.

[34] Reconstructions of such influence are not lacking in the literature. With the single exception of the influence of Orphism on Pythagoreanism, they are wholly conjectural, and amount to nothing more than the detection of certain supposed resemblances between the theological and philosophical cosmogonies. For the best statement of this point of view, see Guthrie, *op. cit.* in n. 55, Ch. VII. I can only record the impression that the ingenious 'parallelisms' which are traced here between, say, Anaximander and the Orphic cosmogony are (*a*) unconvincing at such points as the alleged correspondence between a supposed *gonimon* in Anaximander and the Orphic Egg or between Anaximander's Moist and the Orphic Eros and (*b*) constitute no proof of an 'indelible impression' which the Orphic theogony is here (p. 224) said to have made on Anaximander, and cannot even be taken as evidence of Anaximander's acquaintance with this cosmogony. If we could generalize from the fragments of Xenophanes and Heraclitus, we would have to say that Ionian philosophy ignores the sixth-century theogonies: Xenophanes made Homer and Hesiod the butt of his polemic against the poets (above, note 26); Heraclitus inveighs against the same pair but names also Xenophanes, Hecataeus, and Archilochus (B 40, B 42, B 56, B 57, B 105, B 129); neither of them mentions Orpheus or Musaeus or any of the rest except Epimenides, who is mentioned by Xenophanes as having lived 154 years (B 20).

on any of the theogonies prior to that of Pherecydes.[35] With this one exception, all that remains of their 'close reciprocal relationships' with the philosophers is that they dealt with the common problem of the origin of the world, the nature of the gods, the destiny of man. But their attack on these problems is decidedly different. Is the difference merely that they tell myths, while the philosophers do not? If that were all, Jaeger might be justified in treating them as a half-way house between Hesiod and Ionian *physiologia*. But in so doing he misses—ignores or explains away[36] —the remarkable fact that these theologies are one and all ascribed to men who, as historical or legendary characters, were leading figures in the new religious movements and activities of the time. Orpheus is the founder of mystic rites par excellence;[37]

[35] Nothing in Jaeger to this effect except for (*a*) the conjecture that the two Titans in Epimenides B 5 are Oceanus and Tethys followed by the further conjecture, 'possibly the philosophy of Thales has been influential here' (p. 66), and (*b*) the assertion that 'as in the older [*sc.* Pythagorean] philosophy, Air [in Epimenides B 5] is thought as the void' (p. 65). (*a*) needs no comment. As for (*b*), there is no evidence in the text that 'air is thought as the void', nor, if there were, would it be chronologically plausible to infer Pythagorean influence on a sixth-century theogony; but perhaps Jaeger's statement is not intended as assertion of philosophical influence, which would then reduce the 'close' influence of philosophy on the theogonies prior to Pherecydes to the compound conjecture in (*a*).

[36] On the ground (p. 60) that the nominal authorship is frequently demonstrably false. But what matters here is (*a*) the fact (not the veracity) of the ascription and (*b*) the use to which these writings were put, as, e.g., by Orphic sectaries, prophets, and priests (Euripides, *Hippol.* 925–7; Plato, *Rep.* 364 e and *Meno* 81 a–c).

[37] Euripides, *Rhesus* 943–4, 'Orpheus taught her [Athens] the torch-processions of mystic rites'; Aristophanes, *Frogs* 1032–3, 'Orpheus taught us mystic rites and to abstain from slaughter; Musaeus the healings of diseases and oracles'; Plato, *Prot.* 316 d [ancient 'sophists' assumed various guises, one of them being that of] 'those occupied with mystic rites and oracles, followers of Orpheus and Musaeus'; Ephorus *ap.* Diodorus 5, 64. 4: 'he was the first to introduce mystic rites to the Greeks'. For the interpretation see especially I. Linforth, *The Arts of Orpheus*, Berkeley, 1941, pp. 291 ff. Jaeger's remark (p. 60), 'he [Orpheus] was not a specifically religious figure but rather a mystical singer of primeval times', seems to me to pose a false contrast. Orpheus was both singer and religious figure; one *could* refer to him *qua* singer; but is there any instance where a *theological* doctrine would be referred to him *qua* mere singer? Jaeger himself assumes without question a little later that the account of the soul in the 'so-called Orphic poems' (Aristotle, *de An.* 410 b 22 ff.) is 'Orphic' in the specifically religious sense of the word.

so is Musaeus, and also a patron of cathartic medicine.[38] Of the historical figures Epimenides is the famous purifier of Athens, prophet, founder of shrines;[39] Onomacritus a no less famous expert in oracles;[40] Pherecydes' religious ventures are obscure, but we do know his reputation as a wonder-worker.[41] Is it likely that theogonic writings would be imputed to such figures if there were no connection between the religious speculations contained in these works and the religious enterprises of their reputed authors?

The only way we can account for both the unprecedented proliferation of such a literature and the peculiar authority attached to it by the sectaries of the new cults [42] is to consider how urgently the sponsors of new rites would need to explain and justify their meaning over against the massive authority of the traditional ceremonials sanctioned by long established usage. Thus the new worship of Dionysus produced 'sacred tales' (*hieroi logoi*) which 'explained' to the Greeks 'both the name of Dionysus and the sacrifice and the procession of the phallus'.[43] A similar func-

---

[38] A glance at the fragments in Diels–Kranz will show how persistently he is associated with the foundation of mystic rites, especially those of Eleusis. On his association with religious (purificatory) healing Aristophanes, *Frogs* 1033 is decisive.

[39] See the fragments in Diels–Kranz.

[40] Herodotus, vii. 6, 'a *chresmologos* who set in order the oracles of Musaeus'. I do not know why Diels–Kranz do not include his fragments among those of the theogonists; see the relevant testimonies in Kern, *Orphicorum Fragmenta*, Berlin, 1922, pp. 55–6, and for the interpretation, M. P. Nilsson, 'Orphism and Kindred Movements', *Harv. Theol. Review*, 28 (1935), 195–8.

[41] Arist. Frag. 191 Rose says of Pythagoras: 'and he did not hold back from Pherecydes' miracle-mongering'. Theopompus' *Mirabilia* included a section on Pherecydes (Pherec. A 1 and A 6).

[42] Euripides *Hippol.* 954.

[43] Herodotus, ii. 48, 3 ff. The original explanation Herodotus attributes to the quasi-mythical Melampous who, he thinks, imported the cult from Egypt; but he adds that it was improved by 'subsequent wise men (*sophistai*)'. How close the bond between such 'sacred tales' (*hieroi logoi*) and the cult might be in certain cases we learn from another report in Herodotus where the explanatory 'sacred tale' appears to be actually incorporated in the mystic rite (ii. 51. 4). (One cannot help comparing in this connection his account of Persian sacrifices [i. 132, 3] where the recitation of a theogony by a *Magos* is part of the ritual; this report is now confirmed, I think, by students of early semitic ritual, who show the ceremonial function of Babylonian and Palestinian myths of Creation: for the references, see Cornford's essay, 'A

tion was served by the tales which expounded the Orphic belief in reincarnation: the Platonic Socrates says he heard them from 'men and women wise in things divine' whom he identifies expressly as 'priests and priestesses who have made it their business to give an account of the matters with which they are occupied'.[44] Even more instructive, I think, is Plato's account of the itinerant prophets at *Rep.* 364 b 2: they appeal to Hesiod and Homer for support on some doctrinal generalities; but they produce 'a mass of books by Musaeus and Orpheus' as authorities for their *ritual*.[45] The bond of such a literature with the cult is not only as close as Hesiod's, but closer, since it moves into that area of religious procedure which Hesiod had so largely left alone. But I

---

[44] *Meno* 81 a. The importance of this passage was called to my attention by Linforth, *op. cit.*, p. 294, whose interpretation I am largely following here.

[45] βίβλων δὲ ὅμαδον παρέχονται . . . καθ' ἅς θυηπολοῦσιν, literally, 'they produce a pile of books . . . in accordance with which they perform their ritual'. I follow the general view in taking the 'they' of this sentence, to be the 'mendicant priests and soothsayers' of 364 b 5; I am not convinced by Linforth's suggestion (*op. cit.*, pp. 90–1) that the subject is the holders of the general view introduced at 364 a, since the people in question here are obviously priests, while the general view would be that of the public at large. Incidentally, I believe that Lindsay's and Cornford's rendering for *agyrtai*, 'mendicant priests', is correct and clearly supported by the dictionary (Liddell and Scott, new edn, s.v.): from *ageiro*, to collect, *agyrtes* generally 'beggar', in special contexts 'begging priest'. P. Boyancé, 'Platon et les Cathartes Orphiques', *Revue des Etudes Grecques*, 55 (1942), 225 and ff., rightly insists that there is no ground for taking the word to mean 'charlatan, quack'; Plato takes obviously a very harsh view of these people, but he is not contrasting them as bogus-Orphics with 'real' Orphics. On the other hand, I see no reason to assume that Orphism was anything like a coherent, homogeneous movement; not only was Orphism itself 'but one of the many currents of mystic and cathartic beliefs emerging in the archaic age' (Nilsson, *op. cit.*, p. 185), but there were different currents within it, so that Plato could speak with deep respect of some Orphic functionaries in the *Meno* and adopt its doctrine of σῶμα-σῆμα (*Crat.* 400 c) in the *Phaedo*, yet still feel quite free to vent his scorn on the itinerant soothsayers of the present passage.

Ritual Basis for Hesiod's *Theogony*' in *The Unwritten Philosophy*, Cambridge, 1950, though Cornford's interpretation of Hesiod along similar lines strikes me as forced). That readings from sacred *bibloi* were a part of the ceremonial in some fourth century mystic rites is clear from Demosth. 18. 259.

am not suggesting that we should think of the major theogonies as *ad hoc* fabrications to explain this or that rite. We may certainly credit their authors with vigorous, adventurous minds that would hardly be satisfied with piecemeal aetiologies, but would weave their interpretations of particular myths or rites into a far-flung pattern of creation and salvation.[46] The few surviving fragments attested by good authorities suggest that these theogonies were no less ambitious in scope than Hesiod's epic.[47] Vast canvasses they must have been, thronged with gods and goddesses, drawing the whole universe into their design, accounting in their own fashion for the origin and nature of gods, world, and men. But somewhere along the line their story would make good the claim of the religious enterprise favoured by those who composed or recited it and undermine, by implication or open attack, the claims of their rivals. Such a hypothesis will account for the known facts. And though the dearth of evidence makes it impossible to prove it, it can at least be partially documented in fragments of the one theology whose outlines can be reconstructed with some measure of confidence, that of Pherecydes.

Following Aristotle's famous statement that Pherecydes 'does

[46] I hope this will meet Professor Rose's objection ('Theology and Mythology in Aeschylus', *Harv. Theol. Review*, 39 [1946], 15–16) that Linforth's view (referred to at note 44, above) is not 'the whole truth'. Rose speaks of the theologians as 'minds not so radically tempered as to insist on going to the very foundations of the subject, in this case their own religion . . ., taking nothing for granted and arguing from first principles, yet sufficiently alert to ask themselves what the time-honoured names, legends, and rites meant' (p. 16). This is perfectly acceptable except that in two respects it would hardly apply to the major theogonists who, unlike such poets as Pindar and Aeschylus, (i) *did* go in their own way 'to the foundations of the subject' and (ii) were concerned with more than the 'time-honoured names, legends, and rites' since their data would include new rites, legends, and even (as certainly in Pherecydes) names.

[47] Fully confirmed in the Aristophanean imitation of Orphic theogony in *Birds* 685 ff., which is modelled on Hesiod not only in the scope and style of the theogony but also in the immediately following (709 ff.) parody of *Works and Days*; see e.g. Rogers's notes *ad loc*. The Aristophanean theogony, incidentally, also confirms the general relation of theogony to cult: the Birds' claim to world sovereignty having been asserted against Zeus on the ground that they are 'more ancient and older than Cronus and Titans and Earth' (467-8) and therefore (562) deserve to be worshipped above the (traditional) gods, the theogony in due course puts their claim to cosmic priority into the framework of a full-fledged account of creation.

not say everything in myths',[48] scholars are generally agreed that this comes closer to philosophy than any of the surviving theogonies.[49] But does this justify the statement that the names of his cosmogonic deities 'are merely a transparent archaistic veil which by no means obscures their purely speculative character'?[50] Speculative some of them certainly are. But are they *purely* speculative? Have they no definite connection with the cult? This it seems is what Jaeger is concerned to assert, presumably on the ground of borrowings from the philosophers. He holds that Pherecydes was influenced by Anaximander in substituting the beginningless, ever-living Zas, for the Hesiodic Zeus, great-grandson of Earth, and also in turning the traditional Cronus into the time-god, *Chronos*.[51] But would these transformations,

[48] *Met.* 1091 b 9. But note that Aristotle does not consider him any less of a 'theologian' on this account: he puts him in the same company with the Magi, whose connection with the Persian cult we know from Herodotus (above, note 43).

[49] See, e.g., von Fritz in Pauly-Wissowa *Realencyklopaedie*, s.v.; Kathleen Freeman, *Companion to the Pre-Socratic Philosophers* (Oxford, 1946), pp. 36 ff.

[50] Jaeger, p. 72; asserted (in the concluding paragraph of the chapter) of the sixth-century theogonies generally, but intended (I assume) particularly of Pherecydes, since it would apply much less to any of the rest.

[51] Jaeger I think has a reasonably good case in deriving Pherecydes's doctrine of the eternity of the cosmogonic deities from Anaximander (pp. 67–8), though we cannot exclude the possibility that such an idea occurred independently to Pherecydes. The case for deriving *Chronos* from Anaximander (p. 68 and notes) seems to be quite another matter. There is simply nothing in Anaximander's system to correspond to Time as a substance, still less a cosmogonic one; and this, I think, should be the decisive consideration in our interpretation of the closing words of Anaximander B 1, κατὰ τὴν τοῦ χρόνου τάξιν, on which Jaeger bases his argument. That these words are a verbatim citation has been questioned in an acute paper by F. Dirlmeier, 'Der Satz des Anaximandros', *Rhein. Mus.*, 87 (1938), 376–82, whose arguments, though answered in part by K. Deichgraeber ('Anaximander von Milet', *Hermes*, 75 [1940], 16–17) make it hazardous to base any argument on the assumption that the words in question are Anaximander's own. Assuming that they are, Jaeger insists that the word *taxis* has the active sense, 'ordinance' or 'decree', rather than the merely passive sense 'order' (p. 35 and notes; also earlier in *Paideia*, I, 2nd English edn, (New York, 1945), 455, n. 50; a similar view had been taken still earlier by H. Fränkel, 'Parmenidesstudien', *Goett. Nachrichten* (1930), p. 183.) I concede that if *taxis* was in the original fragment it probably had the active sense; but if so, it could only have been pure metaphor (for the periodic, cyclical order of 'reparation'), part of the 'poetic language' to which Theophrastus so pointedly refers in making the citation. It could not be literally meant

whatever their debt to philosophy, serve 'merely [to] express the recent utterances of speculative thought' (p. 69)? The first thing we are told about Zeus (B 1 and B 2) is that he gave *Gē* (Earth) as a wedding-gift[52] to *Chthoniē* (another name for Earth, here co-original with Zeus and *Chronos*) and that thus *Chthoniē* acquired the 'name' *Gē*. Now Wilamowitz has pointed out that in Mykonos, hard by Pherecydes' native Syros, there is a cult to *Gē Chthoniē*, whose apparent redundancy would be very properly explained here by Pherecydes' theology: dark, barren *Chthoniē* becomes the multi-coloured, fertile Earth when fructified by Zas, the principle of life.[53] Here the Hesiodic bestowal of 'honours' by Zeus to other deities[54] is merged with the notion of a divine marriage (*hieros gamos*), the prototype both of the Greek marriage-rites and of a solemn fertility-festival, the *hieros gamos*, celebrated in various parts of Greece.[55] The deities to which the *hieros gamos* is now referred by Pherecydes, including the explicit reference to them of the presentation of the gifts of Unveiling (the *Anakalyptēria*) in the nuptial rites,[56] would surely be more than 'purely speculative'

---

[52] *Ge* is thus *Chthonie's* 'gift of honour' (γέρας, B 1; τούτῳ σε τιμῶ, B 2). Various cities claimed the honour of having been Zeus's wedding-gift (Acragas, scholiast to Pindar, *Ol.* ii. 10; Thebes, Euphorion *ap.* scholiast to Euripides, *Phoen.* 687; both from Zeus to Persephone εἰς ἀνακαλυπτήρια). Pherecydes extends this idea, making the whole earth a wedding-gift to *Chthonie*.

[53] 'Pherekydes', *Preuss. Akademie der Wissenschaften* (Sitzungsber., Phil.–hist. Klasse, 1926), p. 125: *Glaube der Hellenen*, I, 210.

[54] See above, note 27.

[55] See L. R. Farnell, *op. cit.*, I, 184 ff. and notes; and W. K. C. Guthrie, *The Greeks and their Gods* (London, 1950), pp. 53 ff.

[56] B 2: 'from this arose the custom (*nomos*) among both gods and men'. Rose interprets the presentation of the gifts to Unveiling as 'in itself a rite

---

because the idea of Time as an agent, issuing ordinances and decrees, has absolutely no place in the system as we know it. I conclude, accordingly, that there is no evidence for Jaeger's assumption that Pherecydes borrowed his Chronos from Anaximander, since no one would seriously argue that Pherecydes copied a cosmogonic deity from an incidental metaphor in a physicist. As for the equation of *Chronos*–Cronus, it is *not* asserted in the fragment; but it is in the testimonies (A 9), and parallels the equations Zeus = Zas and *Ge* = *Chthonie*; one may perhaps conjecture that *Chronos* became Cronus through Zas's intervention, as in the transformation of *Chthonie* into *Ge*. I agree with Gomperz ('Zur Theogonie des Pherekydes', *Wiener Studien*, 47 [1929], 16, n. 6) that Wilamowitz's sententious 'Ich halte einen Urgott Zeit im 6. Jahrhundert für undenkbar' is sheer dogmatism.

entities, mere expressions of 'the recent utterances of speculative thought'. As for Cronus, he too is quite different from the Hesiodic figure, since he now fights against the Titans, retains possession of the heavens, and is there crowned king of all.[57] That Cronus is not, as in Hesiod, Zeus' prisoner in Tartarus, but his honoured associate in the upper world, may be asserted on good evidence as Orphic doctrine;[58] and a fragment of Pherecydes explicitly connects the fight of *his* Cronus against the Titans with 'the mysteries about the Titans and the Giants who are said to have made war on the gods and the [*sc.* mysteries] in Egypt about Typhon and Horus and Osiris'.[59] Finally we have the testimonies of Pherecydes' teaching about the soul which Jaeger completely ignores—just why, I do not know. Cicero tells us that his doctrine of the eternity of the soul is the first extant in literature; another

[57] B 4. The leader of the Titans is now Ophioneus, an obscure figure in Greek mythology, but mentioned also (as Ophion) in the theogony sung by Orpheus in Apollonius Rhodius, *Argon.* 1. 496 ff. (= Orpheus B 16 in Diels–Kranz), as 'holding sway on snowy Olympus' before he was expelled by the might of Cronus and 'fell into the waves of the Ocean'.

[58] It occurs in one of our earliest and best sources of Orphic belief: Pindar's Second Olympian Ode (cf. also Pythian iv. 291). It is implied at v. 70, where the souls of the just 'pass by the highway of Zeus unto the tower of Cronus'. The life of the just here (vv. 62 ff.) 'not vexing the soil with the might of their hands, nor the water of the sea, to gain a meagre livelihood' is pictured quite obviously as that of the 'age of Cronus' (Hesiod, *Op.* 111 ff.), no longer a remote antiquity, as an Hesiod, but a perpetual present in the Isles of the Blest. (Hesiod, *Op.* 169 ff. ed. Rzach, where Cronus, reconciled with Zeus, reigns over the Isles of the Blest, is generally recognized as a later interpolation: see Solmsen, *op. cit.*, p. 156, note 142.)

[59] B 4. The 'mysteries about the Titans and the Giants' must be Dionysiac and/or Orphic (Pausanias, viii. 37, 5, 'Taking the name of the Titans from Homer, Onomacritus both composed rites to Dionysus and made the Titans the perpetrators of the sufferings of Dionysus'). For the connection of Dionysiac and Orphic rites, see Nilsson, *op. cit.*, p. 202 and ff. The reference to the Egyptian rites is to be understood in the light of the widespread Greek belief that various Greek divinities and rites, especially Dionysiac and Orphic, came from Egypt; see e.g., Herodotus, ii. 48 (note 43, above), and Hecataeus of Abdera ap. Diodorus, i. 23 and i. 96, the latter including the statement that 'the rites of Osiris and Dionysus are the same'.

of Union, for to give part of one's property is to give a piece of one's self and therefore a kind of communion with the recipient', and adds that traces of the Unveiling-rite still survive in the marriage-rites in modern Chios *Ancient Greek Religion*, pp. 33 and 146).

source that he believed in transmigration; a third that he taught that duality of heavenly and earthly elements in the soul which would be, on any theory, the most obvious corollary to the belief in transmigration.[60] This dualistic conception of man would match and would doubtless be connected in his theology with the 'original [Zeus-*Chthoniē*] dualism' which Jaeger rightly finds 'the distinguishing feature of Pherecydes' theory' (p. 69).

The same belief in transmigration and in a dualistic conception of the world recurs in Pythagoreanism, whose founder is presented by so many of our sources as the junior associate of Pherecydes.[61] Here for the first time we find a chapter of Presocratic philosophy which can be confidently classed as a theology, since its ultimate data were the hopes, rites, and tabus that centred about the doctrine of transmigration.[62] Like Epimenides, Ono-

---

[60] Listed under A 2 and A 5 in Diels–Kranz; Fragments B 6 and B 8 also bear on his doctrine of immortality. The heavenly and earthly parts of the 'soul' (Aponius in A 5) is probably a reference to the dual nature of man's *life*, whose mortal part is earth and returns to earth, while its immortal part is 'heavenly' or 'aethereal' and returns to its heavenly source. There are many fifth-century instances of this belief, some of them listed in Gomperz, *op. cit.*, p. 24, n. 18; also Pindar Frag. 131: the 'body of all men is subject to over-mastering death', but the *eidolon*, which 'alone comes from the gods' remains alive (a clear reference to mystic faith, since the first line mentions the 'rite that releaseth from toil'); also in the well-known Orphic tablets from Petelia and Eleuthernai [Crete], B 17 and 17a in Diels–Kranz, 'I am the son of Earth and starry Heaven.'

[61] The references in W. Rathmann, *Quaestiones Pythagoreae, Orphicae, Empedocleae*, (diss. Halle, 1933), p. 12, n. 10.

[62] In his remarkably learned dissertation (cited in the preceding note) Rathmann has taken it upon himself to dispute the general view that transmigration was certainly taught by Pythagoras. His arguments on this score are completely unconvincing. Thus Dicaearchus' testimony is not discredited (as he suggests, pp. 3 ff.) but on the contrary greatly strengthened by his personal disbelief in immortality and tendency to assimilate Pythagoras to his own preference for the 'practical life'. Rathmann offers no good reason to doubt the reference of Xenophanes, B 7 to Pythagoras in Diogenes Laertius, viii. 36 (see W. Kranz, 'Vorsokratisches II', *Hermes*, 69 [1934], 226–7) which is conclusive contemporary testimony to Pythagoras' belief in transmigration. A more serious argument which has swayed Nilsson is drawn from the conflicts in the testimonies concerning Pythagorean abstinence from flesh, 'some speaking of a general prohibition of certain parts of the animal or certain animals, e.g. the matrix, the heart, the brain, the sea-urchin, especially of such animals as were not sacrificed. If the general prohibition against killing animals and eating their flesh existed

macritus, and Pherecydes, Pythagoras was a religious sage: what is more, he is known to have founded a coherent religious sect.[63] In our best and earliest sources we hear even more of his religious activities than of his philosophy.[64] Herodotus mentions

[63] A prominent feature of all the biographical traditions.

[64] Herodotus' reference to him as 'not the weakest wise man (*sophistes*) among the Hellenes' (4. 95) is, of course, no exception. Burnet wrongly translates *sophistes* here as 'scientific man' (*op. cit.*, p. 85). The context (Pythagoras as a teacher of Salmoxis) makes it clear that Herodotus uses *sophistes* here to mean 'religious sage' as e.g. at ii. 49: Rathmann (p. 47) compares also Euripides, *Rhesus* 949, which refers to Orpheus and Musaeus as *sophistai*; so also Protagoras in Plato, *Prot.* 316 d. But I do not mean, of course, to minimize Pythagoras' encyclopaedic interests in philosophy, mathematics, music, etc., which are amply attested by the general tradition and get near-contemporary witness in Heraclitus B 40 and B 109; the latter is now generally accepted as genuine (*vs.* Diels) and is a good testimony to his wide

---

originally among the Pythagoreans, these special prohibitions would be meaningless'; and if the general prohibition was not original, the belief in transmigration could not have been original either (Nilsson, *op. cit.*, p. 206). This leads Nilsson to think that the belief in transmigration came later, under Orphic influence. But surely, the conflict of our testimonies on this point can be explained in other ways. We know that there were different grades of membership in the Pythagorean order; and there are explicit reports in our sources that the rules for the lower grade (the *akousmatikoi*) were (as we would expect) less stringent than for the inner circle not only in other matters such as the sharing of property (see contract of *koinobioi* with *akousmatikoi* in Iamblichus, *Vita Pyth.* 29–30; and cf. *ibid.* 80–1) and doctrinal proficiency (*ibid.* 81 and 87 ff.) but also quite specifically for the observance of the ritual and dietary tabus (*ibid.* 108–9, 150). Nilsson objects (*Geschichte der Griechischen Religion*, I (Munich, 1941), 666, n. 8) that this resolution of the difficulty assumes that the distinction in grades of membership had been established in Pythagoras' own lifetime. But (i) I see no good reason to doubt the testimonies of the biographical sources on this point, and (ii) even if the distinction did arise in the fifth century after his death, it could still account for conflicting dietary prescriptions in our fourth-century sources. There are other factors, too, especially in the case of Aristoxenus (the most vehement opponent of the tradition of total abstinence), whose testimony is self-contradictory (cf. Frag. 27 Wehrli, where he does concede that the Pythagorean diet was vegetarian after all, but tries to explain it away by giving medical reasons for it) as well as in contradiction to some of the best authenticated original prohibitions (as e.g. that of beans, which Aristoxenus denies, Frag. 25 Wehrli), and can only be explained by his obvious effort to produce a rationalized, prettified portrait of Pythagoras, purged of magical features.

the Pythagoreans only to refer to the peculiar rites they shared
with the Orphics.[65] Plato mentions his name only to speak of him
as the founder of what was still 'the Pythagorean mode of life';[66]
Isocrates, to say that he was distinguished for wisdom in 'sacrifices
and religious rites' as much as 'in the rest of philosophy'.[67] That
he enjoyed quasi-divine status; that sundry miracles were ascribed
to him; that his order observed tabus which savour of primitive
magic—all this is vouched for by Aristotle.[68] The only writings
ascribed to him by an early (fifth century) authority are the verses
he is said to have published under the name of Orpheus.[69] Apart
from the doctrine of transmigration and the belief that 'things are
numbers', the only idea we can credit to him with any measure of
probability is the conception of the world in terms of a duality of
principles, the finite and the infinite, the first being the principle
of the good, the second of evil.[70] Here is something absolutely
without parallel in antecedent or contemporary natural inquiry;[71]

[65] 2. 79, shorter version of the Florentine manuscripts, and Linforth's commentary (*op. cit.*, 38 ff.).
[66] *Rep.* 600 b. Our best commentary on the sense that Plato's words here
would convey to his audience are the numerous references to the way of life
of Pythagorean sectaries in middle comedy (collected in Diels–Kranz,
Pythagoreische Schule, E) where the dietary tabus are most prominent.
[67] *Busiris* 28–9.   [68] Fragments 191 ff. Rose.
[69] Ion of Chios B 2; cf. Iamblichus. *Vita Pyth*, 146. For the interpretation,
see Linforth, *op. cit.*, pp. 110 ff.
[70] Aristotle, *E.N.* 1106 b 28, 'for evil is a [form] of the unlimited, and good
of the limited, as the Pythagoreans imagined'; also *Met.* 986 a 16 ff., 987 a
13 ff., 1093 b 11 ff. What is 'peculiar' to the Pythagoreans says Aristotle
(987 a 13 ff., and cf. W. D. Ross *ad loc.*) is that the infinite and the One (= the
finite) are the 'substance' of things and 'this is why they said that number
is the substance of all things'—a remarkable presentation of the doctrine that
things are numbers as an inference from the ultimate cosmological dualism
of finite-infinite. On this general topic see W. A. Heidel, '*Peras* and *Apeiron*
in the Pythagorean Philosophy', *Archiv für Geschichte der Philosophie* 14
(1901); and for the reliability of the ascription of the *Peras–Apeiron* contras
to the earliest phase of Pythagoreanism, cf. my remarks in my review of
J. Raven, *Pythagoreans and Eleatics*, in *Gnomon*, 25 (1953), 30–1.
[71] The difference would hold even as over against Alcmaeon whose 'opposites
are cited by Aristotle, *Met.* 986 a 27 ff., as a doctrine 'similar' to that of the
Pythagoreans: (i) the finite-infinite duality do not appear in Alcmaeon'

learning, in spite of the fact that the words 'practised inquiry (*historien*
above all men' is a sneer (so Verdenius, 'Notes on the Presocratics', *Mne
mosyne*, S. III, Vol. 13 [1947], pp. 283–4).

and the contrast is all the more striking in that the only Ionian philosophers Pythagoras could have known made the Infinite itself (Anaximander) or the infinite Air (Anaximenes) the ultimate cosmogonic principle and endowed it with the attributes of divinity. Pythagoreanism not only rejects the monistic concept of nature axiomatic in the *physiologoi* but implicitly condemns their highest principle as evil. We can only infer that, whatever its details, this cosmological innovation was the speculative ground for the dualistic conception of man implied by the belief in transmigration which is the one doctrine we can certainly ascribe to Pythagoras.

IV

No one who has ever plunged into the bottomless pit of research into Pythagoreanism will find it in his heart to blame Jaeger overmuch for leaving out this whole chapter from his book.[72] The omission is disconcerting, all the same. For if it is a philosophical *theology* that we are looking for in the Presocratics, it is only here that we shall properly find it.[73] For here we do get a system of thought which, on the evidence, must have served to justify the beliefs and practices of a religious cult. And this is precisely what we do not get in any system of natural inquiry from Anaximander to Democritus. There are no moorings in the cult for any of them from which reason is not free to cut loose. They are free to

[72] There are scattered references to Pythagoreanism in the book (especially at pp. 83 ff. and 151 ff.), but these are only incidental to the discussion of other doctrines. A brief sketch of his view of the teachings of Pythagoras had been offered earlier in *Paideia*, Vol. I (pp. 161 ff. of the 2nd English edn).
[73] Not in Empedocles' *Purifications*, for (as I shall argue in Section V) this work is not a genuinely *philosophical* theology, but a theology (in the more traditional sense) tacked on to the philosophical system of the work *On Nature*.

ist, nor do the implied arithmetical (odd-even) and geometrical (square-oblong) dualities; (ii) Alcmaeon's opposites are not discriminated as 'good' and 'evil' respectively (in spite of Aristotle's citation of 'good and evil' at *Met*. 986 a 34), since Alcmaeon's norm of health is equipoise (*isonomia*, 3 4), not subordination, as would be required if one term in each pair of opposites were held 'good' and the other 'evil'. Alcmaeon was doubtless acquainted with the Pythagoreans at Croton, and may have been on intimate terms with them; but there is no evidence for regarding him as a Pythagorean: see W. A. Heidel, 'The Pythagoreans and Greek Mathematics', *American Journal of Philosophy*, 61 (1940), 3-6 (below, pp. 352-54).

condemn the cult with the savage irony of a Heraclitus, or to explain its foundations away with the relentless persistence of a Democritus.[74] They are also free to ignore it altogether, and this is even more characteristic of them, quite symptomatic of their general temper. Their theme is nature, and their object to explain the how and why of its unfailing order. When they find in this a moral meaning—and they all do before the atomists—they may express the trust and reverence they feel for it by calling it 'god'. But they may not go so far. Thus there is no good conclusive evidence that either Anaximander[75] or Anaxagoras[76] called their

[74] See my 'Ethics and Physics in Democritus', *Philosophical Review*, 54 (1945), 581, n. 24: and 'Religion and Medicine in the Cult of Asclepius', *Review of Religion*, 13 (1949), 284 and notes. When Jaeger (p. 181) says that Democritus 'did not deny the gods altogether', but 'recognized eternity and imperishability as properties belonging to the gods' and retained 'prayer as the most fundamental way of expressing one's faith in the reality of the Divine', he misunderstands B 166. There Sextus clearly tells us that (according to Democritus) the *eidola* were not imperishable and that there was 'no other god [*sc.* other than the *eidola*] having an incorruptible nature'; whence it follows that there are no gods in the recognized sense of the word. When Sextus says that Democritus 'εὔχετο that he might chance to meet lucky *eidola*', εὔχετο can not mean 'prayed' (what sense would there be in praying to Democritean *eidola*?) but only 'hoped, wished for' as e.g. in Aristotle, *E.N.* 1118 a 32 and 1129 b 5. I must also dissent from Jaeger's interpretation (pp. 183–4) of B 30. I cannot see that this projects the style of the Ionian philosophers and their monotheistic doctrine into primitive times. The style of the prayer is at least as old as Homer (cf. *Iliad* iii. 177). The reference to 'Zeus' carries no necessary monotheistic implications.

[75] Jaeger argues at length (pp. 29 ff., 203 ff.) that Anaximander did call the *Apeiron* 'divine'. But the crucial text καὶ τοῦτ' εἶναι τὸ θεῖον may just as wel be (*a*) Aristotle's own interpretation of the view that the all-encompassing *arche* must be divine as (*b*) citation of Anaximander. I see no definite evidence in favour of (*b*), while (*a*) is favoured by two considerations: (i) τὸ θεῖον does not occur as a substantive for 'divinity' in any of the Presocratics or any other text prior to Aeschylus and Herodotus, while it is one of Aristotle's favourite terms; (ii) the ancients did not understand this particular text or any other text at their disposal to say that Anaximander himself taught that the *Apeiron* was τὸ θεῖον: even the chapter in Aetius (i. 7) which generously supplies even Democritus with a god (= fire!), does not say that Anaximander's *Apeiron* was god, but only that 'Anaximander declared that the infinite *ouranoi* were gods'. Cicero (*de Nat. Deorum* = Anaximander A 17) speaks, like Aetius, of the worlds as *nativos deos*, and objects that they cannot be gods, since god *must* be eternal.

[76] As Jaeger observes (p. 161) there is no such statement in the fragments he disregards, I think wisely, such doxographic reports as those of Aetius

cosmogonic principle 'god' or even 'divine'. If they did not, their reticence would be significant and easy to understand from what we know of their position. Consider the case of Anaximander.

When one comes to his fragments fresh from the Theogonies,[77] one moves into a strange new world of thought and feeling. So many of the familiar landmarks have vanished that one can hardly guess which of the old names if any, its discoverer would have wished to conserve. Not only is it true that properties and functions traditionally reserved to the gods are now transferred to an

---

[77] The standard ones, Homer's and Hesiod's, mainly the latter, since it was by all odds the most influential. As for the sixth-century theogonies, I have suggested above (note 34) that there is no *evidence* of Anaximander's acquaintance with them. In any case, they are infinitely closer to Hesiod than to Anaximander, since they continue to assume the generation of the gods. The important exception is Pherecydes, whose cosmogonic gods are explicitly said to be eternal. I have expressed above, note 51, reserved agreement with Jaeger's view that in this respect Pherecydes was probably influenced by Anaximander. This is chronologically permissible on the general view which makes Pherecydes a somewhat younger contemporary of Anaximander. To push Pherecydes towards the end of the sixth century (so Jaeger, p. 67) in order to facilitate the possibility of philosophical influence on him seems to me unwarranted. Incidentally, there is no evidence that Pherecydes 'assimilated the philosophical criticisms of anthropomorphism' (Jaeger, p. 69); the divine marriage and battles which are so prominent in his theogony are definite evidence to the contrary.

. 7, 5 and 12. He nevertheless holds 'that this must have been his doctrine' . . . both (a) from the hymn-like form in which the predicates of Nous are expressed, and even (b) from the content of these statements . . . [e.g.] 'the epithets "infinite", "self-ruling", "unmixed", and "itself by itself"' (p. 161). Both (a) and (b) beg the question which is precisely whether Anaxagoras may not have used just these epithets in just that style, and still held back from calling the *Nous* 'god' or 'divine'. On similar grounds one might have argued even more strongly that Parmenides taught the Divinity of his Being; but there Jaeger respects the silence of the fragments and concludes that Parmenides 'definitely fails to identify Being with God' (p. 107). Though the *ex silentio* argument is always dangerous, I think it unlikely that Plato would not have alluded to the divinity of Anaxagoras' *Nous*, had he known of it, in the crucial passage (*Phaedo*, 97 b ff.: and cf. *Laws* 967 b) which argues that, having said so much ('*nous* is the world-ordering principle'), Anaxagoras should have said more (that 'everything has been disposed for the best'); since the latter would have followed even more strongly from a teaching of the *divinity* of the *Nous*, some reference to such teaching, had Plato known of any in Anaxagoras, would almost certainly have crept into Plato's argument.

utterly different sort of entity; what is more, the properties and functions themselves have changed. In creation the pattern of sexual generation has been replaced by a quasi-mechanical process, which simply sorts out the physical components of an original mixture, and does so not once, to create the single world of traditional thought, but endlessly, to produce innumerable worlds throughout an infinity of time. What is there here that Anaximander would wish to denote by the same noun as that used of Hesiod's Zeus? We simply have no *a priori* way of answering the question; we can only go to the evidence, such as it is. This does not tell us that Anaximander called the *Apeiron* 'god', but that he so called 'the infinite worlds'.[78] This, then, Anaximander may have felt, was the best he could do for the gods in his system, presumably because the gods of the Theogonies were themselves generated.[79] Reserving 'agelessness' to the *Apeiron*,[80] he was taking away from the gods their most characteristic prerogative, but doing so by the compulsion of his logic. In his system whatever has a beginning must have an ending. If the gods have a birth, they cannot be deathless; only the beginningless *Apeiron* can be truly ageless and immortal.

No less different from the popular gods is the *Apeiron* in its role of world 'governor'. Traditionally the justice of Zeus is 'ordained unto men' and, quite explicitly in Hesiod, no further.[81] Only occasionally are the 'beasts' too drawn into the circle of his Justice.[82] The forces of nature, uncertainly personified as earth-born deities, are subdued by Zeus in the battle with the Titans

[78] A 17; see above, note 75. There is a certain analogy here in Parmenides who calls *Dike-Ananke* a divinity in the realm of Becoming (A 37, B 12) but not in the realm of Being.

[79] As implied, of course, by the literal meaning of the word *theo-gonia*. A Jaeger observes (p. 32) the term 'ever being' (αἰὲν ἐόντες), frequently applied to the gods in Homer and Hesiod, 'shows merely that the gods are thought of as immortal, living for ever'. That this usage is continued in the sixth century theogonies is confirmed by the Aristophanean imitation in the *Birds*; v. 688 speaks of the gods as 'the immortal, the ever being', while a v. 691 the theme of the theogony is announced as 'the nature of the birds [= "gods" here], the generation of the gods . . .' Pherecydes' is the first known deviation from the tradition.

[80] B 2, B 3.

[81] Hesiod, *Op.* 276–8. Cf. the citation from Solmsen in note 30 above. See also his remarks at p. 65 and pp. 159–60 of his *Hesiod and Aeschylus*.

[82] Archilochus, Frag. 84, Hiller-Cr.

and brought more or less under his power. But there is no notion of natural *laws* issued and maintained by Zeus. So far from maintaining natural regularities, Zeus himself and the other gods override them right and left. To do so is their prerogative and indeed provides the main medium of omens, oracles, marvels, punitive thunderbolts, storms, plagues, etc., through which they make known their will to men and enforce it upon them. What could be further from the Justice of the *Apeiron* whose laws, fixed in the physical structure of the world, are cosmic in their scope and natural in their execution? When Jaeger tells us that Anaximander's cosmology offers 'the first philosophical theodicy' (p. 36), it is essential to remember that the 'justice' and 'reparation' of Fragment 1 operate simply through the self-regulative periodicities of a physical equilibrium.[83] This is certainly more, as Jaeger observes, that a 'mere explanation of nature' in *our* sense of these words, or the words 'justice' and 'reparation' would be meaningless. But it is both more and less than a 'theodicy' in any sense in which the Justice of the gods had been conceived or, for that matter, ever was conceived, by the clientele of the Greek cult. No theodicy could satisfy the cult which did not include a doctrine of individual providence, and no such doctrine could be squeezed out of Anaximander, or even Xenophanes, Heraclitus, and others who did call nature 'god'.[84] Philosophy could fill the order only by

[83] I offer justification of this view at pp. 168 ff. of the paper cited above, note 17 (this volume, p. 75). I wonder whether Jaeger is true to his own methodological principle (cited above, p. 97) in speaking of 'divine justice' in Anaximander without explicit consideration of the (purely physical) mechanism through which 'justice' and 'reparation' are maintained?

[84] Jaeger takes it for granted that the Justice and Reparation of Anaximander B 1 occur not only in the physical cosmos but also in the world of politics and morals (p. 35: and earlier in *Paideia*, I, 2nd English edn., p. 160). There is no evidence for this assumption, nor is it possible to understand how it could fit Anaximander's physics. How *would* the balanced equalities of hot–cold, dry–moist, etc., enforce reparation of human wrong-doing? Heraclitus goes far beyond Anaximander in annexing 'human' to 'divine' law and justice. But even here the self-regulative execution of the 'common law' inherent in the soul and the state falls far short of a doctrine of individual providence. So does Anaxagoras' *Nous* as, I think, is clear from the disappointment of the youthful Socrates with his cosmology in the *Phaedo*. Jaeger takes Anaxagoras B 12 to mean that the ordering of creation by *Nous* proceeds in accordance with 'preconceived world-plan' (p. 163); but I do not know how he gets this out of ἐκόσμησε ('ordered, arranged') or πάντα ἔγνω νοῦς ('*Nous* knew all things'). Anyhow, I think Jaeger would

grafting Zeus' all-seeing eye on a cosmic power, watchful of every single life to requite its vice and virtue in minute proportion in this life and the next. It was probably the Pythagoreans[85] and after them certainly Plato[86] and the Stoics who performed this remarkable operation, and thus produced a properly theological theodicy.

I hope my argument[87] has made it clear that it concerns more than linguistic propriety, and would not be met had Jaeger dropped the word 'theology' and spoken less provocatively of 'the religious ideas' of the Presocratics. The real issue here is not verbal usage, but historical matter of fact, i.e. the actual relation of the beliefs of the Presocratics to those of contemporary religion. I do not mean to suggest that Jaeger is unaware of the gulf be-

[85] Not explicit in any reliable tradition of early Pythagorean teaching, but implicit in the whole doctrine of transmigration with its teaching of divine judgement and retribution. Cf. Philolaus' doctrine (B 15) that the gods keep a 'guard' over men.

[86] Notably in *Laws* 903 b ff. Cf. F. Solmsen, *Plato's Theology* (Ithaca, 1942), Ch. 9.

[87] I have made no mention of the Eleatics who occupy a unique position among the Presocratics, partly because I have already sketched my interpretation of Parmenides' peculiar blend of mysticism and logic in 'Parmenides' Theory of Knowledge', *Trans. Amer. Philol. Assoc.*, 77 (1946), 74-7 partly too because I find Jaeger's account of Parmenides the most satisfying chapter in the whole book. 'What Parmenides has done,' he writes, 'is to take over the religious form of expression and transpose it to the sphere of philosophy, so that in truth a whole new intellectual world takes shape' (p. 97)—a fine statement, I believe, of the treatment of religious ideas not only by Parmenides but by all the *physiologoi* from Anaximander to Democritus.

---

agree that, so far as we can judge from the fragments, Anaxagoras' *Nous* was not meant to fulfil the function of a personal providence. Neither would the Cosmic Intelligence of Diogenes' Air. Jaeger follows closely W. Theiler (*Zur Geschichte der teleologischen Naturbetrachtung bis auf Aristoteles* [Zurich 1924]) in assuming that Diogenes was the source for the providential arrangements of nature recited by Xenophon (especially at *Mem*. i. 4 and 4, 3), but adds that we cannot read into this source the meaning they now have in Xenophon himself, 'namely, that these are all ways in which the gods provide for man's needs' (p. 168). Theiler's learned and ingenious thesis has never received to my knowledge the criticism it deserves. Earlier S. O. Dickerman (*De Argumentis Quibusdam apud Xenophontem*, etc., [Halle, 1909]) had rejected the hypothesis that Diogenes was Xenophon's source (p. 48); to Dickerman's argument I would add that if Diogenes were as much of a teleologist as Theiler takes him to be, he could hardly have been so completely ignored in Socrates' vain search for a teleological cosmology in the *Phaedo*.

tween the two. He often alludes to it in one way or another, and remarks in one place that the gap which exists in this period 'is never again entirely closed' (p. 174). My point is simply that, taking the gap for granted, he never stops to measure it. The result of this omission is actually, though doubtless unintentionally, an under-estimation of the vast distance between the two *types* of religious belief, and consequently a failure to exhibit the full dimensions of the unique achievement of the Presocratics as *religious* thinkers. This, in a word, lies in the fact that they, and they alone, not only among the Greeks but among all the people of the Mediterranean world, Semitic or Indo-European, dared transpose the name and function of divinity into a realm conceived as a rigorously natural order and, therefore, completely purged of miracle and magic. To *moralize* divinity was not their main, and certainly not their unique contribution.[88] Pindar and Aeschylus here labour in the same cause as Xenophanes and Heraclitus: and the Hebrew prophets were doing the same a good two centuries before Xenophanes, and with a passionate intensity unequalled by any Greek philosopher or poet. But the world of Pindar and Aeschylus is thick with magic of almost every description. The prophets of Israel and Judah fought a valiant rearguard action against wizards, necromancers, and soothsayers. But they lacked the conceptual equipment to see that magic was not only a religious impropriety but a sheer impossibility; and they never cleared their minds of the notion of miracle which is the intellectual foundation of magic. Miracle remained a permanent feature of Hebraic as of Greek[89] and, later, Christian piety. To

[88] The same may be said of their contribution to religious universalism. Jaeger holds (p. 48) that this began in the western world 'neither with the Christian nor with the prophets of Israel, but with the Greek Philosophers'. But the idea of one God who governs nature and all men is already in Amos (i. 3–2, 3; ix. 6–7).

[89] Plato's position here is most instructive. Transmigration itself is a miracle, since the immortal part of the soul is reserved to the reason and is disjoined from the passionate and appetitive parts which are explicitly said to be *mortal* (*Tim.* 69 c ff.); how then could the identity of the *immortal* soul be preserved throughout its incarnations in animals, reptiles, etc., which are conspicuously lacking in reason? It is no use trying to explain away transmigration as a myth, since it is (i) the premise for the epistemological doctrine of Recollection in the *Meno*; (ii) the premise for the metaphysical doctrine of the immortality of the soul in the *Phaedo*; (iii) repeatedly recognized in the cosmology of the *Timaeus*. Plato's attitude to the irrationalities of the public

present the deity as wholly immanent in the order of nature and therefore absolutely law-abiding was the peculiar and distinctive religious contribution of the Presocratics, and it should be put in the forefront of any account of their religious thought. They took a word which in common speech was the hallmark of the irrational, unnatural, and unaccountable[90] and made it the name of a power which manifests itself in the operation, not the disturbance, of intelligible law. The transposition opened new religious possibilities. Had these been realized, Greek religion would have been freed of those evils which Lucretius in retrospect so justly imputes to it.

V

Had Jaeger done justice to this phase of the religious teachings of the Presocratics he would have altered the perspective of much of what he has to say. And the main beneficiary would have been the chapter on 'The Origin of the Doctrine of the Soul's Divinity', which makes Anaximenes, of all people, the bridge between earlier Greek beliefs about the soul and the Orphic doctrine. The argu-

[90] So, e.g., in Herodotus in spite of his very considerable rationalism. Note his use of 'the divine' to denote events such as these: the Cnidian workmen suffer an unaccountably large proportion of injuries (i. 174, 4); the cats in Egypt rush headlong into the fire (ii. 66); Ariston is convinced that not he, but an apparition, has had intercourse with his wife (vi. 69); the wrath of Talthybius descends on the perfectly innocent sons of Spertheias and Bulis (vii. 134). When the event is so strange that it is no use even looking for a natural explanation, then it *must* be 'divine'. *Per contra*, if a thing can be explained by natural means, it cannot be divine (vii. 16. 2). So the author of *On the Sacred Disease* (1): 'men think it [the "sacred disease"] divine (= θεῖον πρᾶγμα, same expression as in Herodotus, ii. 66 and vi. 69) because of their inexperience, and its marvellous character, and the fact that it does not resemble anything else'.

---

cult which his state religion would conserve (*Rep.* 427 bc, *Laws* 738 cd) is a more complicated question. It may be, as E. R. Dodds argues ('Plato and the Irrational', *Journal of Hellenic Studies*, 65 [1945], 22–3) that there is 'little reason, and certainly no necessity, to credit Plato with a serious belief in the personal gods of Greek mythology and Greek cult'. Yet Plato speaks as though he did accept the reality of good and evil daemons with power to intervene unaccountably in human life (*Laws* 877 a, 732 c), and at *Tim.* 71 divination appears as a vehicle of 'some apprehension of reality and truth' which, though quite inferior to reason, may still be due to 'divine possession'.

ment is roughly as follows: We know that the Orphics thought of the soul as (a) divine and (b) independent of the body. Jaeger holds that they also thought it (c) incorporeal (p. 84) which, he thinks, would follow from (b), and (d) air-like, on the strength of Aristotle's reference to 'the account in the so-called Orphic poems, [which] says that the soul comes in from the whole when breathing takes place, being borne in upon the winds'.[91] He thinks that (d) 'already presupposes the philosophical theory [of Anaximenes] that air is the principle of life' (p. 80); and he also finds a connection with Anaximenes at (c), assuming that *his* breath-soul was 'as incorporeal as possible' (p. 84), and also at (a), since Anaximenes taught that Air was divine.[92] This raises more questions than it answers. Briefly:

(i) Chronology: Where is the evidence that the Orphic theory of the soul comes after Anaximenes? But

(ii) Why need Jaeger make such an assumption? He argues convincingly[93] that the breath-soul is an old, pre-Homeric notion, as evidenced in such expressions as 'breathing out one's soul'. Why need the Orphics get from Anaximenes an idea long embedded in their mother tongue?

(iii) If the Orphics thought of the soul as air,[94] would they think of it as incorporeal? Is air incorporeal?

[91] *De An.* 410 b 22 ff. (= Orpheus B 11), in the Oxford translation.
[92] In attributing the doctrine of the divinity of the cosmogonic power to Anaximenes, Jaeger seems to argue (p. 36) mainly from the fact that it was already taught by Anaximander and would thus be conserved by Anaximenes. If, as I have argued, there is no definite evidence for ascribing the divinity of the *arche* to Anaximander, independent grounds for crediting it to Anaximenes must be offered. These I can only find in later testimonies (Cicero, Aetius in A 10), which, however, may be suspected of confusing the doctrine of Anaximenes with that of Diogenes of Apollonia who *did* teach the divinity of the cosmogonic Air. It may be worth noting that our most comprehensive and reliable account of his system, that of Hippolytus (*fidissimum excerptorem*, Diels found him, *Doxographi Graeci*, p. 132) makes no mention of the divinity of Air, but only says that 'gods and things divine' were 'generated' from Air (A 7); and that St Augustine (*Civ. Dei.* viii. 2) seems to agree with Hippolytus, saying that 'the gods arose from the air'.
[93] In agreement with the view of E. Bickel, *Homerische Seelenglaube* (*Schriften der Koenigsberger Gelehrten Gesellschaft* 1 [1925], Heft 1).
[94] I see no good reason to doubt Jaeger's view that they did, though no such conclusion is warranted by one of the sources to which he looks for support (pp. 80 and 84), *sc.* Aristotle's report (*de An.* 213 b 22 ff.) of the Pythagorean

(iv) Anaximenes certainly did not think the soul 'as in-incorporeal as possible', but the reverse. To say that everything, from fire to earth, is air, is to say that soul, as air, is as corporeal as anything else.[95]

But none of this really gets to the heart of the question. The stark, irreconcilable contrast between Ionian naturalism and Orphic dualism would be untouched by any theory of the material composition of the soul the Orphics may have entertained, even if this were borrowed from philosophy. Anaximenes himself may have taught the divinity of the soul, though there is no such statement in either fragments or testimonies. This way of speaking and thinking is quite congenial to the temper of Ionian philo-

[95] Cf. Diogenes of Apollonia B 7: '[air is] an eternal immortal body'. Jaeger says that Anaximenes 'did not identify it [sc. soul = air] with any corporeal substance of the world of experience' (p. 84). I believe that this is precisely what he did (see, B 1, which offers a primitive sort of experimental evidence for the 'warm air' theory of soul), his choice of Air in place of Anaximander's *Apeiron* being dictated by the desire to find a cosmogonic substance *in* 'the world of experience', taking pains to explain the particular physical circumstance under which the air about us is 'imperceptible' (A 7).

view that the *ouranos* 'breathed' in 'air' and 'void' from the surrounding infinity: Aristotle's report does not *say* that this inhalation is soul, nor could it be, since, *qua* infinite, the void would come for the Pythagoreans under the heading of the 'evil' principle which would certainly not be that of the (divine) soul. Aristotle's single reference to the Orphic theogony (n. 91) seems slim ground on which to base the reconstruction of their theory of the soul, but perhaps good enough where positive evidence is so hard to come by. Here, however, we should note that Aristotle's report does not strictly say that in this view soul was air: fire, or the fiery aether, could also be 'borne about' by winds and 'inhaled' (so in the philosophers, e.g. Heracl. A 16, Democr. A 106). Jaeger doubtless means to use 'air' broadly enough to include fiery aether (clearly so in another context, p. 208, n. 63, where he refers to Heraclitus' theory of soul as 'air'), and with good reason since the distinction between air and aether is hazy enough in the philosophers (for Heraclitus, cf. B 31, B 36, B 76; for Empedocles, note that 'air' in B 17. 18 = aether in B 71, etc., while at B 38 aether = fire!) and would be even hazier in popular thought. In Anaximenes soul is *warm air* (B 1 *sub. fin.*). When the mystery cults contrast the *aethereal* soul with the earth-born body (see above note 60) it is safe to assume that the contrast is between the warm, bright aether of the soul and the cold, dark earth of the body no less than between the volatile consistency of the 'breath'-soul and the heavy, compact 'earth'-body.

sophy. We find it in Heraclitus,[96] Diogenes of Apollonia,[97] and even Democritus![98] There is no reason why Anaximenes too would not have welcomed the idea on the same terms. But what would it have meant to him on *these* terms? In Ionian philosophy the divine is nature itself, its basic stuff and ruling principle. To say that the soul is divine is then to naturalize it; it is to say that it is subject to the same sequence of law and effect which are manifest throughout the whole of nature. And this is the very opposite of the Orphic doctrine of the divinity of the soul, whose content is rather obscure, but whose intent is perfectly clear: that the soul is not a natural, but a super-natural, entity. The word 'supernatural' would not, of course, figure in their vocabulary. But it would describe their meaning better than any word at our disposal. When they said that the soul was divine they meant that it is an exile from another world: its stuff is god-stuff; its powers are not bound by the limits of the observable uniformities of nature but include the oracular and other magical powers of divine being;[99] its destiny is determined not by the natural properties of air, fire, etc., but by the mysterious will of superior gods who impose on this lesser *daimon* the penance of transmigration, and prescribe, through their priests and prophets, the necessary purificatory rites

[96] If we may read so much into the equation of θνητοὶ ἀθάνατοι in B 62 (cf. B 77).
[97] In the valuable testimony of Theophrastus (*de sens.* 42) to which Jaeger draws attention, p. 171.
[98] See 'Ethics and Physics in Democritus' (cited above, note 74), pp. 580–2.
[99] For the oracular powers of the soul which 'has come from the gods', see Pindar's famous frag. 131 Schroeder. For the sundry magical powers (including oracles) claimed by the Orphic adept our best texts are Empedocles B 111, B 112, B 129; with Empedocles' claims (in his capacity of Orphic god-man) to control the winds and make rain, cf. those of the magicians and purifiers in *On the Sacred Disease* (4): 'they profess to know how to bring down the moon, eclipse the sun, make storm and sunshine, rain and drought, the sea impassable and the earth barren'. For other instances of Orphic magic, see Euripides, *Cycl.* 647–9; and Plato, *Rep.* 364 bc, which includes black magic (*katadesmoi* here = *katadeseis* in *Laws* 933 a, the *tabellae defixionis*, on which see M. P. Nilsson, *Greek Popular Religion* [New York, 1940], pp. 114–15). Such things were practised no doubt only by the lowest type of Orphic priests who, however, cannot be dismissed as merely 'quack' Orphics (see above, note 45); the fact that priests who invoke the authority of books by Orpheus and Musaeus for their rites practise this kind of magic is a significant commentary on the Orphic concept of the soul.

and tabus. Could one imagine a sharper antithesis to any doctrine of the divinity of the soul that Anaximenes could possibly have taught?

The only answer I can think of would be by way of Empedocles. Here we do have a philosopher, and of the first order, who is also a devotee of Orphic purity. If it could be shown that what his natural philosophy tells us about the soul will square with his doctrine of transmigration, we would have strong, indeed conclusive, grounds for saying that the two doctrines are not as incompatible as we must think them on the strength of all our other evidence. And this is precisely what no one has yet succeeded in showing. Jaeger does not attempt and, if I read him aright, does not intend so much. He recognized the 'basic incompatibility'[100] between the 'mysticotheological' thought-forms of the *Purifications* and the rationalistic logic of the poem *On Nature*. But he still argues for some sort of imaginative coherence between the two: 'In the mythical space of a world pervaded by divine figures, the two attitudes so irreconcilable from our abstract point of view will be seen to fit together as two distinct, but in the last analysis basically homogeneous, spheres for the interplay of divine forces'.[101] I can only say that, after reading this chapter with care and accepting gratefully much of its detail, I do not find that the promised reconciliation comes off. Not only from our 'abstract' point of view, but from Empedocles' own as well,

[100] P. 133. For a sample of the opposite view at its boldest extreme, see Cornford, *op. cit.*, p. 241: 'Empedocles . . . exemplifies, in a most remarkable way, the . . . view that men's cosmological views were almost entirely dictated by, and deduced from, their religious convictions'. A similar view is expressed in more temperate language in Cornford's chapter on 'Mystery Religions and Presocratic Philosophy' in Vol. IV of the *Cambridge Ancient History*, pp. 566–9, (and more recently in C. H. Kahn's 'Religion and Natural Philosophy in Empedocles' Doctrine of the Soul', *Archiv. für Geschichte der Philosophie*, 42 (1960), 1–35].

[101] P. 134. I cannot be sure that I understand exactly what Jaeger means here, but suspect that he reads more into the deification of the four roots in *On Nature* than the evidence allows. All Empedocles means by calling them 'gods' is to call attention to their (*a*) privileged immortality against the mortality of all other physical substances (as I have argued in 'The Physical Theory of Anaxagoras', *Philos. Rev.* 59 [1950], pp. 77–8, and (*b*) joint and equal share along with Love and Strife in the maintenance of the cosmic order (see the paper cited above at note 16, pp. 159–60). This sort of divinity builds no bridges on the *Purifications*.

the two pictures of reality remain not only heterogeneous but contradictory at crucial points; they admit of no rational or, for that matter, even imaginative harmony. Take, for instance, the major fragment of the *Purifications* where the fatality of transmigration is somehow blamed on Strife.[102] 'In this way,' Jaeger remarks, 'the philosopher tries to interpret the fundamental religious facts of the Orphic theory in accordance with the supreme principle of his natural philosophy' (p. 150). But the natural philosophy does not single out Strife as *the* power which sets in motion the wheel of becoming. Love is at least as necessary.[103] What is more, *On Nature* speaks of Love as the creator of 'mortal forms', while on Jaeger's interpretation, this fragment of the *Purifications* assigns just this function to Strife.[104] Again, if the Golden Age of the *Purifications*, as Jaeger interprets it (pp. 150 ff.), stands for a world where Love holds undisputed sway, the imaginative construct would clash badly with that of the physical poem. For without Strife, the cosmologist holds, there could be no world at all, good or bad, only an indiscriminate mixture, no individual gods or daemons or anything else.[105] But the *Purifications* speaks of men, beasts, and birds, as well as gods, when 'the flames of good fellowship glowed' in the Golden Age (B 128). Just

[102] B 115. 13-14, '. . . an exile from the gods and a wanderer, for that I put my trust in insensate Strife' (translation after Burnet) which Jaeger takes for 'a mythical way of expressing its (*sc.* the wandering soul's) entanglement in the cosmic machinery under the rule of Hate' (p. 150). He had offered a different interpretation in *Paideia* (Vol. I, 2nd edn of English translation, p. 169, with reference to B 115. 9 ff.): 'In the cosmos revealed by the physicists, the soul (*sc.* of Orphic piety) can find no home.' But if this is (as I believe) the right interpretation, I do not see how Empedocles may be said to present 'a synthesis which shows very instructively how these two different ways of viewing the world (*sc.* Orphism and *physiologia*) could supplement and complete each other' (*loc. cit.*).

[103] As Jaeger justly observes (p. 140): 'Hate is as necessary as Love to maintain its (*sc.* the world's) dynamic structure, even though Empedocles loves Love and hates Hate'. Hence Hate's 'equality' (B 17. 27) with Love, a powerful testimony to the subordination of religious feeling to the requirements of the physical system in this poem.

[104] Cf. φυομένους παντοῖα διὰ χρόνου εἴδεα θνητῶν, B 115. 7 with θνητ' ἐφύοντο and χεῖτ' ἔθνεα μυρία θνητῶν, παντοίαις ἰδέησιν ἀρηρότα of B 35, 14–17, under the influence of φιλότητος ὁρμή.

[105] Not only men, animals, and plants, but also the 'long-lived gods' come into being only when the world-process is set in motion ἐκ τούτων, *sc.* Love and Strife (B 20. 9 ff.).

how then are the *Purifications* 'in the last analysis basically homogeneous' here with the cosmology?[106]

As for the concept of the soul, Empedocles' natural inquiry presents us with a cardinal doctrine, explicit in the surviving fragments, and enormously influential on Greek medical thought. It is the well-known theory that perception and thought are the functions of the blood, which is conceived as a mixture of the four elements in equal ratio.[107] But blood can hardly exist without 'flesh'; and in the *Purifications* flesh is termed in Orphic fashion an 'alien garment'[108] which the wandering daemon puts on when, and presumably only when, he serves his sentence in the wheel of transmigration. How then does he get along without it in his first and last estate of discarnate blessedness? How does he think the thoughts of love when he has nothing to think with?[109] It is better to drop the question and therewith the assumption that Empedoclean physics and mysticism are 'basically homogeneous'. Jaeger spoke of Empedocles in *Paideia*[110] as a 'philosophical

[106] Two more of the many points which cannot be dealt with here: (1) 'It has already been correctly observed that the theory of the four elements, as it is generally called, is presupposed in the *Katharmoi* as well' (p. 143). This on the strength of B 115. 9 ff., which, however, on Jaeger's earlier interpretation (above, note 102), voices the hostility of the natural universe to the Orphic soul. Is there any suggestion, here or elsewhere, that the four elements would (along with Love and Strife) pervade the whole of reality in the *Purifications*, as they certainly do in *On Nature*? (2) It is not quite clear whether Jaeger means to identify (as he seems to do, pp. 140 ff.) the *Sphairos* of *On Nature* with the 'holy and unutterable mind' of B 134, See K. Reinhardt's arguments against the identification by W. Kranz. *Empedocles* (Zurich, 1949), p. 48, in his review of this book in *Classical Philology*, 45 (1950), 176–7.

[107] B 98, B 105.

[108] B 126. To Jaeger's comment, 'in this image we see corporeality regarded as a mere transient, non-essential wrapping—a conception just as strange to the Greek of Homer's time as it is to the Ionian philosopher' (p. 147), I would merely add: and just as strange to Empedocles himself *qua* philosopher and medical man.

[109] I cannot imagine how this and many other difficulties could be met by Cornford's view (*op. cit.*, p. 239; now revived by H. S. Long, 'The Unity of Empedocles's Thought', *American Journal of Philology*, 70 [1949], 156–7) that the transmigrating soul is a compound of Love and Strife. In any case, such a view remains purely conjectural; there is no support for it in fragments and/or testimonia, which always treat mental processes as functions of the ratio not of Love–Strife but of earth–water–air–fire.

[110] Vol. I, 2nd English ed., p. 295.

centaur, . . . a prodigious union of Ionian elemental physics and Orphic theology'. 'Prodigious' is the right word for the union of physics and theology, as it is for the junction of immortal god and mortal flesh. The one is as much of a miracle as the other, and Empedocles doubtless devoutly believed it to be such. He left us no explanation of either, and it would be futile to try to supply it by rationalizing the theology of the mystic or mystifying the logic of the cosmologist.[110a]

To set the contribution of Presocratic philosophy to the concept of the soul in its just historical perspective we must see how here, as in its concept of God, it is its peculiar genius to transpose a religious idea into the medium of natural inquiry, transforming, but not destroying, its associated religious values. It is the function of high religion to foster man's reverence for himself no less than his reverence for God. In this respect the record of Greek religion can hardly be called a success. The fault lay at least in part with its traditional concept of the soul as the 'image' or 'shadow' of the real man, which was somehow the principle of life but neither of feeling nor judgement.[111] This psyche's ghostly survival after death was a wretched affair; Homer regards with mixed feelings of gloom and contempt the flitting, squeaking, batlike[112] creatures in the 'joyless' regions[113] of nether darkness.[114]

This flimsy support for the sense of reverence for life could be strengthened in one of two opposite ways. The super-natural psyche could be retained and reformed, turned into an infinitely more robust affair, human and superhuman, an incarnate god or

---

[110a] For a thorough treatment, see now A. A. Long, 'Thinking and Sense-Perception in Empedocles: Mysticism or Materialism', *Classical Quarterly*, N.S. 16 (1966), 256–76.

[111] I follow here Jaeger's view (p. 74 and ff. with notes) that *psyche* in Homer refers not only to the ghostly residue which survives death but also to the principle of life in the living person. The latter had been ignored in Rohde's classic on this theme. Jaeger seems to make a judicious synthesis of the best features of Rohde's work with those of his critics.

[112] *Od.* xxiv. 1 ff.

[113] *Od.* xi. 94; an idea repeatedly echoed in tragedy, Aeschylus, *Eum.* 301, 423. Euripides, *Or.* 1082–4.

[114] M. P. Nilsson, 'The Immortality of the Soul', *Eranos* 39 (1941), pp. 1–16, at p. 3: 'The Greek Underworld was a gloomy and terrible place, and its terror consisted just in its emptiness, its nothingness. . . . The afterlife is at most a vacuum, the soul a worthless, useless shadow. It is evaluated accordingly.'

daemon, possessing in life and conserving after death all the powers of thought, will, and passion of the full-blooded man, with an extra load of divine powers thrown in for good measure.[115] This was the way of the mystery cults. The Orphic theogonies, Pythagoras, the Empedocles of the *Purifications*, and finally and most triumphantly Plato, adopted and justified this faith. Plato's influence made it a dominant doctrine of Hellenistic thought; thence it passed with appropriate modifications into Christian theology, as Jaeger observes (p. 73). Whatever our estimate of the wisdom of this conception, we have no right to call it 'the' Greek view of the soul. No less Greek was the radical alternative chosen by the Presocratics. They too merged the psyche with the feeling *thymos* and the thinking *nous*. But they did so without regard to the cult and with no concessions to magic. They assumed from the start [116] that they could apply to the soul the same categories of understanding which formed the framework of their natural inquiry. They thought of it as a part of nature, with a natural origin and a natural ending, but as no less divine for being just that, since it shared the powers of wisdom and justice writ large throughout the universe and could therefore realize within the human microcosm some measure of the order which ruled the infinite worlds. This was its destiny, natural and divine, to be that unique thing, 'a self-increasing logos'.[117] Except for Heraclitus, the Presocratics were too preoccupied with cosmological and physiological problems to develop the potentialities of this idea.

---

[115] See above, note 99.
[116] Anaximander (A 11, A 30), in assuming that man arose from purely natural substances (earth and water) by a purely natural process (heating by the sun); Anaximenes (B 1, B 2), in assuming that the properties of soul are simply those of air. This initiates a tradition in which a dualistic conception of soul–body is unthinkable; soul *is* body, either a particular physical substance *in* the body (air in Anaximenes and Diogenes, fire in Heraclitus and the atomists) or else the mixture (*krasis* of the physical components of the body as a whole (Parmenides) or of the blood (Empedocles). The detachable ghost-soul of Homer or God-soul of the mystery cults is precluded. Immortality is implied or asserted (Heraclitus, Alcmaeon) in quite another sense, i.e. the physical survival of the substance(s) which make it up, but which does not imply the preservation of personal identity so essential for the mystery cults. Anaxagoras' doctrine of the 'unmixed' *nous* is the first break in the tradition, though it is not made the basis of any doctrine of personal immortality.
[117] Heraclitus B 115.

But we can see its vitality in Democritus, where the sense of reverence for man survives the loss of faith in God.[118] He can no longer believe in the divinity of nature, but he still believes in the divinity of the soul.[119]

[118] See above, note 98.
[119] For a thorough criticism of an earlier draft I am indebted to my colleague, Friedrich Solmsen. The opinions in this paper are my own; but many suggestions which have improved it have come from him.

VI

BACK TO THE PRESOCRATICS*

Sir Karl Popper

I

'BACK to Methuselah' was a progressive programme, compared with 'Back to Thales' or 'Back to Anaximander': what Shaw offered us was an improved expectation of life—something that was in the air, at any rate when he wrote it. I have nothing to offer you, I am afraid, that is in the air today; for what I want to return to is the simple straightforward *rationality* of the Presocratics. Wherein does this much discussed 'rationality' of the Presocratics lie? The simplicity and boldness of their questions is part of it, but my thesis is that the decisive point is the critical attitude which, as I shall try to show, was first developed in the Ionian School.

The questions which the Presocratics tried to answer were primarily cosmological questions, but there were also questions of the theory of knowledge. It is my belief that philosophy must return to cosmology and to a simple theory of knowledge. There is at least one philosophical problem in which all thinking men are interested: the problem of understanding the world in which we live; and thus ourselves (who are part of that world) and our knowledge of it. All science is cosmology, I believe, and for me the interest of philosophy, no less than of science, lies solely in its bold attempt to add to our knowledge of the world, and to the theory of our knowledge of the world. I am interested in Wittgenstein, for example, not because of his linguistic philosophy, but because his *Tractatus* was a cosmological treatise (although a

* The Presidential Address, delivered before the meeting of the Aristotelian Society on 13 October 1958; first published in the *Proceedings of the Aristotelian Society*, N.S. 59, 1958–9. The footnotes were added in the revised reprint of the address in *Conjectures and Refutations*.

crude one), and because his theory of knowledge was closely linked with his cosmology.

For me, both philosophy and science lose all their attraction when they give up that pursuit—when they become specialisms and cease to see, and to wonder at, the riddles of our world. Specialization may be a great temptation for the scientist. For the philosopher it is mortal sin.

II

In this paper I speak as an amateur, as a lover of the beautiful story of the Presocratics. I am not a specialist or an expert: I am completely out of my depth when an expert begins to argue which words or phrases Heraclitus might, and which he could not possibly, have used. Yet when some expert replaces a beautiful story, based on the oldest texts we possess, by one which—to me at any rate—no longer makes any sense, then I feel that even an amateur may stand up and defend an old tradition. Thus I will at least look into the expert's arguments, and examine their consistency. This seems a harmless occupation to indulge in; and if an expert or anybody else should take the trouble to refute my criticism I shall be pleased and honoured.[1]

I shall be concerned with the cosmological theories of the Presocratics, but only to the extent to which they bear upon the development of *the problem of change*, as I call it, and only to the extent to which they are needed for misunderstanding the approach of the Presocratic philosophers to the problem of knowledge—their practical as well as their theoretical approach. For it is of considerable interest to see how their practice as well as their theory of knowledge is connected with the cosmological and theological questions which they posed to themselves. Theirs was not a theory of knowledge that began with the question, 'How do I know that this is an orange?' or, 'How do I know that the object I am now perceiving is an orange?' Their theory of knowledge started from problems such as, 'How do we know that the world is made of water?' or, 'How do we know that the

---

[1] I am glad to be able to report that Mr G. S. Kirk has indeed replied to my address; see below, Ch. VII. [Professor Popper's answer to Kirk's criticisms, which could not be included in this volume, is printed as an *Appendix* to his paper, in *Conjectures and Refutations*, pp. 153 ff.]

world is full of gods?' or, 'How can we know anything about the gods?'

There is a widespread belief, somewhat remotely due, I think, to the influence of Francis Bacon, that one should study the problems of the theory of knowledge in connection with our knowledge of an orange rather than our knowledge of the cosmos. I dissent from this belief, and it is one of the main purposes of my paper to convey to you some of my reasons for dissenting. At any rate it is good to remember from time to time that our Western science—and there seems to be no other—did not start with collecting observations of oranges, but with bold theories about the world.

III

Traditional empiricist epistemology and the traditional historiography of science are both deeply influenced by the Baconian myth that all science starts from observation and then slowly and cautiously proceeds to theories. That the facts are very different can be learned from studying the early Presocratics. Here we find bold and fascinating ideas, some of which are strange and even staggering anticipations of modern results, while many others are wide of the mark, from our modern point of view; but most of them, and the best of them, have nothing to do with observation. Take for example some of the theories about the shape and position of the earth. Thales said, we are told, 'that the earth is supported by water on which it rides like a ship, and when we say that there is an earthquake, then the earth is being shaken by the movement of the water'. No doubt Thales had observed earthquakes as well as the rolling of a ship before he arrived at his theory. But the point of his theory was to *explain* the support or suspension of the earth, and also earthquakes, by the conjecture that the earth floats on water; and for this conjecture (which so strangely anticipates the modern theory of continental drift) he could have no basis in his observations.

We must not forget that the function of the Baconian myth is to explain why scientific statements are *true*, by pointing out that observation is the *'true source'* of our scientific knowledge. Once we realize that all scientific statements are hypotheses, or guesses, or conjectures, and that the vast majority of these conjectures (including Bacon's own) have turned out to be false, the Baconian myth becomes irrelevant. For it is pointless to argue that the conjectures of science—those which have proved to be false as well as those which are still accepted—all start from observation.

However this may be, Thales' beautiful theory of the support or suspension of the earth and of earthquakes, though in no sense based upon observation, is at least inspired by an empirical or observational analogy. But even this is no longer true of the theory proposed by Thales' great pupil, Anaximander. Anaximander's theory of the suspension of the earth is still highly intuitive, but it no longer uses observational analogies. In fact it may be described as counter-observational. According to Anaximander's theory, 'The earth . . . is held up by nothing, but remains stationary owing to the fact that it is equally distant from all other things. Its shape is . . . like that of a drum. . . . We walk on one of its flat surfaces, while the other is on the opposite side'. The drum, of course, is an observational analogy. But the idea of the earth's free suspension in space, and the explanation of its stability, have no analogy whatever in the whole field of observable facts.

In my opinion this idea of Anaximander's is one of the boldest, most revolutionary, and most portentous ideas in the whole history of human thought. It made possible the theories of Aristarchus and Copernicus. But the step taken by Anaximander was even more difficult and audacious than the one taken by Aristarchus and Copernicus. To envisage the earth as freely poised in mid-space, and to say 'that it remains motionless because of its equidistance or equilibrium' (as Aristotle paraphrases Anaximander), is to anticipate to some extent even Newton's idea of immaterial and invisible gravitational forces.[2]

---

[2] Aristotle himself understood Anaximander in this way; for he caricatures Anaximander's 'ingenious but untrue' theory by comparing the situation of its earth to that of a man who, being equally hungry and thirsty yet equidistant from food and drink, is unable to move. (De Caelo, 295 b 32. The idea has become known by the name 'Buridan's ass'.) Clearly Aristotle conceives this man as being held in equilibrium by immaterial and invisible attractive forces similar to Newtonian forces; and it is interesting that this 'animistic' or 'occult' character of his forces was deeply (though mistakenly) felt by Newton himself, and by his opponents, such as Berkeley, to be a blot on his theory.

How did Anaximander arrive at this remarkable theory? Certainly not by observation but by reasoning. His theory is an attempt to solve one of the problems to which his teacher and kinsman Thales, the founder of the Milesian or Ionian School, had offered a solution before him. I therefore conjecture that Anaximander arrived at his theory by criticizing Thales' theory. This conjecture can be supported, I believe, by a consideration of the structure of Anaximander's theory.

Anaximander is likely to have argued against Thales' theory (according to which the earth was floating on water) on the following lines. Thales' theory is a specimen of a type of theory which if consistently developed would lead to an infinite regress. If we explain the stable position of the earth by the assumption that it is supported by water—that it is floating on the ocean (*Okeanos*)—should we not have to explain the stable position of the ocean by an analogous hypothesis? But this would mean looking for a support for the ocean, and then for a support for this support. This method of explanation is unsatisfactory: first, because we solve our problem by creating an exactly analogous one; and also for the less formal and more intuitive reason that in any such system of supports or props failure to secure any one of the lower props must lead to the collapse of the whole edifice.

From this we see intuitively that the stability of the world cannot be secured by a system of supports or props. Instead Anaximander appeals to the internal or structural symmetry of the world, which ensures that there is no preferred direction in which a collapse can take place. He applies the principle that where there are no differences there can be no change. In this way he explains the stability of the earth by the equality of its distances from all other things.

This, it seems, was Anaximander's argument. It is important to realize that it abolishes, even though not quite consciously perhaps, and not quite consistently, the idea of an absolute direction —the absolute sense of 'upwards' and 'downwards'. This is not only contrary to all experience but notoriously difficult to grasp. Anaximenes ignored it, it seems, and even Anaximander himself did not grasp it completely. For the idea of an equal distance from all other things should have led him to the theory that the earth has the shape of a globe. Instead he believed that it had the shape of a drum, with an upper and a lower flat surface. Yet it looks as if the remark, 'We walk on one of its flat surfaces, while the other is on the opposite side', contained a hint that there was no absolute upper surface, but that on the contrary the surface on which we happened to walk was the one we might *call* the upper.

What prevented Anaximander from arriving at the theory that the earth was a globe rather than a drum? There can be little doubt: it was *observational experience* which taught him that the surface of the earth was, by and large, flat. Thus it was a speculative and critical argument, the abstract critical discussion of Thales' theory, which almost led him to the true theory of the shape of the earth; and it was observational experience which led him astray.

V

There is an obvious objection to Anaximander's theory of symmetry, according to which the earth is equally distant from all other things. The asymmetry of the universe can be easily seen from the existence of sun and moon, and especially from the fact that sun and moon are sometimes not far distant from each other, so that they are on the same side of the earth, while there is nothing on the other side to balance them. It appears that Anaximander met this objection by another bold theory—his theory of the hidden nature of the sun, the moon, and the other heavenly bodies.

He envisages the rims of two huge chariot wheels rotating round the earth, one twenty-seven times the size of the earth, the other eighteen times its size. Each of these rims or circular pipes is filled with fire, and each has a breathing-hole through which the fire is visible. These holes we call the sun and the moon respectively. The rest of the wheel is invisible, presumably because it is dark (or misty) and far away. The fixed stars (and presumably the planets) are also holes on wheels which are nearer to the earth than the wheels of the sun and the moon. The wheels of the fixed stars rotate on a common axis (which we now call the axis of the earth) and together they form a sphere round the earth, so the postulate of equal distance from the earth is (roughly) satisfied. This makes Anaximander also a founder of the *theory of the spheres*. (For its relation to the wheels or circles, see Aristotle, *De Caelo*, 289 b to 290 b 10.)

VI

There can be no doubt whatever that Anaximander's theories are critical and speculative rather than empirical: and considered as approaches to truth his critical and abstract speculations served him better than observational experience or analogy.

But, a follower of Bacon may reply, this is precisely why Anaximander was not a scientist. This is precisely why we speak of early Greek *philosophy* rather than of early Greek *science*. Philosophy is speculative: everybody knows this. And as everybody knows, science begins only when the speculative method is replaced by the observational method, and when deduction is replaced by induction.

This reply, of course, amounts to the thesis that scientific theories should be defined by reference to their origin—their origin in observations, or in so-called 'inductive procedures'. Yet I believe that few, if any, physical theories would fall under this definition. And I do not see why the question of origin should be important in this connection. What is important about a theory is its explanatory power, and whether it stands up to criticism and to tests. The question of its origin, of how it is arrived at— whether by an 'inductive procedure', as some say, or by an act of intuition—may be extremely interesting, especially for the biographer of the man who invented the theory, but it has little to do with its scientific status or character.

VII

As to the Presocratics, I assert that there is the most perfect possible continuity of thought between their theories and the later developments in physics. Whether they are called philosophers, or pre-scientists, or scientists, matters very little, I think. But I do assert that Anaximander's theory cleared the way for the theories of Aristarchus, Copernicus, Kepler, and Galileo. It is not that he merely 'influenced' these later thinkers; 'influence' is a very superficial category. I would rather put it like this: Anaximander's achievement is valuable in itself, like a work of art. Besides, his achievement made other achievements possible, among them those of the great scientists mentioned.

But are not Anaximander's theories false, and therefore non-scientific? They are false, I admit; but so are many theories, based upon countless experiments, which modern science accepted until recently, and whose scientific character nobody would dream of denying, even though they are now believed to be false. (An example is the theory that the typical chemical properties of hydrogen belong only to one kind of atom—the lightest of all atoms.) There were historians of science who tended to regard as unscientific (or even as superstitious) any view no longer accepted at the time they were writing; but this is an untenable attitude. A false theory may be as great an achievement as a true one. And many false theories have been more helpful in our search for truth than some less interesting theories which are still accepted. For false theories can be helpful in many ways; they may for example suggest some more or less radical modifications, and they may stimulate criticism. Thus Thales' theory that the earth floats on water reappeared in a modified form in Anaximenes, and in more recent times in the form of Wegener's theory of continental drift. How Thales' theory stimulated Anaximander's criticism has been shown already.

Anaximander's theory, similarly, suggested a modified theory—the theory of an earth globe, freely poised in the centre of the universe, and surrounded by spheres on which heavenly bodies were mounted. And by stimulating criticism it also led to the theory that the moon shines by reflecting light; to the Pythagorean theory of a central fire; and ultimately to the heliocentric world-system of Aristarchus and Copernicus.

VIII

I believe that the Milesians, like their oriental predecessors who took the world for a tent, envisaged the world as a kind of house, the home of all creatures—our home. Thus there was no need to ask what it was for. But there was a real need to inquire into its architecture. The questions of its structure, its ground-plan, and its building material, constitute the three main problems of Milesian cosmology. There is also a speculative interest in its origin, the question of cosmogony. It seems to me that the cosmological interest of the Milesians far exceeded their cosmogonical interest, especially if we consider the strong cosmogonical tradition, and the almost irresistible tendency to describe a thing by describing how it has been made, and thus to present a cosmological account in a cosmogonical form. The cosmological interest must be very strong, as compared with the cosmogonical one, if the presentation of a cosmological theory is even partially free from these cosmogonical trappings.

I believe that it was Thales who first discussed the architecture of the cosmos—its structure, ground-plan, and building material. In Anaximander we find answers to all three questions. I have briefly mentioned his answer to the question of structure. As to the question of the ground-plan of the world, he studied and expounded this too, as indicated by the tradition that he drew the first map of the world. And of course he had a theory about its building material—the 'endless' or 'boundless' or 'unbounded' or 'unformed'—the *apeiron*.

In Anaximander's world all kinds of *changes* were going on. There was a fire which needed air and breathing-holes, and these were at times blocked up ('obstructed'), so that the fire was smothered:[3] this was his theory of eclipses, and of the phases of the moon. There were winds, which were responsible for the changing weather.[4] And there were the vapours, resulting from

[3] I do not suggest that the smothering is due to blocking breathing-in holes: according to the phlogiston theory, for example, fire is smothered by obstructing breathing-out holes. But I do not wish to ascribe to Anaximander either a phlogiston theory of combustion, or an anticipation of Lavoisier.

[4] In my address, as it was originally published, I continued here 'and indeed for all other changes within the cosmic edifice', relying on Zeller who wrote (appealing to the testimony of Aristotle's *Meteor.* 353 b 6): 'Anaximander, it seems, explained the motion of the heavenly bodies by the currents of the air which are responsible for the turning of the stellar spheres.' (*Phil. d. Griechen*, 5th edn, Vol. 1 [1892], p. 223; see also p. 220, n. 2; Heath, *Aristarchus* [1913], p. 33; and Lee's edition of the *Meteorologica*, [1952], p. 125.) But I should perhaps not have interpreted Zeller's 'currents of air' as 'winds', especially as Zeller should have said 'vapours' (they are evaporations resulting from a process of drying up). I have twice inserted 'vapours and' before 'winds', and 'almost' before 'all' in the second paragraph of section ix; and I have replaced, in the third paragraph of section ix, 'winds' by 'vapours'. I have made these changes in the hope of meeting Mr G. S. Kirk's criticism on p. 332 of his article (this volume, p. 170).

the drying up of water and air, which were the cause of the winds and of the 'turnings' of the sun (the solstices) and of the moon.

We have here the first hint of what was soon to come: of the *general problem of change*, which became the central problem of Greek cosmology, and which ultimately led, with Leucippus and Democritus, to *a general theory of change* that was accepted by modern science almost up to the beginning of the twentieth century. (It was given up only with the breakdown of Maxwell's models of the ether, an historic event that was little noticed before 1905.)

This *general problem of change* is a philosophical problem; indeed in the hands of Parmenides and Zeno it almost turns into a logical one. *How is change possible*—logically possible, that is? How can a thing change, without losing its identity? If it remains the same, it does not change; yet if it loses its identity, then it is no longer that thing which has changed.

IX

The exciting story of the development of the problem of change appears to me in danger of being completely buried under the mounting heap of the minutiae of textual criticism. The story cannot, of course, be fully told in one short paper, and still less in one of its many sections. But in briefest outline, it is this.

For Anaximander, our own world, our own cosmic edifice, was only one of an infinity of worlds—an infinity without bounds in space and time. This system of worlds was eternal, and so was motion. There was thus no need to explain motion, no need to offer a *general* theory of change (in the sense in which we shall find a general problem and a general theory of change in Heraclitus; see below). But there was a need to explain the well-known changes occurring in our world. The most obvious changes—the change of day and night, of winds and of weather, of the seasons, from sowing to harvesting, and of the growth of plants and animals and men—all were connected with the contrast of temperatures, with the opposition between the hot and the cold, and with that between the dry and the wet. 'Living creatures came into being from moisture evaporated by the sun,' we are told; and the hot and the cold also administer to the genesis of our own world edifice. The hot and the cold were also responsible for the

BACK TO THE PRESOCRATICS

vapours and winds which in their turn were conceived as the agents of almost all other changes.

Anaximenes, a pupil of Anaximander and his successor, developed these ideas in much detail. Like Anaximander he was interested in the oppositions of the hot and the cold and of the moist and the dry, and he explained the transitions between these opposites by a theory of condensation and rarefaction. Like Anaximander he believed in eternal motion and in the action of the winds; and it seems not unlikely that one of the two main points in which he deviated from Anaximander was reached by a criticism of the idea that what was completely boundless and formless (the *apeiron*) could yet be in motion. At any rate, he replaced the *apeiron* by air—something that was almost boundless and formless, and yet, according to Anaximander's old theory of vapours, not only capable of motion, but the main agent of motion and change. A similar unification of ideas was achieved by Anaximenes' theory that 'the sun consists of earth, and that it gets very hot owing to the rapidity of its motion'. The replacement of the more abstract theory of the unbounded *apeiron* by the less abstract and more common-sense theory of air is matched by the replacement of Anaximander's bold theory of the stability of the earth by the more common-sense idea that the earth's 'flatness is responsible for its stability; for it . . . covers like a lid the air beneath it'. Thus the earth rides on air as the lid of a pot may ride on steam, or as a ship may ride on water; Thales' question and Thales' answer are both reinstituted, and Anaximander's epoch-making argument is not understood. Anaximenes is an eclectic, a systematizer, an empiricist, a man of common sense. Of the three great Milesians he is least productive of revolutionary new ideas; he is the least philosophically minded.

The three Milesians all looked on our world as our home. There was movement, there was change in this home, there was hot and cold, fire and moisture. There was a fire in the hearth, and on it a kettle with water. The house was exposed to the winds, and a bit draughty, to be sure; but it was home, and it meant security and stability of a sort. But for Heraclitus the house was on fire.

There was no stability left in the world of Heraclitus. 'Everything is in flux, and nothing is at rest.' *Everything* is in flux, even the beams, the timber, the building material of which the world is made: earth and rocks, or the bronze of a cauldron—they are all in flux. The beams are rotting, the earth is washed away and blown away, the very rocks split and wither, the bronze cauldron turns into green patina, or into verdigris: 'All things are in motion all the time, even though . . . this escapes our senses', as Aristotle expressed it. Those who do not know and do not think believe that only the fuel is burned, while the bowl in which it burns (cf. DK, A 4) remains unchanged; for we do not see the bowl burning. And yet it burns; it is eaten up by the fire it holds. We do not *see* our children grow up, and change, and grow old, but they do.

Thus there are no solid bodies. Things are not really things, they are processes, they are in flux. They are like fire, like a flame which, though it may have a definite shape, is a process, a stream of matter, a river. All things are flames: fire is the very building material of our world; and the apparent stability of things is merely due to the laws, the measures, which the processes in our world are subject to.

This, I believe, is Heraclitus' story; it is his 'message', the 'true word' (the *logos*), to which we ought to listen: 'Listening not to me but to the true account, it is wise to admit that all things are one': they are 'an everlasting fire, flaring up in measures, and dying down in measures'.

I know very well that the traditional interpretation of Heraclitus' philosophy here restated is not generally accepted at present. But the critics have put nothing in its place—nothing, that is, of philosophical interest. I shall briefly discuss their new interpretation in the next section. Here I wish only to stress that Heraclitus' philosophy, by appealing to thought, to the word, to argument, to reason, and by pointing out that we are living in a world of things whose changes escape our senses, though we *know* that they do change, created two new problems—*the problem of change* and *the problem of knowledge*. These problems were the more urgent as his own account of change was difficult to understand. But this, I believe, is due to the fact that he saw more clearly than his predecessors the difficulties that were involved in the very idea of change.

For all change is the change of something: change presupposes something that changes. And it presupposes that, while changing, this something must remain the same. We may say that a green leaf changes when it turns brown; but we do not say that the green leaf changes when we substitute for it a brown leaf. It is essential to the idea of change that the thing which changes retains its identity while changing. And yet it must become something else: it was green, and it becomes brown; it was moist, and it becomes dry; it was hot, and it becomes cold.

Thus every change is the transition of a thing into something with, in a way, opposite qualities (as Anaximander and Anaximenes had seen). And yet, while changing, the changing thing must remain identical with itself.

This is the problem of change. It led Heraclitus to a theory which (partly anticipating Parmenides) distinguishes between reality and appearance. 'The real nature of things loves to hide itself. An unapparent harmony is stronger than the apparent one.' Things are *in appearance* (and for us) opposites, but in truth (and for God) they are the same.

Life and death, being awake and being asleep, youth and old age, all these are the same . . . for the one turned round is the other and the other turned round is the first. . . . The path that leads up and the path that leads down are the same path. . . . Good and bad are identical. . . . For God all things are beautiful and good and just, but men assume some things to be unjust, and others to be just. . . . It is not in the nature or character of man to possess true knowledge, though it is in the divine nature.

Thus in truth (and for God) the opposites are identical; it is only to man that they appear as non-identical. And all things are one— they are all part of the process of the world, the everlasting fire.

This theory of change appeals to the 'true word', to the *logos*, to reason; nothing is more real for Heraclitus than change. Yet his doctrine of the oneness of the world, of the identity of opposites, and of appearance and reality threatens his doctrine of the reality of change.

For change is the transition from one opposite to the other. Thus if in truth the opposites are identical, though they appear different, then change itself might be only apparent. If in truth, and for God, all things are one, there might, in truth, be no change.

This consequence was drawn by Parmenides, the pupil (*pace* Burnet and others) of the monotheist Xenophanes who said of the one God: 'He always remains in the same place, never moving. It is not fitting that He should go to different places at different times . . . He is in no way similar to mortal men, neither in body nor in thought.'

Xenophanes' pupil Parmenides taught that the real world was one, and that it always remained in the same place, never moving. It was not *fitting* that it should go to different places at different times. It was in no way similar to what it appeared to be to mortal men. The world was one, an undivided whole, without parts, homogeneous and motionless: motion was impossible in such a world. In truth there was no change. The world of change was an illusion.

Parmenides based this theory of an unchanging reality on something like a logical proof; a proof which can be presented as proceeding from the single premiss, 'What is not is not'. From this we can derive that the nothing—that which is not—does not exist; a result which Parmenides interprets to mean that the void does not exist. Thus the world is full: it consists of one undivided block, since any division into parts could only be due to separation of the parts by the void. (This is 'the well-rounded truth' which the goddess revealed to Parmenides.) In this full world there is no room for motion.

Only the delusive belief in the reality of opposites—the belief that not only *what is* exists but also *what is not*—leads to the illusion of a world of change.

Parmenides' theory may be described as the first hypothetico-deductive theory of the world. The atomists took it as such; and they asserted that it was refuted by experience, since motion does exist. Accepting the formal validity of Parmenides' argument, they inferred from the falsity of his conclusion the falsity of his premiss. But this meant that the nothing—the void, or empty space—existed. Consequently there was now no need to assume that 'what is'—the full, that which fills some space—had no parts; for its parts could now be separated by the void. Thus there are many parts, each of which is 'full': there are full particles in the world, separated by empty space, and able to move in empty space, each of them being 'full', undivided, indivisible, and unchanging. Thus what exists is *atoms and the void*. In this way the atomists arrived at a *theory of change*—a theory that dominated scientific thought until 1900. It is the theory that *all change, and specially all qualitative change, has to be explained by the spatial movement of unchanging bits of matter—by atoms moving in the void.*

The next great step in our cosmology and the theory of change was made when Maxwell, developing certain ideas of Faraday's, replaced this theory by a theory of changing intensities of fields.

X

I have sketched the story, as I see it, of the Presocratic theory of change. I am of course well aware of the fact that my story (which is based on Plato, Aristotle, and the doxographic tradition) clashes at many points with the views of some experts, English as well as German, and especially with the views expressed by G. S. Kirk and J. E. Raven in their book, *The Presocratic Philosophers*, 1957. I cannot of course examine their arguments in detail here, and especially not their minute exegeses of various passages some of which are relevant to the differences between their interpretation and mine. (See, for example, Kirk and Raven's discussion of the question whether there is a reference to Heraclitus in Parmenides; cf. their note 1 on pp. 193 f., and note 1 on p. 272.) But I wish to say that I have examined their arguments and that I have found them unconvincing and often quite unacceptable.

I will mention here only some points regarding Heraclitus (although there are other points of equal importance, such as their comments on Parmenides).

The traditional view, according to which Heraclitus' central doctrine was that all things are in flux, was attacked forty years ago by Burnet. His main argument (discussed by me at length in note 2 to Ch. 2 of my *Open Society*) was that the theory of change was not new, and that only a new message could explain the urgency with which Heraclitus speaks. This argument is repeated by Kirk and Raven when they write (pp. 186 f.): 'But all Presocratic thinkers were struck by the predominance of change in the world of our experience.' About this attitude I said in my *Open Society*: 'Those who suggest . . . that the doctrine of universal flux was not new . . . are, I feel, unconscious witnesses to Heraclitus' originality, for they fail now, after 2,400 years, to grasp his main point.' In brief, they do not see the difference between the Milesian message, 'There is a fire in the house,' and Heraclitus' somewhat more urgent message, 'The house is on fire.' An implicit reply to this criticism can be found on p. 197 of the book by Kirk and Raven, where they write: 'Can Heraclitus really have thought that a rock or a bronze cauldron, for example, was invariably undergoing invisible changes of material? Perhaps so; but nothing in the extant fragments suggests that he did.' But is this so? Heraclitus' extant fragments about the fire (Kirk and Raven, Frag. 220–2) are interpreted by Kirk and Raven themselves as follows (p. 200): 'Fire is the archetypal form of matter.' Now I am not at all sure what 'archetypal' means here (especially in view of the fact that we read a few lines later, 'Cosmogony . . . is not to be found in Heraclitus'). But whatever 'archetypal' may mean, it is clear that once it is admitted that Heraclitus says in the extant fragments that all matter is somehow (whether archetypally or otherwise) fire, he also says that all matter, like fire, is a process; which is precisely the theory denied to Heraclitus by Kirk and Raven.

Immediately after saying that 'nothing in the extant fragments suggests' that Heraclitus believed in continuous invisible changes, Kirk and Raven make the following methodological remark: 'It cannot be too strongly emphasized that [in texts] before Parmenides and his apparent proof that the senses were completely fallacious . . . gross departures from common sense must only be accepted when the evidence for them is extremely strong.' This is intended to mean that the doctrine that bodies (of any substance) constantly undergo invisible changes represents a gross departure from common sense, a departure which one ought not to expect in Heraclitus.

But to quote Heraclitus: 'He who does not expect the unexpected will not detect it: for him it will remain undetachable, and unapproachable' (DK, B 18). In fact Kirk and Raven's last argument is invalid on many grounds. Long before Parmenides we find ideas far removed from common sense in Anaximander, Pythagoras, Xenophanes, and especially in Heraclitus. Indeed the suggestion that we should test the historicity of the ideas ascribed to Heraclitus—as we might indeed test the historicity of those ascribed to Anaximenes—by standards of 'common sense' is a little surprising (whatever 'common sense' may mean here). For his suggestion runs counter not only to Heraclitus' notorious obscurity and oracular style, confirmed by Kirk and Raven, but also to his burning interest in antinomy and paradox. And it runs counter, last but not least, to the (in my view quite absurd) doctrine which Kirk and Raven finally attribute to Heraclitus (the italics are mine): '. . . that natural changes of all kinds [and thus presumably also earthquakes and great fires] are regular *and balanced*, and *that the cause of this balance is fire, the common constituent of things that was also termed their Logos.*' But why, I ask, should fire be 'the cause' of any balance—either 'this balance' or any other? And where does Heraclitus say such things? Indeed, had this been Heraclitus' philosophy, then I could see no reason to take any interest in it; at any rate, it would be much further removed from common sense (as I see it) than the inspired philosophy which tradition ascribes to Heraclitus and which, in the name of common sense, is rejected by Kirk and Raven.

But the decisive point is, of course, that this inspired philosophy is *true*, for all we know.[5] With his uncanny intuition Heraclitus saw that things are processes, that our bodies are flames, that 'a rock or a bronze cauldron . . . was invariably undergoing invisible changes'. Kirk and Raven say (p. 197, note 1; the argument reads like an answer to Melissus): 'Every time the finger rubs, it rubs off an invisible portion of iron; yet when it does not rub, what reason is there to think that the iron is still changing?' The reason is that the wind rubs, and that there is always wind; or that iron turns invisibly into rust—by oxidation, and this means by slow burning; or that old iron looks different from new iron, just as an old man looks different from a child (cf. DK, B 88). This was Heraclitus' teaching, as the extant fragments show.

I suggest that Kirk and Raven's methodological principle 'that gross departures from common sense must only be accepted when the evidence for them is extremely strong' might well be replaced by the clearer and more important principle that *gross departures from the historical tradition must only be accepted when the evidence for them is extremely strong*. This, in fact, is a universal principle of historiography. Without it history would be impossible. Yet it is

5 This should establish that it makes sense; at any rate, I hope it is clear from the text that I appeal to truth here in order (*a*) to make clear that my interpretation at least makes sense, and (*b*) to refute the arguments of Kirk and Raven (discussed later in this paragraph) that the theory is absurd. An answer to G. S. Kirk which was too long to be appended here (although it refers to the present passage and to the present paragraph) will be found in *Conjecture and Refutations*, pp. 153 ff.

constantly violated by Kirk and Raven: when, for example, they try to make Plato's and Aristotle's evidence suspect, with arguments which are partly circular and partly (like the one from common sense) in contradiction to their own story. And when they say that 'little serious attempt seems to have been made by Plato and Aristotle to penetrate his [i.e. Heraclitus'] real meaning' then I can only say that the philosophy outlined by Plato and Aristotle seems to me a philosophy that has real meaning and real depth. It is a philosophy worthy of a great philosopher. Who, if not Heraclitus, was the great thinker who first realized that men are flames and that things are processes? Are we really to believe that this great philosophy was a 'post-Heraclitean exaggeration' (p. 197), and that it may have been suggested to Plato, 'in particular, perhaps, by Cratylus'? Who, I ask, was this unknown philosopher—perhaps the greatest and the boldest thinker among the Presocratics? Who was he, if not Heraclitus?

XI

The early history of Greek philosophy, especially the history from Thales to Plato, is a splendid story. It is almost too good to be true. In every generation we find at least one new philosophy, one new cosmology of staggering originality and depth. How was this possible? Of course one cannot explain originality and genius. But one can try to throw some light on them. What was the secret of the ancients? I suggest that it was a *tradition—the tradition of critical discussion.*

I will try to put the problem more sharply. In all or almost all civilizations we find something like religious and cosmological teaching, and in many societies we find schools. Now schools, especially primitive schools, all have, it appears, a characteristic structure and function. Far from being places of critical discussion they make it their task to impart a definite doctrine, and to preserve it, pure and unchanged. It is the task of a school to hand on the tradition, the doctrine of its founder, its first master, to the next generation, and to this end the most important thing is to keep the doctrine inviolate. A school of this kind never admits a new idea. New ideas are heresies, and lead to schisms; should a member of the school try to change the doctrine, then he is expelled as a heretic. But the heretic claims, as a rule, that his is the true doctrine of the founder. Thus not even the inventor admits that he has introduced an invention; he believes, rather, that he is returning to the true orthodoxy which has somehow been perverted.

In this way all changes of doctrine—if any—are surreptitious changes. They are all presented as restatements of the true sayings of the master, of his own words, his own meaning, his own intentions.

It is clear that in a school of this kind we cannot expect to find a history of ideas, or even the material for such a history. For new ideas are not admitted to be new. Everything is ascribed to the master. All we might reconstruct is a history of schisms, and perhaps a history of the defence of certain doctrines against the heretics.

There cannot, of course, be any rational discussion in a school of this kind. There may be arguments against dissenters and heretics, or against some competing schools. But in the main it is with assertion and dogma and condemnation rather than argument that the doctrine is defended.

The great example of a school of this kind among the Greek philosophical schools is the Italian School founded by Pythagoras. Compared with the Ionian school, or with that of Elea, it had the character of a religious order, with a characteristic way of life and a secret doctrine. The story that a member, Hippasus of Metapontum, was drowned at sea because he revealed the secret of the irrationality of certain square roots, is characteristic of the atmosphere surrounding the Pythagorean school, whether or not there is any truth in this story.

But among Greek philosophic schools the early Pythagoreans were an exception. Leaving them aside, we could say that the character of Greek philosophy, and of the philosophical schools, is strikingly different from the dogmatic type of school here described. I have shown this by an example: *the story of the problem of change which I have told is the story of a critical debate, of a rational discussion*. New ideas are propounded as such, and arise as the result of open criticism. There are few, if any, surreptitious changes. Instead of anonymity we find a history of ideas and of their originators.

Here is a unique phenomenon, and it is closely connected with the astonishing freedom and creativeness of Greek philosophy

How can we explain this phenomenon? *What we have to explain is the rise of a tradition.* It is a tradition that allows or encourages critical discussions between various schools and, more surprisingly still, within one and the same school. For nowhere outside the Pythagorean school do we find a school devoted to the preservation of a doctrine. Instead we find changes, new ideas, modifications, and outright criticism of the master.

(In Parmenides we even find, at an early date, a most remarkable phenomenon—that of a philosopher who propounds *two* doctrines, one which he says is true, and one which he himself describes as false. Yet he makes the false doctrine not simply an object of condemnation or of criticism; rather he presents it as the best possible account of the delusive opinion of mortal men, and of the world of mere appearance—the best account which a mortal man can give.)

How and where was this critical tradition founded? This is a problem deserving serious thought. This much is certain: Xenophanes who brought the Ionian tradition to Elea was fully conscious of the fact that his own teaching was purely conjectural, and that others might come who would know better. I shall come back to this point again in my next and last section.

If we look for the first signs of this new critical attitude, this new freedom of thought, we are led back to Anaximander's criticism of Thales. Here is a most striking fact: Anaximander criticizes his master and kinsman, one of the Seven Sages, the founder of the Ionian school. He was, according to tradition, only about fourteen years younger than Thales, and he must have developed his criticism and his new ideas while his master was alive. (They seem to have died within a few years of each other.) But there is no trace in the sources of a story of dissent, of any quarrel, or of any schism.

This suggests, I think, that it was Thales who founded the new tradition of freedom—based upon a new relation between master and pupil—and who thus created a new type of school, utterly different from the Pythagorean school. He seems to have been able to tolerate criticism. And what is more, he seems to have created the tradition that one ought to tolerate criticism.

Yet I like to think that he did even more than this. I can hardly imagine a relationship between master and pupil in which the master merely tolerates criticism without actively encouraging it.

It does not seem to me possible that a pupil who is being trained in the dogmatic attitude would ever dare to criticize the dogma (least of all that of a famous sage) and to voice his criticism. And it seems to me an easier and simpler explanation to assume that the master encouraged a critical attitude—possibly not from the outset, but only after he was struck by the pertinence of some questions asked, without any critical intention, by the pupil.

However this may be, the conjecture that Thales actively encouraged criticism in his pupils would explain the fact that the critical attitude towards the master's doctrine became part of the Ionian school tradition. I like to think that Thales was the first teacher who said to his pupils: 'This is how I see things—how I believe that things are. Try to improve upon my teaching.' (Those who believe that it is 'unhistorical' to attribute this undogmatic attitude to Thales may again be reminded of the fact that only two generations later we find a similar attitude consciously and clearly formulated in the fragments of Xenophanes.) At any rate, there is the historical fact that the Ionian school was the first in which pupils criticized their masters, in one generation after the other. There can be little doubt that the Greek tradition of philosophical criticism had its main source in Ionia.

It was a momentous innovation. It meant a break with the dogmatic tradition which permits only *one* school doctrine, and the introduction in its place of a tradition that admits a *plurality* of doctrines which all try to approach the truth by means of critical discussion.

It thus leads, almost by necessity, to the realization that our attempts to see and to find the truth are not final, but open to improvement; that our knowledge, our doctrine, is conjectural; that it consists of guesses, of hypotheses, rather than of final and certain truths; and that criticism and critical discussion are our only means of getting nearer to the truth. It thus leads to the tradition of bold conjectures and of free criticism, the tradition which created the rational or scientific attitude, and with it our Western civilization, the only civilization which is based upon science (though of course not upon science alone).

In this rationalist tradition bold changes of doctrine are not forbidden. On the contrary, innovation is encouraged, and is regarded as success, as improvement, if it is based on the result of a critical discussion of its predecessors. The very boldness of an innovation is admired; for it can be controlled by the severity of its critical examination. This is why changes of doctrine, far from being made surreptitiously, are traditionally handed down together with the older doctrines and the names of the innovators. And the material for a history of ideas becomes part of the school tradition.

To my knowledge the critical or rationalist tradition was invented only once. It was lost after two or three centuries, perhaps owing to the rise of the Aristotelian doctrine of *epistēmē*, of certain and demonstrable knowledge (a development of the Eleatic and Heraclitean distinction between certain truth and mere guesswork). It was rediscovered and consciously revived in the Renaissance, especially by Galileo Galilei.

XII

I now come to my last and most central contention. It is this. The rationalist tradition, the tradition of critical discussion, represents the only practicable way of expanding our knowledge—conjectural or hypothetical knowledge, of course. There is no other way. More especially, there is no way that starts from observation or experiment. In the development of science observations and experiments play only the role of critical arguments. And they play this role alongside other, non-observational arguments. It is an important role; but the significance of observations and experiments depends *entirely* upon the question whether or not they may be used to *criticize theories*.

According to the theory of knowledge here outlined there are in the main only two ways in which theories may be superior to others: they may explain more; and they may be better tested—that is, they may be more fully and more critically discussed, in the light of all we know, of all the objections we can think of, and especially also in the light of observational or experimental tests which were designed with the aim of criticizing the theory.

There is only one element of rationality in our attempts to know the world: it is the critical examination of our theories. These theories themselves are guesswork. We do not know, we only guess. If you ask me, 'How do you know?' my reply would be, 'I don't; I only propose a guess. If you are interested in my problem,

F   151

I shall be most happy if you criticize my guess, and if you offer counter-proposals, I in turn will try to criticize them.'

This, I believe, is the true theory of knowledge (which I wish to submit for your criticism): the true description of a practice which arose in Ionia and which is incorporated in modern science (though there are many scientists who still believe in the Baconian myth of induction): the theory that knowledge proceeds by way of *conjectures and refutations*.

Two of the greatest men who clearly saw that there was no such thing as an inductive procedure, and who clearly understood what I regard as the true theory of knowledge, were Galileo and Einstein. Yet the ancients also knew it. Incredible as it sounds, we find a clear recognition and formulation of this theory of rational knowledge almost immediately after the practice of critical discussion had begun. Our oldest extant fragments in this field are those of Xenophanes. I will present here five of them in an order that suggests that it was the boldness of his attack and the gravity of his problems which made him conscious of the fact that all our knowledge was guesswork, yet that we may nevertheless, by searching for that knowledge 'which is the better', find it in the course of time. Here are the five fragments (DK, B 16 and 15, 18, 35, and 34) from Xenophanes' writings.

The Ethiops say that their gods are flat-nosed and black
While the Thracians say that theirs have blue eyes and red hair.

Yet if cattle or horses or lions had hands and could draw
And could sculpture like men, then the horses would draw their
    gods
Like horses, and cattle like cattle, and each would then shape
Bodies of gods in the likeness, each kind, of its own.

The gods did not reveal, from the beginning,
All things to us; but in the course of time,
Through seeking, men find that which is the better . . .
These things are, we conjecture, like the truth.

But as for certain truth, no man has known it,
Nor will he know it; neither of the gods,
Nor yet of all the things of which I speak.
And even if by chance he were to utter
The final truth, he would himself not know it:
For all is but a woven web of guesses.

To show that Xenophanes was not alone I may also repeat here two of Heraclitus' sayings (DK, B 78 and 80) which I have quoted before in a different context. Both express the conjectural character of human knowledge, and the second refers to its daring, to the need to anticipate boldly what we do not know.

It is not in the nature or character of man to possess true knowledge, though it is in the divine nature . . . He who does not expect the unexpected will not detect it: for him it will remain undetectable, and unapproachable.

My last quotation is a very famous one from Democritus (DK, B 117):

But in fact, nothing do we know from having seen it; for the truth is hidden in the deep.

This is how the critical attitude of the Presocratics foreshadowed, and prepared for, the ethical rationalism of Socrates: his belief that the search for truth through critical discussion was a way of life—the best he knew.

VII

POPPER ON SCIENCE AND THE PRESOCRATICS

G. S. Kirk

IN his presidential address to the Aristotelian Society entitled 'Back to the Presocratics' (*Proceedings of the Aristotelian Society* (1958-9), pp. 1-24)* Professor K. R. Popper gave a partial survey of Presocratic thought, in order to show that it supports his idea that scientific discovery begins not from observation or experiment but from theories or intuitions. For Popper 'the beautiful story of the Presocratics' (p. 131) produced fascinating cosmological explanations, some at least of which were 'staggering anticipations of modern results' (p. 132); and those explanations, which were intuitions or theories and not the result of observation, help to indicate that this is how science actually proceeds. For 'all science is cosmology' (p. 130)—with this quasi-paradox, at least, I do not propose to disagree; it amounts to the sensible and very Heraclitean opinion—though this is not an aspect of Heraclitus' thought upon which Popper touches—that the main philosophical problem is that of 'understanding the world in which we live, including ourselves, who are part of that world, and our knowledge of it' (p. 130). Nor is much comment necessary on the denial that 'it is better to study the problem of the theory of knowledge in connection with our knowledge of an orange rather than in connection with our knowledge of the cosmos' (p. 132)—another reason why Popper approves of the Presocratics. What he is maintaining here (for a more lucid statement of which see the 1958 preface to his *The Logic of Scientific Discovery*) is that what we ultimately want to know about is pre-

* Reprinted with a few changes in K. R. Popper, *Conjectures and Refutations*, and in this volume, Ch. VI. References are given to pages in this volume.

cisely 'the world in which we live, including ourselves', and that it is therefore a mistake to create special branches of philosophy which might envisage the theory of knowledge, for example, in isolation, as pursued only in relation to otherwise subsidiary test-questions like 'What is an orange?' The truth is, though, that no sensible person thinks it absolutely 'better' to examine knowledge of an orange than to examine knowledge of the world as a whole; but he may think it *more helpful* to concentrate at first on deliberately limited acts of perception, as a useful stage on the way to assessing knowledge in its wider aspect, as exercised on our total environment. Again, when Popper asserts of specialization that 'for the philosopher it is the mortal sin' (p. 131) his words should be read against the background of *The Logic of Scientific Discovery* and related to logical positivism and its successors; he means no more than that specialization for its own sake is harmful, since it produces branches of philosophy that claim to be divorced from what Popper terms 'cosmology'. But to imply that *any* philosophical specialization is wrong—that philosophical means cannot be temporarily isolated from ultimate philosophical ends—is clearly mistaken.

The aspects of Popper's paper to be treated here are first (in Section I) his main submission about the nature of scientific discovery, and secondly (in Section II) the narrower question of how far the Presocratics can truly be said to illustrate that submission. I should say at once that in the course of his paper Popper made fairly severe criticisms of an interpretation of Heraclitus, for which I am responsible, in Kirk and Raven, *The Presocratic Philosophers* (Cambridge, 1957). In Section II I take the opportunity of discussing these criticisms at some length; and it was from reflection on them that my wider interest in the paper as a whole, and in *The Logic of Scientific Discovery*, originated.

I. POPPER'S THEORY OF SCIENTIFIC INTUITION

The position is roughly as Popper states it, that 'Traditional empiricist epistemology, and the traditional historiography of science, are still deeply influenced by the Baconian myth according to which science starts from observation and then slowly and cautiously proceeds to theories' (p. 132). He further argues that 'the function of the Baconian myth is to explain why scientific statements are *true*, by pointing out that observation is the "true source" of our scientific knowledge'. This second statement reveals something of Popper's own attitude to scientific methodology, which was formed, as he writes in the 1958 preface to *The Logic of Scientific Discovery*, in reaction against the attempts of the Vienna circle to base all philosophical and scientific truth upon verification by experience. Philosophy of the traditional type had assumed that philosophical truths were metaphysical in content and could be apprehended by intuition. The positivists of the Vienna circle denied this. In disagreeing with them Popper was asserting his belief in something not far distant from the classical conception of the role of philosophy. Yet science, with its emphasis on observation and controlled experiment, seemed from one point of view to be on the side of the new philosophy, which maintained that to go beyond the limits of the verifiable was profitless and meaningless. In this sense science was the enemy of the traditional conception of philosophy as primarily concerned with unprovable hypotheses, intuitions and theories. But what if scientific method should prove to be almost the reverse of what had generally been assumed, proceeding not inductively from observation and experiment to theories, but from theories to the validation, or possible falsification, provided by experimental tests? Then logical positivism would lose a powerful support for its claim to epistemological impregnability. This is what Popper set out to show in his *Logik der Forschung* (1934), recently reissued in an expanded form as *The Logic of Scientific Discovery* (referred to in what follows as *LSD*); and this is still the background of his recent paper 'Back to the Presocratics'. Thus it is not surprising if Popper's own explanation of scientific discovery tends to go to the opposite extreme to what he calls 'the Baconian myth'. It seems possible that his view of science was not the result of an initial objective observation of how scientists proceed, but was itself, in an early application of Popper's developed theory, an 'intuition' closely related to current philosophical difficulties and subsequently compared with actual scientific procedure.

Popper was naturally concerned with the logical difficulties inherent in the theory that science attains true knowledge by proceeding from particular observations to a universal conclusion or law. An induction based on a set of particular instances could not, by Hume's argument, be scientifically true. Popper tried to evade this dilemma by maintaining that science does not, as a matter of fact, proceed in this inductive manner, and that scientific 'truth' cannot in any case be accepted as a datum: 'The old scientific ideal of *epistēmē*—of absolutely certain, demonstrable knowledge—has proved to be an idol. The demand for scientific objectivity makes it inevitable that every scientific statement must remain *tentative for ever*. It may indeed be corroborated, but every corroboration is relative to other statements which, again, are tentative' (*LSD*, p. 280). What scientists produce are theories which may work for the time being and allow further progress, but which may subsequently have to be discarded because of the discovery of one new apparent fact with which they do not accord. Thus in eluding Hume's dilemma Popper abandons the concept of absolute scientific truth. At the same time, though, in making 'falsifiability', or the lack of it, the criterion of whether or not a theory is to be regarded as 'scientific', he implicitly accepts that epistemology is somehow ultimately based, as the positivists required, on the immediate impact of particular experiences. Popper therefore seems to compromise between traditional philosophy and the tenets of linguistic analysts, by arguing that we should retain something like the methodology of the former with something not too different from the epistemology of the latter. The possible internal inconsistencies of this in many ways attractive position may be left to others to assess.

What I wish to examine in particular is Popper's account of the method of scientific discovery. I question what he describes as his 'most central contention' ('Back to the Presocratics', p. 151): that 'there is no way [*sc.* of expanding knowledge] that starts from observation or experiment. In the development of science, observations and experiments play only the role of critical arguments. It is an important role; but the significance of observations and experiments depends *entirely* upon the question whether or not they may be used to *criticize theories*'. Some of this is of course true, and constitutes an important correction of the exaggerated idea that science always proceeds methodically from experiment to theory. But in pronouncements of this kind, which are of course distillations of a more diffuse argument, Popper disguises the fact that science ultimately does start from observation—and thus, though he himself denies this, that it *is* in part inductive, even if not so rigidly inductive as is often suggested.

Naturally, most attempts to extend scientific knowledge start immediately from an idea or intuition, which is then tested 'scientifically' and accordingly approved, modified, or rejected. But the idea or intuition which acted as the starting-point of any such particular process is itself the culmination of a previous process or series of processes which must have been 'inductive' in some valid sense because it must ultimately have been based on an indefinite number of particular observations. Theories can only be founded, whether directly or indirectly, on the basis of a complex of observations or experiences. If those experiences are inadequate in scope or in some other respect, or if they are improperly related to each other, they cannot lead to a satisfactory theory—they will lead to a theory (or better 'intuition', since at this stage the formative mental process is often, admittedly, not deliberate but sub-conscious) which will not survive the tests applied in the second stage, the one which Popper and ordinary usage count as 'the scientific process' proper. What Popper has done, then, in his description of the process of scientific discovery, is to ignore the essential preliminary stage of making observations, of building up a complex structure of experience out of which, by some kind of inductive process, come intuitions or universal theories. Scientific discovery does not differ in this respect from any other kind of theorizing, whether 'true' or 'untrue' in effect. Popper concentrates solely on the second stage, when such an intuition is brought into the open, tested in the laboratory, and, if not contradicted, promoted to the status of a 'corroborated' scientific theory representing a growth of knowledge.

How does Popper attempt to answer this extremely obvious objection to his theory of scientific discovery? He does so—though without discussing the matter at all fully—in two ways which are closely related to each other.

(i) He claims that *how* men arrive at theories cannot be determined, because the process is not entirely a rational one: 'However, my view of the matter, for what it is worth, is that there is no such thing as a logical method of having new ideas, or a logical reconstruction of this process. My view may be expressed by saying that every discovery contains "an irrational element" or "a creative intuition", in Bergson's sense' (*LSD*, p. 32). At the same time he admits some connection between theories and sense-perception: 'I do not wish to deny that there is a grain of truth in the view that mathematics and logic are based on thinking, and the factual sciences on sense-perceptions. But what is true in this view has little bearing on the epistemological problem' (*LSD*, p. 93). But presumably Popper does not think that the whole process from sense-perception to theory is an irrational one; even allowing for the sake of argument that there may be some illogical jump in the process, a large part of the process is still rational and can be studied logically. This part includes some kind of preliminary classification and sorting, leading to the collection in the mind of similar particulars, and since it is logical it cannot be summarily dismissed from the field of epistemology.

(ii) He asserts that the whole question of the origins of a scientific theory is from this point of view unimportant: 'The question of how it happens that a new idea occurs to a man—whether it is a musical theme, a dramatic conflict, or a scientific theory—may be of great interest to empirical psychology; but it is irrelevant to the logical analysis of scientific knowledge' (*LSD*, p. 31). Popper adds these words: 'This latter is concerned not with *questions of fact* (Kant's *quid facti?*), but only with questions of *justification or validity* (Kant's *quid juris?*)'. But in what I have called the first stage of scientific discovery the point at issue is not questions of fact *simpliciter*, but *the interrelation and arrangement of facts*; and this cannot be totally dissociated from 'questions of justification or validity'. All Popper's arguments at this crucial point are based on this confusion, as it seems to me to be, or on the related distinction, to which he attaches great emphasis, between '*the psychology of knowledge* which deals with empirical fact, and the *logic of knowledge* which is concerned only with logical relations' (*LSD*, p. 30). Popper uses this distinction as a weapon against empiricist attempts to examine the first stage of scientific discovery; but all his attacks on what he terms 'psychologism' are weakened by the artificiality of his classification into 'facts' and 'relationships'.

Is it possible to detect an element of circularity in Popper's argument as a whole? This is what he seems to be saying: 'We can overcome the problem of induction (so far as scientific discovery is concerned, and *a fortiori* in other types of theorizing) by a new conception of science—that it starts from theories, not from observations, and then proceeds to test these theories *deductively*. Against the criticism that the theories are themselves formed inductively, from prior observations, I reply that the process by which theories are formed is no business of mine, is no part of the logic of knowledge, since the connection between facts and theories cannot be determined with certainty—partly because I personally feel it contains an irrational step, partly because in any case the theory of induction is unacceptable'.

In his presidential address Popper again decides, at a critical stage, that the question of origins is irrelevant:

I do not see at all why the question of origin should be important. What is important about a theory is its explanatory power, and whether it stands up to criticism and to tests. The question of its origin, of how it is arrived at—whether by an 'inductive procedure' as some say, or by an act of intuition—may be extremely interesting from a point of view of the biography of its originator, but it has little to do with its scientific character ('Back to the Presocratics', p. 136).

Up to a point this is admirable, typical as it is of the practical urge of Popper's epistemology, of his desire to by-pass mere technicalities and concentrate on approaches capable of leading to a positive gain in knowledge. Yet even apart from the logical difficulties outlined above, I am not convinced that the matter of origins is so unimportant as Popper makes out. For one thing, 'the biography of its originator' is obviously relevant to the historical evaluation of a theory, and the philosophy of science makes frequent and essential use of historical examples. And then is it really the case that 'all scientific statements are hypotheses, or guesses, or conjectures' (op. cit., p. 132)? If we accept the premise that science starts from intuitions, and suppress the rest, it may seem legitimate to accept that general conclusion. Yet such a conclusion promotes the misleading assumption that all scientific statements, if 'corroborated' by tests, possess the same degree of 'truth'. Yet if one remembers, as I maintain one should, that all scientific theories are ultimately based on experience, then the relation of a theory to its origins in experience, including its remoteness from those origins, is relevant to the kind of test that should be applied to it, to the effectiveness of that test in terms of validation or invalidation, and to the kind of 'truth' which may ultimately emerge. To claim that all discoveries, including presumably the discovery of axioms, are 'hypotheses, or guesses, or conjectures' is to undervalue the ultimate basis of epistemology, namely agreed experience, and thus to frustrate Popper's own ideal of increasing knowledge of the world in which we live and o ourselves.

This section may be summed up by the claim that Popper's new description of the nature of scientific discovery does not really circumvent, as it professes to do, the problem of induction, since it leaves out of account a vital preliminary stage to scientific or any other kind of theorizing. Thus it does not remove science and philosophy out of range of the critique of the linguistic analysts. As an empirical description of scientific methodology Popper's account, in spite of its merits, is incomplete; and although it simplifies epistemology in one respect, by explaining scientific error, it complicates it in another, by ignoring the empirical background of scientific and philosophical speculation and blurring the distinction between theorizing of different kinds.

In the section which follows a different aspect of Popper's presidential address is considered: his historical assessment of the Presocratic philosophers, and the value of his conviction that they illustrate his theory of the nature of scientific discovery.

II. POPPER ON THE PRESOCRATICS

Some years ago I tried to show (*The Cambridge Journal*, VI [1952–3], 515 ff.) that another philosopher, R. G. Collingwood, in the course of supporting an idea of his own about the philosophy of history, had given a misleading account of the early Greek philosophers. Popper's article now presents a comparable situation, so it seems to me, and it may be salutary to marshal some of the evidence once more in the face of an assessment of certain Presocratics which is interesting but in some respects inaccurate. This is not to say that either account—Collingwood's (especially in *The Idea of Nature*) or Popper's—is without value. It is self-evident that Popper, even apart from his central thesis, has many acute and revealing things to say. It is always useful, in any case, to see how a practising philosopher reacts to his earliest western predecessors. Yet the Presocratics, because of the boldness, simplicity, and variety of their ideas, and also because of the great difficulty of delimiting these with any sort of precision, have fallen victim to some particularly wild interpretations by philosophers (one thinks, for example, of Hegel, Nietzsche, and Heidegger), which if allowed to stand uncriticized could only obstruct the formation of a reasonable historical valuation.

If I seem to be claiming to defend the Presocratics from philosophers, it should be made clear that Popper also considers that they need defence—not from philosophers but from 'the experts', among whom he is kind enough to include myself. He has some hard words for 'the experts', by whom the 'simple straightforward *rationality*' of the Presocratics has been overlaid (p. 130). He asserts that he himself is not an expert: 'I am completely out of my depth when an expert begins to argue what words or phrases Heraclitus might have used, and what words or phrases he could not possibly have used' (p. 131). Popper speaks professedly as 'an amateur, as a lover of the beautiful story of the Presocratics . . . based on the oldest texts we possess' (p. 131); and he states that 'The exciting story of the development of the problem of change appears to me in danger of being completely buried under the mounting heap of the minutiae of textual criticism' (p. 139). Now by all means, if the specialists in any field are getting it all wrong, let them be told so; but the particular trend of Popper's remarks displays an apparently total disregard for the nature of the evidence on the Presocratics and for the inevitable problems of its assessment. As though 'what words or phrases Heraclitus might have used', for example, is irrelevant to the assessment of what he thought! It is these 'words or phrases', and the other *verbatim* fragments of the Presocratics themselves, and not the reports of Plato, Aristotle, and the doxographers, as Popper appears to think, that are 'the oldest texts we possess'. They are extremely valuable as evidence, in many cases of greater value than later and demonstrably one-sided accounts. It should in fact be obvious even to an 'amateur' that the reconstruction of Presocratic thought must be based both upon the later tradition and upon the surviving fragments. In many instances it is difficult, though it is not impossible, to distinguish *verbatim* quotations from paraphrases, or to separate original fragments from the context of the ancient authors who quoted them. Most people would agree that considerable progress has been made in this direction even since Popper formed his views on the Presocratics. To describe this necessary and constructive activity, as he does, as though it were mere obstructive pedantry, to talk scornfully of 'the minutiae of textual criticism' in this context, is little short of absurd. Indeed the whole amusing pose of the amateur *versus* the experts may be thought to impede rather than to promote that constructive interchange of ideas on which Popper himself lays so much stress (e.g. pp. 130 ff.) as the chief means of philosophical and scientific progress. 'The experts' have had a brush with this 'amateur' before, over *The Open Society and its Enemies*; they are not yet so blinded by minutiae that they will not read what he writes on their subject with the closest attention, even without the stimulus of such paradoxes. With this comment we may turn to consider Popper's account of some of the individual Presocratic theories.

Thales

Of the early Presocratics Popper remarks (on p. 132): 'Here we find fascinating ideas, some of which are strange and even staggering anticipations of modern results while many others are, from our modern point of view, wide of the mark; but most of them, and the best of them, have nothing to do with observation'. He then considers Milesian theories of the shape of the earth and the manner of its support. Thales thought that the earth floated on water like a log (so Aristotle) or a ship (so Seneca, representing Theophrastus); earthquakes were caused by the rocking of the water underneath. Popper admits that Thales' ship-analogy must have been based on observation, but maintains that for the conjecture that the earth is supported by water 'he could have no basis in his observations' (p. 132). Later we read that his theory 'though in no sense based upon observation, is at least inspired by an empirical or observational analogy'. The distinction between 'being based on' and 'being inspired by' is a rather fine one, but what is meant is that there is no direct evidence in nature that the earth floats on water (though I would observe that the welling-up of springs from beneath the earth's surface, for example, might be taken as indirect evidence). Let us concede this for the sake of argument. Are we therefore to infer with Popper that Thales' theory must have been based on a non-empirical intuition? Such a supposition, unlikely as it is in itself, shows that Popper leaves out of account all recent discussions of Thales. It is not a question of 'the minutiae of textual criticism' here, but of general knowledge of Near-Eastern mythology and its influence on Greek cosmogony. The creation-myths of the Mesopotamian and

Egyptian river cultures had envisaged the world as built on a raft on the primeval water or as thrusting up from beneath its surface. The latter is the common Egyptian version; it is not hard to see how natural an idea this was for a people whose whole life revolved around the emergence each year of their revitalized fields above the receding waters of the Nile. Though mythical in form, then, this idea was firmly based, for the Egyptians, upon observation and experience. That there were waters under the earth is an elaboration which also appeared widely—in Mesopotamia of course, in Egypt itself (the sun-boat sails under the earth each night), and in the Old Testament (e.g. Tehom is 'the deep that lieth under', *Genesis* xlix. 25). The surrounding river Okeanos in Homer, and its untypical description in book 14 of the *Iliad* as 'origin of all', are, almost certainly, indirect products of this same complex of ideas. The cosmology of Thales, in its main aspect, is another product, but one in which the mythological form has been abandoned. In that, and no doubt in his making explicit what was only implicit before—notably that this is the way the world is supported—lies much of his historical importance. Evidence for Thales is so tenuous, though, that we cannot say with *total certainty* that his theory was based on the earlier mythological accounts—to which, however, he had access through Egypt (a land in which he showed great interest and which he may have visited), possibly through Sardis, and obliquely through the *Iliad*. Yet it is *highly probable* that his theory was so based—or at the lowest evaluation perfectly possible. Would it not have been better for Popper to inform his audience and readers of this possibility? They would then have been able to see more clearly that Thales' 'intuition' may well have been ultimately based, after all, on a very specific experience: not that of Thales himself, but of the influential river-peoples with whom the widely diffused account long ago originated.

Thus Thales' theory of the way the earth is supported is probably based on experience, though perhaps not in the first instance on his own experience. That this experience was crystallized and passed down in mythical form, to be rationalized once again by Thales, does not diminish its empirical nature, although it does diminish the 'scientific' quality of Thales' theorizing at this point. To this extent it makes Thales even less valuable as an example of the intuitive method in scientific discovery which Popper was seeking to illustrate. Yet we may be certain that Thales did not just say to himself, 'I must rationalize a myth or two.' The pragmatic nature of many of his activities, like his feats of mensuration, diversion of a river, and so on, suggests that he would have used his own observations, as well as previous theories, in the isolation and solution of any physical problem. Intuition, too, he would have used—this we may admit; but intuition both based upon and supported by observation and experience.

Popper asserts of Thales' theory that it 'strangely anticipates the modern theory of continental drift'. We must reject this implication that the manner in which his theory was formed consequently has special relevance to a study of scientific method. The coincidence between the ancient and the modern theory is neither sizeable nor significant. It is not even particularly 'strange', given the phenomenon of Presocratic thought. The Presocratics poured out cosmological theories of such variety and imagination that the strange thing would be if some coincidences between those and modern cosmological accounts could *not* be found. Very few of these coincidences are really significant; though that between ancient and modern atomism is an exception up to a point, because, although the motives and essence of each are quite distinct, it was historical knowledge of the ancient theory that promoted the atomistic theories of the eighteenth century. But I doubt if it was Thales who gave Wegener the idea of continental drift.

Anaximander
It is not surprising that Popper lays great stress on Anaximander's idea that the earth remains motionless, to quote Hippolytus, 'because of its equal distance from all things'. This, Popper maintains, is a highly intuitive idea, one which does not even use observational analogies: '. . . the idea of the earth's free suspension in space, and the explanation of its stability, have no analogy whatever in the whole field of observable facts' (p. 133). In part I agree. The only specific experience which might be directly involved in this idea would be of 'Burridan's ass' situations in real life; otherwise the explanation given is very abstract—that is, far removed from specific experiences, even if ultimately generalized from them. Popper further observes, acutely, that in describing the shape of the earth as like that of a column-drum Anaximander

was using an observational analogy; and that it was just this concession to experience that led to a weakness in the theory as a whole namely the inconsistency that a cylinder would not remain in equilibrium in a spherical world. I would add that Anaximander made the earth's surface *flat* because it appeared to be so, at least to the superficial glance which was all that many Presocratics seem to have considered necessary; he made it *circular* because the horizon does seem to encircle us, as indeed mythological tradition, with its surrounding Okeanos, had implied; he gave it *depth* because it seemed very solid below, as the tradition also testified (Tartaros is far below in Homer and Hesiod); and he made it *one-third as deep as it was wide* to fit in with the ratio of the heavenly bodies, which was not opposed to observation and which embodied a traditional symmetry between sky, earth, and the underparts of earth—cf. Homer, *Iliad* viii. 16, etc. Thus Anaximander's arrangement of the cosmos was related to observation both directly and as expressed in mythical or traditional form.

On p. 135 Popper proceeds to argue that Anaximander's account of the heavenly bodies, according to which sun, moon and stars are orifices in wheels of fire enclosed by mist, is designed to preserve the stability of his system: for if sun and moon, for example, were the solid masses that they appear to be, then, when they are both visible on the same side of the earth, the earth could not be in equilibrium. This is an attractive idea; but Popper is not justified in writing of the wheels of the fixed stars that 'together they form a sphere round the earth, in accordance with the postulate that all things are positioned at similar distances from the earth' (cf. p. 135).* For, as I shall explain below, we do not know that the apparent uniformity of distance of the stars did not precede the postulate and help to determine it, rather than *vice versa*. On details of Popper's account of the wheels of the heavenly bodies the following comments may be made. (i) There are difficulties in the assumption that the wheels of the fixed stars rotate round the axis of the earth: see Kirk and Raven, *The Presocratic Philosophers*, p. 136 f. (ii) The fire in the wheels is not 'smothered' (Popper, p. 138) in eclipses, etc., it is merely hidden by the opaque mist or air. (iii) On the same page the assertion that 'fire . . . needed air and breathing-holes', implying (I presume) that the fire

* [Slightly modified by Professor Popper in the later version printed in this volume. Ed.]

in the wheels feeds on the surrounding air, should be put forward merely as a suggestion. There is no specific evidence to support it, and the word used by the doxographers to describe the breathing-holes, ἐκπνοαί, is against it.

Popper also contends (p. 134) that Anaximander's theory of equilibrium contained a deliberate criticism of Thales' idea of how the earth was supported; for the water that supports the earth itself needs support, and so on *ad infinitum*. It was Aristotle, in fact, who first certainly raised this objection: 'as though the same argument did not apply to the water supporting the earth as to the earth itself!' (*De Caelo* B 13, 294 a 28 ff.). This is just the sort of objection that Aristotle would make; we cannot be so sure about Anaximander. Thales would presumably have replied, 'But the water which supports the earth goes down indefinitely, you would never come to its limit, and it does not need any other support' (cf. Xenophanes, Fr. 28 as against Hesiod, *Theog.* 811). To this reply, at least, Anaximander with his 'indefinite' basic substance might not have been totally unsympathetic. It must further be remembered that Anaximander, having rejected water as primary substance for quite different reasons, and having sub-stituted something that had no counterpart in the developed world, could not use Thales' kind of explanation for the support of the earth, based as this was on observational analogies and evidence derived from the developed world, and had to produce an explanation of his own that was inevitably a somewhat abstract one. It must remain a moot point, then, whether or not Anaxi-mander's theory of equilibrium was a conscious correction of his predecessor.[1]

It is obvious from the very nature of Anaximander's originative substance, which was specifically not identifiable with anything in our world, that he was trying to explain things in terms that

---

[1] Thales and Anaximander were fellow-townsmen, admittedly, and probably not too different in age. Contact between them must be presumed. But Popper overstates the probable coherence of the Milesian 'school' and the probable amount of discussion and mutual criticism within it. He is im-pressed (p. 134) by the Suda's description of Thales as Anaximander's 'teacher and kinsman'. But this represents a standard assumption by Alex-andrian biographers and later compilers: that philosopher X, if he came from the same city as philosopher Y and was somewhat older than him, must have been his teacher, and frequently his 'kinsman' also. This is usually a purely speculative piece of schematization.

went beyond those of immediate observation and experience. Even so Popper seems to me to give an extreme and improbable statement of the case, especially in regard to the position of the earth. A different and in my view more probable account can be given of the origins and motives of the theory of equilibrium; one which does not stress nearly so strongly the intuitive, *a priori*, non-observational element in it.

We do not know a great deal about Anaximander's cosmogony, but we do know (from Ps.-Plutarch, *Strom.* 2, DK 12 A 10) that early in the world's history a kind of sphere of flame surrounded a mass of air or mist, the central part of which concreted to form the earth. Then the flame broke away, presumably because of the expansion of the mist, and somehow became enclosed in the latter—presumably in part of that mist which had expanded—so as to form the wheels of the heavenly bodies. Thus both the wheel-like shape of these, and their concentric disposition round the earth, would arise naturally from the initial physical concept of a sphere of flame forming round air or mist, the centre of which becomes the earth. But this concept is itself obviously based on the arrangement of the world of our experience: the bright, fiery sky at the outside, earth in the middle, air and mist in between. What Anaximander has done, apparently, is to imagine a kind of primeval explosion as the cause of the expansion of our world from an original nucleus or core. The elements of this nucleus are 'the hot' and 'the cold', as the doxographers put it, or flame and mist. The disruption and expansion of the surrounding sphere of flame causes the formation of separate circles of fire inclined at different planes: here is probably the basis of the conception of the heavenly bodies. Some correction of Thales is as likely to have been intended here as over the manner of the earth's support; for now the sun, for example, could travel freely under the earth at night, while Thales' conception had presupposed something not too far distant from the old mythopoeic equipment of golden boats or the like, in which the heavenly bodies could sail round Okeanos from west to east. Anaximenes, later, was evidently still exercised by this problem, which must have been a conspicuous one and to which Anaximander had offered a brilliant solution by no means incompatible with what our experience suggests. Now in his expanded world Anaximander was left with the earth at the centre, surrounded by the wheels of the heavenly bodies at great distances. How is the world to remain, as it appears to remain, in its place? Clearly it could not be supported from beneath, since it has no contact with anything that could support it—certainly not the 'indefinite' itself. Some quite new explanation had to be given, and Anaximander hit upon the idea of lack of motive, in a spherical system, to move one way rather than another. A brilliant conjecture, as Popper says; but according to the account given above it was in part suggested by a cosmogonical concept which itself arose from imaginative observation of the ordinary world. This makes the non-observational, *a priori* quality of Anaximander's theory of equilibrium considerably less conspicuous than in Popper's account, according to which that theory came first, as an act of pure intuition, and then the description of the position of the earth and the nature of the celestial bodies was deduced from it.

Nevertheless Anaximander's idea was sufficiently remarkable. It is certainly the best Presocratic example of a potentially productive theory in which the intuitive element was relatively high, the observational element relatively low. I doubt, though, whether this is adequate for the defence of Popper's thesis that all scientific theories are based entirely on intuitions. It is also excessive to claim (as Popper does on p. 133) that the idea 'made possible the theories of Aristarchus and Copernicus', though we must remember Popper's odd conviction that 'there is the most perfect possible continuity of thought between [Presocratic] theories and the later developments in physics' (p. 136). It is almost equally excessive to assert that 'by stimulating criticism, it also led . . . to the Pythagorean theory of a central fire'. This latter theory was in all probability another assumption with a relatively strong *a priori* element unaffected by Anaximander (see Aristotle, *De Caelo* B 13. 293 a 18 ff.). The Pythagorean theory, which achieved great notoriety, may have affected Aristarchus; there is little reason for supposing that Anaximander's theory did so.

It has been seen that much emphasis is laid by Popper on 'the exciting story of the development of the problem of change', which he considers to be 'in danger of being completely buried under the mounting heap of the minutiae of textual criticism' (p. 139). Yet closer attention to the texts would certainly have saved him from some errors in describing change according to Anaximander. It is quite untrue that winds were responsible, as well as for the weather, 'for all other changes within the cosmic edifice' (cf. n. 4, p. 138), or that 'the winds . . . were conceived as the agents of all change' (cf. p. 140). Popper is perhaps misled by Seneca, *Qu. Nat.* ii. 18, DK 12 A 23: 'Anaximandrus omnia ad spiritum rettulit.' But by 'omnia' here Seneca merely means 'all meterological phenomena'; so much is made plain by his context. That this is what Anaximander thought is confirmed by Aetius, iii. 3, 1–2, in a clear reproduction of Theophrastus (DK *ibid.*, cf. Kirk and Raven, *The Presocratic Philosophers*, pp. 137 ff.). Other natural changes in the cosmos, of which there were of course many kinds, were certainly explained in the main, in so far as they were explicitly accounted for, by the operation of the important Anaximandrian principle of cosmological *injustice* being inevitably followed by *retribution*: thus the excess of cold–wet that produces winter is presumably punished by a drastic diminution of this group of substances in summer, and a corresponding new excess of hot–dry. Although Popper devoted much of his paper to the 'development of the problem of change', he curiously said nothing whatever about this important and interesting attempt, suggested in the single extant fragment of Anaximander, to provide some kind of explicit motivation—albeit in a metaphorical or anthropomorphic form—for the major changes in the natural world. On the contrary he asserted that because Anaximander posited an infinity of worlds 'There was . . . no need to explain motion, no need to construct a general theory of change' (p. 139). It is far from clear how Popper envisages these worlds of Anaximander's, or how he thinks that they made a theory of change unnecessary—which they evidently did not do, since Anaximander had such a theory. Nor does he discuss the contradictions in the evidence for innumerable worlds in Anaximander, which have given rise to considerable controversy as to their nature or indeed their very existence as part of Anaximander's thought.

Heraclitus

Popper supports in an extreme form the traditional interpretation of Heraclitus' physics, which goes back to Plato, against the altered emphasis suggested by Burnet on the basis of the fragments and developed by Karl Reinhardt and later by myself.

Popper thinks (see p. 144) that all the 'experts' accept the kind of interpretation advanced in *The Presocratic Philosophers*. He should be relieved to learn that on the question of universal and constant flux many of them do not. There is much room for disagreement here, but it is the grounds for disagreement that count; and it seems to me that Popper, although he usefully develops some objections already raised by others, starts from a position of his own which is in certain respects a demonstrably false one. Yet he has much that is valuable to say, and his general position as a defender of the tradition could be correct, even if not for the reasons which he advances.

The view put forward by Popper is that while the Milesians 'looked at our world as our home . . . for Heraclitus, the house was on fire'; 'there are no solid bodies. Things are not really things, they are processes, they are in flux' (p. 140). This is a somewhat extreme elaboration of Plato, *Cratylus*, 402 A: 'Heraclitus somewhere says that all things are in process and nothing stays still, and likening existing things to the stream of a river he says that you would not step twice into the same river.' Now Popper observed in *The Open Society* (note 2 to Ch. 2) that Burnet had challenged the belief that this was Heraclitus' central doctrine; and he repeats this observation, with much else from the earlier work, in his presidential address. Yet Burnet did not attack the Platonic interpretation in itself; on the contrary he accepted the doctrine of flux, but claimed that 'it is not the most original feature of the system. The Milesians had held a similar view' (*EGP*[3-4], p. 146); and he argued that for Heraclitus the idea of a stability that persists through change was equally or more important. There is some truth in the words quoted from Burnet, but they nevertheless constitute an exaggeration. The Milesians seem to have held a view of change which, though not totally incompatible with that attributed to Heraclitus by Plato, was obviously much less extreme. On p. 144 Popper states that this argument of Burnet's is repeated by Kirk and Raven. This is not, I think, the case. I was and am impressed, as almost all other scholars have been, by Burnet's emphasis on the importance of stability in Heraclitus; but unlike Burnet, and following Reinhardt, I rejected the letter of the Platonic interpretation that everything is literally changing all the time. I also differed significantly from Burnet in writing that 'all Presocratic thinkers were struck by the dominance of change in the world of our experience. Heraclitus was obviously no exception, indeed he probably expressed the universality of change more clearly than his predecessors' (*The Presocratic Philosophers*, pp. 186 f.)—a statement of which Popper quoted the first sentence but not the second.

On p. 145 Popper examines my contention that 'nothing in the extant fragments suggests' that 'Heraclitus really thought . . . that a rock or a bronze cauldron, for example, was invariably undergoing invisible changes of material'. He replies that the fragments about fire [Frags. 30, 31, 90] show that all matter is, somehow, fire—and is therefore constantly changing. In a sense it is true that the totality of matter is envisaged as fire, though it is absolutely untrue that Heraclitus inevitably 'also says that all matter, like fire, is a process', as Popper asserts on p. 145. Fragments 30, 31, and 90 stated that the world-order is an ever-living fire, that fire turns into sea and earth, that all things are an exchange for fire. These sayings also show that it is the world-order as a whole that is a fire—but a fire which is being extinguished in measures so as to become sea, then earth. Sea and earth are what fire 'turns to'; they are not themselves fire, they have been 'exchanged for it', and according to Fragment 36 it is 'death' for soul-fire to become water and for water to become earth. At the same time sea and earth, or, rather, other parts of them, are being 'kindled' back into fire in the same measure as governed their change from it. This 'measure' persists through change: it is an important aspect of the Logos, and is thus intimately connected with the nature of cosmic fire itself.[2]

---

[2] It is extraordinarily difficult, indeed impossible, to describe Heraclitus' views on this subject in precise terms, partly because the evidence is too sparse but partly also because Heraclitus himself, who was not working within the framework of a developed formal logic, was probably extremely loose in his expression, and perhaps also in his very conception of, the relationships between fire, Logos, and the constituents of the manifold world. In the short account in *The Presocratic Philosophers* I deliberately chose a vague word, 'archetypal', to express the vagueness of fire's priority in the world. Popper derides this choice of word (pp. 145 f.)—which, however, quite obviously is not intended to imply *cosmogonical* priority in Heraclitus. The choice of word may not be the best possible, but the problem is a real and an important one—though not for Popper, to whom the wording of the fragments is a pedantic detail.

Many of the objects of our world, then, are not made of fire in any normal physical sense. They are fire which is being, or has been, extinguished; they are exchanged for fire; they are dead fire. Therefore they do not, presumably, share the *continuous* change of fire or flame itself. My argument is that Heraclitus regarded the world-order *as a whole* as a fire, and that this was the important thing for his theory of change. Parts of this cosmic bonfire are temporarily extinguished—mountains and rock, for example, for the most part. Yet not the whole of any of the major divisions of matter is 'dead'—this would destroy both the measure and the 'strife' on which the perpetuation of this measure depends (Frags. 80, 53); nor is it 'dead' for ever, for the world is a place of change, a constant fire, and everything in it must eventually change too. This would allow Heraclitus to accept, what common sense strongly suggests, that many of the things in our world are not changing all the time, though they all change some of the time. Popper argues ably against this position, which I admit is far from certain. He claims, however, not to understand what 'common sense' means here, and adds that we find 'ideas far removed from common sense in Anaximander, Pythagoras, Xenophanes' even before Parmenides, and that we do so too in Heraclitus. But I would deny this: 'gross departures from common sense', as I called them, were carefully avoided by the Presocratics, and this is one of the basic kinds of 'clarity' of early Greek speculation. Naturally many of the conclusions of the early Presocratics were contrary to common sense; but they were not gratuitous departures from it ('gratuitous' expresses my meaning better than 'gross') since *they appeared to be entailed by arguments which themselves depended on observation and common sense*. Thus the Pythagoreans, if they thought that things are made of numbers, were scarcely advancing a common-sense point of view; yet it was a view that arose directly, if mistakenly, from a particular and very striking observation: that the main notes of the musical scale are related to each other in terms of whole numbers. In Anaximander only the theory of innumerable worlds seems gratuitously contrary to common sense, and I have advanced other reasons elsewhere for doubting whether he held any such theory. Xenophanes' more fantastic ideas seem to me best explained as deliberate exaggerations, parodies perhaps of his predecessors. Can we then say that the conclusion that all things separately are in permanent flux is necessarily entailed by any course of reasoning followed by Heraclitus? The answer is surely negative. Against this Popper emphasizes (on p. 145) the paradoxical quality of some of Heraclitus' pronouncements, which he takes to be a sign that Heraclitus was not governed by common sense. But the paradoxes in Heraclitus, most notably that opposites are really 'the same', are carefully worked out and demonstrated, and do not suggest any gratuitous abandonment of common sense; rather the contrary.

At this point the argument becomes somewhat rarefied. I agree, though, that it remains theoretically possible that certain *invisible* changes of our experience, for example the gradual rusting of iron, cited by Popper, struck Heraclitus so forcefully that they persuaded him to assert that all things which were not in visible change were in invisible change. I do not think however, that the extant fragments suggest that this was the case.

Popper justifiably raises, as others have, the question of Plato and Aristotle: are we entitled to go against the ancient tradition about Heraclitus, according to which he said that everything is in flux? Obviously, as Popper insists, this tradition cannot be disregarded unless there is good evidence for doing so. Yet some of this 'good evidence' must be evidence about the nature and reliability of the tradition itself. Popper contents himself with the erroneous reflection that Plato, Aristotle, and the doxographic tradition are 'the oldest texts we possess', and seems unaware of how precarious the ancient tradition is over not one or two, but scores of matters in the history of sixth- and fifth-century Greek thought. Cherniss has shown conclusively that Aristotle often misinterprets his predecessors. It is easy to go too far in denigrating Aristotle as a historian; but that he was capable of serious error in the assessment of his predecessors, including Plato, is beyond dispute. Theophrastus often followed Aristotle; and the doxographical tradition is virtually Theophrastus with compressions, distortions, and omissions. As for Plato, he at least was not attempting to act as an objective historian. These are all well-known facts that need not be laboured. They should not be exaggerated; but they are enough to show the limitations of the attitude that 'What is good enough for Plato and Aristotle is good enough for me.' At the same time it is only the extremity of Popper's position that deserves criticism—that the evidence of

Plato, Aristotle, and Theophrastus must always be treated with extreme care and respect is manifest.

Hitherto I have been discussing whether Heraclitus posited *constant* change in every single physical object, as Popper and many others think, or, as I think, constant change in the world as a whole, with some things having temporary periods of stability. For Popper at least the difference between these two opinions is a vitally important one, since he infers from the traditional interpretation that for Heraclitus 'Things are not really things, they are processes' (p. 141). Few supporters of the traditional interpretation would go so far as this, nor would they find Heraclitus such a useful example of intuition preceding scientific discovery as Popper does. Yet Popper's understanding of the physical nature of the particular changes he envisages for Heraclitus is a reasonable one. The idea to which I was most opposed was that invisible particles of matter were constantly being discharged from any object rather like electrons being discharged from the atomic nucleus. And yet Empedocles, only a generation or two later, advanced something very like this idea in order to explain the mechanism of vision: everything in nature gives off 'effluences' which make contact with the eye. This idea was taken up by the Atomists, who talked of 'images' composed of a transparent layer of atoms. So far as I remember no one has used the Empedoclean theory as a means of defending the plausibility of a constant-flux theory in Heraclitus; yet it would be an argument with at least superficial attractions. All the same, there are factors which suggest that any such theory is post-Heraclitean: it seems to depend upon the discovery of pores in the body by Alcmaeon of Croton; it is associated with the new interest in sense-perception that followed Parmenides, who had also made the abandonment of common sense less repugnant; and it was certainly not used in Heraclitus' own account of perception, such as it was—a use which might be expected if a theory of effluences, of a kind, lay ready to hand. As opposed to this type of interpretation Popper is right to insist that imperceptible changes, some of which seem to have been noted by Heraclitus, would be envisaged as similar in kind to perceptible ones: iron is diminished by rust, the child grows up by assimilating food, and so on. I would suggest, however, that the conclusion Heraclitus drew was not that 'all things are a process', but that 'in spite of the many examples of change and instability in it, the world of our experience is ordered, determinate, and unified'. There is no need to insist that a small alteration of emphasis here makes a great difference. That Plato altered Heraclitus' emphasis is shown even by comparing his version of Heraclitus' river-statement, 'Heraclitus somewhere says that all things are in process and nothing stays still, and likening existing things to the stream of a river he says that you would not step twice into the same river,' with what seems to be a *verbatim* quotation of Heraclitus on the same subject (Frag. 12): 'Upon those that step into the same river different and different waters flow.' The fragments about the Logos and the nature of fire show that the stability or measure which persisted through change was as important for Heraclitus as the change itself, or more so. The 'sameness' of the river is stressed in Heraclitus' river-statement, it may be noted, but in Plato's version not at all; for the 'same' river is implied in Plato's paraphrase to be an impossibility.

Heraclitus accepted change in all its manifest presence and inevitability, but claimed that the unity of the world-order was not thereby prejudiced: it was preserved through the Logos which operates in all natural changes and ensures their ultimate equilibrium. Popper is indeed isolated when he asserts that such an interpretation of Heraclitus is 'absurd' (p. 145). 'If this is Heraclitus' philosophy,' he writes, 'then I see no reason to take any interest in it.' This statement, and others like it, give the clue to Popper's own approach to Heraclitus and to the ancient philosophers in general: it is an essentially unhistorical approach, in which more interest is shown in what an ancient thinker evokes, what he potentially might have been or thought, than in what he actually was or thought. This is a familiar and natural attitude, the ultimate ancestor of which was Aristotle. It can in certain circumstances be fruitful, but is in itself anti-historical. Popper envisages the history of philosophy as the gradual production of a set of basic ideas, each idea being associated particularly with a single known thinker. It is assumed that all the known thinkers of the past must have had important, well-defined ideas which can be reconstructed without difficulty. Thus, in defending his interpretation of Heraclitus' philosophy, Popper writes on p. 147 that it 'seems to me a philosophy that has real meaning and real depth. It is a philosophy worthy of a great philosopher. *Who, if not Heraclitus, was the great thinker who first realized that men are flames and that things are processes?'* [my italics]. Again (*ibid.*): 'Who, I ask, was this unknown philosopher—perhaps the greatest and certainly the boldest thinker among the Presocratics? Who was he, if not Heraclitus?' Here one remembers the curious claim made a few pages earlier: 'As to the Presocratics, I assert that there is the most perfect possible continuity of thought between their theories and the later developments in physics.' That kind of continuity is assumed to exist; someone must first have said that things are processes; therefore that someone must have been Heraclitus. Popper, the enemy of historicism, applies a kind of historicism in reverse: instead of using the past to predict the future he uses the present, or his idea of what constitutes philosophy, to interpret the past. More startling still, he applies the criterion of possible *truth* as the test of the historicity of a theory. On p. 145 he finds that 'the suggestion that we should test the historicity of Heraclitus' ideas . . . by standards of "common sense" is a little surprising'. Shall we not find his own 'test' much more surprising—'But the decisive point is, of course, that this inspired philosophy [i.e. that man is a flame, etc.] is *true*, for all we know' (p. 146)?

Note.—A long and detailed reply by Professor Popper to this article may be found in his *Conjectures and Refutations*, pp. 153 ff.

VIII

THEOPHRASTUS ON THE PRESOCRATIC CAUSES

J. B. McDiarmid

THE most important ancient writing on the history of European thought was the *Physical Opinions* of Theophrastus.[1] In this work of sixteen or eighteen books Theophrastus gave for the first time a systematic treatment of earlier views on the main problems of science and philosophy. Its influence in antiquity is attested by the frequency and respect with which it was referred to by later ancient writers. But its unique position was not fully appreciated by modern scholars until Usener[2] collected the fragments of it and Diels scrutinized these fragments in relation to the large body of other doxographical writings. Diels proved that these writings,

[1] The writer wishes to record his gratitude to Professors H. F. Cherniss and E. A. Havelock, who both urged the undertaking of this study and have generously read the manuscript and made many suggestions for its improvement.

The fragments of the *Physical Opinions* will be cited by page and line in Hermann Diels, *Doxographi Graeci* (Berlin, 1879), which will be referred to in notes as *Dox*. Theophrastus' *De Sensibus* will be cited by section or by page and line of the text in *Doxographi Graeci*. The fragments of the Presocratics will be cited by number or by volume, page, and line of Hermann Diels, *Die Fragmente der Vorsokratiker* (5th edn by W. Kranz, Berlin, 1934-7). The works of Aristotle will be cited by page, column, and line of the Prussian Academy edition (Berlin, 1831); and the Aristotelian commentators, by page and line of the Prussian Academy edition (Berlin, 1882-1909).

Abbreviations of modern books frequently cited are:

Burnet = John Burnet, *Early Greek Philosophy* (4th edn, London, 1945),
Cherniss = Harold Cherniss, *Aristotle's Criticism of Presocratic Philosophy* (Baltimore, 1935).
Zeller = Edward Zeller, *Die Philosophie der Griechen*, I, 1 (7th edn, Leipzig, 1923); I, 2 (6th edn, Leipzig, 1920).

[2] Hermann Usener, *Analecta Theophrastea*, pp. 25-43.

far from being isolated and independent, were virtually all derived directly or indirectly from the *Physical Opinions*.[3] This fact has been of great consequence for the evaluation of both the doxographers and Theophrastus. Statements of such writers as Aetius have been invested with the full authority of Theophrastus, and, on the other hand, this authority has seemingly been enhanced by the very number of the doxographers who accepted it. When a report has been traced back to the *Physical Opinions*, scholars have been satisfied that it has been traced to an 'unimpeachable source' and that it 'must have been based on direct acquaintance' with the original Presocratic writing.

That Theophrastus himself was not isolated has long been common knowledge. Parallels between his statements and those of Aristotle have frequently been noted by Zeller and others. Two years before Diels published his *Doxographi Graeci* Zeller presented a paper in which he called attention to the similarity between certain fragments from the first book of the *Physical Opinions* and Aristotle's survey of earlier causal theories in *Metaphysics* A;[4] and in his notes to the *Physical Opinions* fragments Diels indicated further parallels. Zeller's conclusion was:

'Theophrast habe sich in seiner Übersicht über die Geschichte der Physik, trotz der Selbständigkeit seines Wissens und seines Urteils, die er auch hier an der Tag legt, und trotz der Modifikationen, welche die eigentümliche Natur seiner Aufgabe nöthig machte, an die Übersicht über die philosophischen Principien, die Aristoteles im ersten Buch der Metaphysik gegeben hatte, in umfassender Weise angeschlossen.'[5]

This has been the general view. The similarities between the statements of Theophrastus and Aristotle have been seen not as disproof of Theophrastus' value but, rather, as corroboration of

[3] *Dox.*, pp. 1–263. Diels' main conclusions about the nature and influence of the *Physical Opinions* are stated briefly, along with references to more recent bibliography, by Otto Regenbogen, Pauly-Wissowa, *Real-Encyclopaedia der classischen Altertumswissenschaft, Supplement*, VII, 1535–9. Briefer statements are to be found in Burnet, pp. 33–9, and T. L. Heath, *Aristarchus of Samos*, pp. 1–6. Useful diagrams of the doxographical tradition are given by Heath (*loc. cit.*) and by W. Capelle at the end of his *Die Vorsokratiker*.
[4] E. Zeller, 'Über die Benützung der aristotelischen Metaphysik in den Schriften der älteren Peripatetiker', *Abhandlungen der Königlichen Academie der Wissenschaften zu Berlin* (1877), pp. 145–67.
[5] *Loc. cit.*, p. 155.

Aristotle based on an independent judgement of the original evidence. Indeed, Theophrastus has been regarded as the more trustworthy witness of the two; for, while it is granted that Aristotle's statements about his predecessors may be coloured by his own philosophical bias, it is maintained that Theophrastus is an objective historian and, therefore, free from this fault.

The question of Aristotle's bias has been dealt with exhaustively by H. Cherniss in his *Aristotle's Criticism of Presocratic Philosophy*.[6] Cherniss has found that Aristotle's accounts of earlier doctrines are so inextricably bound up with arguments for his own doctrine that history cannot be easily distinguished from interpretation. Aristotle is not interested in historical facts as such at all. He is constructing his own system of philosophy, and his predecessors are of interest to him only in so far as they furnish material to this end. He believes that his system is final and inclusive and that, therefore, all earlier theories have been groping towards it and can be stated in its terms. Holding this belief, he does not hesitate to modify or distort not only the detailed views but also the fundamental attitudes of his predecessors or to make articulate the implications that doctrines may have for him but could not have had for their authors. His method of dealing with his predecessors is to set up debates between them. Each debate is resolved in the formulation of one of his own theories, and the grouping and sentiments of the participants vary as the predetermined solution of each debate requires. Thus, there is no constancy in the historical value of his comments; nor is there even such a thing as *the* Aristotelian interpretation.

In this respect the survey of *Metaphysics* A is no different from similar passages found elsewhere.[7] There Aristotle marshals the early doctrines in such a way as to establish that all philosophers have been seeking, knowingly or not, to achieve his system of four causes and that none had ever put forward any other type of cause than these. Behind his argument is the assumption that the main problem of earlier philosophy was causality and that the cause that first and chiefly engaged the attention of the Presocratics was the material cause. The Presocratics as a group are set up as champions of matter, and on the opposing side is Plato, who is champion of the formal cause. The opposition is resolved by Aristotle's synthesis of matter and form. As Cherniss has said, Aristotle's

[6] Note especially Cherniss, pp. 347–74.   [7] Cherniss, pp. 218 and 359–61

purpose makes it natural that the details of his account should be unhistorical, and it is not surprising to find that the fragments of the Presocratics do not confirm the view that their interest was primarily in the material constituents into which existence could be analysed. Further, although this particular interpretation of the Presocratics runs through many of Aristotle's discussions, this fact does not lend greater weight to it. Each instance is explicable by the argument in which it occurs, and, when it does not suit the argument, Aristotle modifies or abandons it.

One result of Cherniss' findings is that further investigation must be made of the relationship of Theophrastus to Aristotle. It is no longer possible to suppose that the similarities between their accounts of the Presocratics are due merely to agreement on specific historical data. Nor is it enough to explain these similarities as being due to the influence on Theophrastus of Aristotle's 'bias for the abstract and metaphysical point of view'. In each case the Aristotelian passage that Theophrastus has used must be examined in its context with regard to the purpose of Aristotle's argument, the assumptions on which he is proceeding, and the particular distortion of the early doctrine that has resulted therefrom; and each interpretation must be seen not only in relation to the fragments of the Presocratics themselves but also in relation to the other interpretations of Aristotle which Theophrastus may or may not have adopted. To be complete this investigation must ultimately include the writings of the later doxographers as well as the fragments of Theophrastus. But each doxographer raises individual problems in addition to those that are due to the common dependence on Theophrastus' work. The first step is, therefore, to consider the attested fragments from the *Physical Opinions*. The present study will be further limited to fragments on Presocratic causes from the first book of this work. This choice has been made not only because these fragments have been by far the most important for the reconstruction of Presocratic philosophy but also because they demonstrate most clearly Theophrastus' method of using Aristotle and the types of interpretation and misrepresentation that may come from it.

Before we turn to the fragments a few remarks should be made about their immediate source and their condition. Most of the attested fragments from the first book of the *Physical Opinions* are derived from Simplicius' comments on Aristotle, *Physics* 184 B

15 ff., in which Aristotle is schematizing all the possible views of the physical principles.* The arrangement of doctrines given by Simplicius is dictated by the passage on which he is commenting, and it is clearly not the arrangement of Theophrastus.[8] Furthermore the content of Simplicius' comments has also been influenced by the *Physics* passage. But the fact remains that Simplicius is the best available source for Theophrastus' discussion of the principles.

THALES

A comparison of the account of Thales' principle quoted by Simplicius from Theophrastus with that given by Aristotle in the *Metaphysics* leaves little doubt of Theophrastus' dependence on Aristotle.[9] The similarities between the two accounts are so striking that, if they were not found in the account of Aetius, which is also derived from Theophrastus, it might be suspected that Simplicius had himself copied directly from the *Metaphysics*. Both Theophrastus and Aristotle report that Thales declared water to be the principle of all things; that he arrived at this theory from the observation that the seeds of all things are moist, that nutriment is moist, and that the warm lives by the moist (Theophrastus adds that Thales observed that dying things dry up, and Aristotle, that the warm is generated from the moist); that he held that, since water is the principle, the earth rests on it. Theophrastus concludes his account with the remark that Thales was reported to have been the first to reveal the investigation of nature to the Greeks, and that, although he had many predecessors, he was so superior to them as to eclipse them. This last is a synopsis of an allusion by Aristotle to a tradition that Homer

* [Pp. 88–91 of the original are hereinafter greatly condensed. Eds.]
[8] On the composition of the *Physical Opinions*, see *Dox.*, pp. 102–7, and H. Diels, 'Leukippos und Diogenes von Apollonia', *Rh.M.*, XLII (1887), 7 ff.
[9] Compare the following two passages:
  Physical Opinions, Frag. 1 (= *Dox.*, p. 475, 2–14 = Simplicius, *Phys.*, pp. 23, 22–33);
  Aristotle, *Metaphysics* 983 B 20–30. Cf. also Aetius, i. 3, 1.*
* [The two passages are extensively compared in the original, pp. 135–6 Eds.]

and the early cosmologists had held views about nature similar to that of Thales.[10]

The simple statement that Thales declared water to be the principle of all things does not disclose precisely how Theophrastus is using the word 'principle' nor what assumptions about Thales' doctrine are required by it. Aristotle settles these questions in the prefatory remarks before his account of Thales; and, since the assumptions that he makes there underlie all the accounts of matter that Theophrastus has taken from *Metaphysics* A, it will be well to discuss them at the outset. For Aristotle the ultimate material principle is a substrate which persists but undergoes changes of quality. This concept—or, rather, an approximation of it—was held, Aristotle believes, by all his predecessors, and he asserts that it is found even among the earliest thinkers.[11] He says: 'That of which all things consist, the first from which they are generated, the last into which they are destroyed—the substance remaining, but changing in its modifications—this, they say, is the element and principle of things; and, therefore, they think that nothing is generated or destroyed, since they believe that this sort of entity is always preserved. . . .'[12] The effect of this is that

[10] *Metaphysics* 983 B 27—984 A 3.
Aristotle will not vouch for this tradition, and he is doubtful even of Thales. The tradition referred to is a playful suggestion by Plato that Heraclitus and the other physicists derived their doctrine of flux from Homer (*Cratylus* 402 B, *Theaetetus* 152 E, 160 D, 180 C). That Aristotle can take Plato's humour so seriously prompts the question how much he may have been influenced by Plato to begin the history of philosophy with Thales. He assumes as self-evident that men's first interest was in the material source of things. He may have reasoned that, since the earliest of those who framed myths about the gods (983 B 29) identified this source as water, it was to be expected that the earliest philosophers (983 B 6–7) took this opinion as their starting-point. Aristotle's entire treatment of the early philosophers exhibits a tendency to make history conform to common sense.

In another fragment (*Scholiast to Apollonius Rhodius*, II, 1248 = *Dox.*, p. 475, n. 11), Theophrastus says that Prometheus was the first to share philosophy with men and that for this reason the myth arose that he shared fire with them. This fragment is probably from Theophrastus' Περὶ Εὑρημάτων. As Burnet (p. 40, n. 2) points out, it is 'merely an application of Peripatetic literalism to a phrase of Plato's' (cf. *Philebus* 16 C and Protagoras 321 C).

[11] *Metaphysics* 983 B 6–18.
[12] *Metaphysics* 983 B 8–13. His expression here, τῆς μὲν οὐσίας ὑπομενούσης, τοῖς δὲ πάθεσι μεταβαλλούσης (983 B 9–10), makes certain his identification

all the early thinkers are represented as sharing Aristotle's analytical and abstract concern with matter. Lack of firsthand evidence from the writings of the early physicists prevents the complete resolution of doubts that may be held about the general view of matter that Aristotle attributes to them—though the fact that he can seriously comment on the material theory of Homer in the same context with those of the physicists makes doubt not unreasonable. With regard to the concept of matter that he attributes to them, however, there can be no doubt. This concept rests on the combination of two ideas: the definition of identity and difference as formulated in consequence of Eleatic logic, and the distinction between subject and attribute as developed first by Socrates and Plato.[13] It is, therefore, an obvious historical impossibility that any Presocratic should have held this concept. If Thales did say that all things come from water, he cannot have meant that water is a principle in the sense that Aristotle and Theophrastus use the word. The entire doxographical tradition about his principle is, thus, spoiled at its source by an anachronism, an anachronism that becomes the more deceptive for being removed from its original context.*

Little can have been known of Thales by the fourth century B.C. Aristotle is the earliest writer to represent him as a philosopher, and the cautious tone of Aristotle's few other references to him leaves the impression that Aristotle knows little of him and recognizes the limit of his knowledge.[14] Simplicius reports, probably from Theophrastus, that Thales was said to have left nothing in writing but a work on nautical astronomy;[15] and there

[13] W. A. Heidel, 'Qualitative Change in Pre-Socratic Philosophy', *Archiv für Geschichte der Philosophie*, XIX (1906), 337.

* [Discussion of Hippo, pp. 92–3 of original, is here omitted. Eds.]

[14] *De Caelo* 294 A 29–30; *De Anima* 405 A 19–20, 411 A 8; *Metaphysics* 983 B 22, 984 A 2; *Politics* 1259 A 18–19.

[15] *Dox.*, p. 475, 13–14. Diels (*ad loc.*) treats this sentence as a comment of Simplicius and not as part of the Theophrastus fragment. But, as will be seen, it is the practice of Theophrastus to quote from the Presocratic writings

of the material principle with his substrate. This identification is evident throughout *Metaphysics* A in his references to matter as τὸ ὑποκείμενον or ἡ ὑποκειμένη οὐσία (983 A 30, 983 B 16, 984 A 21–22, 985 B 10). Elsewhere he says more explicitly that those who generate all things from one principle must hold that generation is the qualitative change of the substrate (*De Generatione* 314 A 8–11, 314 B 1–4).

is no evidence that Theophrastus had any information about Thales' views on causality other than what is given in the *Metaphysics*. In its original form Theophrastus' account may have been as guarded as Aristotle's is. But in the quotation of it as given by Simplicius and in the doxographers such caution is absent. What had been for Aristotle at best a conjecture on a very uncertain tradition has become in them a historical fact.

HERACLITUS

In the *Metaphysics* Aristotle says of Hippasus and Heraclitus only that they made their principle fire.[16] To this Theophrastus adds that they held that fire is the substrate from which things are formed by rarefaction and condensation and into which they are again dissolved; for according to Heraclitus, he says, 'all things are an exchange for fire'.[17] With the exception of the last few words, which Theophrastus apparently drew from Heraclitus' works, this addition is merely particularization of Aristotle's general dicta that for all the material monists change was the

---

[16] *Metaphysics* 984 A 7–8.

[17] *Physical Opinions*, Frag. 1 (= *Dox.*, pp. 475, 14—476, 2 = Simplicius, *Phys.*, pp. 23, 33—24, 6).

The account quoted by Simplicius closes with the statement that Heraclitus set a certain order and limited time for the change of the world in accordance with a fated necessity. (*Dox.*, p. 476, 1–2.) This is not evidence that Theophrastus attributes a periodic conflagration to Heraclitus. The language here shows the influence of Stoic interpretation. The word used for fate is εἱμαρμένη, which is a technical Stoic word. Heraclitus would probably use χρησμοσύνη or χρεών (see Heraclitus, Frag. 65 and Heidel *Archiv*, XIX [1906], 351, n. 46), which Theophrastus correctly interpreted as a reference to the order in the continuous generation and destruction of things (cf. Heraclitus, Frag. 30). Later writers take this to mean that there is a periodic general destruction of the universe (Diogenes Laertius, ix. 7–8); but Theophrastus no more ascribes this notion to Heraclitus than he does to Anaximander, in whom he apparently also finds the same concept of ordered change (cf. *Dox.*, p. 476, 10–11 and note 42). He is concerned with fire not in its purely cosmological aspects but in its function as the material cause of all generation and destruction. (On the supposed evidence of Aristotle for the periodic conflagration, see Cherniss, p. 29, n. 108.)

---

in support of his interpretations. It is not unlikely that, when no such writings are available, he should comment on this fact, particularly in the case of such an important figure as Thales.

alteration of a persisting substrate [18] and that they generated other things from the substrate by means of rarefaction and condensation. [19]

The presupposition on which this account of Heraclitus is based is the same as that already noted in connection with Thales, that the material principles of the Ionians were approximations of the Aristotelian prime matter and differed from one another only in the names by which they were called. [20] Even without firsthand evidence from the texts of the Ionians this representation of their notions of matter may be discounted. In the case of Heraclitus it may be disproved by reference to extant fragments of his writings. These show that he did not conceive fire as inert matter. The central point of his doctrine is, on the contrary, the constant flux of all things, including fire. The essential characteristic of fire is not its persistence as a substrate but rather its very impermanence, in which Heraclitus found at the same time both an explanation of the endless change of the phenomenal world and a visible symbol of that change. [21]

Theophrastus' misunderstanding of the nature of the Heraclitean fire as a single material principle causes him to attribute the rarefaction–condensation process to Heraclitus. It has long been recognized that this attribution is false. In making it Theophrastus not only reads into Heraclitus the Aristotelian theory of qualitative change; he also involves his account in a curious difficulty and forces on Heraclitus' words an interpretation they will not bear. For the Peripatetics rarefaction–condensation implied an undifferentiated substrate that is informed by the contrary qualities rare and dense, i.e. hot and cold. Since according to their view fire is the rarest of the four simple bodies, it cannot be subject to rarefaction. In order to attribute both rarefaction and condensation to Heraclitus, therefore, Theophrastus must disregard the primary nature of fire and treat fire as something intermediate between rare and dense, i.e. an approximation of his own prime matter. That he does so seems clear from the distinction he makes between rarefaction–condensation and dissolution into the sub-

[18] See note 12.
[19] *Physics* 187 A 12–16 (here Anaximander is excepted). See also *Physics* 189 B 5–10.
[20] Fire is called the φύσις ὑποκειμένη (*Dox.*, p. 475, 17–18). See note 12.
[21] Heraclitus, Frags. 30, 76, 90, 126. Cf. Cherniss, pp. 380–2.

strate;[22] for, if fire is really fire and not something intermediate in density, dissolution is simply rarefaction. Heraclitus himself said that all things are an exchange for fire, and fire for all things, as wares for gold, and gold for wares.[23] Theophrastus refers to this simile to prove that Heraclitus employed rarefaction–condensation. But, whatever the figure may have meant for Heraclitus, it is not suitable as a description of rarefaction–condensation; for in the exchange of wares for gold the value of the substance remains, but the substance does not.[24]

Theophrastus' account of Heraclitus' theory of change provides an interesting example of the way he may derive his interpretations from Aristotle and yet give an incomplete and erroneous presentation even of Aristotle's views by selecting certain statements and disregarding others. In *Metaphysics* A, which has been Theophrastus' chief source, Aristotle is concerned with Heraclitus' fire only as it squares with his own concept of material causality. And, when he is seeking antecedents for his theory of contrariety, he would certainly hold that for Heraclitus as a monist all change must be due to rarefaction and condensation. When, however, he is concerned with proving the impossibility of any of the four simple bodies as a single principle, he ascribes rarefaction–condensation to those who made their principle water or air or a body midway between air and water in density;[25] but he says Heraclitus held that things are formed from a composition of fire as from the melting down of metal scrapings.[26] How the process of smelting is to be applied to the generation of things from fire is not clear. The figure is at any rate not appropriate to signify rarefaction–condensation, and Aristotle's use of it is certain evidence that he cannot express Heraclitus' doctrine in his usual terms.[27] Similarly, Aristotle asserts that most of his predecessors were agreed that interaction could occur only between unlike or opposite things.[28] Under the influence of this view, in the *De*

---

[22] *Dox.*, p. 475, 15–18.   [23] Frag. 90.   [24] Zeller, I, 819.
[25] *De Caelo* 303 B 13–17.   [26] *De Caelo* 304 A 18–21.
[27] The figure καθάπερ γὰρ ἐκ τῶν ψηγμάτων λεγομένων τὸν χρυσὸν συνεστάναι is used in Diogenes Laertius, ii. 8, for the process of production by aggregation in the theory of Anaxagoras. In Diodorus Siculus, II, 50, gold prepared in the usual way from ore in mines is called ἐκ ψηγμάτων καθεψόμενος. Aristotle probably had this process of smelting in mind and may have taken the figure from the writings of Heraclitus.
[28] *De Generatione* 323 B 3–12; Democritus alone is excepted.

THEOPHRASTUS ON THE PRESOCRATIC CAUSES

Sensibus Theophrastus attributes to Heraclitus the theory that perception is due to the interaction of opposites and involves alteration.[29] When, however, Aristotle comes to an individual consideration of Heraclitus' doctrine of the soul, he implies that Heraclitus believed interaction to be between similars, for he says that according to Heraclitus that which is in motion is known by that which is in motion.[30]*

ANAXIMANDER

According to Simplicius' quotation from Theophrastus, Anaximander held that the Infinite is the principle of things, and he said that this is not water or any of the so-called elements but some other infinite body out of which are generated all the heavens and the worlds in them; things pass away into those things from which they are generated by necessity; for they make reparation and satisfaction to one another for their injustice in accordance with the order of time, as Anaximander said in somewhat poetic words.[31] In the historical synopsis of the *Metaphysics* Aristotle

[29] *De Sensibus*, 1–2.　　　　　　　　　　[30] *De Anima* 405 A 25–8.
* A discussion of Hippasus, pp. 95–6, in the original, is here omitted. [Eds.]
[31] *Physical Opinions*, Frag. 2 (= *Dox.*, p. 476, 3–11 = Simplicius, *Phys.*, p. 24, 13–21).

Theophrastus also says, Ἀναξίμανδρος . . . ἀρχήν τε καὶ στοιχεῖον εἴρηκε τῶν ὄντων τὸ ἄπειρον, πρῶτος τοῦτο τοὔνομα κομίσας τῆς ἀρχῆς. Two main interpretations have been given of this: that, according to Theophrastus, Anaximander introduced the name ἄπειρον of the material cause (Burnet, p. 54, n. 2); and that Anaximander introduced the term ἀρχή and Theophrastus has added στοιχεῖον to define this term in Peripatetic phraseology (W. Heidel, *CP*, VII [1912], 215–16, and W. Jaeger, *The Theology of the Early Greek Philosophers*, pp. 24–8). Other ancient evidence is inconclusive:

(a) Hippolytus, *Refut.*, I, 6, 2: οὗτος μὲν οὖν (Anaximander) ἀρχὴν καὶ στοιχεῖον εἴρηκε τῶν ὄντων τὸ ἄπειρον, πρῶτος τοὔνομα καλέσας τῆς ἀρχῆς. It has been argued that τῆς ἀρχῆς here is against the first view, since τὴν ἀρχήν is required with καλέσας (Jaeger, *op. cit.*, p. 201, n. 27). This objection holds only if it be supposed that Theophrastus originally wrote καλέσας rather than the κομίσας preserved by Simplicius. If he did not, the question is not what Theophrastus meant but only what Hippolytus, or some intermediate writer, thought he meant. In fact, if Theophrastus wrote κομίσας, the τῆς ἀρχῆς in Simplicius is just as embarrassing to the second view; for there τὴν ἀρχήν is expected in apposition to τοὔνομα.

(b) Simplicius, *Phys.*, p. 150, 23: πρῶτος αὐτὸς (Anaximander) ἀρχὴν ὀνομάσας τὸ ὑποκείμενον. This seems to support the second view. Burnet's translation,

188

does not mention Anaximander by name. Elsewhere he gives two distinct and apparently contradictory accounts of Anaximander's

---

'being the first to name the substratum of the opposites as the material cause', not only does not render the Greek (Jaeger, *op. cit.*, p. 201, n. 28); it makes no sense, since Simplicius has already treated the water of Thales as a material substratum of the opposites (*Phys.*, pp. 149, 5-7 and 150, 11-12). If, however, Simplicius means that Anaximander was the first to call the substratum by the name ἀρχή, his remark is not much to the point. He is commenting on Aristotle's division of doctrines into those that explained generation by a single material principle and the opposites and those that explained it not by alteration but by a separation of the opposites from the material principle. Of this latter doctrine he says: ἐνούσας γὰρ τὰς ἐναντιότητας ἐν τῷ ὑποκειμένῳ, ἀπείρῳ ὄντι σώματι, ἐκκρίνεσθαί φησιν Ἀναξίμανδρος, πρῶτος αὐτὸς ἀρχὴν ὀνομάσας τὸ ὑποκείμενον (*Phys.*, p. 150, 22-4). Anaximander is the first philosopher named by Aristotle as holding this doctrine, and it is the fundamental difference between his material principle and those of the other Ionians that interests Simplicius. If the invention of any term is appropriate to the discussion, it is the invention of the Infinite. (The suggestion is offered that where the manuscripts read αὐτός Simplicius may have written οὕτως: 'first by this name (Infinite) calling the substrate a principle'.)

(*c*) Simplicius, *De Caelo*, p. 615, 15: ἄπειρον δὲ πρῶτος (Anaximander) ὑπέθετο. This clearly supports the first view.

If any solution is to be reached it can only be on the basis of what seems probable from the general point of view observed in the other fragments of the *Physical Opinions*. The other fragments reveal no interest in the invention of Peripatetic phraseology. Theophrastus is interested in the nature and function of Presocratic causes; for the most part he speaks as if the Presocratics already used later terminology (e.g. στοιχεῖα in Empedocles [*Dox.*, p. 478, 1-2]), and it is only when the name of a cause is peculiar to a philosopher or the function of it is not self-evident that he makes a point of the name employed by his predecessor (*Dox.*, pp. 478, 4; 479, 8; 485, 2). The question he asks is how the theory of each philosopher differed from that of his predecessors. Each of the earlier philosophers under each heading is the first to hold that doctrine. This is implied when it is not explicitly stated. Thus, Anaxagoras is said to be the first to add the 'missing cause' and Parmenides is the first to say that the world is spheroid (*Dox.*, pp. 478, 19 f.; 482, 17); but it is understood that Thales is the first to make his principle water and Anaximenes, air. In the sentence following the one in question, Theophrastus makes it clearer what Anaximander was first to do: λέγει δὲ αὐτὴν (i.e. τὴν ἀρχήν) μήτε ὕδωρ μήτε ἄλλο τι τῶν καλουμένων εἶναι στοιχείων, ἀλλ' ἑτέραν τινὰ φύσιν ἄπειρον ... (*Dox.*, p. 476, 6-7). Anaximander was the first to make his principle the ἄπειρον, signifying by this name some infinite body other than the elements.

Finally, the suggestion that Theophrastus added στοιχεῖον to define Anaximander's term ἀρχή is answered by Heidel's admission (*loc. cit.*) that such collocations as ἀρχὴ καὶ στοιχεῖον are common in Aristotle (see Bonitz, *Index*

principle: that it is a single body apart from the elements; and that it is a mixture like the mixture of Empedocles.[32]

There is general agreement that the latter part of Theophrastus' account contains a fragment from the work of Anaximander, although there has been much debate as to how far the fragment extends, how much it has been altered in transmission, and what it means. It will be necessary to deal briefly with these questions before discussing the possible connection between Theophrastus' account and those of Aristotle. It may be taken as certain that the reference to Anaximander's 'somewhat poetic words' indicates direct quotation and applies at least to the metaphorical statement that things make reparation and satisfaction to one another for their injustice. The preceding clause, which states that things pass away into those things from which they are generated, has been accepted as substantially, if not verbally, an accurate representation of Anaximander's thought. If this is so, the explanatory 'for' that links this clause to the metaphor permits only one interpretation, namely, that the metaphor is a poetic expression for the process of generation and destruction. Accordingly, the unspecified subject of the metaphor must be the things that are generated and destroyed; the payment of reparation and satisfaction is equated with destruction; and the injustice that is so expiated must be due in some way to generation. Most attempts to reconstruct Anaximander's doctrine depend on some such interpretation of the text as this. But the two clauses cannot be connected in the way supposed. They express two quite distinct relationships which do not explain each other. The dissolution of things into those things from which they are generated involves the relationship of particular things to their source. The metaphorical clause, on the other hand, suggests the opposition of equals in a court of law and the compensation of one equal by the other for a wrong committed. There can be no such equality

[32] *Physics* 204 B 22–29, 187 A 20–26.

Aristotelicus, p. 702 a 26 ff.). One instance is found in a passage of the *Metaphysics* that has already been shown to have influenced Theophrastus: ἐξ οὗ γὰρ ἔστιν ἅπαντα τὰ ὄντα . . . τοῦτο στοιχεῖον καὶ ταύτην ἀρχήν φασιν εἶναι τῶν ὄντων (983 B 8–11). If it is to be maintained that Anaximander used the term ἀρχή and that Theophrastus defined it by στοιχεῖον, there is just as good reason to say that τῶν πρώτων φιλοσοφησάντων οἱ πλεῖστοι, of whom Aristotle is here speaking, used the term στοιχεῖον and Aristotle added ἀρχή to define it.

between particular things and the Infinite, nor can there be any question of the generation and existence of a thing being an injustice against the Infinite.[33] And to say that the dissolution of a particular thing into the Infinite is the same as the payment of reparation to the thing's injured opponent is to ascribe to Anaximander a concept of law that no Greek of his time would have understood. As has frequently been noted, the metaphor refers to the *jus talionis*. According to this the expiation of a wrong is settled between the interested parties and their immediate kin; reparation is made directly to the sufferer and not to some third superior authority, which in this case must be the Infinite.

The key to the problem is the clause about generation and destruction. The observation that on death things are resolved once more into that from which they were generated is a commonplace in Greek literature, and it is definitely attested in

---

[33] Diels ('Anaximandros von Milet', *Neue Jahrbücher*, XXVI [1923], 69) says: 'Ein Unrecht, eine ἀδικίη ist es, wenn das Individuum sich aus dem unendlichen Ganzen loslöst. Diesen Frevelmut zahlt es mit dem Tode, die Geburt des einen ist mit dem Tode des anderen verknüpft.' (Cf. R. Mondolfo, *Problemi del pensiero antico*, Ch. II.) But, as Heidel (*loc. cit.*, p. 234) remarks of this view, 'That were in truth justice with a vengeance'. The fact that reparation is made 'to one another' (ἀλλήλοις, *Dox.*, p. 476, 10) is conclusive evidence against Diels. G. Vlastos ('Equality and Justice in the Early Greek Cosmologies', *CP* XLII [1947], 169–72; above, pp. 56–91) recognizes the difficulty of Diels' position, but his attempt to cope with this difficulty is unsuccessful. He argues that it is the opposites that commit injustice against one another and that their penalty is reabsorption or blending into the Infinite. This reabsorption, he believes, does not really involve destruction; it is 'only a process which insures full reparation among the opposites themselves'. But the text of Theophrastus does not speak of the generation and destruction of the opposites. It speaks of the generation and destruction of things (τοῖς οὖσι, *Dox.*, p. 476, 9); and—if any proof be needed that 'things' include more than the opposites—the preceding sentence of the text refers explicitly to the generation of the heavens and worlds from the principle (*Dox.*, p. 476, 7–8). Certainly it will not be proposed that the heavens and the worlds retain their identity after dissolution into the Infinite; and, since no distinction is made between different kinds of things, presumably all kinds of things suffer the same sort of destruction as the heavens and worlds do. H. Fränkel (*Dichtung und Philosophie des Frühen Griechentums*, p. 345–7) sees rightly that the things generated and destroyed are all things that exist, and he is of the opinion that the sin of a thing is that it seizes on the potentialities of other things that might have come into being in its place. This theory saves the facts of the text but reads more into the text than is there.

philosophical writings as early as Xenophanes.[34] But the language in which it is here cast belongs to a later period, and both the language and form recall similar statements in Aristotle.[35] One of these occurs in a passage of the *Metaphysics* which has influenced Theophrastus' treatment of all the Ionians. Aristotle says that most of the early philosophers thought that the principles in the form of matter were the only principles of all things, for, he says, they thought that the element or principle of things is 'that of which all things consist, that from which they are first generated and into which they are finally destroyed'.[36] In the extant fragments of the *Physical Opinions* this notion of circular change is ascribed to Hippasus and Heraclitus as well as to Anaximander; and in derived doxographical accounts it is ascribed to all the Ionians.[37] With Aristotle's statement may be compared, for example, the following from Aetius: 'Anaximander says that the Infinite is the principle, for all things are generated from this and all things are destroyed into this'.[38] The conclusion is unavoidable. What Theophrastus has done is apply to the Ionians individually what Aristotle has asserted of them as a group.[39] The probability that Theophrastus is quoting or paraphrasing from Anaximander is, therefore, no greater or less than that Aristotle and he are quoting or paraphrasing from any other member of the group. Aristotle does not claim that any of the Ionians formulated the principle of circular change in so many words; and, far from regarding this principle as an unique feature of Anaximander's doctrine, he does not mention Anaximander in *Metaphysics* A at all.[40] He is intimating what he thinks must have been the Ionians'

---

[34] Xenophanes, Frag. 27. [35] Heidel, *loc. cit.*
[36] *Metaphysics* 983 B 6–11. N.B. 983 B 8–9: ἐξ οὗ γίγνεται πρῶτον καὶ εἰς ὃ φθείρεται τελευταῖον. For similar formulations cf. *Physics* 204 B 33–34; *De Generatione* 325 B 18–19; *Metaphysics* 1000 B 25–26, 1066 B 37; *Nicomachean Ethics* 1173 B 5–6.
[37] *Dox.*, p. 475, 16–17. Cf. Aetius, i. 3, 1; i. 3, 3; i. 3, 4; i. 3, 11.
[38] Aetius, i. 3, 3.
[39] This should not need saying, since these parallels were noted long ago by Diels (*Dox.*, p. 179). Like many later interpreters, Diels failed to see fully the significance of the parallels for the fragment of Anaximander.
[40] Aristotle not only assumes that the early philosophers in general employed the principle of circular change; he uses this principle to refute their theories. One of his arguments against Anaximander is that this principle disproves the existence of an infinite body apart from the elements (*Physics* 204 B 29—205 A 1). He does not say that Anaximander recognized this principle but

reasoning about the nature of the material cause.[41] Theophrastus' intention is evidently the same. The generation–destruction clause is not to be connected with the metaphor; and it does not refer to any special view of Anaximander but to the view that he supposes Anaximander held in common with the other Ionians.

This solution does not remove all the difficulties from the passage, but it does clear the way for understanding the function of the metaphor. Reference to the cycle of generation and destruction is made parenthetically to identify the Infinite as the material substratum. The things generated from the Infinite and destroyed into it are things in general, including the heavens and the worlds in them. The things of the metaphor are things of a special sort, things that are opposed and that wrong each other. The only such things of which Theophrastus speaks are the 'so-called elements'. The gist of the passage, then, is this: Anaximander declared the Infinite to be the principle of all things (i.e. that out of which all things are generated and into which they are destroyed); and he said that the Infinite is some body which is not water or any of the other so-called elements, for, as he said, 'they make reparation and satisfaction to each other for their injustice'. Thus, Theophrastus is quoting what appears to be Anaximander's justification of his own doctrine against Thales and any one else who made one of the opposed elements the primordial matter. The thread of the argument has been obscured, probably by

[41] It can hardly have escaped either Aristotle or the Presocratics that, if the stock of primitive matter is infinite, circular change is unnecessary. It is necessary only if matter is finite, as it is in the system of Aristotle; for, if change is not circular, matter must eventually be exhausted. According to Aetius (i. 3, 3), whose testimony on this point is evidently derived from Aristotle (*Physics* 203 B 18–20) through Theophrastus, it was in order to prevent the exhaustion of matter that Anaximander made his principle infinite. In this case, Anaximander did not argue the existence of his infinite material principle from the fact of circular change, as Aristotle would hold in the *Metaphysics*; and whatever he said about circular change was probably limited to change between things already differentiated from the Infinite. Cf. W. Kraus, 'Das Wesen des Unendlichen des Anaximander', *RhM*, XCIII (1950), 371 f.

neglected its consequences; the implication is, rather, that if Anaximander had employed the principle of circular change, he could not have set up his Infinite in the first place.

Simplicius.[42] But it is clear that Simplicius, too, understood the subject of the metaphor to be the elements and took the metaphor as Anaximander's argument for the existence of a separate

[42] The immediate passage containing the fragment of Anaximander reads: ἐξ ὧν δὲ ἡ γένεσίς ἐστι τοῖς οὖσι, καὶ τὴν φθορὰν εἰς ταῦτα γίνεσθαι κατὰ τὸ χρεών, διδόναι γὰρ αὐτὰ δίκην καὶ τίσιν ἀλλήλοις τῆς ἀδικίας κατὰ τὴν τοῦ χρόνου τάξιν, ποιητικωτέροις οὕτως ὀνόμασιν αὐτὰ λέγων (Dox., p. 476, 8–11). Damage to the text has certainly accompanied or caused the confusion of the argument, and no certain reconstruction can be made. The following comments are offered on some details:

(1) ἐξ ὧν δὲ ἡ γένεσίς ἐστι τοῖς οὖσι καὶ τὴν φθορὰν εἰς ταῦτα γίνεσθαι. Cherniss (op. cit., pp. 376 f.) sees in the use of the plurals (ὧν and ταῦτα) evidence that Theophrastus knew that the Infinite was a multitude of bodies and not a single entity. Since, however, the clause is a generally applied formula of Aristotle and is probably not even a paraphrase of Anaximander's words, the plurals cannot have this significance. Probably they have no special significance at all. Aristotle sometimes uses the plural in such statements (Metaphysics 1000 B 25–26, De Generatione 325 B 18–19), and sometimes the singular (Metaphysics 983 B 8, Nicomachean Ethics 1173 B 5–6); and in two otherwise identical passages the manuscripts agree on the singular in one place (Physics 204 B 33–34), while in the other some manuscripts read the singular and others the plural (Metaphysics 1066 B 37, on which see Ross's critical apparatus). The fact that Aetius always expresses the formula in the singular is probable evidence that Theophrastus had done so, as Aristotle does at Metaphysics 983 B 8. It will be noted, too, that immediately before the sentence in question Theophrastus uses the singular ἐξ ἧς of the Infinite (Dox., p. 476, 7). This proves that, even if ἐξ ὧν is from Theophrastus, he does not consistently regard the Infinite as a plurality.

(2) (a) κατὰ τὸ χρεών, (b) κατὰ τὴν τοῦ χρόνου τάξιν. The first of these may be from Anaximander; the second has a Peripatetic flavour (cf. Aristotle, Politics 1261 A 34, Meteorologica 351 A 25–26; Theophrastus, Metaphysics 6 b 27—7 a 15). Dirlmeier ('Die Satz des Anaximandros von Milet', RhM, LXXXVII [1938], 380 f.) suggests that the second is Theophrastus' paraphrase of the first and that Theophrastus is interpreting Anaximander's reference to necessity as meaning that change is not chaotic but is governed by a temporal order. This suggestion is given weight by several other passages derived from Theophrastus. Physical Opinions, Frag. 1 (Dox., p. 476, 1–2): ποιεῖ (Heraclitus) δὲ καὶ τάξιν τινὰ καὶ χρόνον ὡρισμένον τῆς τοῦ κόσμου μεταβολῆς κατά τινα εἱμαρμένην ἀνάγκην.

Diogenes Laertius, x. 7–8 (on Heraclitus): . . . πάντα δὲ γίνεσθαι καθ' εἱμαρμένην . . . (8) . . . γεννᾶσθαί τε αὐτὸν ἐκ πυρὸς καὶ πάλιν ἐκπυροῦσθαι κατά τινας περιόδους ἐναλλὰξ τὸν σύμπαντα αἰῶνα· τοῦτο δὲ γίνεσθαι καθ' εἱμαρμένην.

Diogenes Laertius, viii. 84: ἔφη (Hippasus) δὲ χρόνον ὡρισμένον εἶναι τῆς τοῦ κόσμου μεταβολῆς.

Hippolytus, Refut., i. 6, 1: οὗτος (Anaximander) ἀρχὴν ἔφη τῶν ὄντων φύσιν

Infinite. Immediately after the metaphor he adds the comment that Anaximander observed the change of the elements into one another and thought, therefore, that the substratum must be other than the elements.[43] Theophrastus does not say by what intermediate step he believes Anaximander to have proceeded from the opposition of the elements to the conclusion that the Infinite must be other than the elements. The missing step may be readily supplied: if one of the elements were the Infinite, the other elements could no longer restrain its injustice by compelling it to pay retribution, and they would, consequently, be destroyed by it. The argument is given in full by Aristotle in the first of his interpretations mentioned above. He says that some philosophers set up the Infinite as the source of the elements and other than them because the elements are contrary to one another and, if one of them were infinite, it would destroy the others.[44] He does not mention Anaximander by name, but it is almost certain that he is thinking primarily of him. Theophrastus has accepted Aristotle's reconstruction of Anaximander's reasoning and has submitted Anaximander's

[43] *Dox.*, p. 476, 11–14.   [44] *Physics* 204 B 22–9.

τινὰ τοῦ ἀπείρου, ἐξ ἧς γίνεσθαι τοὺς οὐρανοὺς καὶ τὸν ἐν αὐτοῖς κόσμον ... λέγει δὲ χρόνον ὡς ὡρισμένης τῆς γενέσεως καὶ τῆς οὐσίας καὶ τῆς φθορᾶς.

In all four passages, change is related to some sort of temporal order. In the first two passages the temporal order is linked to necessity or fate; and some reference to fate was probably also found in the source of the third, since Theophrastus seems to have treated the doctrines of Hippasus and Heraclitus as identical in most important details. Finally, the parallel should be noted between the fourth passage and the sentence in Theophrastus immediately before the passage under examination: ἐξ ἧς ἅπαντας γίνεσθαι τοὺς οὐρανοὺς καὶ τοὺς ἐν αὐτοῖς κόσμους (*Dox.*, p. 476, 7–8). No one of these pieces of evidence is conclusive, but taken together they allow a reasonable conjecture that necessity and the temporal order were linked in the original text of Theophrastus also and that they referred to the generation and destruction of the heavens and the worlds in them. Thus, Theophrastus may have written: ἐξ ἧς ἅπαντας ... κόσμους κατὰ τὸ χρεὼν καὶ τὴν τοῦ χρόνου τάξιν or ἐξ ὧν δὲ γένεσίς τοῖς οὖσι, καὶ τὴν φθορὰν εἰς ταῦτα γίνεσθαι κατὰ τὸ χρεὼν καὶ τὴν τοῦ χρόνου τάξιν. W. Jaeger (*Paideia*,[2] trans., p. 159), taking κατὰ τὴν τοῦ χρόνου τάξιν with the justice metaphor, translates τάξις as 'ordinance', and he uses as evidence legal expressions like τάττειν δίκην. The passages noted above, particularly the first, make this interpretation improbable.

metaphor as evidence—possibly the very evidence used by Aristotle in the first place.

Aristotle and Theophrastus assume that by the Infinite Anaximander sought to correct doctrines whose single infinite material principle was one of the elements; he had, like the other Ionians, accepted as real the diversity of the physical world, but he had seen that the consequence of the destruction of opposites by one another must be that in a universe such as Thales' there could never be anything but an infinite mass of one element. Now, the name given by Anaximander to his principle does suggest that he may have reasoned that the infinite diversity of things could be accounted for only by some principle that was no single thing but was the source of all things. But Theophrastus and Aristotle throw no light on what his reasoning was. Their interpretation clearly presupposes that he had subscribed to the specifically Aristotelian notion of the equilibrium of the contraries and the genesis of the four simple bodies through the interaction of the contraries on undifferentiated matter.[45] This interpretation is proved unhistorical if only by the fact—acknowledged by Aristotle himself—that Empedocles introduced the concept of four elements. The further errors in supposing the Infinite to be undifferentiated matter in the Aristotelian sense will be demonstrated presently.

The implication of such a material principle as Aristotle and Theophrastus attribute to Anaximander would for them be that all change must be qualitative.[46] But Simplicius, probably on Theophrastus' authority, says that Anaximander held generation to be not the qualitative change of the material principle but the separation of the contraries due to eternal motion.[47] Simplicius

[45] Cherniss, p. 28.   [46] Aristotle, *De Generatione* 314 A 8–11, 314 B 1–4.
[47] *Dox.*, p. 476, 13–16. (Cf. Aristotle, *Physics* 187 A 26–31.) This is the source of all later doxographical statements that attribute eternal motion to Anaximander. It is impossible to determine what first-hand evidence Theophrastus had for it. Probably he has merely drawn his own conclusion from some of Aristotle's general statements about early views of change. In the *Metaphysics* (984 A 27–9) Aristotle says that the early monists had not troubled to give a cause of motion, the implication being that motion simply exists, without a cause of its beginning or its end. Elsewhere he says that those physicists who posit a single principle declare it to be in motion (*Physics* 184 B 15–18) and that those who hold that there are infinite worlds, some coming into being and some perishing, declare that motion is eternal (*Physics* 250 B 15–20). But, again, he implies that Leucippus was the first to state that motion is eternal (*Metaphysics* 1071 B 26–33; cf. Cherniss, p. 173, n. 128).

notes that this is the reason why Aristotle groups Anaximander with Anaxagoras. In a later passage he says that according to Theophrastus, too, the doctrines of Anaximander and Anaxagoras are similar, for Anaximander said that in the process of separation from the Infinite like is borne to like and that particular things such as gold and earth are not generated but have existed previously in the Infinite.[48] Theophrastus believes that the material principle of Anaxagoras may be considered either as a mixture of infinite particles or as a single body that is indeterminate in kind and size. In either case, he concludes, the material principles of Anaxagoras and Anaximander would appear to be similar.

The meaning of this last passage is obvious: Theophrastus thinks it possible to consider the material principle of Anaximander both as a single indeterminate body and as a mixture. Since these two concepts appear to be incompatible, modern scholars who believe Anaximander to have been a monist have sought to rescue Theophrastus from this difficulty by arguing that he does not mean to attribute a mixture to Anaximander.[49] Their

[48] *Dox.*, p. 479, 2 ff.
[49] E.g. Zeller, I, 279 ff. Zeller's reasoning is throughout strongly influenced by his predisposition to take the accounts of Aristotle and Theophrastus at their face value. A detailed refutation of his view is not necessary. The question is settled by the correct interpretation of ἐκεῖνος (*Dox.*, p. 479, 4). Zeller (I, 280, n. 5) refers this to Anaxagoras (as do Diels [*ad loc.*] and Kranz [*Vors.*, II. p. 15, 24]); but, as Heidel points out (*CP*, VII [1912], 230, n. 3), ἐκεῖνος must be Anaximander. Not only does normal Greek usage require that this word refer to the former of the two names mentioned, i.e. Anaximander; but, unless ἐκεῖνος is Anaximander, the comparison with Anaxagoras breaks down; and the reference to Anaxagoras by name in the following sentence is not needed unless a change of subject is to be indicated. (If with Zeller we take ἐκεῖνος as Anaxagoras, the gist of the argument is: (1) Anaxagoras held the homoeomery theory; (2) and Theophrastus says that Anaxagoras' theory was like that of Anaximander; (3) for Anaxagoras held the homoeomery theory. Even if we allow this curious reasoning to stand, is it not still implied that Anaximander held the homoeomery theory?) Furthermore, there is no basis for Zeller's statement that, according to Theophrastus, the comparison with Anaximander is contingent on the assumption that Anaxagoras' material principle was unitary (*op. cit.*, p. 280). The relevant portion of the text reads: 'καὶ οὕτω μὲν οὖν', φησί (Theophrastus), 'λαμβανόντων δόξειεν ἂν ποιεῖν τὰς μὲν ὑλικὰς ἀρχὰς ἀπείρους, ὥσπερ εἴρηται, τὴν δὲ τῆς κινήσεως καὶ τῆς γενέσεως αἰτίαν μίαν. εἰ δέ τις τὴν μῖξιν τῶν ἁπάντων ὑπολάβοι μίαν εἶναι φύσιν ἀόριστον καὶ κατ' εἶδος καὶ κατὰ μέγεθος, ὅπερ ἂν δόξειε βούλεσθαι λέγειν, συμβαίνει δύο τὰς ἀρχὰς αὐτὸν λέγειν τήν τε τοῦ ἀπείρου φύσιν καὶ τὸν νοῦν, ὥστε πάντως φαίνεται τὰ σωματικὰ στοιχεῖα παραπλησίως ποιῶν Ἀναξιμάνδρῳ' (*Dox.*, p. 479,

argument would make Simplicius guilty of misunderstanding Theophrastus. But there is no reason to doubt that Simplicius is reporting Theophrastus accurately; for Anaximander is treated as a pluralist by St Augustine, who wrote a century before Simplicius and derived material from Theophrastus through a different line of transmission.[50] The seeming contradiction of Theophrastus must stand.

How Theophrastus can treat the Infinite both as a single body and as a mixture becomes apparent from the passage of the *Physics* in which Aristotle gives his second interpretation of Anaximander.[51] He distinguishes Anaximander, Anaxagoras, and Empedocles from the monists on the grounds that, whereas the monists derived plurality by condensation and rarefaction, these three separated the inherent contraries from their material principle. This principle he designates both as a mixture and as the One; thus at the same time he sets Anaximander, Anaxagoras, and Empedocles off from the monists and he reduces them to essential identity with the monists by designating their principle as the One. He is enabled to do so without contradiction because he assumes that the mixture of these three is in fact not a mixture but a homogeneous body in which the four simple bodies are qualitatively suspended through the alteration of each in the direction of its opposite. Hence, although his use of the word 'separate' implies the pre-existence in the mixture of contraries as distinct things, he is thinking of the contraries not as material ingredients but as the limits of the alteration of the prime matter; by the inherence of these contraries in the One he means the potential inherence of the contraries in his chemical mixture; and by separation he means the actualization of these potential contraries.[52] This passage is almost certainly Theophrastus' second source, and his interpretation becomes intelligible in the light of it.

[50] Augustine, *Civitas Dei*, viii. 2.
[51] *Physics* 187 A 20–6. Here it is implied that the material principle of Anaximander was a mixture; it is expressly stated in a similar connection at *Metaphysics* 1069 B 20–2.
[52] Cherniss. pp. 140–42.

9–16). Clearly, the last clause (ὥστε . . . Ἀναξιμάνδρῳ) is meant to go with both its own sentence and the preceding one; the meaning is that, whether Anaxagoras' material principle be regarded as plural or singular, it is similar to that of Anaximander.

By understanding Anaximander's mixture in the special sense in which Aristotle does here Theophrastus may with indifference speak of it now as a unity and now as a plurality, since regardless of the term he uses the result is the same: the Infinite is a unified substratum for alteration, and separation from the Infinite is simply that alteration.

That Anaximander or any of the other Presocratics should have conceived the mixture in this way is highly improbable. Such a mixture presupposes the Aristotelian concept of qualitative change, a concept which, as has been seen, cannot have been held by any Presocratic. The mixture of the Presocratics in general was simply an aggregate of infinitesimal particles of things, and generation from the mixture was the separation of these particles. If Anaximander did speak of inherence in the mixture, then, he meant the inherence of actually existent things and not the inherence of anything like the Aristotelian contraries. If he referred to the Infinite in language that would suggest to the Peripatetics an indeterminate substance, he meant simply that in the Infinite no one thing so predominates as to give the Infinite any one definite character.[53] Very probably he did think of the Infinite as containing particles of contrary things; but, apart from the accounts of Aristotle and Theophrastus and the doxography dependent on them, there is no evidence for the current notion that these contrary things were prototypes of the four simple bodies.

If Aristotle has misinterpreted both the nature of the Infinite and the nature and functions of its constituent parts, and if Theophrastus has merely repeated his misinterpretation, what positive historical value have their accounts? Their attempt to make a monist of Anaximander is on a par with their similar treatment of Anaxagoras and Empedocles and is no more or less credible. But what is significant is that they feel constrained to group Anaximander with the pluralists at all. Since the result of their interpretation is that he turns out to be a monist, there appears to be no reason that they should not have considered him as a monist from the outset if they had any good evidence for doing so.[54] The grouping of Anaximander with the pluralists, then, may be of some importance as a recognition of the fact

53 W. A. Heidel, *AGPh*, XIX (1906), 345 f.
54 Cherniss, p. 366.

that, however his doctrine may have differed from that of Anaxagoras or Empedocles, it was more closely related to theirs than to
the monists'. Furthermore, it should be noted that, although the
interpretations of Aristotle and Theophrastus are responsible for
the emphasis placed on contrariety in later accounts of Anaximander, their interpretations hardly justify that emphasis. In his
second interpretation Aristotle's aim is to prove that Anaximander recognized the function of contrariety in generation. He
therefore fixes attention on the contraries because they are the
only products of the separation from the Infinite that are important for his argument. He may intend to give the impression
that all the products of separation are contrary, but he does not
specifically say that Anaximander himself stated so. He speaks of
the separation of contraries from the mixture of Anaxagoras in
the same context, although a few lines later he makes it clear that
he is aware that the homoeomeries include such things as flesh
and bone.[55] Theophrastus evidently believes that Anaximander's
theory of change was like the homoeomery theory of Anaxagoras,
and he gives as examples of things separated from the Infinite not
only the contrary earth but also gold.[56] Having seen in his account
of Thales and Hippo how he may overinterpret Aristotle's
association of two philosophers, we may doubt that he has any
better authority for attributing the homoeomery theory to Anaximander than Aristotle's statement that both Anaximander and
Anaxagoras employed the process of separation from the mixture.
But at any rate Theophrastus is probably near the truth of the
matter. Despite their attempt to reduce Anaximander to the terms
of their own doctrines, therefore, both Aristotle and Theophrastus give indications of knowing that Anaximander was a
pluralist. And, however questionable may be the basis of Theophrastus' attribution of the homoeomery theory to Anaximander,
the fact that he makes this attribution means that testimony
derived from him cannot be used to support the modern view that
all the ingredients of the Infinite are contrary.

ANAXIMENES AND DIOGENES

Theophrastus says that Anaximenes agreed with Anaximander in
declaring the substrate to be one and infinite but differed from him

[55] *Physics* 187 A 20–3. Cf. 187 B 2–7.   [56] *Dox.*, p. 479, 4–7.

in making it a qualitatively defined substance, air.[57] This principle, Anaximenes thought, varies in density and rareness; as it is rarefied it becomes fire; as it is condensed it becomes wind, cloud, water, earth, and stone according to the degree of condensation; and from these things the others are derived. Like Anaximander, he maintained that motion is eternal and that change is caused by it. The core of this passage is Aristotle's statement in the *Metaphysics* that Anaximenes and Diogenes believed air to be prior to water and to be the most primary of the simple bodies.[58] The rest is for the most part drawn from other statements made by Aristotle regarding the monists in general without special reference to Anaximenes. He says that all the physicists consider the infinite an attribute of one of the elements;

[57] *Physical Opinions*, Frag. 2 (= *Dox.*, pp. 476, 16—477, 5 = Simplicius' *Phys.*, pp. 24, 26—25, 1). Elsewhere Simplicius says ἐπὶ . . . τούτου μόνου (i.e. Ἀναξιμένους) Θεόφραστος ἐν τῇ ἱστορίᾳ τὴν μάνωσιν εἴρηκε καὶ τὴν πύκνωσιν (*Dox.*, p. 477, n. 1 = *Phys.*, p. 149, 32 ff.). This sentence is strange because, on the authority of Theophrastus, Simplicius ascribes rarefaction and condensation to Hippasus, Heraclitus (*Dox.*, p. 475, 15–17) and Diogenes of Apollonia (*Dox.*, p. 477, 9). The suggestions that μόνου = πρῶτον (Diels) and that πρῶτον should be read for μόνου (Usener) are not convincing. If Theophrastus meant πρῶτος there is no reason why he should have risked ambiguity by using μόνος with the meaning πρῶτος; and that Simplicius understood him to mean μόνος is shown by Simplicius' next sentence, δῆλον δὲ ὡς καὶ οἱ ἄλλοι τῇ μανότητι καὶ πυκνότητι ἐχρῶντο (*Phys.*, p. 150, 1–2). It is possible, of course, that Simplicius misunderstood Theophrastus or that Theophrastus simply contradicted himself (for similar contradictions see Theophrastus, *De Sensibus*, 38, and Stratton, *ad loc.*; Aristotle, *De Generatione* 323 B 10–11 and Cherniss, p. 91, n. 387). But if neither is the case, it is difficult to see how Theophrastus could have denied rarefaction and condensation to Diogenes. Probably, as Zeller suggests (I, 322, n. 1), Simplicius is thinking only of the earliest Ionians. Aristotle's assertion that all the monists employed rarefaction and condensation (*Physics* 187 A 12–16; cf. *De Caelo* 303 B 13–17) is only what he considers to be the consequence of a single material principle. Very probably neither he nor Theophrastus had any knowledge of how Thales accounted for change; both ascribe to Anaximander the mechanism of Anaxagoras; and the vagueness of Aristotle's reference to Heraclitus' mechanism of change suggests that he was not sure of Heraclitus' meaning. Theophrastus could attribute rarefaction–condensation to Heraclitus and the other monists on the grounds that this was the only mechanism of change possible in their systems. His statement regarding Anaximenes probably should not be taken to mean that he thinks no other Ionian employed rarefaction–condensation but that Anaximenes was the only one who did so explicitly (cf. *Dox.*, p. 493, 5: μόνος ἢ μάλιστα).

[58] *Metaphysics* 984 A 5–7.

that all the physicists who make the substrate one of the elements generate other things by rarefaction and condensation; that all who employ a single principle such as air or water believe that it is in motion; and that all who believe that there is an infinite number of worlds, some being generated and some being destroyed, assume that motion is eternal.[59]

When Theophrastus speaks of air as a unitary substrate and uses Aristotle's technical word for this, he betrays once more the influence of Aristotle's tendency to interpret the Ionian principles as substrates of alteration; and it is safe to assume that his use of the word implies all the significance attached to it by Aristotle.[60] One consequence of Ionian monism is, according to Aristotle, that generation and destruction must be the qualitative change of the substrate; and, in order to accommodate the Ionian rarefaction and condensation theory to his own theory of qualitative change, he equates the rare and dense with the hot and cold, which are his contrary forces.[61] The result of this for Anaximenes is that air becomes, in fact if not in name, a homogeneous and qualitatively neutral body that is subject to alteration by the hot and cold. As in the case of Anaximander, however, Theophrastus makes statements about Anaximenes' principle which would prove that air is not a substrate in the Aristotelian sense. The very name of Anaximenes' principle shows that he did not conceive it as qualitatively neutral, and Theophrastus makes a point of distinguishing Anaximenes from Anaximander by the fact that air is qualitatively determined while the Infinite is not. And that air is not homogeneous and that the differentiation of air is not alteration is shown by the parallel he finds between the mechanism of change employed by Anaximenes and Anaximander. In saying that Anaximenes, like Anaximander, explained change by eternal motion he must mean that change results not from alteration but from some mechanical process which causes the emergence of things that are differentiated in their degree of extension and compression.[62]

[59] See notes 19 and 47.
[60] Theophrastus calls air ἡ ὑποκειμένη φύσις. See note 12.
[61] *De Generatione* 330 B 7–13.
[62] Despite his interpretation of rarefaction and condensation as qualitative change, Aristotle, too, in one passage recognizes what must have been the general view of the Presocratics on this matter. He says that all affections have their source in condensation and rarefaction, that heavy and light, soft and hard, hot and cold, are considered to be forms of density and rarity, and

It is likely that Anaximenes did consider fire, wind, cloud, water, earth, and stone to be products of the rarefaction and condensation of air. But it is doubtful that, as Theophrastus says, he derived other things from these. Theophrastus apparently supposes that he used two distinct processes of generation: rarefaction and condensation, by which he accounted for certain primary differentiations, and combination, by which he formed compound things from these primary differentiations. But, if Anaximenes was satisfied to explain such seemingly diverse things as stone and cloud by the single process of rarefaction and condensation, it is hard to imagine that he would have felt the need for any kind of secondary process. And, since the sole difference between the supposed primary bodies is one of extension, the difference between the compounds of these bodies would presumably be the same, so that in its effect combination would be identical with rarefaction and condensation. The double process is needed only if the primary bodies are elements. Undoubtedly Theophrastus thinks that they are.[63] Aristotle's theory is that the four simple bodies are produced through the action of the contraries on primary matter and that compound bodies are combinations of the simple bodies. Theophrastus has found both substratum and contrariety in Aristotle's treatment of Anaximenes; and these two originative sources give rise to bodies which, although more numerous, are approximations of the Aristotelian simple bodies. The error in thinking that the differentiations of air are simple bodies of this sort needs no demonstration. It is sufficient to note that the Aristotelian theory involves qualitative change. Indeed, to postulate simple bodies of any sort is possible only if Anaximenes fails to apply his rarefaction–condensation principle rigorously. Either he did so fail, or—what is more likely—the things cited by Theophrastus are not primary differentiations at all but are merely a few striking examples drawn by Anaximenes from the whole scale of density, probably with the purpose of illustrating the operation of his theory.

Theophrastus, like Aristotle, groups Diogenes of Apollonia

[63] Cicero (*Acad.*, ii. 37, 118), who is dependent on Theophrastus, goes even farther than Theophrastus. He names the products of air as fire, water, and earth, and he says that other things are formed from these.

that condensation and rarefaction are combination and separation, by which are caused the generation and destruction of substances (*Physics* 260 B 7–12).

with Anaximenes as holding the theory that air is the principle of things.[64] He says, further, that Diogenes, too, maintained that air is infinite and eternal and that the form of other things comes to be from it when it is rarefied and condensed, i.e. when it changes in its modifications.

In extant fragments Diogenes does describe air as an eternal and undying body, and he does say that there are modifications of air due to differences in heat and cold, dryness and dampness, greater and less mobility, etc., which arise and pass away.[65] Theophrastus probably had the writings of Diogenes available, but his treatment of Diogenes here is essentially the same as his treatment of Anaximenes and is probably from the same source.[66] Diogenes' writings are at any rate no protection against the influence of Aristotle. With Aristotle, Theophrastus infers that, since the principle is referred to in the singular, unity in the Eleatic sense is meant. The eternity of the principle as opposed to the transitoriness of its modifications points to its being a persistent substrate of change. And the identification of rarefaction and condensation with qualitative change is facilitated by the fact that Diogenes seems himself to have equated the rare and dense with the hot and cold.[67] But the air of Diogenes is no more an Aristotelian substrate than is that of Anaximenes. When he refers to air as 'manifold', he is referring not to the qualification of air by the contraries but to the numberless modifications that he says 'are in it'. These modifications are quantitative. He says that all things have a share of air but the share of each thing is not the same as that of any other thing. To be sure, he distinguishes the different forms of air by their heat and cold, etc.; but there can be no question that the basic difference between things is in their density.[68]

[64] *Physical Opinions*, Frag. 2 (= *Dox.*, p. 477, 5–11 = Simplicius, *Phys.*, p. 25, 1–7).

[65] Diogenes, Frags. 5 (*Vors.*, II, 61, 10–14), 7 and 8.

[66] The detailed information given by Theophrastus on Diogenes' psychological theory (*De Sensibus*, 39–48) indicates first-hand knowledge of Diogenes' work. Simplicius (*Phys.*, p. 25, 7–8) says that Diogenes' writings were extant in his time. In preserved fragments Diogenes does not say that air is infinite. Theophrastus may have got this from Aristotle's assertion that all physicists regarded their principles as infinite (*Physics* 203 A 16–18). So too, the description of air as eternal may be from Aristotle's similar statement about the infinite principles of the physicists (*Physics* 203 B 13–15).

[67] Frag. 6 (*Vors.*, II, 65, 13–14).

[68] Frag. 5 (esp. *Vors.*, II, 61, 11–14 and 62, 3–5).

The grouping of philosophers that Theophrastus has taken from the *Metaphysics* has here resulted in a serious misrepresentation of doctrine. Aristotle is convinced that the material monists did not—and could not—answer the problem of efficient causality, and he makes no distinction between the early and late monists in this regard.[69] Thus, Diogenes is represented as differing from Anaximenes only in being after him in time. Aristotle asserts, further, that it is unlikely that one of the elements is the cause of the goodness in things or that the materialists should think that it is.[70] Now, the doctrine that Aristotle here rejects as inconceivable is precisely that maintained by Diogenes. He introduces Intelligence as the cause of motion and of the best possible order in the world, and this Intelligence is a form of air.[71] It must have been as obvious to Diogenes as it was to Aristotle that material monism was no longer tenable if it failed to cope with efficient causality. Diogenes attempted to preserve the earlier doctrine by incorporating in it later notions about the cause of both motion and order. Aristotle's suppression of this part of Diogenes' doctrine, in complete disregard for Diogenes' clear statements, is a criticism based on his own presuppositions about the final-efficient cause. The offhand manner in which he rules out even the possibility that the cause of goodness should be material is intended to dispose of doctrines like that of Diogenes as being not worth further comment. His silence about Intelligence falsifies Diogenes' doctrine, but his motive is clear. Theophrastus acknowledges Diogenes' connection with the late physicists by saying that Diogenes wrote for the most part in an eclectic manner and agreed in some points with Anaxagoras and in others with Leucippus.[72] By the reference to Anaxagoras is probably meant, among other things, Diogenes' adoption of Intelligence as the final-efficient cause, but Theophrastus does not, like Aristotle, give any reason for excluding this cause from his account.

[69] *Metaphysics* 984 A 16–29.
[70] *Metaphysics* 984 B 11–14.
[71] Frags. 3, 4 and 5 (*Vors.*, II, 61, 4–8).
[72] *Dox.*, p. 477, 5–8. Neither Aristotle nor Theophrastus enumerates Diogenes' borrowings from these philosophers. On this see Zeller, I, 354 ff. Theophrastus says that Diogenes was almost the last of the physicists.

EMPEDOCLES

According to Theophrastus, the material principles of Empedocles are four—fire, air, water, and earth—which are eternal but change in number owing to aggregation and segregation.[73] The principles in the strict sense, those by which the four elements are moved, are Love and Strife; for, as Empedocles held, the elements must be continually in alternate motion, being at one time aggregated by the force of Love and at another time segregated by the force of Strife. Theophrastus quotes from Empedocles: 'at one time all uniting in one through Love, at another being borne apart by the repulsion of Strife'.[74] This quotation, we must suppose, is the authority for Theophrastus' report.

If Theophrastus has consulted the works of Empedocles, he has done so, apparently, only to find support for the interpretation of Aristotle; for his account is in all essentials the same as the descriptions of Empedocles' material and efficient principles in *Metaphysics* A.[75] Probably the verses that Theophrastus quotes were

[73] *Physical Opinions*, Frag. 3 (= *Dox.*, pp. 477, 16—478, 15 = Simplicius, *Phys.*, pp. 25, 19—26, 4). Theophrastus says that Empedocles was born not long after Anaxagoras and was the admirer and follower of Parmenides (*Dox.*, p. 477, 17–18. See note 75).

[74] *Dox.*, p. 478, 8–10 (Empedocles, Frag. 17, 7–8).

[75] *Metaphysics* 984 A 8–11; 985 A 21–33.

Aristotle remarks that Anaxagoras was prior to Empedocles in age but later in works (*Metaphysics* 984 A 11–13). He is apparently attempting to justify his treatment of Empedocles before Anaxagoras by showing that in the real sense Empedocles was prior to Anaxagoras just as his four material principles are a logical step between the single principle of the Ionians and the infinite principles of Anaxagoras. Since Aristotle is prone to identify chronological and logical order, the fact that he considers such a remark necessary may indicate that it was generally known that Anaxagoras was born earlier than Empedocles. Theophrastus may have had good reason for adding that the difference in ages was not great; but it is at least equally possible that he has merely drawn his own conclusion from Aristotle's remark (cf. Ross on *Metaphysics* 984 A 12; Cherniss, p. 219, n. 5; and C. E. Millerd, *On the Interpretation of Empedocles*, p. 13). Simplicius says that Empedocles was Παρμενίδου . . . ζηλωτὴς καὶ πλησιαστὴς καὶ ἔτι μᾶλλον τῶν Πυθαγορείων (*Dox.*, p. 477, 18). Of Empedocles' relationship to the Pythagoreans, Diels (*ad loc.*) rightly says, 'narratio de Pythagoreorum disciplina aut aliena est a Theophrasto aut certe immutata redditur a Simplicio'. Diogenes Laertius (iii. 55) states: ὁ δὲ Θεόφραστος Παρμενίδου φησὶ ζηλωτὴν αὐτὸν γενέσθαι καὶ μιμητὴν ἐν τοῖς ποιήμασι· καὶ γὰρ ἐκεῖνον ἐν ἔπεσι τὸν περὶ φύσεως ἐξενεγκεῖν λόγον.

the basis for part of Aristotle's account. The only point at which he differs from Aristotle is in his assertion that the alternate motion caused by Love and Strife was continuous. The source for this is apparently the verse of Empedocles immediately preceding the verses quoted.[76] In *Metaphysics* A Aristotle does not specify whether Empedocles held that motion is continuous or not; but in that context at least he would probably agree with Theophrastus, since the only distinction he makes there regarding motion is that the Eleatics denied it and the other Presocratics accepted its existence with or without stating a cause for it.[77]

Since Aristotle and Theophrastus assume that Empedocles' principles can be adequately expressed in terms of the Peripatetic material and efficient causes, they treat the four elements as permanent, inert masses of substance that are in themselves incapable of motion and they treat Love and Strife as two immaterial, universal motors that act upon the elements. The degree to which Theophrastus has carried this identification of Empedocles with the Peripatetics is shown clearly by his designation of Love and Strife as the 'principles in the strict sense';[78] for this reflects the Peripatetic conviction that the form-efficient cause is more a principle than matter is. Enough of Empedocles' work remains to allow a test of this interpretation. It is obvious from the fragment quoted by Theophrastus that the principles of

---

[76] *Dox.*, p. 478, 4–7. Cf. Empedocles, Frag. 17, 6: καὶ ταῦτ' ἀλλάσσοντα διαμπερὲς οὐδαμὰ λήγει.
[77] *Metaphysics* 984 A 27 ff. [78] *Dox.*, p. 478, 3.

The indebtedness of Empedocles to Parmenides is evident not only in his mode of expression but also in his doctrine. But the use of πλησιαστής by Simplicius—unless, of course, this was written by Simplicius for an original μιμητής preserved by Diogenes Laertius—seems to imply a closer relationship, that of student to teacher. In view of the relationships that Theophrastus attempts to establish between Anaximander and Xenophanes and between Xenophanes and Parmenides, it seems not unlikely that he believes a similar relationship to have existed between Parmenides and Empedocles—and for similar reasons (see p. 119). Just as Aristotle represents the Eleatic doctrine as a development from the Ionian monism but does not suggest a teacher–student relationship between the two schools, so, too, by way of preface to his discussion of Empedocles' theory of efficient casuality, he remarks that Parmenides had given Love an important place in his cosmogony (*Metaphysics* 984 B 23–31; cf. Cherniss, p. 222), but he does not even hint that Empedocles was Parmenides' disciple.

Empedocles had certain resemblances to the Aristotelian material and efficient causes; but it is equally obvious from other fragments that there is no exact correspondence and that Empedocles did not define the nature and operation of his principles as precisely as this interpretation would suggest. And, while he says that Love aggregates and Strife segregates the elements, he also attributes to the elements certain motions of their own.[79] From this it follows that the four roots are not inert matter, and Love and Strife are not the causes of all motion. In fact, the fragments indicate that Empedocles thought of Love and Strife chiefly, if not exclusively, as effecting the formation and dissolution of organic compounds.[80]

In the latter part of his account Theophrastus attempts to show that Empedocles was not consistent in his use of Love and Strife. Not only did Empedocles assign the efficient power to Strife and Love when he said, 'at one time uniting in one through Love, at another being borne apart by the repulsion of Strife'.[81] Sometimes he reduced Love and Strife to the level of the elements and thus posited six elements; for he said, 'And at one time it parted asunder so as to be many instead of one;—fire and water and earth and the mighty height of air and dread Strife, too, apart from these, everywhere of equal weight, and Love, in their midst, equal in length and breadth.'[82] This passage of Theophrastus has been cited as evidence that Theophrastus regards Love and Strife as no less material than the four elements and Empedocles himself so regarded them.[83] That these two forces are never matter in the sense that the four elements are, is, however, shown by their special functions and by the facts that they are seen only with the mind[84] and are never, in the fragments, referred to as constituents of any thing.[85] Furthermore, Theophrastus does not say simply that Love and Strife are elements; his objection is that *sometimes* they are like elements and *sometimes* they are not, i.e. that Empedocles treated them both as material and as immaterial. What Theophrastus means by calling them elements becomes

---

[79] Empedocles, Frags. 17, 30–5; 21, 13–14. Cf. C. E. Millerd, *op. cit.*, pp. 34 ff., and W. A. Heidel, *AGPh*, XIX (1906), 365 f.
[80] Millerd, *op. cit.*, p. 38.   [81] *Dox.*, p. 478, 6–15.
[82] Empedocles, Frag. 17, 17–20.   [83] E.g., by Burnet, p. 232.
[84] Empedocles, Frag. 17, 21 and 25–6.
[85] E.g., Empedocles, Frags. 71 and 96.

clearer from related Aristotelian passages that probably influenced his criticism.

In *De Generatione* Aristotle likewise attributes six elements to Empedocles,[86] and once in the *Metaphysics* he distinguishes Empedocles' Love from Anaxagoras' *Nous* by calling the one an element and the other a principle.[87] In the former passage he differentiates between the two efficient elements, Love and Strife, and the four material elements. The latter passage shows that his reason for calling Love and Strife elements rather than principles is not that he considers them to be of the same nature as the four elements but that they seem less immaterial than such efficient principles as Anaxagoras' *Nous*. In a further passage he objects that Empedocles made Love both an efficient and a material principle;[88] but this no more than the passages already mentioned is proof that he considers Love to be simply a material element. His argument depends solely on his conviction that the Sphere is a homogeneous compound and that Love, being part of it, must be material. The quotation given by Theophrastus indicates that he is following the same line of reasoning. The basis of his argument is not so much the physical attributes of Love and Strife as the fact that these forces are listed along with the four elements as if all six were products of separation from the One. Theophrastus is misinterpreting the verses he quotes; for, when the elements are completely brought together by Love, Strife has withdrawn and is, therefore, not part of the Sphere.[89] Furthermore, although his criticism is right in so far as Love and Strife are not consistently treated as immaterial forces, they are certainly more nearly immaterial than material; for Empedocles held that all space is filled by the elements,[90] and Love and Strife operate on them not from without but from within as they do in living creatures.[91]

The part of Theophrastus' report that is based on the *Metaphysics* reproduces Aristotle's interpretation accurately. But attention should be drawn to Aristotle's other comments made there and elsewhere. To be sure, in the *Metaphysics* he refers, as Theophrastus does, to the four roots as elements, but he also calls them 'the

---

[86] *De Generatione* 314 A 16–17.　　[87] *Metaphysics* 1091 B 11–12.
[88] *Metaphysics* 1075 B 3–4. Cf. Cherniss, p. 108, n. 444.
[89] Empedocles, Frags. 35 and 36.　　[90] Empedocles, Frag. 17, 32–3.
[91] Empedocles, Frags. 35, 9–11; 17, 22–4.

so-called elements in the form of matter', and by this vague expression he signifies that the four roots do not accord exactly with his own concept of matter.[92] He treats Love and Strife as efficient causes, but he places limits on the equation of them with his own efficient cause; for, while he grants that Empedocles had made greater use of these causes than Anaxagoras did, he objects that Empedocles still did not use them adequately or consistently.[93] The interpretation that Theophrastus adopts from *Metaphysics* A is only one of several offered by Aristotle. Although in the *Metaphysics* Aristotle treats Empedocles as a material pluralist for whom apparent generation and destruction are merely the aggregation and segregation of four unchanging and distinct substances, in another context he complains that Empedocles speaks both as a pluralist and as a monist.[94] As a pluralist, he holds, Empedocles must distinguish between generation and alteration.[95] When he makes Empedocles a monist, on the other hand, he treats the Sphere as a homogeneous substrate in which the contraries inhere potentially.[96] On this view the Sphere, not the elements, is ultimate; and this Aristotle considers to have been Empedocles' belief, contrary to what Empedocles himself had said.[97] He holds, too, that, although Empedocles did not express himself clearly, he meant that Love and Strife were also the causes of good and evil, i.e. final causes.[98] Again, he treats Love and Strife not as causes at all but as the states of the world at the moments of complete aggregation and segregation.[99] In *Metaphysics* A he probably considers the operation of Love and Strife to be continuous; but in one passage of the *De Caelo* he makes Empedocles' cosmic cycle start with a precosmical unified body in

[92] Aristotle speaks of Empedocles' elements as τὰ ὡς ἐν ὕλης εἴδει λεγόμενα στοιχεῖα, meaning by this that they do not accord exactly with his own concept of matter (*Metaphysics* 985 A 32; cf. Cherniss, p. 308, n. 67).

[93] *Metaphysics* 985 A 21–23. The inadequacy he has in mind is Empedocles' failure to appreciate the full significance of his principles for the Peripatetics (see, e.g., *Metaphysics* 984 B 32—985 A 10, 1000 A 24 ff.; cf. Cherniss, pp. 230–4).

[94] *De Generatione* 315 A 3–25.

[95] *De Generatione* 314 A 11–13; cf. Cherniss, pp. 106 ff.

[96] *Physics* 187 A 20–6; cf. Cherniss, pp. 50–1.

[97] *De Generatione* 325 B 15–25; cf. Cherniss, p. 96.

[98] *Metaphysics* 984 B 32—985 A 10. Cf. *Metaphysics* 993 A 17–18, where Aristotle finds even the formal cause in Empedocles.

[99] *Metaphysics* 1004 B 29–34; cf. Cherniss, pp. 47–8.

a state of rest.[100] This interpretation is clearly incorrect since it ignores the fact that during both the increase of Love and the increase of Strife both Love and Strife are active. What matters is not that some of these interpretations are in greater or less agreement with the fragments but that each of them has as much claim to being Aristotle's judgement as his interpretation in the *Metaphysics* has. A complete text of the *Physical Opinions* might reveal the same diversity in Theophrastus' interpretations. For, although in his treatment of the principles he understands the activity of Love and Strife to be continuous, in the *De Sensibus* he assumes, as Aristotle does in the *De Caelo*, that only one force is active at one time and that during the period of Love only aggregation takes place.[101]

ANAXAGORAS

Theophrastus says that Anaxagoras was the first to change the opinions about the principles by supplying 'the missing cause' and that his material principles were infinite.[102] He held that all the

[100] *De Caelo* 301 A 13–20; cf. Cherniss, pp. 194–6.
[101] *De Sensibus*, 20 (*Dox.*, p. 505, 10–11).
[102] *Physical Opinions*, Frag. 4 (= *Dox.*, pp. 478, 16—479, 16 = Simplicius, *Phys.*, pp. 26, 31—27, 23).
The account as given by Simplicius is repetitious and inconsistent. Certainly only part of it is an actual quotation from Theophrastus. About this part there can be no doubt, since Simplicius repeats it elsewhere in the same form under Theophrastus' name (*Dox.*, p. 479, 9–16; cf. Simplicius, *Phys.*, p. 154, 16–23). The rest, if not a quotation, is at least an accurate paraphrase, since it is paralleled by doxographers who have derived material from the *Physical Opinions* by other lines of transmission (*Dox.*, pp. 478, 18—479, 5. Cf. *Vors.*, II, pp. 19, 34—20, 8; 20, 13; 20, 37–8; 47, 9–14).
Anaxagoras is said by Theophrastus to have shared the philosophy of Anaximenes (*Dox.*, p. 478, 18–19). The doxographers say that Anaxagoras was the student of Anaximenes (*Vors.*, II, pp. 5, 4–5; 8, 3–4; 8, 36–7; 8, 42–3; 19, 40–1). Anaximenes was probably dead before Anaxagoras was born (Burnet, p. 253). Aristotle connects the doctrine of Anaxagoras with that of Anaximander (*Physics* 187 A 20–6), and Theophrastus follows him in this (*Dox.*, p. 479, 3–16). Theophrastus apparently thinks that the two philosophers were connected by more than the similarity of their doctrines, and he has attempted to fit them into a scheme of teacher–student relationship. Philosophy begins with Thales; Anaximander is the student of Thales (*Dox.*, p. 476, 3–4); after Anaximander, philosophy divides and one of his students, Xenophanes (*Dox.*, p. 482, 14–15), becomes the first of the Eleatics, while the other, Anaximenes (*Dox.*, p. 476, 16–17), continues the tradition of the physicists; Anaximenes, in turn, is followed by Anaxagoras.

homoeomeries, such as water, fire, and gold, are ungenerated and indestructible and that apparent generation and destruction is due only to their aggregation and segregation. All things, he believed, are in all things, and a particular thing, such as gold, derives its character and name from the predominance of one thing in its composition; for he had declared that 'in everything there is a portion of everything' and 'each thing is and was most manifestly those things of which it has most in it'.[103] Theophrastus makes the comment that this theory resembles that of Anaximander, since Anaximander, too, held that in the separation from the Infinite like particles are borne to like and that particles are not generated but are already present in the Infinite. The difference between the two theories is that Anaxagoras posited *Nous* as the cause of motion and generation. Thus viewed, Theophrastus says, Anaxagoras' material principles would appear to be infinite, and the cause of motion and generation would be one. He adds, however, that if the mixture of Anaxagoras were understood as being one thing, indefinite in kind and size, it would appear that Anaxagoras' principles were two, the Infinite and *Nous*. Theophrastus remarks that this latter explanation is what Anaxagoras 'would seem to mean'.

The quotations from Anaxagoras establish that Theophrastus has used at least part of the work on which he is reporting. But the interpretation that he gives is throughout influenced by Aristotle. The statement that Anaxagoras made *Nous* the cause of motion and generation may, for example, have been derived from the text of Anaxagoras.[104] But the statement that Anaxagoras first changed the opinions about causality by supplying 'the missing cause' is an interpretative comment and criticism derived from the *Metaphysics* and is understandable only on the thesis developed there. If this statement is taken by itself, granted the identification of *Nous* as the missing cause, there is still no indication of what the whole is from which *Nous* has been missing. And, even if it be supposed that the whole is the four Aristotelian causes, there is still the difficulty that Theophrastus attributes efficient causality to Parmenides, whom he presumably knew to be earlier than Anaxagoras.[105] In the *Metaphysics* Aristotle states how Anaxagoras

---

[103] Anaxagoras, Frags. 11 and 12 (*Vors.*, II, 37, 22–3 and 39, 6–7).
[104] E.g., Frags. 12 (*Vors.*, II, 38, 5–6 and 10–12) and 13.
[105] *Dox.*, p. 482, 13.

changed the opinions about causes and in what sense the cause that he proposed could be said to fulfil a lack. Parmenides had, according to Aristotle, used fire as an efficient cause; but, since such causes as this and the other elements are inadequate to generate the world, men were compelled by the truth to seek 'the next cause', for neither a material element nor chance could be the cause of the goodness and beauty in things. Anaxagoras, then, seemed like a sober man by comparison with the random talk of his predecessors when he declared that *Nous* is present throughout nature as the cause of order and arrangement, i.e. as the cause both of the goodness in things and of movement.[106] This is undoubtedly what Theophrastus means, too; Anaxagoras was the first to glimpse the final-efficient cause as something that must by its very nature be other than the elements, by which Parmenides and other earlier thinkers like him had explained motion. It should be observed, however, that, although Aristotle praises Anaxagoras as the discoverer of the final-efficient cause, he reports a tradition that Hermotimus had expressed the same views earlier than Anaxagoras.[107] And he goes on to say that one might suspect that the first to seek after such a cause was Hesiod or Parmenides or whoever first made Love a principle and that Empedocles treated both good and evil as principles.[108] He promises that he will decide later how all these thinkers should be arranged with regard to the priority of their discovery.[109] But he does not fulfil this promise, and Theophrastus has been content to accept his enthusiastic acclaim of Anaxagoras as proof that Anaxagoras was the first.

The statement that Anaxagoras' material principles are infinite, ungenerated, and indestructible and that apparent generation and destruction are due only to their aggregation and segregation may likewise be supported by the fragments of Anaxagoras.[110] But the wording follows closely the wording of the *Metaphysics*.[111] Clear

[106] *Metaphysics* 984 B 1–18, 20–2.
Elsewhere Aristotle considers Nous not only as efficient and final (*Metaphysics* 988 A 14–17, 988 A 33–4, 988 B 6–11, 1075 B 8–10; *Physics* 265 B 22–3) but also as formal (*Metaphysics* 989 B 16–19) and as equivalent to his unmoved mover (*Physics* 256 B 24–7. Cf. Cherniss, p. 172, n. 122).
[107] *Metaphysics* 984 B 18–20.   [108] *Metaphysics* 984 B 23—985 A 10.
[109] *Metaphysics* 984 B 31–2.
[110] *Dox.*, p. 478, 21–3; cf. Anaxagoras, Frags. 1 and 17.
[111] *Metaphysics* 984 A 13–16.

evidence that Theophrastus is borrowing from Aristotle is his reference to the principles as 'homoeomeries'. This word does not occur in the fragments of Anaxagoras; it is Aristotle's translation into his own phraseology of Anaxagoras' 'seeds', and it is a possible translation because Anaxagoras included in his seeds substances such as flesh and bone which Aristotle calls by the general term 'homoeomery'.[112] The importance of the word in the present context is that Theophrastus has followed *Metaphysics* A in giving fire and water as examples of the Anaxagorean homoeomeries. These examples are misleading both with regard to the place of the elements in Anaxagoras' philosophy and with regard to the opinion of Aristotle and Theophrastus on this question.[113] Thus far, in presenting earlier notions of matter, when Theophrastus has referred to the elements as principles he has meant the *maxima membra*; and, for lack of warning to the contrary, it is to be assumed that he means the same thing when he speaks of the doctrine of Anaxagoras. Now, Anaxagoras undoubtedly did think that there were seeds of the Empedoclean elements as well as of other things; and, since the Aristotelian term 'homoeomery' is used of the elements as well as of substances like flesh and bone, fire and water may be cited as examples that hold true for both the Aristotelian homoeomeries and the Anaxagorean seeds.[114] But Aristotle himself knows that the seeds of the elements are not the *maxima membra*, and in the *De Caelo* and the *De Generatione* he distinguishes Empedocles from Anaxagoras by the observation that for the former the elements, i.e. the *maxima membra*, were ultimate and for the latter they were compounds of the homoeo-

---

[112] Anaxagoras, Frag. 4 (*Vors.*, II, 34, 6–7); *Dox.*, p. 478, 21; Aristotle, *Metaphysics* 984 A 14 (on which see Ross's note).

Aristotle is careful to say σχεδὸν . . . ἅπαντα τὰ ὁμοιομερῆ, meaning by this, apparently, that there is only a rough correspondence between his homoeomeries and the principles of Anaxagoras.

[113] Burnet (pp. 262 ff.) holds, with Tannery, that the seeds contain portions of the 'traditional opposites' and that, according to Aristotle, the opposites have as much right to be called first principles as the homoeomeries have. This view, while seeming in fact to be substantiated by the passages of Aristotle and Theophrastus referred to above, is based on a misinterpretation of *Physics* 187 A 25 (see note 121). With regard to the fragments of Anaxagoras, it has been refuted in detail by C. Bailey (*The Greek Atomists and Epicurus*, pp. 538–42).

[114] In extant fragments Anaxagoras speaks of αἰθήρ (Frag. 2) but not of fire. Fire is Aristotle's interpretation. Cf. *De Caelo* 302 B 4–5.

meries.[115] And the fact that Theophrastus adds gold along with fire and water as an example of the homoeomeries is tacit recognition that these are not elements in the Empedoclean sense.[116] This being so, it may be asked why fire and water, rather than some unambiguous substances like flesh and bone, are given as examples. The reason, although obscured by the patchwork form of Theophrastus' accounts, is clear in Aristotle's outline of the development of the material cause in the *Metaphysics*. Aristotle believes that all earlier theories of matter resembled his own and were an imperfect expression of it. The material principle towards which the earlier theories evolve is prime matter, and of this the simplest visible forms are the four simple bodies, which the early philosophers thought to be ultimate. The evolution of the material cause is, thus, the emergence of first one, then another, then all four of the simple bodies. The earliest monists each posited one of these as his principle; Empedocles posited all four; and Anaxagoras made his principles infinite.[117] The reference to fire and water as examples of Anaxagoras' principles is meant to show that he does not stand outside of the general evolutionary pattern; his material principles were of the same sort as those of his predecessors and differed only in being numerically infinite.

[115] *De Generatione* 314 A 18—B 1; *De Caelo* 302 A 28—B 3.

Aristotle says that Anaxagoras thought the elements to be compounds of flesh, bone, etc.; but Aristotle does not mean by this that there were no seeds of the elements. The difference between Anaxagoras and Empedocles was that Anaxagoras, by postulating an infinite variety of elementary bodies and asserting that everything contained portions of everything else, eliminated the possibility of such simple bodies as the four roots of Empedocles. Aristotle might merely have said that, while the visible masses of the elements were pure and irreducible entities for Empedocles, Anaxagoras held that they contained portions of each other and of everything else. He makes the contrast sharper by the examples of Anaxagoras' seeds he chooses. Empedocles thought that bone and flesh were compounds of the elements. Anaxagoras would admit that a piece of bone contained seeds of the so-called elements, but he would add that it also contained seeds of gold and stone, etc., and that it was bone not because it contained seeds of the elements but because the seeds of bone in it predominated over the other seeds. In the same way he would maintain that what Empedocles called air contained seeds of bone, flesh, gold, stone, etc., but was air because of the predominance of the seeds of air.

[116] *Dox.*, p. 478, 21.

[117] *Metaphysics* 984 A 2–13.

For his assertion that all things are in all things and that a particular thing such as gold derives its name and character from the predominance in it of one thing, Theophrastus has the evidence of the quotations that he makes from Anaxagoras.[118] It does not follow, however, that he has made an independent evaluation of the evidence. Essentially the same description of the theory appears in *Physics* A in a passage that follows immediately after one that will presently be shown to have influenced the latter part of Theophrastus' account. Aristotle describes the theory thus: everything is mixed in everything; things appear different from one another and receive different names according to the numerical predominance of one of the infinite particles in the mixture; nothing is purely and wholly white, black, sweet, flesh, or bone, but the nature of a thing is that of which it contains the most.[119] This is clearly a paraphrase of the statements of Anaxagoras quoted by Theophrastus or of others similar to them. In this case, again, Theophrastus has apparently adopted the interpretation of Aristotle and has filled in what he thinks is the primary evidence for it. One notable feature of the present descriptions of both Theophrastus and Aristotle is that the homoeomeries are no longer associated with the elements. The example used by Theophrastus is gold; and those of Aristotle are noncontrary things and contrary qualities such as might have been selected to prove the difference between the homoeomeries and the elements.

In the fuller exposition of Anaxagoras' theory to which Theophrastus proceeds in the latter part of his account, he returns to the view implicit in his reference to fire and water as homoeomeries, and he tries to show that Anaxagoras shared the presuppositions on which the theory of the four simple bodies is premised.[120] This is the significance of his remark that the material cause of Anaxagoras is the same as that of Anaximander and may be treated either as plural or single. He says that Anaxagoras 'would seem to mean' that it is single, and from this it may be inferred that he knows that Anaxagoras did not actually say anything of the sort. His authority is now not the text of Anaxagoras but the interpretation set forth in the passage of *Physics* A pre-

[118] *Dox.*, pp. 478, 23—479, 2.
[119] *Physics* 187 B 1–7. See note 121.
[120] *Dox.*, p. 479, 2–16.

ceding that referred to above.[121] This interpretation has been discussed in the section on Anaximander, but it should be reviewed here. Aristotle sets Anaxagoras, Anaximander, and Empedocles apart from those philosophers whose material principle is one, on the ground that for these three things are both one and many and generation is separation from the One of the pre-existent contraries. He knows that for all three the material cause principles are plural. His motive for reducing their principles to a unity is that he wishes to prove that these philosophers had a material principle that resembled his own prime matter. A similar motive is evident in a passage of *Metaphysics* A in which again the material principles of Anaxagoras are shown to be a unity.[122] This latter passage is probably the immediate source of Theophrastus' remark that Anaxagoras 'would seem to mean' a

[121] *Physics* 187 A 20–6.
This passage has been frequently misunderstood. Aristotle says of Anaxagoras and Empedocles: τὸν μὲν (Anaxagoras) ἄπειρα τά τε ὁμοιομερῆ καὶ τἀναντία, τὸν δὲ (Empedocles) τὰ καλούμενα στοιχεῖα (*Physics* 187 A 25–6). Burnet and others have translated τά τε ὁμοιομερῆ καὶ τἀναντία as 'both the homoeomeries *and* the contraries'. This translation cannot be correct. The point of Aristotle's argument is that all the Presocratics made the contraries principles (*Physics* 188 A 19) and the context shows clearly that the contraries are the only products of Anaxagoras' mixture with which he is here concerned. In the phrase, τά τε ὁμοιομερῆ καὶ τἀναντία, he is defining the homoeomeries by hendiadys. The purpose of the whole clause in which it stands is to distinguish Anaxagoras and Empedocles with regard to the number of their contrary principles; the homoeomeries (i.e. the contraries) of Anaxagoras are infinite, but the elements of the latter are finite in number. A few lines later Aristotle says that, according to Anaxagoras, nothing is purely and wholly white, black, sweet, flesh, or bone, but the nature of each thing is that of which it contains the most (*Physics* 187 B 4–7). This has been cited in support of the view that Aristotle believes that *both* the homoeomeries *and* the contraries are ingredients of particular things (G. Vlastos [*Phil. Rev.*, LIX (1950), 52]). But this statement and the one quoted above are not to be taken together as part of a single interpretation. This statement is part of an entirely different argument which is not concerned with contrariety at all but is directed simply against the infinity of Anaxagoras' principles (*Physics* 187 A 26—188 A 18). For the purpose of this argument Aristotle temporarily shifts his point of view and leaves aside the question of contrariety as such. To be sure, he mentions the contraries, white, black, and sweet, but these are not contraries in the sense that was used in *Physics* 187 A 12–26. They are not now principles of generation, but they are, along with flesh and bone, simply some of the infinite ingredients of the mixture.
[122] *Metaphysics* 989 A 30—B 6, B 16–21.

single thing by his material cause. In this instance Aristotle is trying to identify *Nous* and the homoeomeries with his pair of causes, form and matter. He says that, 'if it were assumed that Anaxagoras posited two elements, the supposition would be thoroughly in accord with an argument which Anaxagoras did not state but which he would have accepted if anyone had led him to it'.[123] As Aristotle admits, he is not stating Anaxagoras' doctrine but is giving it a logical development that Anaxagoras had neglected.

At the beginning of his report Theophrastus, following *Metaphysics* A, has said that Anaxagoras explained apparent generation and destruction by aggregation and segregation, and later he has explicitly attributed this theory to him again.[124] But the consequence of the view that Anaxagoras' mixture is a single indeterminate thing is that this mechanism is no longer suitable, since every particle of the mixture will be identical with every other. Theophrastus does not say what he now conceives the generative process to be. But, in the opening sentence of the passage in which this account occurs, Simplicius says that the principles of Anaxagoras are contrary; and, whether or not Simplicius is quoting from Theophrastus, this is undoubtedly how Theophrastus understands the homoeomeries, since contrariety is an essential part of Aristotle's interpretation of the mixture as a single thing.[125] Aristotle states what the contrariety means for Anaxagoras' theory of generation and distinction: the genesis of a specific thing is qualitative change.[126] Thus, the homoeomeries are not physical ingredients of infinite variety, but contrary forces inherent in the mixture; and separation from the mixture is not a mechanical process but the actualization of the inherent contraries. What had started as a correctly and clearly stated doctrine of 'like

---

[123] *Metaphysics* 989 A 30–3.　　[124] *Dox.*, pp. 478, 22–3; 479, 4–6.
[125] *Dox.*, p. 478, 17. The form of Simplicius' statement may have been influenced by *Physics* 184 B 21–2, on which he is commenting. But this does not decrease the likelihood that Simplicius found a similar statement in Theophrastus. Aristotle does not explicitly identify the doctrine meant at *Physics* 184 B 21–2. Simplicius' identification probably comes from Theophrastus.
[126] *Physics* 187 A 29–30. Cf. *De Generatione* 314 A 11–15, where Aristotle says that those who, like Anaxagoras, make the material principles more than one, must distinguish generation from alteration. He objects that Anaxagoras 'failed to understand his own utterance' since he said that generation and destruction are the same as alteration.

to like', in evidence of which Theophrastus produced Anaxagoras' own words, has now turned out to be a doctrine involving the specifically Aristotelian concept of contrariety.[127] With regard to the nature of the error of attributing this sort of contrariety to the Presocratics no more need be said. This instance is, however, particularly interesting, because both Aristotle and Theophrastus admit that their interpretation is possible only on the assumption that Anaxagoras did not understand or mean what he said. It shows, too, how far Theophrastus is prepared to go in accepting Aristotle's interpretations against the known facts of the doctrine interpreted. Further, the contradiction between this interpretation and the first one taken from *Metaphysics* A demonstrates again how Theophrastus can combine two or more of Aristotle's accounts without, apparently, being aware that they are made from fundamentally different points of view.*

PARMENIDES

Theophrastus' account of Parmenides is to be reconstructed from quotations by Alexander, Simplicius, and Diogenes Laertius.[128]

127 In *De Sensibus*, 1–2 and 27 ff. Theophrastus attributes contrariety in sensation to Anaxagoras, apparently finding evidence of this in Anaxagoras' statement that all sensation is accompanied by pain (*ibid.*, 29). This, again, is Aristotelian interpretation. The notion that there is contrast in sensation was probably common among the early philosophers, but it had nothing to do with quantitative change (Cherniss, p. 305, n. 57).

* A discussion of Archelaus, pp. 114–15 in the original, is here omitted, as is a discussion of Xenophanes, pp. 115–21. [Eds.]

128 On Parmenides, Simplicius' quotation from the *Physical Opinions* is limited to the statement that ἐν τοῖς πρὸς δόξαν Parmenides said that the principles are fire and earth (*Physical Opinions*, Frag. 3 [*Dox.*, p. 477, 13–14 = Simplicius *Phys.*, p. 25, 15–16]). More extensive fragments are contained in Alexander and Diogenes Laertius (*Physical Opinions*, Frag. 6 [*Dox.*, p. 482, 5–13 = Alexander, *Metaph.*, p. 31, 7–14]; *Physical Opinions*, Frag. 6a [*Dox.*, pp. 482, 14—483, 7 = Diogenes Laertius, ix. 21–2]).

All these sources say that Parmenides was the follower of Xenophanes (*Dox.*, pp. 480, 5–6; 482, 7–8; 482, 14–15). Theophrastus has made history out of Aristotle's parenthetical remark that Parmenides was *said* to be the student of Xenophanes (*Metaphysics* 986 B 22. See page 119). (Suidas [*Vors.*, I, p. 218, 22 f.] says that, according to Theophrastus, Parmenides was the student of Anaximander. This error is due to a misunderstanding of the statement in Diogenes Laertius [*Dox.*, p. 482, 14–15]: Ξενοφάνους δὲ διήκουσε Παρμενίδης . . . (τοῦτον Θεόφραστος ἐν τῇ Ἐπιτομῇ Ἀναξιμάνδρου φησὶν ἀκοῦσαι). "τοῦτον" here must be Xenophanes and not Parmenides [*Dox.*, p. 103].)

It is as follows. The philosophy of Parmenides took two different directions, the Way of Truth and the Way of Opinion.[129] According to the Way of Truth, the universe is one, ungenerated, eternal, limited, and spherical.[130] Parmenides proved the unity of the whole by this reasoning: That which is besides the existent is non-existent; the non-existent is nothing; therefore the existent is one.[131] To explain the generation of phenomena in accordance with the opinion of the many, however, Parmenides posited fire and earth as the efficient cause and material cause, and he said that from the warm and the cold all things are created.[132]

This is a paraphrase and conflation of elements from two passages in the *Metaphysics*. In the first, Aristotle asserts that the Eleatics, unlike the Ionians, recognized the necessity of an efficient cause to explain motion and that, since they failed to discover this cause, they declared that the unity of being is motionless and denied not only generation and destruction but all change.[133] Among them, he believes, Parmenides alone might be said to have been aware of the efficient cause, and he only inasmuch as he employed in a sense two causes. Recognition of the efficient cause is easier, Aristotle believes, for those who employ more than one principle, e.g. warm and cold, or fire and earth; for they treat fire as the source of movement and the other primary bodies as that which is moved. In the following chapter he repeats that, while the physicists generated the universe from their one principle, the Eleatics asserted that being is motionless.[134] He says that Parmenides seems to have grasped that which is one in definition and therefore said that it is limited. Parmenides had reasoned that, since there is no non-existent, being is one and nothing else is. But, being constrained to follow the phenomena and holding that while only the One exists according to definition many things exist according to sensation, he set up two causes, fire and earth, the former of which he ranked with being and the latter with non-being.

[129] *Dox.*, pp. 482, 8 and 10–14; 483, 3–4; 477, 13–14.
[130] *Dox.*, pp. 482, 10–11; 483, 14–15.   [131] *Dox.*, p. 483, 8–10.
[132] *Dox.*, pp. 482, 11–13; 482, 18—483, 1 (where read αἰτία at p. 482, 20, with Diels, for αὐτόν); 477, 13–14. Cf. Theophrastus, *De Sensibus*, 3 (*Dox.*, p. 499, 13–16).
[133] *Metaphysics* 984 A 27—984 B 8. Cf. Cherniss, p. 221, n. 18.
[134] *Metaphysics* 986 B 14—987 A 2.

The similarities between the accounts of Theophrastus and Aristotle are so obvious as to require no comment. The interpretation given of Parmenides makes him not only a monist who, because of his denial of motion, cannot be properly included in the history of causality,[135] but also a material pluralist who had anticipated the Peripatetic material and efficient causes. The treatment of him as a monist is substantiated by the fragments from the first part of his poem. The treatment of him as a pluralist is based on the supposition that the second part of his poem is as much a presentation of his own views as the first is. This supposition is incorrect; for, at the beginning of the second part, he warns that he has come to the end of his trustworthy speech and thought about the truth, and that henceforth he will give the beliefs of mortals in the deceptive ordering of his words.[136] Furthermore, the principles that Parmenides speaks of in the second part of the poem are not fire and earth, but 'the heavenly fire of flame' and 'dark night'.[137] The identification of night with earth is due to Aristotle's attempt—with complete disregard for Parmenides' words—to find qualitative contrariety in Parmenides by making his supposed principles square with the two limiting terms of the four simple bodies.[138] In order that Parmenides may be treated within the Peripatetic scheme of causality, it is assumed that of the two contrary principles the one must be material and the other efficient. The decision that fire is the active principle rests on the assumption that what Parmenides really meant was the Peripatetic warm; from this it follows that the other principle must be passive. There is nothing in Parmenides' poem to justify this interpretation. He does not say which of the principles is active and which passive, nor does he give any indication that he thinks heat to be the exclusive characteristic of fire and cold of night.

---

135 Aristotle, *Metaphysics* 986 B 10–14, 25–27 (so also *De Caelo* 298 B 15–20; *Physics* 184 B 26—185 A 1). Cf. *Dox.*, p. 480, 4–8 and Theophrastus *apud* Simplicius, *Phys.*, p. 20, 17–26.
136 Parmenides, Frag. 8, 50–53.
137 Parmenides, Frag. 8, 56–9. Simplicius (*Dox.*, p. 477, 14) says the principles were 'fire and earth, or rather light and dark'. The second interpretation is more nearly correct; but it is almost certainly Simplicius' own and is not from Theophrastus, since it does not appear in the excerpts of Alexander and Diogenes Laertius.
138 See Cherniss, pp. 47, n. 187, and 48, n. 192.

Although Theophrastus accepts Aristotle's interpretation of Parmenides' poem as regards the identification of fire and earth with the efficient and material causes, he himself gives evidence against this interpretation. Aristotle says that Parmenides set up fire and earth as causes because he was constrained to follow the phenomena. Theophrastus, on the other hand, says that Parmenides' aim was to explain the generation of phenomena according to the opinion of the multitude; and the care with which he distinguishes the two parts of the poem shows clearly that he is aware that the second part of the poem does not represent Parmenides' orthodox doctrine.¹³⁹ The fact that he nevertheless, like Aristotle, includes the second part of the poem in his historical treatment of Parmenides reveals how much he is disposed to follow the pattern of Aristotle's accounts even when, as here, he appears to know that Aristotle's interpretation is contrary to the Presocratic writings. In the *De Sensibus* he disregards the distinction he has made here between the two parts of the poem and derives his report of Parmenides' psychology from the Way of Opinion without giving a hint that the views he is stating are not Parmenides' own.¹⁴⁰

By his practice of excerpting particular passages from Aristotle, Theophrastus has here again, through the doxographers, given currency to an interpretation that rests on the sole authority of Aristotle but is at the same time only one of several interpretations made by Aristotle. Not only does Aristotle identify fire and night

¹³⁹ Aristotle, *Metaphysics* 986 B 31 ff. says: ἀναγκαζόμενος δ' ἀκολουθεῖν τοῖς φαινομένοις, καὶ τὸ ἓν μὲν κατὰ τὸν λόγον, πλείω δὲ κατὰ τὴν αἴσθησιν ὑπολαμβάνων εἶναι, δύο τὰς αἰτίας καὶ δύο τὰς ἀρχὰς πάλιν τίθησιν, θερμὸν καὶ ψυχρόν, οἷον πῦρ καὶ γῆν λέγων. In all three versions of Theophrastus' account, the two parts of Parmenides' poem are distinguished as being κατ' ἀλήθειαν and κατὰ δόξαν. Alexander, who is probably giving a *verbatim* quotation from Theophrastus, says Parmenides made the principles two 'for the purpose of explaining the genesis of phenomena according to the opinion of most people.' (Alexander, *Metaph.*, p. 31, 11–14 [*Dox.*, p. 482, 10–13]: κατ' ἀλήθειαν μὲν ἓν τὸ πᾶν . . . κατὰ δόξαν δὲ τῶν πολλῶν εἰς τὸ γένεσιν ἀποδοῦναι τῶν φαινομένων δύο ποιῶν τὰς ἀρχάς, πῦρ καὶ γῆν. Simplicius, *Phys.*, p. 25, 16 [*Dox.*, p. 477, 13–14]: ἐν τοῖς πρὸς δόξαν πῦρ καὶ γῆν. Diogenes Laertius, IX, 22 *Dox.*, p. 483, 3–4]: διττήν τ'ἔφη εἶναι τὴν φιλοσοφίαν τὴν μὲν κατ' ἀλήθειαν τὴν δὲ κατὰ δόξαν.)
¹⁴⁰ *De Sensibus*, 3.

with the efficient and material causes; even in one of the passages
from which Theophrastus has borrowed he places in opposition
to fire not earth alone but also water and the other simple
bodies,[141] and he associates fire with being, and earth with non-
being.[142] In another passage, in which he is seeking to establish
Hesiod and Parmenides as forerunners of Empedocles, he equates
Love, not fire, with the efficient cause.[143] The same variation is
found in the treatment of Parmenides' One. Theophrastus evidently takes the One to be corporeal.[144] The corporeality of the
One is certainly implied by Aristotle's attempt in *Metaphysics* A
to establish a historical relationship between the Eleatics and the
Ionian monists.[145] Elsewhere he states explicitly that neither
Parmenides nor Melissus believed that anything exists apart from
sensible substance.[146] But the very fact that he accepts the second
part of the poem as a statement of Parmenides' own doctrine
shows in itself that he thinks the first part is not physical in the
same sense as the second; and when he distinguishes Parmenides
from Melissus he says that the former *seems* to have held that the
One is conceptual, and the latter that it is material.[147] This diver-
gence in his accounts suggests strongly that it is not clear to him
from Parmenides' writings what the nature of the One is.[148] The
first interpretation might seem to be justified by the concrete
language used by Parmenides of the One,[149] and the second might
in part be prompted by the suspicion that the description of the
One is purely metaphorical. Ultimately, however, the first interpretation rests on the assumption that the Eleatic doctrine must
have been a correction of Ionian monism in the direction of his

[141] *Metaphysics* 984 B 5–8. The reference is chiefly to Parmenides. (Cf.
Cherniss, p. 221, n. 18.)

[142] *Metaphysics* 986 B 33—987 A 2; *De Generatione* 318 B 3–7.

[143] *Metaphysics* 984 B 23–31.

[144] N.B. his designation of it as motionless and spherical (*Dox.*, pp. 483, 14
and 482, 11). In the comparison he makes between the Eleatics and Leucippus
the implied basis of the comparison must be that for both schools being was
material (*Dox.*, p. 483, 14–17).

[145] *Metaphysics* 984 A 27 ff.

[146] *De Caelo* 298 B 21–22. Cf. *Physics* 207 A 15 ff., where it is clear that he
treats the One of both Melissus and Parmenides as material.

[147] *Metaphysics* 986 B 18–21.

[148] See Cherniss, p. 23, n. 85.

[149] E.g. Parmenides, Frag. 8, 22 ff.

own system; the second is only his conclusion of what he thinks must logically have been the distinction between Parmenides and Melissus. Neither of his interpretations, therefore, is decisive evidence one way or the other; and what has already been noticed of Theophrastus' technique of compilation does not support the belief that his choice of the one interpretation gives to that interpretation any greater authority.

THE ATOMISTS

Theophrastus reports that Leucippus, according to two different traditions, was said to be an Eleatic and a Milesian, and that he shared the philosophy of Parmenides but took the opposite direction to Parmenides and Xenophanes in his explanation of things.[150] They maintained that the All is one, indivisible, uncreated, and finite, and they agreed not even to investigate nonbeing; but he posited as elements the atoms, which he believed to be in constant motion and innumerable. He made the shapes infinite in number because he thought there was no reason why they should be of one sort rather than of another and because he observed that generation and change are unceasing. He held, further, that being is no more real than non-being but that both are causes in the generation of things; for, supposing the substance of the atoms to be compact and full, he called them being, and he said that they are moved in the void, which he called nonbeing. At this point Theophrastus interrupts his account to say that in like manner Leucippus' associate, Democritus, made his principles the full and the void, calling the one being and the other non-being. Positing the atoms as material, he and Leucippus generated other things by the differences of the atoms. These differences they thought to be three—rhythm, intercontact, and turning, i.e. shape, order, and position.[151] Theophrastus now

[150] *Physical Opinions*, Frag. 8 (= *Dox.*, pp. 483, 11—484, 11 = Simplicius, *Phys.*, p. 28, 4–24).
[151] *Dox.*, p. 484, 1–5. That these lines are a digression is shown by the sentence that follows them: πεφυκέναι γὰρ τὸ ὅμοιον ὑπὸ τοῦ ὁμοίου κινεῖσθαι κτλ. (*Dox.*, p. 484, 5 ff.) This sentence does not refer to the differences of the atoms or to the generation of things by them but to the movement of the atoms in the void, which Theophrastus has been discussing prior to the digression (*Dox.*, p. 483, 22).

returns to the main line of his account with a statement intended to explain the movement of the atoms in the void. Leucippus and Democritus, he says, held that like is naturally moved by like, that things akin are borne to each other, and that when each shape is inserted into a new aggregation it produces a different arrangement. Thus, by their infinite principles, Leucippus and Democritus professed that they alone could give a reasonable explanation of all modifications and substances, as well as of the cause and manner of generation.

It will be seen that Theophrastus' digression on the similarity between the doctrines of Leucippus and Democritus closely follows Aristotle's brief report of atomism in *Metaphysics* A.[152] Aristotle says that Leucippus and his associate, Democritus, made their principles the full and the void, calling the one being and the other non-being.[153] As the monists generated all other things by modification of their principle by the rare and the dense, so these two said that differences in matter are the causes of other things. These differences, they thought, are rhythm, intercontact, and turning, i.e. shape, order, and position.[154] Aristotle ends by saying that, like the others (i.e. the monists), Leucippus and Democritus neglected the cause and manner of motion. This is undoubtedly

---

[152] *Metaphysics* 985 B 4–17. Cf. *Dox.*, p. 484, 1–5. (Commenting on the relationship of these passages Diels [*ad Dox.*, p. 484, 1] says, 'contra de ceteris ὡς γὰρ ὕλην κτλ. [*Dox.*, p. 484, 3–5] accurate Aristoteli respondentibus nihil affirmo'. A comparison of the two passages will show that Diels was unnecessarily cautious.)

[153] *Metaphysics* 985 B 8–10. Cf. *Dox.*, p. 483, 19–21. Aristotle says that the full and the void are causes τῶν ὄντων (985 B 9); Theophrastus says, more accurately, τοῖς γιγνομένοις (*Dox.*, p. 483, 20) but again, probably influenced by Aristotle's sentence, he uses τοῖς οὖσι (*Dox.*, p. 484, 3). Aristotle refers to the full as πλῆρες καὶ στερεόν (985 B 7); Theophrastus, ναστὴν καὶ πλήρη (*Dox.*, p. 483, 21). ναστός is probably a technical term found by Theophrastus in atomistic writings. It does not occur in the *Metaphysics*, but is used in a passage quoted by Simplicius from Aristotle's Περὶ Δημοκρίτου = Frag. 208 (Rose, Teubner edition, p. 166, 5).

[154] *Metaphysics* 985 B 10–13: καὶ καθάπερ οἱ ἓν ποιοῦντες τὴν ὑποκειμένην οὐσίαν τἆλλα τοῖς πάθεσιν αὐτῆς γεννῶσι τὸ μανὸν καὶ τὸ πυκνὸν ἀρχὰς τιθέμενοι τῶν παθημάτων, τὸν αὐτὸν τρόπον καὶ οὗτοι τὰς διαφορὰς αἰτίας τῶν ἄλλων εἶναί φασιν. Aristotle does not say what the analogue of τὴν ὑποκειμένην οὐσίαν is in the atomistic theory. The corresponding sentence in Theophrastus is an explication of what is implicit in Aristotle's sentence: ὡς <γὰρ> ὕλην τὰς ἀτόμους ὑποτιθέντες τὰ λοιπὰ γεννῶσι ταῖς διαφοραῖς αὐτῶν (*Dox.*, p. 484, 3–4). On the διαφοραί cf. *Metaphysics* 985 B 13–17 and *Dox.*, p. 484, 4–5.

what Theophrastus means by saying that they believed that like is *naturally* moved by like; that is, the atomists did not supply a separate cause of motion but, like the Milesians, they simply made motion a property of matter.[155]

With the main body of Theophrastus' account should be compared the passage of the *De Generatione* in which Aristotle gives what he supposes to have been the antecedents of atomism.[156] Aristotle says that some of the ancients believed that being must be one and motionless on the grounds that the void is non-being and that, without the void, motion and plurality would be impossible.[157] The same objection, they asserted, held true not only against the theory that there are many and a void but also against the theory that the universe is discretes-in-contact; for on the latter theory, if the universe is divisible throughout, there is no one and no many but only a void, and at the same time there can be no motion. Reasoning this way they were led to transcend sense-perception and to disregard it on the belief that one should follow the argument.[158] Leucippus, however, thought that he had a theory that harmonized with sense-perception and would not abolish generation and destruction, motion, or plurality; and he made these concessions to phenomena.[159] He conceded that motion is impossible without a void and that the void is non-being; but he held that the full is not one but is composed of units which are infinite in number and are indivisible because of their minuteness. He said that the void exists and that the many move

---

[155] *Metaphysics* 985 B 19–20. Cf. Dox., p. 484, 5–7.

Theophrastus (*De Causis Plantarum*, vi. 7, 2) says that the atomists can explain change in three ways only: that the shapes of the atoms change; that all atoms are inherent but that change is caused by the withdrawal of the atoms that gave the previous complex its character; or that some atoms enter and some go out. The first explanation, he says, is impossible because the atoms are impassive; the second and third are ridiculous because in both cases Democritus must supply the efficient cause. For further criticism of the atomists' failure to give the cause of motion, see Theophrastus, *De Sensibus*, 52; Aristotle, *Physics*, 252 A 32—B 5, 265 B 23–6, *De Caelo* 300 B 8–11, *Metaphysics* 1071 B 33–4.

[156] *De Generatione* 325 A 2 ff.

[157] *De Generatione* 325 A 2–6. Cf. Dox., p. 483, 14–15.

[158] *De Generatione* 325 A 13–15. Cf. Dox., p. 483, 15–16 (καὶ τὸ μὴ ὂν μηδὲ ζητεῖν συγχωρούντων).

[159] *De Generatione* 325 A 23–6. Cf. Dox., p. 483, 18–19 (καὶ γένεσιν καὶ μεταβολὴν ἀδιάλειπτον ἐν τοῖς οὖσι θεωρῶν).

in it.[160] Generation and destruction he believed to be due to the aggregation and segregation of the many (i.e. the atoms), action and passion occurring wherever the many are in contact and generation being caused by their being put together and becoming intertwined.[161]

In these two passages Aristotle is considering atomism from two entirely different points of view and he gives two different representations of the theory. The result is that, by inserting the report derived from the *Metaphysics* into that derived from the *De Generatione*, Theophrastus has made his account self-contradictory. According to the interpretation taken from the *Metaphysics*, the atoms are distinguished by shape, order, and position;[162] in that taken from the *De Generatione*, shape alone is emphasized as if it were the sole distinguishing characteristic of the atoms, and the word 'shape' is used as if it were equivalent to 'atom'.[163] In the account of the *Metaphysics*, all change is said to be due to the differentiation of the material substrate; and, by saying that the atomists substituted shape, order, and position for the rare and dense, Aristotle suggests that the atomists' mechanism of change in some way involved the interaction of contraries.[164] Theophrastus repeats this interpretation, but in his very next sentence —now under the influence of the *De Generatione*—he says that the atomists believed that interaction occurs between similars and that both substantial and qualitative change result from a mechanical reordering of the atoms in the void.[165]

---

[160] *De Generatione* 325 A 26–31. Cf. *Dox.*, p. 483, 16–17. Theophrastus says that the atoms of Leucippus are ἄπειρα καὶ ἀεὶ κινούμενα (*Dox.*, p. 483, 16). On the infinity of motion, see Aristotle, *Metaphysics* 1071 B 31–3, 1072 A 6–7, *De Caelo* 300 B 8–10. In *De Generatione* 315 B 9–11, Aristotle reports that Democritus made the shapes infinite because he thought truth to be in appearance and because phenomena are contrary and infinite. Cf. Theophrastus' statement that Leucippus made the shapes of the atoms infinite because he saw no reason why they should be of one sort rather than another and because he observed the constant generation and change in things (*Dox.*, p. 483, 16–19).

[161] *De Generatione* 325 A 31–4. Cf. *Dox.*, p. 484, 5–8. Aristotle does not here state specifically that like is affected by like, but this principle is presupposed by the process of separation. Elsewhere he does attribute this principle to Democritus (*De Generatione* 323 B 10–15).

[162] *Dox.*, p. 484, 4–5; cf. *Metaphysics* 985 B 13–16.

[163] *Dox.*, pp. 483, 17 and 484, 7. Throughout *De Generatione* A 8 (see 325 B 18, 27–8), as well as in *De Generatione* 315 B 9–12, σχῆμα = ἄτομος.

[164] See note 154.   [165] See note 161.

227

The conflation by Theophrastus of Aristotle's two accounts has had other more serious consequences for the history of atomism. In the opening statement Theophrastus has said that Leucippus was reported to be an Eleatic and a Milesian and that he shared the philosophy of Parmenides. This statement, along with doxographical testimonia to the effect that Leucippus was an Abderite and the student of Zeno,[166] has been used to reconstruct not only Leucippus' own biography but also the personal and doctrinal connections between the schools of the Milesians, Eleatics, and atomists.[167] Lest it be objected that Theophrastus is merely reporting well-known facts, it may be pointed out that Aristotle appears to know nothing of Leucippus' life except that Democritus the Abderite was his associate. Nor does Aristotle appear to know in what way the doctrine of Leucippus was related to that of Democritus or was like or unlike it; he identifies the two men to such an extent that he attributes the same doctrine now to both, now to one alone, and now to the other.[168] This identification has undoubtedly led the doxographers to infer that Leucippus was, like Democritus, an Abderite. The other biographical data reported by Theophrastus and the doxographers have been derived in the same way.

Theophrastus says that Leucippus 'shared' the philosophy of Parmenides; but he proceeds to a statement of the differences between Leucippus and the Eleatics that would make it appear that Leucippus not only did not share any of Parmenides' philosophy but had in fact been utterly opposed to it. The *De Generatione* passage from which he has borrowed indicates what Theophrastus means by 'shared'. He is referring to what Aristotle conceives to have been the starting-point of the atomists, namely, Leucippus' acceptance of the Eleatic axioms that there can be no

166 Diogenes Laertius, ix. 30 (Λ. 'Ελεάτης, ὡς δέ τινες 'Αβδηρίτης, κατ' ἐνίους δὲ Μήλιος [Μιλήσιος should be read]. οὗτος ἤκουσε Ζήνωνος.); [Galen], *Hist. Philos.*, 3 (τούτου [Zeno] δὲ Λ. ὁ 'Αβδηρίτης ἀκουστής κτλ.); Aetius, i. 3, 15 (Λ. Μιλήσιος); Hippolytus, *Refut.*, i. 12, 1 (Λ. δὲ Ζήνωνος ἑταῖρος); Epiphanius, *Adv. Haer.*, iii. 2, 9 (Λ. ὁ Μιλήσιος, κατὰ δέ τινας 'Ελεάτης). Tzetzes (*Chil.*, ii. 980) says that Leucippus was the student of Melissus; the absence of reference to Melissus in the authorities quoted above indicates that Tzetzes is not following the general doxographical tradition.
167 E.g., Burnet, pp. 331 ff.
168 *Metaphysics* 985 B 4–5; *De Generatione* 325 A 1, 23; Frag. 208 (Rose, Teubner edition, p. 166, 1).

motion or plurality without a void and that the void is non-being. Aristotle does not mention any of the Eleatics by name. It is certain, however, that the axioms referred to are those of Parmenides,[169] and the application of these axioms against a universe composed of discretes-in-contact is apparently the attack of Zeno on Empedocles' restatement of the material pluralism that Parmenides had sought to refute.[170] In so far, then, as Leucippus accepted these axioms, he might be said to have shared the philosophy of Parmenides, as well as of Zeno, and he might be said to be in the Eleatic tradition. However, Aristotle also represents Leucippus as attempting to reconcile Eleatic logic with the plurality and change of the phenomenal world and, in *Metaphysics* A, classes him with the Milesian monists, who took motion for granted without troubling to explain it.[171] Leucippus might also, therefore, be said to have shared the philosophy of the physicists. In one fragment Theophrastus makes more explicit the connection that Aristotle believes to have existed between the doctrines of the Milesians and atomists.[172] He says that Democritus advanced his theory of the atoms because he thought the explanations based on the warm, cold, etc., were crude. By this interpretation the atomists are represented as accepting and correcting the physics of the Milesians as they had the logic of the Eleatics. Thus, with regard to the suppositions that Aristotle makes about the background of atomism in his two accounts, Leucippus might be said to be both an Eleatic and a Milesian. There need be no other basis for such a statement than the two Aristotelian passages noted. Theophrastus—or Simplicius and the other doxographers —apparently concluded that relationship of doctrine implied identity of birthplace, and that Leucippus not only owed part of

---

[169] De Generatione 325 A 26–8. N.b. ἀπεφήναντο περὶ τῆς ἀληθείας (325 A 17) and ἐκ τοῦ κατ'ἀληθείας ἑνός (325 A 35).

[170] De Generatione 325 A 6–12. Cf. H. H. Joachim, *Aristotle on Coming-to-be and Passing-away*, pp. 160–1; Cherniss, p. 95, n. 401.

Theophrastus (*Dox.*, p. 483, 13) links Xenophanes with Parmenides as a representative of the Eleatic school. Diels (*Dox.*, p. 483, n. 11) suggests, on the basis of Hippolytus' report, that Zeno should be added after Xenophanes. More probably, Zeno should replace Xenophanes. Xenophanes is not associated in any way with the atomists elsewhere in the doxographers. In De Generatione A 8, Aristotle does not mention Xenophanes by name, nor does he refer to any doctrine that can be identified as that of Xenophanes.

[171] Metaphysics 985 B 10–13, 19–20.

[172] Physical Opinions, Frag. 13 (*Dox.*, p. 491, 19–21).

his doctrine to Parmenides and Zeno but was also a pupil in the supposed Eleatic school. There is nothing in the Aristotelian passages to support these conclusions. Aristotle does not suggest that Leucippus was an Eleatic or Milesian by birth nor even that Leucippus had personal contact with any of the Eleatics. If he had been able to bolster his argument for the doctrinal connection between Leucippus and the Eleatics by reference to known facts of Leucippus' life, he would probably have done so.

But, even if by his double reference to Leucippus as an Eleatic and as a Milesian, Theophrastus intends to refer only to the doctrinal connections suggested by Aristotle, the historical validity of these connections is dubious. That the atomists were influenced by the Eleatics and attempted to answer the objections raised by them is beyond question. The impression given by Aristotle in the *De Generatione* and by Theophrastus in the part of his account derived from that work is, however, that the atomists considered the assertion of the void's existence to be sufficient answer. Clearly it was not, and the atomists can hardly have thought that it was. When Melissus restated Parmenides' doctrine against Empedocles and Anaxagoras, he proved not only that the void is non-being but also that the initiation of movement by such forces as these philosophers had postulated is impossible.[173] To save phenomenal change, therefore, the atomists had also to assert that movement has no beginning but is eternal. Both Aristotle and Theophrastus appear to think that Leucippus did make this assertion.[174] But in the passages discussed here they gloss over this essential feature of Leucippus' doctrine as if it were due to his failure to supply efficient causality rather than to his attempt to defend himself against one of the main attacks to which Empedocles and Anaxagoras had been susceptible. Furthermore, they do not notice that it was not Parmenides or Zeno but Melissus who, while showing the impossibility of such a pluralism as Anaxagoras', had at the same time shown how a plurality could be made consistent with Eleatic logic. He argued that, if there are to be many things, each of them must have the same characteristics as the Eleatic One.[175] It was just this requirement that the atoms of Leucippus were intended to meet. But Aristotle and Theophrastus so underestimate the influence of Melissus on atomism, that Aristotle dismisses him with the comment that 'some'

[173] Melissus, Frag. 2.   [174] See note 160.   [175] Melissus, Frag. 8.

believed the All to be infinite,[176] and Theophrastus makes no reference to him at all. Theophrastus says that the All of Parmenides is one, ungenerated, and finite, while Leucippus declared the atoms to be infinite and in continual movement and observed that change and generation is unceasing.[177] Theophrastus' purpose is to find as complete opposition as possible between the atoms and the Eleatic One, and to do this he must exclude the One of Melissus because it, like the atoms, is infinite. It will be noted, too, that, in so opposing the atomists to the Eleatics, Theophrastus obscures what was in fact a main point of agreement between the two groups; although they held opposed views regarding phenomenal change, they agreed that the principles are incapable of change. Whatever connection the atomistic doctrine may have had with the Milesian on the other hand, it is at least clear that the connection made by Aristotle is due to his belief that, since the atomists had not provided a source of motion comparable to his efficient cause, they must, like the Milesians, have failed altogether to account for motion. It is patently incorrect to imply that the atomists had ignored the question of movement and that by rejecting such forces as Anaxagoras' *Nous* they were simply returning to the Milesian view; and it is equally incorrect to imply that, since they had neglected all the causes but the material, their explanation of change must be essentially the same as that of the Milesians.

Finally, the other reports of Theophrastus and Aristotle should be reviewed briefly in relation to those discussed above. It has been seen that in the *Metaphysics* account the atoms are distinguished by shape, order, and position and in the *De Generatione*, by shape alone. In the *De Sensibus*, however, Theophrastus recognizes, as Aristotle does in the *Physics* and elsewhere, that the atoms are also distinguished by size.[178] The interpretation taken from the *Metaphysics* presupposes that change in some way

---

[176] *De Generatione* 325 A 14–15. Cf. *Metaphysics* 986 B 18–21.

[177] *Dox.*, p. 483, 14–19. Cf. Hippolytus, *Refut.*, i. 12.

[178] *De Sensibus* 60; cf. *Physics* 203 B 1–2, *De Caelo* 303 A 14–15.

Theophrastus says, in the *De Sensibus*, that Democritus distinguished heavy and light by the size of the atoms (61, 68, 71). This may be correct, but it may be derived from Aristotle, *Physics* 326 A 9–10: καίτοι βαρύτερόν γε κατὰ τὴν ὑπεροχήν φησιν εἶναι Δημόκριτος ἕκαστον τῶν ἀδιαιρέτων. If this sentence is Theophrastus' source, then clearly Theophrastus has misunderstood Aristotle. Aristotle does not mean that each atom is heavier in accordance

involves contrariety, and, according to that of the *De Generatione*, change is due to the interaction of similars. But, having thus committed himself so positively on both sides of the question, in the first sentence of his account of Democritus' psychological theory in the *De Sensibus*, Theophrastus says that Democritus did not make it clear whether sense perception is due to the interaction of contraries or similars.[179] This avowal of ignorance is comment enough on the definiteness with which both conflicting notions are attributed to atomists in the *Physical Opinions* fragment. That Democritus did not specifically answer the question asked by Theophrastus in the *De Sensibus* is undoubtedly true; it would simply not occur to him to do so, since in his time all interaction was thought to be between similars. In his closer examination of Democritus in the *De Sensibus*, Theophrastus appears to recognize this fact when he attributes to Democritus the theory that like things best know like;[180] but even then he is so predisposed to interpret Democritus in terms of the Peripatetic theory of sense perception that he cannot refrain from suggesting that Democritus subscribed to the same notion.[181] Lastly, although in both the *Metaphysics* and *De Generatione* interpretations all change is made to result from a single process, in another passage Aristotle claims to find in the atomists the distinction between substantial and qualitative change.[182] He says that generation and destruction are due to the aggregation and separation of the atoms and that alteration is due to order and position.*

[179] *De Sensibus*, 49 (*Dox.*, p. 513, 10–11).
[180] *De Sensibus*, 50 (*Dox.*, p. 513, 27). Cf. Democritus, Frag. 164.
[181] *De Sensibus*, 49, 72. Theophrastus' whole account of Democritus in the *De Sensibus* shows an inclination to assume that Democritus employed contrariety.
[182] *De Generatione* 315 B 6–9.
* A discussion of Metrodorus the Chian, pp. 128–9 in the original, is here omitted. [Eds.]

---

with the excess of its weight, but that each atom has relative weight when compared with any other (cf. Cherniss, p. 97, n. 412). In fact, Aristotle remarks that none of his predecessors had anything to say about absolute weight (*De Caelo* 308 A 9–11). Theophrastus himself seems elsewhere to have excluded weight from the characteristics of the atoms. Aetius (i. 3, 18; i. 12, 6) makes a point of noting that, while the atoms of Epicurus are distinguished by shape, size, and weight, those of Democritus are distinguished only by shape and size.

CONCLUSION

It has been seen that Theophrastus' treatment of Presocratic causes owes not only its general point of view but also much of the detail of its organization and wording to the *Metaphysics* A summary, and that his departures from that summary are usually only for the purpose of gathering additional material from Aristotle's other accounts and from the works of the Presocratics. The improbabilities and demonstrable errors that arise directly from his close adherence to one or other of Aristotle's accounts need not be retold here. I take it as self-evident that, when he merely copies or paraphrases an erroneous or improbable account from Aristotle, his copy or paraphrase is no better or worse than its original. There remains to consider briefly some of the features of his work that, although due to his use of Aristotle, are due to his method of using the text of Aristotle rather than to Aristotle's intentions.

(1) Theophrastus' practice of supplementing the *Metaphysics* summary with statements made by Aristotle in other contexts often causes his accounts to be a bewildering patchwork of ill-fitting pieces. In *Metaphysics* A, Aristotle does not say what mechanism of change was used by the Milesians. In the *Physics* (187 A 12–16) he says that all physical monists accounted for change by rarefaction and condensation. This latter statement Theophrastus applies not only to Anaximenes and Diogenes, of whom it is true; he also applies it to Hippasus and Heraclitus, of whom, as Aristotle knows, it cannot be true (see pp. 187 ff.). Aristotle omits Anaximander from the *Metaphysics* summary. Theophrastus resorts, therefore, to two *Physics* interpretations in one of which Anaximander is a monist and in the other, both a monist and pluralist. The contradiction in the second interpretation, Theophrastus pretends to solve by accepting Aristotle's patently false identification of the primordial mixture with un-differentiated matter (see pp. 198 f.). Similarly, according to the account taken from the *Metaphysics*, Anaxagoras is said to have posited infinite material principles, but by the interpretation just mentioned he becomes, like Anaximander, a monist (see pp. 217 f.). In Empedocles Theophrastus finds the inconsistency that sometimes the material principles are four and sometimes six. This inconsistency, however, is due not to failure on the part of

Empedocles but to Theophrastus' juxtaposition of two separate interpretations of Aristotle, the latter of which rests on the view that Empedocles' Sphere is a homogeneous compound (see pp. 210 f.). The atomists, according to the interpretation of the *Metaphysics*, differed from the Milesians only in substituting shape, order, and position for the rare and dense; but by the interpretation taken from the *De Generatione* their doctrine is related to the Eleatics, and a different account is given of their material principles and of their theory of change (see pp. 227 f.). This sort of confusion and contradiction was probably characteristic of all Theophrastus' doxographical writings; for some of the accounts in the *De Sensibus* are not only inconsistent with the accounts of the principles but also contain inner contradictions (see p. 232).

(2) The interpretations that Theophrastus has borrowed from Aristotle are often only one or two out of several different interpretations that Aristotle offers of a theory. It cannot be said that Theophrastus' use of one interpretation gives that interpretation added weight unless we are prepared to maintain that he has considered the merits of the various possibilities, has chosen one, and has consciously discarded those that do not agree with it. The contradictions observed in the preceding paragraph would be impossible if this were the case. The factor that governed his selection was clearly the availability of material. In *Metaphysics* A he found Aristotle's most comprehensive discussion of causal theories; from this he went to other passages in which Aristotle discusses several doctrines in a small space, notably *Physics* A 4 and *De Generatione* A 8; and he referred to special discussions of individual philosophers only when, as for Anaximander, these general passages were inadequate. This method is almost bound to do injustice both to the author excerpted and to the facts of the doctrines discussed. Even if Aristotle's interpretations are all influenced by his own beliefs, it is clear—and must have been to him—that some are more in accord with the stated doctrines of the Presocratics than others are. As it happens, some of the accounts in the passages that Theophrastus has used are sheer conjecture, whereas some that fall in passages that Theophrastus has not used are undoubtedly nearer the truth, e.g. Aristotle's report of how Heraclitus described change (see p. 187).

234

(3) The fact that Theophrastus extracts Aristotle's interpretations from their contexts is a frequent source of misrepresentation and confusion. Aristotle's interpretations are not doxographical accounts; they are parts of philosophical debates in which he is far from being a disinterested judge (Cherniss, pp. 347–50). The context usually warns us of the particular twist that he is likely to give a doctrine. In Theophrastus there is no such warning, and when he recasts Aristotle's arguments they assume the form of straightforward exposition. Needless to say, our lack of context becomes especially serious when Theophrastus compounds his report from two or more different passages, in each of which Aristotle's argument depends on a different set of assumptions about a doctrine. This difficulty is well illustrated by Theophrastus' double interpretation of Anaximander and Anaxagoras; for without the context of Aristotle we do not know on what grounds the material cause of these philosophers can be regarded as both singular and plural.

(4) Theophrastus does not always reproduce accurately the details of the accounts that he has borrowed. Sometimes the inaccuracies are of slight importance, but they should be noted because they are characteristic of the sort of change that has frequently taken place between the original statement of Aristotle and the statement as it appears in the later doxographers. It has been seen how Aristotle's conjecture about the views of Thales has, through the *Physical Opinions*, hardened into a definite statement that Aristotle deliberately avoided (see pp. 92 f.). One further example should be added. The basis of the doxographical tradition about early notions of matter is the equation with Aristotelian prime matter. This equation is derived by Theophrastus from the *Metaphysics*, but Theophrastus has neglected the qualification that Aristotle attaches to it. Aristotle prefaces his discussion of the early material principles with a reference to them as principles 'in the form of matter' (*Metaphysics* 983 B 7) and thus indicates that these principles, being elements or some other definite bodies, are not primitive matter in his sense at all and that therefore the similarity between these principles and his own is at best very limited.

(5) Two special types of misrepresentation that are caused by Theophrastus' disregard for Aristotle's precise words should be mentioned. First, he tends to overinterpret Aristotle's statements.

When Aristotle says, for example, that the principle of Thales and Hippo was water, that of Anaximenes and Diogenes air, and that of Hippasus and Heraclitus fire, he probably means no more than that. There is no reason to conclude, as Theophrastus apparently does, that when he elsewhere refers to anonymous doctrines whose principles were the elements, he is referring to the members of these pairs. His attribution of rarefaction–condensation to the monists as a group is only what follows from the presuppositions of his own system, and his failure to mention names is perhaps to be explained by his lack of definite evidence. Furthermore, when he links two philosophers with respect to one theory, it does not follow that when he mentions one member of the pair elsewhere he must mean both. So, although Theophrastus was right in understanding him to mean that the material causes of Anaximander and Anaxagoras were similar, it does not necessarily follow, as Theophrastus supposes, that he means that Anaximander subscribes to Anaxagoras' homoeomery theory. Much of the later doxographical tradition relating to little known figures like Thales and Hippasus is probably due to overinterpretation of this sort.

(6) A second kind of overinterpretation is the development of biography from doctrinal affinities. The most striking example of this is the connection that Theophrastus makes between the Milesians, Eleatics, and atomists. From Aristotle's logical reconstruction of the relationship of their doctrines, Theophrastus has produced a scheme of teacher–student relationships: Anaximander–Xenophanes–Parmenides–Leucippus–Democritus (see pp. 224 f. and 228 f.). Similar in origin are probably also the links Parmenides–Empedocles and Archelaus–Socrates (see note 75). The series Thales–Anaximander–Anaximenes–Anaxagoras–Archelaus, which appears consistently in the doxographers, probably starts with Theophrastus and may have been derived in the same way (see note 102). It may be objected that Theophrastus was in the position to know such facts about the lives of at least the later Presocratics. But Aristotle, who might be expected to be no less well informed than Theophrastus, reports only that Parmenides 'is said' to have been the student of Xenophanes and that Democritus was the associate of Leucippus. This fact is significant because one of the premises of the *Metaphysics* summary is the continuity in the evolution of causal theory, and

the biographical connections stated by Theophrastus coincide to a marked degree with what Aristotle imagines the course of this evolution to have been. Those who will not concede that Theophrastus has made history out of logic must explain why Aristotle has failed to confirm his logic by history.

(7) The common supposition that Theophrastus made use of the original writings of the Presocratics is supported, in the fragments studied, by his quotations from almost all the major Presocratics after Thales. The texts of the Presocratics are, however, no protection against the influence of Aristotle, for in almost every instance the meaning of the quotation is distorted in order to yield proof of an Aristotelian interpretation that is clearly impossible. Thus, Anaximander's metaphor about justice is proof of Aristotelian contrariety (see pp. 195 f.); Heraclitus' figure about the exchange of things for fire is interpreted as evidence of rarefaction–condensation (see p. 187); verses from Empedocles are quoted as proof that he posited six material principles (see pp. 208 f.); Anaxagoras is rightly quoted to the effect that the nature of things is due to the predominance in them of one kind of particle, and the process of generation is rightly understood to be the movement of like to like, but a few lines later the primitive mixture is treated as a unified substratum of qualitative change (see pp. 216 ff.); and, although Theophrastus has apparently referred to enough of Parmenides' poem to know that the second part of it is the opinion of the multitude, he nevertheless accepts Aristotle's interpretation which is based on this part (see pp. 222 f.). Furthermore, there is no indication that in compiling his accounts of the causal theories he made use of much more— if any more—of the original writings than he quotes. Several of his quotations appear to be the basis of the Aristotelian interpretation that he repeats. This suggests that he may not have consulted the complete texts of the Presocratics at all but may have referred to a collection of excerpts made for use in the Lyceum.

In sum, the fragments considered disclose no evidence that Theophrastus employed his knowledge of the Presocratics in such a way as to exercise independent judgement about them. Despite his apparent investigation of the original texts, his accounts are in all essentials simply repetitions of some of the interpretations that he found in Aristotle and have, therefore, the same deficiencies.

Further, by his method of selection and adaptation he has frequently misrepresented his source and has exaggerated the faults present in it. It must be concluded that, with regard to the Presocratic causes at least, he is a thoroughly biased witness and is even less trustworthy than Aristotle.

IX

ARISTOTLE AS HISTORIAN

W. K. C. Guthrie

THE work of Cherniss on Aristotle's criticism of the Presocratics may be compared with that of Jaeger on the development of Aristotle's own thought as contained in his *Aristoteles* of 1923. Jaeger modestly described that epoch-making work as a *Grundlegung* or foundation for the history of the philosopher's development, and as such it has been of value not only for itself but in the stimulus it has given to further study, in the course of which the balance of its conclusions has been to some extent altered. Cherniss's own study is of the same pioneer kind, and if I confess to a feeling that it goes rather too far, the comparison with the now classic work of Jaeger will, I hope, make clear my general admiration and appreciation of the fact that it is a permanent contribution with which all future scholarship will have to reckon.

I cannot at this stage even begin to discuss in detail the mass of erudition on which Cherniss's case is built up. Nevertheless, the very widespread acceptance of his strictures on Aristotle's historical sense suggest that anyone to whom they seem extreme should lose no time in giving voice to his misgivings, even in general terms, before they become irrevocably canonical. This thought has been prompted by the recent monograph of Mr J. B. McDiarmid, *Theophrastus on the Presocratic Causes*,[1] at the beginning of which we read simply that 'the question of Aristotle's bias has been dealt with exhaustively by H. Cherniss', whose views then become, without further remark, the starting-point of the younger scholar's own inquiry into the reliability of Theophrastus. Since in what follows I may speak critically of McDiarmid on several points, let me say that his main thesis,

[1] *Harvard Studies in Classical Philology*, LXI (1953), 85–156; above, Ch. VIII.

the dependence of Theophrastus on Aristotle in much of his φυσικῶν δόξαι and the consequent danger of regarding him as a separate authority for Presocratic thought, seems true enough. The derivation of Theophrastus' judgements from those of his master was already beginning to be recognized with fruitful results,[2] and the time was ripe for a general review of the evidence. Here we are concerned with Aristotle himself. The length to which acceptance of Cherniss's criticism as 'exhaustive' may lead is seen in the section on Anaximenes and Diogenes of Apollonia, where we read (above, p. 204) that Theophrastus probably had the writings of Diogenes available, but 'Diogenes' writings are at any rate no protection against the influence of Aristotle'. Now for anyone to whom, as to ourselves, the writings of Diogenes are *not* available, that seems an assertion of unparalleled boldness, matched only by the statement on p. 221, concerning a Peripatetic interpretation of Parmenides' Way of Opinion, that 'there is nothing in Parmenides' poem to justify this interpretation'. If Mr McDiarmid had written what is all that any of us has a right to say—i.e. 'there is nothing in the extant fragments of Parmenides' poem . . .'—we should have been properly reminded of how miserably scanty the surviving fragments of the Way of Opinion are. That he does not do so is due to his antecedent conviction, based on Cherniss, of Aristotle's 'complete disregard' for anything that Parmenides said.

Cherniss's views are summarized by McDiarmid at the beginning of his study as follows (p. 180):

Aristotle is not interested in historical facts as such at all. He is constructing his own system of philosophy, and his predecessors are of interest to him only in so far as they furnish material to this end. He believes that his system is final and conclusive and that, therefore, all earlier thinkers have been groping towards it and can be stated in its terms. Holding this belief, he does not hesitate to modify or distort not only the detailed views but also the fundamental attitudes of his predecessors or to make articulate the implications that doctrines may have for him but could not have had for their authors.

[2] As by Kirk in his *Heraclitus: the Cosmic Fragments* (1954). Cf., e.g., p. 319: 'The theory of an ἐκπύρωσις in Heraclitus was perhaps directly derived by Theophrastus (*like most of his historical judgements*) from Aristotle.' [Italics mine.]

240

Cherniss himself says:[3]

> Aristotle as a philosopher is, of course, entirely justified in inquiring what answer any of the Presocratic systems could give to the problem of casuality as he had formulated it; but to suppose that such an inquiry is historical, that is, to suppose that any of these systems was elaborated with a view to the problem as formulated by Aristotle, is likely to lead to misinterpretation of those systems and certainly involves the misrepresentation of the motives and intentions of their authors.

Now if Aristotle's interpretation of the Presocratics is entirely unhistorical, it is scarcely worth while our continuing to study them. Through Theophrastus he influenced the whole doxographical tradition, and as Cherniss remarks, not only do we possess no single complete work of any Presocratic thinker but such fragments as we have are a selection determined by the interpretations and formulations of Presocratic philosophy in the post-Socratic philosophers for their own philosophical purposes, chiefly by Aristotle. 'If', asks McDiarmid with reference to Anaximander (p. 199), 'Aristotle has misinterpreted both the nature of the Infinite and the nature and functions of its constituent parts, and if Theophrastus has merely repeated his misinterpretation, what positive historical value have their accounts?' He tries to answer his own question, but the only reasonable answer would be that we should have no possible means of knowing. If Aristotle and Theophrastus were capable of distortion to this degree, our independent sources are quite insufficient for an assessment of it. We should be in the position of the (doubtless apocryphal) theologians who having proved the Pauline Epistles one by one to be spurious, found themselves left with no criterion by which to recognize a genuine epistle if they met one.

Those who dismiss Aristotle's statements about his predecessors as unhistorical should at least be aware of what they are doing. They probably agree that Aristotle's was one of the greatest intellects

---

[3] 'Characteristics and Effects of Presocratic Philosophy', *Journal of the Hist. of Ideas*, XII (1951), 320. (See above, Ch. I.) This article contains a most valuable and lucid summary of some of the results of his book on *Aristotle's Criticism of Presocratic Philosophy* (Baltimore 1935), and in making what at present can be no more than some *prolegomena* to a commentary on his views, I hope it is legitimate to refer to its statements rather than to the detailed analysis in the major work.

of all time. They probably agree that he founded formal logic, grasped the principles of scientific method in an even more systematic way than Plato had done, and applied these principles to zoology with such success that his achievement in this sphere can even now excite the admiration of an expert and considering the limited facilities of his age was nothing short of prodigious. They know that he was greatly interested in the historical study of political constitutions, and so aware of the need to have a solid basis of fact underlying any edifice of political theory that he promoted and supervised a series of separate studies of the constitutions of the Greek states, some of which he wrote himself. Moreover, he composed several monographs devoted to separate Presocratic philosophers or schools (and some of us would give much for a sight of his work on the Pythagoreans), in addition— and perhaps preparatory—to the discussion of them in his own philosophical works. I have not yet mentioned his more strictly philosophical greatness, the intellectual force with which he attempts the perhaps impossible task of mediating between Platonism and the scientific outlook, between the conflicting demands of λογικῶς and φυσικῶς ζητεῖν. But I think it would be agreed that no philosopher has shown himself more determined to reduce to a minimum the distorting effects of temperament and prejudice from which not even the most rational of human beings can be entirely free.

After the test of over two thousand years, there is something faintly ridiculous about defending one of the world's greatest philosophers as being on the whole clear-headed and methodical, sane and cautious. Yet it is evidently not superfluous, for we are now asked to believe that whereas on other topics he generally displays these qualities in the highest degree, as soon as he comes to assess his predecessors in the philosophical tradition he is so blinded by the problems and presuppositions of his own thought that he loses all common sense and even any idea of the proper way to handle evidence. Nor is the implication of dishonesty absent. ('His silence about Intelligence falsifies Diogenes' doctrine, but his motive is clear', McDiarmid, above, p. 205.)

Book A of Aristotle's *Metaphysics*, says Cherniss (see above, Ch. I, p. 2), 'interprets all previous philosophy as a groping for his own doctrine of fourfold causality and is, in fact, intended to be a dialectical argument in support of that doctrine'. But we do not need Professor Cherniss to point this out. Aristotle tells us it himself, and indeed repeats it more than once, so alive is he to the danger of our forgetting it. In the *Physics*, he says (*Meta.* A, Ch. 3), I have dealt adequately with the subject of the four causes. Nevertheless it will be a useful check on the rightness and sufficiency of this classification of the modes of causation if we run through what earlier philosophers have had to say on the subject. Either we shall find that they adduce some different type of cause, or if we do not, it will give us more confidence in our own results.[4]

This respect for the work of earlier thinkers is shown in his writings on other subjects too. The point of view is well brought out in *Metaphysics a*, 993 b 11–19:

We should in justice be grateful not only to those whose opinions it is possible to share, but also to those whose accounts are more superficial. These too made their contribution, by developing before us the habit of thought. Without Timotheus, we should lack much lyric poetry; but without Phrynis, there would have been no Timotheus. The same holds good among those who expressed themselves on the truth. From some of them we have accepted certain views, whereas others were responsible for the existence of these some.

τὴν ἕξιν προήσκησαν ἡμῶν expresses a proper and historical attitude to earlier thought, and there is no doubt that it was Aristotle's. To treat one's predecessors like this, instead of (like many scientists and philosophers) dismissing them out of hand as immature, ill-informed or otherwise out of date, is a mark of intellectual maturity. It is not a premise which encourages the conclusion that he will go on to cook their results in order to make them square with his own. He is indeed less likely to do this than the man who conceals, or is unconscious of, his own real intention. The application of this kind of test in addition to his own reasoning shows a stronger historical sense than most original philosophers possess.

In addition to the four causes, another conception fundamental to Aristotle's philosophy is that of natural and violent motion. Each of the elements has for him its natural place in the universe

---

[4] For a repetition of his intentions, see Ch. 5, 986 a 13: ἀλλ' οὐ δὴ χάριν ἐπερχόμεθα, τοῦτ' ἐστιν ὅπως λάβωμεν καὶ παρὰ τούτων τίνας εἶναι τιθέασι τὰς ἀρχάς, καὶ πῶς εἰς τὰς εἰρημένας ἐμπίπτουσιν αἰτίας.

and it is its nature to move towards that place and, once arrived there, to remain still. He therefore divides all movement into natural and enforced. Cherniss (*ACP*, 196–209) complains that here too he criticizes his predecessors only from the standpoint of his own theory. He refers particularly to the discussion of the shape and position of the earth in *De Caelo*, ii. 13. Yet at the conclusion of this discussion Aristotle says (294 b 30):

'But our quarrel with the men who talk like that about motion does not concern particular points, but an undivided whole' (i.e. the behaviour of a particular element, earth, must not be considered in isolation, but only as a part of the cosmos with its universal laws). 'I mean that we must decide from the very beginning whether bodies have a natural motion or not, or whether, not having a natural motion, they have an enforced one. And since our decisions on these points have already been made' (this refers to discussion in chapters 2–4) 'so far as our available powers allowed, we must use them as data.'

The reader could not ask for a clearer warning from the philosopher himself that he is proceeding on certain assumptions of his own, of which he is fully conscious; and in the words 'so far as our available powers allowed' we have a becoming admission that his results may not be final.

There is, of course, much plausibility in the argument that because he was already convinced of the validity of his own scheme of causation he could not but distort his predecessors to fit it, thus 'thoroughly concealing and misrepresenting' their thought (Cherniss, p. 2), but at the same time we must remember the mote and the beam. We are all to some extent at the mercy of our own philosophical presuppositions, and Aristotle had at least the advantages over us that he was an Ionian Greek like the men of whom he was writing and that he was judging them on fuller evidence than we are. He sometimes says of one or other of them that if one seizes what we must suppose him to have meant, instead of judging by the inadequate language at his disposal, one will see that he was trying to say this or that (e.g. of Empedocles at *Meta.* A 985 a 4, of Anaxagoras, 989 a 30). This practice of his can easily be held up to derision as an obvious case of distorting what the philosopher actually said in order to make it fit what Aristotle thinks he ought to have said. But can any of us hope to do better? The arrogance, if such it be, of assuming that one knows what a man wanted to say better than he did himself, is an arrogance from which none of us is free. It was Whitehead who wrote: 'Everything of importance has been said before by someone who did not discover it,' and this statement represents Aristotle's attitude very fairly.

It may be replied that today our aim in studying the Presocratics is purely historical, to find out the truth about them, whereas Aristotle's was the substantiation of his own philosophical views. But in the first place, this again is to underrate the quality of Aristotle's mind as it appears clearly enough in other parts of his works. He did not feel about his philosophical views as an evangelist does about his religion. His interest was in the truth, and he was more capable than most of discarding irrational presuppositions in its pursuit. 'Amicus Plato sed magis amica veritas' is *bien trouvé*; 'Amica veritas sed magis amicum quattuor esse genera causarum' is, for a man of Aristotle's stature, nonsense.

Further, is it such an advantage that in studying the Presocratics we have only historical considerations in mind? Aristotle at least knew that he was investigating a particular question, namely, how far they anticipated his fourfold scheme of causation (or, it may be, his conception of the nature of motion or the *psyche*). Indeed the full consciousness and frankness with which he sets about the task is an excellent guarantee that he will not unduly distort their views. The modern interpreter, just because he is not thinking of his own philosophical presuppositions, is much more likely to be influenced by them unconsciously; and it is absurd to say that because we are not philosophers we have no philosophical presuppositions. It is the philosopher who, because his view of things is framed consciously, is best able to free himself from the preconceptions of his time. The rest of us are more likely to apply them without realizing it.

Here is an example from a scholarly modern discussion of a Presocratic philosopher, Mr J. E. Raven's article on Anaxagoras in the *Classical Quarterly* for 1954. The instance is all the more telling because the writer conforms to the highest standards of scholarship.[5] On p. 133 he writes: 'Whereas every single one of the Presocratics was striving after an incorporeal principle . . . one and all they ended in failure'; and on the next page he adds: 'Anaxagoras . . . in the last resort failed too.' Here we look back,

[5] The appositeness of this parallel was pointed out to me by my daughter, Anne Guthrie, of Somerville College.

from the standpoint of an age to which the distinction between corporeal and incorporeal is familiar, to an age before such a distinction was known, and we say that the men of that age were 'striving' to reach that distinction. Were they? That is a difficult question to answer, but no blame attaches to Mr Raven for putting it in that way, since we can only study these philosophers in the light of our own conceptions, nor would the study be of much value if we did not. But let us at least grant Aristotle a similar freedom without accusing him of distorting his sources any more than we are. He looked at them in the light of his own view of reality, and like the modern scholar (only with much more evidence at his disposal) saw them as 'striving' to reach the same view.

In Cherniss's criticism much less than full weight is given to Aristotle's extreme conscientiousness in reporting the views of others. His statements about Empedocles and Anaxagoras in *Metaphysics* A, already mentioned, are often taken as an instance of his 'reading into' their words what they did not say. If we would justly assess his trustworthiness, it is even more important that he himself is careful to let us know when he ceases to quote the 'stammering utterance' and puts his own interpretation on it. Criticizing his interpretation of Anaxagoras at 989 a 30, McDiarmid writes (above, p. 218): 'As Aristotle admits, he is not stating Anaxagoras' doctrine but giving it a logical development that Anaxagoras had neglected.' He does not seem to see what an enormous debt we owe to the historical sense of the man who so long before the age of scholarship takes the trouble to warn us explicitly [6] when he departs from the text of his author and goes on to his own interpretation. It justifies a certain confidence when we approach the interpretation itself.

In this connection may be cited what, if too much respect were not due to its author, one might be tempted to call the *reductio ad absurdum* of Professor Cherniss's view. Thales, Aristotle tells us (*Meta.* A 983 b 20), said that the ἀρχή, or source of all things, was water, and for this reason he also said that the earth rests upon water. A little later (984 a 2), Aristotle's historical conscience leads him to put the original statement more cautiously: Thales, he repeats, *is said to have* declared himself thus about the first cause. He is, however, sufficiently satisfied on the point himself

[6] λόγον ὃν ἐκεῖνος μὲν οὐ διήρθρωσεν. . . .

to regard Thales as the first figure in the Ionian philosophical tradition which ascribed the ultimate origin af all things to a single principle, this principle being, as Aristotle saw it, a material one. Thales was the originator of this kind of philosophy'. This will not do for Professor Cherniss.

What we know, [he writes (above, p. 4)] of Aristotle's general method of interpreting his predecessors, however, and the specific purpose of his dialectical history in this book arouses the suspicion that Thales was not led from the general doctrine that all things come to be from water to draw the conclusion that the earth rests upon water, but conversely from the tradition which ascribed to Thales the notion that the earth rests upon water Aristotle inferred that he had made water the origin of everything.

I would draw particular attention to this passage because it is far from my intention to argue that Aristotle was a faultless historian or that we can never be in a position to see his faults. He can certainly be detected in misinterpretation, and sometimes in self-contradiction, on the subject of an earlier philosopher.[7]

---

[7] An obvious example is the contradictory senses which he gives to the word φύσις in the same passage of Empedocles (Frag. 8) in *Gen. et Corr.* A 314 b 5 and *Meta.* Δ 1014 b 35. Change and revision of his opinions, and even forgetfulness of what he has said before, are not surprising in writings 'many of which', as Düring has recently reminded us ('Aristotle the Scholar', *Arctos*, 1954, p. 66), are 'continually revised series of lectures' and were never prepared by their author for publication. Cherniss's book provides many instances, though he sometimes exaggerates Aristotle's inconsistency, e.g. in his strictures on the general treatment of Empedocles (*ACP*, 196 n. 211, 352–3). Aristotle's complaint that 'Empedocles does not allow one to decide whether the Sphere or the elements were prior' (*Gen. et Corr.* 315 a 19, Cherniss, n. 211) was from his own point of view justified, and does something to mitigate the heinousness of interpreting in different ways what was to him a self-contradictory system. Some instances offered are not inconsistencies at all. Thus *ACP* 357 says: 'The theory of Anaxagoras may be praised as "modern" when νοῦς is interpreted as final cause and yet held to be inferior to that of Empedocles when Aristotle is arguing that a finite number of principles is preferable to an infinite number.' But why should Aristotle not have regarded it as superior in some respects but inferior in others? Again (same page) 'Anaximander is at one time just another Ionian monist, yet elsewhere he is linked with Anaxagoras and Empedocles.' The inconsistency here may lie in the nature of Anaximander's somewhat primitive ideas rather than being imposed on them by Aristotle. Whether τὸ ἄπειρον, from which things could be 'separated out', was originally a single substance or a mixture, is a question which he had not faced. 'Uncertainty on Aristotle's

But to put it at its lowest, he was intellectually mature, and the fault must in each case be proved before it can be assumed. Here, on the other hand, we are asked to suspect him of an elementary blunder for which there is not a shred of evidence, solely on the prior assumption that he 'is not interested in historical facts as such at all'.

If Aristotle were capable of playing fast and loose with facts to this extent, it would hardly be worth while to consult such a slipshod author on any subject, whether the previous history of philosophy or anything else; so let us look at the manner of his references to Thales. They should throw an important light on his methods and consequent trustworthiness, since in this case we know him to have been relying on intermediate sources only. If Thales ever wrote anything, it was lost before Aristotle's day.

As already noted, the statement about the first cause is given as what 'is said' about Thales. But can we trust Aristotle to distinguish between what he has found in tradition and what is merely his own conjecture? A further glance at his practice should help us to decide. Having repeated the simple statement, he goes on to suggest a reason which may have influenced Thales in making it. His words are (983 b 21): 'He said that the ἀρχή is water, *getting this idea perhaps from* (λαβὼν ἴσως ταύτην τὴν ὑπόληψιν ἐκ τοῦ) seeing that the nourishment of all things is moist and that heat itself arises out of moisture and lives by it . . . and because the seed of all creatures is of moist nature.' The reason for the statement is clearly distinguished from the statement itself as a conjecture of Aristotle: we are not left wondering. I would add, because though not directly relevant to the present point it has a bearing on Aristotle's general trustworthiness as an interpreter of early thought, that Mr McDiarmid does no service to the history of philosophy by simply repeating Burnet's statement that 'arguments of this sort are characteristic of the physiological speculations that accompanied the rise of scientific medicine in the fifth century B.C. At the time of Thales the prevailing interest appears to have been meteorological'. Terms like 'physiological' and 'meteorological', with their sugges-

---

part as to what Anaximander really meant' (p. 25) is very probable, but is not the same as the kind of self-contradiction that is attributed to him elsewhere.

tion of modern scientific departmentalism, are highly anachronistic. No technical interest in physiology is implied in the simple explanation given by Aristotle, and a general curiosity about the origin and maintenance of life far antedates the rise of scientific thought. As Professor Baldry showed in an important article, 'interest in birth and other phenomena connected with sex is a regular feature of primitive societies long before other aspects of biology are even thought of . . . There is every reason for supposing that the Greeks were no exception to this rule.'[8]

The statement that the earth rests on water is referred to again in *De Caelo* (294 a 29) as one which 'they say Thales made' (ὅν φασιν εἰπεῖν Θ. τὸν Μιλήσιον). In *De Anima* we find an interesting form of words whereby Aristotle lets us know with admirable precision (*a*) that he has found something in his authorities about Thales, and (*b*) that he feels justified in drawing a conclusion from it which nevertheless rests on no authority but his own inference: 'It looks, from what is recorded about him, as if Thales too thought of the soul as a kind of motive power, if he said that the loadstone has a soul because it attracts iron.'[9] Later in the same treatise we have another of Aristotle's conjectures, clearly distinguished as such from the statements which he has found in earlier sources: 'Some say that soul is mingled in the whole, which is perhaps the reason why Thales believed that all things are full of gods.'[10] The careful wording of these passages is, for its period, remarkable, and provides the valuable information that in sources available to Aristotle the following statements were attributed to Thales: (i) water is the ἀρχή; (ii) the earth rests on water; (iii) the loadstone has a soul because it attracts iron; (iv) all things are full of gods. To doubt this is to abandon all critical standards and stultify any study of the Presocratics. I would go further, and suggest that the caution and sanity exhibited by Aristotle compel us also to pay serious attention to his own conjectures, and I have tried to show that one of these has been much too hastily dismissed.

---

[8] *Embryological Analogies in Presocratic Cosmogony, Class. Quart.*, XXVI (1932), 28. Baldry refers to Aristotle's version of Thales's motive on p. 33.

[9] 405 a 19: ἔοικε δὲ καὶ Θ. ἐξ ὧν ἀπομνημονεύουσι κινητικόν τι τὴν ψυχὴν ὑπολαβεῖν, εἴπερ τὴν λίθον ἔφη ψυχὴν ἔχειν ὅτι τὸν σίδηρον κινεῖ.

[10] 411 a 7: καὶ ἐν τῷ ὅλῳ δέ τινες αὐτὴν μεμῖχθαί φασιν, ὅθεν ἴσως καὶ Θ. ᾠήθη πάντα πλήρη θεῶν εἶναι.

In considering a so-called fragment, says Professor Cherniss (above, pp. 1–2), one must take into consideration the whole context in which it has been preserved, 'a context which is sometimes as extensive as a whole book of Aristotle's *Metaphysics*'. I would go even further, and say that in judging Aristotle's account of any of his predecessors one must take into consideration his whole philosophical and historical outlook, which can only be understood by a wide and deep reading of his works on a variety of subjects. Mr McDiarmid, for instance, holds that doubts about the view of matter which Aristotle attributes to the early physicists are made antecedently not unreasonable 'by the fact that he can seriously comment on the material theory of Homer in the same context with those of the physicists' (above, p. 184). This is a very misleading statement. It is true that Aristotle is remarkably patient with the views of even poets and mythographers (to whom he once stretches out a hand in a sudden flash of sympathetic insight: 'so the lover of myth is in a sense a philosopher'—διὸ καὶ ὁ φιλόμυθος φιλόσοφός πώς ἐστιν, *Meta.* A 982 b 18), owing to his unshakable and attractive conviction that there must be *some* grain of truth in any sincerely held belief. But there is much in that 'in a sense'. The lover of myth shares with the philosopher the all-important gift of curiosity, but no more. This is the same critic who could write, 'But it is not worthwhile to consider seriously the mythologists' subtleties; one must inquire of those who offer demonstration' (*Meta.* B 1000 a 18: ἀλλὰ περὶ μὲν τῶν μυθικῶς σοφιζομένων οὐκ ἄξιον μετὰ σπουδῆς σκοπεῖν, παρὰ δὲ τῶν δι᾽ ἀποδείξεως λεγόντων δεῖ πυνθάνεσθαι), and who reveals himself in the passage of *Metaphysics* A which McDiarmid is discussing. There is no question of Aristotle's putting Homer on a level with the Milesian philosophers; otherwise he could not designate Thales with clear-cut emphasis as 'the originator of this kind of philosophy'. Only after the serious part of his exposition is over does he add that 'there are some who say' that the old 'theologians' like Homer took this view of nature, then immediately dismissing that as something scarcely susceptible of verification and not worth further thought, he returns to Thales as the earliest thinker relevant to his inquiry. It is sad to be forced into such heavy-handed exegesis of the expressive dryness with which, after the mention of Homer's Okeanos and Tethys, Aristotle continues (983 b 33): 'Whether this really is an ancient view of nature may perhaps be uncertain, but Thales is said to have spoken thus about the first cause.' Homer and Thales in the same context?[11]

To substitute uncritical rejection for sympathetic criticism of Aristotle's account leads, in the absence of any better source of information, to the erection of a purely modern dogmatism in its place. Many examples could be quoted, but space will scarcely permit of more than one. Of the origin of motion in the system of Leucippus and Democritus, Aristotle says in *Metaphysics* A (985 b 19) that they 'like the others, lazily shelved' this question. In *Physics* (265 b 24) he refers to them as those who 'make the void the cause of motion'. Mr McDiarmid notes (above, p. 230 ff.) that Aristotle and Theophrastus where he is dependent on him, give the impression that the Atomists considered the assertion of the void's existence to be sufficient answer to the Eleatic denial of motion, and continues: 'Clearly it was not, and the atomists can hardly have thought that it was.' By this unsupported assertion he closes the door against any use of Aristotle's hint as an aid to reconstructing the problem as the Atomists saw it. If, instead, we follow that hint, we may discover the ingenious way in which they safeguarded their system from the objections to which those of Empedocles and Anaxagoras were open. Parmenides had finally condemned any system which, like the Milesian or Pythagorean, combined the notions of a one and a many. An original one could never become many, for change and motion were impossible because, among other reasons, true void was an inadmissible concept. Empedocles and Anaxagoras had tried to save the phenomena by abandoning the original unity. Positing an everlasting plurality, and accepting the Parmenidean denials of (*a*) generation and destruction and (*b*) void, they evidently thought they could retain the possibility of locomotion by a kind of reciprocal replacement (the motion which later writers compared to that of a fish through water, Simplicius, *Physics* 659. 26 Diels).

For motion even to start in such a plenum, an external cause

---

[11] It may be, as Ross suggests, that Aristotle's introduction of the ancient *theologi* here is a reminiscence of Plato's remarks in the *Cratylus* (402 d) and *Theaetetus* (152 e, 160 d, 180 c), though Plato is quoting them as forerunners of Heraclitus rather than of Thales. In any case, if Plato, as Ross says, is 'jesting', may we not allow Aristotle to have his joke too?

seemed necessary. Otherwise it would remain locked in a solid, frozen mass. Thus whereas to blame the Milesians for omitting to provide a motive cause is anachronistic, to demand it in any post-Parmenidean system is right. The need was there and was known to be there. Hence the Love and Strife of Empedocles and the Mind of Anaxagoras. But to an age for which there was still only one type of entity (that which we should call corporeal, though this term could not come into use until its contrary, the incorporeal, had been conceived), the introduction of Mind over the mixture must have seemed suspiciously like the reintroduction of unity, of a one behind the many, by a back door, thus laying Anaxagoras' system wide open once more to criticism of the Eleatic type.

What is difficult for us to realize is the complete *novelty* of the idea that a true void might exist. Before Parmenides the concept had not been grasped, so that the Pythagoreans could actually identify void and *pneuma* (Aristotle, *Phys.* IV. 213 b 22). Later it had been understood only to be denied as impossible. I suggest, therefore, that the Atomists had consciously faced the problem of the origin of motion and considered that they were providing a new, sufficient, and positive answer by attributing it to the existence of void.[12] The difficulties which had faced the pluralist attempts to rescue phenomena from the grip of Eleatic logic were the difficulties of accounting for a beginning of motion in a mass of matter heterogeneous indeed, but locked together without the smallest chink of empty space between its parts. Substitute for that picture the alternative of an infinite number of microscopic atoms let loose, as it were, in infinite empty space, and it is at least as reasonable to ask 'Why should they stay still?' as 'Why should they move?'

Eleatic logic compelled the Atomists to describe the void as 'what is not' (τὸ μὴ ὄν); but this had an advantage of its own. 'What is' (τὸ ὄν) being still what we should be inclined to call some form of body, space was something different, a mere blank; it is μὴ ὄν. Yet, Leucippus insists, in its own way it exists, it is there (Aristotle, *Meta.* A. 985 b 4 ff.), and not only that, but it is what makes motion possible. Thus Leucippus played on

<hr>

[12] One must remember that Melissus had argued directly from the non-existence of void to the impossibility of motion, in contradiction of Empedocles and Anaxagoras. (Frag. 7, sect. 7, Cherniss, *ACP*, 402.)

Parmenides the kind of trick which Odysseus played on the Cyclops. When asked what started motion, Anaxagoras replies 'Mind', i.e. a positive ὄν somehow different in kind from the matter of which the cosmos is composed. Asked the same question, Leucippus replies, first, that motion has been from all time, but secondly, that what makes it possible is τὸ μὴ ὄν. If 'No man is killing me', the neighbours cannot expect to catch the murderer.

Aristotle is often astonishingly close to our own point of view. Like Mr McDiarmid, he thinks the existence of void is no sufficient explanation of the possibility of motion. It is a *sine qua non*, but not the positive cause—e.g. weight—which his own (incidentally erroneous) mechanics demanded. Hence although he records that they gave this answer, it does not in his eyes absolve them from the charge of 'light-mindedness' (ῥαθυμία) in this respect. But if we use the evidence which he is a good enough historian to give us, we may succeed in overcoming both our own preconceptions and his and getting nearer to the mind of a pre-Platonic thinker. The Atomists came at a stage in the history of thought when the need for a positive cause of motion was bound up with the lack of a true conception of void. The setting free of the atoms, therefore, though to Aristotle it appeared as no more than a *sine qua non*, seemed to them a sufficient explanation, a positive αἴτιον, of their motion. They combined it with the assertion that motion was from eternity, and considered that no further, more positive, cause was required. In this the physics of Leucippus and Democritus are more nearly in accord with the views of motion current in Europe since Galileo and Descartes than with the imperfect theories of Aristotle. He is certainly open to criticism, but not to immediate dismissal on the grounds that the Atomists could never have thought of the void as a sufficient answer to the Eleatic denial of motion.

The proper treatment of Aristotle's evidence is vital for the whole history of Presocratic thought. Here I have done no more than suggest a few reasons for believing that it calls for further investigation. Professor Cherniss has not so much 'dealt exhaustively' with the subject as opened our minds to new and fruitful possibilities—perhaps a greater service. As an historian Aristotle has serious failings, but he deserves less wholesale condemnation than he is at the moment in danger of receiving. Too hasty rejection of some of his judgements may be of less service than sympathetic criticism if we wish to see through his mind to those of his predecessors. A small contribution towards this sympathetic understanding will, I hope, be an acceptable tribute to the great Aristotelian in whose honour it is written.[13]

[13] This paper first appeared in a volume in honour of Sir David Ross. I should like to express my thanks to Mr D. J. Allan for helpful comments and suggestions made while this paper was in draft.

X

HOT AND COLD, DRY AND WET IN EARLY GREEK THOUGHT

G. E. R. Lloyd

IN a previous article (*JHS*, LXXXII (1962) 56 ff.) I examined some of the theories and explanations which appear in Greek philosophy and medicine in the period down to Aristotle, in which reference is made to right and left or certain other pairs of opposites (light and darkness, male and female, up and down, front and back), and I argued that several of these theories are influenced by the symbolic associations which these opposites possessed for the ancient Greeks. In the present paper I wish to consider the use of the two pairs of opposites which are most prominent of all in early Greek speculative thought, the hot and the cold, and the dry and the wet. My discussion is divided into two parts. In the first I shall examine the question of the origin of the use of these opposites in Greek philosophy. How far back can we trace their use in various fields of speculative thought, and what was the significance of their introduction into cosmology in particular? And then in the second part of my paper I shall consider to what extent theories based on these opposites may have been influenced by assumptions concerning the values of the opposed terms. Are these opposites, too, like right and left, or male and female, sometimes conceived as consisting of on the one hand a positive, or superior pole, and on the other a negative, or inferior one? How far do we find that arbitrary correlations were made between these and other pairs of terms, that is to say correlations that correspond to preconceived notions of value, rather than to any empirically verifiable data?

On the problem of the origin of the use of these opposites in various types of speculative theories, it is as well to begin by reviewing the incontrovertible evidence for the post-Parmenidean period before turning to the much less certain and more difficult evidence for earlier writers. The first extant philosophical texts in which the hot and the cold, the dry and the wet are explicitly described as being present at the first stage of cosmological development are certain fragments of Anaxagoras. Fragment 4, for instance, specifically mentions these opposites, along with the bright and the dark, 'much earth' and 'innumerable seeds', as being present in the original mixture when 'all things were together', and the same three pairs of opposites, together with the rare and the dense, are described in Fragment 12 as separating off from one another in the περιχώρησις initiated by *Nous*. The first extant text in which we find a physical theory based on the hot and the cold, the dry and the wet as the *four* primary elements or components of other things appears to be in the Hippocratic treatise *On the Nature of Man*, Ch. 3 (L. vi. 36, 17 ff.)[1] where the author states that on death each of the components of a man's body returns to its own nature, 'the wet to the wet, the dry to the dry, the hot to the hot, the cold to the cold. Such is the nature both of living things and of everything else.'[2] In other fifth- and fourth-century texts these opposites are associated with the elements, rather than named as elements themselves. In Fragment 21, 3–6, Empedocles connects certain pairs of opposites (hot and

[1] The reference to Melissus in Ch. 1 (34, 6) provides a *terminus post quem* for Chs. 1–8 of this composite treatise, and to judge from the report in Anon. Lond., xix. 1 ff., its author was Polybus, the son-in-law of Hippocrates (the theory of veins in Ch. 11, 58, 1 ff., may also be ascribed to Polybus on the authority of Aristotle, *HA* 512 b 12 ff.). While most scholars date this work in the second half of the fifth century (e.g. L. Bourgey, *Observation et Expérience chez les médecins de la collection Hippocratique* [Paris, 1953], pp. 31 f.), F. Heinimann for one (*Nomos und Physis*, Basel, 1945, 158 ff.) puts it at the very end of that century or the beginning of the fourth, on the grounds that the antithesis between νόμος and φύσις is already drawn quite sharply in Chs. 2 and 5.

[2] In Ch. 4 (38, 19 ff.) the writer describes the components of the body in terms of the four humours, blood, phlegm, bile, and black bile, but these are in turn correlated both with the opposites and with the four seasons in Ch. 7 (46, 9 ff.): e.g. blood, like the season spring, is said to be wet and hot.

cold, bright and dark) with certain of his 'roots',[3] though how far he went in working out a comprehensive schema of such associations, it is much more difficult to say.[4] But in the Hippocratic work *On Fleshes*,[5] for example, we find a quite elaborate schema (Ch. 2, L. viii. 584, 9 ff.). Here too there is a four element theory, the most important element being the hot itself ('what the ancients called *aether*'). Of the other three elements, earth is said to be cold and dry, *aer* is hot and wet, and 'that which is nearest the earth' (the sea?) is 'wettest and thickest'. Another such theory is found in *On Regimen* i.[6], where the writer asserts that there are two component elements of all living creatures, namely fire and water

[3] 'Sun' (i.e. fire) is undoubtedly described as bright and hot in verse 3 (ἠέλιον μὲν λευκὸν ὁρᾶν καὶ θερμὸν ἁπάντῃ) and 'rain' (i.e. water) as dark and cold in verse 5 (ὄμβρον δ' ἐν πᾶσι δνοφόεντά τε ῥιγαλέον τε), and when Aristotle quotes these lines at *GC* 314 b 20 ff., he adds that Empedocles 'characterizes the other elements too in a similar way'. But in the more complete version of the fragment quoted by Simplicius (*in Ph.* 159. 13 ff.) the interpretation of the lines which refer to the other two elements is far from clear. Verse 6 (ἐκ δ' αἴης προρέουσι θελεμνά τε καὶ στερεωπά) seems to associate earth with solidity particularly (but not, apparently, with hot or cold): Aristotle, at least, took Empedocles' theory to have been that earth is heavy and hard (*GC* 315 a 10 f.). Verse 4 is even more obscure: ἄμβροτα δ' ὅσσ' εἴδει τε καὶ ἀργέτι δεύεται αὐγῇ. If we take this to refer to air (though this had been doubted by some scholars), it seems to imply that this element, too, like fire apparently, is warm and bright.

[4] C. H. Kahn, *Anaximander and the Origins of Greek Cosmology* (New York, 1960), p. 127, has suggested that 'if the complete poem of Empedocles had survived, we might see that his theory was as fully articulated as that of Aristotle' (in which each of the four simple bodies is constituted by two of the four primary opposites, hot, cold, dry, wet, e.g. fire by the hot and the dry), but this is a very doubtful conjecture. Kahn points out that 'other fragments permit us to catch a glimpse of the causal roles ascribed to the hot and cold, the dense and rare, and to the qualities of taste—bitter, sweet and others', and he instances Fragments 65, 67, 75, 90 and 104. But there is nothing in these fragments to suggest that these opposites are associated with specific 'roots'. Empedocles' theory of these associations survives in Fragment 21 alone, and there the doctrine seems to be still in quite a rudimentary form.

[5] On the date of this treatise, see K. Deichgräber, *Hippokrates, über Entstehung und Aufbau des menschlichen Körpers*, Leipzig, 1935, 27, n. 4, who concludes that it belongs to the end of the fifth century. It should be remembered, however, that the date of this, as of almost every other, Hippocratic treatise cannot be determined with any degree of precision.

[6] This treatise is now generally agreed to be more probably a fourth- than a fifth-century work (see, e.g., J.-H. Kühn, *System- und Methodenprobleme im Corpus Hippocraticum*, Hermes Einzelschriften, 11 [1956], 80, n. 1).

but 'the hot and the dry belong to fire, and the cold and the wet to water', though 'there is some moisture in fire' and again 'there is some of the dry in water' (Chs. 3 and 4, L. vi. 472, 12 ff., 474, 8 ff.).[7]

The evidence for the post-Parmenidean period is clear enough. In the late fifth and early fourth centuries the hot and the cold, the dry and the wet, whether alone or in conjunction with other pairs of opposites, were used in at least two types of physical theories, (1) where they figure as elements themselves, i.e. as the primary substances of which other things are composed (as in *On the Nature of Man*) and (2) where they are associated with the elements, when these were conceived in the form of other substances (as in *On Fleshes*).[8] In addition, there are, of course, innumerable pathological theories in the Hippocratic Corpus, in which diseases are attributed either to these opposites directly, or to their effect on other substances or parts of the body. To mention just two typical examples, in *On the Places in Man* the writer says that 'pain is caused both by the cold and by the hot, and both by what is in excess and by what is in default' (Ch. 42, L. vi. 334, 1 ff.), and the author of *On Affections* puts it that 'in men, all diseases are caused by bile and phlegm. Bile and phlegm give rise to diseases when they become too dry or too wet or too hot or too cold in the body' (Ch. 1, L. vi. 208, 7 ff.). The author of *On Ancient Medicine* (writing after Empedocles, as we know from Ch. 20) attacks the extreme version of such a theory in which the hot, the cold, the wet or the dry was postulated as the sole cause of diseases, and it would appear from a text in Aetius, at least (v. 30, 1, *DK* 24 B 4) that the use of these opposites in theories of disease goes back as far as Alcmaeon, who is

---

[7] Anon. Lond. xx. 25 ff. attributes a neat schema of elements and 'powers' to Philistion: there are four elements and each of these has its own 'power', fire hot, air cold, water wet and earth dry. The dates of *On Fleshes* and of Philistion are, of course, known only very imprecisely, but it seems possible that the theories of Empedocles, *On Fleshes*, Philistion and Aristotle represent a gradual and continuous progress towards a doctrine of elements and opposites that is at once simple and comprehensive.

[8] We should also note theories of the type found in Diogenes of Apollonia in which there is a single primary element (in his case Ἀήρ) but hot and cold, dry and wet and so on are mentioned as its differentiations (see Frag. 5: ἔστι γὰρ πολύτροπος (sc. ὁ ἀήρ) καὶ θερμότερος καὶ ψυχρότερος καὶ ξηρότερος καὶ ὑγρότερος καὶ στασιμώτερος καὶ ὀξυτέρην κίνησιν ἔχων).

reported to have held that health depends on the *isonomia* of certain factors in the body, and that the *monarchia* of one of these causes disease: as examples of the factors, or as he calls them the 'powers', in question, Aetius mentions wet, dry, cold, hot, bitter and sweet.

Hot and cold, dry and wet seem to have been used in pathological theories as early as Alcmaeon, but how far back can we trace their use in cosmological doctrines? With the exception of some fragments of Heraclitus (notably Frag. 126), we rely on the testimony of Aristotle and Theophrastus, and sources which were in turn dependent on them, for our evidence concerning the role of these opposites in pre-Parmenidean writers. For many years these authorities were thought quite reliable enough by the majority of scholars. What might be described as the traditional view of the role of these opposites in the early stages of Greek philosophy is expressed by Cornford, for example (*Principium Sapientiae*, Cambridge, 1952, 34): 'in studying Anaximander's system we shall find the four cardinal opposites mentioned by Hippocrates [Cornford has just referred to the treatise *On Ancient Medicine*] —hot and cold, moist and dry—playing a leading role in cosmogony. They can be identified with the four seasonal powers of summer and winter, rain and drought; and, in the order of space, they become the four elements of Empedocles, fire, air, water, earth.' Yet first Heidel[9] and Cherniss[10] and then more recently McDiarmid[11] have seriously impugned the accuracy of both Aristotle's and Theophrastus' accounts of Presocratic philosophy. Moreover it was just at this point, in his attribution of theories based on opposites to the Presocratics, that Aristotle's interpretation was particularly attacked on the grounds that in Physics A, for example, he is attempting to show that all earlier thinkers held the opposites as principles in order to establish that his own theory of Form and Privation is both final and inclusive. Commenting on the accounts of Anaximander given by Aristotle and Theophrastus, McDiarmid put it that 'their interpretation clearly presupposes that he had subscribed to the specifically Aristotelian notion of the equilibrium of the contraries

---

[9] W. A. Heidel, 'Qualitative Change in Presocratic Philosophy', *Archiv f. Gesch. d. Philos.* XIX (1906), 333 ff.

[10] H. Cherniss, *Aristotle's Criticism of Presocratic Philosophy*, Baltimore, 1935.

[11] J. B. McDiarmid, 'Theophrastus on the Presocratic Causes', *Harvard Studies in Classical Philology*, LXI (1953), 85 ff.; above, Ch. VIII.

and the genesis of the four simple bodies through the interaction of the contraries on undifferentiated matter' (above, p. 176), and Hölscher,[12] too, remarked, with reference to the report on Anaximander in Pseudo-Plutarch *Stromateis* 2 (*DK* 12 A 10), that 'die gegensätzlichen Qualitäten Heiss und Kalt können als solche nicht anaximandrisch sein'. Nevertheless both Kahn[13] and most recently Guthrie[14] have upheld the general reliability of our evidence concerning the role of opposites in the systems of the Milesians. The general problem of the reliability of our sources for Presocratic philosophy cannot be entered into here. But since there is a quite fundamental disagreement, among those who have studied the matter, on whether the hot and the cold, and the dry and the wet themselves were used in cosmological theories as early as Anaximander, a brief re-examination of the evidence that is relevant to this particular question must be undertaken.

The problem hinges on our interpretation of the evidence concerning Anaximander, and first of all we should grant a general point to McDiarmid and others, that on certain occasions when Aristotle or the doxographers have attributed a theory based on contraries, or on the hot and the cold in particular, to one or other of the Presocratic philosophers, they have undoubtedly reformulated the theory in question. A clear example is *Ph.* 188 a 20 ff. (cf. *Metaph.* 986 b 34) where, indeed, Aristotle himself makes it plain that he has reformulated the doctrine of Parmenides. 'Parmenides posits hot and cold as *archai*', he says, and then goes on 'he calls them fire and earth'.[15] The report in Hippolytus

[12] U. Hölscher, 'Anaximander und die Anfänge der Philosophie', *Hermes*, LXXXI (1953), 266; below, Ch. XI.

[13] *Op. cit.*, especially Ch. 2, 119 ff.

[14] W. K. C. Guthrie, *A History of Greek Philosophy*, I, Cambridge, 1962. See also Guthrie's article, 'Aristotle as a Historian of Philosophy', *JHS*, LXXVII (part 1) (1957), 35 ff.; above, Ch. IX.

[15] It may be noted that in this instance later writers refer to Parmenides' principles more often as fire and earth than as hot and cold, e.g. Theophr. *Phys. Op.* Frag. 6 (Alex. in *Metaph.* 984 b 3, p. 31, 7 [Hayduck], *DK* A 7), Hippolytus *Ref.* i. 11, 1, *DK* A 23, D.L. ix. 21, *DK* A 1, but contrast τὸ θερμὸν καὶ τὸ ψυχρόν in D.L. ix. 22, and at Aetius, ii. 20, 8 a, *DK* A 43, what is 'rarer' is described as hot, and what is 'denser' as cold. Aristotle's reference to Parmenides' second principle (Νύξ) as 'earth' has been taken as a typical misinterpretation (McDiarmid, *op. cit.*, 120 f.), but it seems probable enough, to judge from the description of night as 'dense' and 'heavy' (Frag. 8, 59), that this principle was associated with earth, if not actually identified with it.

(*Ref.* i. 7 3, *DK* 13 A 7) on Anaximenes' cosmology contains what seems to be a similar rationalization of an original theory in terms of the hot and the cold, for having described the changes which air undergoes as it rarefies and condenses (becoming fire on the one hand, and wind, clouds, water, earth, and stones on the other), Hippolytus concludes with the inference: 'Hence the chief factors in generation are opposites, hot and cold.'[16] As regards Anaximander himself, the main sources of evidence on which we must base our interpretation of the role of opposites in his system are (1) the reports in Aristotle and Simplicius, (2) the account of his cosmology in Pseudo-Plutarch and (3) the extant fragment. We may consider these in turn to see how far they enable us to determine the nature of his cosmological theories and the terms in which they were expressed.

Anaximander is rarely mentioned by name in Aristotle,[17] and of the passages in question only one (*Ph.* 187 a 20 ff.) is relevant to the problem of his use of opposites. At *Ph.* 187 a 12 ff. Aristotle divides the theories of the φυσικοί into two groups. One group of philosophers postulated a single element and derived other things from this by condensation and rarefaction, and the other group is described as follows: 'The second group are those who hold that the opposites are separated out (ἐκκρίνεσθαι) of the One of which they are constituents, as Anaximander says, and also those who assert that One and Many exist, like Empedocles and Anaxagoras; for they too separate the rest out of the mixture'. Now with regard to Empedocles and Anaxagoras, the accuracy

---

[16] Contrast the testimony of Plutarch (*de prim. frig.* 7 947 F, *DK* 13 B 1) which suggests that Anaximenes reduced differences of temperature to differences of density (and this accords with the frequent mention of 'the rare' and 'the dense' in other reports on Anaximenes, e.g. Theophrastus, *Phys. Op.* Frag. 2, Simplicius, in *Ph.* 24, 26 ff., *DK* A 5). Kahn, however, apparently takes the evidence of Plutarch in precisely the contrary sense, as if Anaximenes reduced differences of density to differences of temperature, for he comments (*op. cit.*, 160) 'Anaximenes seems in fact to have made use of these two (viz. Hot and Cold) in their classic function, as powers of rarefaction and condensation (B 1, A 7.3).'

[17] Four times in all (*Ph.* 187 a 20 ff., 203 b 14, *Cael.* 295 b 12, *Metaph.* 1069 b 22), excluding the valueless reference in the spurious *de Melisso* (975 b 22). On the passages which refer to unnamed philosophers who postulated an element intermediate between fire and air, or between air and water, see the full discussion in G. S. Kirk, 'Some problems in Anaximander', *CQ*, N.S. V (1955), 24 ff.; below, Ch. XII.

of this statement can be checked by referring to the extant fragments of the philosophers themselves. Anaxagoras, at least, undoubtedly refers to a 'separating off' of certain pairs of opposites (the term used in the extant fragments being ἀποκρίνεσθαι), though, as Aristotle himself points out at *Ph.* 187 a 25 f., it is not only the opposites, but also what Aristotle calls the *homoiomere* that are present in the original mixture and separate off from it. In Empedocles, on the other hand, the principal substances that are described as coming together and separating off are the 'roots' (between which there are, it is true, certain oppositions),[18] rather than such opposites as hot and cold, or wet and dry themselves. It would seem, then, that when Aristotle groups these three philosophers together and suggests that they all 'separate out the opposites that are present in the one', this is only true as a broad generalization, and indeed there is a further reason not to press the term 'opposites' (ἐναντιότητες) too far here, in that throughout this chapter Aristotle is arguing towards the general conclusion that *all* previous philosophers 'make the opposites in some way the principles of all things' (*Ph.* 188 a 26 f., cf. also a 19 and b 27 ff.). It is true, of course, that the theory of the separating-out of opposites is *particularly* associated with Anaximander at *Ph.* 187 a 20 ff., but if this passage is good evidence that he referred to opposed substances of some sort in his cosmological theory, it leaves the problem of the precise nature of those substances still unresolved.

The interpretation that the substances that separate off from the Boundless were the hot and the cold, the dry and the wet themselves rests, rather, on the testimony of Simplicius. First there is a passage which contains not so much a direct report on Anaximander's theory, as a generalizing comment on it. We are told that Anaximander 'does not explain generation as due to the changing (ἀλλοιουμέων) of the element, but to the separating off (ἀποκρινομένων) of the opposites because of the eternal motion' (*in Ph.* 24, 23 ff., *DK* 12 A 9).[19] The use of the term ἀλλοιοῦσθαι

---

[18] See above, note 3, on Frag. 21, 3 ff. The main opposition referred to there is that between fire and water, and this is an obvious fact of experience. As Kahn points out, *op. cit.*, 160, the enmity between these two was proverbial, e.g. Theognis, 1245 f., Aeschylus, *Ag.* 650 f. and cf. the fight between Hephaestus and the river Xanthus at *Iliad*, xxi. 342 ff.

[19] This text occurs in a passage in which Simplicius first quotes Anaxi-

shows that this comment is made in part, at least, in the light of Aristotle's analysis of different types of change, and once again it would be rash to try to press the term 'opposites' too far. Elsewhere, however, Simplicius specifies the opposites in question as 'hot, cold, dry, wet, and the rest' (*in Ph.* 150, 24 f., *DK ib.*). Yet this passage occurs in a commentary on the text of Aristotle which we have already discussed (*Ph.* 187 a 20 ff.), and it is quite clear, as indeed Kahn grants, that Simplicius is, here, 'more concerned to explain Aristotle's text than to describe Anaximander's doctrine in detail'. Kahn goes on to suggest, however (*op. cit.*, 41), that while the second pair of opposites, dry and wet, may or may not have been supplied by Simplicius, the first pair, hot and cold, was certainly given by Theophrastus. He cites two pieces of evidence for this, which we must now consider, namely a text of Aetius and the account of Anaximander's cosmology in the *Stromateis*, and these do indeed suggest, quite strongly, that the hot and the cold were mentioned in Theophrastus' account of Anaximander. This still leaves the much more difficult question of whether Theophrastus mentioned the hot and the cold in an attempt to elucidate Anaximander's theory, or in a direct report on it, and while it is, no doubt, impossible to achieve certainty on this problem, some light is thrown on it by examining the context of the reference to these opposites in the two texts in question. Thus at ii. 11, 5 (*DK* 12 A 17 a) Aetius reports: 'Anaximander [*sc.* says the *ouranos* consists of] a mixture of hot and cold.' As the context in Aetius shows, the theory reported here is not a general cosmological doctrine, but one that concerns the substance of the heavenly sphere (*ouranos* means 'heavens' rather than 'universe' here). Now we do not lack other reports on Anaximander's theory of the nature of the heavenly *bodies*, the stars, sun and moon. Hippolytus *Ref.* i. 6, 4–5 (*DK* A 11), Aetius, ii. 13, 7 (*DK* A 18), ii. 20, 1

---

mander's fragment and then goes on to *conjecture* the motives which may have led him to postulate τὸ ἄπειρον (δῆλον δὲ ὅτι τὴν εἰς ἄλληλα μεταβολὴν τῶν τεττάρων στοιχείων οὗτος θεασάμενος οὐκ ἠξίωσεν ἕν τι τούτων ὑποκείμενον ποιῆσαι, ἀλλά τι ἄλλο παρὰ ταῦτα· οὗτος δὲ οὐκ ἀλλοιουμένου κτλ.), and while this conjecture is plausible enough (cf. also Aristotle, *Ph.* 204 b 22 ff.), it is obvious that Anaximander cannot have argued in precisely the way in which Simplicius suggests since this argument depends on the anachronistic doctrine of the four elements.

(*DK* A 12) and ii. 25, 1 (*DK* A 22) all agree in the main features of the theory of the heavenly bodies which they attribute to Anaximander, which is that they are circles of fire which are enclosed in *aer* but which have certain openings at which the stars, sun and moon appear. When we have a set of reports that tell us that according to Anaximander the heavens contain a series of circles composed of *fire* and *opaque mist*, and when we also know that Aristotle and the doxographers do sometimes reformulate the theories of the Presocratics in terms of the neater opposites hot and cold (see above), there is clearly a distinct possibility that the report in Aetius, ii. 11, 5, which refers to the heavens themselves as being composed of a mixture of hot and cold is just another such reformulation, especially since Aristotle's interpretation of Parmenides' principles *fire* and *earth/night* as hot and cold sets such a close precedent.

The second passage in which the hot and the cold are mentioned is in the fullest account of Anaximander's cosmology which we possess, Pseudo-Plutarch *Stromateis* 2: 'He says that at the birth of this cosmos "the" [or "a"][20] germ of hot and cold was separated off from the eternal substance, and out of this a sphere of flame grew about the vapour surrounding the earth like the bark round a tree; when this was torn away and shut off in certain rings, the sun, moon and stars came into existence' (*translator*, Guthrie). The comparison between this passage and Simplicius *in Ph.* 24. 23 ff. is instructive. Where Simplicius refers quite generally to a 'separating off of opposites', the author of the *Stromateis* specifies that what separates off from the Boundless (or the Eternal) is, as he puts it, γόνιμον θερμοῦ τε καὶ ψυχροῦ, i.e. that which is 'capable of generating hot and cold'.[21] But Kirk and Raven[22] rightly point out that 'the nature of the hot (substance) and cold (substance) thus cryptically produced appears from what follows: they are flame and air-mist (the inner part of which is assumed to have condensed into earth)'. And thereafter the account des-

---

[20] τὸ ἐκ τοῦ ἀιδίου γόνιμον. Diels (*Doxographi*, 579 note *ad loc.*) suggested τι as a possible alternative, and this is preferred by Kahn. DK and Kirk and Raven retain τό, however.

[21] Hölscher, Kahn and Guthrie understand the term γόνιμον (rightly, I believe) on the analogy of the similar expression γόνιμος καὶ ζῴων καὶ φυτῶν which is used of the heat of the sun in Theophrastus, *de Igne* 44.

[22] *The Presocratic Philosophers* (Cambridge, 1957), p. 133.

cribes how the flame is broken up into circles (surrounded by mist, though this is not stated here) to form the heavenly bodies. Here too, then, there seems to be a distinct possibility that the reference to 'hot and cold' is in the nature of a comment on Anaximander's theory, rather than a verbally accurate report.

To recapitulate the evidence for Anaximander considered so far: on the one hand, Aristotle and Simplicius refer quite generally to a separating off of opposites in Anaximander's cosmology, and Simplicius certainly reports in one passage that the substances in question are 'hot, cold, dry, wet, and the rest'. Again, the hot and the cold at least are referred to in one text of Aetius (ii. 11, 5) and again in the phrase 'germ of hot and cold' in the *Stromateis*. On the other hand, Aristotle and the doxographers do sometimes reformulate Presocratic theories in terms of the opposites (such as hot and cold); against Aetius, ii. 11, 5, it may be argued that elsewhere Anaximander's theory of the heavenly bodies is much more often described in terms of *fire* and *mist*, and the reference to hot and cold in the phrase quoted in the *Stromateis* seems simply to anticipate the fuller and more precise description that follows: in effect what is produced from the original 'germ' is a *flame* which grows round the *mist* that encircles the earth. On this evidence, the view adopted by Hölscher, that what was produced from the Boundless was not 'the hot' and 'the cold' as such, but rather such substances as (e.g.) flame and mist,[23] seems, to my mind to have the balance of probabilities in its favour; and it seems to derive some support from the fact that in the earliest physical and cosmological theories which have survived in original fragments (those of Xenophanes, Heraclitus, and Parmenides in the Way of Seeming) the primary elements of which other things are composed are such substances as water and earth,[24] fire, light, and night, and not the hot, the cold, the dry, and the wet themselves.[25]

[23] Hölscher refers tentatively to 'Feuer und Luft', but stresses that the question must remain open.
[24] E.g. Xenophanes Frags. 29 and 33, though neither of these fragments necessarily implies a general physical theory (see Guthrie, *HGP*, i. 383 ff.).
[25] These opposites are, however, mentioned in Heraclitus Frag. 126. But this simply refers (like many other fragments in Heraclitus) to the *interconnection* between these opposites (we might compare the mention of day and night, winter and summer, war and peace, satiety and hunger in Fragment 67, for example), and does not suggest that these opposites have any

Yet if the likelihood is that Anaximander's cosmological theory was stated in terms of such substances as e.g. fire and mist, there is surely no reason to doubt that an important and original feature of that theory was that the relationship between the substances in question was conceived as some sort of *opposition*. This seems clear from the one major piece of evidence that we have yet to consider, the fragment itself, where he says 'they pay the penalty and recompense to each other for their injustice according to the ordering of time'. If we assume, as we surely must, that 'they' here refers to cosmological factors of some sort, the sentence tells us nothing about the nature of those factors, but what it does illuminate is Anaximander's conception of the relationships between them, which are described in terms of alternating aggression and reconciliation. As Kirk and Raven, among others, have noted (*op. cit.*, 118) 'the things which commit injustice on each other must be equals, different and correlative', and they continue 'these are most likely to be the opposed substances which make up the differentiated world'. Now the parallels between the known features of Anaximander's cosmology and the system which Parmenides describes in the Way of Seeming are quite striking. Whether or not we hold (with Gigon)[26] that the substances that separate off from the Boundless are Light and Darkness themselves, there seems to be a close similarity between the *fire* or *flame* and *opaque mist* which appears in the reports of Anaximander's theory of the heavenly bodies and in the early stages of the cosmology attributed to him in the *Stromateis*, and the two principles which Parmenides calls 'heavenly fire of flame' (Frag. 8, 56) or 'light' (Frag. 9) or 'flame' (Frag. 12) and 'blind night' or 'obscure night' (Frag. 8, 59, Frag. 9, 3),[27]

[26] *Der Ursprung der griechischen Philosophie*, Basel, 1945, 75.
[27] This is not to say, of course, that in choosing Light and Night as his principles in the Way of Seeming Parmenides may not have been influenced by other philosophers besides Anaximander. It has often been remarked that this pair figures in the Pythagorean συστοιχία given by Aristotle at *Metaph*. 986 a 22 ff., though we cannot be certain whether this represents a pre- or a post-Parmenidean theory. It may be added that the question of whether, or in what sense, the cosmology of the Way of Seeming represents

special role in Heraclitus' physical or cosmological theory. To judge from Fragments 31 and 36 that theory was stated in terms of fire, earth and sea (water), and not in terms of the opposites as such themselves.

and it has often been noticed that the obscure system of inter-woven rings, composed of fire or light and darkness, which Aetius (ii. 7. 1, *DK* 28 A 37) attributes to Parmenides and which is referred to briefly in Frag. 12, bears a marked resemblance to Anaximander's system of the heavenly bodies, with its series of rings compounded of fire and mist.[28] But it is the account of the relationships between major cosmological factors which especially concerns us here. Where we *infer* from Anaximander's fragment that certain cosmological factors (whether two or more than two in number) are opposed to one another, but of equal status, Parmenides' description of his principles in the Way of Seeming is *explicit*: they are *opposites* (τἀντία δ' ἐκρίναντο δέμας Frag. 8, 55, τἀντία v. 59) and 'both of them are *equal*' (ἴσων ἀμφοτέρων Frag. 9, 4). There is, of course, no need to suppose that Anaximander is the only, or even the most important, influence which can be detected in the Way of Seeming. Parmenides' own claim that it is the best cosmology of its kind (which is implied by the remark 'so that no opinion of mortals may outrun you' Frag. 8, 61) suggests that whatever influences he has undergone, or whatever the sources from which he has drawn, he has modified and developed his predecessors' theories in the Way of Seeming, not simply copied them, and indeed there appear to be certain specific points of difference between the theories reported from the Way of Seeming and those ascribed to Anaximander in particular (see above, note 28). But if we ask what form the opposition between cosmological factors took in Anaximander, the Way of Seeming suggests one *possible* answer. The things whose acts of aggression are referred to in Anaximander's fragment were certainly oppo-sites in the original sense of hostile to one another. But if the

[28] There is a full discussion of Parmenides' highly obscure theory in Heath, *Aristarchus of Samos* (London, 1913), pp. 66 ff., who notes that it 'seems to be directly adapted from Anaximander's theory of hoops or wheels'. Yet Parmenides' theory was clearly an adaptation, rather than simply a copy, of Anaximander's, for while each of Anaximander's wheels consisted of fire enclosed in mist, Parmenides apparently distinguished between three different kinds of rings, one sort made of 'the rare' (light) alone, a second made of 'the dense' (darkness) alone, and a third composed of both elements combined.

Parmenides' own beliefs is irrelevant to the present issue in that whatever view we adopt on that problem, the cosmology in question may exhibit resemblances to Anaximander's system.

things in question were not the hot and the cold, the dry and the wet themselves, it seems probable enough that they were conceived as possessing certain specific opposite characteristics, just as in Parmenides' Way of Seeming Night is described as dense and heavy and Fire is, no doubt, conceived both as rare and light (though the test of Frag. 8, 57, is corrupt). In conclusion, we may agree with Hölscher and others that the reports in Aristotle and Simplicius that refer to a separating off of opposites have to some degree reformulated Anaximander's ideas, and yet the actual extent of that reformulation may not have been very great. Whatever the substances were that separate off from the Boundless in the early stages of cosmological development, the notion of some *opposition* between them certainly seems to have been part of Anaximander's theory.[29] If the evidence suggests that these substances were, e.g., fire and mist rather than the hot and the cold themselves, it nevertheless seems possible, and indeed quite probable, that Anaximander himself distinctly associated hot and cold and other pairs of opposites with the substances in question, just as Parmenides associated certain pairs of opposites (rare and dense, light and heavy) with Fire and Night in the Way of Seeming.

A note should be added on the originality and significance of Anaximander's theory of the interactions between opposed cosmological factors. It is well known that certain Presocratic cosmological doctrines are foreshadowed, though often only quite dimly foreshadowed, in Homer and Hesiod. The notion of 'elements', i.e. primary component parts, is, perhaps, implicit in the myth of the making of Pandora out of earth and water,[30] and

---

[29] A similar doctrine of the interaction between opposed substances of various sorts can be traced not only in the fragment and in the theory of the formation of the world reported by Pseudo-Plutarch where (hot) flame and (cold) mist separate off from the Boundless, but also in several of the biological and geophysical theories attributed to Anaximander. Thus according to Hippolytus, *Ref.* i. 6, 6 (*DK* A 11) he held that living creatures arose from the *wet* acted upon by the *sun* (cf. Aetius, v. 19, 4, *DK* A 30), and according to the theory described in Aristotle, *Mete.* 353 b 6 ff. and attributed to Anaximander by Alexander and Aetius (*DK* A 27) he may have represented the sea as what is left of the original *moisture* in the region round the earth, after this had been dried by the *sun*.

[30] Hesiod, *Op.* 60 ff. *Iliad*, vii. 99, is also usually mentioned in this context, though its interpretation is, to my mind, quite doubtful.

Kahn[31] has recently attempted to trace how Empedocles' doctrine of the four elements may have developed out of references to the four world-areas, sky, sea, earth, and underworld (or night) in such passages as *Iliad*, xv. 189 ff., Hesiod, *Theogony* 106 f., 736 f., although this seems at best a remote possibility. It has been noted, too, that opposed factors of various sorts appear quite prominently in the *Theogony*. Emphasis is sometimes laid on the reference to Night (and Erebos) and Day (and Aither) at 123 ff. (a passage which implies the priority of Night); even more important, no doubt, is the role ascribed to Earth and Heaven (132 ff., 147 ff.) as the parents of various creatures, and the use of sexual imagery, the pairing of *male* and *female* personifications, recurs, of course, throughout the *Theogony*. Yet what the *Theogony* contains is merely an account of the *origins* of the various entities mentioned: it is not concerned with the *present* interactions, changes or relationships between them. Anaximander, on the other hand, attempted, it seems, not only to describe the formation of the universe from the Boundless, but also to give an account of the *continuing interactions* between things in the world as we know it. Unlike Earth and Heaven in the *Theogony*, which unite simply to produce a series of offspring, but whose subsequent relationship is left undefined, the unnamed subjects of Anaximander's fragment are involved in a continuous self-regulating interaction, an alternating cycle of 'justice' and 'injustice'. This is a new and undoubtedly most important conception, the introduction of which may be said to mark the beginning of cosmology as such, as opposed to cosmogony or theogony.[32] Moreover, we should note that it is in connection with theories of a type broadly similar to Anaximander's that the hot and the cold, the dry and the wet are most often used in later philosophical and medical writers. The first philosophical text in which these four opposites appear (Heraclitus Frag. 126) describes their *inter*actions: 'cold things grow hot, hot is cooled, wet is dried, dry becomes wet'. Anaxagoras, too, stresses the *inter*dependence of hot and cold in Fragment 8, and there are, of course, many medical theorists who connected health, or the natural state of the body, with the balanced interaction of these and other opposites, and disease with their

---

[31] *Op. cit.*, 134 ff. cf. also M. C. Stokes, 'Hesiodic and Milesian Cosmogonies', Pt. 1, *Phronesis*, VII (1962), 1 ff.
[32] See G. Vlastos' article, 'Isonomia', *AJP*, LXXIV (1953), 337 ff.

temporary imbalance. We find, then, that while the first extant physical theory based on the hot and the cold, the dry and the wet as the four primary elements of other things appears in *On the Nature of Man*, the doctrine of the balanced interaction of opposed substances occurs in various forms in earlier theorists and goes right back to Anaximander himself. Furthermore, while we cannot be certain of the exact terms in which his cosmological theory was expressed, it is likely enough that he referred to some interaction between hot and cold substances, at least, if not between the hot and the cold as independent entities.

II

The hot and the cold, the dry and the wet appear particularly often, though not exclusively, in theories of a general type which can be traced back as far as Anaximander, in which the relationship between opposed factors is conceived as one of a continuous, balanced interaction. Unlike right and left, male and female, or light and darkness, these four opposites do not figure in the Pythagorean 'co-ordinate columns' ($\sigma\upsilon\sigma\tau o\iota\chi\iota\alpha$)[33] and it may seem unlikely that any of the theories in which they appear should be affected by preconceived notions of value such as influence many of the doctrines which were based on right and left. Yet these two pairs are undoubtedly correlated often enough with other opposites, and moreover some of the correlations which were proposed quite clearly correspond not to any empirically verifiable data, so much as to assumptions concerning the values of these opposite terms. Several of the theories which were based on these opposites can, in fact, only be explained on the hypothesis that they too sometimes possessed certain positive and negative values, though these may be neither so pronounced, nor so stable, as those of the pair right and left. First, however, we should consider to

[33] Hot and cold, dry and wet are, however, described as being $\iota\sigma\acute{o}\mu o\iota\rho\alpha$ in the world in the cosmology reported to have been found by Alexander Polyhistor in certain 'Pythagorean notebooks' (Diogenes Laertius, viii. 24 ff., *DK* 58 B 1a) though the value of this evidence is disputed (see most recently Guthrie, *HGP*, i. 201, n. 3). As Kahn notes (*op. cit.*, 190) the doctrine of the equality of hot, cold, dry, and wet resembles that which is found in, for example, *On the Nature of Man*, Ch. 7 (L. vi. 48, 20 ff.). The conception of the special importance of the hot, and its connection with life, in Chs. 27 f., may also be paralleled elsewhere, e.g. in the theory attributed to Philolaus in Anon. Lond. xviii. 8 ff., and *On Fleshes*, Ch. 2, L. viii. 584, 9 ff.

what extent these opposites, hot, cold, dry, and wet, had any marked symbolic associations for the ancient Greeks as a whole, in so far as we can judge from the pre-philosophical texts. Like ourselves, the ancient Greeks connected warmth not only with life itself, but also with such emotions as joy and relief.[34] Conversely, cold is associated, naturally enough, with death, and then also with such emotions as fear.[35] As regards the pair dry and wet, several usages suggest that the Greeks conceived the living as 'wet' and the dead as 'dry'. In the *Odyssey* (vi. 201) we find the expression διερὸς βροτός ('wet mortal') used apparently as the equivalent of ζωὸς βροτός (e.g. xxiii. 187) to mean 'living mortal' (cf. ix. 43, where the same adjective evidently means 'active'), and there seems no good reason to suppose that διερός here is anything other than the common Greek word which literally means 'wet' (e.g. Hesiod, *Op.* 460).[36] Conversely, dead or dying things are 'dry'. This is obviously true of dead wood (e.g. ἀζόμενος used of a poplar dying after it has been felled, *Iliad,* iv. 487), but 'dead' parts of the body, such as the nails, are also described as 'dry' (e.g. Hesiod, *Op.* 743). The dead themselves were called ἀλίβαντες (e.g. Plato, *Rep.* 387 c) which was taken to mean 'without moisture',[37] and the old, too, were apparently thought of as 'dry' for when Athena is about to transform Odysseus into an old man at *Od.* xiii. 392 ff. she says she will 'dry up' his fine skin (κάρψω μὲν χρόα καλόν 398, cf. 430).[38]

[34] Thus the basic meaning of ἰαίνω seems to be to warm (e.g. *Od.* x. 359, cf. melt, *Od.* xii. 175), but when applied to the θυμός, for example, it comes to mean 'comfort', e.g. *Od.* xv. 379, *Iliad,* xxiv. 119, cf. ἰαίνομαι, *Od.* xix. 537.
[35] Among the objects to which the epithets κρυερός and κρυόεις are applied in Homer or Hesiod are Hades (*Op.* 153), fear (*Iliad,* ix. 2), war (*Th.* 936) and γόος (*Iliad,* xxiv. 524).
[36] Cf. Onians, *Origins of European Thought,* Cambridge, 1951, 254 ff. Onians (Ch. 6, 200 ff.) also discusses the expression κατείβετο δὲ γλυκὺς αἰών (e.g. *Od.* v. 152) and collects certain evidence which suggests that sexual love and desire may have been associated with moisture by the ancient Greeks (e.g. Hesiod, *Th.* 910, Alcman 59 Page, Anacreon 114 Page, *h. Hom.* xix. 33 f.).
[37] Cf., Aesch. Frag. 229 which speaks of the dead in whom there is no moisture (ἰκμάς). In the Orphic fragment 32 (*a*) and (*b*) (in *DK* as 1 B 17 and 17a) the dead man who speaks describes himself as αὖος, and the belief that the dead are thirsty evidently underlies the widespread Greek practice of offering them libations.
[38] Cf. e.g. Sophocles, *El.* 819, where Electra, foreseeing her old age, says αὐανῶ βίον.

These usages are, for the most part, clearly derived from such obvious facts of experience as the dryness of dead wood, the warmth of living animals, and the cold of the dead. From this largely biological point of view, hot and wet are together opposed to cold and dry. Yet from another point of view a different correlation naturally suggests itself. The Greek summer is unmistakably hot and dry, the Greek winter unmistakably cold and wet. The contrast between the season of cold and rains and the season when 'Sirius dries the head and the knees and the skin is parched by the burning heat' is vividly described by Hesiod (*Op.* 504 ff., 582 ff.).[39] If the antithesis between Heaven and Earth is particularly important in early Greek religious beliefs, the hot and the dry are naturally associated with the sun and so with Heaven. Unlike right and left, neither hot and cold, nor dry and wet, it seems, possessed any strong positive or negative values *in themselves*, though they acquire such values *by association* in different contexts. But while hot and cold have uniformly positive, and negative associations respectively, the dry and the wet, on the other hand, appear to have ambivalent associations. On the one hand, hot and wet are both connected with what is alive, and cold and dry with the dead, and here wet acquires certain positive, dry certain negative, overtones; but on the other hand, observation of the seasons naturally suggested a different correlation, in which the *dry* and the hot are the positive terms set over against the negative cold and *wet*.

In the philosophers, these opposites are correlated sometimes from a 'cosmological', sometimes from a 'biological', point of view. Anaxagoras, for instance (Frag. 15), separates on the one side cold and wet and dense and dark (associating these, in all probability, with earth) and on the other side hot and dry and rare (connected with aither), and Parmenides, too, very probably associated hot, as well as rare, with fire and light, and cold, as well as dense and heavy, with night of darkness, as the scholion reported by Simplicius (*in Ph.* 31. 3 ff.) explicitly suggests. On

---

[39] It is to be noted, however, that there is no sign in Hesiod, or anywhere else in pre-philosophical literature, of any schematic correlation between the four seasons and the four opposites, such as we later find in, for example, *On the Nature of Man*, Ch. 7 (L. vi. 46, 9 ff.), where winter is wet and cold, spring wet and hot, summer dry and hot, and autumn dry and cold.

the other hand, there is plenty of evidence that the belief in the connection between life and the hot and the wet continued in Greek philosophy and medicine.[40]

Each of the two types of correlations which we have noted so far draws on a different set of observations, on the one hand such meteorological phenomena as the alternation of summer and winter and day and night, and on the other such biological phenomena as the warmth of living creatures and the coldness, and in some cases the dryness, of what is dead. But when we turn to some of the more detailed doctrines which were based on these opposites, we find theories which apparently have no basis in empirical evidence at all. Thus it was widely assumed that the difference between the two sexes was in some way to be connected with a difference between hot and cold (and sometimes, too, between dry and wet), though there was no general agreement as to which opposites corresponded with which sex. The view that women are hotter than men is mentioned by Aristotle at *PA* 648 a 28 ff., where he ascribes it to Parmenides among others. Furthermore the *grounds* on which this theory was adopted are clear from Aristotle's text and from the Hippocratic treatise *On the Diseases of Women* (Book i, Ch. i, L. viii. 12, 17 ff.), namely that menstruation is due to an abundance of (hot) blood and is, therefore, a sign of the greater heat of women. But if this was one opinion that was put forward, the contrary view, that men are hotter than women, was maintained, for example, by Empedocles (Arist. *ib.*, cf. Frags. 65 and 67). If we ask why *this* position was adopted, the answer lies not so much in any empirical data that could be adduced, as in the belief that male and hot are inherently superior to their respective opposites female and cold. True, both the authors of *On Regimen* and Aristotle feel it necessary to defend this view with arguments, though on examination

---

[40] The idea that living creatures originated in the wet when acted upon by the sun is attributed to Anaximander at Hippolytus, *Ref.* i, 6, 6 (*DK* 12 A 11) and a similar theory occurs in the cosmology reported in Diodorus (i. 7, 3 ff., *DK* 68 B 5. 1) (cf. also the view mentioned by Aristotle when he discusses the possible reasons which may have led Thales to make water the principle, namely that 'the hot itself comes to be from this and lives by this', *Metaph.* 98 b 23 f.). *On Regimen*, i, Chs. 32 f. (L. vi. 506, 14 ff.) develops the theory that generation takes place from an interaction between the hot and the wet (or Fire and Water) and the connection between humidity and vital heat is also pointed out in *On Fleshes*, Ch. 9 (L. viii. 596 9 ff.).

their arguments can be seen to consist largely of special pleading. (1) At *On Regimen*, i, Ch. 34 (L. vi. 512, 13 ff.) the writer suggests that males are hotter and drier (*a*) because of their regimen, and (*b*) because females purge the hot from their bodies every month. But (*a*) depends on the writer's schematic, *a priori* analysis of the effects of food and exercise, and (*b*) is clearly a case of special pleading, since if the effect of menstruation is taken to be that females become colder, then by the same reasoning they should also become *drier* on the loss of blood. Yet in the writer's view *males* are hotter and *drier* (conforming to the element Fire) and females are colder and wetter (conforming to the element Water). These opposites are, in fact, arranged according to the writer's notions of fitness (hot, dry, male, and fire each being the positive terms), rather than according to his observation of the differences between the two sexes. (2) Aristotle shares a similar doctrine, but the arguments he uses to defend it are no more convincing. At *GA* 765 b 8 ff. he distinguishes males and females by their ability, or inability, to concoct the blood, assuming that that which becomes the menses in females, becomes semen in males. He notes once again (as at *PA* 648 a 28 ff.) that other theorists took menstruation as a sign of the greater heat of the female sex, but he suggests that this view does not take into account the possibility that blood may be more or less pure, more or less concocted, and he argues, or rather asserts, that semen, though smaller in quantity, is purer and more concocted than the menses.[41] While it is interesting that Aristotle refers here to qualitative, rather than to purely quantitative, differences, in order to determine what is 'hot', his view that males are hotter than females depends first on the notion that semen and menses are the end-products of strictly comparable processes, and second, and more important, on the quite arbitrary assumption that semen is the *natural* product of the process of concoction, and the menses are an *impure* residue. Aristotle believes that the female is, as it were, a deformed male, and it is this conviction, rather than any empirical con-

---

[41] There is an obscure comparison with the production of fruit at *GA* 765 b 28 ff. ('the nutriment in its first stage is abundant, but the useful product derived from it is small'). The idea seems to be that as a plant turns its food first into leaves, then into fruit, so animals turn theirs first into blood, and then (in males) into semen (see Platt's note in the Oxford translation, *ad loc.*).

siderations, that underlies his doctrine that males are hotter than females.[42]

One clear instance where certain theorists correlated hot and cold, dry and wet and other opposites according to preconceived ideas of fitness or value has now been considered, and other less interesting examples could be given from fifth- and fourth-century writers.[43] But the most striking evidence of the tendency to treat these pairs as consisting of a positive and a negative pole comes from Aristotle, whose theories should now be considered in more detail. First we should note how he defines these four terms at *GC* 329 b 26 ff. 'Hot' is 'that which combines things of the same kind' (τὸ συγκρῖνον τὰ ὁμογενῆ); 'cold' 'that which brings together and combines homogeneous and heterogeneous things alike' (τὸ συνάγον καὶ συγκρῖνον ὁμοίως τά τε συγγενῆ καὶ τὰ μὴ ὁμόφυλα); 'wet' is 'that which, being readily delimited (i.e. by something else), is not determined by its own boundary' (τὸ ἀόριστον οἰκείῳ ὅρῳ, εὐόριστον ὄν) and 'dry' 'that which, not being readily delimited (i.e. by something else), is determined by its own boundary' (τὸ εὐόριστον μὲν οἰκείῳ ὅρῳ, δυσόριστον δέ). These definitions are highly abstract and convey no hint that these opposites had any positive or negative associations for Aristotle. It is all the more surprising, then, that in other contexts these pairs are clearly conceived as divided into a positive, and a negative, pole. This is particularly obvious in the case of hot and cold. As we have just seen, Aristotle's belief that the male sex is hotter than the female has no empirical basis, but merely reflects his preconceived notion of the superiority of *male* and *hot*. The doctrine that the right hand side of the body is hotter than the left is another theory that derives from assumptions concerning

---

[42] E.g. *GA* 737 a 27 ff. τὸ γὰρ θῆλυ ὥσπερ ἄρρεν ἐστὶ πεπηρωμένον, καὶ τὰ καταμήνια σπέρμα, οὐ καθαρὸν δέ. Cf. further E. Lesky, *Die Zeugungs- und Vererbungslehren der Antike und ihr Nachwirken*, Wiesbaden, 1951, 151 f.

[43] Thus there is an elaborate schema in which the four ages of man are correlated with pairs of opposites in *On Regimen*, i, Ch. 33 (L vi. 510, 24 ff.), the first age being hot and wet, the second hot and dry, the third cold and dry, and old men cold and wet. But this schema seems dictated in part, at least, by the author's desire to associate the second age, that of the young man, with the male sex and the superior element Fire, and old age with the inferior element Water (cold and wet): his view that the old are cold and *wet* in particular runs counter to the generally accepted Greek notions though it also appears in *On Regimen in Health* Ch. 2 (L. vi. 74, 19 ff.).

the values of these terms and has no basis in fact (see *JHS*, LXXXII (1962) 62 ff.). Then again in *PA* B 2 647 b 29 ff. he suggests certain correlations between the temperature and the purity of the blood, and the strength and intelligence of different species of animals or even of different parts of the same animal. Thus thick and hot blood is conducive to strength, and thinner and colder blood to sensation and intelligence,[44] but 'best of all are those animals whose blood is hot and thin and clear: for such are favourably constituted both for courage and for intelligence'.[45] Elsewhere the association between heat and perfection is again apparent when he suggests at *PA* 653 a 27 ff. that the region round the heart and the lung is hotter and richer in blood in man than in any other animal (and in males more so than in females), for this too is a doctrine for which he can have had no direct evidence.

In Aristotle's theory hot is clearly the positive term, cold the privation: indeed this is explicitly stated on several occasions (e.g. *Cael.* 286 a 25 f., *GC* 318 b 16 f.). His attitude towards the pair dry and wet is, however, less clear. At *PA* 670 b 18 ff. where he correlates hot and right on the one hand, and cold and left on the other, the inferior left side of the body is said to be both cold and *wet*. Again at *GA* 766 b 31 ff. he says that parents who have a 'wetter or more feminine' constitution tend to produce female children, and this suggests that wet is also associated with the inferior female sex.[46] On the other hand at *GA* B 1 (732 b 15 ff.) he defines the main genera of animals according to their methods of reproduction (which correspond to differences in their constitutions) and here the most perfect animals, the Vivipara, are said to be 'hotter and wetter and less earthy by nature' (732 b 31 f.). The second group, the 'ovoviviparous' animals (e.g. cartilaginous fishes) are cold and wet, the third and the fourth (the Ovipara which lay perfect, and those which lay

---

[44] One of the facts which he has in mind when making this latter suggestion is that some bloodless animals (e.g. bees) are more intelligent than many sanguineous animals which are hotter than them (*PA* 648 a 5 ff.).

[45] He goes on to suggest that the upper parts of the body are distinguished in this respect (i.e. in the heat and purity of their blood) from the lower, as also are males from females, and the right side of the body from the left (*PA* 648 a 11 ff.).

[46] The view that men are dry and hot, and women wet and cold is also often expressed in the Pseudo-Aristotelian *Problemata* (e.g. 879 a 33 ff.).

imperfect, eggs) are hot and dry, and cold and dry respectively, and the fifth and final group (insects) are 'coldest of all' (733 b 10 ff.). Greater perfection clearly corresponds, in this schema, to a combination of greater heat and greater 'humidity'. Again at *Long.* 466 a 18 ff. he says that 'we must assume that the living animal is by nature wet and hot, and life too is such, while old age is cold and dry, as also is that which is dead: for this is plain to observation'. Yet he goes on to note that both the quantity and the *quality* of the humidity of animals affect their length of life: 'for not only must there be a lot of the wet, but it must also be hot' (a 29 ff.). The pair dry and wet occupies, then, a somewhat ambivalent position in Aristotle's philosophy, as indeed it had also done, to some extent, in earlier Greek speculative thought. On the one hand he notices a connection between humidity and life, and between dryness and death (and here he develops a notion which can be traced back to Homer and Hesiod). Yet this does not prevent him from suggesting, in other contexts, that the wet is the inferior, private term, when he correlates it with female, left and cold.

The evidence we have considered shows that the tendency to divide opposites into a positive and a negative pole is by no means confined, in early Greek speculative thought, to the use of such pairs as right and left, or light and darkness, but is found also in some of the theories based on the much more common pairs hot and cold, dry and wet. This is all the more striking since the symbolic associations which these two pairs possessed for the ancient Greeks were not particularly marked (compared with those of right and left and certain other opposites) and indeed in the case of dry and wet these associations were rather ambivalent. Hot and cold, dry and wet do not figure in the Pythagorean συστοιχία as reported by Aristotle: moreover when they are introduced into cosmology and medicine, they are used most often in theories in which their *balance* and *continuous interaction* are stressed, which certainly do not imply, though they do not exclude, the idea that these pairs are each divided into a positive and a negative pole. Yet on several occasions we find theorists proposing correlations between these and other opposites which have no basis in empirical evidence at all, but merely reflect certain preconceived notions of the values of the contrasted terms. Several theorists maintained, for example, that the male sex is hotter than the female, and Empedocles, for one, took the difference in temperature to be the origin or source of the difference between the two sexes (Frags. 65, 67). If this may have been the traditional view, or rather that view that accords with the generally accepted notions concerning the values of these opposites, other theorists rejected it and reversed the correlation. In discussing the use of right and left, I noted that some of the *a priori* theories which were proposed, were rejected by later writers on empirical grounds: thus Aristotle refuted the belief that males are formed on the right side of the womb by referring to the evidence of anatomical dissections (*GA* 765 a 16). So too it would seem that some theorists (of whom Parmenides may well have been the first) argued from the fact of menstruation that females, and not males, are the hotter sex. Among later philosophers, the tendency to divide hot and cold, and dry and wet, each into a positive and a negative pole is particularly marked in Aristotle, even though the abstract definitions which he gives of these four terms at *GC* 329 b 26 ff. give no hint of this. Although he never presents his theory in the form of a complete συστοιχία, his Table of Opposites, if we reconstructed it from remarks scattered through the physical works, would be almost as extensive as that which he attributed to the Pythagoreans. Right and male and up and front and hot and dry would certainly appear on one side, set over against left, female, down, back, cold, and wet on the other, and such other pairs as light and heavy, rare and dense, might also be included in the list, correlated with hot and cold or dry and wet—the Table as a whole reflecting both empirical and *a priori* considerations.[47] Even where the facts

---

[47] At *Cael.* 286 a 26 ff. 'heavy' is said to be the privation of 'light', and at *Ph.* 217 b 17 ff. and *Cael.* 288 b 7 ff. 'heavy' and 'dense' are associated together, and so too 'light' and 'rare' (for this reason, perhaps, as well as because of the association between 'thin' and 'clear', the blood of males is said to be 'thinner' than that of females, *PA* 648 a 11 ff.). Yet with such a pair as 'soft' and 'hard' we find different types of correlation proposed in different contexts: on the one hand 'hard' is associated with 'dense' (e.g. *Ph* 217 b 17), but on the other it is assimilated to 'dry' at *GC* B 2 330 a 8 ff. in a chapter in which he reduces various types of opposites to 'hot' and 'cold' or 'dry' and 'wet' while at the same time pointing out some of the ambiguities of these terms. From other passages (e.g. *Ph.* 259 a 6 ff.) it would appear that like the Pythagoreans, Aristotle thought 'one' superior to 'many' and 'limited' to 'unlimited'.

appeared to conflict with his correlations, he did not abandon his belief that these pairs of opposites may be arranged in a single systematic schema. This is apparent from his firm correlation of wet with left, female and cold, even though he recognized the connection between humidity and warmth and life, and between dryness and cold and death. Indeed, on the subject of hot and cold, he explicitly remarked on the extent of the disagreement that existed between different theorists as to which things are hot and which cold. As he puts it at *PA* 648 a 33 ff. (cf. also a 24 f.) 'if there is so much dispute about the hot and the cold, what are we to think about the rest? For the hot and the cold are the most distinct of the things which affect our senses'. One instance of such a dispute, concerning the temperature of the two sexes, has already been discussed, and Aristotle mentions several others.[48] Yet we saw that while there was no agreement as to which sex was hot, which cold, *both* parties in this dispute seem to have assumed that *some* correlation may be established between male and female on the one hand, and hot and cold on the other. Some at least of those who rejected the view that males are hotter than females, were not content simply to reject that view, but proposed the contrary, but equally erroneous, theory that the female sex is uniformly and essentially hotter.[49] It is, then, one of the notable features of the use of hot and cold and dry and wet in early Greek speculative thought, that while there was little agreement about their particular application to different problems, the assumption that *some* correlation was to be set up between these and other pairs of opposites was sometimes shared

[48] E.g. the dispute as to whether land-animals are hotter or colder than water-animals, and the disagreement about which 'humours' are hot and which cold. Cf. also the opposite views about the nature of the ψυχή mentioned at *de An.* 405 b 24 ff. We know little about the arguments used on each side in these controversies, but it seems unlikely that *a priori* considerations affected the discussion to any great extent. Thus Philolaus seems to have held that the phlegm is hot (as opposed to the generally accepted view that it is cold) simply on the grounds of a suggested etymology of the word φλέγμα from φλέγειν (see Anon. Lond. xviii. 41 ff.).

[49] It is strange that the fact of menstruation was taken by both sides in this dispute to be significant of a difference in the temperature of the two sexes (though they disagreed about how this evidence was to be interpreted). Yet while the temperature of the female certainly rises and falls according to the menstrual cycle, the fact of menstruation provides no evidence concerning the *relative* temperature of *males* and females at all.

both by those who put forward views based on *a priori* considerations, and by those who rejected those views on empirical grounds.[50] And it is, perhaps, particularly surprising that the tendency to incorporate these opposites into a single systematic, but often quite arbitrary, schema should survive in Aristotle, even though he was fully aware of the lack of agreement among his predecessors on the subject of the hot and the cold and the dry and the wet, and drew attention, on several occasions, to some of the ambiguities which the use of these terms involved.[51]

---

[50] The writer of *On Ancient Medicine* provides something of an exception to this general rule, for he notices the difficulties which arose concerning the application of the doctrine of the hot and the cold, the dry and the wet to problems of diagnosis and cure (Ch. 13, *CMG* i. 1, 44, 8 ff.) and then suggests that hot and cold are the least important of the δυνάμεις in the body (Ch. 16, 47, 12 ff.).

[51] I must express my thanks to Mr G. S. Kirk for reading and criticizing an earlier draft of this paper. The faults that remain are, of course, entirely my own responsibility.

XI

ANAXIMANDER AND THE
BEGINNINGS OF
GREEK PHILOSOPHY*

Uvo Hölscher

HERMANN FRÄNKEL'S proposition, that all doxographical statements are indefinite if they do not include the original wording,[1] is, to a certain extent, also true in reverse. For although it was actually in connection with Anaximander that this remark was made, discussion of the Anaximander fragment has shown how ambiguous a sentence remains when examined in isolation, as well as how helpful it is to analyse the tradition which transmits it. Some things are still drawn from the latter without adequate enquiry into their origin. In so far as the following deals once again with the doctrine of opposites,[2] I am less interested in arguing the rights of each single *placitum*, than in recognizing something of the nature of the rather inaccessible archaic way of thinking. This will be done firstly by continuing an investigation which has already proved its worth: that is, criticism of Aristotle's accounts. After that, an attempt is made to establish what this way of thinking was like by examining the assumptions from which Anaximander developed his conception of the origin of things.

* I gained important insights and the opportunity to write the following paper during a term as visitor at University College London, which I owe to the generosity of the British Council.

¶ The footnote numbers in this abbreviated version (see p. 310 and pp. 313-14) correspond with those of the reprint of this article by the Wissenschaftliche Buchgesellschaft.

[1] H. Fränkel, 'Parmenidesstudien', *Nachr. Gött. Ges.* (1930), p. 181; see Vol. II of this collection.
[2] This article replaces my outline published in the last volume of *Philologus* published during the war.

I. Simplicius, *Phys.*, 150, 24: ἐναντιότητες δέ εἰσι θερμὸν ψυχρὸν ξηρὸν ὑγρὸν καὶ τὰ ἄλλα ('oppositions are hot, cold, dry, wet, and the rest'). In Diels this sentence is printed with the *Testimonia* (A 9). Zeller treated it likewise, and so, most recently, did Deichgräber.[3] It does not come from Aristotle, and thus it has the value of a *testimonium* only if it comes from Theophrastus. That is Diels' opinion, and he cites the sentence as a fragment of Theophrastus (*Dox.*, p. 134). But the context in Simplicius—the interpretation of Aristotle's *Physics A* 4—contains no indication that Simplicius had here returned to Theophrastus as his source. It is true that Theophrastus is quoted on p. 149, 32—from the intermediary source or from memory from p. 24, 29—but only to be refuted immediately by citing Aristotle. Simplicius disputes the listing of the ancient *Physikoi* (149, 7) by referring to *Metaphysics* 984 a 2 and 989 a 5–15, and the succeeding argument against Alexander and Porphyry also relies entirely on references to Aristotle; it is the division of the *Physikoi* according to *alloiosis* (change of quality) and *ekkrisis* (separating out) which Simplicius rightly emphasizes in this passage of the *Physics*—again on p. 154, 2—and this is especially Aristotelian, discussed in *De gen. et corr.* A 1. After dealing at length with the first group, Simplicius comes on p. 150, 20 to *ekkrisis* and Anaximander. Here, in every way, including his formulation, he is following Aristotle. There is no reason to join Diels and Burnet in considering this passage Theophrastean,[4] since it is a mere paraphrase of *Physics A* 4. The inserted information about the first use of the word *arche* cannot serve as proof: Simplicius remembered it from his own doxography (p. 24, 15), even though the wording and context differ here. And when he finally interprets the 'opposites' with the aid of the Aristotelian qualities, he does so from his knowledge of Aristotle.[5] No trace of Theophrastus. For these reasons this sentence does not belong among the *testimonia*.

II. Simplicius, 24, 13 ff. (= Diels A 9). Deichgräber cites the entire passage, without differentiation, as Theophrastean.[6] Kranz

[3] Zeller, *Philos. d. Griechen*, I⁶, 295 A 1; Deichgräber, *Hermes*, 75 (1940), 16.
[4] Diels, *Dox.*, pp. 134 and 476n; Burnet, *Early Gr. Phil.*, Section 13.
[5] So too Zeller, *op. cit.* That in spite of this he considers the pair of opposites 'hot and cold' to be Anaximandrian rests on his interpretation of the account of Pseudo-Plutarch, see below, p. 290.
[6] *Op. cit.*, p. 11.

(in *DK*) considers only the first three sentences to be Theophrastean, while Diels (*Dox.* p. 476) attributes to Theophrastus, in addition to these, the words towards the end ἀποκρινομένων τῶν ἐναντίων διὰ τῆς ἀιδίου κινήσεως ('the opposites being separated off through the eternal movement'). I do not know of any justification for either judgement on the text. We must attempt an analysis.

At line 21 the account is interrupted by an explanation: δῆλον δὲ ὅτι . . . Theophrastus seems to write δῆλον ὡς: cf. *De sensibus*, §§ 13, 39, 52, 70. On the other hand, δῆλον ὅτι is common in Simplicius to introduce an interpretation. Most comparable is p. 24, 6, where the Theophrastean account is likewise broken off with καὶ δῆλον ὅτι. The explanations thus introduced offer suggestions, partly taken from Aristotle, as to how the philosopher could have arrived at his *arche*. They consist partly of general characterizations, partly of particular arguments. Both prove to be un-Theophrastean: the former in style—long lists of abstract qualities in the form of adjectives used as nouns, permeated also by Stoic terminology (cf. above all the long list of such adjectives, p. 36, 9–14); the latter in their purely Aristotelian content. Thus on p. 24, 6–11, after the list of qualities comes the argument from Aristotle, *Metaph.* 988 b 35; on p. 25, 10–12, again after the qualities, comes the argument from *Metaph.* 989 a 5. The closeness of the two Aristotle passages, together with the verbal echoes in Simplicius of the words of Aristotle, where he would also have found the general characterizations, are sufficient proof that Simplicius is here drawing on Aristotle himself. Thus he expressly refers to Aristotle when he states the reason for the *arche* of Anaxagoras and Archelaos, p. 27, 28. Therefore in writing this doxography, Simplicius always had Aristotle, in addition to Theophrastus (and Alexander), at hand.[7]

Thus it becomes clear that in the report of Anaximander also, from line 21 on, it is no longer Theophrastus speaking, but Simplicius. He repeats, in order to explain it, what he has previously copied out from Theophrastus (cf. ἀλλ᾽ ἑτέραν τινὰ φύσιν . . . ἀλλά τι ἄλλο παρὰ ταῦτα). The thought in this sentence is purely Aristotelian; compare Simplicius' statement about Aristotle on p. 35, 25, which agrees with it almost word for word.

[7] My previous doubts as to the Theophrastean origin of Simplicius, 23, 24 f. (*Hermes*, 81, 259) will not be repeated here. Convincing argument by McDiarmid, *Harv. Stud. Cl. Phil.* 67 (1953), pp. 135 f.

He goes on to say that Anaximander did not, like those previously named (Thales, Heraclitus, etc.), and as the last sentence about *metabole* might also suggest, hold the doctrine of a transformation of an original material, but that of the separation of opposites. This again is Aristotle's division from *Physics A* 4. Theophrastus did not use this schema in his doxography: there was no mention of *alloiosis* in Thales, the only possible predecessor to Anaximander; and condensation, which is attributed by Simplicius on p. 24, 2 to Heraclitus, was, according to his own testimony (149, 32), limited in Theophrastus to Anaximenes. But since Simplicius, disagreeing with Theophrastus but agreeing, as he thinks, with Aristotle, attributes condensation also to 'the others' (p. 150, 1), one cannot avoid the conclusion that the passage about condensation and rarefaction in Heraclitus (p. 24, 2) was added by Simplicius. It supports the same division into *alloiosis* and *ekkrisis* which he applies to Anaximander. Finally, that in so doing he has Aristotle's *Physics A* 4 before him, is shown by his last sentence: 'for that reason Aristotle groups him with those around Anaxagoras.' Thus, for the time being, Aristotle and not Theophrastus must be regarded as the source for 'the opposites being separated off'.

III. There remains 'eternal motion'. According to Hippolytus (= A 11), Theophrastus mentioned it also. For Simplicius it is the confirmation and basis of a division which he uses throughout his doxography and which likewise comes from Aristotle. Diels (*Dox.*, p. 105) thought it possible that Theophrastus, too, followed it in his chapter on the *arche*. But the following reflection shows that to be unlikely. Aristotle's division, according to *Physics A* 2, was:

	one *arche*		several	
unmoved	moved	finite		infinite (in number)

Alexander had remarked that the subdivision of the 'several' could also be applied to the two groups of the 'one', and vice versa (though meaninglessly), but had dismissed this idea as superfluous (Simplicius, 21, 34 and 41, 23). But Simplicius cannot refrain from trying out at least the first on his doxography (cf. p. 41, 10) and renounces the second possibility only with obvious regret. This leads to the following arrangement (I omit the 'several'):

One			
unmoved		moved	
infinite	finite	finite	infinite
(Melissos)	(Parmenides)	(Thales, Heraclitus)	(Anaximander, Anaximenes)

Even without Simplicius' explicit assurance (p. 28, 30) that 'this abbreviated survey is not chronological but according to affinity of doctrine', it is clear that this arrangement is his own work and is oriented to Aristotle's *Physics*, not to Theophrastus. Thus, too, the reason given for considering Hippasus' and Heraclitus' *archai* as finite obviously comes from Simplicius (p. 24, 8).

Thus in each case the introductory words (e.g. p. 24, 13, 'Of those who say [*sc.* the *arche* is] one' etc.) belong to Simplicius, as Diels saw. This does not, of course, mean that the *kinesis* in Anaximander comes from him. He probably ascribed finiteness to Thales on his own initiative, but motion is already part of the Aristotelian concept of the *Physikoi* and thus would have been found in Theophrastus too. This leaves only the question of the sense in which Theophrastus spoke of 'eternal motion'. For Simplicius it is the cause of the separation of opposites. It is clear that he imagines this, as in Anaxagoras, as caused by a rotary motion (cf. p. 35, 15). It is probable that he imagines it in the same way in Anaximenes (p. 24, 31). In Aristotle *kinesis* is not limited to movement in space, and it is precisely when he attributes it to the *Physikoi* that he primarily means changeability. It is also linked with transformation in Anaximenes by Theophrastus (Simplicius p. 24, 31), and moreover, if we can trust the actual words, not as its mechanical but its immanent cause: 'through which *metabole* occurs'. Thus it must be considered possible that in speaking of 'eternal motion' Theophrastus had in mind something other than the separation of opposites. And this becomes certain when other evidence is adduced.

IV. But first Aristotle on the separation of opposites, *Physics A* 4. Aristotle has here a particular aim: to show that all earlier philosophies amount to the recognition of opposing principles, and thus to prepare the way for his own doctrine of form and its privation. The division of the *Physikoi* into two groups, according to transformation and separation of the original material, was not made for this passage; where it belongs in context, in *De gen. et corr.* A 1, it is presented as being identical with the other division into 'monists' and 'pluralists'. As representatives of *ekkrisis*, Empedocles, Anaxagoras and Democritus are named. Anaximander is noticeably absent; he really could not be counted among the 'pluralists'. But he is treated together with them in the *Physics*, where both groups are manipulated slightly to make them acknowledge the One. And here it is even possible for him to be named first in order, for the 'unity' of the beginning is far more evident in his case than with the two others, who are added with an explanatory 'For these, too, . . .', *mixis* in their case being made equivalent to the One.

However, what both the *alloiosis* group and the *ekkrisis* group have in common above all is the opposites. In this sense, condensation and rarefaction in Anaximenes (who is typical of the one group) are explained as opposites—we shall show later that this is forcing the interpretation of Anaximenes too. Aristotle, faced by the alternatives of his own division, clearly had reason to place Anaximander in the *ekkrisis* group, and since he is concerned with opposites, he writes that 'the opposites contained in the One separate out'. Moreover this sentence refers not only to Anaximander, but equally to the other two; the extract in Diels (A 16) is misleading here. In the following passage Aristotle criticizes only Anaxagoras for his doctrine that everything is 'contained' in everything, i.e. the opposites mutually in one another. In fact, 'contained in' (ἐνεῖναι) is his term and his central thought. It could not be thought until the Eleatics had criticized the concept of becoming—as Anaxagoras puts it: 'It does not come to be, but already was in existence inside'. The 'opposites' 'separate' by means of their oppositeness from the 'One' in which they are 'contained': each of these four concepts can be exemplified from fragments of Anaxagoras [8] and each recurs in Aristotle's criticism (most notably 187 a 32 and b 23). Thus it is clear that Aristotle is primarily criticizing Anaxagoras when he disputes the sentence which holds true for the whole group: 'out of the One, in which they are contained, the opposites are separated'. The One occurs also in Empedocles; we know enough about him to be able to say with what reservations the rest of the formulation

[8] The opposites Frag. 4, 8 and 15; their *diakrisis* Frag. 13, 15 and 16; the One Frag. 1, 4 and 8; being contained Frags. 4 and 6.

applies to him. For Anaximander, on the other hand, one may claim only what is firmly attested from other sources or what the words demand. For this, *ekkrisis*, the main concept which characterizes the one group as opposed to the *alloiosis* of the other, is quite sufficient. If, according to that concept, in Anaximander the world came into existence through 'separating out', there could be no doubt for Aristotle as to *what* separated: the opposites themselves, into which Empedocles' and Anaxagoras' original mixture divided, and which he tries to show constituted the leading thought of all his predecessors. Thus the sentence represents a generalization by Aristotle, in which he transfers the doctrine of the separation of opposites from the one who expressed it most clearly, to the whole *ekkrisis* group. But that, far from being a quotation from Anaximander, is an *ad hoc* interpretation.

V. For Aristotle, the concept of *ekkrisis* is linked with that of mixture. That is why in *Physics A* 4 Anaximander's 'One' is grouped with Empedocles' and Anaxagoras' 'mixtures'. Thus too, in *Metaph.* 1069 b 20 it is actually called mixture, though by means of a loose zeugma with Empedocles' mixture.[9] In both cases the question is whether the concept of mixture is Aristotle's interpretation, or whether it belongs to the source material for his interpretation. *Physics A* 4 is easier to decide: 'For these too separate the rest out of the mixture'. What they have in common is not the mixture but *ekkrisis*[10] and the One is only tacitly interpreted as mixture. Not so in *Metaph.* 1069: there it is the other way round and the mixtures are interpreted as the One,[11] and that obviously presupposes that they really were mixtures.

Now Aristotle can perfectly well even in the sense of his own terminology give the name 'mixtures' to these compounds interpreted as unities. His concept of mixture is developed in *De gen. et Corr. A* 10. There, to be contained in a genuine mixture is called 'to be *potentially*' (327 b 25). The mixture is 'the unification of the things mixed when they have been changed' (328 b 22): so, too, its separation happens by *alloiosis*. Thus in *De Caelo* 302 a 21 he

---

[9] See Zeller, I[6], 279 A 1.
[10] *Contra* W. A. Heidel, 'Qualitative Change in Pre-Socratic Philosophy', *Arch. f. Gesch. d. Philos.*, 19 (1906), pl. 345 A 24.
[11] I follow the emendation of Ross.

speaks of the *ekkrisis* of fire and earth from flesh and wood, in which they are contained *potentially*, which implies *alloiosis*. The two concepts which are contraries in his criticism of his predecessors are united in his own physics. That makes sense. The *alloiosis* group offered him this very thought of the transformation and unity of the material, whereas the *ekkrisis* group offered the conceptual stability and immutability of the opposites. In the doctrine of potentiality the contradictions of the earlier philosophers converge.

We are familiar with Aristotle's efforts to make both groups agree with respect to this doctrine—most clearly in *Physics A* 4— and particularly his attempt to interpret Anaxagoras' 'all things together' as unity, and inherence in the mixture as potentiality, not actuality.[12] The same concern is the reason for his criticism of Empedocles' *sphairos*: 'Taken as material from which the other substances come into existence by transformation, the One is the element; but in as far as it comes into existence through the coming together of substances, and the latter from its dissolution, the latter are the elements and more fundamental.'[13] His interpretation is always ultimately blocked by the mechanical descriptions of those mixtures.[14] But there is no similar criticism of Anaximander. In fact, the unity of his *apeiron* fitted Aristotle's idea of potentiality so much better that in the third book of the *Physics* he developed the concept of matter directly from his criticism of the *apeiron*.[15] And it is not for nothing that in *A* 4 he contrasts Anaximander's One with the others 'who teach the multiplicity of the One', and limits the term mixture to the latter.

From this we may conclude that the text of Anaximander, apart from the *ekkrisis* analogy, gave no grounds for regarding the *apeiron* as a mixture.

---

[12] *Met.* 989 a 30, 1063 b 29.   [13] *De gen. et corr.* 315 a 21.

[14] Cherniss's valuable book, *Aristotle's Criticism of Pre-Socratic Philosophy*, suffers mostly from the fact that he considers that Aristotle's interpretation is due to a large extent to misunderstanding. Thus in this case he presupposes that Aristotle simply could not think of Empedocles' One as a compound; to him it would be the material substrate from which the opposites came into being by qualitative change. But at the same time Aristotle's distinction between change and separation, and his placing of Empedocles in the *ekkrisis* group, shows that he was not blind to the 'ancient' mechanistic mixture doctrines.

[15] Particularly 207 a 21.

The comparison of Anaximander with Anaxagoras was taken over from Aristotle by Theophrastus (Simplicius, 27, 11)—but with a characteristic refinement: whereas Aristotle placed Anaximander's original material among the mixtures of the later philosophers (*Phys. A* 4), and vice versa interpreted these mixtures as the One material (*Metaph.* 1069), Theophrastus allows the comparison to hold good only in the second case, i.e. in the view, which he shares, of Anaxagoras' 'all things together' not as a compound but as a unity having no qualities.[16] It must be remembered, however, that the comparison is not in the paragraph on Anaximander but in the one on Anaxagoras. Simplicius, too, makes the distinction most strikingly, on p. 24, 25, 'Aristotle put Anaximander among those around Anaxagoras'; p. 154, 14, 'Theophrastus put Anaxagoras with Anaximander', i.e. Aristotle (*Phys. A* 4) makes Anaximander a 'pluralist', Theophrastus (agreeing with Aristotle *Metaph.* 1069) makes Anaxagoras a 'monist'. Theophrastus had Anaximander's text in front of him; his explanation would have been impossible, if the latter had allowed one to imagine a mixture. Thus, led by the prudent criticism of Theophrastus, we shall dissociate Anaximander from Anaxagoras again.*

VI. About the nature of Anaximander's *ekkrisis* we have information from Theophrastus. The first half of Simplicius' account of Anaximander is sufficiently guaranteed to be Theophrastean by the parallel reports in Hippolytus and Pseudo-Plutarch. The passage about the origin of the worlds from the *arche* runs, in more or less the same words in each: . . . τινὰ φύσιν ἄπειρον, ἐξ ἧς ἅπαντας γίνεσθαι τοὺς οὐρανοὺς καὶ τοὺς ἐν αὐτοῖς κόσμους ('. . . a certain infinite nature, out of which come to be all the

---

[16] Thus already Zeller, I[6], 280. Heidel ('Qual. Change . . .', p. 345) first shared this interpretation of the passage and therefore rejected Theophrastus (*Apeiron* as unity) in favour of Aristotle (*Apeiron* as mixture). Later ('On Anaximander', *Classical Philology*, 7 [1912], 230) he tried to withdraw from this position, saying that the parallels between Anaxagoras and Anaximander were almost all intended for both cases. But Simplicius' second introduction of the Theophrastus quotation, p. 154, 14, proves that it only holds good in *one* case: 'Although Theophrastus groups Anaxagoras and Anaximander together, nevertheless he also understands the words of Anaxagoras in such a way that by substrate he can mean a unified material.'
* [A paragraph on Augustine, *De civ. dei.* viii. 2, is here omitted. Eds.]

heavens and the *kosmoi* that are in them'). The expression is unusual enough to give a clue to Anaximander's actual thought.[17] In Pseudo-Plutarch it is clearer in one detail: ἀποκεκρίσθαι ('have been separated off') is preserved instead of γίνεσθαι ('come to be'). Theophrastus also spoke of the 'eternal motion', in the course of which the separation occurs (Hippolytus = A 11).[18] In view of Simplicius' 'the opposites being separated off through the eternal motion', it is here, if anywhere, that one would expect the opposites. Instead, the 'heavens'; and the '*kosmoi*' in them. Thus Simplicius has obviously smuggled in the separation of the opposites. What led him to do this is clear from the above: since on the whole he follows the Aristotelian interpretation of *ekkrisis* (separating out), he has combined this with his source. Theophrastus, where he also found the expression *apokrinesthai* (to be separated off). One should not underestimate Simplicius' independence in the doxographical chapters.

Pseudo-Plutarch has preserved a part of the Anaximandrian cosmogony from Theophrastus. The whole account divides into four sections, also marked outwardly by a repeated 'he says', and corresponding to Books I (Principles), IV (Geology), II (Cosmology) and VI (Physiology) of the *Vetusta Placita* which Diels (*Dox.*, p. 181) inferred. The same order is preserved in Hippolytus, who adds to the four information from Book III (Meteorology), and the time at which he lived, thereby indicating the arrangement in the 'biographical' intermediary source.

The third section runs:

φησὶ δέ τι [ms τὸ] ἐκ τοῦ ἀιδίου γόνιμον θερμοῦ τε καὶ ψυχροῦ κατὰ τὴν γένεσιν τοῦδε τοῦ κόσμου ἀποκριθῆναι καί τινα ἐκ τούτου φλογὸς σφαῖραν περιφυῆναι τῷ περὶ τὴν γῆν ἀέρι ὡς τῷ δένδρῳ φλοιόν· ἥστινος ἀπορραγείσης καὶ εἴς τινας ἀποκλεισθείσης κύκλους ὑποστῆναι τὸν ἥλιον καὶ τὴν σελήνην καὶ τοὺς ἀστέρας.

('He says that something productive of hot and cold was separated off from the eternal at the genesis of this world and out of this a sphere of flame grew around the air which is round the earth, like bark round the tree; when this (*sc.* the sphere) was broken

[17] Reinhardt, *Parmenides*, p. 74, detects in the formulation a trace of Anaximander's own words. Hippolytus and Pseudo-Plutarch clearly did not understand the 'worlds in the heavens'; the former replaced them with the singular, the latter took them for the same as the heavens.
[18] Cf. Simplicius, *Phys.* 41, 17.

off and shut off into certain circles, there persisted the sun and the moon and the stars.')

The pair of opposites, hot and cold, linked with the term 'separated off', has been seized upon to support previously formed opinions without regard to the rest of the text. There have even been attempts to alter the text.[19] But even when the text is kept to, the prevailing scheme of thought is usually that of the 'division' or the 'separating off' of the opposites.[20] Let us attempt to base our examination on the certainties offered by the text.

(1). The section does not offer a complete cosmogony, but deals only with the arrangement of the sky. The origin of Earth, Sea, and Air is not described.

(2). What 'separates' is not the opposites but the *gonimon*. This separation is not a splitting but a separating off. There does not seem to be any immediate statement that it is the separation from the Infinite. 'To be separated off' (*apokrinesthai*) previously used of the heavens and also occurring elsewhere, may be taken as Anaximandrian.[21]

(3). The expression τὸ ἐκ τοῦ ἀιδίου γόνιμον is strange; ἐκ τοῦ ἀιδίου as an attribute of duration would have no parallel[22] and no satisfactory meaning. On the other hand, if it refers to the place of origin, the definite article τό is surprising, since what is referred to only forms by the separation and is unknown to us until then. But the substantival γόνιμον in itself is a stumbling-block; to translate it 'the germ' may suit the sense, but grammatically it is 'the thing strong in begetting' or 'the power of begetting'; the separation would refer to the quality 'γόνιμον' and mean that something loses its power of begetting. If so, γόνιμον can only be used attributively. Thus Burnet translates, without comment, 'something able to produce'.[23] In *Doxographi Graeci*, Diels sug-

---

[19] Zeller, I⁶, 295, n. 1, suggested γόνιμον θερμόν τι καὶ ψυχρόν. Kranz, *Vorsokr. Denker* 42 changed ἀποκριθῆναι to διακριθῆναι, with the translation 'zerspalten'.
[20] E.g. H. Fränkel, 'Parmenidesstudien', p. 184 [see Vol. II of this collection]; R. Mondolfo, *l'infinito nel pensiero dei Greci*, p. 239.
[21] So already Zeller, I⁶ 294.
[22] What Heidel, 'On Anaximander', p. 229, A 2, adduces, ἐκ παντὸς τοῦ χρόνου, etc., is scarcely comparable. Moreover, Pseudo-Plutarch writes about Anaximenes (= DK A 6) ἐξ ἀιῶνος.
[23] Burnet, Section 19.

gested the indefinite τι instead of the definite τό; this is very plausible. It would also make the hitherto missing[24] connection 'was separated off . . . from the eternal'.[25] 'The eternal' seems to be the same as Anaximander's 'indestructible and deathless'.

(4). 'Something from the eternal . . . was separated off' has a parallel in 'out of this a sphere of flame grew around . . .' where 'this' refers to *gonimon*. The two processes match each other in the same way: the germ comes from the eternal, the fire from the germ. It seems that these two phases are also meant by the expression 'the heavens and the worlds in them'. The first process is described as separation, the second as growing-around and tearing-off: the basis of each is the idea of a spatial detaching.[26]

(5). The simile which illustrates this idea may be taken as Anaximander's own.[27] The vital character of the simile does not necessarily mean that the cosmos is thought of as a living being: other similes used to explain the cosmos are taken from the technical sphere. But the process itself is spontaneous, rather than mechanical and passive. The concept of an eddy as in Anaxagoras,[28] or of winnowing and sieving as in Democritus,[29] is thus excluded.

(6). Diels claimed the expression *gonimon* for Theophrastus, referring to Porphyry, *De abstin.* ii. 5. Better proof is Theophrastus' *De igne* 44, where the warmth of the sun is called 'productive (*gonimos*) of animals and plants'.[29a] Diels also surmised that the word might even be Anaximander's. In any case it suits the image of the growing tree.

(7). The opposite qualities, Hot and Cold, cannot be Anaxi-

---

[24] So that Heidel (*Proceed. of the Amer. Ac. of Arts and Sciences* [1913], p. 687) believed ἀπὸ τοῦ ἀπείρου had dropped out.

[25] ἀποκρίνεσθαι ἔκ τινος, e.g. Plato, *Republic* 564 e.

[26] Reinhardt, *Parmenides*, p. 74, stresses the spatial interpretation of ἀποκρίνεσθαι.

[27] Cf. Kranz, 'Gleichnis und Vergleich . . .', *Hermes*, 73 (1938), 117.

[28] A. Heidel, The δίνη in Anaximenes and Anaximander, *Class. Philol.*, 1 (1906), 281.

[29] Burnet, Section 17, not before the 2nd edn; Gigon, *Ursprung der griech. Philos.*, p. 78.

[29a] Cf. also Irenaeus, *adv.* Haereses ii. 18, 2 (also 2, 14), who describes Anaximander's 'immensum . . . omnium initium, *seminaliter* habens in semet ipso omnium genesin'.

mander's as such.[30] We must ask what their equivalent was in
Anaximander. The context at first suggests Fire and Air, the
only elements which are named here and which, according to
other references, form the wheels of the constellations. The second
mention of the same pair of opposites is in Aetius, ii. 11, 5
(= A 17 a): 'Anaximander [made it] of hot and cold mixture.'
Here the subject is not a Primary Mixture, but the substance of
the sky; so this does not belong next to the supposed Theophrastus fragment, where it stands in *Doxographi*, p. 134. It also
raises the question of what Theophrastus was rendering with the
two qualities. Gigon did not hesitate to translate them into
'archaic' as in Parmenides (or Hesiod) and call them 'light and
night'.[31] It is obvious how they then become 'powers': their relation to each other could only be described as complementary, as
opposites which condition each other. Pseudo-Plutarch gives no
decisive help; φλόξ (flame), in the text, is as archaic as φῶς (light).
It would be extremely strange if this characteristic pair of fundamental powers were not mentioned in the surviving doxography.
The question must remain open for the time being.

(8). Περιφυῆναι means, besides spontaneous growing forth,
that the ball of flames 'fits closely'. Then ἀπορραγείσης describes
how the fire of the heavens was set so far away, past a wide,
empty space. ἀποκλεισθείσης denotes, according to Hippolytus,
the splitting (ἀποκριθέντα again) of the heavenly fire into three
rings, and their enclosure in air. Burnet (§19) translates the following ὑποστῆναι 'came into existence'. But, first, it can hardly mean
that, and, second, to be precise, the stars have not come into
being by the enclosure. Kranz[32] translates: 'seien Sonne, Mond
und Sterne dafür eingetreten'; but what this could mean is not at
all clear. A more probable meaning is 'survive, continue to exist'.[33]

---

[30] It is true that W. Kraus (*Rh. Mus.*, 93 [1950]) thinks this possible. But see
Reinhardt, *Parmenides*, pp. 21 and 24. τὸ ἄπειρον is different: indicative not
of a quality (like the Hot), but of an appearance (like Fire).

[31] O. Gigon, *Ursprung d. gr. Phil.*, p. 75.   [32] *Vorsokrat. Denker*, p. 43.

[33] The word occurs frequently in Aetius, and never means 'to take up a
position', let alone 'arise', but always 'exist, last, survive, settle'. The sentence about Anaximander's apeiron, too: ἵνα μηδὲν ἐλλείπῃ ἡ γένεσις ἡ
ὑφισταμένη—often quoted thus but incomprehensible to me—can only mean:
'so that Becoming does not cease existing', i.e. the second ἡ should be deleted.

According to W. Kraus, *Rh. Mus.*, 93, [1950], 367[8], ὑφισταμένη should
have 'post-Christian' significance here—how does that get into Aetius?

This would mean that 'sun, moon and stars had stood firm' against the enclosure; of the First Fire only they survived.

The manifold obscurities in the text have until now militated against its significance. But now we may regard it as a more or less faithful passage from Theophrastus, which, moreover, preserves much of the actual form of Anaximander's thought.

VII. Aristotle clearly twisted Anaximander's concept of *apokrisis* by putting it under his rubric of *ekkrisis*. It became the separation of opposites in the same sense as that in which in Anaxagoras the qualities separate from each other by virtue of their opposing principles, thereby creating the cosmos.

Now, Heidel and Cherniss have attempted in a very different way to free Anaximander from the Aristotelian categories.[34] In the concept of *alloiosis* Heidel recognized the specifically Aristotelian idea, which implies the doctrine of potentiality, and he therefore discounted for all the Presocratics the idea of transformation of a substance. He was right in so far as he contradicted the Theophrastean interpretation of the *apeiron* as a substance having no qualities. But he remained ensnared in the Aristotelian schema: in place of *alloiosis* he put *ekkrisis* and the allegedly ancient idea of a mechanical mixture of unchangeable substances. It is also Cherniss's opinion that Aristotle no longer understood this way of thinking, in which the qualities were still thought of as substantial, and that he therefore transferred his conception of abstract qualities to the earlier thinkers and misinterpreted the archaic mixtures as unified substratum and the separation as transformation.[35]

Now this is certainly wrong. Aristotle's interpretations of Anaxagoras and Empedocles in the light of his new doctrine clearly show that he understood the mechanical character of their mixture and separation. As for the qualities, he was likewise much too well aware of the novelty of his discovery to impute it involuntarily to his predecessors.[36] Qualities as substances were traditional, and Aristotle was well able to imagine them. It would be easier to accuse him of having misinterpreted the ancient δυνάμεις, which the qualities were too, as mere substances.

[34] Heidel, 'Qualit. Change . . .' (see above, n. 10); Cherniss, *Arist. Crit.*, pp. 358 ff.

[35] Cherniss, p. 366.   [36] Cf., e.g., *Gen. et Corr.* A 2 (317 a 17).

This would not really need to be said, except that Cherniss does not always avoid the danger of reading Aristotle's accounts of the Presocratics too straightforwardly.[37] It is true that Aristotle forces his questions on the ancients, but for that reason his statements about them always preserve the character of a philosophical discussion which takes every proffered thought as a possibility to be pursued further. From the multiplicity of levels in Platonic speech there still remains a lightness, almost a conversational quality, in quoting and interpreting, which should not be overlooked. The method that consists of finding the 'genuine' by eliminating the Aristotelian can also lead one astray.

Now if one says that the Ionians had already thought of the mixtures of Empedocles and Anaxagoras, one has missed the polemical sense of these mechanistic doctrines: they contradict the Milesians—and indeed the prevailing view of mankind— who credited substance with an unlimited but also unexamined capacity for transformation. 'There is no transformation'—such a denial was only possible after and because of Parmenides, who also introduced the concept of mixture.[38] Thus Aristotle does not *invent* transformation, but brings the ancient phenomenon back into a respectable position, in opposition to the mechanical systems. To the latter systems there also belongs the mechanical concept of Primary Motion. But Anaximander's *kinesis* means, above all, power of transformation, as it still does for Parmenides. This transformation is neither a 'qualitative changing' of a substratum in the Aristotelian sense, nor a 'separating out' in Anaxagoras' sense, but both at once, as the growth of bark round a tree is both. In this early thought, which appears to be still closely linked to myth, the process of transforming a primary substance into other substances is clearly not yet a problem. Anaximander believed completely in a genuine coming-into-being. Against whom would the Eleatic axiom otherwise be directed, that nothing comes of nothing? The physical idea of the preservation of substances arose only from the Eleatic concept of being.

VIII. It is more difficult to judge the role which the so-called Hot and Cold could have played in Anaximander's world-view. One could say that the meaning of *apokrisis* which is shown by

37 See n. 13, and n. 34.   38 Reinhardt, *Parmenides*, p. 74.

interpretation of the text of Theophrastus does not exclude the sense that opposing powers are created from the 'germ', even if this creation did not take the form of the separating of a unity. As for example in Hesiod, to whom Gigon's interpretation in terms of 'day and night' is oriented; there it is not a separation of day and night but a begetting of day by night. But the two are still by no means conceived as opposing cosmic powers; at most the mother is nearer chaos than the daughter. In Parmenides, on the other hand, the creation of the opposing 'forms' is, for the first time, division of the One. The duality serves to explain a universal condition—διὰ παντὸς πάντα περῶντα (B 1, 32: 'permeating all things everywhere'). There is no trace of this in Anaximander. It is clear that the opposites belong to the *diakrisis* schema.

However it is true that the doxography often mentions violent processes, which have led to the present state of the world, and violence is still clearly dominant in the present arrangement. The Pseudo-Plutarchean account speaks of a tearing off, probably a bursting, of the balls of fire, and enclosure of the rings of fire— in air, according to Hippolytus. Ὑποστῆναι, denoting the growth of the constellations, represented resistance to force. And the air still succeeds from time to time in enclosing the fire (A 21). It is also with force (βιασάμενον) that the air bursts from the cloud and causes thunder (A 23). It is forcefully (*violentus*) that the air penetrates and shakes the earth (A 28). The burning of the once water-covered earth (A 27) can only be imagined as violent and unwillingly suffered; and the enclosure of the sun by air and the τροπαί, which it undergoes from the water-vapours, sound like a payment for violence. This tone becomes more distinct when Anaximander speaks of human life; Plutarch understood it: 'As the fire devours the wood from which it burns—that is, its own father and mother—thus Anaximander spoilt fish for eating by calling it mankind's father and mother' (A 30).

One can hardly doubt that all this information about violent deeds and encroachments shaped Anaximander's world-view as he expressed its law in the surviving fragment:

Ἀναξίμανδρος . . . ἀρχὴν . . . εἴρηκε τῶν ὄντων τὸ ἄπειρον . . . ἐξ ὧν δὲ ἡ γένεσίς ἐστι τοῖς οὖσι, καὶ τὴν φθορὰν εἰς ταῦτα γίνεσθαι κατὰ τὸ χρεών· διδόναι γὰρ αὐτὰ δίκην καὶ τίσιν ἀλλήλοις τῆς ἀδικίας κατὰ τὴν τοῦ χρόνου τάξιν.

(Anaximander . . . said the *arche* of existing things is the *apeiron* . . . from whatever things beings have their genesis, their destruction also is into these according to necessity; for they pay the penalty and recompense to each other for their injustice according to the ordering of time.) (Simplicius, *Physics*, 24, 13.)

The law consists, according to Theophrastus, in the necessary succession of becoming and decaying. The context in Simplicius shows what kind of becoming was primarily in Theophrastus' mind: with ἐξ ὧν δὲ he takes up ἐξ ἧς from the previous sentence, extracting the general law like Aristotle's *Metaph.* 983 b 24 (τὸ δ' ἐξ οὗ γίγνεται τοῦτ' ἐστιν ἀρχὴ πάντων); thus the sentence explains the rise of the worlds and their kosmoi. In the Pseudo-Plutarchean extract the rise of the worlds and their kosmoi is similarly followed by a sentence about becoming and decaying; it says that both are eternal, whereas all kosmoi return periodically. This is clearly only another version of the same sentence which introduces the fragment in Simplicius; its sense is: the worlds come into being and decay eternally according to the law of certain time-circuits. The periodical return in Pseudo-Plutarch must be equivalent to κατὰ τὸ χρεών ('in accordance with necessity'), since this is interpreted as 'arrangement of time'. Thus the parallel account confirms that it is Theophrastus' interpretation.[39]

The cycle of return also throws a light on the significance of the *kosmoi*. For ἀνακυκλουμένων demands as subject a concept referring to time, which the 'worlds' can hardly be.[40] And yet the word can only refer to κόσμους. So the 'kosmoi in the worlds' must be the time-concept that is required, namely the cyclically recurring states of world-forming, as Reinhardt has explained the word.[41]

[39] See Fr. Dirlmeier, *Rh. Mus.*, 87 (1938), 376, and *Hermes*, 75 (1940), 329. *Chronos* interpreted as a personification by W. Jaeger, *Theology of the Early Greek Philosophers*, p. 35. Dirlmeier's reference to Simplicius, *Phys.*, 24, 5, τάξιν τινὰ καὶ χρόνον ὡρισμένον is a convincing argument against this.

[40] See the difficulty in which Burnet (Section 18, note) therefore finds himself. W. A. Heidel, *Class. Phil.*, 6 (1911), 86, wants to make αὐτων refer to φθοράν and γένεσιν, which necessitates deleting πάντων; not very illuminating.

[41] Reinhardt, Parmenides, p. 174. Kranz's interpretation of the *kosmoi* as the rings of the galaxies ('Kosmos als philos. Begr.', *Philologus*, 93 [1939], 430 ff.) would not explain their return. His support of this interpretation in archaic language rests only on Pythagoras (DK 28 A 44) and Pseudo-Hippocrates π. ἑβδομάδων. The sky as cosmos may be early Pythagorean, but the word was used there at first not as a substantive and absolute, but predicatively

Pseudo-Plutarch gives 'the *kosmoi* being infinite', which, although he himself misunderstood it, seems then very plausible.[42] The fragment is quoted for the rise and decay of the worlds, but expresses a general law; this is clear from the neuter plural.[43] The *periodos* of the *kosmoi* would have been matched by other periods within the present *kosmos*. One would think first of the cycle of years and days. It is tempting to interpret the alternation of day and night and of summer and winter in the sense of a pair of cosmic opposites, but there are other periods which were certainly not included in this schema in Anaximander, the life of earthly beings. Here the only alternation is between life and death or life and other life. Balance is not achieved by an equal pull of opposites, but by the fact that each has an allotted span. It is characteristic that the cycles do not remain constant, but develop dominance of one aspect: the sea, once occupying the whole space of the earth, is said to 'become, because of the drying out (by the sun), smaller and smaller, and finally quite dry'. That would be the end of the cause of the τροπαί, and therefore also the end of summer and winter (and day and night also perhaps, because the mist-veils of the rings of fire would be consumed?). The 'opposites' are not eternally equal;[44] one devours the other. But the 'injustice' which brings the cycles to an end is compensated

---

[42] See above, n. 17.

[43] Cherniss, p. 377, thinks, wrongly, that the plural ἐξ ὧν indicates the plurality of the ἀρχή, which would then be a mixture of all materials as in Anaxagoras.

[44] Cherniss, p. 379, accepts the cosmic opposites to such an extent that he maintains that 'Hot and Cold have existed as such eternally'.

('the sky is a well-arranged order'). That does not yet go beyond the Homeric use (ἵππου κόσμον), and it is a far cry from the ὅλος ὁ κόσμος of Pseudo-Hippocrates. But in our case the problem begins where several cosmoi are mentioned, as in Pseudo-Hippocrates. There it does not come from Ionian physics, but from Pythagoreanism, and hardly the earliest. It presupposes the opposition of Above and Below, the gradation of the regions, which is alien to the Milesians. As certainly as the archaizing cosmology of π. ἑβδομάδων contains Ionian elements, it is equally doubtful that the whole thing can be up-dated accordingly (Kranz, 'Kosmos und Mensch . . .', *Nachr. Gött. Ges.*, [1938], pp. 121 ff.). In particular, that with the *kosmoi* we have an archaic use is again supported only from Pythagoras and Anaximander. The examples which Kranz adduces from Herodotus, etc. (*Philol.*, p. 431) are instructive, for they show that it is always a question of an arrangement, in contrast to other possible arrangements.

in a larger cycle, which has its beginning and end in the 'limitless' which 'directs everything'. We know nothing of how Anaximander pictured the end of the worlds; but it seems certain that the drying out of the sea is part of a *metakosmesis*, and that it happens by a victory on the part of the sun. Heraclitus will say later: 'the sun will *not* overstep its measures . . .'. And the thought authorizing this will be the opposites.

Anaximander's doctrine seems to have included a similar change of periods in the history of mankind; he says that the first men 'only survived for a short time' the change to dry.[45] The thought seems to me to be connected with Hesiod's fable of the Ages. The expression in Aetius echoes *Opera* 133 verbally; and the context proves to be similar: it deals with the men of the Silver Generation, who remain children for a hundred years and are nourished by their mother, but then only live a short time as adults because they destroy each other by their own folly and hybris. The counterpart of these are the men of the last generation: they are scarcely born before they turn grey, there is no limit to their sins, even their own parents they would no longer respect. That represents the future; we stand between the two—even if dangerously near the end. A period is described between the earliest and the last; it is possibly a cycle, since Hesiod complains that he would wish to have been born earlier or later, if this phase were only past. In Anaximander too a view of the final period must have supplemented the history of the beginning, since man must share the fate of the earth from the water of the beginning to its drying out. Other motifs of the narrative also recur: long suckling period, death soon after weaning, ingratitude towards the nurse, injustice to one another, hybris and punishment. Now if in Anaximander men at first 'only survived for a short time' after becoming adult, clearly they gradually lengthened their life-span or exchanged the length of the different phases of their life. By what encroachment they succeeded in doing this, after they had 'set foot on land' and

45 DK A 30: ἐπ' ὀλίγον χρόνον μεταβιῶναι can hardly mean anything else. Burnet, Section 21: 'they changed in a short while their mode of living', is linguistically impossible. Kranz (*Vors. Denker*, p. 43), 'for a short time took on a different form of life'; the 'different form of life' would be the human one; what does 'for a short time' mean then? On μεταβιῶναι = super-vixisse, cf. Heidel, *Proc. Amer. Acad.* (1913), p. 687, and Liddell and Scott.

'could already feed themselves', is shown by the context in Plutarch: (A 30) they devour the fish, their 'own parents'. If this connection with Hesiod is valid, it is a rare opportunity to observe the transition from myth to philosophy. Hesiod's fable is also intended to explain the world: the condition in which we live in the world. But the narrator of myths and the moralist is himself involved; while interpreting he condemns. Anaximander views from a distance; his insight culminates not in a complaint but in contemplation of a law, and in the philosophical contemplation the prophetic element found in Hesiod completely vanishes.

Naturally much in this outline is hypothetical—any attempt to refer the fragment's abstract formula to its cosmological content rests unfortunately on a particularly weak basis. But on the whole the picture is not of a schema of complementary opposites, but the 'arrangement of time', in which conquest is paid for with downfall. The schema of Anaximander's thought was the contrast of the Finite with the Eternal.[46] He sees finiteness not in the image of the balance of opposites, but under the aspect of hybris: encroachment of the Finite on the Finite. The *portion* which is therefore allotted to the Finite by fate is its 'time'. Fate is sent not by χρόνος but by τὸ χρεών. From this position, right measure and excess in Heraclitus look like traditional motifs; 'war' belongs to the tradition, the new element is 'harmony'—created by the idea of the opposites. And as in Anaximander finiteness goes with hybris, so in Heraclitus the immortality of the mortal goes with 'right measure'.

To return to Theophrastus' opposites of Hot and Cold: as opposites they have no place in this world-picture. That becomes clear in the light of a further consideration. Air plays a significant role in Anaximander. But we should not yet think of it as atmosphere; the expression in Pseudo-Plutarch, 'the air around the earth', follows a later view. *Aer* is wind and vapour. It seems to be in the process of being discovered as an element, but it is still vaporized water, *anathymiasis* between sea and sun. The doctrine of the four elements has not yet been developed,[47] in fact the

---

[46] On this, see Gigon, *Ursprung*, pp. 62 f.

[47] The number four for the elements must be older than Empedocles; but it is questionable whether one may interpret Hesiod, *Theog.*, 735/6, as referring to four elements (Kranz, in DK, on Emped. Frag. 6). The ancestors of the elements are the parts of the world; but the Air does not come from Tartaros

schema which is the basis of Anaximander's cosmos seems to have been the same scale of three elements, or rather world-parts, as in Heraclitus: Earth, Sea, and Fire. At the same time we have, in Fragment 126 of Heraclitus, the four qualities as in Aristotle: one can see how Heraclitus has imposed his doctrine of opposites on some traditional physics which had not been conceived according to a schema of pairs of opposites. The cosmogonic sequence in Anaximander is: Sea, Fire, Earth; so it may have been Sea and Fire which Theophrastus named, as the two original cosmic elements, the Cold and the Hot. In another place he found his Aristotelian pair of opposites in the fiery vapour mixture, which formed the bowl of the sky in Anaximander. But that does not mean that Anaximander too regarded this from the aspect of fundamental opposites. His world-picture was not drawn from a logically—or morally—experienced duality.

IX. Let us glance at Anaximenes merely for the purpose of comparison. What Anaximander did not examine, the transformation of substances, becomes his problem, and for the first time the answer is really to do with physics. From the point of view of atomism we are inclined to conceive the process of condensation only as a compression in space, as Aristotle does in *Categ.* 10 a 16: he says that thick and thin do not actually belong to the category of quality but of quantity.[48] But we should be misrepresenting Anaximenes if we applied the Aristotelian alternative to him. Aristotle himself, in spite of his own conception,[49] did not count Anaximenes' condensation under *synkrisis* but under *alloiosis*, thus at least interpreting it more correctly than Heidel and Cherniss,[50] who regard the air as a mixture of all substances.

[48] Cf. also *De caelo* 299 b 7.
[49] *Physics* 260 b 11. Against this: *Gen. et corr.*, 314.
[50] According to W. A. Heidel, 'Qualit. Change . . .', p. 203, n. 3, Air is a mixture from which the materials separate. Cherniss, *Arist. Crit.* . . . pp.

---

but from the area of the superterrestrial winds and vapours, and in Hesiod that is still the area of the sky (*Theog.*, 697). There is a further piece of archaeological evidence which has been interpreted as referring to the four elements, the 'Three-bodied figure' in the pediment of the Old Temple of Athena on the Acropolis. The interpretation presupposes that the fourth element, Earth, would be expressed in the serpent-figure of the monster. Cf. Brommer, *Marb. Winck. Progr.*, 1947.

It is significant that in the doxography about Anaximenes the pair of opposites, Hot and Cold, also occurs. The context should be noted: Hippolytus (= A 7): The air, 'when it is condensed and rarefied, appears different in each case; for when it dissolves into the thinner it becomes fire, the winds on the other hand are condensed air; in the course of (further) felting air becomes cloud; when more condensed, water; more, it becomes earth; and, when most compressed, stone; so that the highest opposites, which condition becoming, are Hot and Cold'. The final sentence, to go by its form, could just as well be Anaximenes' own chain of reasoning, as Theophrastus'. To a certain extent it is refuted by the preceding account: all difference of 'appearance' depends only on a greater or lesser amount of compression. All limits, and finally the opposites themselves, are wiped out, since the doctrine is held of the complete transformability of substances. Thin and Thick are not realities, transforming the primary substance in one direction or the other, and even condensation and rarefaction are not opposite principles, whose combined effect makes the multiplicity of things, but they are only the fluctuating of the infinitely volatile element. It is true that in this Fire and Stone are contrasted with one another as the two final states of the process of transformation; but it is just this which indicates clearly that for Anaximenes the opposites are the *result* of the transformation, not, as in Anaxagoras, its principle and cause. If this conclusion was already drawn by Anaximenes, its sense could only have been that Stone and Fire, though opposites, are actually one and the same. However it is more probable that the whole schema of transformation in two directions comes from Theophrastus, who wanted to give more concrete proof from Anaximenes of the opposites discovered by Aristotle, *Physics A* 4. His dependence on the Aristotelian interpretation for this point also throws a light on his exposition of the opposites in Anaximander.

X. It is true that my interpretation would scarcely be tenable if Anaximander had already described his Boundless as an inter-

---

379 f., feels that he has to contradict Aristotle, since he misunderstood the transformation of Air in Anaximenes as the qualifying of an indifferent material.

mediate between two opposites. Gigon attempts to show this by taking Aristotle's mentions of an 'intermediate element' as referring to Anaximander. The controversy about this is long-standing (see Simplicius, p. 149). Most commentators claimed the intermediate element for Anaximander, although Nikolaos and Porphyry claimed it for Diogenes of Apollonia. Simplicius wavers (p. 25, 9 and 203, 3). None of them knew any more than we do.[51] So there only remain the passages in Aristotle. They divide into two groups, one speaking of an intermediate between Air and Water, the other between Air and Fire; sometimes Aristotle only says 'the intermediate' or 'that which is beside the elements'. He makes no distinction in treatment. His stubborn silence about the author is remarkable; he only speaks of an un-determined plurality of Physikoi. Burnet (Section 15) thought that the changes in the two descriptions proved that they come from Aristotle, as alternative interpretations of Anaximander's *apeiron*. Gigon goes one step further: he considers the 'inter-mediate', but not the further definitions, to be Anaximandrian. However, the plural is a sure indication that at least the reference is not to Anaximander alone. Thus Aristotle is also thinking of some other unknowns of the fifth century. It is not impossible that Anaximander is one of those referred to in the more general formulation 'beside the elements' *Gen. et Corr.* 329 a 9; but the 'intermediate element' clearly belongs to others. In *Physics* 187 a 14 (189 b 9 belongs to it) and in *De caelo* 303 b 12 condensation and rarefaction are ascribed to them, putting them in Anaximenes' circle: for Aristotle, Anaximander belongs to the *diakrisis* group.[52] But if one wished to attribute to Anaximander the 'intermediate' merely as idea, whether spatial or conceptual, it would require two *opposites* between which to be in the middle. Gigon reconstructs 'between Light and Night'; but the two elements which Aristotle would have had to substitute for Light and Night are not opposites but any pair of substances which are adjacent in the scale of elements. Did Aristotle, then, not have opposites available, to reproduce 'Light and Night' suitably in *his* language? In fact, Aristotle's formulations clearly indicate various attempts among Anaximenes' followers, because of the new interest in the elements, to define the quality of the *apeiron* for the first time, and to define it as something extremely changeable.

[51] Cp. Zeller, I⁶, 287 f.   [52] Thus also Cherniss, p. 13.

An argument such as that preserved in Aristotle's *Physics* 204 b 22 (= A 16)—a one-sided, infinite quality would annihilate the others by its infiniteness—cannot be Anaximandrian for several reasons. First, Anaximenes could scarcely then have trumped the 'undefined' element with his Air; moreover, the argument is familiar with the qualities and their opposites, and the intermediate element is conceived on *that* basis; finally and most important: the infiniteness of the primary substance is already presupposed here; the argument is only about its quality. It is true that I do not believe the remark to be Aristotelian [53] either; it appears to be completely archaic and not as serious about the concept of the Infinite as Aristotle would be: the Infinite is the 'surrounding', which, if it were Air or Water or Fire, would devour the finite substances by its superior quality. In any case it should be taken out of the evidence for Anaximander.

Moreover we have the evidence of Theophrastus, that Anaximander 'did not say what the Boundless is, whether it is Air or Water or Earth or some other substances'. [54] And even if we grant that Aristotle, by asking about the quality, had missed an original concrete and spatial sense of μεταξύ, how could the 'encompasser' [55] be described as an 'intermediate' at all?

If, therefore, we have to agree with Zeller's interpretation, that Anaximander in no way qualified the Boundless as an element, [56] yet, on the other hand, it appears that the Moist occupied a special position in his cosmogony: the 'begetter' which split off from the Boundless is the 'first moisture' from which Fire grew. So it could in fact be easy enough to imagine the Infinite itself as 'wet vapour' or as 'fiery vapour' or, more pertinently, as an intermediate between Water and Fire (if one may trust *Physics* 189 b 2). Once one had interpreted Anaximander's *arche* thus, it had to follow that the rise of the 'first moisture' from the 'vapour' was thought of as condensation. Perhaps Anaxi-

---

[53] As Cherniss thinks, p. 28, n. 106.
[54] Aetius, i. 3, 3 = DK A 14. The formulation in Simplicius, p. 24, 16, 'he says it is neither . . . nor . . .' is clearly a distortion; the correct phrase in Diogenes, οὐ διορίζων. Otherwise there could have been no discussion about it at all.
[55] Περιέχειν as an Anaximandrian term: cf. W. Jaeger, 'Theology . . .', p. 202, n. 39.
[56] Zeller, I, 291.

mander would not have contradicted this. The concept just had not yet been coined by him; he pictured it as separation. One sees how close Anaximander and Anaximenes are in their basic conception, and how it is only Aristotle's schema which makes them representatives of opposite principles. But their followers prove to be completely dependent on the two original philosophers, and it is understandable that Aristotle quotes them anonymously. At the same time it becomes clear why the intermediate element appears in Aristotle in such proximity to the interpretation of Anaximander's *apeiron*.

XI. The above-mentioned argument in Aristotle (*Physics* 204 b 22 f.), which has proved to be non-Anaximandrian, raises the question of what other reasons or considerations could have led Anaximander to his conception of the *arche*, and whether the first philosophers mentioned reasons at all. The reason which Aristotle (*Metaph.* 983 b 22) attempts to give for Water in Thales is clearly given as his own reflection. The other, which Simplicius (p. 24, 21) presents as Anaximander's thought, has likewise proved to be his own explanation. It is a disputed question, whether we possess in the Anaximenes fragment Anaximenes' original reasons. Clearly all these arguments also contain an *interpretation* of the *arche*.

However, one reason for the 'Boundless' is adduced as Anaximander's, which might well be his own: 'so that Becoming might not cease'.[57] Aristotle offers it among the five traditional reasons for the Infinite, in a context where he has Anaximander in mind—he has quoted him in the previous sentence (203 b 14); and Theophrastus seems to have read it in Anaximander (Aetius = A 14). The reason differs from later ones in that it does not consider the quality (in the sense of Theophrastus' ἀόριστον) but rather the extent of the Infinite; or more precisely, the concept itself.

The appearance of this concept is startling, and it would be a good thing if we could pick out its forerunners in Greek thought. In Homer Sea and Earth are called 'immeasurable' (ἀπείρων), but in Anaximander the word has a stricter meaning

[57] Zeller, I, 274; cf. above, n. 33. I can scarcely follow any of the remarks of W. Kraus, *Rh. Mus.*, 93 (1950), 364 ff. The subject of ἐλλείπῃ is γένεσις, not τὸ ἄπειρον. Ἐλλείπῃ ὑφισταμένη means the same as ἐπιλείπῃ.

and stands independently, as concept and idea. The other concept connected with it, the 'Immortal', is exemplified in the Homeric gods, and therewith the contrast with the Finite in time, so that the concept of Being could easily develop from the concept of divinity. But 'Boundlessness' seems so opposed to the Greek concept of the divine that Parmenides could actually deny it for the true 'Being'; not to speak of Aristotle. Inexplicable as the creation of new thoughts always is, yet it is improbable that they ever come into existence without any preparation. What picture existed before Anaximander, from which he could develop his conception of the Boundless? This question must also be of great importance for the interpretation.

As long as Hesiod's Chaos was taken in the sense of Ovid's *indigesta moles*, it could be regarded as the forerunner of Anaximander's *arche*, taken as the *Undefined*. Neither interpretation is now held, except by a few. But even where other interpretations of Chaos are attempted, philosophy is often taken as beginning with Hesiod.[58] H. Fränkel explains Chaos as the Nothing, in contrast with the Universe as Being. *Apeiron*, as the successor to Chaos, is then interpreted as the 'possible' in contrast to the Existing. Gigon sees in Chaos the 'split or cavity' between earth and heaven, taking it that Hesiod made a bold abstraction from the last concrete beings, 'between' which the 'world cavity' lies, Earth and Sky. The *apeiron* would then be the undefined 'intermediate' which divides into day and night.

On the other hand, as long as one joined Aristotle in regarding early philosophy as a tentative groping for the material cause, Thales could count as the first to search for the element. Then *apeiron* became the 'undefined element'. But what was Thales' Water actually? Aristotle himself presumed a meaning which is not oriented to the 'elementary' character of Water, i.e. things do not 'consist' 'of water' but 'exist because of water' ($\tau o \dot{\nu} \tau \omega \ \zeta \tilde{\omega} \nu$); it does not matter if he nevertheless formulates this explanation with the ambiguous $\dot{\epsilon} \xi \ o \tilde{\upsilon} \ \gamma \dot{\iota} \gamma \nu \epsilon \tau a \iota$ to suit his theme (983 b 24).

From what I have said it is clear how important it is for the interpretation to establish the true background of Anaximander's conception of *arche*. Let us begin with Thales.

---

[58] H. Fränkel, *Parmenidesstudien*, p. 182 [see Vol. II of this collection]; *Dichtung und Philosophie des frühen Griechentums*, pp. 142–9, 341–8; O. Gigon, *Ursprung der griechischen Philosophie*, esp. pp. 34 f. and 78.

XII. Of the four sentences which have survived from Thales' 'philosophy', only one is not of doubtful sense: that the earth floats on the water. The report is reliable, because Aristotle quotes it only in support of his statement that Water is the origin; also because in another place [59] he cites the simile of the floating piece of wood, which has parallels in the numerous similes in the Ionians. We should begin with this certainty and argue back to the other sentence about Water as origin, which is quite uncertain for us at first—not vice versa, as Burnet does. But the concept of the floating earth does not occur anywhere else in Greece.[60] How did Thales come upon it?

It has been convincingly shown that the sea originally was alien to the Greeks and had no place in their myth. The concept of the encircling stream flowing round the earth was apparently taken over by them from the more ancient peoples of the Eastern Mediterranean.[61] This water was not necessarily a sea bearing the earth. However, streams flow out of Okeanos and join beneath the earth in a hidden net-work, breaking out as springs.[62] Thus the waters of the deep already belong to the world-picture with the encircling stream. Nor would it be true to say that the sea is Eastern and the Stream Greek; Babylonians and Egyptians also called the outer water 'river'. With both Greeks and Easterners the encircling river became an encircling sea— however, the difference is that Okeanos, answering to a deeply rooted idea of the Greeks, remained a water of the earth, or, speaking mythologically, the son of Gaia; whereas the 'bitter river' and the 'great encircler' were deepened to the idea of an all-embracing and supporting sea. Only in this sense could Water receive the rank of Origin.

This role of water is common to several Babylonian creation myths. The *Eridu* poem, of which the text comes from the seventh century, though going back farther, [63] narrates that in the beginning there was no temple, no tree, no city, and no living being, 'all lands were sea'; the dwellings of the gods were first built;

[59] *De Caelo* 294 b 28 (= A 14).
[60] Floating islands (*Od.* x. 3, Lucian *Dial. mar.* 10) are fairy-tale islands.
[61] Cf. A. Lesky, *Thalatta*, p. 64; Wilamowitz, *Kronos und die Titanen*, p. 10.
[62] *Iliad*, Φ 195 ff. Plato, *Phaed.* 112.
[63] H. Gunkel, *Schöpfung und Chaos in Urzeit und Endzeit*, p. 419. Text also in Jeremias, *Hdb. d. orient. Geisteskultur*, p. 123.

then 'Marduk built a raft of reeds on the surface of the water, he created dust and shook it out over the reed-raft', that is the Earth. The Earth resting on the Water, and Water as Origin—both concepts are closely related here. They belong to the general Babylonian world-picture as it is also portrayed in the creation-epic *Enuma elish*: beneath the surface of the Earth is Apsu, the watery deep, and Apsu is, with Tiamat, the world sea, the origin of the gods. But above the firmament of the heavens is the same water, part of Tiamat, which Marduk split and divided into the waters of the heavens and of the deep. Similar beliefs are found in the Old Testament: Psalm 136, 6 'Jahwe, who made firm the earth over the water'; Psalm 24, 2, 'He hath founded the earth upon the seas, and established it upon the floods'; Psalm 104, 3, 'Jahwe . . . who layeth the beams of his chamber in the waters.' And this water is Tehom, 'the deep', above which 'in the beginning . . . the spirit of God brooded'. God divided it into the waters above and the waters of the deep, the dividing firmament is 'in the midst of the waters'. From the heavenly waters comes the nourishing rain, 'many blessings' come 'from the watery deeps which lie below'.[64] Finally, in Egypt the concept is similar in essentials: the earth is a flat disc with a high rim, its pictogram represents its shape.[65] It rests on the water which surrounds it.[66] The Nile springs from this subterranean water and makes the earth fertile. On the earth's rim or on pillars there rests the heavenly vault; water encircles the heavens in the form of a second Nile, from which life-giving rain pours. Over the heavenly waters the sun-god travels in his boat, continuing his journey in the evening through the subterranean waters in another boat. This all-embracing and all-supporting water is, according to the cosmogony of Heliopolis, the oldest god, Nun;[67] from him Atum, the sun-god, is born. From his seed, falling on the water, came the first stone or first hill, on which the god took a firm stand and spat Schu and Tefnut from

[64] *Genesis,* 49, 25, *Deuteron.,* 33, 13.
[65] Schafer, *Antike,* 3 (1927), 97 and 100.
[66] J. A. Wilson in H. Frankfort, *The Intellectual Adventure of Ancient Man,* pp. 38 and 45 (English edn. under the title *Before Philosophy*); H. Bonnet, *Reallexikon,* p. 586; S. A. B. Mercer, *The Religion of Ancient Egypt,* pp. 260 f.; A. Erman, *Die Religion der Aegypter* (1934), pp. 14 ff.
[67] Erman, pp. 89 ff., Mercer, pp. 275 ff.; Schafer, p. 116, Fig. 31, Nun represented as all-surrounding element and sun-bearing god.

his mouth, i.e. Air (or emptiness) and Mist. These two beget Geb and Nut, i.e. the male Earth and the female Sky: Schu steps beneath the goddess of the sky and holds her bent in a curve over the earth.

These concepts, which dominated the lands of the south-eastern Mediterranean during the first Greek centuries, were not taken over by the Greeks. One may object that Okeanos and Tethys in the *Iliad* (XIV, 201) bear witness to similar beliefs for Greece. But this shows the very opposite: to name Thales' predecessors, later writers never quoted anything but this line from the *Iliad*, together with the Orphic theogony. They were never able to refer to Greek myths. In actuality, Greek mythology is entirely lacking in the cosmological character which belongs to the eastern myths. Okeanos and Tethys did not have anywhere else in Greek thought the rank allotted them by the line of the *Iliad*; and Hesiod did not join in. Also they are unique in the *Iliad*, and there is no choice but to regard them as eastern or 'Aegean' intrusions, as the name of Okeanos certainly is. But what is left of the ancient pair of gods in the *Iliad* in the end? They belong there to a story of the generations, the fight of Zeus against Kronos, and the marital dispute of the ancestors probably stems from their taking different sides in this fight. How little cosmology there is in the attributes of the 'ancients'! The wide background of the alien world-picture disappears behind the idyll. Is a foreign myth not being misused here to provide colour for a divine prank? The 'origin' remains an incidental title, still a stranger in Greek thought.

A few other details penetrated along with Okeanos: in Mimnermos the concept of the sun's chariot is linked with the sun's nightly boat-journey over the water;[68] however the idea actually belonging to Helios remains that of the sun-chariot.

XIII. I believe that after this it is impossible to agree with Zeller that 'everything develops naturally from the presuppositions of the Greek people',[69] in so far as this sentence is asserting the autarky of Greek philosophy. Thales could not have been drawing on any Greek tradition when he raised Water to the rank of

[68] Mimnermos Frag. 10, cf. Stesichoros Frag. 6. That may go back to the Titanomachy: Athen. 9, 470 b.
[69] Zeller, I⁶, 39.

arche. Of course he knew the line of the *Iliad,* and if we knew nothing else we should have to believe that he developed this mythological fragment into his cosmological theory.[70] But his doctrine, that the earth floats on the water, is too unusual and too similar to the dominant concept in the East for us not to have to use a comparison with those myths in our explanation.

For from the beginning these contained a speculative element which was lacking in the Greek myths. So both Babylonians and Egyptians were led early by the cosmic character of their gods to a kind of speculation about nature.*

If one considers this early cosmological speculation, in whose world-picture Thales' two cosmological images—Water as *arche,* and water supporting the earth—are foreshadowed, it becomes far more probable that Thales was inspired to conceive his *arche* by a new contact with the south-east, than that he developed the sparse conceptions which had already penetrated, in a direction which had hardly been started upon in Greece. The similarity was already noticed in ancient times and it was surmised that Thales' teaching stems from Egypt.[74] If one collects the mentions of Thales, there is much evidence that he does indeed owe this inspiration to Egypt. His observations about the pyramids can hardly be doubted; he had his own theory about the flooding of the Nile;[75] his fixing of the rise of the Pleiades to the twenty-fifth day after the spring equinox (A 18) only holds good for Egypt.[76] So the report that he had been in Egypt seems fairly reliable; it was noted down by the Alexandrian biographers (Aetius, 1. 3, 1). The historical requirements for it are there: there were close links between Egypt and Ionia, Ionian soldiers had served in the Egyptian army since Psammetichos I, and Naukratis was founded

---

[70] Also dismissed by Wilamowitz, *Kronos u. d. Titanen,* p. 10, n. 2.
* [Supporting material, drawn especially from the meaningful names of Babylonian and Egyptian mythological figures, is here omitted. Eds.]
[74] Simplicius, *De caelo,* p. 522, 14, Plutarch, *Is. et Os.,* DK 34 (= A 14). Thales' dependence on Egyptian ideas has, after Roth's uncritical attempts, attacked by Zeller, been considered by Maspero, *Histoire ancienne des peuples de l'Orient,* p. 27, and by Tannery, *La géometrie Grecque.* Kranz, *Nachr. Gött. Ges.,* (1938), p. 156, acknowledges dependence for the idea of the floating earth, but not for Water as first thing.
[75] Herodotus, ii. 20, cf. DK A 16.   [76] Zeller, I, 258.

in 650 by Thales' home-city. Of course language was no hindrance to the exchange of thoughts,[77] and since Psammetichos there was a separate class of interpreters.[78] Thales' prediction of the solar eclipse of 585 rests on knowledge of an eclipse-period which could only have been gained by several centuries' observations. These were not carried out in Greece, but can be traced back to 721 in Babylon, as can the first documented prediction of a lunar eclipse to 568.[79] It is still an open question whether it was the Babylonians who developed this science, or the Egyptians: Gundel supported Egypt's priority.[80] And can Thales have been there, and exchanged views (certainly not limited to commercial affairs), and heard nothing about the earth floating on water, and Water as the Origin?[81]

XIV. For the interpretation of Thales' *arche* it follows that we have no reason to regard Water as the primary substance in the sense that it changes into all substances, nor to assume that Thales was led to his conception by observation of vaporization or silting. Such things may have been part of it, but we do not know. Even Aristotle, who according to his tendency insists on the 'changeability' of Water, imagines quite other reasons for Thales. And he seems to be right. The idea which was given to Thales is that of the First Sea, which supports the earth and is the basis of all life; a new idea for the Greeks, to whom the sea was the 'unfruitful'. The floating earth certainly also *rose from* the sea, but not even Aristotle knew that Thales had said that, or he would have mentioned it.

The mythological idea becomes physical in Thales. But peculiarly Greek as the contrast thus indicated is, this process is still linked with the meeting with the East. The Egyptian idea of the First God had an essentially elementary character matched by no Greek *god*, only by the Sea. The rationalistic turn, the demythologizing, thus happened merely by the transference, and

---

[77] Zeller raises this objection, I⁶, 43. [78] Herodotus, ii. 154.
[79] Fotheringham in *The Observatory*, 51 (1928), Nr. 653, 304.
[80] W. Gundel, *Dekane und Dekansternbilder*, pp. 327 ff., 338 f.; Fr. Boll, *Kl. Schriften*, p. 253, for Babylonian origin.
[81] That Thales was inspired by Egypt is also accepted by R. Mondolfo (*Riv. di Filologia*, 93, 1935, p. 145), but he has him mainly depend on Greek tradition. The concept of the floating earth is not taken into consideration.

one may surmise that it was furthered by meeting those cosmic divinities.

The divinity of the element is something else again. After Anaximander one is tempted to ascribe this character to Thales' *arche* also. But what is preserved about it in the doxography is wrapped completely in Stoic terminology and arguments, and where they can be traced to their source in Aristotle they are merely conjectures based on the dictum about the soul of the magnet.[81a] This does not lead us anywhere.

How much the connection with Egypt reveals for other propositions of Thales cannot be decided here. The following is added merely as a question, to illustrate how questionable Thales' whole philosophy is. I do not know how one could ignore Diogenes' statement, that Thales was the first to designate the soul as immortal. Gigon surmises that Choirilos faked it, in order to dispute Pythagoras' claim to fame for this thought;[82] but even if this were his intention, it does not make a deceit any more probable. On the other hand, his teaching is not simply a formulation of older Greek ideas of the soul. These were certainly something very complex, and people probably always believed in a further existence in some form. But immortality is another thing again. The 'spiritual' soul is originally and essentially not living, but the image of the dead, it 'lives' in Hades. But immortality is what the earlier Greeks, simply by their conception of 'mortals', did not admit in man at all. And thus the new teaching arises, with the promise or claim that man becomes a god. Thus when Thales said 'immortal', he said something very new. In itself it is not impossible that he himself had developed his new 'teaching' from the earlier belief, as it existed in his century. If he were only a kind of Epimenides; if this *placitum* did not stand in such desperate isolation among the others! However, the most probable is stimulus from outside. Once one admits his sojourn in Egypt one cannot deny that belief in the immortality of the soul could not escape his attention. Herodotus is of the opinion that the Egyptians originated this belief,[83] which is found

[81a] Cf. Snell, *Philologus*, 98 (1944), 173 ff.
[82] *Ursprung d. gr. Phil.*, p. 57.
[83] Herodotus, ii. 123. Although in the same passage he wrongly attributes the migration of souls to the Egyptians, his information on belief in immortality is reliable.

among the Semites no more than it is among the Greeks. The pyramid texts bear witness to how ancient and dominant the belief was in Egypt.[84] The fact that life on the other side was thought of as corporeal does not contradict the idea of the soul, for resurrection happens by the very return of the body to the soul. Thus Man becomes a god among gods.[85]

Finally there is the other sentence about the soul: there are souls in amber and magnets. Has it anything to do with the first sentence? Even if one takes it as pure physics one can hardly imagine a connection. And 'Everything is full of gods (or demons)': Aristotle links these sentences into an attractive conjecture, but in Thales they stand like rudiments of a primitive animism, long overtaken by the times,[86] which was probably never native to Greece in this form. They too look like something brought in from abroad, however rationally he used them.

From this point of view, Thales' philosophy offers a doubtful picture. Not so much because of its dependence on foreign concepts, as because of its lack of context. It does not seem permissible to separate from the other *placita* the sparse utterances about Water and call them his 'philosophy'. It is difficult to say in what sort of a work one is to think of them collected. It is quite credible that he did not write any comparable to the later περὶ φύσεως.[87] Nevertheless he appears to be the first who, more through imported information than by his own speculative thought, awakened in his home-city an interest in cosmogony.

[Sections XV–XIX (*Hermes* 81, 1953, pp. 391–411) are omitted, since they deal with the detail of the mythological background to Presocratic philosophy, rather than with the philosophers themselves. Professor Hölscher argues that the cosmogonical passages in Hesiod cannot stem from wholly Greek origins, but must be explained by knowledge of Near Eastern myths. He draws parallels between the Kronos story in Hesiod, and the Hittite

---

[84] Erman, *Die ägypt. Rel.*, pp. 101 ff.; H. Bonnet, *Reallexikon*, pp. 347 ff.

[85] The decision in the case of Thales does not touch the more general issue of the origin of the belief in immortality of sixth-century Greece. E. R. Dodds, *The Greeks and the Irrational*, traced the connections with Thrace. All the same, deification is an essential point, and the Shamanism of the north does not seem to include it.

[86] A trace in Homer, but even there it is a formula left from earlier times: the arrow which 'desired to eat meat', *Il.* XI. 573. Od. 317. XXI, 168.

[87] Cf. Gigon, *Ursprung der gr. Philos.*, p. 58.

Kumarbi epic (see J. B. Pritchard, *Ancient Near Eastern Texts*, pp. 120 ff.), and suggests also that the discovery of this epic gives more plausibility to the alleged Phoenician cosmogony, attributed to Sanchunjaton, in Philo of Byblus *apud* Eusebius *Preparatio Evangelica* 1, 10. Hölscher finds in the Near Eastern myths the ultimate sources of Hesiod's notion of Chaos (the abyss within which the world was formed), and the inclusion of the origin of the world in the myth of the succession of world-rulers. Ed.]

XX. This would all seem to indicate that we should remove Hesiod somewhat from the beginnings of philosophy. The speculative element in him shows him less as a cosmologist than as a moralist. The religious motif of a call by the divinity, which is at the same time a call *to* the divinity to witness, has close parallels in prophetic literature, such as Epimenides, or Ezekiel, Isaiah, and Jeremiah,[181] and, as a guarantee of truth, is more closely related even to the priestly call on Taaut in Sanchunjaton than to that of Parmenides on the Logos. It is true that the religious form has left an effect on it, as on Heraclitus too,[182] but now it becomes the clothing for something new, for the power of convincing comes no longer from revelation but from thought. Thus Parmenides, even in the speech of the goddess, created dialectical proof, and Heraclitus, in analogy with the divine oracle's utterance, the proving simile. The Milesians did not yet argue much,[183] but the appeal to examination and understanding indicates a new relationship to truth there too. On the other hand, Hesiod's proclamation claims to be true because the goddesses proclaimed it. Even the thing which looks so new in comparison to Homer, and which links Hesiod with the philosophers, the stepping-forward of the person, the contrast with the others, when compared with the east appears to be an essential constituent of the genre. On the other hand, Hesiod's own Greek contribution stands out more clearly against this background: in place of secret temple-wisdom and time stretching back to the beginning, he stresses the Charis of the moment; in place of distance and

[181] Schwartz compares Hesiod with Hosea, *Charakterköpfe*, 19. H. receives the baton also not as a poet, but as a priest and prophet.

[182] Cf. Diller, 'Hesiod u. d. Anf. d. gr. Phil.', *Antike u. Abendl.*, II 142 f.

[183] Although there is Anaximenes' example of compressed air (B 1).

fear, authority and obedience, he has the intimacy of nearness to the gods.

My concern was to illuminate the background. For now Hesiod moves towards the Ionians again in a tradition of speculative thought. Just as the face of Greece was turned from the beginning towards the East, it is characteristic that the Ionians turned to the East in search of the 'True': not, like late antiquity, to receive secret revelation, but critically, interested by its different aspect. Their own mythos was the first sacrifice. That is how it was that contact with the mythological cosmogonies of the East gave the main impetus to the creation of the unmythological systems of early philosophy. But we must remember that even the mythological concepts of the East were permeated with a sense of reality about the cosmos, even a technical prosiness, which is completely absent in the Greek examples: the path of the ship of the sun could be measured, the earth, although a god, could be depicted as a bath tub. Both Babylonians and Egyptians developed a kind of practical science which through all the centuries never came into conflict with the myth and it is significant that both, myth and 'science', lay in the hands of the same class, the priests. It is a world-picture both mythological and 'exact'.[184] It was these practical arts, together with the cosmic speculations, which made the Greeks feel like children. Representations of the cosmos are almost as completely absent in archaic art as they were common in Babylonia and Egypt.[185]

[184] Cf. Br. Meissner, *Babylonien und Assyrien*, II, pp. 380 ff.
[185] The single exception, the shield of Achilles with the depiction of Heaven and Earth and of Okeanos as the All-surrounding, proves the rule: there was nothing like it in Greece. The nearest comparison with the scene-pictures is found in Phoenician and Egyptian art (H. L. Lorimer, *Homer and the Monuments*, p. 487), and comparisons with the cosmic representations are found on two Phoenician bronze bowls, which show in the middle the starry heaven, surrounded by a garland of hills with trees and animals, and on the rim a strip with mythological scenes (Layard, *The Monuments of Niniveh*, II, Plates 61 and 66). But just as the picture of the beleaguered city has also been found in a Mycenaean shaft-grave, so have the heavens with sun and moon been found on a Mycenaean gold ring (Evans, *Palace of Minos*, IV, Fig. 385). In this respect, too, the Mycenaean–Minoan culture touches the East. Where there are single examples of sun, moon, and star appearing on an archaic gem (Parrot, IX, Plate II, 12), Poulsen (*Der Orient und die frühgriechische Kunst*, p. 50) doubts whether it is a case of Mycenaean tradition or of Phoenician influence. Cf. also Wilamowitz, *Glaube der Hell.*, I, 258.

Helios and Selene, if they were thought of as actual nature divinities, were still felt to be barbaric in Aristophanes' time.[186] The Greek gods were unsuited from the beginning to rise to the cosmic level.[187] The mingling of the ways of thinking—one may even call it identity—seems to me to be Eastern, separation Greek. It was the separation which first made philosophy possible. But the same separation also freed the myth from the priestly domain for the poetic.

Perception of these connections has often been distorted by discrediting attacks, and also not infrequently by a disbelief that the Greeks should owe their most peculiar achievement to alien influences. Such formulations overgeneralize and do not do justice to the process of borrowing and transformation. Philosophy is not Eastern; it is truer to say that the discovery of the East was itself already part and function of this Ionian science.

XXI. Anaximenes, coming later, in certain respects shows greater dependence on the East. His world-model is perhaps too close to nature for it to be necessary to draw comparisons with similar ideas from the East: the bell of the sky set on the outermost rim of the earth. But in his conception the result is that the sun and moon circle not under the earth but round the earth: that is the Babylonian conception.[188] The comparison of the fixed stars with *zographemata* must refer only to the constellations: [189] they were discovered by the Babylonians or the Egyptians and reached the Greeks only from them.[190] It is worth remarking, however, that what was once a mythological way of viewing them has now become a comparison. The same is true of the other comparison of the stars with nails fastened to the sky.[191]

---

[186] Aristophanes, *Peace*, v. 406.

[187] Cp. Fr. Boll, *Kl. Schriften*, p. 93, and Wilamowitz, *GL. d. H.*, I, 254.

[188] Fr. Boll, *Zeitschr. f. Assyr.*, 28 (1914), p. 361, n.

[189] DK A 14, cf. Gigon, *Urspr.*, p. 115.

[190] Boll's view of the Babylonian origin of the zodiac pictures (*Sphaera*, p. 181) has been disputed by W. Gundel, who traces them to Egypt, *Dekane und Dekansternbilder im alt. Aeg.*

[191] Although I cannot point to any examples from the East, I believe that this idea is not Greek. The architectonic thought, which belongs to the demiourgos motif, is alien to Greek mythology. On the contrary, stars as shining nails seem to belong to a picture of the Sky as temple-roof. This idea is found in Egypt (Schäfer, *Antike*, 3, pp. 95 f.).

These are examples of the Greek separation of the ways of thinking: how perception of Nature from its beginning separated from myth.

There is nothing further to say about the similarity of Anaximenes' *arche* with the Phoenician. But the comparison is illuminating for the cosmogony. According to Hippolytus' report[192] it seems at first as if Anaximenes thought that the world came into being by transformation of Air in two opposite directions—into Fire, and into Water–Earth–Stone. But a few sentences later he reports that Fire, and from that the stars, come into being from the moisture of the earth. Similarly Pseudo-Plutarch:[193] the first thing created by 'felting' of Air is Earth, and from that Sun, Moon, and Stars. In Sanchunjaton there rises 'from the intertwining of the wind' Mot, that is Earth in its watery prime condition, and from Mot rise 'sun and moon, stars and constellations'. But that means that the transformation in two directions was only a schema of Theophrastus and had nothing to do with cosmogony.[194] And thus this too shows that one cannot speak of an original division into Thin and Thick, or Hot and Cold, or Light and Night.

But what might be more important: the concept of condensation may be present already in Sanchunjaton. For 'intertwining' there and 'felting' here describe the same process with the same metaphor. But before accepting this one should weigh every possibility, as to whether Philo, in presenting Sanchunjaton's cosmogony, had here borrowed the Milesian, or rather the atomistic concept. His text is not free of suspicion of distortion. Instead of narrating mythologically the birth of 'Desire' from the 'self-desire' of the Pneuma, he speaks of the rise of a 'mixture' which 'was called Pothos'. That sounds like a philosophical interpretation. If one also takes into consideration that the interpretative words spoil the pure parallelism of the sentence, it seems sensible to imagine them absent in the original and to leave to the Ionian the discovery of the physical concept.

XXII. Anaximander at last. He cannot be separated from the context we have explored. But he is the first who deserves the name of a philosopher, independent and bold.

[192] DK A 7.   [193] DK A 6.
[194] Both also distinguished by Zeller (I, 1, 322 and 324) and Gigon (pp. 100 and 111), but the contradiction unexplained.

With his heavenly globe, whether a real model or only de-scribed,[195] he stands in the tradition of Eastern pictures of the cosmos, pictures whose model-like character is clear from the cosmic representations.[196] But Anaximander is the first to separate the disc of the earth from the rim of the sky, indeed he even dissolves the solid bowl of the sky into a mixture of air and fire.[197] The most significant thing about this is that it makes directions relative, in that the mythological 'Beneath' loses its meaning; then the change of dimensions: whereas for the East, and thus the Greeks, the sky did not lie very far above the earth, the distance of the sun's sphere is now fixed at twenty-seven times the earth's radius.[198] And all former dimensions are ex-ceeded as other worlds join the World.[199] Obviously Babylonian, too, is the order of the spheres of the stars: lowest, the fixed stars, then the moon, the sun highest.[200] And the equality of the inter-vals—again due to thinking from a model—is also already found in Babylon: the divine eagle flying upwards reaches the next sky every two hours.[201]

[195] Gigon considers a real model probable, *Urspr.*, p. 86.

[196] H. Schäfer, *Antike*, 3, 94 ff.; cf. above, n. 191.

[197] That Anaximander imagined the sky as a solid bowl (Gigon, p. 85), is hard to accept from Theophrastus' description. From that Anaximander seems rather to have contradicted the traditional view. Also, the 'open sky' seems to harmonize better with the cosmogony, growth from a nucleus, and the expansion of the world (if it is Anaximandrian, Aristotle, *Meteor.* 325 a 25), and finally with the end of the world, however it is imagined. One cannot say that it does not suit archaic thought, since Xenophanes even imagined the sky to be boundless (A 41 a).

[198] If one may rely on Diogenes (= DK 11 A 1, 24), Thales was ahead of him in that he determined the ratio of the size of the sun and moon to the extent of their courses as the same figure 1 : 27—according to Anaximander the size of the sun is equal to that of the earth (A 21).

[199] I doubt whether Anaximander spoke of 'infinitely' many worlds (i.e. Pseudo-Plutarch (A 10), Simplicius, Augustine, Aetius, ii. 1, 3, and Cicero (A 17) speak of the 'countless cosmoi' always in connection with Eternal Recurrence, i.e. the cosmoi are the never-ceasing *diakosmeseis*. Aetius, i. 7, 12 (A 17) belongs here too. Against this we have only Aetius, ii. 1, 8, which carries, however, little weight, because Anaximander is only named there as one of the group of 'those who declare the cosmoi to be infinite'. Where the οὐρανοί are mentioned (A 9, 10, 11) it is at the most 'all heavens'. The change in the meaning of *kosmos* also necessarily caused confusion.

[200] Diodorus, ii. 30, 6, cf. Boll, *Real Encyclop.*, 'Hebdomas' 2565.

[201] Br. Meissner, *Babylonien und Assyrian*, II, 108.

Anaximander was the first Greek to draw a model of the earth's surface as well. But one can point to a surviving example of its Babylonian predecessors, the small terrestrial map in the British Museum,[202] which represents Mesopotamia as a round disc, with the broad Euphrates flowing through it from north to south, and surrounded by the circular 'Bitter River' (cf. Herodotus' mockery of the circular Okeanos on Hekataios' terrestrial map, 4, 36). Names are written in for the cities, rivers, and mountains. If, as Gigon has plausibly argued, Anaximander imagined the earth as a bath-tub,[203] this also clearly shows dependence on the East.[204] But the earth is no longer floating on the water: the sea moves into the middle, a 'remnant' of the primary moisture— again a changed dimension. It remains questionable, whether Anaximander imagined that Okeanos flowed around the mountains of the rim; in any case it is no longer the 'surrounding' (περιέχον) like the Babylonian 'Bitter River'.

Anaximander was the first to build a sundial. Sundials had been, according to Herodotus, invented by the Babylonians and copied from them by the Greeks.[205] Anaximander was also the first to teach the angle of the ecliptic. This was discovered by Babylonians and Egyptians and made known to the Greeks from there.[206]

So much is only to list the known facts. But one would be misjudging the nature of this Ionian science if one attempted to separate these discoveries, which it owed to the East, from actual 'philosophy', saying that the discoveries were isolated practical tricks.[207] Nor did their speculative and their practical side draw on two different sources—Hesiod and Ionian technical science.[208] Just as in the East speculation about the cosmos and observation of nature were functions of the same priestly spirit, so did the Ionians come into contact with both at once. It became philosophy while becoming science.

[202] Br. Meissner, *Klio*, 19 (1925), pp. 97 ff.
[203] Gigon, *Urspr.* p. 88.
[204] The view, that Diodorus, ii. 31, 7, referred to an inverted bath-tub—as, e.g., Meissner II 107—has been refuted by Schäfer, *Antike*, 3, p. 98.
[205] A 4; Herodotus, ii. 109.
[206] A 5; Diodorus, i. 98; W. Gundel, 'Dekane . . .', pp. 338 f.
[207] Zeller, I, 1, 28; Burnet, *Early Gr. Phil.*, Introd. 10–12.
[208] Gigon attempts to prove two essentially separate traits in Presocratic philosophy, speculation about the cosmos, stemming from Hesiod. and the examination of problems by the Ionians.

* 319

It is true that it is as impossible to determine a source for Anaximander as it is for Hesiod. But *his* cosmogony too fits into a tradition, as is shown by the comparison with Anaximenes and Sanchunjaton. In both of them the first thing to form from the origin is the Moist, that is Earth in its primary condition. From that there rise the stars. In Anaximander we have the First Moisture and the sphere of flames which grows out of it. According to Anaximenes, the winds also rise from the water and drive the Fiery, which has gathered above as stars, at great speed in a circular course (A 19). The winds rise from the water according to Sanchunjaton too, namely by the heat of the sun. They 'separate' and 'divide themselves from the original place' and when they 'collide again' there rises a kind of First Storm, which summons the first beings to life. In Anaximander the winds likewise rise through the heat of the sun—Aetius writes of 'the fire', and this must have mainly meant a cosmogonic event. Burnet's conjecture, that by this process the fire was 'torn off' the water, is thus supported. In Egyptian mythology, 'Air' lifts the 'Sky' from the Earth.[209] What inspired Anaximander in his cosmogony to assign to water the role of a kind of *arche* within the world was therefore not only the example of Thales but a traditional order of creation.

Equally traditional was the triple gradation of the parts of the world: Water, Earth, and Fire. They dominated the Babylonian world-picture;[210] thus in the Old Testament too the entirety of the cosmos is embraced with the triple formula: 'anything that is in heaven above, or that is in the earth beneath, or that is in the water under the earth.'[211] Heraclitus still follows the triple division. With one significant difference: Water comes between Fire and Earth. Anaximander was the cause of that, when he had the 'Prime Moisture' become a 'remnant', at the same time translating the Eastern schema into Greek, where Earth had precedence.

Anaximander's conception of the *arche* belongs in the line of pictures of the Origin which we have discussed. It can be seen that the *apeiron* was not—as it would seem from Asistotle—(any more than Thales' Water) discovered by speculation on the unity

[209] See above, p. 308.
[210] Jensen, *Kosmologie der Babylonier*, p. 3.
[211] *Exodus* 20, 4.

and quality of the material cause of all things, but has its roots in a given cosmogonic view which is essentially of a spatial nature. In itself there is no reason why it should not be put together with Hesiod's Chaos, since both spring from the same root. The comparison shows above all that the Boundless has its mythological predecessors not in the World Cavity but in the Infinite Depth. But it is improbable that Anaximander developed his concept from that of Hesiod's Chaos; for the Boundless is the highest Director and stands in place of Zeus, whereas Chaos is against the gods. And something else which *apeiron* has in common with the Eastern concepts of the Origin is not expressed in Hesiod's Chaos: that it is the Encompasser. The concept of the Boundless is linked with it everywhere, and everywhere in a different way: in Sanchunjaton as that for which no limit has yet been set; in the Old Testament as infinite depth and source of abundance; in Babylon as monstrous First Mother, giving birth inexhaustibly; in Egypt as all-embracing Origin and oldest god. But it is clear that under all the variations there lies a basic conception of the Origin, which shows different facets at different times. The Greeks, too, understood it in different ways: in Hesiod it became an anti-Olympian domain; Thales understood it perhaps to the greatest extent in its cosmic reality; Anaximenes, more in its substantiality, the later concept of the element being foreshadowed in him. In this transmitted concept of the Origin there lies also the real reason for the fact noted by Aristotle and explained in his own way:[212] that nobody chose Earth as *arche*; this would have been quite possible after Hesiod; but Earth could not be the Encompasser.

Anaximander's view is the most complex. It contains the begetting-power of the Origin, its inexhaustibility and its divinity. But what gives it its philosophical character is its conceptual quality. This was helped by the spirit of the Greek language, which managed to catch the abstract in adjectives made nouns.[213] That Anaximander had an ear for language, we may deduce from Theophrastus' quotation and his judgement on it. He, above all the others, was the first artist in prose. Now philosophy was made from language, and the 'Boundless' became a concept: it drew the temporal sense of 'Eternal' along with it,

---

[212] *Met.* 989 a 5.
[213] B. Snell, *Entdeckung des Geistes*, pp. 217 ff.

together with its opposite, the Finite.[214] Now, too, the 'surrounding', which was only contained in the older pictures as a mythological view, became independent, cosmologically and conceptually, as the thing which simultaneously 'surrounds' the whole world and 'surpasses' and 'guides' all finite things. This concept was not discovered by searching for the primary substance, but in continuing traditional thinking about the Origin. But mythological thought had already prepared the conceptuality of the *Apeiron*, by personifying this special aspect of the Origin in figures such as the 'Infinite' or the 'Depths', and linking them in pairs or triads with such other 'abstractions' as 'Darkness' or 'Water'. Personification is the mythical form of the abstract. Thus while it is true that in Anaximander the *arche* had entirely divested itself of the mythological form, yet its peculiar being came in the end from the myth, i.e. its character as a power, its religious dignity and the living reality of the concept.

[214] K. Reinhardt, *Parmenides*, p. 253.

XII

SOME PROBLEMS IN ANAXIMANDER

G. S. Kirk

THIS article deals with four almost classic problems in Anaximander. Of these the first is of comparatively minor importance, and the second is important not for what Anaximander thought but for what Aristotle thought he thought. Problem 1 is: Did Anaximander describe his τὸ ἄπειρον as ἀρχή? Problem 2: Did Aristotle mean Anaximander when he referred to people who postulated an intermediate substance? Problem 3: Did Anaximander think that there were innumerable successive worlds? Problem 4: What is the extent and implication of the extant fragment of Anaximander? Appended is a brief consideration of the nature of Theophrastus' source-material for Anaximander; on one's opinion of this question the assessment of the last two problems will clearly depend.

The present article was read as a paper to the Oxford Philological Society in November 1953, and has been slightly emended as a result of the helpful discussion on that occasion. Recently there has appeared a study of considerable interest and importance, J. B. McDiarmid's 'Theophrastus on the Presocratic Causes', *Harvard Studies in Classical Philology*, LXI (1953), 85–156 (above, Ch. VIII). In his brief discussion of Anaximander McDiarmid has a good deal to say which bears on my problems 1, 2, and 4. In the first two cases, and up to a sharply defined point in problem 4 (after which there is a radical difference of interpretation), his views complement my own. It seemed more useful, therefore, to leave my main text unaltered (except for the addition of the present paragraph), and to refer to McDiarmid's views, where necessary, in additional footnotes—one or two of them of some length. It might be added that the suggestions at the end of this paper about

Theophrastus' access to original Presocratic sources may now be judged in the light of McDiarmid's general thesis (which he seems to me to have proved),[1] that Theophrastus is heavily dependent on Aristotle's Presocratic interpretations, and should not be unthinkingly accepted as an independent source.

In the table on the following page will be found the main evidence, set out in corresponding columns, for the reconstruction of Theophrastus' abridged account of Anaximander's *arche*. Simplicius appears to give a more or less exact quotation from the two-volume abridgement of Φυσικῶν δόξαι. Hippolytus and the Pseudo-Plutarchean *Stromateis* give looser paraphrases. In the right-hand column I have placed some extracts from Aristotle which illustrate Theophrastus' dependence on him at some points. If one compares the language of λέγει δ' αὐτὴν . . . φύσιν ἄπειρον in column 1 with Aristotle's οἱ δὲ περὶ φύσεως πάντες κτλ. in column 4 (where the sense is notably different), one sees that Theophrastus was so soaked in Aristotle that he tended on occasion to express (and to distort) his meaning by means of the mere rearrangement of complex Aristotelian terms.

1. DID ANAXIMANDER DESCRIBE HIS τὸ ἄπειρον AS ἀρχή?

It is now generally agreed[2] that the words πρῶτος τοῦτο τοὔνομα κομίσας τῆς ἀρχῆς, in the Simplicius column of the following table, mean that Anaximander first used the word ἀρχή of the originative substance, in his case τὸ ἄπειρον. I merely wish to revive and

---

[1] See also my *Heraclitus, the Cosmic Fragments*, 20–5, 30.

[2] Not, however, by McDiarmid, who on pp. 138–40 (above, n. 31 on p. 188) argues in favour of the conclusion put forward here. However, he rejects Burnet's interpretation of πρῶτος αὐτὸς ἀρχὴν ὀνομάσας τὸ ὑποκείμενον (see p. 189), and tentatively suggests reading οὕτως for οὗτός. His objections to that interpretation are: (1) it 'does not render the Greek, as Jaeger claims': with this I disagree (see note 3). (2) 'It makes no sense, since Simplicius has already treated the water of Thales as a material substratum of the opposites (*Phys.*, pp. 149, 5–7 and 150, 11–12).' This objection seems to me to be met by my submission below that 'Anaximander would be singled out here as the first explicit holder of the idea in question because opposites were actually named by him (and not of course by Thales) as emerging from the *arche*.' But McDiarmid would not accept this: see note 8. He usefully calls attention to another passage in Simplicius, *de Caelo* p. 615, 15 Heiberg, which possibly supports the minority view: ἄπειρον δὲ πρῶτος (Anaximander) ὑπέθετο.

Simplicius *in Phys.*, p. 24. 13 Diels (DK 12 A 9)	Hippolytus, *Ref.* 1. 6. 1–2 (DK 12 A 11)	[Plutarch] *Stromateis* 2 (DK 12 A 10)	Aristotle parallels
... Ἀναξίμανδρος ... ἀρχήν τε καὶ στοιχεῖον εἴρηκε τῶν ὄντων τὸ ἄπειρον,	(2) οὗτος μὲν ἀρχήν τε καὶ στοιχεῖον εἴρηκε τῶν ὄντων τὸ ἄπειρον,	... Ἀναξίμανδρον ... τὸ ἄπειρον φάναι τὴν πᾶσαν αἰτίαν ἔχειν τῆς τοῦ παντὸς γενέσεώς τε καὶ φθορᾶς,	
πρῶτος τοῦτο τοὔνομα κομίσας τῆς ἀρχῆς.	πρῶτος τοὔνομα καλέσας τῆς ἀρχῆς.		
λέγει δ' αὐτὴν μήτε ὕδωρ μήτε ἄλλο τι τῶν καλουμένων εἶναι στοιχείων, ἀλλ' ἑτέραν τινὰ φύσιν ἄπειρον,	(1) οὗτος ἀρχὴν ἔφη τῶν ὄντων. φύσιν τινὰ τοῦ ἀπείρου,		*Phys.* Γ4. 203ᵃ16: οἱ δὲ περὶ φύσεως πάντες ὑποτιθέασιν ἑτέραν τινὰ φύσιν τῷ ἀπείρῳ τῶν λεγομένων στοιχείων, οἷον ὕδωρ ἢ ἀέρα ἢ τὸ μεταξὺ τούτων.
ἐξ ἧς ἅπαντας γίνεσθαι τοὺς οὐρανοὺς καὶ τοὺς ἐν αὐτοῖς κόσμους.	ἐξ ἧς γίνεσθαι τοὺς οὐρανοὺς καὶ τὸν ἐν αὐτοῖς κόσμον.	ἐξ οὗ δή φησι τούς τε οὐρανοὺς ἀποκεκρίσθαι καὶ καθόλου τοὺς ἅπαντας ἀπείρους ὄντας κόσμους.	*de Caelo* Γ5. 303ᵇ10: ἔνιοι γὰρ ἓν μόνον ὑποτίθενται, ... ὃ περιέχειν φασὶ πάντας τοὺς οὐρανοὺς ἄπειρον ὄν.
	ταύτην δ' ἀίδιον εἶναι καὶ ἀγήρω, ἣν καὶ πάντας περιέχειν τοὺς κόσμους.		*Phys.* Γ4. 203ᵇ11: (τὸ ἄπειρον) περιέχειν ἅπαντα καὶ πάντα κυβερνᾶν ... καὶ τοῦτ' εἶναι τὸ θεῖον· ἀθάνατον γὰρ καὶ ἀνώλεθρον, ὥσπερ φησὶν Ἀναξίμανδρος καὶ οἱ πλεῖστοι ...
ἐξ ὧν δὲ ἡ γένεσίς ἐστι τοῖς οὖσι, καὶ τὴν φθορὰν εἰς ταῦτα γίνεσθαι κατὰ τὸ χρεών.	λέγει δὲ χρόνον ὡς ὡρισμένης τῆς γενέσεως καὶ τῆς οὐσίας καὶ τῆς φθορᾶς.	ἀπεφήνατο δὲ τὴν φθορὰν γίνεσθαι καὶ πολὺ πρότερον τὴν γένεσιν ἐξ ἀπείρου αἰῶνος ἀνακυκλουμένων πάντων αὐτῶν.	*Phys.* Γ5. 204ᵇ33: ἅπαντα γὰρ ἐξ οὗ ἐστι, καὶ διαλύεται εἰς τοῦτο.
διδόναι γὰρ αὐτὰ δίκην καὶ τίσιν ἀλλήλοις τῆς ἀδικίας κατὰ τὴν τοῦ χρόνου τάξιν,			
ποιητικωτέροις οὕτως ὀνόμασιν αὐτὰ λέγων.	(λέγει δὲ χρόνον)		

reinforce Burnet's view (*EGP* 4, 54, n. 2) that, on the contrary, what is meant is that Anaximander was the first to call his material principle (for which ἀρχή was the normal Peripatetic term) by the name τὸ ἄπειρον. The Simplicius version seems to me to mean *that and nothing else.* The Hippolytus version, printed in column 2, is odd as it stands: I know of no good parallel for the genitive of the name given, after the phrase ὄνομα καλεῖν. Burnet suggested that τοῦτο was omitted by haplography before τοὔνομα, which seems probable enough in itself; compare another corruption in the Hippolytus passage, τὸν . . . κόσμον for τοὺς . . . κόσμους. As for καλέσας, it is possible as it stands, or it may have replaced an original κομίσας (which indeed is more likely in view of the greater accuracy elsewhere of Simplicius' version): note that Hippolytus omits τῶν καλουμένων στοιχείων, which he nevertheless probably read in his source. If this interpretation is correct, Theophrastus was simply developing Aristotle's judgement at *Phys.* Γ 4,203 a 16 (the first passage in the right-hand column above), that all the φυσικοί assumed an ἄπειρον: Anaximander was the first actually to use the expression, and as a complete description of the *arche.*

The real objection to the Burnet interpretation, however, is based on another passage of Simplicius, *in Phys.*, p. 150, 20 Diels: ἕτερος δὲ τρόπος καθ᾽ ὃν οὐκέτι τὴν μεταβολὴν τῆς ὕλης αἰτιῶνται οὐδὲ κατὰ ἀλλοίωσιν τοῦ ὑποκειμένου τὰς γενέσεις ἀποδιδόασιν, ἀλλὰ κατ᾽ ἔκκρισιν· ἐνούσας γὰρ τὰς ἐναντιότητας ἐν τῷ ὑποκειμένῳ, ἀπείρῳ ὄντι σώματι, ἐκκρίνεσθαί φησιν Ἀναξίμανδρος, πρῶτος αὐτὸς ἀρχὴν ὀνομάσας τὸ ὑποκείμενον. I accept that the obvious meaning of the last clause is 'having been the first to call the substratum of opposites ἀρχή'. Yet leaving aside the possibility that Simplicius might merely have misunderstood Theophrastus, this piece of information is quite gratuitous and irrelevant in the place where it stands. Burnet's interpretation of the clause was: 'being the first to name the substratum of the opposites as the material cause'. I accept this as a possible, though not the obvious, meaning of these words.[3] What seems important is that such a meaning would be absolutely relevant, instead of absolutely

___

[3] At any rate Jaeger's objection, *The Theology of the Early Greek Philosophers*, 201, n. 28, that ὀνομάζειν must mean literally 'to give the name of', is not cogent. This verb is sometimes used loosely to mean 'specify as', 'identify as'; e.g. Plato, *Rep.* 4, 428 e . . . ὅσοι ἐπιστήμας ἔχοντες ὀνομάζονταί τινες εἶναι . . .

irrelevant, to Simplicius' commentary here, the sense of which is that the φυσικοί made their originative substance a substratum of Aristotelian change. Admittedly this is assumed to be true, also, of Thales *qua* φυσικός: but Anaximander would be singled out here as the first explicit holder of the idea in question because opposites were actually named by him (and not of course by Thales) as emerging from the *arche*.

Three final points. First, Theophrastus, like Aristotle, was content to use the word ἀρχή, without special comment, in his remarks on *Thales*, and Simplicius had actually quoted those remarks only about 250 words before the passage on Anaximander. Secondly, if Simplicius had really understood from Theophrastus that Anaximander pioneered this sense of ἀρχή, he might be expected to have introduced this information somewhat earlier, in his long expansion of Aristotle's discussion of ἀρχαί at the very beginning of his commentary (*in Phys.*, pp. 3–7 Diels, esp. p. 6, lines 31 ff.). Thirdly, it is admitted that Anaximander *could* perfectly well have used ἀρχή, meaning 'source'; compare, for example, νείκεος ἀρχή in the *Iliad*. In any case I should have expected him, like most cosmogonists, to have used phrases like ἀπ᾽ ἀρχῆς or κατ᾽ ἀρχήν. But ἀρχή used by itself, and not in prepositional phrases, does not occur in the surviving fragments of any other Presocratic thinker, as a description of the primary and originative substance. I find this *silentium* odd, though of course by no means conclusive. In sum, I do not think that Burnet's view can be proved to be correct; but I suggest that it is at least as likely to be right as the accepted view, and should certainly not regarded as liquidated.[4]

II. DID ARISTOTLE MEAN ANAXIMANDER WHEN HE REFERRED TO PEOPLE WHO POSTULATED AN INTERMEDIATE SUBSTANCE?

It is well known that in nine places Aristotle, when listing the material principles of monistic physicists, mentions a substance intermediate between the so-called elements: either denser than fire and finer than air, or denser than air and finer than water, or once, oddly and no doubt by error, intermediate between water

---

[4] With McDiarmid's support I now feel inclined to claim rather more than this.

and fire. Of the ancient commentators, Alexander referred all and Simplicius most of these passages to Anaximander. Zeller, however, followed Simplicius in noting that one of them clearly places Anaximander in a quite separate group from whoever postulated an intermediate substance: *Physics A* 4, 187 a 12 'ὡς δ' οἱ φυσικοὶ λέγουσι, δύο τρόποι εἰσίν. οἱ μὲν γὰρ ἕν ποιήσαντες τὸ σῶμα τὸ ὑποκείμενον, ἢ τῶν τριῶν τι ἢ ἄλλο ὅ ἐστι πυρὸς μὲν πυκνότερον ἀέρος δὲ λεπτότερον, τἆλλα γεννῶσι πυκνότητι καὶ μανότητι πολλὰ ποιοῦντες . . . οἱ δ' ἐκ τοῦ ἑνὸς ἐνούσας τὰς ἐναντιότητας ἐκκρίνεσθαι, ὥσπερ Ἀναξίμανδρός φησι, καὶ ὅσοι δ' ἕν καὶ πολλά φασιν εἶναι, ὥσπερ Ἐμπεδοκλῆς καὶ Ἀναξαγόρας· ἐκ τοῦ μίγματος γὰρ καὶ οὗτοι ἐκκρίνουσι τἆλλα. This crucial passage states that 'the physicists may be divided into two groups. Those (οἱ μέν) who make the corporeal substratum *one*, either one of the three (*sc.* fire, air, water) or something else denser than fire and finer than air, generate the rest by thickening and thinning . . . while the others (οἱ δέ) say that the opposites are separated out from the one, in which they inhere, *as Anaximander says.* . . .' On the strength of this passage Zeller (Z-N I. i. 283 ff.) held that Anaximander can *never* be meant when an intermediate is mentioned. A few, for example Burnet (*EGP* [4], 55 f.) and Joachim (*Aristotle on Coming-to-be and Passing-away*, 193 and 225), clung to Alexander's view, but Zeller has carried the day and it is now widely taken for granted (for example by Ross, *Aristotle, Physics,* 482 f.) that the intermediate substance has nothing to do with Anaximander.[5] One of the characteristics of this highly academic dispute is the freedom with which each side has simply ignored hostile evidence. Thus Burnet ignored the crucial passage already quoted; while those, on the other hand, who maintain that the references must be to some unknown thinkers *intermediate between Anaximenes and Heraclitus,* for example (!) (cf. Ross, *loc. cit.*), neglect the damaging fact that the description of the nature of the intermediate body varies from passage to passage, apparently at random. Burnet remarked: 'This variation shows at once that he [*sc.* Aristotle] is not speaking historically'. If this were

---

[5] McDiarmid has a good discussion (*op. cit.*, pp. 100 ff; above, pp. 197 ff.) of the way in which Aristotle and then Theophrastus were able to treat Anaximander as both a monist and a pluralist. He does not go into the particular difficulties of the intermediate-substance terminology, but obviously assumes that Anaximander is sometimes meant.

modified so as to mean that Aristotle did not always have in mind a specific intermediate actually postulated by a specific thinker, I should agree unreservedly.[6]

Once again, the commonly discarded view seems the more correct. The idea of intermediate substances surely arose in the first instance out of Aristotle's obvious bewilderment at Anaximander's concept of an originative material qualified only as ἄπειρον (which Aristotle took to mean, primarily, spatially infinite), and as divine and all-encompassing. Himself committed to the four simple bodies and to the theory of change as between opposites, and accepting 'the elements' as the key-note of primitive physics, Aristotle normally assumed that Anaximander must have meant his ἄπειρον to have *some* relation to one or more of the στοιχεῖα—especially since it evidently gave rise to the opposites. Thus at *Phys.* Γ 4, 203 a 16 (quoted in the right-hand column on p. 325), in the course of his discussion of infinity, Aristotle asserted that *all* the φυσικοί, obviously including Anaximander, attach to the infinite some other substance from the so-called elements, for example water or air or something intermediate between the two. Here we may pertinently ask what substance Anaximander attached to the ἄπειρον, in Aristotle's present judgement, if not an intermediate.

The conviction that there should be some relationship, even if not one of simple identity, between τὸ ἄπειρον and the Presocratic elements underlies the use of Aristotle's phrase τὸ παρὰ τὰ στοιχεῖα, 'that which is other than the elements, is not identifiable with any of them'. Some at least of the passages in which this phrase occurs, although no formal mention is made of Anaximander (whom Aristotle names only four times in all), almost certainly refer to him. (i) *de Generatione* B 5, 332 a 18 ὁ δ' αὐτὸς λόγος περὶ ἁπάντων, ὅτι οὐκ ἔστιν ἐν τούτων ἐξ οὗ τὰ πάντα. οὐ μὴν οὐδ' ἄλλο τί γε παρὰ ταῦτα, οἷον μέσον τι ἀέρος καὶ ὕδατος ἢ ἀέρος καὶ πυρός, ἀέρος μὲν παχύτερον καὶ πυρός, τῶν δὲ λεπτότερον. ἔσται γὰρ ἀὴρ καὶ πῦρ ἐκεῖνο μετ' ἐναντιότητος, ἀλλὰ στέρησις τὸ ἕτερον τῶν ἐναντίων, ὥστ' οὐκ ἐνδέχεται μονοῦσθαι ἐκεῖνο οὐδέποτε,

---

[6] Nevertheless, Nicolaus and Porphyrius suggested Diogenes of Apollonia, whose *arche* was indubitably air and not an intermediate; while Zeller and Diels hit infelicitously upon one Idaeus of Himera, about whom we are told one thing and no more by antiquity, that he, too, believed the *arche* to be air.

ὥσπερ φασί τινες τὸ ἄπειρον καὶ τὸ περιέχον . . . Here τὸ ἄπειρον καὶ τὸ περιέχον, which is implied to be 'something other than the elements', τί γε παρὰ ταῦτα (and a μέσον or intermediate), seems almost certainly intended as a reference to Anaximander. He at any rate is the only one who can have held that the indefinite surrounding stuff (cf. *Phys.* Γ 4. 203 b 11) may be considered as existing by itself (μονοῦσθαι,), without reference to specific forms of matter ('the elements'). (ii) *de Generatione* B 1, 329 a 8 ἀλλ' οἱ μὲν ποιοῦντες μίαν ὕλην παρὰ τὰ εἰρημένα, ταύτην δὲ σωματικὴν καὶ χωριστήν, ἁμαρτάνουσιν. ἀδύνατον γὰρ ἀνεῦ ἐναντιώσεως εἶναι τὸ σῶμα τοῦτο αἰσθητὸν ὄν· ἢ γὰρ κοῦφον ἢ βαρὺ ἢ ψυχρὸν ἢ θερμὸν ἀνάγκη εἶναι τὸ ἄπειρον τοῦτο, ὃ λέγουσί τινες εἶναι τὴν ἀρχήν. 'But those who assume a single corporeal and separate material beyond those specified, παρὰ τὰ εἰρημένα, are in error. For it is impossible for this body, being perceptible, to be without contrariety; for this infinite thing, which some say is the ἀρχή, is necessarily light or heavy or hot or cold.' The argument is that this substance is corporeal, and therefore perceptible, by definition: hence it must have the properties of perceptible bodies, lightness or weight, etc., and so be bound up with the opposites and positively related to the elements. The description τὸ ἄπειρον τοῦτο, ὃ λέγουσί τινες εἶναι τὴν ἀρχήν must, I think, be intended to refer to Anaximander. (iii) *Phys.* Γ 5, 204 b 22 declares that some people say that there is an infinite body beside the elements, τὸ παρὰ τὰ στοιχεῖα, to avoid the consequence that derivative bodies would be destroyed by the infinite stuff if both it and they were characterized by opposites. This reason for the avoidance of an actual constituent of our differentiated world as originative substance, although expressed in typically Aristotelian terms, may well have been substantially Anaximander's,[7] *contra* Cherniss, *Aristotle's Criticism of Presocratic Philosophy*, 376. It accords with the implication of the extant fragment, to be discussed later, which cannot be said of the other motive suggested by Aristotle for the hypothesis of an infinite *arche*—'that becoming might not fail', ἵνα ἡ γένεσις μὴ ἐπιλείπῃ. Admittedly a motive resembling this latter one was assigned to Anaximander by Aetius and presumably, therefore, by Theophrastus: but Theophrastus may simply have picked the wrong one of the two motives suggested by his master, or he may have thought that both were relevant.

[7] See also McDiarmid, above, pp.195-96.

In view of the above instances we may accept the opinion of many scholars that in some at any rate of the passages concerning a substance *other than the elements* Aristotle appears to have Anaximander in mind. If this is so, then we may take it that on occasions at least Aristotle thought of Anaximander's τὸ ἄπειρον as τὸ παρὰ τὰ στοιχεῖα.

Now the formulation τὸ παρὰ τὰ στοιχεῖα is presumably a deliberate one. One notices that it is wide enough to embrace not only intermediate substances, if such were really to exist, but also other postulable forms of matter not identical with fire or air or water or earth. Normally, it is true, the phrase appears to refer to an intermediate. It may be significant, however, that in one passage, *Phys. Γ* 5, 204 b 29 (continuing the passage cited at (iii) above), the idea expressed by the phrase in question is refuted by an argument appreciably wider than (though not precluding) that regularly brought to bear against any intermediate substance: not that it is an element, merely, with excess or deficiency of one contrary (as, for example, at *de Generatione B* 1, 332 a 22, quoted under (i) above), but that if it were originally perceptible body we should still be able to perceive it, since things are destroyed into that from which they came.

Theoretically, then, a *mixture* or *fusion* of the so-called elements, in addition to an intermediate between them, might come under the broad heading of τὸ παρὰ τὰ στοιχεῖα. Now that Aristotle was inclined on occasion to class Anaximander with Empedocles and Anaxagoras, as *separating out* the opposites from an original One, we know both from *Phys. A* 4, 187 a 20 (quoted on p. 328) and from *Met. Λ* 2. 1069 b 21: τὸ Ἀναξαγόρου ἓν . . . καὶ Ἐμπεδοκλέους τὸ μίγμα καὶ Ἀναξιμάνδρου. It is not difficult to guess why Aristotle considers Anaximander in this light: it is because he knew that Anaximander used a term like ἀποκρίνεσθαι or ἔκκρισις, or because he knew that Anaximander somehow produced opposed substances in a secondary stage of the world-forming process.[8] In either case, Aristotle would have assumed, τὸ ἄπειρον

---

[8] U. Hölscher, *Hermes*, LXXXI (1953), 261 f. (cf. 265–7) [above, pp. 287, 291–294], thinks that it was Aristotle who supplied the opposites in Anaximander, because he took Anaximander's use of ἀποκρίνεσθαι (which need not imply opposites) to imply the ἔκκρισις of Aristotle's own opposites and the four simple bodies. One should certainly be cautious here, but I think that Hölscher's attempt to deny the concept of opposites to Anaximander has no indisputable foundation, and that it is contrary to the probable implica-

must, for Anaximander, have potentially or actually contained the opposites. According to the present suggestion, then, Aristotle, by thinking of Anaximander as postulating a first principle which was not identifiable with any of the traditional elements, which was παρὰ τὰ στοιχεῖα, was enabled by the ambiguity of this formulation and the concept which it expresses to concentrate on either of two alternative interpretations of τὸ ἄπειρον—as an *intermediate*, or as a *mixture*. Passages have been adduced in which each interpretation is used; though it must be admitted that the two mixture-interpretation passages do not use the παρὰ τὰ στοιχεῖα formulation. Thus it may be that in the crucial passage *Phys. A* 4, 187 a 12 (on p. 328), where Aristotle divides the φυσικοί into two classes, those who generate out of the one by condensation and rarefaction, and those who generate by separation from a mixture, Anaximander appears explicitly in the second class; but Aristotle is led to associate with the first class, also, a type of substance, for the sake of exhaustivity, which he elsewhere normally connects with Anaximander.

tions of the fragment and to Heraclitus' implicit correction of Anaximander. McDiarmid now adds his warning (*op. cit.*, pp. 101 f.; above, pp. 199 f.) to Hölscher's, and in particular calls attention to Simplicius *in Phys.* p. 27, 11 Diels (*Dox.*, 479, 2), where Simplicius may assert that, according to Theophrastus, Anaximander separated *gold* and *earth* out of his ἄπειρον. The question is whether ἐκεῖνος here refers to Anaximander or to Anaxagoras (the two are being compared). Both views have been taken, and I am not convinced that McDiarmid is right in saying that ἐκεῖνος *must* be Anaximander. We have to take into account that the choice of the strong demonstrative may have been determined by the lost context in Theophrastus himself, or even in Alexander, and not by the extant context in Simplicius' version. In this extant context, it is true, ἐκεῖνος should refer to Anaximander: and this is important evidence so far as it goes. In any event, I do not maintain that what is separated off from Anaximander's ἄπειρον must *only* be the two important pairs of opposites mentioned by Heraclitus, canonized by Empedocles, and taken over by Aristotle—though these were the most obvious cosmological (and meteorological) oppositions at any date. Nor would I insist that only objects defined by their names as opposites (e.g. τὸ θερμόν and τὸ ψυχρόν, or τὸ σκληρόν and τὸ μαλακόν) are separated off. We can see from Anaxagoras Frag. 4 that no one kind of classification would necessarily be used. *If* Anaximander (and not only Anaxagoras) mentioned gold and earth among the things separated from the Indefinite, this does not mean that he did not feel all those things to possess contrary δυνάμεις in one way or another; though some would have a more obvious polarity (and would perhaps be more important cosmologically) than others. See also p. 342 below.

That an intermediate substance should be named on occasion simply for the sake of exhaustivity, and be devoid for the time being of any specific historical association for Aristotle, may seem improbable on first consideration. Yet the casual way in which the intermediate may be introduced is exemplified by *Meta. A* 8, 989 a 12: κατὰ μὲν οὖν τοῦτον τὸν λόγον οὔτ᾽ εἴ τις τούτων τι λέγει πλὴν πυρός, οὔτ᾽ εἴ τις ἀέρος μὲν πυκνότερον τοῦτο τίθησιν ὕδατος δὲ λεπτότερον, οὐκ ὀρθῶς ἂν λέγοι. Here Aristotle's argument is that he who explains γένεσις by accretion should postulate as *arche* the finest form of matter, that is, fire; 'otherwise, if he specifies anything but fire, even if he made it denser than air and finer than water, he would be at fault'. Clearly the second-best to fire here is the intermediate between fire and air, and Aristotle should have said 'denser than *fire* and finer than *air*'.[9] He also varies in his treatment of intermediates as a class. At *Phys. A* 6, 189 b 5 he asserts that τὸ μεταξύ is *less* bound up with the opposites than the elements are, but elsewhere there is held to be no distinction between them in this respect. At *de Generatione B* 5, 332 a 20 (quoted on p. 329 above), and in other passages, it is plain enough that it is the intermediate as such and not any particular intermediate that is under consideration. These factors lead to the conclusion that Aristotle did not on any occasion have any objective historical use of an intermediate substance in mind, and that he usually specified one or other intermediate almost at random, merely for the sake of example.[10] At the same time the variation in his treatment and the fact that the intermediate is mentioned not once but several times, when the *archai* of the Presocratics are in question, indicate that he thought the possibility of the existence of such substances to deserve attention, if only by refutation. The conception of the intermediate is really his own, but it arose out of a feeling that Anaximander must have meant his ἄπειρον to be somehow qualified in terms of opposites. Aristotle assumed (to recapitulate) that Anaximander must have met this problem in one of the two ways

[9] A slip by Aristotle, or a displacement in the text-tradition, is a possibility, of course, but hardly more probable than not. We have allowed him one such slip already—the intermediate between water and fire (omitting air) at *Phys. A* 6, 189 b 1.
[10] The intermediate between water and earth is not mentioned, since it would be liable to the same obvious objections as earth, though to a lesser degree.

which Aristotle himself suggested, both of which are covered by the description of the ἄπειρον as 'not identical with any of the elements'. When it was Aristotle's purpose to enumerate the single *archai* of the monists he tended to include τὸ μεταξύ, which arose out of his consideration of Anaximander and which he sometimes but not always associated with him. When, on the other hand, he turned to consider cosmogonies which made explicit use of the opposites, he was able to treat Anaximander's ἄπειρον as being παρὰ τὰ στοιχεῖα to the extent of *containing* the opposites, like Empedocles' σφαῖρος and Anaxagoras' ἦν ὁμοῦ πάντα. On one occasion this latter interpretation of Anaximander is formally opposed to the postulation of an intermediate. This should persuade us not that the intermediate never had any association with Anaximander, but that it is simply a rather vague formulation by Aristotle which, though in the first place applied to Anaximander, is often repeated with no thought of him in mind and merely to satisfy Aristotle's own requirements of exhaustivity.[11]

---

[11] Before leaving this problem mention should be made of an hypothesis propounded by O. Gigon in his *Der Ursprung der griechischen Philosophie*, pp. 68 ff. In our nine Aristotelian passages which refer to an intermediate he distinguishes between those that describe it as denser than one element and finer than another, and those (four in number) which simply call it μεταξύ and do not mention density. These latter passages, Gigon asserts, are accurate references by Aristotle to Anaximander; while the others are classed as 'a later interpretation' on the dubious ground that the idea of rarefaction and condensation does not antedate Anaximenes. On this criterion the crucial passage *Phys. A* 4, 18 a 12 is 'a later interpretation'. But this does not explain the opposition in that passage between Anaximander and the intermediate; for the so-called later interpretation, of a substance intermediate in density, was at any rate an interpretation of Anaximander, and must have been to some extent associated by Aristotle with him. The suggestion that, in those passages where *as it happens* (as I would contend) Aristotle does not mention density in connection with the intermediate, we are face to face with a genuine undistorted account of Anaximander is surely rather extravagant. This suggestion is made in order to support a theory that many will find implausible, that Anaximander's ἄπειρον was intermediate between light and night, in a manner not so much physical as metaphysical or ideal! As so often an apparently promising initial examination of the evidence is followed by highly speculative conclusions which lie far beyond the range of that evidence.

III. INNUMERABLE WORLDS

Cornford demonstrated in *CQ* XXVIII (1934), 1 ff., that Burnet's assignment (*EGP*⁴, 58 ff.) of coexistent innumerable worlds to Anaximander rested on a false assessment of the doxographical evidence on this point, as well as on the misinterpretation of several later Presocratics. References in the doxographers to coexistent *kosmoi* were due, Cornford thought, partly to a confusion with Anaximander's κύκλοι of sun, moon, and stars, partly to a post-Theophrastean application of Atomistic arguments to *all* who postulated unlimited matter.

Cornford accepted Zeller's contention (Z-N I. i. 305 ff.) that the plural worlds which all scholars accept in Anaximander were successive and not coexistent. His chief objection to coexistent worlds was that there is 'nothing in the appearance of nature' to suggest them (except perhaps the stars, obviously excluded by the character of Anaximander's account of them). But the same objection, I submit, applies to the *successive* separate worlds accepted by Zeller and Cornford—'separate', that is, as opposed to local κόσμοι or periodical rearrangements of our earth's surface. The total destruction of the world and its reabsorption into the originative material, followed by the birth of a new world, and so on, were for long accepted in Heraclitus on the strength of the Stoic *ecpyrosis*-interpretation (see my *Heraclitus, the Cosmic Fragments*, 335 ff.), and its acceptance has perhaps unconsciously conditioned many modern scholars to countenance successive separate worlds in Anaximander. But the idea of different worlds in time would be, surely, an absolutely extraordinary one for an early Ionian thinker, whose object, judging from the other evidence, was to explain *our* world and account for its coherence. This necessitated, as it seemed to the Milesians, the description of a cosmic evolution from a single kind of matter. It did *not* necessitate the irrelevant and bizarre hypothesis of the world disappearing again into that same kind of matter. The material of the world was divine; it possessed its own life and movement, perhaps, but the life was the unending life of the immortal gods and not the terminable life of R. G. Collingwood's cosmic cow (*The Idea of Nature*, 32).[12] As for the argument that what was born must die,

[12] Collingwood's interpretation here is influenced by his tendency to view archaic Greek speculation through the medium of later thought. In this

one has only to think of the widely scattered myths of the birth of Zeus, for example, to dispose of *that*. This world is assumed to have had a birth because only so, it seemed, could its intuited unity be rationally explained.

At the same time there was undoubtedly a widespread tendency among the Greeks to believe that our world has undergone in the past, and will undergo again in the future, periods or cycles of drastic physical alteration. I refer not to the analogous idea of culture-periods like Hesiod's five ages, but to the belief in catastrophes by extensive fire and flood, a belief well illustrated in the course of the μῦθος at *Timaeus* 22 c–e: 'Many are the destructions of men and of many kinds that have been and shall be, the greatest of them by fire and water, the rest shorter and from countless other causes.' The Egyptian priest who speaks these words goes on to say that the story of Phaethon conceals a truth, that periodically the earth is scorched when the heavenly bodies incline too near in their orbits. The Deucalion myth, too, may be placed in a comparable context. These mythical traditions arose in part, no doubt, from a residual folk-memory of floods and droughts in, for example, Egypt and Mesopotamia. But in the sixth century B.C. supporting evidence of a more tangible kind was at hand. In Ionia there seemed to be incontrovertible signs that the sea was slowly drying up: the great river-mouths were silting at surprising speed, and the harbours of Ephesus and Miletus were in danger. Further, Xenophanes, who was not much junior to Anaximander, had access to reports of fossils from many parts of the Aegean world, from which he concluded that the land must once have been sea and is gradually drying out. In time, he thought, the process would be reversed and everything would turn into mud, and so on. Anaximander, too, might have heard of these marine fossils, which would naturally be a source of general curiosity. At all events Alexander of Aphrodisias, in his commentary on Aristotle's *Meteorologica*, asserted that according to Theophrastus a reference there (*Meteor. B* 1, 353 b 6) to 'those who think that the sea is diminishing and drying up, and that eventually it will all be dry' was to Anaximander and Diog-

---

case he is projecting the ideas of the *Timaeus* on to the Ionians (cf. *op. cit.*, 72).

enes of Apollonia.[13] It is possible, therefore, that Anaximander did, like Xenophanes, postulate long-term changes in the constitution of the earth's surface—changes in heat and cold, dryness and wetness, which might alternate like summer and winter though at much longer intervals.[14]

If Anaximander held this kind of view—and we have Alexander's word for it, and no more, that Theophrastus thought he did—then it is easy to see how his theory of successive states of the earth's surface, perhaps involving the near-destruction of animal life, could have been later expanded into one of successive separate worlds. This type of distortion might be particularly easy because of the ambiguity of the word κόσμος, which could signify either the world as a whole or more localized arrangements within it.

Our direct evidence for successive separate worlds in Anaximander is entirely based upon Aristotle and Theophrastus. According to Simplicius' version of Theophrastus (in the left-hand column of the table on p. 325) he wrote of 'all the heavens and the worlds in them'; these, we are told, came from the Boundless. It is clear that this contention is meant to be supported by the fragment of Anaximander, which Theophrastus evidently went on to quote. I shall argue below that this fragment cannot in fact be concerned with the relation between successive worlds and the Boundless. If that is so, then the reliability of Theophrastus' testimony[15] on the question of innumerable worlds falls very much under suspicion. In fact, the phrase τοὺς οὐρανοὺς καὶ τοὺς ἐν αὐτοῖς κόσμους looks like a reminiscence of a remark by Aristotle at de Caelo Γ 5, 303 b 10: ἔνιοι γὰρ ἓν μόνον ὑποτίθενται, καὶ τοῦτο οἱ μὲν ὕδωρ, οἱ δ᾽ ἀέρα, οἱ δὲ πῦρ, οἱ δ᾽ ὕδατος μὲν λεπτότερον ἀέρος δὲ πυκνότερον, ὃ περιέχειν φασὶ πάντας τοὺς οὐρανοὺς ἄπειρον ὄν. Here the reference to 'all the heavens'

[13] Of course, Theophrastus might simply have referred this opinion to Anaximander because he thought that he at any rate postulated successive worlds; but on such grounds he might have referred it also to, for example, Empedocles. It would fit in, too, with Anaximander's known anthropogonical theories, to which the suggestion of Alexander is not opposed.

[14] Aristotle called such periods 'great summer' and 'great winter' (Meteor. A 14. 352 a 30), though he himself argued that changes in climate and in the conformation of land and sea were localized, and were balanced by reverse changes elsewhere.

[15] Or the coherence of Simplicius' account of Theophrastus, I might now add in view of McDiarmid's interpretation discussed in n. 24.

is puzzling on any interpretation.[16] Conceivably it is intended to cover those φυσικοί who might in Aristotle's view have posited plural worlds—possibly Heraclitus, and also Empedocles and the Atomists, although formally the reference is limited to monists. If, as some think, Aristotle's phrase points particularly to Anaximander (for the intermedate substance has just been mentioned), we have to consider whether πάντας τοὺς οὐρανούς might be intended to describe Anaximander's plural rings of the heavenly bodies: this at least is what Cornford thought. I must confess I find this difficult, and I do not think that Cornford adequately demonstrated that οὐρανός might be used in precisely such a sense (*CQ*, XXVIII (1934), 10–12). At any rate Theophrastus seems to have decided to clarify Aristotle's phrase by adding the words 'and the worlds in them'. Cornford held that he meant successive worlds, but this was certainly not implied by the Aristotle text, where περιέχειν if anything (though not by any means inevitably) suggests coexistent worlds. A further possibility is that Aristotle was thinking of his own development of the Callippean system of concentric spheres (which might properly be termed οὐρανοί), and by a slip applied the language proper to these to the early monists. At *Phys. Γ* 4, 203 b 11 he wrote simply τὸ ἄπειρον . . . περιέχειν ἅπαντα καὶ πάντα κυβερνᾶν.[17]

When we turn to the post-Theophrastean doxographical tradition we find confusion: sometimes Anaximander's worlds are coexistent, sometimes they are successive, sometimes they are both. Simplicius consistently treats them as both coexistent and successive, as though they were the worlds of the Atomists. Consider *in Phys.*, p. 1121, 5 Diels: οἱ μὲν γὰρ ἀπείρους τῷ πλήθει τοὺς κόσμους ὑποθέμενοι, ὡς οἱ περὶ Ἀναξίμανδρον καὶ Λεύκιππον καὶ Δημόκριτον καὶ ὕστερον οἱ περὶ Ἐπίκουρον, γινομένους αὐτοὺς καὶ φθειρομένους ὑπέθεντο ἐπ' ἄπειρον ἄλλων μὲν ἀεὶ γινομένων ἄλλων δὲ φθειρομένων, καὶ τὴν κίνησιν ἀίδιον ἔλεγον . . . Here Simplicius applies to Anaximander, as well as to the Atomists, Aristotle's assertion at *Physics* Θ 1, 250 b 18 that 'All who say that there are innumerable worlds, and that some worlds are coming into existence and others perishing, say that motion is eternal'. Further, in Aristotle's enumeration of the causes of the concept of infinity comes the following passage: *Phys. Γ* 4. 203 b

[16] Less so, if one stomachs coexistent worlds in Ch. 6.
[17] I owe this suggestion to Professor R. Hackforth.

23 διὰ γὰρ τὸ ἐν τῇ νοήσει μὴ ὑπολείπειν καὶ ὁ ἀριθμὸς δοκεῖ ἄπειρος εἶναι καὶ τὰ μαθηματικὰ μεγέθη καὶ τὸ ἔξω τοῦ οὐρανοῦ. ἀπείρου δ' ὄντος τοῦ ἔξω, καὶ σῶμα ἄπειρον εἶναι δοκεῖ καὶ κόσμοι· τί γὰρ μᾶλλον τοῦ κενοῦ ἐνταῦθα ἢ ἐνταῦθα ('If that which is outside the heaven is infinite, then there seems to be infinite body, too, and infinite worlds: for why should there be more of the void in one place then another?') The actual reference is to the Atomists, but the same argument might seem to apply to Anaximander with his ἄπειρον primary substance. Cornford thought that only Simplicius drew this false conclusion; but can we be sure that Theophrastus himself was not swayed by Aristotle's formulation, or the familiar Atomist arguments which determined it? In this case Simplicius' judgement would not be independent, but would depend, as often, upon the doxographical tradition stemming from Theophrastus.[18] Certainly the division in the two versions of Aetius (see Cornford, *CQ* XXVIII (1934), 4 f.) about the nature of Anaximander's worlds could be easily accounted for on the hypothesis that Theophrastus, himself lacking special information (except, he thought, for the fragment, which he misinterpreted), assigned Leucippean worlds passing away and coming to be throughout space to Anaximander. It is infuriating of Cicero not to have made himself clearer at *de nat. deorum* 1.10.25: 'Anaximandri autem opinio est nativos esse deos longis intervallis orientis occidentisque, eosque innumerabilis esse mundos, sed nos deum nisi sempiternum intellegere qui possumus?' In this comparatively early offshoot of the Theophrastean tradition the point at issue is concealed in the ambiguous words *longis intervallis*. Are these intervals spatial or temporal? If spatial, they show that the assignment of Atomistic-type worlds to Anaximander probably derives from Theophrastus himself. Unfortunately there is no way of settling the question on the basis, at least, of Cicero's language.[19]

---

[18] It is important that St Augustine, whose source for Theophrastus is separate from Simplicius', attributed Atomistic-type worlds to Anaximander: *CD*, 8, 2 (DK 12 A 17).

[19] Burnet thought it 'much more natural' to understand intervals of space rather than of time. Cornford wrote as follows: 'That Cicero himself took "intervals" to refer to time seems probable from Velleius' next words, "sed nos deum nisi *sempiternum* intellegere non possumus".' Here is an example of special pleading almost as notable as anything Burnet ever perpetrated: for the contrast implied in 'deum . . . sempiternum' is adequately provided by *nativos* and *orientis occidentisque*.

My suggestions on the question of innumerable worlds in Anaximander may be summarized as follows. (1) The concept of successive separate worlds is a very difficult one, and is unlikely to have occurred before Parmenides forced scientific dogmatism to become more extreme, and to exceed by far the range of common sense, in the effort to overcome his criticisms. Empedocles, with his theory of successive states of the cosmic σφαῖρος, may have mediated the idea of entirely separate successive worlds. (2) Cycles of alteration of the earth's surface, however, were accepted in ancient legend and were further suggested by the changing relation of land and sea. In one source it is implied that, according to Theophrastus, Anaximander believed in such cycles. (3) We do not know for certain what Aristotle thought; but Theophrastus may have been persuaded (*a*) by an illegitimate extension of the application of natural cycles in Anaximander, (*b*) by a misinterpretation of the extant fragment, and (*c*) by an application of Atomistic arguments to *all* who explicitly postulated (as it seemed) infinite matter, to credit Anaximander with innumerable worlds of the Atomistic type. This would account for peculiarities in the later tradition.

IV. THE EXTENT AND IMPLICATION OF THE EXTANT FRAGMENT

Simplicius *in Phys.*, p. 24, 17 Diels (for what precedes see column 1 of the table on p. 325) . . . ἑτέραν τινὰ φύσιν ἄπειρον, ἐξ ἧς ἅπαντας γίνεσθαι τοὺς οὐρανοὺς καὶ τοὺς ἐν αὐτοῖς κόσμους. ἐξ ὧν δὲ ἡ γένεσίς ἐστι τοῖς οὖσι, καὶ τὴν φθορὰν εἰς ταῦτα γίνεσθαι κατὰ τὸ χρεών· διδόναι γὰρ αὐτὰ δικὴν καὶ τίσιν ἀλλήλοις τῆς ἀδικίας κατὰ τὴν τοῦ χρόνου τάξιν, ποιητικωτέροις οὕτως ὀνόμασιν αὐτὰ λέγων. Where the quotation begins has been much disputed; but the words ἐξ ὧν δὲ . . . εἰς ταῦτα γίνεσθαι are probably not by Anaximander, *contra* Cornford, Jaeger, Kranz in DK, etc. Cornford (*CQ*, XXVIII (1934), 11, n. 2) held that Theophrastus would have written γίνεται and not ἡ γένεσίς ἐστι, and φθείρεσθαι and not τὴν φθορὰν . . . γίνεσθαι. But the nouns γένεσις and φθορά had become Aristotelian technical terms and this is precisely why they are used. They do not occur at all (for what this is worth) in extant Presocratic contexts. (In Anaximander, too, we might perhaps have expected πᾶσι or πᾶσι χρήμασι and not τοῖς οὖσι the dative case of which appeared to Deichgräber, in *Hermes*, lxxv (1940), 13, to be 'alt'). The statement seems to be a Peripatetic variant on a common formula applied by Aristotle to the φυσικοί, simply expressed, for example, at *Phys. Γ* 5. 204 b 33: ἅπαντα γὰρ ἐξ οὗ ἐστι, καὶ διαλύεται εἰς τοῦτο.[20] The words κατὰ τὸ χρεών, on the other hand, look like part of the *verbatim* quotation. χρεών is the most plausible conjecture for MS. χρεώμενα in Heraclitus Frag. 80, to give κατ᾽ ἔριν καὶ χρεών, and χρεών is used by itself, meaning 'necessity', in Euripides and Plato. It is a rather poetic word except in the common phrase χρεών ἐστι, and it is this special usage alone which is found in Aristotle, six times. We should readily accept χρεών ἐστι in Theophrastus, but not κατὰ τὸ χρεών. What may have happened, therefore, is that Theophrastus paraphrased the preceding sentence in Anaximander, by substituting for it a familiar Peripatetic formulation which seemed equivalent; yet he retained the original closing phrase κατὰ τὸ χρεών to connect his paraphrase with the direct quotation which follows, διδόναι γὰρ αὐτὰ δίκην κτλ., which contained a narrower restatement, and a justification, of the preceding assertion.[21]

Now it has been argued by Heidel, Cherniss, and Vlastos that αὐτά and ἀλλήλοις must refer to more or less equal partners, because of the nature of the legal situation depicted: as Heidel put it (*CP*, VII. (1912), 234), '*dike* obtains between peers'. This is, of course, an over-simplification. Dike as a personification regulates the behaviour of man to man, but also, on occasion, man to gods. Yet *mutual* δίκη, that is, an established reciprocal relation, was assumed to operate only between members of a single social group: there was no point, for example, in a man exemplifying his concept of *dike* by offering not to attack a lion. It is absurd to think, therefore, as used to be thought, that it is the world on the one hand and the Boundless on the other that stand in this relation (which is specified as a reciprocal one) to each other. How could the divine ἄπειρον be said to commit injustice? Rather the subject of αὐτά is the opposed world-masses of (primarily) the predominantly hot stuffs and the predominantly cold stuffs, the wet and the dry, the first pair of which Theo-

[20] Similarly McDiarmid, above, pp. 191–93.
[21] See Theophrastus' *de sensibus* for his tendency to quote isolated words and short phrases.

phrastus, according to the Pseudo-Plutarchean *Stromateis* quoted on p. 349, said were somehow *produced*[22] from the Boundless at the beginning of the world. That this analysis into opposed substances, or into groups of objects possessing contrary δυνάμεις, was applied not only to a stage in cosmogony but also to the continual natural processes of the developed world is not unlikely in itself.[23] Whether Anaximander actually called these opposed conglomerates 'the hot' and 'the cold' and so on, or whether he was content normally to use more specific terms like winter and summer (which are, however, opposed to each other and mutually exclusive), is immaterial. According to this interpretation, then, our fragment means that cosmological events are maintained by a fluctuating balance of power between opposed masses. The legalistic metaphor of excess and deprivation, κόρος and χρησμοσύνη (these words occur as Frag. 65 of Heraclitus), accounts not only for the *balance* of natural cycles like day–night, winter–summer, heat–cold, perhaps great winter–great summer, it also explains the *continuity* of these cycles by providing a metaphorical, anthropomorphic motive for action and reaction.

The essentials of the interpretation outlined above were stated both by Burnet and by Heidel, who failed, however, to establish any satisfactory relation between this continuing cosmological balance and the odd hypothesis of innumerable coexistent worlds. If the worlds are successive, however, the difficulties become intolerable. How does the world pass away, if it forms a self-perpetuating system? And how are we to reconcile the fragment,

[22] I deliberately do not emphasize any possible biological meaning in γόνιμον It *may* have such a meaning here, it *may* imply that Anaximander used here, like the *Theogony*, the metaphor of sexual generation. Yet these are at least two instances in Plutarch where γόνιμος means simply 'productive of', in a purely metaphorical and weakened sense and without any noticeable implication of sexual generation: *Qu. conviv.*, 7, 715 f; *Maxime cum princ.*, 3, 978 c. We simply cannot be sure, therefore, of its exact connotation in the Pseudo-Plutarch passage.

[23] The analysis into 'opposites', in the developed world, was certainly made shortly after Anaximander, most notably by Heraclitus; we are told that Anaximander used opposites at some stage in cosmogony (though see note 2 on p. 26); it is reasonable to assume, therefore, quite apart from the evidence of the fragment, that he did not simply ignore their future history but retained them as constituents of our developed world of experience. It is from this world, after all, that the analysis into opposites must originally have been derived.

as Theophrastus tries to do, with the idea of innumerable worlds? Vlastos (*CP*, XLII (1947), 172; above, p. 80) followed Cherniss in developing an ingenious but laborious answer to this problem: 'the damages are paid (*sc.* by the opposites) not to the Boundless but to each other', but they are only paid in full when the world is reabsorbed into the Boundless. The Boundless itself is a fusion of opposites, as is shown by the plural form of ἐξ ὧν δὲ ἡ γένεσις (Vlastos, above, p. 77, after Cherniss, *Aristotle's Criticism of Presocratic Philosophy*, 377 ff.).[24] It is clear that the whole argument

---

[24] McDiarmid, *op. cit.*, p. 97 (above, p. 190f.), agrees that the payment cannot be between the world and the ἄπειρον; and also shows that the Cherniss–Vlastos suggestion is untenable. But he goes on to argue that the subject of διδόναι γὰρ αὐτά is not pairs of opposed substances, but is τὰ ὄντα, the existing things of the separated world—as is shown by τοῖς οὖσι in the preceding sentence in Simplicius (see above, n. 33 on p. 191). I would reply that these very existing things are in fact opposites, in the sense suggested in note 8, but that it is illegitimate to use sentence-sequence here in order to determine the precise reference of αὐτά, since on any interpretation, and particularly on McDiarmid's, there is confusion in the sequence of Theophrastean generalization and direct quotation. Indeed, McDiarmid himself states on p. 98 (p. 193 above) that 'The generation–destruction clause is not to be connected with the metaphor'. His own interpretation of the whole passage is ingenious. He argues that in διδόναι . . . ἀδικίας Theophrastus 'is quoting what appears to be Anaximander's justification of his own doctrine against Thales and any-one else who made one of the opposed elements the primordial matter'. The world-constituents, I take this to mean, pay the penalty *to each other*, i.e. each to all the others, and not all to *one* constituent material, the ἀρχή in the Thales-type theory. The gist of the Theophrastean extract according to McDiarmid is, then, as follows: 'Anaximander declared the Infinite to be the principle of all things (i.e. that out of which all things are generated and into which they are destroyed); and he said that the Infinite is some body which is not water or any other of the so-called elements, for, as he said, "they make reparation and satisfaction to each other for their injustice".' This interpretation deserves a fuller examination than can be given it here, and is in many ways an attractive one which cannot be lightly dismissed. I will only say that its plausibility is severely diminished by the necessity of assuming that, in McDiarmid's words, 'The thread of the argument has been obscured, probably by Simplicius'. If the meaning were as proposed, we should expect ἐξ ὧν γάρ (not δέ), and διδόναι δ' ἐκεῖνα (or another strong demonstrative), not διδόναι γὰρ αὐτά. In addition, the sentence-order would be different. But why should Simplicius or any intermediary have ruined the emphasis by tampering with pronouns and connecting particles—a far profounder change than the mechanical shift of a sentence or two? Further, the addition of κατὰ τὴν τοῦ χρόνου τάξιν, whether by Theophrastus or by Anaximander himself, removes the heavy emphasis on ἀλλήλοις (which is not, in any case,

here depends upon the assumption that the Boundless itself somehow contains the opposites. That this is incidentally implied is undeniable; but that it should have been explicitly argued by Anaximander is contrary to the whole conception of τὸ ἄπειρον, which is presumably so called just because its nature cannot be properly defined. The minor argument from ἐξ ὧν is too improbable to merit discussion.[25]

I fall back, therefore, on the view that the fragment has nothing to do with worlds perishing into the Boundless, but that it describes cosmological changes in the one continuing world. The assertion that originally preceded κατὰ τὸ χρεών, and which Theophrastus was able to paraphrase by an Aristotelian formula which suited his own cosmological interpretation of the fragment, might have been to the effect that each opposite changes into its own opposite and into no other, for example the hot is replaced by the cold and not by the wet or the soft. This is a necessary hypothesis for Anaximander's theory of cosmic stability, obvious to us but not so obvious then, since Heraclitus also emphasized it for his own special purposes. The axiom may easily have been

---

[25] It might be argued that Aristotle *Phys.* Γ 4, 203 b 11, τὸ ἄπειρον . . . περιέχειν ἅπαντα καὶ πάντα κυβερνᾶν, καὶ τοῦτ᾽ εἶναι τὸ θεῖον, needs some explaining. How does the Boundless 'govern' or 'steer' all things? By virtue, obviously, of surrounding or containing them; but what actual control can it exercise within the cosmos, if the idea of innumerable destructions and recreations is rejected? The question is difficult to answer on any hypothesis; we cannot be absolutely sure, of course, that περιέχειν . . . καὶ κυβερνᾶν, though perhaps an archaic phrase, is taken from or refers specifically to Anaximander. Heraclitus' fire steers all things (Frag. 64), but that of course exists *within* the cosmos, to some extent. We cannot suppose that the Boundless as such interpenetrates the differentiated world. But presumably it may have been thought of by Anaximander as the ultimate source of the δίκη between opposites on which the stability of the world depends. By enclosing the world, the Boundless prevents the expansion of differentiated matter; if there is thought to be any loss (which is doubtful), the Boundless would make it good. Possibly, if Anaximander thought of the Boundless as divine, he automatically gave it control, without determining precisely how this control was to take effect.

---

in a particularly emphatic position), which is demanded if the argument is to be that which McDiarmid suggests. In any case, it seems difficult to exclude from the injustice-metaphor the implication that the things of the world are opposed to each other.

stated in terms so general that Theophrastus was able to mistake its proper application.

The final words, κατὰ τὴν τοῦ χρόνου τάξιν, are treated by Theophrastus as belonging to Anaximander, since the stylistic judgement ποιητικωτέροις οὕτως ὀνόμασιν αὐτὰ λέγων would naturally follow directly upon the quotation and not upon an insertion or paraphrase by Theophrastus. Admittedly, we find superficially similar phraseology in Theophrastus himself; for example, of Heraclitus, τάξιν τινὰ καὶ χρόνον ὡρισμένον.[26] There may be an unconscious echo here, but what marks the phrase in Anaximander as original is the personification of χρόνος. There is a very close parallel for this, as Jaeger has pointed out, in Solon Frag. 24 Diehl, lines 1–7:

> ἐγὼ δὲ τῶν μὲν οὕνεκα ξυνήγαγον
> δῆμον, τί τούτων πρὶν τυχεῖν ἐπαυσάμην;
> συμμαρτυροίη ταῦτ᾽ ἂν ἐν δίκῃ Χρόνου
> μήτηρ μεγίστη δαιμόνων Ὀλυμπίων
> ἄριστα. Γῆ μέλαινα, τῆς ἐγώ ποτε
> ὅρους ἀνεῖλον πολλαχῇ πεπηγότας·
> πρόσθεν δὲ δουλεύουσα, νῦν ἐλευθέρα.[27]

The idea of the 'trial conducted by time' is similar to that of the 'retribution according to the assessment of time' in Anaximander. With κατὰ τὴν τοῦ χρόνου τάξιν one might compare, for example, κατὰ τὴν Ἀριστεί[δου τάξιν in the Athenian tribute-lists.[28] What

[26] McDiarmid, 141 f. (above, n. 42 on p. 194), is won over by such similarities, and accepts the view of Dirlmeier, RhM LXXXVII (1938), 380 f., that κατὰ τὴν τοῦ χρόνου τάξιν is Theophrastus' paraphrase of κατὰ τὸ χρεών.

[27] Bergk's conjecture ἐν Δίκης θρόνῳ in line 3 is unnecessary, improbable in itself, and entirely lacking in textual warrant. It is approved by Dirlmeier, RhM, LXXXVII (1938), 378.

[28] Whether τάξις in the fragment means 'act of assessing' or 'objective assessment' (i.e. the result of an act of assessment) makes no material difference, as it happens, to the meaning. Jaeger approved the translation 'ordinance' (e.g. Paideia², English translation³, Oxford, 1946, 159 f. and note 50 on p. 455). A consideration of the meaning of nouns in -σις in the Iliad and Odyssey suggests that the active meaning is more likely here. Professor D. L. Page drew the following conclusion from a review of the Homeric evidence which he kindly sent me: 'It is strongly suggested that a new -σις formation, such as τάξις, will have been intended to denote the action of the verb, not its result, at least in archaic Greek'. But Jaeger's assumption that active uses were necessarily legal is discredited by the use of the verb,

is assessed in the present case, however, is not so much the *amount* of retribution, for this is fixed on a pre-established proportional quantitative basis of restitution in full plus an indemnity. In any case Time does not control the *amount*, but rather the *period* in which the fixed proportion must be paid. Again, this does not imply, what would be improbable in itself, that that time-limit for payment must be fixed once and for all, the period the same and unchanging in every case.[29] Rather it implies one or both of two things: (*a*) that Time on each occasion will make an assessment of the period for repayment, for example a short period for an encroachment of night on day, a longer one for an encroachment of winter on summer; and (*b*) that Time has made a general assessment once and for all, to the effect that *sooner or later* in time the compensation must be paid. These ideas have partial analogies in Aeschylus; *Choephoroe* 648 ff., τέκνον δ' ἐπεισφέρει δόμοις | αἱμάτων παλαιτέρων | τίνειν μύσος χρόνῳ κλυτὰ | βυσσόφρων 'Ερινύς: here χρόνῳ means 'in the fullness of time, sooner or later'; *Supplices* 732 f., χρόνῳ τοι κυρίῳ τ' ἐν ἡμέρᾳ | θεοὺς ἀτίζων τις βροτῶν δώσει δίκην: here χρόνῳ, 'in time', is limited by the addition of κυρίῳ τ' ἐν ἡμέρᾳ, 'the day fixed for payment'. In neither case, however, is Time itself in control. Earlier, in Solon, it is the *inevitability* of retribution that is stressed again and again—payment sooner or later, πάντως: so at line 8 of Frag. 1 Diehl, πάντως ὕστερον ἦλθε δίκη, or again at line 28, of the retribution of Zeus, πάντως δ' ἐς τέλος ἐξεφάνη. So too in Frag. 24, quoted above, the indubitable meaning is that Earth justifies Solon's actions, because *with the lapse of time* she has become free. This, and not any predetermined time-limit, is what the δίκη χρόνου implies there: *formerly* Earth was enslaved, *now* she is free. No more specific chronology is either implied or required. The analogy of Solon persuades me that this idea of *inevitability* lies also behind Anaximander's κατὰ τὴν τοῦ χρόνου τάξιν, though not, perhaps, to the exclusion of separate individual assessments.

[29] As, for example, in Empedocles fr. 30.2: ἐς τιμάς τ' ἀνόρουσε τελειομένοιο χρόνοιο. Vlastos, *CP*, XLII (1947), 161, n. 48 (above, n. 45 on p. 64), has no grounds for his assumption that Anaximander's phrase must have had an equivalent application to that of Empedocles here.

and the necessary supplement of the noun, in the tribute-lists; though even there (as indeed in Jaeger's examples from Plato, *Politicus* 305 c and *Laws* 925 b) it cannot be proved that the sense of the noun is active.

According to such an interpretation δίκη, retribution, comes sooner or later, inevitably, among men according to Solon and among natural events according to Anaximander. No single mechanical time-cycle is in question; there are variations in the length of day and night, of summer and winter, of which Anaximander would be well aware. What mattered was that a particular encroachment should earn, eventually, an equivalent retribution: a drought, for example, be made good either by a series of wettish winters or by a single flood. So too Heraclitus allowed for flexibility in the balance of his natural changes, provided only that the total equilibrium of fire, water, and earth was not disturbed.

So much, for the time being, for the problems; but clearly the assumption that Theophrastus was sometimes mistaken in his interpretation of Anaximander requires justification. Theophrastus is regarded as infallible because, it has always been maintained, he had Anaximander's book in front of him. This is, in fact, nowhere asserted by Theophrastus or any other ancient source, and I shall outline some reasons for doubting whether Theophrastus had access to the complete works of a sixth-century Milesian like Anaximander. None of these reasons is compelling in itself, and the case must be regarded as a cumulative one.

1. We know from the catalogue of his works preserved in Diogenes Laertius (v. 42–50) that Theophrastus wrote special monographs on Anaximenes, Empedocles, Anaxagoras, Archelaus, Diogenes, and Democritus, but not on Thales, Anaximander, or Heraclitus. It is at least a possibility that one motive for neglecting the last three was a dearth of original evidence. Of the thinkers to whom Theophrastus did devote monographs, only Anaximenes and Empedocles might not be obviously familiar in the Athens of the Sophists, and interest in Anaximenes was no doubt revived by Diogenes of Apollonia; while Empedocles had the advantage of using an easily propagated and less perishable verse medium. With the decline of Miletus in the fifth century Anaximander's book might very well have gone out of direct circulation, especially if it had never gained popularity on the mainland.

2. We do not know how much *Thales* committed to writing, but, whatever it was, neither Aristotle nor Theophrastus had direct knowledge of it.

3. The surviving fragment of *Anaximenes*, on whose Ionic dialect and style Theophrastus commented, is not only not in Ionic but also partly reworded. This may be due to Aetius, but it might well mean that Theophrastus did not always use the most original version of Anaximenes.

4. Theophrastus did not write a special study on *Heraclitus*: indeed, he appears to have been comparatively ill-informed about him, and to cling loosely to the Aristotelian interpretation. He ventured a stylistic or logical judgement, however: some of the things Heraclitus wrote were half-finished, ἡμιτελῆ, others were inconsistent. To us Heraclitus' surviving fragments do not give an impression of shoddiness: perhaps Theophrastus was handicapped by the nature of his source, which may well have been a mechanically arranged selection of the odder sayings. Heraclitus is said to have deposited his book in the temple of Artemis at Ephesus; possibly this was an aetiological story to explain its absence from the Alexandrian library, since it would have been destroyed when the temple was burnt down in 356 B.C.[30]

5. In his *de sensibus* we possess a long extract from Theophrastus' doxographical work. It is surprising that he could not find more to say about Heraclitus' views on sensation than he actually did, if he had a book by Heraclitus, or a complete collection of his pronouncements, in front of him. It is also plain that Alcmaeon, at all events, must have had more to say on the subject than he is credited with in the few lines on him in Theophrastus.

6. Diogenes Laertius mentions a summary exposition by Anaximander which he supposes Apollodorus to have come across, since the latter knew that Anaximander was sixty-four in 546 B.C. This does not prove, of course, that the whole of Anaximander was extant. On the contrary, Diogenes' statement that Anaximander πεποίηται κεφαλαιώδη τὴν ἔκθεσιν (ii. 2) suggests that Apollodorus somehow mentioned that his source for him was not, in Apollodorus' opinion, the original work.

7. It is clear that Theophrastus was relatively well informed on the astronomy, meteorology, and anthropogony of Anaximander. Yet on his *arche* Theophrastus was evidently vague. This is suggested (*a*) by the inadequacy of his account of the nature of

[30] See the index of *Heraclitus, the Cosmic Fragments*, s.v. 'Book' and 'Theophrastus'. Whether Heraclitus himself ever 'wrote a book' in the usual sense seems doubtful.

348

τὸ ἄπειρον; (b) by what I have proposed to be a misinterpretation of the fragment; and (c), perhaps, by the apparently puzzled phraseology in Pseudo-Plutarch's version of Theophrastus, on the subject of Anaximander's cosmogony: [Plut.] *Stromateis* 2 φησὶ δὲ τὸ ἐκ τοῦ ἀιδίου γόνιμον θερμοῦ τε καὶ ψυχροῦ κατὰ τὴν γένεσιν τοῦδε τοῦ κόσμου ἀποκριθῆναι καί τινα ἐκ τούτου φλογὸς σφαῖραν περιφυῆναι . . .

These considerations indicate that we are not entitled automatically to assume that prose works written in Ionia in the sixth or early fifth century were still available in their entirety to Theophrastus. In the case of Anaximander I would suggest that what Theophrastus might have had in front of him was not a complete book but a collection of extracts, in which emphasis was laid upon astronomy, meteorology, and anthropogony rather than upon the nature and significance of τὸ ἄπειρον, which might always have seemed confusing. In respect of his *arche*, indeed, Anaximander must assuredly have been considered obsolete and unimportant by the end of the fifth century. The extant fragment could be quoted by Theophrastus, of course, because it really came among the cosmological-meteorological extracts.

XIII

THE PYTHAGOREANS AND GREEK MATHEMATICS

W. A. Heidel

HISTORIANS are not agreed regarding the relevancy of the history of mathematics to the general history of science and philosophy. While Zeller treated it as negligible, except as mathematical concepts entered expressly into a system, some recent historians have regarded it as far more important, some going so far as to assign it to a leading role in the story. A story, of course, requires a hero, and Pythagoras would naturally play that part, were it not for the critical examination of the tradition that began, say, with the publication of Zeller's monumental work. In default of so imposing a figure, historians now tend to fall back upon the 'Pythagoreans', as one might tell the story of a nation as that of a reigning dynasty; for the Pythagoreans are conceived as the mathematicians *par excellence* of Greece down to the middle of the fourth century B.C.

Obviously this view has certain formal advantages, which it is not necessary to emphasize. Moreover, the candid student will gladly acknowledge that the concentration on mathematics that favours and accompanies this point of view has been fruitful in many ways. To be sure it is no uncommon observation that the positive contribution of any discussion is apt to be incidental and nearly or quite independent of the preconceived notion as to the angle from which the subject should be approached. It is important, therefore, to determine with what right and in what measure the critical historian may single out the Pythagoreans as especially worthy of playing the leading role, even if one grants the pre-eminent importance of mathematics.

Though our present concern is with the Pythagoreans as

mathematicians, one cannot altogether ignore certain data on which historians rely as evidence of scientific achievements on the part of Pythagoras himself. In this regard contemporary evidence, which we should value highly, is negligible when closely examined. Xenophanes alluded to his belief in the transmigration of souls, significant in reference to his religious views, but of philosophic importance only on certain assumptions that we have no right to make for Pythagoras himself. Much is made of a statement of Diogenes Laertius[1] that Xenophanes denied that God breathes, it being assumed that he was rejecting the Pythagorean doctrine, attested by Aristotle,[2] that the cosmos inhales time and empty space from the surrounding infinite. If one adopts this view one does so in spite of several important considerations. For, first of all, the authority of Diogenes is not in itself great, and the passage in which the statement occurs is confused and in part certainly inaccurate, since it asserts that Xenophanes held the doctrine of the four elements. This alone, without other considerations, suffices to show that we have to do with a source on which one may not well rely. However, assuming that Xenophanes really said that God does not breathe, it is not necessary to suppose that he had a philosophical statement to the contrary in mind. He presumably had in mind rather the popular anthropomorphism; for he said that God in no wise resembles man, either in body or in mind—He is all sight, all hearing, all thought.[3] That implies that God has neither eyes nor ears. Why should He have lungs? The reference to Pythagoras presupposes that Xenophanes identified God with the cosmos, an assumption that rests on a dubious interpretation of a statement by Aristotle;[4] but even if one accepts that interpretation as true, there is as good reason to think that he was criticizing Anaximenes as Pythagoras.

Heraclitus also referred to Pythagoras, but in ways that do not warrant one in supposing that he thought of him as in any

---

[1] IX. 19.

[2] *Phys.* 213 b 22 ff., Frag. 201 Rose.

[3] The text of Diogenes apparently presupposes this context, for it continues σύμπαντά τε εἶναι νοῦν καὶ φρόνησιν καὶ ἀΐδιον.

[4] *Metaph.* 986 b 24, εἰς τὸν ὅλον οὐρανὸν ἀποβλέψας τὸ ἓν εἶναί φησι τὸν θεόν. Aside from the fact that the Laurentian omits τὸν θεόν, the word ἀποβλέψας raises questions. It is natural to suppose that here, as at 991 a 23, it means 'looking at a model', the usual meaning in Plato.

sort concerned with science or mathematics. 'Learning of many things,' he says,[5] 'teacheth not understanding, else would it have taught Hesiod and Pythagoras, and again Xenophanes and Hecataeus.' Another fragment,[6] of doubtful authenticity, asserts that Pythagoras practised inquiry more than all other men, and constructed for himself a wisdom that was only a knowledge of many things and an imposture. One suggestion of the text, as it has come down to us, is that Pythagoras culled his wisdom from many books. That might indeed be true, but what we otherwise have grounds for believing regarding him would hardly suggest it. The only real clue to the meaning of Heraclitus is the company in which he places the sage; and one will hardly contend that it suggests scientific inquiry in the sense in which it was practised by Pythagoreans in later times. Certainly it is difficult to associate the imposture charged to him with mathematics or mathematical theories.

On the other hand, Epicharmus at a somewhat later date is seriously invoked as a witness to the mathematical interest of Pythagoras or his Order; for a fragment of his refers to odd and even numbers.[7] Whether the text is genuine or not, it seems to me incredible that one should think of these terms or of the practice of counting with pebbles as originating with Pythagoras. No doubt odd and even numbers, square and oblong figures were almost as old in his day as they are in ours. To make plausible a reference to a particular thinker it does not suffice to point out something that was presumably the common property of many, if not most men; what one has a right to require is something distinctive, for example, in the connection of ideas.

When one comes to Alcmaeon the case is not quite so simple. There is no doubt that he was a physician of Croton, where according to tradition Pythagoras first established his Order. Of the date at which the medical school[8] of Croton originated we have no definite knowledge, though certainly it existed before the arrival of Pythagoras; neither is it certain whether it had a filiation to any other school, though a relation to the Cnidian is

[5] Frag. 40 Diels, tr. Burnet. [6] 129. [7] Frag. 2 Diels.
[8] This term, commonly used, is apt to prove misleading. We must not think of an organized society in the sixth century. Wherever there were physicians who taught their art to their sons or to others whom they approved, there was a 'school'.

not improbable. As a physician Alcmaeon would most naturally derive whatever medical or physiological presuppositions he made from the school to which he belonged, and there is the best of evidence for the belief that in his time as well as later a physician was generally interested in such scientific researches as were being pressed, as the employment of Democedes and Ctesias by the Kings of Persia well illustrates. Alcmaeon dedicated his treatise to three men reported to have been Pythagoreans, but about whose attainments and achievements we know little or nothing. We may assume, therefore, that he was at least on intimate terms with members of the Order, as would be natural in any case since all concerned presumably belonged to the intellectually more conspicuous group of citizens. This association need not of course imply any formal relation to the Pythagorean Order, nor does it afford any grounds for attributing to it any special interest or direction of research considered as a whole. Later tradition, to be sure, regarded Alcmaeon as a Pythagorean, and that view is still generally accepted. So far as one can see, this assumption can be justified only by a statement in Aristotle's *Metaphysics* which, however, proves upon examination to be at least very dubious. After speaking of certain Pythagoreans who set up a table of ten pairs of contraries —limited and unlimited, odd and even, etc.—he proceeds,[9]

In this way Alcmaeon of Croton seems to have conceived the matter, and either he got the view from them or they got it from him; for he expressed himself similarly to them. For he says most human affairs go in pairs, meaning not definite contrarieties such as the Pythagoreans speak of, but any chance contrarieties, e.g. white and black, sweet and bitter, good and bad, great and small. He threw out indefinite suggestions about the other contrarieties, but the Pythagoreans declared both how many and which their contrarieties are.

In justice to those who regard Alcmaeon as a Pythagorean it must be added that this version of Aristotle's statement omits a clause asserting that he was ⟨young⟩ in the old age of Pythagoras, which is found in some good manuscripts but wanting in the best. I fully agree with Ross in bracketing it, not only because it is omitted by the Laurentian and is quite ignored by Alexander and is besides otherwise contrary to the usage of Aristotle, but because the text of the MSS. that contain the clause is imperfect,

[9] *Metaph.* 986 a 26 ff., tr. Ross.

since it does not give the inevitable word 'young' (νέος). This seems to me strongly to suggest that we have here a marginal note carelessly embodied in the text. One may even conjecture with some confidence the source of the marginal note; for it may well be derived from Porphyry's *Life of Pythagoras* (c. 104), where a long and ill-assorted list is given of the most ancient Pythagoreans who were contemporaries or pupils of Pythagoras, young in his old age (συγχρονίσαντες καὶ μαθητεύσαντες τῷ Πυθαγόρᾳ πρεσβύτῃ νέοι), including Alcmaeon. If that were true, one readily understands why Alexander could not take account of it.

Now, if we consider the matter more in detail the data regarding Alcmaeon fail to give us much real information. Aristotle, on this view, affords no indication of his date, and Porphyry is as always, except where we can certainly make out his authorities, quite untrustworthy. In this instance he groups as contemporaries and personal pupils of Pythagoras, along with Alcmaeon, such men as Philolaus and his pupil Eurytus as well as Lysis, the teacher of Epaminondas, who must be dated near the turn of the fifth and fourth centuries. Furthermore it is natural to infer that Aristotle had no knowledge whether Alcmaeon was actually a member of the Pythagorean Order; and the way he speaks of the possible relation of their respective doctrines is quite noncommittal. To this one must add that from Zeller onward the consensus of scholars has strongly tended to regard the table of ten contrarieties as a relatively late creation of certain Pythagoreans. It is clear, then, that Alcmaeon affords no criterion for determining what is early and late in Pythagoreanism.

What he had in common with certain Pythagoreans of unknown date is, according to Aristotle, a tendency to look upon things as characterized by contraries. Just why Aristotle should have thought it necessary to ask whether such a natural point of view had been borrowed by either from the other remains a profound mystery, because he himself had emphasized the role of certain contrarieties in the thought of the Ionians, especially Anaximander. Not to mention the common Greek practice of setting one state in contrast to its opposite,[10] it was

[10] See Burnet, *Early Greek Philosophy*,[3] p. 8. Heraclitus only emphasizes what was a common Greek point of view. His merit lies in his attempt to reconcile the oppositions which everyone felt.

inevitable that Alcmaeon as a physician should concern himself with such phenomena as heat and cold, the opposite effects of summer and winter on his patients. If there was anything distinctive of either Alcmaeon or Pythagoras in this respect we have no knowledge of it. Burnet, to be sure, in his notes on Plato, *Phaedo* 86 b f., would have us believe that the doctrine was Pythagorean, though the special form of it there set forth must have been influenced by Empedocles and the Sicilian School. What one may infer from Aristotle's statement is perhaps only that he was aware that Alcmaeon was sometimes regarded as a Pythagorean or, because of the dedication of his book, in close touch with the Order, but that he was not prepared to commit himself on the question of their relations. That, at least, appears to have been his general attitude towards the Pythagorean tradition as we see it reflected in the works of his maturity.

Our present concern being with the history of Greek mathematics and the role played by the Pythagoreans in it, it is clear that so far what we know about Alcmaeon throws no light on the subject. It is true that in the Pythagorean table of contrarieties there are several pairs of mathematical concepts; but none of these is attested for Alcmaeon, and the uncertainty respecting his date and that of the table deprives the question of all possible evidential value. The same is obviously true of the only other datum that may be thought to have a bearing on Pythagorean science. Aetius states[11] that certain *mathematikoi*, presumably Pythagoreans, held that the planets moved in a sense contrary to that of the fixed stars, i.e. from west to east, and that Alcmaeon agreed with them. While this would not directly throw light on Pythagorean mathematics, if accepted and interpreted as implying that the theory of the *mathematikoi* was at least as old as Alcmaeon, it would confirm one's belief in the scientific interest of Pythagoreans at a date presumably before the middle of the fifth century. The character of the text of Aetius, however, is such as hardly to warrant one in accepting the statement as a fact or in so interpreting it, if it were true; for Aetius is lavish of statements about Pythagoras that sober criticism must reject, and perhaps the earliest dependable evidence regarding the date of Alcmaeon comes from Greek medical writers of the 'Hippocratic' and

[11] II. 16, 2–3. The other astronomical views attributed to Alcmaeon are, as Burnet, *EGP*[3], p. 110, n. 1, truly says, extremely crude.

Sicilian schools in the latter half of the fifth century. The earliest of the 'planets' (excluding sun and moon) mentioned are the morning and evening stars, the discovery of their identity being attributed to Parmenides or to Pythagoras. Disregarding the latter, it is possible that the former actually referred to their identity. As for the supposed retrograde motion of the planets, including sun and moon, we know that Plato in the *Laws* still thought it worth while to declare that it was false. We are told that Anaxagoras and Democritus held that all the stars moved from east to west. On the other hand Plato in the *Timaeus* and the myth of Er in the *Republic* represented the planets as moving from west to east. It may very well be true, therefore, that the notion was originated or at least held by Pythagoreans.

It is certain that Plato and his school owed much to the Pythagoreans, and that Socrates had among his associates men who were somehow affiliated with them. It was, however, a revived Pythagoreanism in both cases, and many questions that cannot be confidently answered arise in connection with it. On the surface it would appear that the associates of Socrates were chiefly concerned with religious and moral problems, while Plato and his school debated mathematical questions with Pythagoreans. This appearance may be deceptive. In any case, as we shall presently see, it is difficult if not impossible for the most part to distinguish between what is Platonic and what is Pythagorean. Above all, we obtain from Plato no certain criteria by which one could differentiate between the fifth and the fourth centuries in Pythagorean thought. Since the revived Pythagoreanism died out at the end of the fourth century one turns expectantly to Aristotle and his pupils for information, the more hopefully because Aristotle and his school diligently studied the earlier history of the several sciences. There were, however, marked differences among them, and unfortunately Aristoxenus of Tarentum, who was most deeply interested in Pythagoreanism, appears in general to deserve little confidence. It seems probable that he was responsible for a good deal that is reported by later writers.

To begin with Aristotle, there are those who confidently cite a statement made by Apollonius, a writer not earlier than the second century B.C., in his *Historiae Mirabiles*, 6: 'After these (*sc.* Epimenides, Aristeas, Hermotimus, Abaris, Pherecydes) came Pythagoras the son of Mnesarchus. At first he busied him-self with mathematics, i.e. with numbers,[12] but after a time he did not refrain from the miracle-working of Pherecydes.' It will be noted that at best we have here witness to concern about numbers on the part of Pythagoras, entirely credible in itself, but giving no real information, because we are left in the dark regarding the way he was supposed to deal with numbers. So much might probably have been said of any man at the time. The circumstance that makes it worth while to cite the remark is that it is supposed to be derived from Aristotle, who would presumably mean that Pythagoras already began the speculations about numbers mentioned as characteristic of Pythagoreans in his extant treatises. There is, however, no reason whatever to think that the statement derives from Aristotle,[13] who is expressly cited only as authority for several statements in the sequel. It is interesting, however, to note that from the context it would seem to follow that Pythagoras took up Miracle-working after the fashion of Pherecydes after arriving at Metapontum, whereas his occupation with numbers would thus have begun (and ended?) in Ionia.[14] This would be poor evidence for Pythagoras and his Order as the prime movers in the study of mathematics among the Greeks. We may confidently dismiss this datum as of no significance. Elsewhere Aristotle attributed not a single scientific achievement to Pythagoras. Apollonius is known to have quoted as genuine works admitted to be falsely attributed to Aristotle, and in the present case, where no authority is actually cited, it is more likely that he derived the notion from Heraclides of Pontus or a similar source. It is characteristic of a certain kind of the search for sources that this particular state-ment should be attributed to Aristotle simply because it precedes several others expressly referred to him. There is no doubt that he had written a special treatise about the Pythagorean

---

[12] καί is here, as often, defining.

[13] Rose includes it in Aristotle, Frag. 191.

[14] The supposed connection of Pythagoras with Pherecydes is referred by some to his earlier, by others to his later years. Iamblichus, *Vit. Pyth.*, 184, represents Pythagoras as returning from Italy to attend him in his last illness. This is very improbable. Whether this statement derives from Aristoxenus, who said that he buried Pherecydes in Delos (Diogenes Laertius, i, 118), is not certain, though not improbable.

doctrines,[15] but there remain some difficult questions regarding its scope.

Perhaps the most precise statement regarding the date of the Pythagoreans known to Aristotle occurs in the *Metaphysics*:[16] 'Contemporary with these philosophers and before them the Pythagoreans, so-called, devoted themselves to mathematics; they were the first to advance this study, and having been brought up in it they thought its principles were the principles of all things.' Of the nature of this study we shall speak presently; for the moment we are concerned chiefly with the temporal relation of the Pythagoreans. It seems clear that the philosophers to whom they were to be compared as to date were Leucippus and Democritus, who had just been mentioned, not the entire series of thinkers previously enumerated. Unfortunately the statement leaves much to be desired, because it is very vague. Assuming that Aristotle meant that the Pythagoreans were contemporaries of both Leucippus and Democritus and in part earlier than either of them, the time indicated might extend from a date before the middle of the fifth century far into the fourth. That is doubtless true as to the later period, and it may have been the case so far as the earlier date is concerned; but it is not certain that Aristotle meant to say just that. It is quite possible that he meant that the first ones were contemporary with Leucippus and earlier than Democritus, for his expression is singularly wanting in precision. What does he imply in saying that they were the first to advance the study of mathematics? Conceivably he might have meant that the study long antedated them and that their merit lay in notably advancing it; but if so, one learns nothing from him that one could not safely infer from a general knowledge of Greek civilization, which had already attained a high degree of advancement. Again, the statement that they had been brought up in the study implies either that it existed as such before they took it up, or that those who advanced it were not the earliest Pythagoreans. At all events careful attention to Aristotle's statement actually assures us that in the latter part of the fifth century Greek mathematics had attained considerable development, which the Pythagoreans were credited with promoting. The precise date would then depend on that of Leucippus, which is unknown.

[15] *Metaph.* 986 a 12.   [16] *Ibid.*, 985 b 23 ff.

Another statement similarly vague also occurs in the same work. 'Socrates,' we are told,[17] 'occupied himself with the excellences of character, and in connection with them became the first to raise the problem of universal definitions—for in the realm of physics the problem was only touched on by Democritus, who defined, after a fashion, the hot and the cold;[18] while the Pythagoreans had before then treated of a few things, whose definitions[19] they connected with numbers—e.g. opportunity, justice, or marriage.' We may ignore the reference to definitions by predecessors of Socrates, as they were not definitions at all in the logical sense; but it is worth noting that Aristotle at least affords no comfort to those who attribute definitions of geometrical terms to Pythagoreans before the time of Zeno. What interests us here is that Socrates is dated after Democritus and the Pythagoreans are set down before the latter. If this order is accepted as historically true, the occupation of Socrates with universal definitions must be referred to his last years, and the Pythagoreans who proposed the identification of concepts like justice or marriage need not have been earlier than the last third of the fifth century.

In many passages Aristotle either expressly couples Pythagoreans with Plato or Platonists or else makes statements that may sometimes apply to both and sometimes distinguish between them. Doubtless in his lectures he would make it clear to whom he specifically referred; we cannot always distinguish, and even his ancient commentators were often at a loss. What this means is at once obvious. For Aristotle the Pythagoreans were generally of interest chiefly because of their relation to the teachings of the school of Plato in which he was brought up. The subjects of prime importance to him were those debated in the Academy, while he belonged to it, and between him and the leading

[17] *Metaph.* 1078 b 17 ff., tr. Ross.
[18] Aristotle apparently refers to such things as the description of the fire atoms as little spheres.
[19] Cf. *Metaph.* 985 b 29, 987 a 19 ff. It is curious that Aristotle should regard such identifications as definitions. One should expect him somewhere to refer to the definition of mathematical terms, e.g. such as are required in geometry, but he never does so. At best the statement, *Eth. Nic.* 1132 b 21 ff. ὡρίζοντο γὰρ ἁπλῶς τὸ δίκαιον τὸ ἀντιπεπονθὸς ἄλλῳ might be compared with attempts of interlocutors in Platonic dialogues. See in general, *De Part. An.* 642 a 24 ff.

Platonists, after he had set up his own school. As has already been said, we are frequently unable to assign the various views to their advocates, just because those who heard his lectures were presumably themselves engaged in the debates and hardly needed to be told whose views were being criticized. Though we cannot hope to go far in solving the historical and personal questions involved in these discussions, a general presumption does seem to be created by this state of the record. Whatever may have gone before (the very point that chiefly concerns us at the moment) it is difficult to accept the view, now tacitly assumed by some scholars, that the debates in the Academy, during Aristotle's connection with it, were chiefly concerned with Pythagorean theories and definitions proposed a century or more earlier. When in search of teachings that might seem to foreshadow his own doctrine Aristotle was often compelled to reinterpret the record, not only in regard to the four kinds of causation but also in regard to other matters. One might easily point out instances where a rather primitive doctrine is set into a very different light because the point of view had radically changed. Unless one bears this in mind one is likely to misconceive entirely the historical development or at least to build a structure of unverifiable and improbable hypotheses.

So far as concerns the chronology of Pythagorean mathematics it seems to be clear that Aristotle does not warrant us in going beyond the middle of the fifth century. Of course one may conjecturally go much farther back, and many have done so and doubtless will continue to do so. That is a privilege any scholar has, provided he is himself aware, and keeps his readers aware, of the basis of his statements. We have therefore to consider the view of the Pythagorean mathematics as Aristotle saw it. It is surprising how little positive information he gives us on this head, and some of his definite, and repeated, statements are open to the justifiable suspicion of actual misrepresentation.

His most general statement[20] tells us that the Pythagoreans were the first to advance the study of mathematics. He does not say what he means by the term, but it is natural from the context to infer that he was thinking principally of their preoccupation with *numbers*. They thought numbers, as the first

[20] *Metaph.* 985 b 22 ff.

principles of mathematics, were the principles of all things. Because they saw in numbers resemblances to things about them, and because the attributes and ratios of the musical scales could be expressed in numbers, and all other things were modelled after numbers, they thought the elements of numbers were the elements of all things and that the whole heaven was a musical scale and a number. As for the elements of number he elsewhere [21] tells us that they were the odd and the even, or the limited and the unlimited. The examples he gives of the way in which they noted resemblances in numbers to parts of the heavens and how they identified numbers with certain abstract concepts do not add to our knowledge of mathematics, but rather suggest that their method was fantastic and futile, as were the 'definitions' he mentions. If these were the best they could offer, they required little serious attention, and there would be no reason to suspect that their geometry afforded examples of terms properly defined. The same may be said of his report regarding the nature of the One and of the Infinite. [22] We are repeatedly told that they

---

[21] *Metaph.* 986 a 18.

[22] Aristotle repeatedly says that the Pythagoreans, like Plato, regarded the One (τὸ ἕν) and the Infinite (τὸ ἄπειρον) as substance and not as attribute, and yet divided the latter (*Phys.* 203, a 4–6; 204 a 20–34; cf. *Metaph.* 987 a 134; 1001 a 3 ff.; 1053 b 9–16). One wonders what basis there was for his statements so far as the Pythagoreans were concerned. Possibly he was transferring Platonic expressions to them. One suspects that he had only the expressions τὸ ἕν and τὸ ἄπειρον to go on, and interpreted these as implying the substantial existence of the One and the Infinite apart from any entity of which they might be predicated. This interpretation might well be captious; for, when he professes to cite an actual opinion of theirs, he says (*Metaph.* 1091 a 13 ff., tr. Ross), 'There need be no doubt whether the Pythagoreans attribute generation to them (i.e. things) or not; for they obviously say that when the One had been constructed (whether out of planes or of surface or of seed or of elements which they cannot express [rather, about which they don't know what to say]), immediately the nearest part of the Infinite began to be constrained [rather, reading εἰσείλκετο, "inhaled"] and limited by the limit.' Whatever their *language* might imply, it is fair to assume that they thought of the Infinite, not as a substance, but as an attribute of something that could be inhaled, say breath, or air. Cf. Diels, *Vorsokr.*[5], I, 460, 4 ff. The passage above enclosed in parentheses is explained by *Metaph.* 1080 b 20, ὅπως δὲ τὸ πρῶτον ἕν συνέστη ἔχον μέγεθος, ἀπορεῖν ἐοίκασιν. In any case, whatever basis he had for the supposition that the One and the Infinite were substances seems to have referred to cosmology, and so had reference to mathematics only on the assumption that *the cosmos was actually constituted of*

knew only one kind of number, the 'mathematical' or abstract, but that it also had magnitude, or was spatial. Aristotle is apparently puzzled by this contradiction, and it is difficult to believe that any one consciously held these contradictory views regarding the same thing. One is tempted to think that Aristotle combined two classes of expressions, (1) those relating to mathematics and (2) those used in their cosmology. In their reckonings and in their theory of numbers the numerals they employed were naturally those used by everyone else, whether or not they were expressly characterized as abstract. The difficulty, real or factitious, arose from their use of numbers in cosmology. Here the different way in which Aristotle represents their views raises the question whether he does them justice, for it is hardly possible to regard as synonymous the statements that the concrete things are made of numbers and that they display resemblances to or are imitations of numbers. There are, of course, ways in which one may explain the different statements without impugning Aristotle's veracity or the fairness of his interpretation; but, when all is said, there remains a reasonable doubt as to the actual views of the Pythagoreans that is not removed by referring to the figurate representation of numbers or to the practice of Eurytus. It is more to the point to note that in any case this practice of Eurytus makes it impossible to distinguish between early and late conceptions of numbers among Pythagoreans. To say, as is sometimes said, that Eurytus 'still' used the primitive method merely begs the question. We know that, as the pupil of Philolaus, he was approximately contemporary with Plato.

In all this we discover little that goes beyond the concern of the Pythagoreans about numbers. The table of ten contrarieties contains several mathematical terms, but they may all relate to numbers rather than to geometry. The same is true of the musical intervals and concords and of the harmony of the spheres. As for Pythagorean geometry proper, in which historians of mathematics are naturally most interested, there is, so far as I can see, no certain reference to it in Aristotle. One naturally thinks of the proposition that the square on the hypotenuse of a right-

---

numbers. In so far as the Pythagoreans meant that to be taken quite literally, his argument would of course hold good; but it throws no light on their mathematical conceptions.

angled triangle is equal to the sum of the squares on the other two sides, which no one, probably, doubts that we owe to the Pythagoreans; but, in the first place, though Aristotle alludes to it,[23] he does not say that it was Pythagorean, and secondly he states the matter as concerned with numbers, using it as an example of demonstration by a *reductio ad absurdum*: the proof that the diagonal is incommensurable results from the fact that odd must be equal to even numbers. He speaks of Pythagoreans as earlier than Plato, but he provides no criterion by which to distinguish later from earlier or to determine the age of a single achievement.

When we come to his pupil Eudemus, who wrote the history of the mathematical sciences, we naturally have great expectations. Unfortunately little remains of his work, and that little has in part to be reconstructed from late sources. In the reconstruction, moreover, due care has not always been taken to avoid unjustifiable assumptions; for it does not follow from the fact that the later tradition dealing with the history of mathematics ultimately depends on Eudemus that it did not suffer additions as well as losses. The situation here seems to be quite parallel to that of the doxographic tradition which ultimately derives from Theophrastus, for it is plain in the latter case that the phase represented by Aetius was strongly influenced by the school of Posidonius, who followed the Stoic practice of 'accommodation' or assimilation of earlier to later doctrines. We know, for example, that Posidonius thought that Parmenides knew the geographical zones.[24] When it is reported[25] that Pythagoras and Parmenides regarded the earth as spherical, it is obvious that these views go together. Since every other indica-

[23] *Anal. Pr.* 41 a 26.

[24] Strabo, i. 94, repeated by Aëtius, iii. 11, 4. Aëtius, ii. 12, 1, says that Pythagoras and his followers knew the five celestial zones. This looks like another inference to Pythagoras from (late) Pythagoreans, such as we might expect Posidonius to make. Aëtius, ii. 24, 9, even attributes the notion of zones to Xenophanes.

[25] Diogenes Laertius, viii. 48; ix. 21. From the former passage it seems clear that Theophrastus merely said that Parmenides (first?) used the term στρογγύλη as describing the form of the earth. Though it *may* mean spherical, it need not be so interpreted, because it is used in the description of the earth by Diogenes of Apollonia, who thought it a circular disk. Favorinus was the authority of Diogenes Laertius.

THE PYTHAGOREANS AND GREEK MATHEMATICS

tion points definitely to the conclusion that the sphericity of the earth was first proposed about the end of the fifth century, one has good reason to suspect that we have in these statements an example of the historical method of Posidonius, of which Galen gives us a good illustration. He says[26] that Posidonius ascribed the doctrine of the tripartite soul to Pythagoras, 'inferring it from what some of his disciples have written, though no treatise of Pythagoras himself has survived to our time'. There being no evidence of Pythagorean writings before the time of Philolaus,[27] who lived at most a generation before Plato, the Pythagoreans on whom he relied dated presumably from the fourth century or later, and it is not even necessarily implied that these attributed the doctrine in question to Pythagoras. Probably Posidonius merely found the doctrine stated by some Pythagorean and from its source inferred that Pythagoras himself had held it, because, as he thought, his followers religiously adhered to his views.

It is obvious to any critical student that the reports of Aëtius regarding Pythagoras and the Pythagoreans are so compounded of earlier and later data that they are for historical purposes entirely useless except as they can be checked by reference to others that inspire greater confidence. This does not, of course, mean that Posidonius himself is to be credited with every statement about Pythagoras and Pythagoreans in Aëtius. It is enough for our purposes to know that his method has infected the mass. It is important to bear this in mind in dealing with the history of mathematics, which, as has just been said, derives ultimately from Eudemus, as the doxographic tradition derives from Theophrastus. There is good reason to suspect that the former was subjected to the same influences as the latter. Tannery made out a strong case for the thesis that the summary account of the development of Greek mathematics given by Proclus was directly or indirectly derived from Geminus, and we chance to know that Geminus wrote a commentary on Posidonius. These facts suffice to cast suspicion on the statement of Proclus regarding the mathematical achievements of Pythagoras, which owe their supposed authority to the presumption that they derive from Eudemus. While there are many historians who hold that view,

[26] *De Hippocr. et Platone*, p. 478.
[27] Demetrius Magnes *ap.* Diogenes Laertius, viii, 85.

it has been rejected of late by several leading scholars. That it may be questioned is enough for our present purpose. I may add, however, that in my opinion it is certainly not derived from Eudemus. There is, in fact, no satisfactory evidence that Aristotle, Eudemus, or Theophrastus attributed a single scientific achievement to Pythagoras himself: such things they always referred to 'Pythagoreans'. If other members of Aristotle's school represented Pythagoras as the originator of the interests that marked the scientific pursuits of his Order, it becomes a pertinent question why they did so. We should be especially grateful if we could be quite sure that it was really Dicaearchus, one of the best pupils of Aristotle, who said[28] of Pythagoras:

What discourses he held with his associates, no one can affirm, for they observed exceptional silence. Nevertheless what is best attested by all is, first, that he said that the soul is immortal; next, that it migrates into other species of living beings; and in addition, that according to certain periods the things that once were come about again, and nothing is absolutely new; and that all beings that have souls must be considered akin. For it seems that Pythagoras was the first to introduce these beliefs into Greece.

Proclus, then, after saying that Thales first went to Egypt and thence introduced geometry into Greece, himself discovering many propositions and preparing the way for his successors to discover the principles of many others, approaching some solutions in a more general (i.e. abstract), others in a more visual manner, and saying that Mamercus, the brother of the poet Stesichorus was mentioned[29] as having interested himself in geometry, proceeds:[30] 'Following these Pythagoras converted geometrical philosophy[31] into the form of a liberal education, contemplating its principles deductively and investigating its theorems in an immaterial and rational way. It was he who discovered the theory of proportions (?) and the construction of the (five) regular solids.' As I have already said, I cannot believe

[28] Porphyry, *Vit. Pyth.*, 19. Diels (*Vorsokr.*[5], I, 100, 36 ff.) holds, with most scholars, that this statement is part of the text which Porphyry refers to Dicaearchus (c. 18).
[29] This expression suggests Proclus' dependence on general literature rather than on a serious history of mathematics.
[30] *In Eucl.*, p. 65, 11, Friedlein (ed.).
[31] Eudemus would hardly have used this expression.

that this truly represents Eudemus, however much in detail may have been ultimately derived from him. Judging by what we otherwise know of him we may be sure that he did not so speak of Pythagoras; but he may have characterized the method of the *Pythagoreans* in some such terms, which seem to reflect the ideals of Plato as set forth in the *Republic*. Even so, however, the method of (Pythagoras or) the Pythagoreans, as here described, does not differ essentially from that attributed to Thales. We know, to be sure, that Eudemus did credit Thales with the knowledge of certain fundamental propositions of geometry;[32] but it is plain that his knowledge of them was inferred from feats with which tradition credited him. The question naturally arises, since we have here no verbatim quotations from Eudemus, whether he attributed these discoveries to Thales unconditionally or merely said that he must have known the propositions *if the traditions were true*. Either view is, of course, possible. In any case, however, the statement of Proclus and the known inferences of Eudemus make it certain that the mathematical tradition did not regard Pythagoras as the *founder* of the science in Greek lands. One must add that the statement that Pythagoras discovered the construction of the cosmic (Platonic) solids is certainly not true. The laboured efforts of certain scholars to find some justification for it are based on the indefensible view that we are here dealing with Eudemus rather than with Proclus. If the latter's immediate source was Geminus we may really have to thank Posidonius for the view generally accepted by historians of Greek mathematics.

We are fully justified, then, in disregarding the supposed testimony of Eudemus to the mathematical achievements of Pythagoras; but of course that does not eliminate the Pythagoreans. If we take the statements of Proclus as applying to them, we have essentially the same view as we obtain from Aristotle. But Eudemus, fortunately, compensates us for the loss of spurious data regarding the founder by giving precious information about specific achievements of those who called themselves Pythagoreans. It is not necessary for our present purpose to review and evaluate the precious data of Eudemus as reported by Proclus in his *Commentary on the Elements of Euclid*. That may safely be left to more competent mathematicians. It is only necessary to emphasize the need of guarding against the same

[32] Diels, *Vorsokr.*[5], I. 79, 8 ff.

temptation to which Eudemus may have succumbed—the temptation to infer too much from what we may safely accept as fully attested. If that precaution is fully observed we arrive at a body of propositions and demonstrations at least as early as Eudemus and presumably earlier. One wishes that one might add that all this body may be certainly referred to the time before Hippocrates of Chios,[33] who is said to have written the first *Elements of Geometry*; for then we should have an approximate *terminus ante quem*. Obviously this cannot be done, because there were Pythagoreans who lived contemporary with and after him, and we know almost nothing about the contents of his treatise.

To sum up the situation, we may say that from Aristotle and Eudemus we learn that from the middle of the fifth century onward there were Pythagoreans busily and fruitfully occupied with mathematics, especially with the theory of numbers and geometry. Between the middle of the fifth century and Aristotle there are a few data of considerable importance; but about the part played by Pythagoreans (excepting the specific achievements mentioned in Eudemus, all without dates or names of individual geometers) we have no satisfactory evidence. It is one of the most singular facts in the history of Greek thought that individual Pythagoreans are rarely mentioned except by later writers whom one has every reason to suspect. Aristotle, indeed, mentions among others Hippasus, but only to say[34] that he, like Heraclitus, made fire the material cause. Whether he wrote a book or not we do not know, but we incline to doubt it because it is expressly stated that he did not[35] and that Philolaus was the first Pythagorean to do so. Even if he did, however, we should infer from Aristotle's reference that his book did not deal with mathematics. In later times he became the Judas of the Order, who betrayed his master's secrets and was deservedly destroyed by the gods. He obviously cannot afford firm footing for a reconstruction of the

---

[33] There exists no evidence for his date, which is commonly put about 450 B.C. This seems to me too early; on the other hand Erich Frank, *Platon und die sogen. Pythagoreer*, p. 227, probably goes too far in the opposite direction in saying that he lived scarcely before 400.

[34] *Metaph.* 984 a 7. Theophrastus (Diels, *Vorsokr.*[5], I. 109, 6 ff.) repeats this with amplification probably based only on Aristotle's statement that Hippasus and Heraclitus made fire their ἀρχή.

[35] Diogenes Laertius, viii. 84, citing Demetrius Magnes as his authority. Cf. note 27.

development of Greek mathematics. Aristotle's other references to individual Pythagoreans—to Paron, Xuthus, Eurytus—tell us nothing of importance.[36] Philolaus is cited in the *Eudemian Ethics*,[37] but not for mathematics. The contention of some scholars that Aristotle in the *Metaphysics*[38] refers to a statement of his is more than dubious. While I believe that Erich Frank has tried to prove too much, I fully agree with Burnet in regarding the so-called fragments of Philolaus as spurious, or at least as pseudepigraphic. What we may safely say about his views depends on Plato, Eudemus,[39] and Menon, and that throws no light on his mathematics. Even if one accepts the 'fragments', however, there is little gain in this respect, unless they are interpreted and combined with texts dating from later centuries. What remains for the would-be historian are inferences. Besides Aristotle and Eudemus, Plato and the Platonists contemporary with Aristotle inevitably demand consideration; but here, as has already been stated, the information is in general rather vague and subject to different interpretations. Above all, it affords no definite chronological data and no assured references to individuals. Even about Archytas we know too little to be of much service. In fine, we may be said to have positive knowledge only of a considerable body of mathematics in which Pythagoreans were certainly concerned; and some of these Pythagoreans were earlier than Plato; how much older, we do not know, and one is strongly inclined to infer from the polemical tone of many references, that the questions at issue were, at least for the most part, the subjects of debate in the schools of Plato and of Aristotle and therefore presumably not dating back a century or more.

Though this state of our actual knowledge is rarely, if ever, frankly confessed, it has evidently troubled the more conscientious historians. That is why so much stress is laid on the con-

---

[36] Diogenes Laertius, viii. 46, mentions as the last of the Pythagoreans, whom Aristoxenus knew, Xenophilus, Phanto, Echecrates, Diocles, and Polymnastus, pupils of Philolaus and Eurytus. None of these, so far as we know, contributed anything to mathematics. Ecphantus appears as an astronomer who combined opinions of Democritus and Anaxagoras. Perhaps he was only an imaginary person, playing a role in a dialogue of Heraclides Ponticus. We know nothing about his mathematics.

[37] 1225 a 33.

[38] 1080 b 6: cf. Philolaus, Frag. 8 Diels.

[39] That is, provided the *Eudemian Ethics* was written by him (300 B.C. ?).

nection of the Eleatics with the Pythagoreans. Burnet [40] confesses that the only means of distinguishing between what is earlier and what is later in Pythagoreanism is furnished by the Eleatics. This assumes, what one has tried to prove, that there are in the doctrines and arguments of the Eleatics adequate proofs of the existence of Pythagorean doctrines. If that can be shown, the student does indeed have a sure foundation for his reconstruction of the history of Greek mathematics, though even so it must remain in good part conjectural. Much as this is to be desired, we must not permit our wishes to influence our judgement as to what we may infer from the evidence at our command. On the other hand we may not lightly regard the theses of such eminent scholars as Tannery, Baumker, and those who have accepted their conclusion. If we cannot agree with them, we may derive a little comfort from the fact that they often confess that their accounts are largely conjectural.

There is much to be said for the view that the Eleatics had relations more or less intimate with Pythagoreans. This need not be disputed, though there remain certain difficulties that may not be ignored. By way of illustration one may cite Parmenides. One statement [41] has it that he was 'converted to peace' not by Xenophanes but by the Pythagorean Ameinias, to whom he erected an heroön after his death. This implies that Parmenides was converted to Pythagoreanism, and one would naturally think of this occurring in his youth. If there is any basis for this statement, the evidence for it, one would suppose, was the monument to Ameinias and the inscription it bore. Alongside this datum, however, we must place another. In the proëm of his work Parmenides himself tells of being conducted by the Sun-maidens from Darkness into Light, even to a goddess who reveals to him the unshakeable heart of Truth. If this means anything, it must symbolize another conversion, again presumably in his youth. [42] This conversion is taken to be a renunciation of Pythagorean

[40] *Greek Philos. Thales to Plato*, pp. 43 f.
[41] Diogenes Laertius, ix. 21.
[42] I should not insist, as Burnet did, on the fact that the goddess addresses him as κοῦρος, for that is hardly decisive. But the tone of the poem is so uncompromising that I can think of it only as the work of a young man fond of paradoxes; its crude form also suggests a first attempt. If this view is right it has obvious bearings on the question of Parmenides' relation, for example, to Heraclitus.

369

dualism. He thus appears to be (rather strangely for a 'stabilizer') as volatile as Schelling and an apostate from the faith of the Order. Though this cannot be regarded as in any way conclusive, it inevitably suggests caution regarding a person and a situation about which unfortunately we know far less than we would wish. We need not dwell upon Parmenides, however, because the only aspect of his teaching that even remotely concerns mathematics is that dealing with the One and the Many, which is the theme of Zeno's arguments.

It is really in Zeno that we have to look for reference to Pythagorean mathematics, if it is to be found in the Eleatics. Now it must appear strange, in view of the assurance of many modern scholars, that there is not, so far as I know, a single hint in our sources that the Greeks themselves were aware of the purpose of Zeno to criticize the fundamental doctrines of the Pythagoreans. Of course our historians have a ready answer to this objection to their thesis. Are we not told[43] that Zeno wrote *Against the Philosophers* and that he meant to pay off with interest those who ridiculed or travestied the view of his master, Parmenides, that All is One? As for the title of Zeno's book, may one confidently assume that it was not given by the Alexandrians but by Zeno himself? The latter supposition is extremely improbable if we date the work *c.* 465 B.C. With that assumption falls also the presumption that it was specifically directed against the Pythagoreans as the only 'philosophers' at the time prominent in Italy. But why should one think especially of 'philosophers'? The paradoxical doctrine of Parmenides that All is One and that motion is impossible must have made him the butt of many a ribald remark. Philoponus says,[44] 'Those who introduce plurality are confident of it because of its self-evidence, for there is a horse and a man, etc.' Surely Parmenides, as a man, was not a horse? One imagines that Antisthenes the Cynic was not the first to answer the arguments against motion by getting up and walking away.[45] That is still the way the man of the world answers philosophers and professors. Indeed, if we are to depend on the titles of books attributed to Zeno, why should we not rather think of Empedocles, on whose work he is reported to have written a commentary? Assuming that the Pythagoreans were the profound

[43] Suidas, *s.v. Ζήνων* (after Hesychius), and Plato, *Parm.* 128 c.
[44] *Phys.*, 42, 18, Vitelli (ed.).   [45] Diels, *Vorsokr.*[5], I. 251, 20 ff.

philosophers we are given to understand, we should hardly think of them as indulging in the kind of ridicule that Plato's statement implies.

It is clear that nothing reported about the purpose of Zeno's book affords the least presumption in favour of the view that it was directed against the Pythagoreans. If there is any evidence pointing to such a conclusion it must therefore be discovered in the arguments themselves. It would be tedious and useless to review the arguments in detail. They are familiar to every student of Greek thought and their subtlety still exercises the student of logic and mathematics. We need only to direct attention to their general assumptions and the form in which the arguments have been handed down to us. Regarding the latter it is important to observe that we have at most three statements [46] that can be plausibly regarded as preserving the actual words of Zeno, whereas the variant versions of his arguments themselves prove that we have for the most part to deal with paraphrases dating from later times, from which we can at best infer only the drift of the argument. If this is obvious at first glance, it is emphasized also by Aristotle's reference [47] to those who urge the antinomies of Zeno and by the certainty that at times he is thinking quite as much of Plato as of the Pythagoreans.[48]

It is sometimes urged that Zeno was attacking an hypothesis. But there is really no reason whatever to single out the Pythagoreans as the proponents of the fundamental hypothesis of all his arguments, to wit, that things are a plurality. Whatever specious considerations may be offered in favour of the supposition that Zeno had Pythagoreans in mind are all due to incidental statements in later authors, who are manifestly *interpreting* and not reporting what he said. So far as we know Zeno did not mention the word 'number' at all, though he does *imply*

[46] Diels, *ibid.*, p. 255, 14, prints εἰ μὴ ἔχοι μέγεθος τὸ ὄν, οὐδ' ἂν εἴη as *ipsissima verba* of Zeno. This is in itself improbable and is further indicated as not true by comparing with προδείξας the passages p. 257, lines 3 and 6 introduced by προδείξας and δεικνύς. Except when it is expressly stated that a passage is given *verbatim* it is rarely possible to distinguish between a quotation and a paraphrase, which may be quite free and is in fact very often entirely misleading.
[47] *Phys.* 263 a 5 ff. It is obvious that no inferences can safely be drawn regarding the original intention of an argument from later applications of it.
[48] E.g. *Metaph.* 1001 a 29–b 13.

a reference to numbers.[49] In doing so, moreover, he implies no special conception of number but only such as anyone must have who enumerates objects of any sort. Most of the difficulties he raises are connected with the notion of infinity. What we actually know about the Pythagorean notion of infinity, in relation to number, is *nil*. Taking infinity in the strict sense,[50] Zeno evidently regards a realized or realizable infinite, that is, a numerable infinite, as a *contradictio in adjecto*. Either things are just as many as they are, in which case they are finite in number, or if they are not, they are not numerable at all, and plurality has no meaning. Parmenides has said that what is is One and at least distinctly implied that it is extended. That statement would naturally provoke criticism; for what has extension must have limits that do not coincide and consequently presuppose an interval between them. This criticism is so obvious that it requires no great mathematician to make it. Zeno recognizes the difficulty [51] and, as Plato says, pays the critic off with interest. We may imagine him retorting, Yes, there is a difficulty here, but is your assumption of plurality any less obnoxious to objection? You insist that the extended is divisible. Well and good: supposing it to be divisible, it must be divisible *ad infinitum*, for so long as it is extended (and parts of the extended must themselves be ex-

[49] E.g. Frag. 3 Diels.

[50] Zeno is the true Parmenidean in doing so; for much of the significance of Parmenides arises just from the insistence on a single and strict sense in the use of the terms τὸ ἕν and τὸ ὄν. It was this tendency, especially emphasized by the Eleatics, that created and promoted dialectic by requiring the distinction and definition of terms.

[51] This is certainly implied in the statement Plato represents Zeno as making (*Parm.* 128 d) that the hypothesis that there is a plurality leads to *still more ludicrous consequences* than the Parmenidean hypothesis that the One only exists. Similarly Plato frankly admitted difficulties in his theory of ideal forms. I think it is unwarranted to say, as is often said, that Zeno's arguments against an indivisible unit (ἕν) do not touch the One of Parmenides, but apply only to an atomic unit, supposed to be Pythagorean; for the One of Parmenides, if extended, as is clearly implied in describing it as continuous, is liable to the same objections as the atom. I cannot otherwise understand the statement attributed to Zeno by Eudemus (Diels, *Vorsokr.*[5], I. 251, 25) εἴ τις αὐτῷ τὸ ἕν ἀποδοίη τί ποτέ ἐστιν, ἕξειν τὰ ὄντα λέγειν, for here τὸ ἕν *must* refer to the Parmenidean One. The only way of escape would lie in regarding the One as incorporeal; but neither Parmenides nor Zeno took that way.

tended) there is no limit to division. The only alternative is that the parts shall not have extension, in which case they will be nothing, and no multiplication of them can produce an extended body. The horns of the dilemma are equally fatal, and once one takes the conception of infinity seriously the dilemma must be obvious to any man of intelligence. The difficulty thus posed is logical rather than mathematical, and I, for one, cannot see why we need to look beyond Zeno for the author of the alternatives. If one says he must have been attacking someone who held that reality is composed of indivisible entities, why should one think of contemporary Pythagoreans, rather than of Democritus, Plato, and Xenocrates? If the latter could accept, after the dilemma had been stated, the latter horn, why may not Pythagoreans of a later age have done the same? The burden of proof rests with those who contend that Pythagoreans, Zeno's predecessors or contemporaries, held that view. *His* argument cannot take the place of such proof.

As has already been said, the supposed reference to the Pythagoreans finds its only documentary support from later writers. There we find such terms as *monad, henad, point,* etc., but not in Zeno's own statements. He doubtless spoke, as did Parmenides, of the *one* (ἕν); *monad*[52] and *henad,* which are not known to occur before Plato's time, are obviously abstract terms, suited to a conception of number directly opposed to the view attributed to the Pythagoreans by Aristotle, who insists that their numbers had magnitude. He does, to be sure, say that they were mathematical, but apparently only because they used numbers in ordinary calculations, as one does in every mathematical operation. Moreover, he expressly declares that their numbers were not *monadic.* That, it would seem, should dispose of the supposition that they used the term monad.[53] As for the contention that Zeno

---

[52] Theo Smyrnaeus, p. 20, 19, says 'Αρχύτας δὲ καὶ Φιλόλαος ἀδιαφόρως τὸ ἕν καὶ μονάδα καλοῦσι, καὶ τὴν μονάδα ἕν. One can well believe this statement, for that brings us down to Plato's time; but why should it be made, if Zeno had already used the terms interchangeably?

[53] *Metaph.* 1080 b 18 τὸν γὰρ ὅλον οὐρανὸν κατασκευάζουσιν ἐξ ἀριθμῶν, πλὴν οὐ μοναδικῶν, ἀλλὰ τὰς μονάδας ὑπολαμβάνουσιν ἔχειν μέγεθος. From any point of view this statement is curious. I take it that Aristotle in the last clause was falling into current terminology, which consequently signifies nothing. (Alexander, *In Metaph.*, p. 746, 1, Hayd (ed.), says μοναδικὸν τὸ ἀμερὲς καὶ ἀσώματον ἐνταῦθα δηλοῖ.) I think, however, that he could not have said that

was attacking a view that identified the monad with the point, it is clear that there is really no evidence to support it. Simplicius does indeed twice [54] quote Eudemus on this matter, but when it is stated that Zeno identified the point with zero this is expressly given as a conjecture (ὡς ἔοικε); in other words, it is an *interpretation* Eudemus offers of Zeno's argument. That an interpretation in terms of mathematics was called for would seem to be strong evidence that Zeno's statement was couched in *logical* terms. After the manner of the commentators Simplicius [55] gives as a fact what Eudemus conscientiously stated as a conjecture.

Much is made of the supposed identification by the Pythagoreans of the unit (monad), point, and atom. That Pythagoreans at some time may have made this identification need not be denied, though the evidence has not been produced. Those who see criticism of Pythagoreans here regard them as maintaining the contradictory positions (*a*) that space (body) is extended

---

[54] *Phys.*, pp. 97, 13 ff.; 138, 32. Aristotle, *Metaph.* 1001 b 7 ff. had given a similar interpretation. If Eudemus had found in Zeno anything to justify the identification he would hardly have contented himself with conjecture. Tannery, *Pour l'histoire de la science hellène*, p. 252, says that Eudemus did not know Zeno's arguments except through tradition. This supposition is difficult to credit, since Simplicius still had the original text at hand. As the historian of mathematics Eudemus would, it seems, certainly have consulted and carefully read the book, had he believed it dealt specifically with the fundamental concepts of mathematics. Tannery there calls attention to another significant fact—that Eudemus, so far as we know, did not mention Zeno in his history of mathematics, but only in his *Physics*. I can account for this only on the supposition that he, like Aristotle, regarded the Eleatic arguments as essentially logical and as concerned with the fundamental concepts of the physical sciences generally rather than with the particular question of number or geometry.

[55] *Phys.*, p. 99, 7 ff. Burnet, *EGP*³, p. 315, n. 3, quotes part of this statement as if this were actually a quotation from Eudemus. That is hardly fair dealing. Similarly, *ibid.*, p. 314, he says, 'Plato (*Parm.* 128 c f.) tells us that the premises of Zeno's arguments were the beliefs of the adversaries of Parmenides.' The only premise stated is that *things are many*. That premise was certainly not peculiar to Pythagoreans!

---

the Pythagoreans' numbers were *not monadic* if he had evidence of their using μονάς for ἕν. Cf. *De Caelo* 300 a 14 ff. In *Phys.* 227 a 27 ff. he speaks of those who describe point and monad as separate (κεχωρισμένας), and says that on this view monad and point cannot be identical. If these were Pythagoreans, we have no means of dating them; more probably they were Platonists. Cf. note 56.

and therefore divisible, and (*b*) that division may be halted at a given point, leaving discrete ultimate units, which however are equivalent to geometrical points. It is important to observe, however, that Zeno does not say, or imply, that anyone took both these positions, but regards them as *alternative* possibilities under the general hypothesis of a plurality conceived as parts of an extended whole. The conception of non-extended units (points) is itself an alternative under the head of ultimate units. The argument purports to show that each of the conceived possibilities leads to absurd consequences. How difficult it is to determine the special target of these arguments, supposing that there was one, is shown by the fact that they apply perfectly to the Atomists, whom Aristotle (*De Gen. et Corr.* 324 b 25 ff.) represents as trying to meet the Eleatic logic. Similarly *Phys.* 187 a ff. might well be taken as referring to the Atomists; the ancient commentators, however, thought of Plato and Xeno-crates, and Ross, *Metaphysics*, I, p. xc, thinks there is an evident reference to Plato's *Sophist*. The equation of the monad and the point having position is attested only by a quite late writer.[56] Now it is obvious that Zeno did consider, only to reject, the indivisible unit, most pointedly, perhaps, in the 'Arrow', where time and space are each conceived as composed of indivisible units. Why one should think this was Pythagorean doctrine I am unable to discover. To make the supposition plausible one must produce evidence that Pythagoreans, and Pythagoreans of Zeno's time, held such a view of time, space, and motion. In the 'Stadium' also we have the same elements, only even more sharply defined; for there space, time, and motion are conceived as com-posed of indivisible units, each precisely corresponding to each. The refinement of the argument is truly wonderful; but what grounds have we for thinking that Pythagoreans expressly held such a view? If Zeno constructed his subtle argument on the sole basis of an extended (spatial) unit, such as Aristotle supposes

---

[56] Proclus, *In Eucl.*, p. 95, 20. If Aristotle, *Phys.* 227 a 27 ff. and *Metaph.* 1002 a 36 ff., represent Pythagorean doctrine, rather than an interpretation of it by Platonists (cf. Plato, *Parm.* 148 d ff.), there is no way of dating the notion that the point and the monad may be identified. Cf. note 54. In any case we should have to assume, from the usage of Parmenides and Zeno, that the Pythagoreans of the first half of the fifth century spoke of τὸ ἕν and not of the *monad*.

their numbers to have been, he was presumably capable of conceiving without help from anyone else *a continuum of any sort* as composed of discrete units, which would be a natural way of regarding plurality. Plato makes Zeno say that his arguments were intended to show that the hypothesis of plurality led to even more absurd conclusions than monism *if one adequately followed it out*. I take it, it was Zeno himself [56a] who analyzed the assumption of plurality into its elements, purely as a logical problem,[57] presenting the alternatives under which it could be made. I would not deny that one or the other of the possibilities he considers had already been stated by others, for it is of course possible: if one holds it to be a fact, one must produce the evidence for thinking so.

Lest the position of this survey be mistaken, it should be clearly stated that we have no satisfactory evidence for the view that Zeno was attacking a particular theory, that is to say, the Pythagorean. There is no pretence, on the other hand, that there is clear evidence that he was not doing so. It suffices for our purpose to point out that the arguments he advanced were, as Plato implies, the result of a thorough canvass of the implications of plurality considered as referred to a world having the property of extension

[56a] When Plato, *Phaedrus* 261 d, called Zeno the Eleatic Palamedes he obviously had in mind the *inventiveness* of Palamedes celebrated in several dramas. Clearly Diogenes Laertius, ix. 25, or his source, so understood the matter, for it is coupled with the statement of Aristotle that Zeno was the inventor of dialectic, as Empedocles was of rhetoric. The acknowledged originality of Zeno and the fact that no ancient authority suggests that he was criticizing views of the Pythagoreans create a strong presumption that he alone is responsible for both the form and the presuppositions of his arguments.
[57] It seems clear that Aristotle so regarded the Eleatic method: *De Gen. et Corr.* 325 a 13 ὑπερβάντες τὴν αἴσθησιν καὶ παριδόντες αὐτὴν ὡς τῷ λόγῳ δέον ἀκολουθεῖν, cf. *De Caelo*, 298 b 20–3. On the other hand, in his Δόξα Parmenides, according to Aristotle, *Metaph.* 986 b 31 ff., set up two causes and principles, ἀναγκαζόμενος ἀκολουθεῖν τοῖς φαινομένοις, καὶ τὸ ἓν μὲν κατὰ τὸν λόγον, πλείω δὲ κατὰ τὴν αἴσθησιν ὑπολαμβάνων εἶναι. The dialectic of Plato's *Parmenides* clearly presupposes the same purely *logical* approach. Where numbers are mentioned, e.g. 143 a ff., 149 b, this is done incidentally, and in no way suggests that the subject was of special importance. If it be true, as some contend, that the *Parmenides* is partly a criticism of the atomism of Democritus, it is such only by implication, the logical problem of the 'one' being the essential point. If, as it would appear, Theophrastus did not discuss Zeno in his Φυσικῶν δόξαι, he also presumably took the position that the arguments were purely logical.

that Parmenides admitted. There is no express reference to number, or if there is, certainly none to a particular conception of number; for, though the arguments are applicable to number, the analysis seems to have been conducted as a dialectical exercise, noting and drawing the necessary conclusions from the alternative forms the primary assumption of plurality may take. If one contends that there were stated hypotheses of schools opposed to Parmenides, it is fair to ask whether one is to assume that every hypothesis of Plato's *Parmenides* is likewise to be so considered. Is it not possible, indeed highly probable, that in that dialogue Plato was imitating the method of Zeno? If so, is it not fairly arguable that the latter also was himself setting up the hypotheses in order to point out their necessary implications?

It is clear that Zeno or others who repeated and applied his arguments might have used them against the theories of Anaxagoras and the Atomists; for they fit their theories as perfectly as the supposed Pythagorean doctrine of numbers. These philosophies did in fact accept the horns of Zeno's dilemma, Anaxagoras adopting the view that matter may be infinitely divisible without therefore being reduced to o; Leucippus and Democritus, that matter is ultimately constituted of discrete indestructible particles;[58] and we must assume that both schools applied their principles to mathematics. We need not now inquire how they met the inevitable problems of continuity and infinity. Both these problems continued to exercise the schools of the fourth century; and it is more than likely that Pythagoreans engaged in the

[58] Aristotle pointed out (*De Caelo*, 303 a 8) that the atoms were quasi-numbers, and he represented the theory of the Atomists as an answer to the Eleatic logic (*De Gen. et Corr.* 324 b 24 ff.). It is notable that the dependence of Atomists on the Pythagoreans, which must be evident if the reconstruction of Burnet is sound, was apparently never thought of (Aristotle, *De An.* 404 a 1 ff., 16 ff., really has no significance, even if the text be sound, which, like Diels, I doubt), just as no one hinted at the supposed Pythagorean doctrine as the target of Zeno's devastating arguments. In fact Burnet, *EGP*[3], p. vi, insists that 'the vital point' of his argument is his contention that Atomism was derived from Eleaticism. That one ignored even the Atomists, again shows how preoccupied one was with the debates in Platonic circles. On the other hand, if one takes Aristotle's view that the Pythagorean numbers had magnitude, one finds it difficult to understand how it could be asserted (cf. Aëtius, i. 3, 9) of Ecphantus (who, if an historical person, must have lived in the fourth century), τὰς Πυθαγορικὰς μονάδας οὗτος πρῶτος ἀπεφήνατο σωματικάς, thus making the (numerical) unit virtually an atom.

debates. Unfortunately we have no satisfactory evidence for them, more especially about the middle of the fifth century.

One readily understands the motives of those who press the claims of Pythagoreanism and seek by all means to reconstruct its doctrines during the obscure period between the times of Parmenides and Plato. We know that there were members of the school who busied themselves with mathematics and contributed much to the advancement of the science, but except for specific discoveries and their necessary implications we actually know little more; above all, we have no chronological data except the fact that a good deal had been achieved before the time of Aristotle and Eudemus. Even respecting the necessary implications of the specific achievements with which Eudemus credits the Pythagoreans we can confidently affirm no more than that they must have been known to them; for it by no means follows that they *discovered* them.

We are thus brought to a point that has been strangely ignored in the reconstruction of Greek mathematics. We have seen that we have no dependable evidence of mathematical achievements of Pythagoras himself, and we know that in later times one inferred his teachings from opinions held by those who were known as Pythagoreans. The best-informed Greeks did not regard him or his followers as the creators of Greek mathematics, but thought of them as being active in promoting the science. Eudemus credited Thales with a knowledge of some fundamental geometrical problems: since he did so, as we gather from one instance, by inference from practical achievements traditionally attributed to the sage of Miletus, we may refuse to accept his conclusion; but it is not without significance that the first general historian of mathematics found no difficulty in assuming such knowledge on the part of an Ionian earlier than Pythagoras. We know, moreover, that Anaximander also framed a picture of the cosmos that was essentially geometrical and in principle not unlike that involved in the later Pythagorean theory of the 'harmony of the spheres'. Indeed, the engineering feat of Eupalinas in constructing the tunnel of Samos implies certain definite geometrical propositions. We thus know that mathematics was cultivated in Ionia before the time of Pythagoras, who left his native Samos about the time the tunnel was built. One readily surmises that Pythagoras had learned some of its rudiments before he went to Italy, whether he and his earliest associates did or did not devote themselves to the study.

There is, in fact, much to be said for the view that mathematics was intensively cultivated by the Ionians from the sixth century onward. Aside from the geometrical pattern of the cosmos, Anaximander and his successor Hecataeus evidently applied similar principles in the construction of their maps of the earth, and later Ionians applied the same methods in laying out cities. Plato evidently had these schemes in mind, perhaps consciously combining them with cosmological patterns, in describing the capital city of the Atlantians. This aspect of Ionian research should not in the least surprise us when we reflect that almost all the Presocratic thinkers, who laid the foundation of Greek science in all fields, were Ionians. But we are not restricted to general considerations and probabilities. Whereas we cannot name a single Pythagorean before Archytas who made a notable contribution to mathematics, we have considerable evidence regarding others whom it will repay one to consider briefly, without attempting to appraise their several merits.

We have referred to Thales, Anaximander, Hecataeus, and Hippodamus of Miletus. Agatharchus of Samos is mentioned [59] as a scene-painter for Aeschylus in a way to suggest that he was interested in the problem of perspective, which was taken up and advanced by Anaxagoras of Clazomenae and Democritus of Abdera. We have every reason to think that the latter two contributed principles of fundamental importance to the solution of geometrical problems. Oenopides, the astronomer, and Hippocrates, the author of the earliest known handbook of geometry, were natives of Chios, and Leodamas of Thasos is mentioned as a contemporary of Plato and Archytas among those who contributed to the improvement of geometry.[60] One notes with interest that all these were Ionians. One cannot pass over Hippias of Elis, who not only concerned himself with astronomy, but attempted the solution of difficult geometrical problems and touched on the history of mathematics. Though he was presumably not an Ionian (we know nothing of his antecedents), he

---

[59] Vitruvius, *Praef.* 7.

[60] Proclus, *In Eucl.*, prol. II, p. 66, 14, ἐν δὲ τούτῳ τῷ χρόνῳ (i.e. Plato's) καὶ Λεωδάμας ὁ Θάσιος ἦν καὶ Ἀρχύτας ὁ Ταραντῖνος καὶ Θεαίτητος δ Ἀθηναῖος, παρ' ὧν ἐπηυξήθη τὰ θεωρήματα καὶ προῆλθεν εἰς ἐπιστημονικωτέραν σύστασιν.

shared all the interests of the Ionians and in character resembled them rather than the Pythagoreans. Meton was an Athenian, as was Theaetetus. The latter, as a pupil of Theodorus of Cyrene, has of course been thought to belong to the Pythagorean line, though we have no good reason to think of Theodorus as connected with the school. Iamblichus, in his list of Pythagoreans,[61] mentions a Theodorus of Tarentum, but he may quite well have been a different person. In his commentary on Euclid's *Elements* Proclus[62] gives a list of precursors of Euclid in the composition of geometrical handbooks, each surpassing his predecessor in the number of propositions and the excellence of the demonstrations. Going backward from Euclid he names Hermotimus of Colophon, Theudius of Magnesia, Leon the pupil of Neoclides, and Hippocrates of Chios. Again, where we know anything about the men he names, we are faced with a group of Ionians.

This is certainly a remarkable showing, which it is difficult to understand except on the supposition of a continuous tradition of strong interest in geometry among the Ionians from early times. As against this indisputable evidence it appears reckless to suggest that we owe the entire development of mathematics to the Pythagoreans and to assume that all the necessary implications of the specific achievements credited to Pythagoreans by Eudemus constitute 'Pythagorean geometry'. Even Iamblichus, who was inclined to claim nearly everything for that school, lends no support to such pretentions, for he says[63] that when the mathematical secrets of the Order had been divulged by Hippasus, two men, Theodorus of Cyrene and Hippocrates of Chios did most to advance the science. If we disregard the discredited

[61] *Vit. Pyth.*, 265. [62] P. 67, Friedlein (ed.).

[63] Diels, *Vorsokr.*[5], I. 108, 10 ff. Aristotle, *Meteor.* 342 b 29 ff., compares and contrasts the views of certain "Italians" (Pythagoreans) and Hippocrates of Chios regarding the comet. The passage decides nothing about the question of their relations. Erich Frank, *Platon und die sogen. Pythagoreer*, p. 233, holds that Aristotle meant to set Hippocrates apart from the Pythagoreans; Loria, *Scienze Esatte*, p. 74, thinks he classed them together. Such instances of partial agreement, with differences in detail, seem to me natural where there is a common interest in a problem. In order to decide whether one thinker depended on the other we should have to know more than we do, especially regarding their chronology. By the end of the fifth century, it seems, many minds were contributing to a more or less common stock of knowledge and opinion.

story of Hippasus and the secret teachings of Pythagoras, we have here a confession that neither of these celebrated men belonged to the Order.

If one is to believe that the Ionians above mentioned learned their mathematics from the Pythagoreans one must make some extremely improbable assumptions; for the connection of the individual philosophers and scientists with Pythagoreanism, though often asserted, cannot generally be accepted as based on anything better than the same wishful thinking that inspires some historians of the present day. Iamblichus, to be sure, furnished a long list of 'Pythagoreans' assigned to various cities, including Ionian Paros, Cyzicus, and Samos, but Melissus is the only person otherwise known, and he could be connected with Pythagoreanism only through the apostate Parmenides. We do not even know when the Order, originally at home in Italy, was scattered. Zeller thought it could not have been before the middle of the fifth century; and what dependable sources tell us of such representatives as Lysis, Philolaus, and the Pythagoreans who associated with Socrates rather suggests that their interests lay in other directions.

The conclusion to which we are driven by our study is that it is impossible to reconstruct the history of Greek mathematics, as one may to a certain extent tell the story of the development of Greek scientific thought in general, by focusing attention upon individual men or groups. Regarding our knowledge of details and also with respect to the necessary inferences from known facts nothing is changed; but the role of the Pythagoreans must appear to have been much exaggerated. If we are to exercise our imagination in order to supplement our knowledge it would seem that we must reckon with the probability of a continuous mathematical tradition in Ionian lands from an early date. Supposing that to be true, the question arises how the achievements of individuals and groups were communicated, so that it became possible from time to time to sum up and integrate the whole. To that question, which arises in other fields of Greek thought also, there is no satisfactory answer.

XIV

THE DISCOVERY OF
INCOMMENSURABILITY BY
HIPPASUS OF METAPONTUM*

Kurt von Fritz

THE discovery of incommensurability is one of the most amazing and far-reaching accomplishments of early Greek mathematics. It is all the more amazing because, according to ancient tradition, the discovery was made at a time when Greek mathematical science was still in its infancy and apparently concerned with the most elementary, or, as many modern mathematicians are inclined to say, most trivial, problems, while at the same time, as recent discoveries have shown, the Egyptians and Babylonians had already elaborated very highly developed and complicated methods for the solution of mathematical problems of a higher order, and yet, as far as we can see, never even suspected the existence of the problem.

No wonder, therefore, that modern historians of mathematics have been inclined to disbelieve that ancient tradition which dates the discovery in the middle of the fifth century B.C.,[1] and that there has been a strong tendency to date the event much later, even as late as the first quarter of the fourth century.[2] But the

---

* This article owes much to discussions of the early history of Greek mathematics which were carried on more than ten years ago between the author and Professor S. Bochner, now of Rice University. This does not mean, of course, that Dr. Bochner has any part in whatever deficiencies the present article may have.
[1] This tradition will be discussed below, pp. 385 ff.
[2] The first to make an attempt to show that the discovery of incommensurability was 'late', and certainly later than ancient tradition indicates, was Erich Frank in his book on *Platon und die sogenannten Pythagoreer* (Halle,

question can hardly be decided on the basis of general considerations. It is the purpose of this paper to prove: (1) that the early Greek tradition which places the second stage of the development of the theory of incommensurability in the last quarter of the fifth century, and therefore implies that the first discovery itself was made still earlier is of such a nature that its authenticity can hardly be doubted; (2) that this tradition is strongly supported by indirect evidence; (3) that the discovery can have been made on the 'elementary' level which, even according to E. Frank and O. Neugebauer,[3] Greek mathematics had reached in the middle of the fifth century; (4) that the character of scientific investigation as developed in the early part of the fifth century makes it not only possible but very probable that the discovery was made at the time in which the late ancient tradition places it; and (5) that this late tradition itself contains some hints as to the way in which the discovery, in all likelihood, actually was made.

The earliest precise and definite tradition concerning a phase in the development of the theory of incommensurability is found in Plato's dialogue *Theaetetus*, 147 b. This dialogue was written in the year 368/67 B.C., shortly after the death of the mathematician Theaetetus after a battle in which he had been fatally wounded.[4] The fictive date of the dialogue is the year 399 B.C., that is, the year of the death of Socrates. In the first part of the dialogue the old mathematician Theodorus of Cyrene is represented as

---

[3] See the preceding note.
[4] This was proved by Eva Sachs in her dissertation *De Theaeteto mathematico* (Berlin, 1914). Her results in this respect seem absolutely certain and have been universally accepted.

Max Niemeyer, 1923). He does not commit himself to a definite date, but contends that the discovery cannot have been made before the last years of the fifth century (p. 228 ff.). O. Neugebauer, the most outstanding living authority on the earliest history of mathematics, goes even farther. In a letter to the author of the present paper he expressed the opinion that the discovery could not have been made before Archytas of Tarentum. Since Archytas was head of the government of Tarentum in 362 B.C., this seems to indicate that in his opinion the discovery was not made before the early fourth century at the earliest. It was also he who based his opinion on the 'trivial' character of fifth-century Greek mathematics. In the present paper an attempt will be made to show that Greek mathematics in that period was in fact very elementary in many respects when compared with contemporary or earlier Babylonian and Egyptian mathematics, but by no means 'trivial'.

demonstrating to a group of young men, among them young Theaetetus, who is represented as a youngster of about seventeen, the irrationality of the square roots of 3, 5, 6, etc., up to 17. Though the dialogue itself is, of course, fictive, it seems hardly possible to assume that Plato, in a dialogue dedicated to the memory of a friend who has just died prematurely and who had had a very important part in the development of the theory of incommensurability and irrationality,[5] would have attributed to someone else what was really his friend's own accomplishment. The inevitable conclusion, therefore, is that what Theodorus demonstrates in the introduction to the dialogue was actually known when Theaetetus was a boy of seventeen.[6]

Theodorus of Cyrene is represented as an old man in Plato's dialogue. According to an extract from Eudemus' history of mathematics[7] he was a contemporary of Hippocrates of Chios and belonged to the generation following that of Anaxagoras and preceding that of Plato. Since Anaxagoras was born in *c.* 500, and Plato in 428, this implies that Theodorus was born about 470 or 460, which agrees with Plato's statement that he was an old man in 399. Plato does not say that what Theodorus demonstrated to Theaetetus and the other youngsters in 399 was at that time an entirely new discovery, though the fact that he gave a proof for each one of the different cases separately shows that the theory had not yet reached a more advanced stage.[8] But even if we assume that Theodorus' demonstrations had been

---

[5] For details, see my article *Theaitetos* in Pauly-Wissowa *Realencyclopädie*, Vol. V A, pp. 1351–72.

[6] E. Frank (*op. cit.*, pp. 59, 228, and passim) and others have quoted a passage in Plato's *Laws* (819 c ff.) as a proof of their assumption that the discovery of incommensurability cannot have been made before the end of the fifth or the beginning of the fourth century. In this passage 'the old Athenian', who is usually identified with Plato, says that he became acquainted with the discovery of incommensurability only late in his life and that it is a shame that 'all the Greeks' are still ignorant of the fact. It is quite clear that the latter statement is a rhetorical exaggeration since 'all the Greeks', if taken literally, would include the Athenian himself, who by now obviously does know. The passage then proves nothing but that even striking mathematical discoveries in the fifth century did not become known to the general educated public. But this is also true of the fourth and third centuries.

[7] In Proclus' commentary to Euclid's *Elements*, p. 66 Friedlein.

[8] Concerning the probable steps from the first discovery to the theory of Theodorus, see *infra*, pp. 398 ff.

worked out for the first time not so very long before, Plato's dialogue would still indicate that the irrationality of the square root of 2, or the incommensurability of the side and diameter of a square had been discovered by someone else. For it is difficult to see why he should have made Theodorus start with the square root of 3, unless he wished to give an historical hint that this was the point where Theodorus' own contribution to mathematical theory began. This in itself then would be quite sufficient to show that the discovery of incommensurability must have been made in the earlier part of the last quarter of the fifth century at the very latest, and since mathematical knowledge at that time travelled very slowly, may very well have been made earlier.[9]

What can be inferred from Plato's dialogue *Theaetetus* receives strong confirmation from indirect evidence which has been presented by H. Hasse and H. Scholz.[10] It is perhaps not necessary to accept their interpretation of the doctrines of Zeno of Elea in every detail. But there can hardly be any doubt that they have proved conclusively that there must have been a connection between some of Zeno's famous arguments against motion, and the discovery of incommensurability.[11] Since Zeno was born not later than 490 B.C., acceptance of the results of the treatise quoted would lead to the conclusion that the discovery of incommensurability must have been made not later than the middle of the fifth century, which is also the date indicated by ancient tradition.

In contrast to the tradition concerning the second phase of the development of the theory of incommensurability the tradition concerning the first discovery itself has been preserved only in the works of very late authors, and is frequently connected with

9 See note 6.
10 H. Hasse and H. Scholz, *Die Grundlagenkrisis der griechischen Mathematik*, Charlottenburg, Kurt Metzner, 1928, pp. 10 ff.
11 In contrast to this, E. Frank (*op. cit.*, pp. 219 ff.) has contended that the mathematical philosophy of the Pythagoreans which *preceded* the discovery of incommensurability presupposes the atomistic theory of Democritus and a fully developed theory of 'the subjectivity of sensual qualities'. The analysis of the early form of Pythagorean philosophy attempted below will, I hope, show that it has nothing whatever to do with Democritus' atomism, and is certainly no more dependent on a fully developed theory of the subjectivity of sensual qualities than the philosophy of Parmenides, who was born at least sixty years earlier than Democritus.

stories of obviously legendary character.[12] But the tradition is unanimous[13] in attributing the discovery to a Pythagorean philosopher by the name of Hippasus of Metapontum.

Ancient tradition concerning the life and chronology of Hippasus is scanty. Iamblichus in his treatise *De communi mathematica scientia*[14] says that early Greek mathematical science made great progress through the work of Hippocrates of Chios and Theodorus of Cyrene, who followed upon Hippasus of Metapontum. Since Hippocrates and Theodorus are also mentioned together in the extract from the history of mathematics of Eudemus of Rhodes,[15] it seems likely that Iamblichus' note also goes back to the very reliable work of this disciple of Aristotle. According to this work Hippasus belonged to the generation preceding that of Theodorus (according to ancient usage this means an average difference of age of about thirty to forty years), who in his turn was a contemporary of Hippocrates of Chios.

According to Iamblichus' *Life of Pythagoras*,[16] Hippasus had an important part in the political disturbances in which the Pythagorean order became involved in the second quarter of the fifth century, and which ended in the revolt of *c.* 445, which put an end to Pythagorean domination in southern Italy.[17] This agrees perfectly with the tradition which places him in the generation before Theodorus, who, as shown above, was born between 470 and 460. This confirmation is all the more valuable because the tradition of the political history of the Pythagoreans which was first collected by Aristoxenus of Tarentum and Timaeus of Tauromenium is, on the whole, quite independent from the ancient tradition of early Greek mathematics, which was first collected by Eudemus of Rhodes.

---

[12] For instance, the story told by Iamblichus, that he was drowned in the sea, and that this was a divine punishment for his having made public the secret mathematical doctrines of the Pythagoreans [DK 18, 4].

[13] The one seeming deviation from the unanimous tradition in Proclus, *op. cit.* (see note 7), p. 67, is obviously due to a corrupt reading (ἀλόγων for ἀναλόγων or ἀναλογιῶν) in some manuscripts.

[14] Iamblichus, *De communi mathematica scientia*, 25, p. 77 Festa.

[15] See note 7.

[16] Iamblichus, *De Vita Pythagorea*, 257, pp. 138 f. Deubner.

[17] For the date, see K. von Fritz, *Pythagorean Politics in Southern Italy* (Columbia University Press, 1940), pp. 77 ff.

The mathematical achievements—apart from the discovery of incommensurability—ascribed to Hippasus by ancient tradition, are the following:

1. An anonymous scholion on Plato's *Phaedo*,[18] quoting a work on music by Aristotle's disciple Aristoxenus, says that Hippasus performed an experiment with metal discs. He had four metal discs of equal diameter made in such a way that the second disc was $1\frac{1}{3}$ times as thick, the third $1\frac{1}{2}$ times as thick, and the fourth twice as thick as the first one. He then showed that by striking any two of them the same harmony of sounds would be produced as by two strings whose lengths were in the same proportion as the thicknesses of the discs. Theon of Smyrna[19] attributes to him a similar experiment with four tumblers, the first of which was left empty, while the others were filled $\frac{1}{4}$, $\frac{1}{3}$, and $\frac{1}{2}$ with water.

2. Boethius[20] attributes to him a theory of the musical scale showing how the different musical harmonies can mathematically be derived from one another.

3. Iamblichus[21] says that Hippasus concerned himself with the theory of proportions and 'means' and was the first to change to 'harmonic mean' the name of what previously had been called the contrary, or, as some translate, the sub-contrary, mean, the formula of which is $\dfrac{a}{c} = \dfrac{a-b}{b-c}$. But Nicomachus attributes this change in terminology to Philolaus.

4. According to Iamblichus,[22] Hippasus was also the first to draw or construct[23] the 'sphere consisting of 12 regular pentagons', or, as he says in another passage,[24] to inscribe the regular

---

[18] Schol. in Plato *Phaedo* 108 d; see *Scholia Platonica*, W. Chase Greene (ed.) (Philol. Monographs publ. by Am. Philol. Assoc., Vol. VIII, 1938), 15. All the passages quoted in notes 18–24 are also collected, though sometimes in a slightly abbreviated form, in H. Diels, *Vorsokratiker*, Vol. 1.

[19] Theon Smyrnaeus, *Expos. Rerum Mathem.*, p. 59 Hiller.

[20] Boethius, *De Institutione musica*, 11, 10.

[21] Iamblichus, *In Nicomachi arithmet. introd.*, p. 109 Pistelli.

[22] Iamblichus, *De communi mathem. scientia*, 25 (p. 77 Festa) and *Vita Pythag.* 18, 88 (p. 52 Deubner).

[23] The Greek term γράψασθαι has both meanings.

[24] *Vita Pyth.*, 34, 247 (p. 132 Deubner). The name of Hippassus is not mentioned in this passage, but since the same story is connected with the divulgation of the discovery as in the first passage, there can be no doubt that the reference is to Hippasus.

dodecahedron in a sphere and to make this construction public, which was considered a criminal divulgation of Pythagorean secret knowledge.

Of these four statements the first and fourth are of special importance and must be carefully analyzed, while the second and the third are of a certain importance for our problem mainly in connection with the first one.

In regard to Hippasus' experiments it seems relevant to point out that in the period in which Hippasus lived other Greek philosophers also conducted scientific experiments, while after that time, with one possible exception,[25] we do not again hear of scientific experiments until the third century. In fact, the philosopher to whom most of these experiments are attributed, Empedocles (*c.* 490 to *c.* 430 B.C.), was a native of Sicily, lived for some time in southern Italy, and though not a Pythagorean himself, was undoubtedly influenced by Pythagorean thought.

The experiments attributed to Empedocles are the following: (1) an experiment to show that drinkable water could be extracted from the sea, in order to show that fish did not 'feed on' salt water, but on sweet water which could be extracted from it;[26] (2) an experiment with small open vessels filled with water and swung around on a cord, in order to prove the existence of what we would call a centrifugal force, which in his opinion prevented the celestial bodies from falling to the earth,[27] (3) an experiment with pulverized ore of various kinds and colours, in order to show that the different elements when mixed in this way become inseparable, and their original qualities indistinguishable in the mixture;[28] (4) an experiment with a *clepsydra* or water-clock, in order to prove that seemingly completely empty vessels are actually filled with air.[29] This experiment and a similar one with

[25] See *infra.*
[26] Empedocles, Frag. A 66 in H. Diels, *Die Fragmente der Vorsokratiker*, Vol. 1.
[27] *Ibid.*, A 67.
[28] *Ibid.*, A 34.
[29] *Ibid.*, B 100. Here the description of the experiment is given in its original wording. Empedocles in fact does not describe it as an experiment made by himself but as an illustrative analogy derived from the observation of a young girl playing with a water-clock. But this belongs to the poetical style, since Empedocles expounded all his philosophical and scientific theories in verse. The minute description of the process leaves no doubt whatever that Empedocles must have made the experiment himself.

leather bags is also attributed to Anaxagoras[30] (born in *c.* 500 B.C.).

The one possible exception to the statement that the known scientific experiments of the Greeks belong to the fifth and third (and later) centuries, but not to the fourth, is found in a passage from a work of Archytas, quoted literally by Nicomachus and Porphyrius.[31] In this fragment Archytas propounds the theory that sound is produced by a concussion of the air, that the pitch of the sound depends on and is proportional to the velocity of the motion producing it, and that if the velocities producing two sounds are in certain simple numerical ratios, well known musical harmonies result. The arguments by which these theories are supported are based on observations which *can* be made in everyday life, and without experimentation; but the way in which the observations are introduced strongly suggests that, though originally they may have been made incidentally, they were at least checked by being repeated in an experimental fashion. Archytas, however, does not claim to be the author of these theories and to have made personally the observations or experiments from which they are derived, but attributes them to mathematicians whose names he does not give. At the same time it is obvious that these theories and observations represent an advanced stage of scientific development as compared with the experiments of Hippasus and their results. For in the Archytas fragment Hippasus' demonstration of a way in which the same musical harmonies can be produced by any conceivable kind of sound-producing instrument is integrated with a general physical theory of sound. Since, on the other hand, both Hippasus and Archytas were Pythagoreans living in southern Italy, since Archytas, as shown above,[32] belonged to the second generation after Hippasus, and since, nevertheless, Hippasus and Archytas are sometimes mentioned together in ancient tradition[33] as having contributed to the development of a physical theory of sound, there really seems to be no reason to doubt that there actually existed a scientific tradition in one branch of the Pythagorean school through which a theory of sound was gradually developed.

[30] Anaxagoras, Frag. A 68/69 in H. Diels , *op. cit.*
[31] Archytas, Frag. B 1 (Diels, *op. cit.*).
[32] See *supra*, p. 382 and note 2.
[33] For instance, Iamblichus, *In Nicom. arithm. intr.*, p. 109 Pistelli.

Since, finally, the authenticity of the fragment from Archytas' *Harmonikos* can hardly be doubted, and as far as I can see never has been doubted, and since he clearly implies that the theory of sound had reached a rather advanced stage before he himself began to contribute to it, it is difficult to see how some scholars [34] could claim that ancient tradition projected into a much earlier time the accomplishments of a later period, when it attributed to Hippasus, a man belonging to the second generation before Archytas, the first beginnings of a theory which had reached a much more advanced stage before Archytas wrote his work.

Everything then seems to confirm the assumption that the experiments attributed to Hippasus by ancient tradition actually can have been made, and most probably were made, in southern Italy in the middle of the fifth century, that is, when Hippasus is supposed to have lived in that region. To that extent, at least, the late tradition, which according to E. Frank and others, is of no value whatever, seems to be vindicated.

But what can Hippasus' experiments with discs and tumblers possibly have to do with the discovery of incommensurability? In order to show the inter-connection which is, of course, very indirect, it will be necessary to make a further analysis of the purpose and meaning of these experiments.

All the experiments ascribed to philosophers of the fifth century, as their description clearly shows, were obviously undertaken not so much in order to find out something new, but rather in order to support and verify an already existing theory, for instance, that the fish do not consume salt water as such, but extract sweet water from it, that the celestial bodies do not remain in the sky because they are lighter than air, etc. The same is true of the experiments attributed to Hippasus. That certain musical harmonies would be produced if the lengths of two strings of the same kind were in certain ratios had always been known. It had also been known in regard to flutes. From this double knowledge, then, the general assumption was derived that it would be so in all cases. What Hippasus did was, in a way, nothing but a verification of this assumption by means of various sound-producing bodies which were not ordinarily used as musical instruments. But two things are significant. Strings have, so to speak, only one dimension. In regard to flutes, too, especially if the different

[34] See E. Frank, *op. cit.*, p. 69 and *passim*.

tones are produced on the same flute, one will not always think of the other two dimensions. When Hippasus used tumblers and discs, however, he had to point out that the discs, for instance, must be equal in two dimensions and differ only in the third if the musical harmonies are to be produced, but that it did not matter whether the third dimension was what usually was called length or thickness. In this way, then, the result can be most clearly formulated, namely, that the musical harmonies are completely independent of the material of which the sound-producing body consists, and of the special quality or colour of the tones produced, and that the production of these harmonies depends exclusively on simple one-dimensional numerical ratios. We hear then, further,[35] that Hippasus was not content with having proved this point but also investigated the mathematical relations between the ratios producing the most outstanding harmonies and tried to derive them mathematically from one another.

As long as Hippasus remained within the limits of the theory of music, all this, of course, could not lead to the discovery of incommensurability. But there are strong indications that he and his associates did not confine themselves to this special field.

Aristotle very frequently mentions the Pythagoreans or so-called Pythagoreans, and attributes to them the doctrine that 'all things are number'.[36] According to E. Frank these so-called Pythagoreans are not Pythagoreans at all,[37] but contemporaries of Plato who were deeply influenced by his philosophy.[38] If this

[35] See *supra*, n. 20.
[36] The doctrine is expressed and explained in a great many different ways by Aristotle; for instance, that 'the elements of numbers are the elements of all things' (*Metaph.* 986 a 1 ff.), or that 'all things are composed of numbers' (*ibid.*, 1080 b 16 f.), or that 'the things themselves are numbers' (*ibid.*, 987 b 29 f.), or that 'number is the essence of everything' (*ibid.*, 987 a 19). But the last expression uses specific Aristotelian terminology and is obviously an attempt to explain what appeared too odd in its original wording.
[37] *Op. cit.*, p. 68 ff.
[38] E. Frank lays great stress on the fact that Aristotle speaks often, though not in the majority of cases, of the 'so-called' Pythagoreans, and infers from this that he meant that they were not really Pythagoreans. In fact, there was an excellent reason for the use of the word 'so-called', namely, that in Aristotle's time 'Pythagoreans' was the only name designating the adherents of a philosophical school or sect that was derived from the name of the founder; that is, it was an unusual expression. Confirmation of this can also

were so it would be difficult to see why Aristotle, who should have known, never says a word about it, and always seems to imply that Plato's theory of numbers is later. It would also be possible to show that the comparatively very primitive Pythagorean theory cannot possibly be later than Plato's very complicated one. But this would require an analysis of considerable length, which fortunately is not necessary for the present purpose, since there is more direct evidence to show that there must have been Pythagoreans in the fifth century who had a doctrine similar to that ascribed to them by Aristotle.

Archytas in the long fragment quoted above[39] says that the same men who elaborated a theory of sound had also attained 'clear insight' into problems of astronomy, geometry, and arithmetic. Again, of course, he refers to what others had done before he wrote his work. Unfortunately, the passages in which he described the achievements of his predecessors in astronomy and geometry have not come down to us. But since he speaks of the clear insight which they had attained, it is not likely that it was only in music that they had arrived at a stage so advanced that it must have required a considerable time to attain it. Moreover, Archytas says that the sciences mentioned are intimately related to one another because all of them 'turn back' to 'the first (or fundamental) form of everything that is'. This seems a very advanced form of the doctrine which Aristotle attributes to the 'so-called Pythagoreans'. Again, everything seems to indicate that the close connection between arithmetic, geometry, astronomy, and musical theory, as well as the somewhat crude theory that 'all things are numbers' must have been considerably older than Archytas, that is, at least as early as the middle of the fifth century.

In order to understand the origin and meaning of this latter doctrine, an analysis of the Greek terminology of the theory of proportions will be helpful. The Greek expression for proportion means literally 'the same ratio'. For our term 'ratio' the Greeks have two expressions: *diastema*, which means literally 'interval',

[39] See *supra*, p. 389 and note 31.

be found in the fact that the only analogy to the name 'Pythagoreans' found in pre-Aristotelian literature (Heracleiteans in Plato's *Theaet.* 179 e) is obviously used in fun.

and *logos*, which means literally 'word'. The first term clearly shows the connection of the early theory of proportions with musical theory.[40] But the second term is even more significant. The Greeks had two terms for 'word': *epos* and *logos*.[41] *Epos* means the spoken word, or the word which appeals to the imagination and evokes a picture of things or events. This is the reason why it is also specifically applied to epic poetry. *Logos* designates the word or combination of words in as much as they convey a meaning or insight into something.[42] It is this connotation of the term *logos* which made it possible for it in later times to acquire the meaning of an intrinsic law or the law governing the whole world.

If *logos*, then, is the term used for a mathematical ratio, this points to the idea that the ratio gives an insight into a thing or expresses its intrinsic nature. In the case of musical harmonies the harmony itself would be perceived by the ear, but it was the mathematical ratio, which, in the mind of the Pythagoreans, seemed to reveal the nature of the harmony, because through it the harmony could be both defined and reproduced in different media.

It is easy to see how this general idea could be extended to astronomy, especially to the regular motions of the celestial bodies and the interrelations between their various cycles.[43] But it is the extension of the theory to geometry which is of special importance for our problem.

The mathematical theorem which is in tradition most closely connected with Pythagoras and the Pythagoreans, is the theorem that in a right-angled triangle the sum of the squares on the sides

[40] This is also the case with the word *horos* designating the terms of a ratio or a proportion. See K. von Fritz, *Philosophie und sprachlicher Ausdruck bei Demokrit, Platon und Aristoteles* (New York, Stechert, 1938), p. 69.
[41] As to the question of how early the term *logos* was used in the sense of ratio, see *infra*, pp. 407 f.
[42] This is also characteristic of the corresponding verb *legein*. In consequence, the Greeks can form the following sentence: N. N. says (there follows a literal quotation of his words) saying (there follows an interpretation of their meaning). It is clear that 'saying' in this sentence really means 'meaning'. The verb *eipein*, which corresponds to *epos* cannot be used in the latter sense. It is also significant that those stories which Herodotus, for instance, calls *logoi* are always stories with a moral, that is, with a meaning.
[43] For details, see my article on Oinopides of Chios in Pauly-Wissowa, *Realencyclopaedie*, Vol. 17, pp. 2260–7.

including the right angle is equal to the square on the side sub-tending the right angle. Nobody who knows anything about the early history of Greek mathematics has ever doubted that the proof of this theorem given by Euclid in the first book of his Elements cannot have been found by Pythagoras or his early followers. This is also what the best ancient tradition says, since Proclus attributes this proof to Euclid himself.[44] Though at the time when, in the last quarter of the fifth century, Hippocrates of Chios elaborated his famous theory of the *lunulae*, the 'Pythagorean theorem' must have been considered valid for right-angled triangles whose sides are commensurable with one another and for triangles whose sides are incommensurable, and furthermore must have been extended to cover all similar figures erected on the sides of a right-angled triangle, it is not possible for us to find out exactly how the early Greek mathematicians proved or tried to prove the theorem in this general form, since there exists no tradition about it.[45] Fortunately, it is not necessary for our purpose to have this knowledge.

Again, the theory must have started from an observation which had been generally known long before the beginning of Greek philosophy, namely, that if one puts together three pieces of wood of the respective lengths of 3, 4, and 5, a right-angled triangle will result. In fact, this is an old form of a carpenter's square. Since the size of carpenter's squares was not standardized, it must also have been a matter of common knowledge that the absolute length of the sides of the triangle was irrelevant, and that all triangles whose sides were in that proportion were not only right-angled but also 'similar' in shape. Finally, it seems to have been known of old that the sum of the squares of 3 and 4 was equal to the square of 5.

Even if we had no tradition about it we would have to conclude that the Pythagoreans must have been impressed by these facts as soon as they had begun to suspect that the nature of a good many things might be found in or expressed by numbers, especially since there is indirect evidence to show that even before Pythagoras the philosopher Thales (*c.* 620 to *c.* 540 B.C.) and his

[44] Proclus, *In primum Euclid. elem. librum Comment.*, p. 426 Friedlein.
[45] For the various possibilities, see the lucid exposition of Th. Heath in his commented translation of Euclid's *Elements* (Cambridge, 1926), Vol. 1, pp. 352 ff.

followers had concerned themselves with what we may call the ornamental shape of geometrical figures [46] and also seem to have connected this ornamental appearance especially with the angles. The fact, at least, that according to Proclus [47] they used the term 'similar angles' for what later was called 'equal' angles can hardly be explained otherwise. [48]

On the basis of this earlier development the Pythagoreans can hardly have failed to notice that any two triangles will be similar in shape if their sides are in proportion, though in actual fact in the earliest period this knowledge can have been an exact knowledge only in regard to triangles whose sides are commensurable with one another. Though this assumption is not supported by any direct tradition—probably because it was too obvious to be especially mentioned—it follows not only from the general situation, but especially from the close analogy of the Pythagoreans' theory of music and their earliest theory of geometrical figures, which is attested everywhere. For just as they declared that the musical harmonies which are perceived by the ear 'are' really the numbers by which the proportionate lengths of the strings, etc., producing them are measured, so the geometrical figures, whose shape is perceived by the eye but cannot otherwise be either exactly determined or expressed in language, 'are' really the numbers or sets of numbers constituting the ratios of the lengths of their sides by which their shape is determined and can therefore be expressed. [49]

According to ancient tradition, the theory, before the discovery of incommensurability, was further extended in two directions. Proclus [50] credits Pythagoras with a formula which makes it

[46] For the evidence, see Th. Heath, *A History of Greek Mathematics* (Oxford, 1921), Vol. 1, pp. 130 ff.

[47] *Op. cit.*, p. 250 Friedlein.

[48] It is perhaps pertinent to observe that the historian Thucydides (I, 77) also uses the term 'similar' where he means equality of form (or in this case: procedure). For he uses the expression 'similar laws' where, as the context shows, he does not mean similar laws but what otherwise was called *isonomia* or equality before the law.

[49] The Pythagoreans were, of course, aware that triangles are the only rectilineal figures whose shape is definitely determined by the proportionate length of their sides. That they realized the importance of this fact for their theory seems proved by Theon's statement (*op. cit.*, pp. 40 ff.) that they divided all other rectilineal figures into triangles.

[50] *Op. cit.* (see note 44), p. 428 Friedlein.

possible to form any number of different rational right-angled triangles by finding pairs of numbers the sum of the squares of which is equal to a square number.[51] It is irrelevant for our purpose whether this formula is rightly attributed to Pythagoras personally, but one can safely assume that it belongs to the very oldest period of Pythagorean mathematics. For Proclus usually relies on the very excellent history of mathematics of Aristotle's disciple Eudemus of Rhodes; and in this case what he says seems all the more worthy of credit in that he does not claim too much and rather implies a criticism of the common tradition that Pythagoras 'proved' the 'Pythagorean theorem' in its general geometrical form.

Nevertheless, the formula marks a great advance. One has to interpret it in terms of Pythagorean philosophy in order to understand its importance in regard to our problem. In the theory discussed before, the shape of figures which are similar in the mathematical sense of the word is directly related to a definite set of integers. Two triangles, with the sides 3, 4, 5 and 8, 15, 17 respectively are not, on the other hand, *similar* in the sense of the (modern or Euclidean) mathematical term. But they are still 'similar' in regard to the ornamental element of one right angle; and this 'similarity' is not related to or expressed in one definite set of integers, but is related to the fact that the two sets of integers related to the two triangles enter into the same mathematical formula. What is important for our problem in this extension of the theory is merely that it shows how the Pythagoreans were not content with a simple theory but, with an extraordinarily inquisitive spirit, adapted this theory to ever more complicated problems.

The second extension of the Pythagorean theory which is important as a preparation for the discovery of incommensurability is the theory of polygonal numbers. This theory, the beginnings of which ancient tradition, starting with Aristotle,[52] attributes also to the early Pythagoreans, was many centuries later

[51] The formula, though expressed in a somewhat more complicated way, amounts to the statement that if m be any odd number,

$$m^2 + \left(\frac{m^2 - 1}{2}\right)^2 = \left(\frac{m^2 + 1}{2}\right)^2.$$

[52] The relevant passages have been collected by Heath, *History* (see note 46), 1, 76 ff.

developed by Diophantus to what is now called indeterminate analysis. But for a long time it remained rather sterile from a purely mathematical point of view. This is probably the reason why Euclid disregarded it in the arithmetical section of his Elements and why other high-ranking mathematicians from the fourth century onwards have done likewise.

Just like the other geometrical theories of the Pythagoreans discussed so far, this theory is concerned with interrelations between numbers and geometrical figures. But in this case the figures are not drawn and formed by straight lines of certain proportionate measures, but are built up from dots. The theory then is concerned with the question from what numbers of dots arranged in a certain order the different polygons can be built.[53] It seems perfectly clear from the evidence presented so far that this theory is a natural product of the development of Pythagorean thought. It, therefore, certainly need not, as E. Frank contends,[54] be dependent on or, in its original form, even be influenced by the physical atomism of Democritus, which has an entirely different origin. Whatever chronological inferences E. Frank draws from this incidental affinity are, therefore, absolutely unwarranted.[55]

Though the 'atomism' of the theory of polygonal numbers seems most remote from the discovery of incommensurability it is here that we come nearest to our problem. All the Pythagorean doctrines discussed so far either are based on or result in a search for numbers, i.e. integers, from which geometrical figures with certain properties can be built up. In the course of these efforts the Pythagoreans can hardly have failed to wonder what numbers might be hidden in certain well-known figures which had not

[53] Triangular numbers, for instance, are (1), 3, 6, 10, 15, like this:

etc.

[54] Op. cit. (see note 2), pp. 52 ff.
[55] The passage in Aristotle, De Anima, 409 a 10 ff., where Aristotle quite correctly says that if one replaces Democritus' material atoms by immaterial dots the result is very similar to the quantitative theory of the Pythagoreans, need certainly not have chronological implications. But even if it had such implications, this would not prove anything, since Aristotle in this passage does not refer to the earliest form of the Pythagorean doctrine.

been built up in this way, for instance, the isosceles right-angled triangle, which was of special importance to the Pythagoreans because it was one-half of the square, the latter figure having become a mystical symbol in the Pythagorean community. In the case of the isosceles right-angled triangle, however, it is not possible to express the ratio between its sides in integers. It is perhaps not too far-fetched a speculation if one assumes that the early development of the theory of polygonal numbers was partly due to an attempt to overcome this difficulty by building up the polygons from dots rather than from straight lines. In fact, this seems all the more likely because here again the division of polygons and polygonal numbers into triangles and triangular numbers is one of the main points of the theory. Theon, for instance, points out [56] that an oblong number can be divided into two equal triangular numbers while a square number is made up of two unequal triangular numbers whose sides differ by one unit, namely,

FIG. 1

But however this may be, men of the inquisitive spirit which characterized Hippasus and some of his Pythagorean contemporaries [57] can hardly have been satisfied with these arithmetical theorems as a substitute for the solution of the real problem, namely, the problem of the ratio between the sides of an isosceles right-angled triangle. This is again confirmed by ancient tradition; for what Plato says about Theodorus' demonstration of the irrationality of the square of roots of 3, 5, 6, 7, etc., presupposes,

[56] Op. cit., p. 41 Hiller.
[57] See supra, pp. 386 ff. and p. 396.

as shown above,[58] that the irrationality of the square root of 2 had already been proved.

Fortunately, the original demonstration of the irrationality of the square root of 2 has been preserved in an appendix to the tenth book of Euclid's elements;[59] and that this demonstration is actually, at least in its general outline, the original one is attested by Aristotle. One glance at this demonstration[60] shows that it does not presuppose any geometrical knowledge beyond the Pythagorean theorem in its special application to the isosceles right-angled triangle, which, as is well-known, can be 'proved' simply by drawing the figure in such a way that the truth of the theorem in that particular case is immediately visible.[61] Apart

[58] See *supra*, p. 385.

[59] Euclid, *Elementa*, X, Append. 27, pp. 407 ff. (This appendix is not included in Heath's translation of Euclid's *Elements*.)

[60] In literal translation this demonstration runs as follows: Let $ABCD$ be a square and AC its diameter. I say that AC will be incommensurable with AB in length.

For let us assume that it is commensurable. I say that it will follow that the same number is at the same time even and odd. It is clear that the square on AC is double the square on AB. Since then (according to our assumption) AC is commensurable with AB, AC will be to AB in the ratio of an integer to an integer. Let them have the ratio $DE:F$ and let DE and F be the smallest numbers which are in this proportion to one another. DE cannot then be the unit. For if DE was the unit and is to F in the same proportion as AC to AB, AC being greater than AB, DE, the unit, will be greater than the integer F, which is impossible. Hence DE is not the unit, but an integer (greater than the unit). Now since $AC:AB = DE:F$, it follows that also $AC^2:AB^2 = DE^2:F^2$. But $AC^2 = 2AB^2$ and hence $DE^2 = 2F^2$. Hence DE^2 is an even number and therefore DE must also be an even number. For if it was an odd number its square would also be an odd number. For if any number of odd numbers are added to one another so that the number of numbers added is an odd number the result is also an odd number. Hence DE will be an even number. Let then DE be divided into two equal numbers at the point G. Since DE and F are the smallest numbers which are in the same proportion they will be prime to one another. Therefore, since DE is an even number, F will be an odd number. For if it was an even number the number 2 would measure both DE and F, though they are prime to one another, which is impossible. Hence F is not even, but odd. Now since $ED = 2EG$ it follows that $ED^2 = 4EG^2$. But $ED^2 = 2F^2$, and hence $F^2 = 2EG^2$. Therefore F^2 must be an even number, and in consequence F also an even number. But it has also been demonstrated that F must be an odd number, which is impossible. It follows, therefore, that AC cannot be commensurable with AB, which was to be demonstrated.

[61] For examples, see Heath, *The Thirteen Books of Euclid's Elements*, Vol. 1, p. 352.

from this the demonstration remains in the purely arithmetical field; and since the early Pythagoreans speculated a good deal about odd and even numbers [62] the demonstration itself cannot have been beyond their reach. [63]

Yet if this demonstration of the irrationality of the square root of 2 was the only way in which incommensurability can have been discovered, one might still agree that there are good reasons for Frank's and Neugebauer's hesitation to attribute the discovery to the middle of the fifth century. The demonstration requires not only a good deal of abstract thinking, but also of strict logical reasoning. Apart from this, the laboured language of the demonstration as given in the appendix in Euclid shows clearly with what difficulties the early Greek mathematicians had to struggle when elaborating a proof of this kind. In fact, this conclusion is all the more cogent because the demonstration, though somewhat more archaic in form than Euclid's own demonstrations, uses a form of presenting the argument in short concise sentences which has no parallel in Greek literature of the fifth century. [64] If, then, the proof as such, as the combined passages in Plato and Aristotle seem to indicate, [65] belongs to the fifth century, it seems safe to assume that in its original form it was still more laborious. Most significant, however, is the fact that the whole proof, as presented, uses the terms *commensurable* and *incommensurable*, just as Theodorus did in Plato's *Theaetetus*, as something already known. This seems to presuppose that incommensurability was already known when the demonstration was elaborated.

Since the form of the proof as it appears in the appendix to Euclid may not be the original one, the form of the proof in

---

[62] See, for instance, Aristotle, *Physics*, 203 a 5 ff.; *Metaph.*, 986 a 22 ff.

[63] Concerning the arithmetical premises of this demonstration and the probable deficiencies of its original form, see my article on Theodorus of Cyrene in Pauly-Wissowa, *RE*, Vol. VA, pp. 1817 and 1820 ff.

[64] In order to illustrate this, one may compare the literal fragments of Zeno of Elea which show a very high degree of abstract thinking and also of close logical reasoning, but at the same time are written in a laboured language with long and cumbrous sentences, while Aristotle (in the fourth century) and later writers who give an account of Zeno's theory, reproduce the same arguments in a sequence of very short sentences very similar to those found in the appendix to Euclid.

[65] Plato, *Theaetetus*, pp. 147 B ff. and Aristotle, *Analytica Priora*, 41 a 26–31 and 50 a 37. See also *supra*, pp. 385 and 394.

Euclid's appendix may not be sufficient to show with certainty that when the irrationality of the square root of 2 was demonstrated, the discovery of incommensurability as such had already been made, probably in a different mathematical object. But if one considers the further evidence presented above, the suspicion that such was the case becomes very strong. For it is difficult to believe that the early Greek mathematicians should have discovered the incommensurability of the diameter of a square with its side by a process of reasoning which was obviously so laborious for them if they had no previous suspicion that any such thing as incommensurability existed at all. If, on the other hand, they had already discovered the fact in a simpler way, it is perfectly in keeping with what we know of their methods to assume that they at once made every effort to find out whether there were other cases of incommensurability. The isosceles right-angled triangle in that case was the natural first object of their further investigations.

It is at this point that the tradition concerning Hippasus' interest in the dodecahedron, or 'the sphere out of 12 regular pentagons' has to be considered. There can be no doubt that Hippasus was not the author of the mathematical construction of the dodecahedron, as Iamblichus claims in one place.[66] Quite apart from other considerations, this is proved by the fact that the better tradition implies that this was an achievement of Theaetetus,[67] who belonged to the second generation after Hippasus. And in another passage, Iamblichus[68] himself claims merely that Hippasus 'drew' the regular dodecahedron, which is probably the original tradition.

That Hippasus was interested in the dodecahedron and in the dodecahedron as a 'sphere made of 12 regular pentagons' is very likely. For regular dodecahedra occurred in Italy as products of nature in the form of crystals of pyrite.[69] With the Pythagoreans'

66 See note 24.
67 For details, see the article quoted in note 5, pp. 1364 ff.
68 See notes 22 and 23.
69 See F. Lindemann in *Sitz.-Berichte Akad. München, math.-phys. Klasse*, Vol. 26, pp. 725 ff. Lindemann gives also evidence to show that dodecahedra were used as dice in Italy at a very early time, and that the regular dodecahedron seems to have had some religious importance in Etruria. Especially the latter fact, if known to the Pythagoreans, would naturally have increased their interest in the figure.

interest in geometrical forms these crystals must certainly have attracted their attention and evoked a desire to analyze their form mathematically. In addition, we know that the Pythagoreans used the pentagram, i.e. a regular pentagon with its sides prolonged to the point of intersection,[70] as a token of recognition.

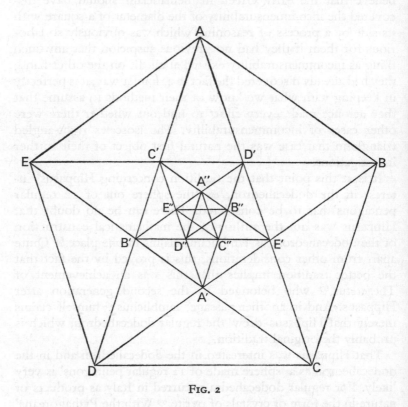

FIG. 2

It is absolutely in the character of Hippasus as we now know him that he should have tried to find out about the numbers and ratios incorporated in the pentagram and regular pentagon. Could it then really be a mere coincidence that the same Hippasus is credited with the discovery of incommensurability and with an

[70] See Lucian, *De lapsu in salutando*, 5, and schol. Aristophanes, *Nubes*, 609.

interest in the 'sphere consisting of 12 regular pentagons', and that the regular pentagon is exactly the one geometrical figure in which incommensurability can be most easily proved?

How would the Pythagoreans have gone about it if they wanted to know the ratio between the lengths of two straight lines? Again, the method was an old one, known by craftsmen as a rule of thumb many centuries before the beginning of Greek philosophy and science, namely, the method of mutual subtraction,[71] by which one finds the greatest common measure. It is, of course, impossible to discover incommensurability by applying this method in the way in which craftsmen do it: with measuring sticks or measuring ropes. But if one looks at the pentagram or at a regular pentagon with all its diameters filled in—and we have seen that the Pythagoreans were interested in diameters—the fact that the process of mutual subtraction goes on infinitely, that therefore there is no greatest common measure, and that hence the ratio between the diameter and side cannot be expressed in integers however great, is apparent almost at first sight. For one sees at once that the diameters of the pentagon form a new regular pentagon in the centre, that the diameters of this smaller pentagon will again form a regular pentagon, and so on in an infinite process (see fig. 2).

It is then also very easy to see that in the pentagons produced in this way $AE = AB'$ and $B'D = B'E'$ and therefore $AD - AE = B'E'$, and likewise $AE = ED' = EA'$ and $B'E' = B'D = B'E$ and therefore $AE - B'E' = B'A'$, and so forth ad infinitum, or, in other words, that the difference between the diameter and the side of the greater pentagon is equal to the diameter of the smaller pentagon, and the difference between the side of the greater pentagon and the diameter of the smaller pentagon is equal to the side of the smaller pentagon, and again the difference between the diameter of the smaller pentagon and its side is equal to the diameter of the next smaller pentagon and so forth in infinitum. Since ever new regular pentagons are produced by the diameters it is then evident that the process of mutual subtraction will go on for ever, and that therefore no greatest common measure of the diameter and the side of the regular pentagon can be found.

[71] For evidence to show that the Pythagoreans used this method in mathematical theory, see *infra*, p. 405.

One may, of course, still ask how the Pythagoreans could prove that $AE = AB'$ and $B'D' = B'E'$, etc. Now Proclus, probably getting his information from Eudemus of Rhodes, states[72] that Thales was the author of the theorem that in an isosceles triangle the base angles are equal. In connection with this it is important to note that Aristotle[73] refers to an archaic proof of this proposition. He does not quote all the steps of this proof, but what he quotes shows that 'mixed angles', i.e. angles formed by a straight line and the circumference of a circle, were used in the demonstration, and that in all likelihood the proof was based on a rather primitive method of superimposition.[74] It is clear that with this latter method the converse of the proposition could be proved without difficulty. It follows that the equality of AE with AB' and of $B'D$ with $B'E'$ could be derived from the equality of $\angle AEB'$ with $\angle AB'E$ and of $\angle B'DE'$ with $\angle B'E'D$, if these angles could be proved to be equal respectively.

As to this latter proof, the evidence is somewhat less definite. But Eudemus of Rhodes[75] attributes to the early Pythagoreans the proof that the sum of the internal angles in any triangle is equal to two right angles. From this theorem the general theorem that in any polygon the sum of the internal angles is equal to $2n - 4$ right angles can very easily be derived, if one divides the polygon into triangles,[76] and we know[77] that the Pythagoreans constantly experimented with dividing polygons into triangles. The proposition furthermore that in any polygon the sum of the external angles is equal to four right angles is a mere corollary of the preceding proposition.[78] On the basis of these propositions, finally, the equality of the angles figuring in the demonstration suggested above can be very easily shown.

It follows that there is no reason whatever to disbelieve that Hippasus was able to demonstrate the incommensurability of the side with the diameter of a regular pentagon. For what is

[72] Op. cit., pp. 250 f. Friedlein.   [73] Aristotle, Analyt. Pr., 41 b 13 ff.
[74] For details, see Heath, Elements (see note 45), 1, 253.
[75] Quoted by Proclus, op. cit., 379 Friedlein.
[76] The proof is quoted by Proclus, op. cit. After the polygon has been divided into triangles, the proposition about the sum of the angles of a triangle being known, the remainder of the proof is a simple addition.
[77] See supra, note 49.
[78] Aristotle refers to this proof as to something very well known in Analyt. Post. 99 a 19 ff. and 85 b 38 ff.

needed for the proof suggested is nothing but two fundamental geometrical propositions which concern the isosceles triangle and the sum of the angles in any triangle, and in addition the old time-honoured method of finding the greatest common measure by mutual subtraction. All the rest is nothing but the simplest addition, subtraction, and division. Of the two geometrical propositions, the first had undoubtedly been 'proved' in a very primitive way even before Pythagoras.[79] The second one was probably also proved in some such way, though we do not know exactly how.[80] But there can be no doubt whatever that its truth was known long before Hippasus. That the proofs of these theorems as existing in the middle of the fifth century did not come up to the Euclidean conception of a satisfactory proof is not to the point. For the question is not whether Hippasus could give a demonstration which in all its steps would have satisfied Euclid or Hilbert, but whether he was able to find a proof which at the level which mathematical theory had reached in his time was considered absolutely convincing, and as to this there can be no doubt. It is, perhaps, not unnecessary to point out specifically that the demonstration of incommensurability

[79] It is an interesting fact that all the theorems which ancient tradition attributes to Thales are either directly concerned with problems of symmetry and 'provable' by superimposition, or of such a kind that the first step of the proof was obviously based on a consideration of symmetry and the second step, which brings the proof to its conclusion, is a simple addition or subtraction. The much discussed Euclidean proof of the first theorem of congruence by superimposition seems, then, the last remnant of a method which once had been widely applied and with which Greek scientific geometry had started.

[80] The proof attributed to the Pythagoreans by Eudemus seems to presuppose the famous fifth postulate of Euclid. But Aristotle (*An. Pr.*, 65 a 4) indicates that there existed an old mathematical demonstration about parallels and angles which involved a vicious circle. It seems, then, quite possible that the equality of alternate angles on parallels cut by a straight line was at first considered self-evident on the basis of considerations of symmetry, that then a faulty attempt to prove the proposition was made, and that finally Euclid tried to give the whole theory a sound foundation by his famous postulate. In this case the proof of the proposition concerning the sum of the angles of a triangle attributed to the early Pythagoreans by Eudemus may really be very old. But Geminus (in Eutocius' commentary on the *Conica* of Apollonius of Perge; Vol. II, 170 of Heiberg's edition of Apollonius) mentions a still older demonstration in which the proposition was proved first for the equilateral, then for the isosceles, and finally for the scalene triangle.

suggested above does not presuppose any geometrical construction in the strictly mathematical sense at all, as long as the Pythagoreans were able to draw a reasonably accurate regular pentagon in some way, and this can hardly be questioned, for a quite beautiful pentagram can be seen on a vase of Aristonophus which belongs to the seventh century B.C. This vase was found at Caere in Italy and is now in a museum in Rome. Neugebauer's argument, therefore, that the discovery of incommensurability could not have been made by Hippasus since Oinopides, who belonged to the succeeding generation, was still concerned with the most 'trivial' mathematical constructions, has no validity.[81]

There is, then, perhaps some justification for the claim that the analysis so far has proved what was promised in the introduction to this paper, namely, that the discovery of incommensurability can have been made in the middle of the fifth century, that the development of the Pythagorean doctrine of numbers as the essence of everything naturally led to this discovery, that ancient tradition contains strong hints as to the way in which the discovery actually was made, and last but not least, that Greek mathematics in that early period may have been very elementary,[82] but certainly was not trivial. It was not trivial because the Greeks had two peculiarities which the Egyptians and Babylonians obviously lacked. They were very prone to build up sweeping general theories on very scanty evidence. Of this the Pythagorean theory that 'all things are numbers' is a striking example. Yet at the same time they were not content with having such a theory, but made unremitting efforts to verify it in all directions. It was

[81] In my article on Oinopides (see note 43) I have tried to show that Oinopides' mathematical constructions were not 'trivial' either, if viewed in connection with the problems which he tried to solve. But the solution of the present problem is quite independent from the acceptance or rejection of this suggestion.

[82] In the present article only so much mathematical knowledge has been attributed to the early Greek mathematicians as can be ascribed to them with the greatest approximation to certainty which a historical inquiry can attain. The attempt has then been made to show that *even if* their knowledge did not go beyond this, they nevertheless can have discovered incommensurability and by the nature of their theories and methods were naturally led to this discovery. But this does not imply that their knowledge must necessarily have been as limited and elementary as has been assumed in this paper.

on account of this second peculiarity that they discovered incommensurability in a very early period.

It is perhaps advisable to add a brief survey of the immediate consequences of the discovery of incommensurability for the further development of the theory of proportions. For this will confirm both the opinion concerning the general character of the early scientific investigations of the Greeks and some special suggestions which have been made in the course of the present inquiry.

The discovery of incommensurability must have made an enormous impression in Pythagorean circles because it destroyed with one stroke the belief that everything could be expressed in integers, on which the whole Pythagorean philosophy up to then had been based. This impression is clearly reflected in those legends which say that Hippasus was punished by the gods for having made public his terrible discovery.

But the consequences of the discovery were not confined to the field of philosophical speculation. *Logos* or ratio, as we have seen,[83] meant the expression of the essence of a thing by a set of integers. It had been assumed that the essence of anything could be expressed in that way. Now it had been discovered that there were things which had no *logos*. When *we* speak of irrationality or incommensurability we mean merely a special quality of certain magnitudes in their relation to one another, and we speak even of a special class of irrational numbers. But when the Greeks used the term *alogos*, they meant originally, as the term clearly indicates, that there was no *logos* or ratio.

Yet this fact must have been very puzzling. It had been generally assumed that two triangles which were similar, i.e. which had the same ornamental appearance, though differing in size, had the same *logos*, i.e. that they could be expressed by the same set of integers. In fact, this is clearly the original meaning of the term ὁ αὐτὸς λόγος (the same *logos*), which we translate by 'proportion'. But two isosceles right-angled triangles had still the same ornamental appearance, and therefore should have had the same *logos*. In fact, it seemed evident that their sides did have the same quantitative relation to one another. Yet they had no *logos*.

The way in which the Greeks amazingly soon after the stunning discovery of incommensurability began to deal with this problem

[83] See *supra*, pp. 392–93.

is a much greater proof of their genius for and their tenacity in the pursuit of scientific theory than the discovery of incommensurability itself. For very soon[84] they began not only to extend the theory of proportion to incommensurables, but also established a criterion by which in certain cases it can be determined whether two pairs of incommensurables (which in the old sense have no *logos* at all) have the same *logos*. The terminological difficulty created by this seeming contradiction in terms is reflected by the fact that for some time the term *alogos* for irrational was replaced by the term *arrhetos* (inexpressible) which is merely another way of expressing what the term *alogos* originally meant. It is also interesting to see how the term *alogos* gradually came back. First the term *rhetos* (rational) is created in contrast to *arrhetos*. Then the term *arrhetos* disappears; and Theaetetus, who developed the theory of irrationality further, reintroduced the term *alogos* but used it only for 'higher' irrationalities, for instance of the form $\sqrt{a\sqrt{b}}$, while he called the simple irrationalities of the form $\sqrt{a}$ *dynamei monon rhetoi* (literally: rational only in the square). Finally, when *logos* had become a technical term and the incongruity of the statement that two pairs of *alogoi* have the same *logos* was no longer felt, the Greek mathematicians returned to the old terminology and called all irrationals *alogos*.[85] The fact that Theaetetus, who died in 369 B.C., had already begun to return to the old terminology is a very strong confirmation of the view that the discovery of incommensurability must have been made long before, and that the term *logos* for ratio, from which *alogos* is derived, must certainly have been used by the Pythagoreans before the middle of the fifth century.

The extension of the theory of proportion to incommensurables required an entirely new concept of ratio and proportion and a new criterion to determine whether two pairs of magnitudes which are incommensurable with one another have the same *logos*. The early solution of this problem is most ingenious. Instead of making the result of the process of mutual subtraction the cri-

---

[84] The famous demonstrations of Hippocrates of Chios, who belonged to the same generation as Theodorus of Cyrene, clearly presuppose that the theory of proportions at his time had already been adapted to incommensurables. See F. Rudio, *Der Bericht des Simplicius über die Quadraturen des Antiphon und des Hippocrates* (Leipzig, Teubner, 1907), and *infra* p. 409.

[85] For details, see my article on Theaetetus (see note 5), pp. 1361 f.

terion of proportionality, namely the two sets of integers determined by measuring two commensurable magnitudes with the greatest common measure found by mutual subtraction, they used the character of the process of mutual subtraction itself as the criterion of proportionality. They established this criterion by giving a new definition of proportionality which made it applicable to commensurables and incommensurables alike. In literal translation this definition says: *magnitudes have the same logos if they have the same mutual subtraction.*[86] It is interesting to see that in this definition the term *logos* has lost its original meaning. The sense of the definitions is, then, that two sets of magnitudes are in proportion if in each case the process of mutual subtraction, even if going on in infinitum, nevertheless can be proved always to go in the same direction.

To show this is especially easy in the case of the diameters and sides of all regular pentagons, since in this case, the diameter being cut in the so-called golden section, it is evident that the process will always go exactly one step in each direction. But if the practical applicability of the new definition had been limited to this case it would have been of little use for the further development of mathematical theory. The most important case in which it is very easy to prove on the basis of the new definition that two pairs of magnitudes are in proportion is the proposition that rectangles and (since parallelograms can very easily be converted into rectangles of the same area) parallelograms of the same altitude are in proportion with their bases.

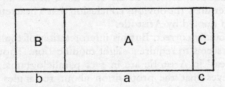

For it is easy to see that if *b* can be subtracted 5 times from *a*, *B* can also be subtracted 5 times from *A*, and if the remainder *c* can be subtracted 8 times from *b*, so can *C* from *B*, and so forth in infinitum.[87] This proportion is the foundation of the famous theorems of Hippocrates of Chios.

[86] See Aristotle, *Topica*, 158 b 32 ff.
[87] In literal translation the passage in Aristotle runs like this: 'It seems that in mathematical theory some propositions cannot easily be proved on account

Yet the usefulness of this new definition for the demonstration of geometrical propositions is still restricted to a rather limited field. The further expansion of the theory of proportions was made possible through the new and even more ingenious definition which was invented by Eudoxus of Cnidus and which runs as follows: *Magnitudes are said to be in the same logos, the first to the second and the third to the fourth, when, if any equimultiples whatever be taken of the first and the third and any equimultiples whatever of the second and the fourth, the former equimultiples alike exceed, are alike equal to, or alike fall short of, the latter equimultiples respectively taken in corresponding order.*[88]

---

of the lack of a definition (or: as long as the proper definition is lacking), as for instance the fact that a straight line cutting an area parallel to its side cuts the area and its base in the same proportion (literally: similarly). But as soon as the definition has been found (the truth of the proposition is at once manifest). For the areas and their bases have the same mutual subtraction; and this is the definition of proportion (ὁ αὐτὸς λόγος)! It seems strange that O. Becker in an article published in 1933 (Quellen und Studien zur Geschichte der Mathematik, Abteilung B, vol. 2, pp. 311 ff.) was the first to give the correct interpretation of the expression 'have the same mutual subtraction' in the passage quoted, while Heath, for instance, still called the definition 'metaphysical', and said that it was difficult to see how any mathematical facts could be derived from the definition.

O. Becker in a most excellent analysis has also proved that the greater part of the 10th book of Euclid's *Elements* which contains a very elaborate theory of irrationals can be proved by means of this definition, while some of the propositions specifically ascribed to Eudoxus cannot be proved on the basis of this definition and presuppose the new definition Euclid V, def. 5. Since the most important propositions of the 10th book of Euclid are ascribed to Theaetetus, Becker drew the obvious conclusion that Theaetetus worked with the old definition quoted by Aristotle.

This is undoubtedly correct. But his interpretation of the rest of the passage in Aristotle seems to require a slight modification. Though Becker has seen that the 'areas' in Aristotle are in fact parallelograms, or rather, rectangles, he believes that the proposition about rectangles was from the beginning proved by an elaborate process of reasoning, which required that several other propositions had been proved first (*op. cit.*, p. 322). This is certainly not what Aristotle indicates, when he says that the truth of the proposition is manifest as soon as the definition is found. For this expression shows clearly that originally a direct application of the definition to the figure given above was considered sufficient proof of the proposition. This is an interesting parallel to the first demonstration of incommensurability in the pentagon as suggested above.

[88] See Euclid, *Elements*, V, def. 5 and *Scholia in Euclid. Element.*, V, 3 (Euclidis Opera, I. L. Heiberg (ed.), Vol. V (Leipzig, Teubner, 1889), p. 282).

If one compares the discovery of incommensurability (assuming that it was made in the manner suggested above) with these extensions of the theory of proportions, it seems evident that the discovery of incommensurability was by far the easiest step. For once the Pythagoreans became interested in the pentagram and the regular pentagon, anyone might be struck by the fact that the diameters will always form a new regular pentagon in the centre; and if, furthermore, the general Pythagorean doctrine required the determination of the *logos* of diameters and sides, all the rest followed very easily. Of the two new definitions of proportion, that of Eudoxus is perhaps the most ingenious inasmuch as it required the greatest effort in abstraction. But the older definition of proportion, by which the original concept of *logos* was replaced by a new one, which made it possible to apply the theory of proportion to incommensurables, was certainly by far the most important step in the development.

The fact that the development from the discovery of incommensurability to Eudoxus took this course has also chronological implications. Eudoxus was born in 400 and died in 347 B.C.[89] His last work, which he left uncompleted, was a large geographical work in many volumes.[90] He was also the author of the method of exhaustion, of the theorem that the volume of a cone is one-third of the volume of a cylinder with the same base and altitude,[91] and undoubtedly of other stereometric theorems which must have been used in the proof of that proposition. All this would have been impossible without the new definition of proportion invented by Eudoxus. He therefore must have created this definition comparatively early in his life, hardly later than 370. It would, then, be little less than miraculous if the first discovery of incommensurability had been made 'in the time of Archytas' who, since he was head of the government of Tarentum in 362, can hardly have been born before 430. It is certainly much easier to believe that the discovery was made in the middle of the fifth century, as ancient tradition claims.

But the solution of the chronological problem is of importance

[89] See K. von Fritz, 'Die Lebenszeit des Eudoxos von Knidos' in *Philologus*, 85 (1930), 478 ff.

[90] See F. Gisinger, *Die Erdbeschreibung des Eudoxos von Knidos*, pp. 5 ff.

[91] See Archimedes, *Ep. ad Dositheum in De sphaera et Cylindro*, p. 4 Heiberg, and *Ad Eratosth. Methodus*, p. 430 Heiberg.

mainly because it makes it possible to acquire a deeper insight into the way in which the Greeks laid the foundations of the science of mathematics and into the special qualities which enabled them within an amazingly short time to make a discovery which their Babylonian and Egyptian predecessors with all their highly developed and complicated methods had not made in many centuries of mathematical studies.

XV

ON HERACLITUS*

Gregory Vlastos

I OFFER here remarks on (*a*) the authenticity of the whole or part of some of his fragments (Part I), and (*b*) the historical relation of his thought to that of those who influenced him most directly, Anaximander and Anaximenes (Part II). The immediate stimulus for these reflections I owe to the study of G. S. Kirk's recent book, *Heraclitus: The Cosmic Fragments*.[1] A work as serious and thorough as this compels one to reconsider many things one has previously taken for granted, to ask new questions, look afresh at the texts, and push through to a finish some hitherto half-finished trains of thought. For this I must express my sincere thanks to Kirk and also the hope that he will see in my many criticisms of his views a mark of esteem, not the reverse. Only a fundamental work is worthy of extensive criticism. And if I have said little on matters in which I agree with him, it is because I could not hope to improve on his own treatment of them.

* After completing the first draft of this paper I had the benefit of comments on it by Professor Friedrich Solmsen and of a detailed discussion of the fragments of Heraclitus made by Professor Harold Cherniss in his seminar at Princeton (Spring Term, 1955). I learned much from both, and made many revisions and corrections accordingly. But it must not be inferred that either or both of them would share all the views I express here; I alone am responsible for any opinion not credited by name to another. With two minor exceptions, I have not even undertaken to *mention* the interesting suggestions put forward by Professor Cherniss in his seminar; original ideas are better presented to the public by their originator, and I hope he may publish them himself. I also wish to thank the Institute for Advanced Study for enabling me to pursue studies on this and other topics under ideal conditions during the year 1954–5.
1 Cambridge University Press, 1954. See my brief review in *AJP*, 76, 1955, pp. 310–13.

PART I

[Part I of the original article is a detailed study of the Greek text of some of the fragments of Heraclitus. The following is a summary of its conclusions, made by the editors.

(*a*) B 91a 'It is not possible to step twice in the same river' (ποταμῷ . . . οὐκ ἔστιν ἐμβῆναι δὶς τῷ αὐτῷ).

B 49a 'In the same rivers we step and do not step, we are and are not' (ποταμοῖς τοῖς αὐτοῖς ἐμβαίνομέν τε καὶ οὐκ ἐμβαίνομεν, εἶμέν τε καὶ οὐκ εἶμεν).

B 12 'On those who step in the same rivers, different and again different waters flow' (ποταμοῖσι τοῖσιν αὐτοῖσιν ἐμβαίνουσιν ἕτερα καὶ ἕτερα ὕδατα ἐπιρρεῖ).

Professor Kirk took B 12 to be the only genuine one of these three. Professor Vlastos argues that B 12 is, of the three, the least likely to be genuine. He suggests that B 91a and the second part of B 12 perhaps come from an original which read: 'You could not step into the same river twice, since different and again different waters flow'. He also defends B 49a.

(*b*) B 89 'To men awake, there is one common world, but men asleep turn away, each to his own' (τοῖς ἐγρηγορόσιν ἕνα καὶ κοινὸν κόσμον εἶναι, τῶν δὲ κοιμωμένων ἕκαστον εἰς ἴδιον ἀποστρέφεσθαι).

Kirk treated this as 'a later paraphrase, partly of the last clause of Fragment 2 and partly of the last sentence of Fragment 1'. Vlastos defends B 89, including the use of *cosmos* in the sense of 'world' here and in B 30.

(*c*) B 51 'They do not understand how being at variance it agrees with itself: a back-turning connection, as of bow and lyre' (οὐ ξυνιᾶσιν ὅκως διαφερόμενον ἑωυτῷ ὁμολογέει· παλίντροπος ἁρμονίη ὅκωσπερ τόξου καὶ λύρης).

Vlastos defends the reading παλίντροπος against Kirk's preference for παλίντονος, 'back-stretched'.

(*d*) B 41. 'Wisdom is one thing: to understand the *gnome* [judgement] which has steered all through all' (ἓν τὸ σοφόν, ἐπίστασθαι· γνώμην, ὁτέη ἐκυβέρνησε πάντα διὰ πάντων).

Vlastos raises objections against Kirk's proposal to take ἐπίστασθαι γνώμην as a periphrasis for γιγνώσκειν and suggests reading ὁτέη κυβερνᾶται.]

PART II*

A prime requisite of the historical interpretation of any philosopher, ancient or modern, is to determine the nexus with those of his contemporaries or predecessors who did the most both to supply him with a working-stock of basic concepts and also to provoke new questions in his own mind, calling for new answers and therewith new concepts. Who are the most likely candidates for the role in the case of Heraclitus?

A proper answer to this question would call for a much more extensive investigation than I could carry out in this paper. All I can do here is to propound a *hypothesis*, and follow it out, in the hope that the results so obtained will commend it to others. It is that the main historical influences on Heraclitus' thought were the great Milesians, Anaximander and Anaximenes, and that our best chance to understand the problems which confronted him and the meaning of his own answers to them is to discover as best we can the links which connect his thought with theirs. Though, I repeat, this is only a hypothesis, it is only fair to add that it is not an implausible one. For think of the suggested alternatives: Parmenides, Xenophanes, Pythagoras. Each of the first two has found powerful exponents, but with results disproportionate to the resources expended on either hypothesis. Reinhardt's brilliant sponsorship of the view that Heraclitus' 'roots' are in Parmenides was condemned to failure at the start by the indefensible chronology on which it was based.[1a] Gigon's attempt to link him with Xenophanes[2] sheds

---

* Minor revisions have been made in Part II by the author.
[1a] For the most recent criticism of his chronology, see Kirk, pp. 1–3. That in spite of this mistake Reinhardt's work has done so much to stimulate Heraclitean studies in the last forty years is a tribute to the vigour of his thinking, the incisiveness of his writing, and the breadth of his knowledge. The same qualities make his later papers (to the first of which I shall continue to refer), 'Heraklits Lehre vom Feuer,' and 'Heraclitea,' *Hermes*, LXXVII (1942), 1 ff. and 225 ff., outstanding contributions.
[2] O. Gigon, *Untersuchungen zu Heraklit* (Leipzig, 1935). For a critique of his theory of Heraclitus' dependence on Xenophanes see W. Broecker, *Gnomon*,

some light on Heraclitus' religious views but almost none on his cosmological and metaphysical conceptions. As for Pythagoras, he is easily the candidate least likely to succeed, since what we know of his doctrine is so meagre in itself, almost infinitesimal in comparison to what we know of Heraclitus; how can our ignorance of the former improve our knowledge of the latter?[3] So by a process of elimination one is led back to the Milesians, where one should have started anyway. That Heraclitus knew their books has high antecedent probability, and is confirmed, quite apart from all the things I shall discuss below, by some meteorological details in which he followed them.[4] That he

[3] If this sounds unduly pessimistic, consider the possible borrowings: (I) *metron* (so Kirk, p. 403). But did this figure in the Pythagorean scheme? We don't know. Our evidence, such as it is, speaks of *peras* (in opposition to *apeiron*), not *metron*. But suppose *metron* was used as an alternate to *peras*; it would then refer, like the latter, to (a) ratios of odd–even numbers such as those of the concordant musical intervals (cf. *Gnomon*, XXV [1953], 33–4) and/ or (b) whole integers, applied to things like justice, the soul, etc. (Aristotle, *Met.*, 985 b 29–31 and Ross *ad loc.*). Where does Heraclitus employ ratios as at (a) or numbers as at (b) in any comparable way? (II) *logos*. What is there analogous to either (a) or (b) in Heraclitus when he speaks of *logos*, e.g., at B 1 or B 31 b? A more interesting suggestion has come from Fränkel, *AJP*, LIX (1938), 309 ff., and Minar, *CP*, XXIV (1939), 338 ff., who take the sense of *logos* borrowed from Pythagoras to be 'proportional mean', i.e. the X:Y::Y:Z ratio. But though a convincing case has been made by Fränkel for Heraclitus' *use* of this 'thought-pattern', there is no evidence that he derived it from Pythagoras, whose use of it is purely conjectural, and, if historical, would not have endeared it to one who thought him a charlatan (B 81). Moreover, though *any* proportion would be a *logos*, there is no evidence that when Heraclitus spoke of *the logos* or 'the same *logos*' he was thinking of a proportional mean at all (cf. my elucidation of B 31 b in the text below, where the required relation is equality, not geometric proportion) nor, conversely, that when he did use the three-term proportion (e.g. at B 83, ape:man::man:god) he was thinking of this relation as a manifestation of what *he* called *logos*.
[4] His explanation of thunder–lightning is that of Anaximander as modified by Anaximenes (Aetius, iii. 3, 1, 2, and 6): Anaximander explained this as a cloud-burst; Anaximenes, likening the phenomenon to the 'sea, which flashes when divided by the oars', added the notion of external impact (which could be only that of wind on cloud) as the cause of the rending of the cloud; Heraclitus' explanation of thunder has both wind-impact on cloud

XIII (1937), 530 ff. Though only a doctoral dissertation Gigon's is a challenging book, and Kirk has done well to devote so much time to the detailed discussion of its views.

had plenty of respect for them we may assume from the fact that they never figure in his vitriolic broadsides against prominent contemporaries and predecessors (B 40, B 42, B 56, B 57, B 81). To be known and not abused by a man of Heraclitus' temperament is tantamount to the receipt of a certificate of merit.

Of B 80, 'one must know that war is common, and right (*dike*) is strife, and that all things come to pass by strife and necessity (*chreôn*)', Kirk rightly remarks that it is 'almost certainly a criticism of Anaximander' (p. 401). Both *dike* and *chreôn* occur also in Anaximander's famous fragment; and the thrice repeated reference to 'war/strife' could hardly fail to allude to Anaximander's notion of the mutual aggression of the elements.[5] But what is the criticism? Kirk's answer—that while Anaximander held that 'change between opposites involves a kind of injustice: on the contrary, *he* (Heraclitus) held that strife between opposites was "the right way", normal and just' (p. 240)—takes us part of the way towards the answer; but not the whole way. To begin with we must notice the enormous difference of the role which 'strife' plays in Heraclitus: '*All* things happen in accordance with strife' (B 80); 'war is the father of *all* and king of all' (B 53). What is only occasional and intermittent, though recurrent, in Anaxi-

---

[5] For my interpretation of Anaximander I must refer to 'Equality and Justice in Early Greek Cosmologies', *CP*, XLIII (1947), 168 ff. (pp. 168–73 on Anaximander) (see pp. 73–83 of this volume). Cf. also F. Dirlmeier, 'Der Satz des Anaximandros', *Rhein. Mus.*, LXXXVII (1938), 376 ff., K. Deichgraeber, 'Anaximander von Milet', *Hermes*, LXXV (1940), 10 ff., and H. Cherniss, 'The Characteristics and Effects of Pre-Socratic Philosophy', *Journal of the Hist. of Ideas*, XII (1951), 319 ff. (pp. 323–8 on Anaximander, see pp. 5–10 of this volume).

(ἐμπτώσεις πνευμάτων εἰς τὰ νέφη) and compression (συστροφάς) of cloud by wind; and there is no reason to think that he offered a different explanation for lightning as the confusing statement in Aetius might suggest. His 'bowls' theory of the heavenly bodies follows Anaximander in attempting to provide for containers of their fiery substance, altering the shape of the holders to suit the disc-shaped bodies postulated by Anaximenes. Heraclitus must also have known the physical theories of Xenophanes but made only one important borrowing from them: the doctrine that 'the sun is new every day' (B 6), though this apparently meant for him that each day's sun is extinguished at night (Kirk, p. 267), while for Xenophanes it meant its 'travelling on *ad infinitum*' (Aetius, ii. 24, 9). An interesting linguistic link between Heraclitus and Anaximenes is pointed out by Reinhardt (*Hermes* 77, 1942, p. 16), διαχεῖσθαι (Anaximenes A 7, A 8; Heraclitus, B 31 b).

mander, becomes universal and invariant in Heraclitus. Why this difference? We cannot answer this question without granting the obvious implication of the river-fragments which Kirk formally denies (p. 367 *et passim*), the universality of change.[6] That strife is universal follows from the assumption that whatever exists is in change with the added assumption that all change is strife, neither of them made by Anaximander. What happens now to the latter's conviction that the world is a realm of 'justice'? Anaximander could hold, and did, that there is both 'injustice' and 'justice' in the world, strife being injustice, and justice consisting in the eventual reparation of the encroachments gained by strife. To Heraclitus this presented an intolerable compromise. Concluding as he did that strife is universal, he would have to infer that, if strife itself were unjust, there could be nothing but injustice. For him there could be no half-way house: either all is injustice, or all is justice, in the physical world. He chose the second alternative, which he could only do by affirming, as he does in B 80, that 'strife *is* justice'. The last clause of this fragment—that 'all things happen in accordance with strife and rightful necessity'—is the completion of the thought which is affirmed in *each* of the preceding clauses.[7]

Thus so far Heraclitus' thought is more intimately connected

[6] For my criticism, see my review of Kirk's book in *AJP*, 76 (1955), 310–13.
[7] Kirk fails to see that πόλεμον . . . ξυνόν in the first makes the same point as δίκην ἔριν in the second. He says that 'in Homer and Archilochus Ares is described as impartial, but here war is said to be universal; this surely must be the sense in view of frr. 2 and 114 and of the description of war as father and king of all in fr. 53' (p. 241). But this misses (a) the perfect connection between the Homeric reference to war as ξυνός *because* 'it kills the killer', *Iliad*, xviii. 309, and Heraclitus' *reason* for saying that strife is just (see the following paragraph in the text); (b) the fact that at B 2 and B 114 ξυνός does indeed have the sense of a *norm* (note 23, above); and (c) that the same sense is even present at B 53 which, of course, accents the universality of war in the strongest terms but also refers to its function as creator (πατήρ) and governor (βασιλεύς), a function which Heraclitus surely regards as just since he says that war establishes the distinction, unquestionably right for him, between gods and men, free and slave. Even the full significance of δίκην ἔριν is not brought out by Kirk, for he makes no mention of usages of ἔρις, νεῖκος which would lend substance to their conception as instruments of justice (cf. latter half of note 134, *CP*, XLII [1947], 170; and Fränkel's fine elucidation of B 80 in *Dichtung und Philosophie des frühen Griechentums* [New York, 1951], pp. 481–2).

with Anaximander's than Kirk or any of the modern interpreters have recognized. Two of the fundamental ideas in Anaximander —that there is strife among the elements, and that a just order is *nevertheless* preserved—are reasserted in a form which universalizes both of them and thereby resolves the opposition between them: what is a 'nevertheless' in Anaximander, becomes a 'therefore' in Heraclitus. The result is that no part of nature *can* 'over-step its measures', which is surely the point of B 94,[8] and not, as Kirk takes it, that 'long-term excess is punished (and reduced)' (p. 402), which is precisely what Anaximander had taught, not Heraclitus. There can be no excess at all, long-term, or short-term either, if '*all* things happen in accordance with strife and rightful necessity'. But when we turn to the next question, 'Why is justice preserved in strife?', we find that Heraclitus stands in a very different relation to Anaximander. For the maintenance of justice the latter had relied immediately upon the equality of the elements. Now, as Kirk notes repeatedly, the notion of nature as an equilibrium of opposing forces does find a place in Heraclitus, though with the difference that the processes of encroachment and reparation are not successive, as in Anaximander, but concurrent: at every moment the main world-masses of fire, water, and earth are each giving up exactly as much as they take, each compensating constantly by the 'death' they suffer (B 36) for the one they inflict.[9] So much, I believe with Kirk, follows from B 31 a: 'the turnings of fire are first sea, and of sea the half is earth, half *prester*': the second clause can only mean that equal amounts of water are turning back into fire and forward into earth, whence it would follow (*a*) that the total mass of water remains constant, consequently (*b*) that the total masses of fire and earth are also constant, since either of these can only change into or from water, and hence, for the same reason, (*c*) that fire and earth must also display the equipollence of change asserted of water in B 31 a—an inference explicitly confirmed in the case of fire by the balancing expressions, 'kindling according to measures, and extinguished according to measures', in B 30.

---

[8] As Reinhardt (*Hermes*, LXXVII [1942], 244, n. 2) has remarked, εἰ δὲ μή in this fragment 'drückt eine Unmöglichkeit aus, einen Fall, der nie eintreten wird, wie in fr. 121: "Und wenn, dann . . .", worauf eine Negation folgt.'
[9] Cf. above, note 7.

But note how short all this falls of preserving (let alone, extending) Anaximander's concept of equality as the guarantee of justice. For one thing, nothing is said to the effect that fire, water, and air are equal to one another. The assumption of the equality of the physical components of the world, reasserted by Parmenides and Empedocles, is quietly dropped by Heraclitus; for Anaximander's equilibrium of elements he substitutes an equilibrium of processes of change. And even the latter is only a special case of 'back-turning adjustment' (παλίντροπος ἁρμονίη). It applies only to those systems which do maintain themselves in a stable equilibrium. The world as a whole is such a system, and so is a river or, for that matter, the humblest candle-flame, so long as its mass remains constant. But many, indeed most, things within the world are not of this kind; there are rivers that dry up and flames that are put out. To uphold the justice of *all* strife Heraclitus must fall back on another notion, more fundamental in his scheme than that of equipollent change: the constancy of a *logos* or *metron* preserved in all changes whatever. This is conveyed, in part, in B 31 b, whose sense is not correctly rendered by Kirk. '(Earth)[10] is dispersed as sea and is measured in the same *logos* as existed before [it became earth]'[11] does not say or of itself

[10] I agree with Kranz, Kirk, and others that ⟨γῆ⟩ is justified by the probability that it was in the text followed by Theophrastus (πάλιν τε αὖ τὴν γῆν χεῖσθαι, Diogenes Laertius, ix. 9). This expansion is rejected by Walzer (*Eraclito*, Florence 1939), Snell (*Hermes*, 76 [1941]), Reinhardt (for the latter's defence, see *Hermes*, 77 [1942], 16, n. 1; and cf. note 12, below). I fail to see what is gained by dropping ⟨γῆ⟩ if θάλασσα διαχέεται is to be understood to mean, as by Reinhardt (*loc. cit.*) 'the sea passes from a solid to a liquid state'; its 'solid state' *is* earth, so we are right back to the meaning of ⟨γῆ⟩ but now without warrant from the text. If one is to forego the initial ⟨γῆ⟩, one should accept the only meaning which Clement's text will then permit, i.e. that the sea is dispersed as *fire*. This makes excellent sense, especially if taken in conjunction with the suggestion in the following note. For my part, I prefer to stick by ⟨γῆ⟩ on the probability that this was in the text known to Theophrastus. But nothing of any great consequence depends on this. The general conclusion I reach from my interpretation of B 31 b and B 90 (towards the close of the paragraph in the text above) would be exactly the same if B 31 b referred to the change from sea to fire instead of from earth to sea.
[11] I am inclined to accept a suggestion made by Cherniss (in his seminar) and treat ἢ γενέσθαι γῆ as a gloss: its presence makes for unnecessary stylistic clumsiness, and its absence would make no difference to the sense; retaining (here contrary to Cherniss) the initial γῆ, the new text would still allow, indeed favor, the same reference of 'before', sc. to the earth's antecedent liquid state.

imply that 'sea is being constantly replenished by the liquefaction of earth proportionally with its diminution by condensation into earth' (p. 331). Heraclitus believes this, but it is not what he says *here*. What he does say is that any part of earth which becomes water has the same *logos* which it had before it had become earth, i.e. when a part of water, w_1, becomes a part of earth, e_1, and then e_1 changes back into a part of water, w_2, then w_2 is 'measured in the same *logos*' as w_1, or $w_2 = w_1$, for short.[12] B 90, 'all things are an exchange for fire, and fire for all things, as wares (are exchanged) for gold and gold (is exchanged) for all things', identifies fire as the thing that remains constant in all transformations and implies that *its* measure is the same or common measure in all things. Thus, in the preceding instance, the same measure would obtain not only between w_1 and w_2, but also between each of these and e_1, and similarly between all previous transformations of which w_1 is the last and all subsequent transformations of which w_2 is the first, and in all cases for the same reason: each member of the whole series represents the same amount of fire which is the common thing—τὸ ξυνόν—in all the different things that compose the series. Thus the ultimate guarantee of cosmic justice is fire: the invariance of *its* measures is what accounts for the observance of the *metron* in all things, and fire is therefore that which 'governs' or 'steers all things' (B 41, B 64, and note 35 in Part I of the original article).

Towards the end of his discussion of B 90 Kirk remarks:

[12] Another possibility on the text suggested in the preceding note is that 'before' refers to the earthy state before it turns into water, in which case it would be e_1 which is said to have the same *logos* as w_2. A variant of this is permitted by the Diels text, sc. that the logical subject of μετρέεται is earth before it turns into sea, in which case the equation would be $e_1 = w_1$. For obvious reasons, neither of these is as likely as the one suggested above, though the latter would avoid completely Reinhardt's objection that on the expansion ⟨γῆ⟩ 'διαχέεται καὶ μετρέεται verschiedenes Subjekt erhalten', since the subject of μετρέεται (as well as διαχέεται) would be γῆ. On the former interpretation here and that of my text above, γῆ would still be the grammatical subject of μετρέεται, but not the logical one; this I do not find absurd, or even difficult, in this context.

(But cf. also the following note.) Incidentally, I would argue that, if ἢ γενέσθαι γῆ is a gloss, it must have been put in by someone who did have an initial γῆ in his text; for, if he did not, it would have been natural to take θάλασσα as the subject, and, in that case, his gloss would probably have been ἢ γενέσθαι θάλασσα.

'There remains one slight difficulty. . . . Fire is said to be an exchange for "all things"; but fire itself must be one constituent of "all things" . . .' (p. 348). There is indeed a difficulty; but is it 'slight' and is it 'simply due to an unavoidable looseness of speech' (*loc. cit.*)? If the trouble were merely verbal, Heraclitus could easily have avoided it by saying that all *other* things are an exchange for fire and fire for all *other* things. The real difficulty is of quite another order. It is why Heraclitus should give to fire so unique and pre-eminent a place, when it is after all just one of three components of the cosmos whose mutual trans- formations are symmetrical. Why should not water or earth have as good a claim to the place of the 'common', since either one of them becomes in due course each of the others? Indeed why should any of them be singled out as the 'common'? And why should the whole world be 'ever-living *fire*'? Are not water and earth also 'ever-living', each of them, like fire, ever- lastingly 'living' and 'dying'?[13]

When Kirk faces up to this problem he thinks he can solve it as follows: 'The fire in question (in B 30) is not simply that which burns in the hearth, because this has no claim to be more important or more primary than sea or earth. The cosmological fire must be thought of primarily as *aether*, that purer kind which in popular thought fills the upper region of the heavens and is considered to be divine and immortal' (p. 316). Whether popular

[13] I cannot understand how the earth could be for Heraclitus 'das Starre, Gegensatzlose, Tote' (W. Broecker, *Gnomon*, 13 [1937], 532). How could anything be *gegensatzlos* in Heraclitus' world, and fail to exemplify both terms of the polarities, change-stability, life-death? Kirk refers approvingly (p. 342) to the remark of H. Gomperz that life, for Heraclitus, consists in passing from a more solid to a more fluid state, while death is the reverse. This too is surely wrong as a generalization; true enough in the case of fire, it would be, e.g., false in the case of earth, for which it would be death to pass into the more fluid state of water. The more common view is that while Heraclitus would exempt nothing from change, he would (*a*) think of fire as changing more rapidly than anything else and (*b*) choose fire as his *arche* for this reason. We need not doubt that Heraclitus believed (*a*), i.e. that the rate of 'exchange' between fire and water is higher than of that between water and earth, though he never says this. Nor do I think that (*b*) is wrong, though I do think it an incomplete answer to the question raised in the text above. Certainly fire makes a better *symbol* of permanence through change and life in death than does anything else. If he were *only* a poet, the superbly evocative power of this symbol would be an ample answer to my question.

thought at this time made this distinction between our fires and the fire of the celestial regions we do not know. What we do know is that it is not to be found in Heraclitus[14] nor in any presocratic fragment, and that no Ionian philosopher thought of 'cosmological' fire, air, etc., as different in kind from that we see and handle ever day. The first surviving text in which this peculiar notion is asserted is in Plato. It is he, not Heraclitus, who says that the fire in the heavens is 'pure', as well as 'fairest', 'most honourable', etc., while ours is 'not at all pure in any way', *Phil.*, 29 B–30 B.[15] But even if Heraclitus had made this distinction, how would it help to answer our question? 'Cosmological' fire would still be on a par with water and earth in the series of natural transformations, and the question why *it* should be elevated above the rest would remain unanswered. It cannot be answered, I submit, without taking account of a powerful historical influence which passes unnoticed in Kirk's book: that of Anaximenes.[16] It is here that Heraclitus found the cosmological pattern we are looking for and superimposed it upon the one he derived and developed from Anaximander. This pattern, in sharp opposition to Anaximander's, explains all the things that compose the world as a differentiation of just one of them. Anaximenes' preference for this type of explanation must have been due partly (*a*) to a genuinely empirical impulse, eschewing an *arche*, like Anaximander's, which must lie forever beyond experience, to put in its place one which is indisputably *in* this world, as well as out of it, and whose relation to experience can be properly explained (Hippolytus, *Ref.*, i. 7, 2), and partly (*b*) to the conviction that the *arche* must be of the same stuff as that of the human soul,[17] doubtless because he held with Anaximander

---

[14] Nor the parallel one between an *Urfeuer* and its *Erscheinungsformen* in sun, *prester*, etc., assumed by Reinhardt, p. 16—an odd vestige of Zeller's theory, who needed an *Urfeuer* as a prop for the *ekpyrosis*.

[15] Where this distinction in respect of the superior 'purity', etc., of τὸ ἐν τῷ παντί over τὸ παρ' ἡμῖν (or τὸ ἐνθάδε) is extended to all the στοιχεῖα, including earth (29D). Cf. *CP* XLII (1947), 176, n. 173 (n. 147 on p. 87 above).

[16] All I can find in Kirk by way of reference to any major relationship between Anaximenes and Heraclitus is the casual remark, pp. 343–4, 'It may be that Heraclitus' omission of air is a direct criticism of Anaximenes' acceptance of it.'

[17] Which is air: A 22 and 23; also Aetius, i. 3, 4, listed as B 2 in *Vors.*⁶, on which see note, 19 below.

that the *arche* which creates the world also governs it,[18] and is therefore intelligent. Though both motives are discernible in Heraclitus, the second far outweighs the first and provides, in my view, the main explanation of the dominant role of fire in his cosmos.

What may have led Kirk to ignore this link is his insistence that 'the parallel between man and cosmos is first explicitly drawn by medical speculation in the fifth century' (p. 312). But it *is* drawn in Anaximenes, B 2; though much of the wording of this fragment is doubtful, there is no good reason to doubt that it paraphrases an analogy drawn by Anaximenes himself.[19]

---

[18] Aristotle, *Phys.*, 203 b 11 ff.: καὶ περιέχειν ἅπαντα καὶ πάντα κυβερνᾶν, ὡς φασι ὅσοι μὴ ποιοῦσι παρὰ τὸ ἄπειρον ἄλλας αἰτίας οἷον νοῦν ἢ φιλίαν, which would certainly include Anaximenes. That air περιέχει the world is also in Anaximenes, B 2. Cf. W. Jaeger, *The Theology of the Early Greek Philosophers* (Oxford, 1947), pp. 29–30 and notes; and on the significance of the ascription of περιέχειν to the *arche* cf. also n. 127 on p. 81 above.

[19] The upshot of the controversy about this fragment—for the best on either side see Reinhardt, *Kosmos und Sympathie* (Munich, 1926), pp. 209–13, and Kranz, *Hermes*, LXXIII (1938), 111, and *Gött. Nachr.* (1938), p. 145—is surely that it should now be regarded as a *testimonium* which does not retain the original wording. How can συγκρατεῖ be defended for Anaximenes when there is no known use of the word prior to the Christian era? Nor is there any presocratic parallel for the notion that the soul holds the body together while, as Reinhardt points out, this was a common Stoic view. On the other hand, there can be absolutely no objection to the statement that the air περεέχει the world (cf. n. 18, above); τὸν ὅλον κόσμον is doubtful (Kranz cites its occurrence in Philol., B 1) but this is not conclusive), though possible. Moreover, the comparison of a human with a cosmic phenomenon is also reported for Anaximenes at A 7, 6; Kranz compares ὡσπερεὶ περὶ τὴν ἡμετέραν κεφαλήν there with οἷον ἡ ψυχὴ ἡ ἡμετέρα here. Finally, the man-world analogy is also implied by Anaximenes' close follower, Diogenes of Apollonia, when he argues that the same thing, air, is that by which man lives and thinks (B4; B5 *sub fin.*; A19, 42 *sub fin.*) and that which governs and thinks in the world. As to what stood for the improbable συγκρατεῖ ἡμᾶς in the original, the simplest guess is ἡμῶν κρατέει. Fränkel (*Dichtung und Philosophie*, p. 348, n. 20) thinks it anachronistic to credit Anaximenes with the notion of the soul ruling man or his body. Certainly there is no known *elaboration* of this idea before Plato. But it would be taken for granted from the moment the *psyche* was identified with the thinking, willing self and hence accorded the power of controlling the body or its functions expressed by κρατέειν and its derivatives (cf. σκελέων τε καὶ χειρῶν ἀκρατέες, Hippocrates, *Art.*, 48; γλώσσης ἀκρατής, Aeschylus, *PV*, 884; αὐτοῦ κρατέειν for the self-control which is lost in drunkenness, Antiphon, *Or.*, v. 26). This concept of the *psyche* is amply documented in Heraclitus (cf. especially B 118 with B 117), and there is no reason why it cannot go back to Anaximenes.

And even if we were to throw it all out, we would still have the fact, independently attested, that Anaximenes made air both the *arche* of all things and the stuff of the human soul, and this suffices for our purpose, for this is precisely what Heraclitus does, merely substituting fire for air. A variety of convergent reasons would prompt this substitution in the case of the soul. As the principle of life, soul would be naturally thought of as fire, since the warmth which persists throughout life and fails only after death, was a fact of ordinary experience.[20] As the principle of thought, soul would be connected both (*a*) with the heat of fire, since that lapse of intelligence which looms so large in Heraclitus' psychological reflections, sleep, was generally regarded as due to a reduction of organic heat,[21] and (*b*) with its light, because of the inevitable association of truth and knowledge with light, of error or ignorance with darkness.[22] Now since his cosmos is 'ever-*living*' and 'governed' by a *gnōmē*, what would be more natural for him than to ascribe the principles of life and intelligence in the cosmos to the same stuff to which

[20] Anaximenes himself would have had to take account of this fact. Cf. Diogenes, B 5, ἡ ψυχή . . ., ἀὴρ θερμότερος τοῦ ἔξω ἐν ᾧ ἐσμεν. This would make the transition (from 'hot air' to 'fire') all the easier for Heraclitus. It is possible, perhaps probable, that Anaximenes had also anticipated Heraclitus in explaining sleep and drunkenness as due to the moistening of the soul, for we know that Diogenes οι Apollonia held this view (A 19, 44). In an interesting paper (*Hermes*, LXXVI [1941], 359 ff.) Diller attributes these and other similarities between Heraclitus and Diogenes to the direct influence of the former upon the latter. This I very much doubt, since the true affinities of Diogenes—in style (cf. Anaximenes, A 1, κέχρηται . . . λέξει . . . ἁπλῇ καὶ ἀπερίττῳ, with Diogenes, B 1, τὴν ἑρμηνείαν ἁπλῆν καὶ σεμνήν), main cosmological doctrine (the same *arche*, air, infinite, giving rise to an infinity of worlds), and primarily 'scientific' bent of mind with no discernible ethical or political interests—are with Anaximenes. It is most unlikely that Diogenes would take over the details noticed by Diller from a thinker with whose temper and fundamental doctrine he was so much out of line. Things common to Heraclitus and Diogenes are much more likely to be derived by Heraclitus from Anaximenes, and by Diogenes either directly from Anaximenes or from intermediaries other than Heraclitus.

[21] Parm., 46 b, somnum . . . Emp. et Parm. refrigerationem. Emp., A 85, E. τὸν μὲν ὕπνον καταψύξει . . . τῇ δὲ παντελεῖ θάνατον, Hippocrates, *De Flat.*, 14, ὁ ὕπνος πέφυκεν ψύχειν.

[22] Attested, e.g. in φαίνω, originally 'shine', derivatively, 'bring to light, disclose, reveal'. Parmenides speaks of his dark form as νύκτ' ἀδαῆ (unknowing), B 8, 59.

he assigned them in the case of man? That the analogy between this cosmic fire and man's fiery soul was so complete for him that it amounts to identity we know from B 36, where he says 'souls' when he *means* 'fire'; as Kirk rightly remarks (p. 341), 'Heraclitus has here put soul in the place of cosmic fire'. Renouncing the Milesian concept of an *arche* which 'contains' the world, he would have to give a physical explanation of the world's 'government' by the *arche* in terms of the physical relation of fire to everything else in the world; and this he did, as we have seen, by imputing to fire the source of the common measure whose preservation throughout all change ensures the 'justice' of all 'strife'. This reconstruction, I submit, explains why fire should have in his system its otherwise inexplicable pre-eminence over water and earth; and it does so by showing how an idea, derived initially from Anaximenes, was grafted upon a concept of justice-in-strife developed from ideas supplied by Anaximander.

Two other cosmological doctrines—his affirmation of the eternity of the world (B 30), and his denial of the infinity of fire and therewith of the sum-total of existence[23]—tell against both Anaximander and Anaximenes. Their significance is best appreciated in terms of his rejection of the Milesian axiom that the world is derived from and 'governed' by an everlasting and infinite substance which 'contains' it. For Anaximander the creative source of the world is wholly outside of it; for Anaximenes it is both in and beyond the world; for Heraclitus it is wholly within the world, which is itself the theatre of the ceaseless and regular transformations of fire, therefore self-creating, self-governing, self-contained. He could thus transfer to the world that eternal life and youth which was always for the Greeks the unique privilege of divinity. To express this he employs in B 30 not only the solemn, traditional formula, 'ever was and is and shall be',[24] but also the new and proud affirma-

---

[23] Arist., *Phys.*, 205 a 1–4; Theophrastus, *Phys. Op.*, Frag. 1 (*Dox. Graeci*, p. 475); Diogenes Laertius, ix. 8. It is strange that this important doctrine should be so seldom noticed in the modern literature; Kirk is typical in ignoring it completely. It is briefly recognized in Zeller–Nestle, *op. cit.*, pp. 862–3, but with the suggestion that Heraclitus did not assert this doctrine explicitly; I see no reason for this opinion: he would have every reason for doing so against Anaximander and Anaximenes, if he did not believe in the infinity of fire.

[24] Reinhardt, pp. 10–11; also in his *Parmenides* (Bonn, 1916), p. 176, n. 2.

tion, 'ever-living', in place of the canonical negatives, 'death-less, ageless' (Anaximander, B 2, B 3) for which he had no use anyhow, since for him the condition of life everlasting is not deathlessness but life endlessly renewed by death in a process where youth and age are 'the same' (B 88). We do not know what form of expression he gave to his denial of the infinity of fire and the totality of being; all we learn from Aristotle and Theophrastus is that he did, without even a hint of his reasons. These we must reconstruct, and our only clue to them is in his new, anti-Milesian concept of the relation of the world-creating *arche* to its creatures. If the two are one, as in Heraclitus, then the *arche* neither need, nor can, be infinite. It need not, for no matter how limited may be its mass, its energy, ever-renewed by reabsorbing its own creatures, is inexhaustible, and thus suffi-cient to maintain it for all time to come. It can not, for it is interdependent with its creatures, and can be no more infinite than they; if it were, the balance of their mutual 'exchanges' would be completely upset.[25]

Finally, what of that doctrine in which his claim to originality centred, according to a widespread belief in antiquity,[26] the unity of the many and the sameness of opposites? If, as Kirk says from time to time (e.g. pp. 121, 344, 402), this only meant for Hera-clitus that 'opposites are essentially connected' or 'not really disconnected', how could we think of it as Heraclitus' 'great discovery' (Kirk, p. 344)? That the many and different things which compose the world are all essentially connected, so much so, that they are all one and the same thing, is the rudimentary truth about the world as conceived by Anaximenes.[27] When

[25] One might still ask why the creatures too could not be infinite. The question could hardly have bothered Heraclitus. He must have assumed, as did every known thinker of classical Greece, that the visible world is finite in extension; the only thing ever held to be infinite was something either beyond the visible world, as for the Milesians and many others after them, or of a different order of being from it, as for Melissus, who was also the first to offer a formal argument against the possibility of more than one infinite being (B6).

[26] Cf. Philo, *Quis rer. div. haer.*, 212–13 ἐν γὰρ τὸ ἐξ ἀμφοῖν τῶν ἐναντίων . . . οὐ τοῦτ' ἔστιν ὅ φασιν "Ελληνες . . . 'Ηράκλειτον κεφάλαιον τῆς αὐτοῦ προστησάμενον φιλοσοφίας αὐχεῖν ὡς ἐφ' εὑρέσει καινῇ;

[27] And is spelled out in the only exposition of this type of cosmology avail-able to us in extant fragments, that of Diogenes (at B 2).

Heraclitus declared that 'all things (come) from one and one from all' (B 10) or even that 'all things are one' (B 50), he was saying something with which Anaximenes would have agreed as a matter of course. But the difference would still be enormous. The sense of the unity of all things would be both lucid and prosaic for Anaximenes: simply, that all things are differentiations of air.[28] Heraclitus' speculative imagination transforms this straightforward cosmological theorem into an assertion of the unity of all differences whatever, including moral ones, and pursues its consequences to that reckless and bewildering conclusion that 'for god all things are fair and good and just' (B 102) which, if true, would be fatal for all morality, not excepting his own.[29] I cannot discuss here the fragments which assert this and other aspects of the most paradoxical of all his doctrines and explore its connection with the doctrines of the justice of all strife and *palintropos harmonia*. Of Kirk's interpretation of these fragments I shall merely remark that it is sober and sensible throughout, and that its only fault is to discount that part of their sense which is inherently obscure and, so far as it is clear, profoundly disturbing not only to the moralist but also to the logician. It proved disturbing enough to the latter to provoke in Parmenides a reaction, violent in the extreme,[30] yet immensely fruitful, for it issued in a doctrine of Being which served as the foundation

---

[28] For an excellent statement of this aspect of Heraclitus' relation to Anaximenes, see Cherniss, pp. 14–15 of this volume.

[29] Kirk (pp. 180–1), following Wilamowitz and others, argues that the second part of the fragment, ἄνθρωποι δὲ ἃ μὲν ἄδικα ὑπειλήφασιν ἃ δὲ δίκαια, can hardly be wholly authentic; ὑπειλήφασι, though barely possible, is most unlikely for Heraclitus. Kirk underwrites Mazzantini's suggestion that the original read something like ἀνθρώποις δὲ ἃ μὲν ἄδικα ἃ δὲ δίκαια. With all this I agree. But what follows for the sense of the whole fragment; Man's wisdom is to god's what an ape's is to man's (B 83); since men's moral distinctions do not exist for god (first sentence of B 102), must they not be ultimately illusory? I fail to see how this difficulty is solved by Kirk's elucidation: moral distinctions, he says, submerged only for (god's) 'synthetic' view, are still 'necessary' and 'legitimate' for the 'analytical' view (man's), pp. 180–1. But what Kirk calls the 'synthetic' view is 'wisdom' for Heraclitus (B 50)—not only for god, but for man too so far as he can reach it. Hence the wiser man becomes, the closer he comes to the view that 'all things are fair and good and just', and if this does not make moral distinctions illusory, I do not know what would.

[30] Cf. Cherniss, pp. 19–22 of this volume.

of the great cosmological constructions of Empedocles, Anaxagoras, and the atomists. In a singularly Heraclitean turn of events, Heraclitus, ignored in Ionia [31] by the best minds of the generation that followed him, lived in them only through the death of his own system in Parmenides.

[31] I say 'Ionia' to allow for some Heraclitean influence on Empedocles (see pp. 67–69 above), though it is subordinate to that of Parmenides. In Ionia itself not one of Heraclitus' distinctive doctrines is conserved by Anaxagoras or Leucippus; so far as we know, they do not even acknowledge their existence by a word of refutation. Democritus must have known intimately Heraclitus' book, for it influenced his style (E. Norden, *Antike Kunstprosa*, I [Berlin, 1915], 22–3) and doubtless also some of his ethical reflections, but he too writes cosmology and ontology as though Heraclitus had never existed. The only possible anti-Heraclitean polemic is Melissus, B 8 (so Kirk, p. 140), a feeble echo of Parmenides' great assault.

International Library of Philosophy & Scientific Method

Editor: Ted Honderich

List of titles, page two

.

International Library of Psychology Philosophy & Scientific Method

Editor: C K Ogden

List of titles, page six

ROUTLEDGE AND KEGAN PAUL LTD
68 Carter Lane London EC4

International Library of Philosophy and Scientific Method
(*Demy 8vo*)

Allen, R. E. (Ed.)
Studies in Plato's Metaphysics
Contributors: J. L. Ackrill, R. E. Allen, R. S. Bluck, H. F. Cherniss, F. M.
Cornford, R. C. Cross, P. T. Geach, R. Hackforth, W. F. Hicken, A. C. Lloyd,
G. R. Morrow, G. E. L. Owen, G. Ryle, W. G. Runciman, G. Vlastos
464 pp. 1965. (2nd Impression 1967.) 70s.

Armstrong, D. M.
Perception and the Physical World
208 pp. 1961. (3rd Impression 1966.) 25s.

A Materialist Theory of the Mind
376 pp. 1967. (2nd Impression 1969.) 50s.

Bambrough, Renford (Ed.)
New Essays on Plato and Aristotle
Contributors: J. L. Ackrill, G. E. M. Anscombe, Renford Bambrough,
R. M. Hare, D. M. MacKinnon, G. E. L. Owen, G. Ryle, G. Vlastos
184 pp. 1965. (2nd Impression 1967.) 28s.

Barry, Brian
Political Argument
382 pp. 1965. (3rd Impression 1968.) 50s.

Bird, Graham
Kant's Theory of Knowledge:
An Outline of One Central Argument in the *Critique of Pure Reason*
220 pp. 1962. (2nd Impression 1965.) 28s.

Brentano, Franz
The True and the Evident
Edited and narrated by Professor R. Chisholm
218 pp. 1965. 40s.

The Origin of Our Knowledge of Right and Wrong
Edited by Oskar Kraus. English edition edited by Roderick M. Chisholm.
Translated by Roderick M. Chisholm and Elizabeth H. Schneewind
174 pp. 1969. 40s.

Broad, C. D.
Lectures on Physical Research
Incorporating the Perrott Lectures given in Cambridge University in 1959
and 1960
461 pp. 1962. (2nd Impression 1966.) 56s.

Crombie, I. M.
An Examination of Plato's Doctrine
1. Plato on Man and Society
408 pp. 1962. (3rd Impression 1969.) 42s.
II. Plato on Knowledge and Reality
583 pp. 1963. (2nd Impression 1967.) 63s.

International Library of Philosophy and Scientific Method
(*Demy 8vo*)

Day, John Patrick
Inductive Probability
352 pp. 1961. 40s.

Dretske, Fred I.
Seeing and Knowing
270 pp. 1969. 35s.

Ducasse, C. J.
Truth, Knowledge and Causation
263 pp. 1969. 50s.

Edel, Abraham
Method in Ethical Theory
379 pp. 1963. 32s.

Fann, K. T. (Ed.)
Symposium on J. L. Austin
Contributors: A. J. Ayer, Jonathan Bennett, Max Black, Stanley Cavell,
Walter Cerf, Roderick M. Chisholm, L. Jonathan Cohen, Roderick Firth, L. W.
Forguson, Mats Furberg, Stuart Hampshire, R. J. Hirst, C. G. New, P. H.
Nowell-Smith, David Pears, John Searle, Peter Strawson, Irving Thalberg,
J. O. Urmson, G. J. Warnock, Jon Wheatly, Alan White
512 pp. 1969.

Flew, Anthony
Hume's Philosophy of Belief
A Study of his First "Inquiry"
269 pp. 1961. (2nd Impression 1966.) 30s.

Fogelin, Robert J.
Evidence and Meaning
Studies in Analytical Philosophy
200 pp. 1967. 25s.

Gale, Richard
The Language of Time
256 pp. 1968. 40s.

Goldman, Lucien
The Hidden God
A Study of Tragic Vision in the *Pensées* of Pascal and the Tragedies of Racine.
Translated from the French by Philip Thody
424 pp. 1964. 70s.

Hamlyn, D. W.
Sensation and Perception
A History of the Philosophy of Perception
222 pp. 1961. (3rd Impression 1967.) 25s.

2*

International Library of Philosophy and Scientific Method
(Demy 8vo)

Kemp, J.
Reason, Action and Morality
216 pp. 1964. 30s.

Körner, Stephan
Experience and Theory
An Essay in the Philosophy of Science
272 pp. 1966. (2nd Impression 1969.) 45s.

Lazerowitz, Morris
Studies in Metaphilosophy
276 pp. 1964. 35s.

Linsky, Leonard
Referring
152 pp. 1968. 35s.

MacIntosh, J. J., and Coval, S. C. (Ed.)
The Business of Reason
280 pp. 1969. 42s.

Merleau-Ponty, M.
Phenomenology of Perception
Translated from the French by Colin Smith
487 pp. 1962. (4th Impression 1967.) 56s.

Perelman, Chaim
The Idea of Justice and the Problem of Argument
Introduction by H. L. A. Hart. Translated from the French by John Petrie
224 pp. 1963. 28s.

Ross, Alf
Directives, Norms and their Logic
192 pp. 1967. 35s.

Schlesinger, G.
Method in the Physical Sciences
148 pp. 1963. 21s.

Sellars, W. F.
Science, Perception and Reality
374 pp. 1963. (2nd Impression 1966.) 50s.

Shwayder, D. S.
The Stratification of Behaviour
A System of Definitions Propounded and Defended
428 pp. 1965. 56s.

Skolimowski, Henryk
Polish Analytical Philosophy
288 pp. 1967. 40s.

International Library of Philosophy and Scientific Method
(*Demy 8vo*)

Smart, J. J. C.
Philosophy and Scientific Realism
168 pp. 1963. (3rd Impression 1967.) 25s.

Smythies, J. R. (Ed.)
Brain and Mind
Contributors: Lord Brain, John Beloff, C. J. Ducasse, Antony Flew, Hartwig Kuhlenbeck, D. M. MacKay, H. H. Price, Anthony Quinton and J. R. Smythies
288 pp. 1965. 40s.

Science and E.S.P.
Contributors: Gilbert Murray, H. H. Price, Rosalind Heywood, Cyril Burt, C. D. Broad, Francis Huxley and John Beloff
320 pp. about 40s.

Taylor, Charles
The Explanation of Behaviour
288 pp. 1964. (2nd Impression 1965.) 40s.

Williams, Bernard, and Montefiore, Alan
British Analytical Philosophy
352 pp. 1965. (2nd Impression 1967.) 45s.

Winch, Peter (Ed.)
Studies in the Philosophy of Wittgenstein
Contributors: Hidé Ishiguro, Rush Rhees, D. S. Shwayder, John W. Cook, L. R. Reinhardt and Anthony Manser
224 pp. 1969.

Wittgenstein, Ludwig
Tractatus Logico-Philosophicus
The German text of the *Logisch-Philosophische Abhandlung* with a new translation by D. F. Pears and B. F. McGuinness. Introduction by Bertrand Russell
188 pp. 1961. (3rd Impression 1966.) 21s.

Wright, Georg Henrik Von
Norm and Action
A Logical Enquiry. The Gifford Lectures
232 pp. 1963. (2nd Impression 1964.) 32s.

The Varieties of Goodness
The Gifford Lectures
236 pp. 1963. (3rd Impression 1966.) 28s.

Zinkernagel, Peter
Conditions for Description
Translated from the Danish by Olaf Lindum
272 pp. 1962. 37s. 6d.

International Library of Psychology, Philosophy, and Scientific Method
(*Demy 8vo*)

PHILOSOPHY

Anton, John Peter
Aristotle's Theory of Contrariety
276 pp. 1957. 25s.

Black, Max
The Nature of Mathematics
A Critical Survey
242 pp. 1933. (5th Impression 1965.) 28s.

Bluck, R. S.
Plato's Phaedo
A Translation with Introduction, Notes and Appendices
226 pp. 1955. 21s.

Broad, C. D.
Five Types of Ethical Theory
322 pp. 1930. (9th Impression 1967.) 30s.
The Mind and Its Place in Nature
694 pp. 1925. (7th Impression 1962.) 70s. See also Lean, Martin

Buchler, Justus (Ed.)
The Philosophy of Peirce
Selected Writings
412 pp. 1940. (3rd Impression 1956.) 35s.

Burtt, E. A.
The Metaphysical Foundations of Modern Physical Science
A Historical and Critical Essay
364 pp. 2nd (revised) edition 1932. (5th Impression 1964.) 35s.

Carnap, Rudolf
The Logical Syntax of Language
Translated from the German by Amethe Smeaton
376 pp. 1937. (7th Impression 1967.) 40s.

Chwistek, Leon
The Limits of Science
Outline of Logic and of the Methodology of the Exact Sciences
With Introduction and Appendix by Helen Charlotte Brodie
414 pp. 2nd edition 1949. 32s.

Cornford, F. M.
Plato's Theory of Knowledge
The Theaetetus and Sophist of Plato
Translated with a running commentary
358 pp. 1935. (7th Impression 1967.) 28s.

6

International Library of Psychology, Philosophy, and Scientific Method
(*Demy 8vo*)

Cornford, F. M. (*continued*)
Plato's Cosmology
The Timaeus of Plato
Translated with a running commentary
402 pp. Frontispiece. 1937. (5th Impression 1966.) 45s.

Plato and Parmenides
Parmenides' *Way of Truth* and Plato's *Parmenides*
Translated with a running commentary
280 pp. 1939. (5th Impression 1964.) 32s.

Crawshay-Williams, Rupert
Methods and Criteria of Reasoning
An Inquiry into the Structure of Controversy
312 pp. 1957. 32s.

Fritz, Charles A.
Bertrand Russell's Construction of the External World
252 pp. 1952. 30s.

Hulme, T. E.
Speculations
Essays on Humanism and the Philosophy of Art
Edited by Herbert Read. Foreword and Frontispiece by Jacob Epstein
296 pp. 2nd edition 1936. (6th Impression 1965.) 40s.

Lazerowitz, Morris
The Structure of Metaphysics
With a Foreword by John Wisdom
262 pp. 1955. (2nd Impression 1963.) 30s.

Lodge, Rupert C.
Plato's Theory of Art
332 pp. 1953. 25s.

Mannheim, Karl
Ideology and Utopia
An Introduction to the Sociology of Knowledge
With a Preface by Louis Wirth. Translated from the German by Louis Wirth
and Edward Shils
360 pp. 1954. (2nd Impression 1966.) 30s.

Moore, G. E.
Philosophical Studies
360 pp. 1922. (6th Impression 1965.) 35s. See also Ramsey, F. P.

7

International Library of Psychology, Philosophy, and Scientific Method
(*Demy 8vo*)

Ogden, C. K., and Richards, I. A.
The Meaning of Meaning
A Study of the Influence of Language upon Thought and of the Science of Symbolism
With supplementary essays by B. Malinowski and F. G. Crookshank
394 pp. 10th Edition 1949. (6th Impression 1967.) 32s.
See also Bentham, J.

Peirce, Charles, *see* Buchler, J.

Ramsey, Frank Plumpton
The Foundations of Mathematics and other Logical Essays
Edited by R. B. Braithwaite. Preface by G. E. Moore
318 pp. 1931. (4th Impression 1965.) 35s.

Richards, I. A.
Principles of Literary Criticism
312 pp. 2nd Edition. 1926. (17th Impression 1966.) 30s.

Mencius on the Mind. Experiments in Multiple Definition
190 pp. 1932. (2nd Impression 1964.) 28s.

Russell, Bertrand, *see* Fritz, C. A.; Lange, F. A.; Wittgenstein, L.

Smart, Ninian
Reasons and Faiths
An Investigation of Religious Discourse, Christian and Non-Christian
230 pp. 1958. (2nd Impression 1965.) 28s.

Vaihinger, H.
The Philosophy of As If
A System of the Theoretical, Practical and Religious Fictions of Mankind
Translated by C. K. Ogden
428 pp. 2nd edition 1935. (4th Impression 1965.) 45s.

Wittgenstein, Ludwig
Tractatus Logico-Philosophicus
With an Introduction by Bertrand Russell, F.R.S., German text with an English translation en regard
216 pp. 1922. (9th Impression 1962.) 21s.
For the Pears-McGuinness translation—*see page 5*

Wright, Georg Henrik von
Logical Studies
214 pp. 1957. (2nd Impression 1967.) 28s.

International Library of Psychology, Philosophy, and Scientific Method

(Demy 8vo)

Zeller, Eduard
Outlines of the History of Greek Philosophy
Revised by Dr. Wilhelm Nestle. Translated from the German by L. R. Palmer
248 pp. 13th (revised) edition 1931. (5th Impression 1963.) 28s.

PSYCHOLOGY

Adler, Alfred
The Practice and Theory of Individual Psychology
Translated by P. Radin
368 pp. 2nd (revised) edition 1929. (8th Impression 1964.) 30s.

Eng, Helga
The Psychology of Children's Drawings
From the First Stroke to the Coloured Drawing
240 pp. 8 colour plates. 139 figures. 2nd edition 1954. (3rd Impression 1966.) 40s.

Koffka, Kurt
The Growth of the Mind
An Introduction to Child-Psychology
Translated from the German by Robert Morris Ogden
456 pp 16 figures. 2nd edition (revised) 1928. (6th Impression 1965.) 45s.

Principles of Gestalt Psychology
740 pp. 112 figures. 39 tables. 1935. (5th Impression 1962.) 60s.

Malinowski, Bronislaw
Crime and Custom in Savage Society
152 pp. 6 plates. 1926. (8th Impression 1966.) 21s.

Sex and Repression in Savage Society
290 pp. 1927. (4th Impression 1953.) 30s.
See also Ogden, C. K.

Murphy, Gardner
An Historical Introduction to Modern Psychology
488 pp. 5th edition (revised) 1949. (6th Impression 1967.) 40s.

Paget, R.
Human Speech
Some Observations, Experiments, and Conclusions as to the Nature, Origin, Purpose and Possible Improvement of Human Speech
374 pp. 5 plates. 1930. (2nd Impression 1963.) 42s.

Petermann, Bruno
The Gestalt Theory and the Problem of Configuration
Translated from the German by Meyer Fortes
364 pp. 20 figures. 1932. (2nd Impression 1950.) 25s.

International Library of Psychology, Philosophy, and Scientific Method
(*Demy 8vo*)

Piaget, Jean
The Language and Thought of the Child
Preface by E. Claparède. Translated from the French by Marjorie Gabain
220 pp. 3rd edition (revised and enlarged) 1959. (3rd Impression 1966.) 30s.

Judgment and Reasoning in the Child
Translated from the French by Marjorie Warden
276 pp. 1928. (5th Impression 1969.) 30s.

The Child's Conception of the World
Translated from the French by Joan and Andrew Tomlinson
408 pp. 1929. (4th Impression 1964.) 40s.

The Child's Conception of Physical Causality
Translated from the French by Marjorie Gabain
(3rd Impression 1965.) 30s.

The Moral Judgment of the Child
Translated from the French by Marjorie Gabain
438 pp. 1932. (4th Impression 1965.) 35s.

The Psychology of Intelligence
Translated from the French by Malcolm Piercy and D. E. Berlyne
198 pp. 1950. (4th Impression 1964.) 18s.

The Child's Conception of Number
Translated from the French by C. Gattegno and F. M. Hodgson
266 pp. 1952. (3rd Impression 1964.) 25s.

The Origin of Intelligence in the Child
Translated from the French by Margaret Cook
448 pp. 1953. (2nd Impression 1966.) 42s.

The Child's Conception of Geometry
In collaboration with Bärbel Inhelder and Alina Szeminska. Translated from the French by E. A. Lunzer
428 pp. 1960. (2nd Impression 1966.) 45s.

Piaget, Jean, and Inhelder, Bärbel
The Child's Conception of Space
Translated from the French by F. J. Langdon and J. L. Lunzer
512 pp. 29 figures. 1956. (3rd Impression 1967.) 42s.

Roback, A. A.
The Psychology of Character
With a Survey of Personality in General
786 pp. 3rd edition (revised and enlarged 1952.) 50s.

Smythies, J. R.
Analysis of Perception
With a Preface by Sir Russell Brain, Bt.
162 pp. 1956. 21s.

10

International Library of Psychology, Philosophy, and Scientific Method
(*Demy 8vo*)

van der Hoop, J. H.
Character and the Unconscious
A Critical Exposition of the Psychology of Freud and Jung
Translated from the German by Elizabeth Trevelyan
240 pp. 1923. (2nd Impression 1950.) 20s.

Woodger, J. H.
Biological Principles
508 pp. 1929. (Re-issued with a new Introduction 1966.) 60s.

PRINTED BY HEADLEY BROTHERS LTD 109 KINGSWAY LONDON WC2 AND ASHFORD KENT